KARL MARX
FREDERICK ENGELS

COLLECTED WORKS

VOLUME

13

KARL MARX
FREDERICK ENGELS

COLLECTED WORKS

LAWRENCE & WISHART
LONDON

FROM THE PREPARATORY MATERIALS

APPENDICES

NOTES AND INDEXES

ILLUSTRATIONS

TRANSLATORS:

SUSANNE FLATAUER: 17, 18, 19, 20, 24, 25
HUGH RODWELL: 89, 93, 94, 95, 96, 97, 102, 106, 108, 109, 111, 114, 115
PETER and BETTY ROSS: 4, 55, 82, 98, 133
BARBARA RUHEMANN: 9, 10, 11, 13, 14, 16, 26, 27, 28, 31, 32, 33
SALO RYAZANSKAYA: 21, 80, 84, 90 (I, II), 100, 113, 116, 120
BARRIE SELMAN: 37, 41, 43, 45, 47, 48, 49, 52, 53, 56, 57, 58, 59, 61, 63, 64, 67, 68, 69, 71, 90 (III, IV, V, VI), 99
CHRISTOPHER UPWARD: 2, 3, 5, 6, 7
JOAN and TREVOR WALMSLEY: 36, 50, 72, 73, 75, 77, 78, 81, 85, 86, 88

Preface

Volume 14 of the *Collected Works* of Marx and Engels contains articles and newspaper reports written between February 9, 1855 and April 25, 1856. Most of these items were published in the American newspaper the *New-York Daily Tribune* (and often reprinted in its special issues—the *New-York Semi-Weekly Tribune* and the *New-York Weekly Tribune*), and also in the German democratic newspaper, the *Neue Oder-Zeitung*. As in previous years some items were published in the Chartist weekly *The People's Paper*. In the spring of 1856 Marx began to write occasionally for periodicals published by David Urquhart and his supporters—*The Free Press* (London) and *The Sheffield Free Press*.

Writing for the comparatively progressive bourgeois press was the only effective means available to Marx and Engels at that time to communicate with a mass readership, and to influence public opinion in favour of proletarian communist ideas. Since a properly working-class and revolutionary democratic press was still so weak, they attached great importance to this channel of communication. The possibility of addressing the German reader through the *Neue Oder-Zeitung*, the most radical of all the newspapers that remained in Germany in the mid-1850s, was particularly important. Marx wrote for the *Neue Oder-Zeitung* from December 1854 (the relevant section of his articles for this newspaper is published in Volume 13 of the present edition) until November 1855, when due to serious financial difficulties and pressure from the censorship the editorial board was compelled to reduce the number of foreign correspondents and later to cease publication of the newspaper entirely. He also sent to the *Neue Oder-Zeitung* military reviews written at his request by Engels for the *New-York Daily Tribune*, translating them into German and often shortening them and adapting them to the requirements of the German reader. In a number of cases Marx included the texts of the military reviews in his own contributions, supplementing them with other material (reviews of international and domestic events, parliamentary debates, etc.).

The editorial board of the *Neue Oder-Zeitung* printed the material Marx sent them in its authentic form. On the other hand, the interference of the *New-York Tribune* editors with the text of articles by Marx and Engels, including arbitrary cuts and insertion of passages which contradicted the original content, became particularly frequent during this period. Thus, Marx's pamphlet *Lord John Russell* was published in the *Tribune* in an abridged form, one of Engels' articles on Pan-Slavism was arbitrarily revised, and many articles were supplemented with introductory, and sometimes also concluding, paragraphs to give them the appearance of having been written in the United States of Northern America (all these cases of editorial interference are indicated in the notes). Eventually the editorial board of the *Tribune* ceased almost entirely publishing articles by Marx under his name, printing them instead in the form of its own editorials. Although angered by such cavalier treatment, Marx and Engels nevertheless continued to write for the *Tribune*. They could not renounce the opportunity of contributing to this widely circulated newspaper, read not only in America but also in Europe.

The present volume is largely a continuation of Volumes 12 and 13 of the present edition. Among the numerous events which attracted the attention of Marx and Engels in 1855 and early 1856, the central place was still held by the Crimean War, which had entered its final stage and was accompanied, as in the preceding stages, by a bitter diplomatic struggle. They continued to analyse in their articles the economic condition of the European countries—England in particular—the domestic and foreign policy of the ruling classes, the state of the working-class and democratic movements, and the prospects for their development.

Marx's and Engels' journalistic activity in this period was also closely intertwined with their theoretical researches, in particular, with Marx's studies in both political economy and foreign policy and diplomacy, and Engels' in military science, the history of the Slavonic peoples, and linguistics. At the same time, through their journalistic activities they accumulated new facts and observations which were then generalised in their scientific writings. Thus, the material Engels used in his regular reports on the Crimean War was summarised by him in important works on military theory, like his series of articles, *The Armies of Europe* written for the American journal *Putnam's Monthly* and published in the present volume. Reports by factory inspectors and information on agrarian relations in Ireland, quoted in Marx's articles for the *Neue Oder-Zeitung*, were later incorporated by him in *Capital*.

Marx's and Engels' journalistic work played an important part in crystallising their sociological views. By analysing current events in their articles, they acquired an increasingly profound understanding of the interconnection between historical processes, the laws of social development and class struggle. This is well illustrated by the contents of the present volume. Its articles and reports present a broad panorama of European social and political life during the mid-1850s against the background of continuing political reaction. They give a clear idea of the class structure of society at that time, the domestic and international conflicts of the day, the characteristic features of the state and its various forms, the position of the political parties, of various organs of the press as their ideological mouthpieces, and the customs and morals of the ruling classes. Serious attention is devoted in these articles to the working-class and national liberation movements.

The main aim of Marx's and Engels' journalistic writings during this period, as in previous years, was to provide the theoretical basis for the strategy and tactics of proletarian revolutionaries on cardinal questions of domestic and international policy, taking into account that in a large part of Europe the transition from the feudal system to capitalism had by no means been completed. The over-riding task was to effect the abolition of the vestiges of feudalism, the unification of politically divided countries, the liberation of oppressed nationalities. And this meant the revolutionary overthrow of the counter-revolutionary regimes which stood in the way of these transformations, and principally the Austrian, Prussian and Russian monarchies, the Bonapartist Second Empire, and the British bourgeois-aristocratic oligarchy. This was the way, in the opinion of Marx and Engels, to prepare for the working class winning political power in the capitalist countries.

The revolutionary approach to current events is seen clearly in those articles by Marx and Engels in which they continued to analyse the causes of the outbreak and the true character of the Crimean War. The final stage of the war confirmed the conclusions of their previous articles and reports, during the period when the conflict between the European powers was coming to a head, and in the early stages of the military operations against Russia by the Anglo-Franco-Turkish coalition, which was later joined by Piedmont. Marx and Engels became even more firmly convinced of the falseness of the official attitude of the West European governments and press, which was that the war of England and France against Russia was being waged in the "national interest" to defend "freedom" and "civilisation" against the encroachments of "despotism". They showed convincingly in their articles that the war was the result of a clash of economic and military interests of the ruling classes of the states engaged in it—the struggle for the partition of the Ottoman Empire and for dominion in the Balkans and the Black Sea straits. Marx and Engels came to the conclusion that the counter-revolutionary standpoint and class self-interest of the West European bourgeoisie made it increasingly incapable of expressing and defending any national interests. "As soon as the effects of the war should become taxable upon their pockets," Marx wrote in the article "Prospect in France and England", "mercantile sense was sure to overcome national pride, and the loss of immediate individual profits was sure to outweigh the certainty of losing, gradually, great national advantages" (see this volume, p. 143).

Marx and Engels concluded that bourgeois-aristocratic England and Bonapartist France, while striving to weaken Tsarist Russia as a rival in the Near East and the Balkans, to capture Sevastopol, to take the Crimea and the Caucasus away from Russia, and to destroy the Russian navy, had no interest whatever in the collapse of Tsarism. The conservative forces in Europe, headed by the governments of the West European states, needed the Tsarist autocracy as an instrument for repressing popular movements and so as one of the bulwarks of the system of capitalist exploitation. Above all, Western politicians feared the revolutionary consequences of the collapse of the Russian autocracy, which would lead to the destruction of the foundation of the political system in Europe laid down by the Congress of Vienna in 1815. The Crimean War, Marx stressed in the article "Eccentricities of Politics", "is undertaken with a view not to supersede but rather to consolidate the Treaty of Vienna by the introduction, in a supplementary way, of Turkey into the protocols of 1815. Then it is expected the conservative millennium will dawn and the aggregate force of the Governments be allowed to direct itself exclusively to the 'tranquillization' of the European mind" (see this volume, p. 284).

In the articles "From Parliament", "Napoleon's War Plans", "The Debate on Layard's Motion.—The War in the Crimea", "The Local War.—Debate on Administrative Reform.—Report of the Roebuck Committee" and others Marx and Engels showed that these counter-revolutionary aspirations of the ruling circles in Britain and France had left a profound imprint on their diplomacy, military plans and methods of warfare. Seeking to avoid any revolutionary consequences, the Allied states had launched military operations in one of Russia's outlying areas, away from the possible centres of the revolutionary and national liberation struggle. Marx and Engels revealed the hidded purpose behind the plan of "local war for local objects" put forward by the French Government and supported by the British Government (see this volume, p. 272). They showed that this strategy was by no means prompted by the desire to reduce the number of casualties and scale of destruction. The "local" Crimean War had inflicted enormous losses and bitter tribulations on the armies and peoples of the belligerents. The Anglo-French strategic plan was aimed at preventing the Crimean War from turning into a war of the peoples against Tsarism, a war which would have threatened the very existence of the anti-democratic system of government in Western Europe.

To change the character of the war, and turn it into a war for the democratic reconstruction of Europe and the liberation of the oppressed nationalities, including the peoples of the Balkans who were under Turkish rule, depended on the level of activity of the proletarian and revolutionary-democratic masses. In place of anti-popular governments, Marx wrote, "other powers must step on to the stage" (see this volume, p. 289). In the articles "The Crisis in England", "Prospect in France and England" and others, Marx and Engels continued to show the working class and the revolutionary democrats how advantage could be taken of the military conflict to develop the movement against the existing counter-revolutionary regimes. Marx hoped that a revolutionary turn of events would "enable the proletarian class to resume that position which they lost, in France, by the battle of June, 1848, and that not only as far as France is concerned, but for all Central Europe, England included" (see this volume, p. 145).

Marx and Engels placed special hopes on the initiative of the French working class. In the article "Fate of the Great Adventurer" Engels wrote openly about the possibility of "the fourth and greatest French revolution" capable of producing an outbreak of powerful revolutionary and national liberation movements all over the continent of Europe. "Germans, Hungarians, Poles, Italians, Croats are loosened from the forced bond which ties them together, and instead of the undetermined and haphazard alliances and antagonisms of today, Europe will again be divided into two great camps with distinct banners and new issues. Then the struggle will be only between the Democratic Revolution on one side and the Monarchical Counter-Revolution on the other" (see this volume, p. 89).

The idea that the way out of the war lay in a popular revolution was the theme running through many articles by Marx and Engels. They sought to show the real instability not only of the domestic, but also of the foreign-policy positions of the counter-revolutionary ruling circles, the contradictions between them in the international arena, and the vulnerability of their diplomacy.

In particular, Marx and Engels revealed deep splits in the coalition of the European powers opposing Tsarist Russia. They noted the constant friction between its main participants, Britain and France, both in the conduct of military operations and in diplomatic talks (see the articles "Some Observations on the History of the French Alliance", "A Critique of the Crimean Affair.—From Parliament", "From the Crimea", "Another British Revelation", "The Reports of Generals Simpson, Pélissier and Niel", "The American Difficulty.—Affairs of France" and others). The collapse of the Anglo-French Alliance predicted by them soon took place, during the Congress of Paris in 1856, at which Russian diplomacy skilfully exploited the differences between the Western powers.

Marx's article "Palmerston.—The Physiology of the Ruling Class of Great Britain", his pamphlet *The Fall of Kars* and Engels' military review "The War in Asia" revealed the colonialist aims underlying the policies of the Western powers, and their treachery in relation to their junior coalition partner—Turkey. Taking advantage of Turkey's backwardness, Marx noted, the governments of Britain and France, under the guise of defending the unity of the collapsing Ottoman Empire, had taken a new step towards its colonial subjection. They had set up effective control over its foreign policy, intervened in its internal affairs, and were laying a hand on Turkish finances (see this volume, p. 368). In *The Fall of Kars,* which has survived in several versions, Marx showed on the basis of facts and diplomatic material how frequently the Western statesmen—the British, in particular—took decisions concerning Turkey behind the back of the Turkish Government, using the weak Turkish army at their discretion and exposing it to attack. The moves of Western diplomacy in relation to the Ottoman Empire, Marx noted, constituted a web of intrigue and provocation aimed at using Turkey as small change in the diplomatic game of the great powers and increasing even more its dependence on the West.

A number of articles in the present volume ("The European War" and others) were written by Marx and Engels when the outcome of the Crimean War was already predetermined. They could already sum it up to a certain extent: "The Anglo-French war against Russia will undoubtedly always figure in military history as 'the *incomprehensible* war'. Big talk combined with minimal action, vast preparations and insignificant results, caution bordering on timidity, followed by the foolhardiness that is born of ignorance, generals who are more than mediocre coupled with troops who are more than brave, almost deliberate reverses on the heels of victories won through mistakes, armies ruined by negligence, then saved by the strangest of accidents—a grand ensemble of contradictions and inconsistencies. And this is nearly as much the distinguishing mark of the Russians as of their enemies" (see this volume, p. 484).

Marx's and Engels' hopes that the Crimean War would be turned into a war for revolutionary change in Europe were not realised. Apart from its influence on the internal development of Russia, it brought about no significant changes in the social and political structure of the European states. The question of the national independence of the peoples subject to the Ottoman Empire also remained unsolved. Nor did the war resolve the contradictions which existed between the European powers on the Eastern and other questions. The Treaty of Paris in 1856 not only failed to settle the points of dispute, but engendered new, even more bitter conflicts. Marx called it a "sham peace" (see this volume, p. 623).

Many of the journalistic works of Marx and Engels dealt with the effect of the war on the economic and social life in the main European countries. Participation in this large-scale military conflict, they noted, had put the existing anti-popular regimes to a serious test, which revealed their defects and inability to meet the new social requirements. War "puts a nation to the test", wrote Marx in the article "Another British Revelation". "As exposure to the atmosphere reduces all mummies to instant dissolution, so war passes supreme judgment upon social organisations that have outlived their vitality" (see this volume, p. 516).

Marx's main attention was devoted to capitalist Britain, where the contradictions between the bourgeoisie and the proletariat were more developed than in any other country at the time. In the articles "Questions of Finance", "The Commercial and Financial Situation", "The Crisis in England" and others, Marx analysed the state of the British economy. It provided, he stressed, a striking example of the operation of the general economic laws of capitalist society, in particular, the cyclical nature of capitalist production, the inevitable alternation of phases of prosperity and crisis. Marx showed that even within the limits of a given cycle the capitalist economy develops unevenly, in fits and starts, and is subject to the emergence of crisis phenomena. Thus, the period of economic prosperity which began at the end of the 1840s was repeatedly interrupted by stagnation in certain branches of industry and commerce in England, particularly in the textile industry. Marx noted an economic decline in late 1853 and early 1854 and another one in 1855. Analysing the tendencies which he had discovered in the economic life of Britain, and also on the world market, Marx predicted that in the near future Britain would undergo a more serious economic crisis than it had ever experienced before. This prediction was fully borne out in 1857, when the first world economic crisis broke out.

Marx's articles "Palmerston", "The British Constitution", "*The Morning Post* versus Prussia.—The Character of the Whigs and Tories", "The House of Lords and the Duke of York's Monument" and a number of others contain an accurate description of Britain's traditional two-party system under which power was held in turn by the Whigs and Tories. "The British Constitution," Marx wrote, "is indeed nothing but an antiquated, obsolete, out-of-date compromise between the bourgeoisie, which *rules not officially* but in fact in all decisive spheres of civil society, and the landed aristocracy, which *governs officially*" (see this volume, p. 53).

One of the main supports of the regime of the bourgeois-aristocratic oligarchy, Marx pointed out, was the aristocracy's monopoly of the key state offices. In many of his articles Marx showed that the oligarchical political system was an obstacle to the country's progressive development. The debates held in both houses of Parliament on various questions, which Marx closely analysed, showed clearly enough what was the class essence of the British Parliament. He revealed the hypocrisy and cupidity of the representatives of both the main political groupings, the obstacles they raised to the exposure of the scandalous abuses in the various departments of the state machine and to progressive reforms.

An important contribution to his vivid description of the ruling oligarchy was the pamphlet *Lord John Russell* (see this volume, pp. 371-93). It provided an addition to Marx's gallery of portraits of leading nineteenth-century British politicians. In this pamphlet Marx showed that Russell's false, ostentatious liberalism, his political wiliness and time-serving, were fully in keeping with the whole character of the Whigs, that party of careerists who, like the Tories, were striving to strengthen the oligarchical regime, but in doing so showed greater flexibility and a readiness to make certain concessions to the industrial bourgeoisie. The struggle between the Whigs and Tories, Marx pointed out, was merely a quarrel between the two ruling factions of the aristocratic upper crust of the exploiting classes; the differences in their policies were becoming less and less marked. Bitter attacks on the government by one or other party when it was in opposition were a means of removing the rival party from power. Once in power, however, each party continued to follow the political course of its predecessor.

Marx discovered more and more signs of the political disintegration of both the Whig and Tory parties, which he had noted when he first began to write for the *Neue Oder-Zeitung* (see present edition, Vol. 13). It was manifest in the bankruptcy of the political doctrines of these old aristocratic parties, their division into separate groupings, the increasing need to resort to manoeuvres and parliamentary alliances. Political instability was giving rise to the tendency to strengthen the personal power of the head of the government, which Marx noted, in particular, in the policy of Palmerston during the formation of his ministry in 1855 and in following years. In the article "Palmerston" Marx drew attention to the way in which this leader of the Right wing of the Whigs had assured by skilful manoeuvring such a composition of his Cabinet as left all the most important threads of government in his own hands. "This time we have not a Cabinet at all, but Lord Palmerston in lieu of a Cabinet" (see this volume, p. 50).

The phenomena detected by Marx reflected a process that had begun under the influence of the drawing together of the interests of industrial capital and of the landed aristocracy and the commercial and financial magnates—the transformation of the Tories into the party of the big bourgeoisie, the Conservatives, and of the Whigs, around whom the middle and petty bourgeoisie were grouped, into the Liberal party. The latter were soon joined by representatives of the bourgeois opposition—the Free Traders.

In his articles of this period Marx continued his trenchant criticism of the ideology and political positions of the Free Traders, using them to expose the class limitations of bourgeois liberalism as a whole. He again showed the illusions of the Free Traders' argument that capitalism could develop without crises, and exposed their hypocritical protestations about love of peace which concealed the striving of the British bourgeoisie to dominate the world market. The Manchester School, Marx stressed, was striving for peace "in order to wage industrial war at home and abroad" (see this volume, p. 258). Cobden, Bright and the other leaders of the Free Traders, he pointed out, while proclaiming themselves "champions of liberty" and "defenders" of the interests of the masses, in fact supported the cruel exploitation of the working class. Evidence of this was their encroachments on the institution of factory inspectors, who to a certain extent restrained the arbitrariness of employers, and their attempts to repeal the laws which limited the working day for women and children.

In contrast to the false statements of the Free Traders about the "prosperity" of the English workers, Marx made use of reports by factory inspectors to show the terrible working conditions at capitalist factories and the constant growth in the number of industrial accidents, particularly among women and children. "The industrial bulletin of the factory inspectors," he wrote, "is more terrible and more appalling than any of the war bulletins from the Crimea. Women and children provide a regular and sizeable contingent in the list of the wounded and killed" (see this volume, p. 370).

Bourgeois-aristocratic Britain was confronted by the working masses, first and foremost, the English industrial proletariat. Marx followed carefully every manifestation of discontent and revolutionary ferment among the masses both in Britain itself and in its colonies. Thus, in the article "The Buying of Commissions.—News from Australia" he noted that in the Australian state of Victoria resistance had been "initiated by the workers against the monopolists linked with the colonial bureaucracy" (see this volume, p. 65).

Marx, who never ceased to take an interest in the fate of the oppressed Irish people, regarded Ireland, which was the arena of bitter social antagonism, as one of the permanent centres of popular discontent (see the article "Ireland's Revenge").

Opposition tendencies among the various social strata in Britain, including the working class, were also being promoted by David Urquhart and his supporters, who, despite their conservative world outlook, criticised the foreign policy of the ruling oligarchy. Marx continued to attack Urquhart's views in the press. But nevertheless he thought it expedient to devote attention in his articles to the comparatively progressive activity of the committees on foreign affairs set up by Urquhart and his followers, which also included representatives of the workers ("The Late Birmingham Conference", "The Committee at Newcastle-upon-Tyne").

Marx's main attention was directed to the English working-class movement—first and foremost, to the continuing attempts, despite the general decline of Chartism, of the leaders of its revolutionary wing to revive mass political agitation under the banner of the People's Charter. In the articles "Anti-Church Movement.—Demonstration in Hyde Park", "Clashes between the Police and the People.—The Events in the Crimea" Marx noted that the Chartists had succeeded in reviving to a certain extent the political activity of the working class, which found expression in mass popular demonstrations in London in the summer of 1855 against the parliamentary ban on Sunday trading. Marx praised the refusal of Ernest Jones and other Chartists to follow the lead of the bourgeois radicals, instead of which they continued to defend the independent positions of the working class and retain its political progamme in full, in spite of the radicals' intentions to replace the latter with "moderate" demands for administrative and other reforms.

In the article "The Association for Administrative Reform.—People's Charter" Marx explained the historical significance of the Chartist programme, the central point of which was the demand for universal suffrage. Adopting a historical approach to political slogans, he showed that whereas in France and on the Continent in general the demand for universal suffrage did not extend beyond the framework of bourgeois democracy, it had a different significance in England. "There it is regarded as a political question and here, as a social one," Marx noted. In England, where the working class constituted the majority of the population, he pointed out that the implementation of this and other points of the People's Charter could lead to a radical democratic transformation of the whole parliamentary system and the country's political structure by the proletarian masses, which would mean "the assumption of political power as a means of satisfying their social needs" (see this volume, pp. 242, 243). From these arguments it is clear that Marx at that time admitted the possibility of the English proletariat coming to power by peaceful means, unlike the countries on the Continent where, in his opinion, the working class could triumph only as a result of the forcible destruction of a military-bureaucratic state machine.

The Chartists' attempts to instil revolutionary energy in the English proletarian masses could not, however, arrest the decline of the Chartist movement, which was increasingly on the wane. This was due to the peculiarities of the development of British capitalism. The British bourgeoisie had succeeded by means of colonial conquests and profits and monopolies on the world market in chaining a significant section of the higher-paid skilled workers to the capitalist system, thereby splitting the working class and strengthening reformist tendencies in the British working-class movement. Nevertheless right up to the end Marx never tired of encouraging his Chartist friends and urging them not to give way to difficulties and to keep faith in the coming proletarian revolution.

On April 14, 1856 at a banquet in honour of the fourth anniversary of the publication of *The People's Paper* Marx delivered a speech full of revolutionary optimism. He spoke of the inevitable collapse of capitalism and the world historic mission of the working class as the social force called upon to overthrow the exploiting system. "History is the judge—its executioner, the proletarian" (see this volume, p. 656).

Continuing to regard the struggle against Bonapartism as one of the most important tasks of the working class and revolutionary democracy, Marx and Engels sought to expose in their articles the close connection between the Bonapartist state's foreign and domestic policy. "It would be easy to demonstrate," we read in the article "Criticism of the French Conduct of the War" by Marx and Engels, "that the pretentious mediocrity with which the Second Empire is conducting this war is reflected in its internal administration, that here, too, semblance has taken the place of essence, and that the 'economic' campaigns were in no way any more successful than the military ones" (see this volume, p. 93). In this article, and also in the articles "Fate of the Great Adventurer", "Napoleon's Last Dodge", "The Local War.—Debate on Administrative Reform.—Report of the Roebuck Committee", "The American Difficulty.—Affairs of France" and others, Marx and Engels stressed that military adventurism was an intrinsic feature of Bonapartist policy, that conquest and aggression were one of the principles on which the political rule of the Bonapartist circles in France itself rested.

Marx's article "The France of Bonaparte the Little" revealed the glaring contrast between official France, which was recklessly squandering the nation's wealth, and the France of the people, to whom the Bonapartist regime had brought poverty and police repression. In the heart of this France of the people, Marx emphasised, revolutionary ferment was maturing against the Bonapartist dictatorship, which betokened "the downfall of the Empire of Agio" (see this volume, p. 620). In the articles "The Reports of Generals Simpson, Pélissier and Niel" and "The Bank of France.—Reinforcements to the Crimea.—The New Field-Marshals", Marx and Engels noted the deterioration of the political situation in France, drawing attention to the signs of growth in the revolutionary mood of the working class, the students and other strata of the population, and to the discontent displayed by a certain section of the bourgeoisie and even of the army, which had up till then served as a bulwark of the Second Empire.

Marx and Engels continued to analyse in the press the events in Prussia, Austria and Tsarist Russia. The Crimean War had exposed the profound contradictions between these states and at the same time confirmed the common counter-revolutionary aims of their ruling circles, united by the attempt to preserve intact the reactionary systems within each of these countries and the corresponding pattern of international relations. Thus, as Marx repeatedly pointed out, the neutrality in the war proclaimed by the Prussian Government was dictated by fear of the revolutionary consequences of transferring the theatre of military operations to Central Europe. In the article "Prussia", Marx dealt with the political system of the Prussian monarchy, in which the formally proclaimed constitution served merely as a cover for the continuation of absolutism and its product—an all-powerful bureaucracy. He notes the lack of rights of the majority of the population, the oppression of the peasantry which remained, as before, "under the direct yoke of the nobility", both administratively and judicially (see this volume, p. 661). At the same time Marx pointed to the rapid growth of industry and commerce, and the unprecedented wealth of the Prussian propertied classes—the Junkers and the bourgeoisie. But the latter remained, as always, politically passive and servile, which confirmed the opinion expressed by Marx and Engels as early as 1848-49 that the German bourgeoisie was incapable of playing a leading role in the struggle for radical bourgeois-democratic demands.

As to the ruling circles in the Austrian Empire, they were striving to obtain Turkish possessions in Europe, and so adopted a hostile attitude towards Russia as their main rival in the Balkans. In his reports "On the Critique of Austrian Policy in the Crimean Campaign" and "Austria and the War" Marx quoted documents that revealed the duplicity of the Austrian government's foreign policy. Marx and Engels saw the cause of this in the internal weakness of the reactionary Habsburg Empire, which stemmed not only from the backwardness of its social system, but also from profound national antagonisms. Reaping the fruits of the centuries-old oppression of the peoples who made up the Empire and fanning national enmity between them, the rulers of the Austrian Empire were in constant fear of an upsurge of the national liberation movements. It was these fears that held them back from open intervention in the military conflict.

Quoting information in their articles about the situation in Russia, Marx and Engels drew attention to the difficulties experienced by the Tsarist autocracy in the course of the war, the exhaustion of its material resources, which were in any case limited by the serf system and the economic backwardness it engendered (see Engels' article "The State of the War" and other items). As Marx and Engels soon realised, the consequences of the Crimean War had a serious effect on the internal development of the Russian Empire. The defeat sustained by Tsarism, which showed, in the words of Lenin "the rottenness and impotence of feudal Russia" (V. I. Lenin, *Collected Works*, Vol. 17, p. 121), created the prerequisites for the maturing of a revolutionary situation in the country, which compelled the ruling classes to introduce reforms. "The Russian war of 1854-55," Marx remarked in a letter to Engels of October 8, 1858, "...has ... obviously hastened the present turn of events in Russia" (see present edition, Vol. 40). Later, in 1871, in a draft of *The Civil War in France* Marx again emphasised the connection between the abolition of serfdom in Russia in 1861 and other transformations. The Crimean War revealed the profound crisis of the whole social and political system of Tsarist Russia, even though it had "saved its honour by the defence of Sevastopol and dazzled foreign states by its diplomatic triumphs in Paris".

Marx and Engels continued throughout the final period of the war to point out that, despite numerous military defeats, Tsarist despotism still represented a serious threat to the European working-class and democratic movement. As one might have expected, they remarked, the changes on the Tsarist throne did not lead to any substantial changes in the foreign policy of the Russian autocracy. Nicholas I's successor Alexander II and his government did not renounce aggressive intentions—in particular, the attempts to exploit Pan-Slavist propaganda as an instrument of aggrandizement.

Engels' article "Germany and Pan-Slavism", together with its English versions, "The European Struggle" and "Austria's Weakness", showed how reactionary were current Pan-Slavist ideas, and Alexander II's Pan-Slavist sentiments. The dissemination of these ideas by the monarchistic elements of certain Slavonic national movements, Engels noted, played into the hands of the Habsburg monarchy and Russian Tsarism in their struggle against the revolution in Germany and Hungary in 1848-49.

Marx and Engels resolutely attacked all nationalistic ideology, whatever form it took, whether Pan-Germanism, Pan-Slavism, or any other form. They stressed that this ideology fanned national differences, that it was deeply alien to the interests of democratic development and the national and social liberation of all peoples, including the Slav peoples.

In his polemic with Pan-Slavism, however, Engels repeated certain theses which have not been borne out by history, about the alleged loss by a number of Slav peoples who formed part of the Austrian Empire (Czechs, Slovaks, and others) of the ability to lead an independent national existence—theses which were expressed by him earlier in the works "Democratic Pan-Slavism" and *Revolution and Counter-Revolution in Germany* (on this see the prefaces to Volumes 8 and 11 of the present edition). The process of social development, which up to the 1860s was dominated by tendencies towards centralisation, the creation of large states, had not yet provided sufficient objective evidence for revising this mistaken view. It was only subsequently that another historical tendency manifested itself fully, namely, the striving of oppressed small peoples, including the Slav peoples of the Austrian Empire, for national independence, and their ability not only to create their own states but also to march in the van of social progress.

The present volume contains a large number of military articles by Engels, who regularly analysed the whole course of the Crimean War, and also his military survey *The Armies of Europe*. These works constitute an important part of his studies on military theory.

Although based on contemporary reports primarily in the English and French press, which contained many omissions and inaccuracies, Engels' military reviews show great insight and a profound understanding of the nature of the military operations in the various theatres of the war—the Caucasus, the Crimea and the Baltic—and of the decisive role of the siege and defence of Sevastopol in the overall course of the military operations, which by then had reached culmination point. Engels found increasing confirmation in the development of the military events of his basic propositions on the theory of warfare, the dependence of warfare on the social and political system, the interconnection between military strategy and the policy of the ruling classes, and the influence of the general state of the organisation of the armed forces on the mode of waging war. He held that the organisation of the army was an integral part of the system of state administration and reflected its characteristic class features.

Thus in the articles "The Struggle in the Crimea", "The War that Looms on Europe", "The Punishment of the Ranks" and others Engels shows the connection between the crude blunders of the British military command, the wretched state of the British expeditionary forces and the conservatism of the British military system as such. He noted the routine nature of the organisation of the British army, the caste spirit and favouritism that prevailed in the War Office, the quartermaster service and the officer corps, the practice of selling commissions and other defects engendered by the oligarchical political regime. The article "The Reports of Generals Simpson, Pélissier and Niel" by Marx and Engels states openly that "the miserable leadership of the British Army is the inevitable result of rule by the antiquated oligarchy" (this volume, p. 542).

In many articles Engels points to the pernicious consequences for the French and Allied armed forces of interference by the ruling clique of the Second Empire and Emperor Napoleon III himself in the conduct of military operations, and also of the effect of the counter-revolutionary aims for which the Bonapartist circles sought to use the army. Under pressure from Paris the operations by the Allied troops were often determined not by military, but by totally unrelated political and dynastic considerations (see the article "From Sevastopol" and others).

Describing the armed forces of Tsarist Russia, in the article "The Russian Army", the relevant section of *The Armies of Europe* and in other works, Engels noted the weakness of the economic base and the archaic nature of the social base of the Tsarist military system. The technological backwardness of the Tsarist army, he emphasised, the almost total absence of modern means of transport, the old-fashioned methods of recruiting and training troops, the substitution of parade-ground drilling for proper military training, the length of military service, the corruption and embezzlement of public funds in the military and civilian administration—all this was the product of the social and political order of the Russia of autocracy and serfdom.

At the same time Engels constantly emphasised the military qualities of the rank and file participants in the armed struggle. He paid tribute to the initiative and élan of the French officers and men, and the stamina and resolve of the English in battle. He invariably spoke with respect of the traditional courage of the Russian soldier. "The Russian soldier is one of the bravest men in Europe", he wrote in *The Armies of Europe* (see this volume, p. 444).

However, the description of the Russian army which Engels gave in these and other works, for all the aptness of his assessment of the state of the army in the Russia of serfdom, was influenced by his sources of information at that time, the anti-Russian bias of the West European press and the tendentious works of Western historians. This, and to a certain extent also the political slant of his articles against Russian Tsarism, explains the presence in his works at that time of certain exaggerations and one-sided opinions, which he revised to a large extent in his later works (*Po and Rhine,* see this edition, Volume 16, and others). Such opinions include, in particular, his statements on the passivity of Russian soldiers, the special role of foreigners in the Russian army due to a lack of native talent, and that Russia in the past had triumphed only over weak opponents and suffered defeat from those equal to it in strength.

It must be said, however, that even though he possessed biased information, Engels assessed the operations of the belligerent powers objectively in the overwhelming majority of cases. This is demonstrated most strikingly by his many articles on the heroic eleven-month defence of Sevastopol by Russian troops. In the articles "The Siege of Sevastopol", "A Battle at Sevastopol" and others, the brilliant operations of the defenders, the skill of the military engineers of the Sevastopol garrison, including the head of the engineering service Todtleben, and the excellent arrangement of the line of fire are contrasted by Engels with the Allied siege operations. He rates the latter very low, emphasising that "not a single siege can be shown in the annals of war, since that of Troy, carried on with such a degree of incoherence and stupidity" (see this volume, p. 155).

Noting the heroism and military fervour of the defenders of the Russian fortress, Engels praised their successful sorties in which they acted "with great skill combined with their usual tenacity" (see this volume, p. 116). He regarded as unprecedented in the history of warfare the creation by the besieged garrison during the defence of new fortifications which they set up in front of the first line, and commented most favourably on the Russians' use of a tiered arrangement of batteries which enabled them to make good use of the terrain.

In the article "Progress of the War" Engels sums up his assessments of the operations by the organisers of and participants in the defence of Sevastopol as follows. "The justness and rapidity of glance—the promptness, boldness, and faultlessness of execution, which the Russian engineers have shown in throwing up their lines around Sevastopol—the indefatigable attention with which every weak point was protected as soon as discovered by the enemy—the excellent arrangement of the line of fire, so as to concentrate a force, superior to that of the besiegers, upon any given point of the ground in front—the preparation of a second, third and fourth line of fortifications in rear of the first—in short, the whole conduct of this defense has been classic" (see this volume, pp. 134-35). Later Engels often returned to the analysis of the Sevastopol campaign (in his articles on the national liberation uprising in India of 1857-59 and in his "Notes on the War" in 1870-71), regarding it as an outstanding example of active defence.

The experience of the defence of Sevastopol enabled Engels to make important generalisations in his articles on the art of warfare, especially with respect to the significance of fortresses in nineteenth-century warfare and their use in conjunction with field armies. From his analysis of other battles of the Crimean War and its general lessons he drew conclusions concerning the advantages of an offensive strategy and the concentration of forces in inflicting the main blow on the enemy's principal groupings, and on the often ephemeral nature of the surprise factor in cases when the consolidation and development of successes achieved in such a way are not ensured by corresponding means, etc.

In short, Engels in his work *The Armies of Europe* gave a broad picture of the level of development of warfare and the state of the armed forces in the middle of the nineteenth century. He analysed the equipment, recruiting method and special tactics of the armies of the different states to show the operation in this sphere of the basic laws of social development. This was to apply the basic principles of historical materialism by showing how the fighting efficiency of an army is determined primarily by the economy and the social and political system of the given country. Thus Engels pointed out that in the Prussian army, for example, the promising principle of recruiting and training of troops by means of a comparatively short period of military service for all those capable of it was frustrated by the representatives of the reactionary political system in order to have a "disposable and reliable army to be used, in case of need, against disturbances at home" (see this volume, p. 433). Again, Engels stressed that the fanning of national strife characteristic of the Habsburg monarchy was also reflected in the Austrian army and had an adverse effect on its fighting efficiency. Engels similarly noted the influence of the surviving feudal relations on the armies of Russia, Turkey and a number of other states. Stressing that the general laws of the evolution of the armed forces manifest themselves in each country in a specific form, Engels showed the importance of national characteristics and traditions in the development of each army. At the same time he pointed out that the general progress of military technology and improvements introduced into warfare induce each army to take into account and use the experience of all the others. An important place in his work is occupied by criticism of the nationalistic tendencies in the treatment of military history by the ruling classes, in particular, in the thesis about the invincibility of this or that army at all times.

* * *

The present volume contains 135 works by Marx and Engels. Seventy-six of the articles are published in English for the first time (six of them have been published in English in part). These include the great majority of articles published in the *Neue Oder-Zeitung*, among them versions of items in the *New-York Daily Tribune* which Marx adapted for the German newspaper, and also the rough draft of Engels' "Crimean War", which is included in the section "From the Preparatory Materials". Thirty-seven of the articles contained in the present volume have not been reproduced in English since their first publication in English and American newspapers. Previous English publications of individual articles by Marx and Engels, in particular in *The Eastern Question*, London, 1897, are indicated in the notes.

In the absence of Marx's notebook for this period with entries concerning the dispatching of items to New York, authorship of articles by Marx and Engels in the *New-York Tribune*, which were usually printed anonymously, has been established mainly on the basis of information contained in correspondence, simultaneous publication in the European and American press, and peculiarities of content and style. During preparation of the articles the date when they were written was checked and most of the sources used by the authors were established.

Discrepancies of substance between the versions of the articles published simultaneously in the *New-York Daily Tribune* and the

Neue Oder-Zeitung are indicated in the footnotes. The same applies to other parallel publications (in the *New-York Daily Tribune* and *The People's Paper*, Engels' work *The Armies of Europe* which was published in *Putnam's Monthly* and the extracts from it that were translated into German by Marx for the *Neue Oder-Zeitung*, and other items). When the versions differ considerably, their texts are given in full. In quoting, Marx sometimes gives a free rendering rather than the exact words of the source. In the present edition quotations are given in the form in which they occur in Marx's text.

Misprints in quotations, proper names, geographical names, figures, dates, etc., discovered during the preparation of the present volume have been corrected (usually silently) on the basis of the sources used by Marx and Engels.

In the case of newspaper articles without a title, or of a number of those which formed part of a series, a heading or number has been provided by the editors in square brackets.

The volume was compiled, the text prepared and the preface and notes written by Stanislav Nikonenko and edited by Lev Golman (Institute of Marxism-Leninism of the CC CPSU). The name index, the index of periodicals and the glossary of geographical names were compiled by Natalia Martynova, the subject index by Marlen Arzumanov, and the index of quoted and mentioned literature by Yevgenia Dakhina (Institute of Marxism-Leninism of the CC CPSU).

The translations were made by Susanne Flatauer, Hugh Rodwell, Peter and Betty Ross, Barbara Ruhemann, Barrie Selman, Christopher Upward, Joan and Trevor Walmsley (Lawrence and Wishart) and Salo Ryazanskaya (Progress Publishers), and edited by Nicholas Jacobs, Frida Knight, Sheila Lynd (Lawrence and Wishart), Salo Ryazanskaya, Tatyana Grishina, Natalia Karmanova and Victor Schnittke (Progress Publishers), and Vladimir Mosolov, scientific editor (Institute of Marxism-Leninism of the CC CPSU).

The volume was prepared for the press by the editors Yelena Kalinina, Alla Varavitskaya and Lyudgarda Zubrilova (Progress Publishers).

KARL MARX
and
FREDERICK ENGELS

WORKS

February 1855-April 1856

New-York Daily Tribune.

VOL. XIV......No 4.323 NEW-YORK. MONDAY. FEBRUARY 26. 1855. PRICE TWO CENTS.

Frederick Engels

THE STRUGGLE IN THE CRIMEA [1]

Immediately after the battle of the Alma,[2] and the march of the Allies on Balaklava, we expressed the opinion that the ultimate result of the Crimean campaign must depend on which of the contending parties should first bring up new forces sufficient to render it superior to its antagonist in numbers and efficiency.[a] The aspect of affairs has, since then, greatly altered, and many illusions have been destroyed; but, throughout the whole time, both the Russians and the Allies have been engaged in a sort of steeple-chase at reenforcements, and, in this effort, we are compelled to say that the Russians have the advantage. In spite of all the boasted improvements in mechanical skill and the means of transport, three or five hundred miles of road are still far easier traversed by an army of Russian barbarians than two thousand miles of sea by an army of highly-civilized French and English—especially when the latter make it a point to neglect all the advantages which their high civilization places at their disposal, and when the Russian barbarians can afford to lose two men to the Allies' one, without impairing their ultimate superiority.

But what can be in store for the Allies when one of their armies—the British—despairing of being destroyed by the Russians, deliberately sets about destroying itself with a systematic consistency, an eagerness, and a success which beat all its former achievements in any line whatever? Yet such is the case. The British force, we are now informed, has ceased to exist as an army. There are a few thousand men left, under arms, out of 54,000,

[a] See Engels' article "The Battle of the Alma" (present edition, Vol. 13, pp. 492-97).—*Ed.*

but they themselves are reported "fit for duty" merely because there is no hospital-room for them to die in. Of the French, some 50,000 may be still under arms, out of twice that number; and, at all events, they have managed to keep in a serviceable state at least five times as many, in proportion, as the British. But what are fifty or sixty thousand men to hold the Heracleatic Chersonese the winter through; to keep Sevastopol blockaded on the south side; to defend the trenches, and—what may be left of them—to take the offensive in spring?

For the present, the British have ceased to send reenforcements. In fact Raglan, despairing of his army, does not appear to wish for any, not knowing how to feed, house and employ even what is left to him. The French may be preparing a fresh set of divisions for embarkation in March, but they have plenty to do to prepare against the eventuality of a great continental spring campaign, and there are ten chances to one that what they send will either be too weak or come too late. To remedy this state of things two steps have been taken, both of which denote the utter helplessness of the Allies to avert the fate which seems inevitably, though slowly, to approach their armies in the Crimea. First, in order to redress the colossal blunder of having attempted this expedition four months too late, they commit the incommensurably greater blunder of sending to the Crimea, four months after their own arrival, and in the depth of winter, the only remnant of a decent army which Turkey still possesses. That army which was already being ruined and dissolving itself at Shumla under the neglect, incapacity and corruption of the Turkish Government, once landed in the Crimea, will melt away, by cold and hunger, at a ratio which will put to the blush even the achievements of the English War-Office in this branch—that is, if the Russians have the sense to leave the Turks, for a time, to themselves, without attacking them. If the weather permits an attack they will be destroyed at once, though at a greater cost to the Russians, and with hardly any advantage, except a moral one.

Then the Allies have taken into their pay—for that is the only way to express it—fifteen to twenty thousand Piedmontese,[3] who are to fill up the thinned ranks of the British army, and to be fed by the British Commissariat. The Piedmontese showed themselves brave and good soldiers in 1848 and '49. Being mostly mountaineers, they possess an infantry which, for skirmishing and fighting in broken ground, is naturally adapted in even a higher degree than the French, while the plains of the Po furnish cavalry soldiers whose tall, well-proportioned stature reminds one of the crack regiments of British horse. They have, besides, not passed through the severe campaigns of the revolution without profit. There is no doubt that these two Piedmontese divisions will turn out as good a "foreign legion" as will figure in this war. But what are these light-footed, agile, handy little fellows to do under the command of an old British martinet,[a] who has no idea of maneuvering, and who expects nothing from his soldiers but the dogged stubbornness which is the glory and at the same time the only military quality of the British soldier? They will be placed in positions unsuited to their mode of fighting; they will be prevented from doing what they are fit for, while they will be expected to do things which no sensible man would ever set them to. To lead a British army in that senseless, point-blank, stupid way to the slaughter-house, as was done at the Alma, may be the shortest way to make them settle the business before them. The old Duke[b] generally took matters quite as easy. German troops may be made to do the same thing, although the high military education of German officers will not stand such want of generalship in the long run. But to attempt such things with a French, Italian or Spanish army—with troops essentially fitted for light-infantry duty, for maneuvering, for taking advantage of the ground—with troops whose efficiency, in a great measure, is made up by the agility and quick glance of every individual soldier—such a clumsy system of warfare will never do. The poor Piedmontese, however, will probably be spared the trial of fighting in the English way. They are to be fed by that notorious body, the British Commissariat, which could never feed anybody but themselves. Thus they will share the fate of the fresh arrivals of British troops. Like them, they will die at the rate of a hundred a week, and furnish three times that number to the hospitals. If Lord Raglan thinks that the Piedmontese will stand his and his Commissaries' incapacity as quietly as the British troops, he will find himself sadly mistaken. There are none but British and Russians who would remain in submission under such circumstances; and, we must say, it is not to the credit of their national character.

The probable development of this melancholy campaign—as melancholy and bleak as the muddy plateau of Sevastopol—will be this: The Russians, when fully concentrated, and when the weather permits, will probably attack the Turks of Omer Pasha

[a] Raglan.—*Ed.*
[b] Wellington.—*Ed.*

first. This is expected by British, French and Turks, so well aware are they of the unenviable position assigned to the latter; it shows, at all events, that the Turks are sent to the North with open eyes; and no better proof of the desperate condition of the Allies can be conceived than is contained in this involuntary admission of their own Generals. That the Turks will be beaten may be taken for certain. Then what will be the fate of the allied and Piedmontese armies? The bluster about an assault on Sevastopol is now pretty much abandoned. On this head we find in the London *Times* of Feb. 6, a letter from Col. E. Napier, to the effect that if the Allies attack the south side of Sevastopol, they will most likely get into it; but they will be pounded into dust by the overwhelming fire of the north forts and batteries, and at the same time besieged by the Russian army in the field. That army, he says, should first have been defeated, and then both the north and south sides of the place invested. As an instance in point, he recalls the fact that the Duke of Wellington twice raised the siege of Badajoz, in order to march against a relieving army.[4] Col. Napier is quite right, and the *Tribune* said quite as much, at the time of the famous flank march to Balaklava.[a] As to the Allies getting into Sevastopol, however, he appears to overlook the peculiar nature of the Russian defenses, which make it impossible to carry the place at one single assault. There are first, outworks, then the main rampart, and behind this the buildings of the town converted into redoubts; streets barricaded, squares of houses loopholed; and, finally, the loopholed rear walls of the strand-forts, every one of which, in succession, will require a separate attack—perhaps a separate siege, and even mining operations. But beside all this, the successful sorties of the Russians of late have sufficiently proved that the town has been approached to a point where the forces of the opponents are fully balanced, and the attack deprived of any superiority except in point of artillery. As long as sorties cannot be made impossible, all idea of an assault is preposterous; the besieger who cannot confine the besieged to the space of the actual fortress, is much less able to take that fortress by a hand-to-hand encounter.

Thus, the besiegers will continue to vegetate in their camp. Confined to it by weakness and the Russian army in the field, they will continue to melt away, while the Russians are bringing up

---

[a] Presumably a reference to Engels' article "The Siege of Sevastopol" published in the *New-York Daily Tribune* on November 15, 1854 (see present edition, Vol. 13, pp. 505-09).—*Ed.*

fresh forces; and unless the new British Ministry brings into play some quite unexpected resources, the day must come when British, French, Piedmontese and Turks are swept from Crimean soil.

Written about February 9, 1855

First published in the *New-York Daily Tribune*, No. 4323, February 26, 1855 as a leading article

Reproduced from the newspaper

Neue Oder-Zeitung.

Mittagblatt. | In Breslau bei der Expedition und den Commandisten pr. Quartal 1 Thaler 20 Sgr. | Breslau, Montag, den 12. Februar 1855. | In Preußen bei allen königlichen Post-Anstalten pr. Quartal 2 Thaler. | № 71.

Karl Marx and Frederick Engels

PALMERSTON.—THE ARMY[5]

London, February 9. Following their acceptance of new ministerial posts, Palmerston and Sidney Herbert have to submit to the formality of re-election to their parliamentary seats. For this reason both Houses were yesterday adjourned for a week. The statements by Lord Derby and the Marquis of Lansdowne in the House of Lords concerning the secret history of the ministerial crisis merely retold an oft-told tale.[a] The sole item of importance was a remark by Derby which contained the key to Lord Palmerston's position. Palmerston is known to have no parliamentary party behind him, or any clique masquerading under that name. Whigs, Tories and Peelites[6] regard him with equal suspicion. The Manchester School[7] is in open conflict with him. His personal supporters among the Mayfair Radicals[8] (as distinct from the Manchester Radicals) number a dozen at the most. Who and what, then, enables him to impose himself on the Crown and on Parliament? His popularity? No more so than unpopularity prevented Gladstone, Herbert, Graham and Clarendon from again seizing the helm of state. Or is the man who never belonged to a party, served all of them alternately, deserted them all in turn and invariably held the balance between them, is he the natural leader of defunct parties which seek to stem the tide of history by forming a coalition? This fact proves nothing at the *present* moment, since it was insufficient to put Palmerston rather than Aberdeen at the head of the coalition in 1852.

Derby has supplied the answer to the riddle. Palmerston is evidently Bonaparte's friend. His premature recognition of the

---

[a] Derby's and Lansdowne's speeches in the House of Lords on February 8, 1855 were reported in *The Times,* No. 21973, February 9, 1855.—*Ed.*

coup d'état in December 1851 was then ostensibly the reason for his expulsion from the Whig Ministry.[9] Bonaparte therefore regards him as *persona grata*, and a trustworthy man. The alliance with Bonaparte is therefore decisive at the moment. Palmerston has thus used foreign affairs to tip the balance of ministerial groupings—and not for the first time, as closer examination of the history of British ministries between 1830 and 1852 would show.

Since at present the situation of the Crimean army can no longer be exploited for the purpose of cabinet intrigues, Lord John Russell went back on his pessimistic opinion in yesterday's sitting in the Commons, allowed the strength of the British army to grow by some 10,000 men and exchanged congratulations with the God-fearing Gladstone.[a] Despite this "parliamentary resurrection" of the British army, there can be no doubt that at the present moment it has ceased to exist as an army. Some few thousand are still listed as "fit for service" because there is no room in the hospitals to receive them. Out of 100,000 the French still number some 50,000, but what are 50,000 or 60,000 men to hold Heracleatic Chersonese through the winter, to blockade the south side of Sevastopol, to defend the trenches and to take the offensive in the spring with those who are left? The French may hold in readiness fresh divisions for embarkation in March, but they are busy preparing for a spring campaign on the continent, and there is every probability that their shipments will be too few or will arrive too late.

That the English and French governments are helpless, indeed have given up the army in the Crimea for lost, is apparent from the two measures to which they have resorted in order to remedy their misfortunes.

In order to make good the error of having undertaken the expedition four months too late, they are committing the incomparably greater error of sending to the Crimea, the only remnants of the Turkish army that are still serviceable, four months after their own arrival and in mid-winter. This army, already broken and in the process of disintegration at Shumla as a consequence of the neglect, incompetence and corruption of the Turkish government, will in the Crimea melt away with cold and hunger to an extent which will even surpass British achievements in this field.

---

[a] Lord John Russell's speech in the House of Commons on February 8, 1855. *The Times*, No. 21973, February 9, 1855.—*Ed.*

As soon as the Russians have attained their full concentration and the weather permits field operations, they will probably first attack the Turks under Omer Pasha. This is expected by the British and French. Thus conscious are they of the unenviable position they have assigned to them. Thus clearly do they show that the strategic error of now throwing the Turks in on the northern side was committed with open eyes. The Turks would only be able to save themselves from ultimate destruction by the most incomprehensible errors on the part of the Russians.

Secondly, the Anglo-French have hired 15,000 Piedmontese for the purpose of swelling the sparse ranks of the British; they are to be fed by the British Commissariat. In 1848 and 1849 the Piedmontese showed themselves to be brave and good soldiers. For the most part mountain-dwellers, their infantry surpasses even the French in skirmishing, sniping and fighting on broken terrain. The plains of the Po on the other hand have produced a cavalry which bears comparison with the British Horse Guards. Finally, they have had a hard schooling in the most recent revolutionary campaigns. These fleet-footed, mobile, adroit little fellows are fit for anything, but not to be British soldiers, which is what they are to be turned into, nor for the direct, ponderous frontal attacks which are the only tactics Raglan knows. And on top of that, to be fed by a British Commissariat whose only previous experience was of feeding itself! The 15,000 Piedmontese will therefore probably prove to be a further blunder.

British reinforcements have been suspended for the present. Raglan himself appears to be refusing them, as he cannot even cope with the remnants he still has. It is hardly believable that the more the British camp is afflicted with disease, overwork and lack of rest, the more prevalent becomes the admirable practice of corporal punishment. Men who are fit only to be sent to hospital, who for weeks have slept and been on duty in wet clothes and on wet ground and have borne all this with almost superhuman tenacity—if these men are caught dozing in the trenches, they are treated to the cat-o'-nine-tails and the birch. "Fifty strokes for every vagabond!"—that is the only strategic order that Lord Raglan occasionally issues. Is it any wonder then that the soldiers of the perpetrator of the famous "flanking-march" to Balaklava follow suit and evade the birch with a "flanking-march" to the Russians? Desertions to the Russian camp are becoming more numerous every day, as *The Times* correspondent reported.[a]

---

[a] Report by W. H. Russell in *The Times*, No. 21971, February 7, 1855.—*Ed.*

All the big talk about storming Sevastopol has of course ceased. The Russian army would first have to be beaten in the field. Thus Wellington twice raised the siege of Badajoz to march against a relief army. We have furthermore already seen that the newly-erected Russian defence works make it impossible for the place to be taken by storm.[a] Finally, the most recent Russian sorties prove that the allied army is at present superior to the Russians only in artillery. As long as sorties cannot be prevented, any idea of storming is absurd; besiegers who are incapable of confining the besieged to the area of the actual fortress are even less capable of seizing the fortress in hand-to-hand combat. Thus the besiegers will continue to vegetate, confined to their camp by their own weakness and by the Russian army in the field. They will continue to melt away, whilst the Russians bring up fresh forces. The prelude to the European war being enacted in the Crimea will end with the destruction of the allied troops unless some completely unexpected resources, which cannot be foreseen, are discovered.

Written on February 9, 1855

First published in the *Neue Oder-Zeitung*, No. 71, February 12, 1855

Marked with the sign ×

Printed according to the newspaper

Published in English for the first time

[a] A reference to Engels' article "Critical Observations on the Siege of Sevastopol" (see present edition, Vol. 13, pp. 593-95).—*Ed.*

Karl Marx

FROM PARLIAMENT.
[—GLADSTONE AT THE DISPATCH-BOX]

London, February 10. Gladstone, Chancellor of the Exchequer of dogmatism and Duns Scotus of finance, has provided a further demonstration of the old saying that faith moves mountains. By faith, Gladstone has resurrected the dead, and by faith increased the strength of the British army in the Crimea from 11,000 to 30,000 men.[a] He is demanding the same faith from Parliament. Unfortunately the report from Dr. Hall, head of the medical department in the camp at Sevastopol, has just arrived.[b] Not only has the 63rd Regiment entirely vanished, according to this report, and of the 46th, which left Britain last November 1,000 men strong, only 30 are still fit for service, but Dr. Hall declares that half of the troops still on active service should be in hospital and that there are at most 5,000-6,000 men really fit for service in camp. Anyone who is familiar with the tricks performed by pious apologists will not doubt that, like Falstaff, Gladstone will turn 6,000 rogues in buckram[c] into 30,000. Has he not already told us in last Thursday's sitting that the two estimates arose from different points of view, e.g. the minimisers of the army in the Crimea were not counting the cavalry as he was, as though there had been any cavalry worth mentioning since the battle of Balaklava.[10] For Gladstone it is a simple matter to count in those who are "not there". It would be hard to outdo the unction with which in last Thursday's sitting he concluded his "budget" on the

---

[a] Gladstone's speech in the House of Commons on February 8, 1855. *The Times*, No. 21973, February 9, 1855.—*Ed.*

[b] Published in *The Times*, No. 21972, February 8, 1855.—*Ed.*

[c] Shakespeare, *Henry IV*, Part I, Act II, Scene 4.—*Ed.*

strength of the army—in which every debit figures as credit and every deficit as surplus—saying that "he forgave the opponents of the government their exaggerations". It would be equally hard to outdo the tone and posture with which he exhorted the Members of Parliament not to let themselves be carried away by "emotions". To bear the woes of *others* with humility and equanimity—so runs the God-fearing Gladstone's motto.

Written on February 10, 1855

First published in the *Neue Oder-Zeitung*, No. 73, February 13, 1855

Marked with the sign ×

Printed according to the newspaper

Published in English for the first time

Karl Marx

LORD PALMERSTON[11]

[*Neue Oder-Zeitung*, No. 79, February 16, 1855]

London, February 12. Lord Palmerston is incontestably the most interesting phenomenon of official England. Although an old man, and almost uninterruptedly upon the public stage since 1807, he has contrived to remain news and to keep alive all the hopes commonly associated with promising and untried youth. With one foot in the grave, he is supposed to be still on the threshold of his true career. Were he to die tomorrow, all England would be surprised to learn that he had been a Minister for half a century. Though he is not a universal statesman, he is certainly a universal actor—equally successful in the heroic and the comic, the sublime and the vulgar style, in tragedy and in farce, although the last is, perhaps, better attuned to his nature. He is not a first-class orator, but is accomplished in debate. With a wonderful memory, great experience, consummate tact, never-failing presence of mind, refined flexibility and the most intimate knowledge of parliamentary artifices, intrigues, parties and personalities, he handles difficult cases with winsome ease, adapting himself to the prejudices of each audience in turn, shielded against all surprise by his nonchalance, against all self-betrayal by his egoistical facility, against impassioned ebullitions by his profound frivolity and aristocratic indifference. His happy wit enables him to insinuate himself with all and sundry. Because he always remains cool-headed, he impresses hot-headed opponents. If a general standpoint be wanting, he is ever prepared to spin a web of elegant generalities. If incapable of mastering a subject, he contrives to toy with it. If afraid to join issue with a powerful foe, he contrives to improvise a weak one.

Submitting to foreign influence in practice, he combats it in words. Since he has inherited from Canning—who, however, warned against him on his death-bed—England's mission of disseminating constitutional propaganda on the Continent, he never, of course, lacks a theme with which to flatter national prejudice while simultaneously keeping alive the jealous suspicions of foreign powers. Having thus conveniently become the *bête noire* of continental courts, he could hardly fail to figure at home as a "truly English Minister". Although originally a Tory, he has succeeded in introducing into his conduct of foreign affairs all those "shams"[a] and contradictions that constitute the essence of Whiggism. He contrives to reconcile democratic phraseology with oligarchic views; to offset the bourgeoisie and their advocacy of peace with the overbearing language of England's aristocratic past; to seem an aggressor when he assents and a defender when he betrays; to spare an ostensible enemy and embitter an alleged ally; to be at the decisive moment of the dispute on the side of the stronger against the weak, and to utter courageous words in the very act of turning tail.

Accused by one side of being in Russia's pay, he is suspected by the other of Carbonarism.[12] If, in 1848, he had to defend himself in Parliament against a motion calling for his impeachment for acting in collusion with Russia, he had the satisfaction in 1850 of being the object of a conspiracy between foreign embassies which succeeded in the House of Lords but came to grief in the House of Commons.[13] When he betrayed foreign nations, it was always done with extreme courtesy. While the oppressors could always count on his active support, the oppressed never wanted for the pageantry of his noble rhetoric. Poles, Italians, Hungarians, etc., invariably found him at the helm when they were vanquished, but their conquerors always suspected him of having conspired with the victims he had allowed them to make. Having him for a foe has, in every instance up till now, spelled a likelihood of success, having him for a friend, the certainty of ruin. But though the art of his diplomacy is not manifest in the actual results of his negotiations abroad, it shines forth all the more brightly in the manner in which he has succeeded in [inducing] the English people to accept phrase for fact, fantasy for reality and high-sounding pretexts for shabby motivation.

Henry John Temple, Viscount Palmerston, was appointed

[a] Marx uses the English word.—*Ed.*

Junior Lord[a] of the Admiralty in 1807, when the Duke of Portland formed his administration. In 1809 he became Secretary at War[a] and retained this post until May 1828 in the Ministries of Perceval, Liverpool, Canning, Goderich and Wellington. It is certainly strange to find the Don Quixote of "free institutions", the Pindar of the "glories of the constitutional system", as an eminent and permanent member of the Tory administration which promulgated the Corn Laws,[14] stationed foreign mercenaries on English soil, every now and then—to use an expression of Lord Sidmouth's—"let the people's blood", gagged the Press, suppressed meetings, disarmed the nation at large, suspended regular courts of justice along with individual freedom—in a word declared a state of siege in Great Britain and Ireland! In 1829 Palmerston went over to the Whigs who, in November 1830, appointed him Secretary for Foreign Affairs. Save for the intervals between November 1834 and April 1835 and between 1841 and 1846, when the Tories were at the helm, he was in sole charge of England's foreign policy from the time of the revolution of 1830 to the *coup d'état* of 1851. We shall survey his achievements during that period in another letter.

[*Neue Oder-Zeitung*, No. 83, February 19, 1855][b]

London, February 14. In recent weeks *Punch* has been wont to present Lord Palmerston in the guise of the clown of the puppet show. As everyone knows, that clown is a mischief-monger by profession, who loves noisy ructions, a concocter of pernicious misunderstandings, a virtuoso of rowdyism, at home only in the general hurly-burly he has created, in the course of which he throws wife, child and, at last, even the police out of the window, ending up, after much ado about nothing, by extricating himself from the scrape more or less intact and full of malicious glee at the turn the rumpus has taken. And, from a picturesque point of view, Lord Palmerston does indeed appear thus—a restless and untiring spirit who seeks out difficulties, imbroglios and confusion as the natural element of his activity and hence creates conflict where he does not find it ready-made. Never has an English Foreign Secretary shown himself so busy in every corner of the earth—blockades of the Scheldt, the Tagus, the Douro,[15]

---

[a] Marx uses the English term.—*Ed.*
[b] The second instalment was published under the heading "Palmerston".—*Ed.*

blockades of Mexico and Buenos Aires,[16] Naples expeditions, Pacifico expeditions, expeditions to the Persian Gulf,[17] wars in Spain for "liberty" and in China for the importation of opium,[18] North American border disputes,[19] Afghanistan campaigns, bombardment of Saint-Jean-d'Acre,[20] squabbles over the right to search shipping off West Africa,[21] discord even in the "Pacific", and all this to the accompaniment of and supplemented by innumerable minatory notes, stacks of minutes and diplomatic protests. On average, all this noise would seem to dissipate itself in heated parliamentary debates which provide as many ephemeral triumphs for the noble lord. He appears to handle foreign conflicts like an artist who is prepared to go so far and no further, withdrawing as soon as they threaten to become too serious, and have provided him with the dramatic stimulus he requires. In this way, world history itself takes on the air of a pastime expressly invented for the private satisfaction of the noble Viscount Palmerston of Palmerston. This is the first impression Palmerston's chequered diplomacy makes on the impartial observer. A closer examination reveals, however, that, strange to say, one country has invariably profited from his diplomatic zigzag course, and that country was not England but Russia. In 1841 [Joseph] Hume, a friend of Palmerston's, declared:

"Were the Tsar of Russia[a] to have an agent in the British Cabinet, his interests could not be better represented than they are by the noble Lord."

In 1837 Lord Dudley Stuart, one of Palmerston's greatest admirers, apostrophised him as follows:

"How much longer [...] did the noble lord propose to allow Russia thus to insult Great Britain, and thus to injure British commerce? [...] The noble lord was degrading England in the eyes of the world by holding her out in the character of a bully—haughty and tyrannical to the weak, humble and abject to the strong."[b]

At any rate it cannot be denied that all treaties favourable to Russia, from the Treaty of Adrianople to the Treaty of Balta-Liman[22] and the Treaty of the Danish Succession,[23] were concluded under Palmerston's auspices. True, the Treaty of Adrianople found Palmerston in opposition, not in office; but for one thing he was the first to give the treaty his blessing, though in an underhand way and, for another, being then the leader of the

---

[a] Nicholas I.—*Ed.*

[b] From Stuart's speech in the House of Commons on March 17, 1837. *Hansard's Parliamentary Debates*, third series, Vol. XXXVII, London, 1837.—*Ed.*

Whig Opposition, he attacked Aberdeen for his Austro-Turkish bias and declared Russia to be the champion of civilization. (Cf., for instance, the sittings of the House of Commons of June 1, 1829, June 11, 1829,[a] February 16, 1830, etc.) On this occasion, Sir Robert Peel told him in the House of Commons that "he did not know whom Palmerston really represented".[b] In November 1830 Palmerston took over the Foreign Office. Not only did he reject France's offer of joint intervention on Poland's behalf because of "the relations between the Cabinet of St. James and the Cabinet of St. Petersburg"; he also forbade Sweden to arm and threatened Persia with war should she fail to withdraw the army she had already dispatched to the Russian frontier. He himself helped to defray the cost of Russia's campaign in as much as, without parliamentary authorisation, he continued to pay out principal and interest on the so-called Russian-Dutch loan after the Belgian revolution had invalidated the stipulations governing that loan.[24] In 1832 he allowed the mortgage on state demesnes which the National Assembly of Greece had guaranteed the English contracting party to the Anglo-Greek Loan of 1824, to be repudiated and transferred as security for a new loan effected under Russian auspices. His despatches to Mr. Dawkins, English representative in Greece, invariably read: "You are to act in concert with the agents of Russia."[c] On July 8, 1833, Russia extorted from the Porte the Treaty of Unkiar-Skelessi whereby the Dardanelles were closed to European warships, and Russia (cf. second article of the treaty) was assured of an eight years' dictatorship in Turkey.[25] The Sultan[d] was forced to sign the treaty by the presence of a Russian fleet in the Bosphorus and of a Russian army outside the gates of Constantinople—allegedly as a protection against Ibrahim Pasha. Palmerston had repeatedly refused Turkey's urgent plea that he intervene on her behalf, and had thus forced her into accepting the help of Russia. (He himself said as much in the House of Commons on July 11, August 24, etc., 1833 and March 17, 1834.) When Lord Palmerston entered the Foreign Office he found English influence clearly preponderant in Persia. His standing order to English agents was that they should "in all cases act in concert with

---

[a] Presumably an error in the *Neue Oder-Zeitung*. On June 11, 1829, Parliament did not sit. The reference is to Palmerston's speech on February 5, 1830 (see present edition, Vol. 12, p. 355).—*Ed.*

[b] From Peel's speech in the House of Commons on February 16, 1830.—*Ed.*

[c] P. I. Rickmann.—*Ed.*

[d] Mahmud II.—*Ed.*

the Russian Ambassador". With his support, Russia placed a Russian pretender on the Persian throne.[a] Lord Palmerston sanctioned the Russo-Persian expedition against Herat.[26] Only when this had failed did he order an Anglo-Indian expedition into the Persian Gulf, a stratagem that strengthened Russia's influence in Persia. In 1836, under the noble lord, Russia's usurpations in the Danubian Delta, her quarantines, her customs regulations,[27] etc., were recognized by England for the first time. In the same year the confiscation of a British merchant vessel, the *Vixen*—and the *Vixen* had been sent out at the instigation of the British government—by a Russian warship in the Circassian Bay of Soujouk-Kale was used by him as a pretext to accord official recognition to Russian claims to the Circassian littoral. It transpired on this occasion that, as much as six years previously, he had secretly recognized Russia's claims to the Caucasus. On this occasion the noble Viscount escaped a vote of censure in the House of Commons by a slender majority of sixteen. One of his most vehement accusers at the time was Sir Stratford Canning, now Lord Redcliffe, English Ambassador at Constantinople. In 1836 one of the English agents[b] in Constantinople concluded a trade agreement with Turkey which was advantageous to England. Palmerston delayed ratification and, in 1838, substituted another treaty so greatly to Russia's advantage and England's detriment that a number of English merchants in the Levant decided they would in future trade under the aegis of Russian firms. The death of King William IV gave rise to the notorious *Portfolio* scandal. At the time of the Warsaw revolution[28] a collection of secret letters, despatches, etc. by Russian diplomats and ministers had fallen into the hands of the Poles when they captured the palace of the Grand Duke Constantine. Count Zamoyski, Prince Czartoryski's nephew, took them to England. There, on the orders of the King and under Urquhart's editorship and Palmerston's supervision, they were published in *The Portfolio*. No sooner was the King dead than Palmerston denied all connection with *The Portfolio*, refused to pay the printer's[c] bills, etc. Urquhart published his correspondence with Backhouse, Palmerston's Under-Secretary of State.[d] Upon this *The Times* (26 January, 1839) comments:

---

[a] Mohammed-Shah.—*Ed.*
[b] David Urquhart.—*Ed.*
[c] F. J. Shoberl.—*Ed.*
[d] *The Times*, No. 16948, January 25, 1839.—*Ed.*

"It is not for us to understand how Lord Palmerston may feel, but we are sure there is no misapprehending how any other person in the station of a gentleman, and in the position of a Minister, would feel, after the notoriety given to the correspondence...."

Written on February 12 and 14, 1855

First published in the *Neue Oder-Zeitung*, Nos. 79 and 8 February 16 and 19, 1855

Marked with the sign ×

Printed according to the newspaper

Published in English for the first time

Karl Marx

HERBERT'S RE-ELECTION.—THE FIRST MEASURES OF THE NEW MINISTRY.—NEWS FROM INDIA

London, February 16. The farce of Mr. Sidney Herbert's re-election as Member of Parliament for the southern division of Wiltshire took place yesterday in Salisbury Town Hall.[a] Even among the English counties Wilts is notorious for a concentration of land-ownership which has turned the whole area into the property of fewer than a dozen families. With the exception of some districts in Northern Scotland, the land has nowhere been so thoroughly "cleared" of inhabitants, nor the system of modern agriculture applied so consistently. Except when family feuds happen to break out among its few landlords, Wilts never sees an electoral campaign.

No rival candidate had been put up against Sidney Herbert. The High Sheriff,[b] who presided over the election, therefore declared him re-elected by all the forms of law at the very beginning of the meeting. Sidney Herbert then rose and addressed a number of very worn-out platitudes to his tenants and vassals. Meanwhile there had gradually gathered in the Town Hall an audience of townspeople who were not entitled to vote but whom the English Constitution fobs off with the privilege of boring the candidates at the hustings.[c] Scarcely had Sidney Herbert sat down than a barrage of questions volleyed about his venerable head. "What about the green coffee-beans served to our soldiers?", "Where is our army?", "What did *The Times* say of

[a] A report on the re-election was published in *The Times*, No. 21979, February 16, 1855.—*Ed.*
[b] E. L. Clutterbuck.—*Ed.*
[c] Marx uses the English word.—*Ed.*

you yesterday?",[29] "Why did you spare Odessa?", "Does your uncle, the Russian Prince Vorontsov, own palaces in Odessa?", etc. Naturally not the slightest notice was taken of these unparliamentary questioners. On the contrary, Sidney Herbert availed himself of the first lull to propose a vote of thanks to the Sheriff for his "impartial" conduct of the "proceedings". This was accepted amidst applause from the parliamentary audience, and hissing and groaning from the unparliamentary. There then followed a second volley of ejaculatory questions: "Who starved our soldiers? Let him go to war himself! etc." No more result than before. The Sheriff then declared the play, which had lasted little more than half an hour, to be over, and the curtain fell.

The first measures of the re-constituted ministry were by no means received with approval. As Lord Panmure, the new Secretary for War, is an invalid, the main burden of his administration falls to the Under-Secretary for War. The appointment of Frederick Peel, the younger son of the late Peel, to this important post arouses all the more displeasure since Frederick Peel is a notorious mediocrity. Despite his youth, he is the living incarnation of routine. Other men become bureaucrats. He came into the world as one. Frederick Peel owes his post to the influence of the Peelites. It was therefore necessary to balance the scales with a Whig in the other pan. Sir Francis Baring has therefore been appointed Chancellor of the Duchy of Lancaster. He was Chancellor of the Exchequer in Lord Melbourne's Whig administration and at that time bore the well-deserved nickname of "Mr. Deficit". The most recent army appointments all remain true to the system of gerontocracy. Thus the octogenarian Lord Seaton has been appointed to the command of the army in Ireland. Lord Rokeby, old, gout-ridden, and deaf, has been dispatched to the Crimea as commander of the Brigade of Guards. Command of the Second Division there—formerly under Sir de Lacy Evans—has fallen to General Simpson, who is no Samson but on the contrary occupied a fitting retirement-post as veteran Lieutenant-Governor of Portsmouth. General Somerset, already a Brigadier in 1811, has been sent to India as commanding General. Finally Admiral Boxer, "that anarch old", as *The Times* calls him,[a] who threw the whole transport service into utter confusion in Constantinople, has now been ordered to Balaklava to put that harbour into "proper order".

---

[a] *The Times*, No. 21979, February 16, 1855. The passage quoted below is from the same issue.—*Ed.*

"We fear," says *The Times*, "we must look elsewhere for Ministerial vigour. [...] It is vain for us to appeal to those who do these things against such cruel and wanton squandering of the best resources of the nation. Were they not infatuated by a long course of power, which only shifted from one portion of their own [...] class to another, they would scarcely have chosen this moment at least for the exhibition of such wanton and short-sighted selfishness. The instinct of self-preservation would have taught them better, but we solemnly ask the people of England whether they will suffer their countrymen to be thus sacrificed at the shrine of cruel apathy or helpless incapacity." *The Times* threatens: "It is not a Government, nor is it even a House of Commons. It is the British Constitution that is under trial."

The latest news from India is important because it describes the deplorable state of business in Calcutta and Bombay. In the manufacturing districts the crisis is slowly but surely advancing. The owners of spinning-mills of fine yarn in Manchester decided at a meeting held the day before yesterday only to open their factories four days a week from February 26 and in the meantime to call on the manufacturers in the surrounding area to follow their example. In the factories in Blackburn, Preston and Bolton notice has already been given to the workers that there will henceforth only be "short time". The fact that in the past year many manufacturers have tried to force the markets by circumventing the commission-houses and taking their export business into their own hands means that bankruptcies will be all the larger in number and in size. *The Manchester Guardian* admitted last Wednesday[a] that there was *overproduction* not only of manufactured goods but also of factories.

Written on February 16, 1855

First published in the *Neue Oder-Zeitung*, No. 85, February 20, 1855

Marked with the sign ×

Printed according to the newspaper

Published in English for the first time

[a] February 14, 1855.—*Ed.*

Karl Marx

PARLIAMENT

London, February 17. Parliament re-assembled yesterday. The House of Commons was obviously displeased. It appeared to be distressed by the conviction that the transactions of the last three weeks had completely broken its authority. There sat the old ministry once more, only reburnished. Two elderly Lords[a] who could not abide each other had disappeared from it, but a third elderly Lord who had shared the vote of no-confidence with those two had not fallen down a rung, but simply up to the top rung. Lord Palmerston was received in solemn silence. No "cheers",[b] no enthusiasm. Contrary to custom, his speech was received with visible indifference and ill-tempered scepticism. For once, too, his memory played him false, and he hesitated, hunting through the notes he had before him, until Sir Charles Wood in a whisper restored the broken thread. His audience seemed not to believe that the change of firm would save the old house from bankruptcy. His whole manner recalled Cardinal Alberoni's verdict on William of Orange:

> "He was a strong man while he held the balance. He is weak now that he has used his own weight to tip the scales."

The most important fact however was undoubtedly the appearance of a new coalition in opposition to the new version of the old one—the coalition of the Tories under Disraeli and the most outspoken section of the Radicals, men like Layard, Duncombe, Horsman, etc. It was precisely amongst the latter, the Mayfair

---

[a] Lord Aberdeen and Lord John Russell.—*Ed.*
[b] Marx uses the English word.—*Ed.*

Radicals,[30] that Palmerston hitherto counted his loudest supporters. Layard had been disappointed in his hopes of receiving a junior post in the Ministry for War, so mutters one government paper. Let him have a post!—hisses another.

Lord Palmerston began the announcement of his new ministry with a brief account of the ministerial crisis. Then he praised his own creation. The ministry he had formed

> "contains sufficient administrative ability, sufficient political sagacity, sufficient liberal principle, sufficient patriotism and determination to [...] fulfil its duties".[a]

Lord Clarendon, Lord Panmure, Mr. Gladstone, Sir James Graham—each was duly complimented. Excellent though the ministry was, it had one great difficulty staring it in the face. Here was Mr. Roebuck, insisting on having his Committee of Inquiry nominated next Thursday. Why had the House need of a committee? He would remind them of an anecdote from the days of Richard II at the time of Wat Tyler's uprising. The young monarch is said to have encountered a troop of rebels, whose chief had just been slain before their eyes. Boldly going up to them, he is said to have exclaimed: "You have lost your leader; my friends, I will be your leader." "So I say" (the young (!) dictator Palmerston), "if you, the House of Commons, now forego this committee, the Government itself will be your committee."

This somewhat irreverent comparison of the House to a band of "rebels" and the unblushing demand of the cabinet to be appointed judge in its own cause, were received with ironical laughter. What do you want, cried Palmerston, raising his voice and tilting his head into that attitude of Irish audacity for which he is known. What is the purpose of a Committee of Inquiry? Administrative improvements? Very well! Hear all the things we intend to improve. Previously you had two Ministers of War, the Secretary at War[b] and the Minister for War. Henceforth you shall have but one, the latter. In the Department of Ordnance, the military command will be transferred to the Commander-in-Chief (Horse Guards[c]) and the civil administration to the Secretary for War. The Transport Board will be enlarged. Previously, under

---

[a] Excerpts from the speeches by Palmerston and other participants in the House of Commons debate of February 16 are quoted from *The Times*, No. 21980, February 17, 1855.—*Ed.*

[b] Marx uses the English term.—*Ed.*

[c] Horse Guards, the English term given by Marx, was used to denote the Commander-in-Chief of the British army, since he and his personnel were housed in what was originally the barracks of the Horse Guards.—*Ed.*

the Act of 1847, the term of service was 10 years. It will now be made optional for men to enlist for any number of years they wish, from 1 to 10. No man will be enlisted below the age of 24 nor over 32. Now to the theatre of war! In order to introduce uniformity, vigour and order into the conduct and management of the war, Palmerston has chosen the unusual device of providing each post with a controller with unspecified powers. Lord Raglan remains Commander-in-Chief but General Simpson becomes Chief of Staff, and Raglan "will feel it his duty to adopt his recommendations". Sir John Burgoyne is recalled to service, and Sir Harry Jones becomes Chief of the Commissariat, with unspecified dictatorial power. At the same time however a civilian, Sir John MacNeill (author of the famous pamphlet *Russia's Progress in the East*), is ordered to the Crimea to inquire into misappropriation, incompetence and dereliction of duty by the Commissariat. New hospital arrangements in Smyrna and Scutari; reform of the medical department in the Crimea and at home, transport vessels for sick and wounded plying every 10 days between the Crimea and Britain. At the same time however the Minister for War[a] will borrow three civilians from the Minister of Health[b] and send them to the Crimea to make the necessary sanitary arrangements for the prevention of pestilence when the spring weather comes and to organise inquiries into the staff and management of the medical department. As one can see, there is excellent opportunity for conflicts of authority. In order to compensate Lord Raglan for his "command hedged about by constitutional institutions", he receives full authorisation to negotiate in Constantinople for a corps of 300 Turkish street-sweepers and grave-diggers whose task will be to consign the army of dead, the decaying horses and other ordure into the sea when the warm season comes. A separate department of land transport will be set up in the theatre of war. Whilst thus on the one hand, preparations are made for waging the war, in Vienna peace will be prepared by Lord John Russell, if that is expedient.

Disraeli: When one has heard the noble Lord extolling his colleagues' "administrative ability and political sagacity", it is [hard] to believe that he is speaking of the same "unparalleled blunderers" whom the House condemned 19 days before[c]!

---

[a] F. M. Panmure.—*Ed.*
[b] B. Hall.—*Ed.*
[c] A reference to the House of Commons debate of January 29, 1855. *The Times*, No. 21964, January 30, 1855.—*Ed.*

Supposing that the promised improvements are implemented and are what they are given out to be, what a satire they were on the ministry which alone had opposed them and which had declared a Commons inquiry into the previous mismanagement to be a vote of no-confidence in itself. Even Lord John Russell had declared he found the mysterious disappearance of the army inexplicable and an investigation of its secret causes to be unavoidable.[a] Was the House to delude itself into rescinding the decision it had reached only 10 days ago? By so doing, it would irrevocably forfeit its public influence for years. What was the argument of the noble Lord and his reburnished colleagues to induce the House of Commons to stultify itself? Promises which would never have been made, had it not been for the threat of a Committee of Inquiry. He would insist on a parliamentary inquiry. Palmerston was commencing his new post by threatening Parliament's freedom of movement. Never had a ministry met with such support and willingness from the opposition as had Lord Aberdeen's, the "late" ministry, or how should he call it! There were two Dromios[b] that confounded him; he would therefore say "the late Ministry and their present faithful representatives—their identical representatives on the government bench".

Roebuck declared that next Thursday he intended to table a list of names for the Committee, which the House had already adopted. The administration was the old one, only the cards had been shuffled but had fallen into the same hands again. Nothing short of the direct intervention of the House of Commons could break the shackles of routine and remove the obstacles which prevented the government from carrying out the necessary reforms, even if it wished to do so.

T[homas] Duncombe: The noble Lord had told them, he and the government would like to be their committee. They were mightily grateful! What the House wanted to do was to inquire into the conduct of the noble Lord and his colleagues! He had promised reforms, but who was to institute them? The very men whose administration had created the necessity for reforms. There had been no change in the administration. It was the *status quo ante*[c] Roebuck. Lord John Russell had deserted his post in cowardly fashion. Lord Palmerston himself might be said to be the "faded

[a] John Russell's speech in the House of Commons on February 8, 1855. *The Times*, No. 21973, February 9, 1855.—*Ed.*

[b] Characters from Shakespeare's *The Comedy of Errors*.—*Ed.*

[c] The position as before [the motion by].—*Ed.*

gem" of 13 bygone administrations, from that of Lord Liverpool down to the present one. Therefore he must undoubtedly be possessed of "great experience as well as of high administrative talent". His Lord Panmure was not even the equal of the Duke of Newcastle. The appointment of the committee was not a censure. It was a question of inquiry. Censure would probably follow on its heels. Concerning the negotiations in Vienna, here too the government was in opposition to the people. The people was demanding a revision of the treaties of Vienna of 1815 in the interests of the Poles, Hungarians and Italians. By war against Russia however, it understood the literal destruction of Russian preponderance.

One can see that Palmerston's ministry is continuing from the point where Aberdeen's ministry ended—with the fight against Roebuck's motion. Between now and next Thursday every effort will be made to obtain by hook or by crook a ministerial majority against the Committee of Inquiry.

Written on February 17, 1855

First published in the *Neue Oder-Zeitung*, No. 88, February 22, 1855

Marked with the sign ×

Printed according to the newspaper

Published in English for the first time

Karl Marx

THE COALITION BETWEEN TORIES AND RADICALS

London, February 19. The coalition between Tories and Radicals, the first signs of which we reported in our last contribution,[a] is today being talked of as a *fait accompli* by the whole of the London daily press. The government *Morning Chronicle* observes on the subject:

"Yet there never yet was a *revolution* which was not accelerated from pique, wounded vanity, misplaced ambition, or sheer folly, by its predestined and unconscious victims; and the motley combination of Derbyites and Liberals who have coalesced with Mr. Roebuck are treading in the very footsteps of those members of the Chamber of Deputies who, when getting up the Reform banquets of 1848, sought only to displace a Ministry, and ended by upsetting a throne."[b]

Roebuck, it asserts, is ready to play the part of a Robespierre *or* (a most remarkable or!) of a Ledru-Rollin. His intention is to form a "committee of public safety". He had had no qualms about proposing the following names for the committee which he had requested: Roebuck, Drummond, Layard, Sir Joseph Paxton (who built the palace for the Great Exhibition[31]), Lord Stanley (Derby's son), Ellice, Whiteside, Disraeli, Butt, Lowe (a member of *The Times*' secret council) and Miles.

"It is useless," continues *The Morning Chronicle*, "to disguise that we are openly threatened with a revolutionary crusade against the aristocracy of this country. [...] The demagogues [...] are seeking the overthrow of Lord Palmerston's Administra-

---

[a] See this volume, pp. 24-25.—*Ed.*

[b] "The prudence, fairness and consistency of nominating Mr. Roebuck's committee...", *The Morning Chronicle*, No. 27504, February 19, 1855. The item containing the passage "It is useless to disguise..." which is quoted below was published in the same issue.—*Ed.*

tion, by skilfully playing off against it the associated, though not combined, forces of Mr. Disraeli and Mr. Roebuck. Democracy is seeking to bring about a revolution by methodically overthrowing one cabinet after another."[a]

Finally, a government paper threatens the dissolution of Parliament, [an] "appeal to the people", as Bonaparte did a few months before the *coup d'état*.

The Economist, whose publisher *Wilson* is Secretary of the Treasury, declares "a representative Constitution" to be incompatible with the conduct of war.[b] The former hat-maker Wilson therefore proposes that Members of Parliament who accept offices of state should be released from the obligation of re-election and cabinet ministers should *ex officio* be granted a seat and voice in the House of Commons. Thus the ministry is to become independent of electors and the House of Commons, but the House would become dependent on the ministry. With regard to this, *The Daily News* warns:

"The people of England must be on their guard, and prepared to make a resolute stand in defence of their representative institutions. [...] An attempt is about to be made to render Government more independent of the House of Commons. [...] This [...] would bring the [...] Government into conflict with the House of Commons. The result would be a *revolution*."[c]

And in fact in Marylebone—considered to be one of the most radical districts of London—a meeting has been called for next Wednesday,[d] to pass resolutions on "the government's attempt [...] to resist the parliamentary inquiry".[e]

Whilst *The Morning Chronicle* is thus prophesying revolution and *The Daily News* an attempt at counter-revolution, *The Times* also is making reference to the February Revolution, although with regard not to the reform-banquets but to Praslin's murder. For a few days ago, in the Irish Court of Chancery, an inheritance case was brought in which the Marquis of Clanricarde—an English peer, ambassador at the court of St. Petersburg during Melbourne's administration and Postmaster-General during Russell's—

---

[a] The concluding sentence given by Marx is not a direct quotation from *The Morning Chronicle*, but rather summarises the gist of several paragraphs.—*Ed.*

[b] "Two Much Needed Reforms", *The Economist*, No. 599, February 17, 1855.—*Ed.*

[c] *The Daily News*, No. 2731, February 19, 1855.—*Ed.*

[d] February 21, 1855.—*Ed.*

[e] From a letter written by parishioners to the St. Marylebone churchwarden, and published in *The Times*, No. 21982, February 20, 1855.—*Ed.*

appeared as the principal actor in a truly Balzacian drama of murder, adultery, legacy hunting and fraud.[32]

"In the gloomy autumn of 1847," observes *The Times*, "when the mind of France was disturbed by the indefinable presage of approaching revolution [...] a great scandal in the very highest circles of Parisian life startled still further the already excited public and contributed most powerfully to accelerate the then impending catastrophe. Those who contemplate with attention the highly excited state of the public mind at this moment cannot contemplate without similar emotion the great scandal which has been disclosed to the public [...] in the Irish Court of Chancery."[a]

Crimes within the ranks of the ruling caste, revealed at the same time in their arrogant helplessness and impotence, the destruction of the flower of the British army, the dissolution of old parties, a House of Commons without a majority, ministerial coalitions based on outlived traditions, the expense of a European war coincident with the most fearful crisis in commerce and industry—here are symptoms enough of an imminent political and social upheaval in Great Britain. It is of particular significance that the wreck of political illusions is taking place at the same time as the wreck of free-trade illusions. Just as the former ensured the government monopoly of the aristocracy, so the latter ensured the legislative monopoly of the bourgeoisie.

Written on February 19, 1855

First published in the *Neue Oder-Zeitung*, No. 92, February 24, 1855

Marked with the sign ×

Printed according to the newspaper

Published in English for the first time

[a] *The Times*, No. 21981, February 19, 1855.—*Ed.*

New-York Tribune.

Vol. X......No 1,022. NEW-YORK, TUESDAY, MARCH 13, 1855. THREE DOLLARS A YEAR.

Frederick Engels

THE WAR THAT LOOMS ON EUROPE[33]

A few weeks more, and unless peace is made at Vienna[34] with a promptitude that nobody in Europe now seems to expect, we shall witness the opening on that Continent of a war in comparison with whose events the Crimean campaign will sink into that insignificance which, in a war between three of the greatest nations on the face of the earth, it always ought to have worn. The hitherto independent operations in the Black Sea, and in the Baltic, will then be connected by a line of battle extending across the whole breadth of the Continent which separates those two colossal inland lakes; and armies whose magnitude is adequate to the almost boundless extent of the Sarmatian plain, will contend for its dominion. Then, and then only, can the war be said to have become truly a European one.

The Crimean campaign requires but a short additional notice at our hands. We have so often, and in such detail, described its character and its chances, that we have merely to record a few fresh facts in confirmation of our statements. A week ago we observed[a] that it had degenerated into a steeple-chase of reenforcements, and that the Russians were likely to get the best of this race. There is now hardly a doubt that by the time when the season admits of uninterrupted operations, followed up according to a preconcerted plan, the Russians will have from 120,000 to 150,000 men in the Peninsula, to whom the Allies can, with superhuman efforts, oppose, perhaps, 90,000. Supposing, even, that both France and England had troops sufficient to send there, where are the transports to be found, as long as out of

[a] See this volume, p. 3.—*Ed.*

every four steamers sent to the Black Sea, three are kept there under all possible pretexts? England has already completely disorganized her transatlantic mail steam service, and nothing is at present in greater demand there than ocean steamers; but the supply is exhausted. The only thing which could save the Allies, would be the arrival in the Crimea exactly at the time it is wanted, of an Austrian corps of some 30,000 men, to be embarked at the mouth of the Danube. Without such a reenforcement, neither the Piedmontese corps, nor the Neapolitan corps, nor the driblets of Anglo-French reenforcements, nor Omer Pasha's army, can do them any real good.

Now let us see what part of their respective forces England and France have already engaged in the Crimea. We shall speak of the infantry only, for the proportions in which cavalry and artillery are attached to such expeditions are so variable that no positive conclusions respecting them can be established. Besides, the whole active force of a country is always engaged in proportion as its infantry is engaged. Of Turkey we speak not, for with the army of Omer Pasha she engages her last, her only army, in this struggle. What is left to her in Asia is no army; it is but a rabble.

England[a] possesses, in all, 99 regiments, or 106 battalions of infantry. Of these, at least 35 battalions are on Colonial service. Of the remainder, the first five divisions sent to the Crimea took up about 40[b] battalions more; and at least eight battalions have been sent since as reenforcements. There remain about 23 battalions, hardly one of which could be spared. Accordingly, England fairly acknowledges, by her last military measures, the peace establishment of her army to be entirely exhausted. Various devices are brought forward in order to make up for what has been neglected. The militia, embodied to the number of some 50,000, are allowed to volunteer for foreign service. They are to occupy Gibraltar, Malta, Corfu, and thus to relieve about twelve battalions on Colonial service, which then may be sent to the Crimea. A foreign legion is decreed; but, unfortunately, no foreigners seem to come forward for enlistment under the rule of the cat-o'-nine-tails. Finally, on the 13th February, orders were issued to create second battalions for 93 regiments—43 of 1,000 men and 50 of 1,200 men each. This would give an addition of 103,000 men,

[a] The text of this paragraph was used by Marx in his report "Parliamentary and Military Affairs" (see this volume, pp. 41-42).—*Ed.*

[b] Here the *New-York Daily Tribune* has a misprint: 46. The correct figure is given in the German version of this article published in the *Neue Oder-Zeitung* of April 23, 1855.—*Ed.*

besides about 17,000 more men for the cavalry and artillery. But not one of these 120,000 men has as yet been enlisted; and then, how are they to be drilled and officered? The admirable organization and general management of the British army has contrived to engage, one way or another, between the Crimea and the colonies, almost the whole of the infantry, with the exception of depot companies and a few depot battalions—not only the men, but the *cadres* too. Now, there are plenty of half-pay generals, colonels and majors on the British army list [who] can be employed for this new force; but of captains on half-pay, as far as we know, there are none, or very few, while lieutenants, ensigns and non-commissioned officers are nowhere to be had in the manufactured state. Raw material there is in plenty; but raw officers to drill raw recruits would never do; and old, experienced, steady non-commissioned officers, as everybody knows, are the mainstay of every army. Besides this, we know from the best authority—Sir W. Napier—that it takes full three years to drill the tag-rag-and-bobtail of Old England into what John Bull calls "the first soldiers of the world" and "the best blood of England." If that is the case when the *cadres* are at hand waiting to be filled up, how long will it take, without subaltern or non-commissioned officers, to manufacture heroes out of the 120,000 men who are not yet found? We may consider the whole military force of England so far engaged in this war that, for the next twelvemonth, the utmost the British Government can do will be to keep up a "heroic little band" of forty or fifty thousand men before the enemy. That number could only be exceeded for very short periods, and with essential derangement of all preparation for future reenforcements.

France,[a] with her larger army and far more complete organization, has engaged a far inferior proportional part of her forces. France possesses 100 regiments of infantry of the line, 3 of Zouaves, and 2 foreign legions, at 3 battalions each; beside 20 battalions of rifles, and 6 African battalions—together 341 battalions. Of these, 100 battalions, or one to each regiment of the

[a] Here begins the text that was reproduced by Marx, with abridgements and alterations, in his report "Condition of the Armies" in the *Neue Oder-Zeitung* of February 24, 1855. The passage beginning with the words "France, with her larger army..." is preceded by the following paragraph: "We have seen that in the next twelve months England can put up against the enemy no more than 50,000 of her own troops, a fighting force which despite its numerical weakness is not to be despised given good leadership and sound administration. One need only recall the battle of Inkerman."[35]—*Ed.*

line, are considered as dépôt-battalions, for the reception and drilling of recruits; the two first battalions only are sent out for active service, while the dépôt prepares the reenforcements destined to keep up their full strength. Thus, 100 battalions must be at once struck off the number. If subsequently these dépôt-battalions are made use of as the groundwork for a third field battalion, as was more than once done under Napoleon, they can do so by having an extraordinary number of recruits made over to them, and then it is some time before they are fit for the field. Thus, the available force of the French army, at the present time, does not exceed 241 battalions. Of these, 25 at least are required for Algeria. Four are at Rome. Nine divisions of infantry, or at least 80 battalions, have been sent to the Crimea, to Constantinople and to Athens. Altogether, say 110 battalions engaged, or very nearly one half of the available infantry of France, upon the peace establishment; minus the dépôts. Now, the arrangements in the French army, the dépôt-battalions organized beforehand, the calling in of the soldiers dismissed on furlough during their last year of service, the faculty of calling out the full number of every year's conscription, beside extraordinary recruitings, and finally the aptitude of the French for military duty, allow the Government to double the number of their infantry in about a twelvemonth. Considering the quiet but uninterrupted armaments made since the middle of 1853, the establishment of ten or twelve battalions of Imperial Guards, and the strength in which the French troops mustered in their respective camps last autumn, it may be supposed that their force of infantry at home is now fully as strong as it was before the nine divisions left the country, and that, as regards the capability of forming third field battalions out of the dépôt-battalions, without much impairing their efficiency as dépôts, it is even stronger. If we estimate, however, at 350,000 men, the infantry force which France will have on her own territory by the end of March, we shall be rather above than below the mark. With cavalry, artillery, &c., such an infantry force would, according to the French organization, represent an army of about 500,000 men. Of these, at least 200,000 would have to remain at home, as *cadres* for the dépôts, for the maintenance of tranquillity in the interior, in the military workshops, or hospitals. So that by the 1st of April, France might take the field with 300,000 men, comprising about 200 battalions of infantry. But these 200 battalions would, neither in organization nor in discipline and steadiness under fire, be upon a par with the troops sent to the Crimea. They would contain many young recruits, and many battalions composed for the occasion. All corps where officers and men are strangers to each other, where a hasty organization upon the prescribed plan has but just been completed in time before they march out, are vastly inferior to those old established bodies in which the habit of long service, of dangers shared together, and of daily intercourse for years, has established that *esprit de corps* which absorbs very soon, by its powerful influence, even the youngest recruits. It must, then, be admitted that the eighty battalions sent to the Crimea represent a far more important portion of the French army than their mere number indicates. If England has engaged, almost to a man, the best part of her army, France, too, has sent to the East nearly one-half of her finest troops.

We need not here go into a recapitulation of the Russian forces, having very recently stated their numbers and distribution.[a] Suffice it to say that of the Russian active army, or that destined to act upon the western frontier of the Empire, only the third, fourth, fifth and sixth corps have as yet been engaged during the war. The Guards and Grenadiers corps are quite intact, as is the first corps also; the second corps appears to have detached about one division to the Crimea. Beside these troops, eight corps of reserve, equal in number of battalions, if not in numerical strength, to the eight corps of the active army, have been, or are still being formed. Thus, Russia brings up against the West a force of about 750 battalions, 250 of which, however, may be still forming, and will always be weak in numbers, while 200 more have suffered great losses during two campaigns. The Reserve, as far as the fifth and sixth battalions of the regiments are concerned, must principally consist of old soldiers, if the original plan of organization has been followed up; but the 7th and 8th battalions must have been formed of recruits, and be very inefficient, as the Russian, in spite of his docility, is very slow to learn military duties. The whole reserve, besides, is badly officered. Russia, therefore, has engaged at the present time about one-half of her regularly organized active army. But then, the Guards, Grenadiers, first and second corps, forming the other half, which has not yet been engaged, are the very flower of her army, the pet troops of the Emperor, the efficiency of which he watches over with especial care. And, moreover, by engaging

[a] See Engels' article "The European War" (present edition, Vol. 13, pp. 609-14).—*Ed.*

one-half of her active army, what has Russia obtained?[a] She has almost annihilated the offensive and defensive strength of Turkey; she has forced England to sacrifice an army of 50,000 men, and has disabled her for at least a twelvemonth; and she has, besides, forced France to engage a similar proportion of troops to those she herself engaged. And while the best African regiments of France are already before the enemy, Russia's own *élite* has not yet fired a shot.

So far, then, Russia has had the best of it, although her troops employed in Europe cannot boast of a single success, but have had, on the contrary, to give way in every action of moment, and to abandon every one of their enterprises. But the matter will change entirely as soon as Austria joins in the war. She has an army of some 500,000 men ready for the field, beside 100,000 more in the dépôts, and 120,000 more in reserve; an army, which, by very little extraordinary recruiting, may be brought to some 850,000 men. But we will take its number at 600,000, inclusive of dépôts, and omitting the reserve, which has not yet been called in. Of these 600,000 men, 100,000 are in the dépôts, about 70,000 more in Italy and other portions of the interior not menaced by Russia. The remaining 430,000[b] are assembled in several armies, from Bohemia through Galicia to the Lower Danube, and 150,000 men could be in a very short time concentrated upon any given point. This formidable army at once turns the balance against Russia, so soon as Austria begins to act against her; for since the whole of the late Russian army of the Danube has been drafted into the Crimea, the Austrians are superior to the Russians on every point, and can bring their reserves to the frontier quite as soon, in spite of the start the Russians have now got. There is only this to notice: that the Austrian reserve is far more limited in its number than that of the Russians, and that the 120,000 reserve soldiers once called in, all further increase must arise from fresh recruiting, and, therefore, be very slow. The longer, therefore, the Austrians hold back a declaration of war, the more advantage they give to Russia. To make up for this, we are told, a French auxiliary army is to march into Austria. But the road from Dijon or Lyons to Cracow is rather long, and unless matters are well

---

[a] Instead of this sentence the German version published in the *Neue Oder-Zeitung* has: "Only the effect of diplomacy on the Western Powers' conduct of the war explains the results already achieved by Russia."—*Ed.*

[b] Here the *New-York Daily Tribune* has a misprint: 330,000. The correct figure is given in the German version published in the *Neue Oder-Zeitung*.—*Ed.*

arranged, the French army may arrive too late, unless the intrinsic value of the reorganized Austrian army should render it a match for even a moderately superior number of Russians.[a]

Austria, then, is the arbiter of the situation. Ever since she took up a military position on her Eastern frontiers, she has maintained her superiority over the Russians. If well-timed arrivals of Russian reserves should for a moment deprive her of it, she may trust to her experienced generals—the only ones, save a very few Hungarians, who of late years have shown military genius—and to her well-organized troops, most of whom have been under fire. A few skilful maneuvers, a very slight step backward, would force her opponent to such detachments as to assure her a fair field. Militarily speaking, Russia is thrown completely on the defensive the very moment Austria moves her armies.[b]

Another point must be mentioned. If France raises her domestic army to 500,000 men, and Austria increases her total forces to 800,000, either of these countries is capable of calling, within a twelvemonth, at least 250,000 men more under arms.[c] On the other hand, the Czar, if ever he completes the seventh and eighth battalions of his infantry regiments, thereby raising his total active force to say 900,000 men, has done almost everything in his power for defense. His late recruiting is said to have everywhere met with considerable difficulties; the standard of hight has had to be lowered, and other means resorted to, to get the requisite number of men. The decree of the Emperor, calling the whole of the male population of Southern Russia[36] under arms, far from being an actual increase of the army, is a plain confession of the impossibility of further regular recruiting. This means was resorted to on the French invasion of 1812, when the country was actually invaded; and then in seventeen provinces only. Moscow then furnished 80,000 volunteers, or one tenth of the population of the province; Smolensk sent 25,000 men, and so forth. But, during the war they were nowhere; and these hundreds of thousands of volunteers did not prevent the Russians from arriving on the Vistula in as bad a state, and in as total a

---

[a] Instead of the passage beginning with the words "and unless matters are well arranged" and ending with the words "a moderately superior number of Russians", the version published in the *Neue Oder-Zeitung* has: "The longer the diplomats procrastinate the less the likelihood that it will arrive on time."—*Ed.*

[b] The *Neue Oder-Zeitung* further has: "Even a short-lived successful offensive could not alter this result."—*Ed.*

[c] The *Neue Oder-Zeitung* further has: "while England's contingent would continually grow from the second year onwards."—*Ed.*

dissolution as the French themselves.[a] This new levy *en masse* means, besides, that Nicholas is resolved on war to the utmost.

But if Austria's participation in the war, throws Russia, militarily speaking, on the defensive, this is not necessarily the case, politically speaking. The Czar's great political means of offense—we have called attention to it more than once—is the raising of the Austrian and Turkish Slavons and the proclamation of Hungarian independence. How greatly these measures are dreaded by Austrian statesmen is known to our readers. No doubt, in case of necessity, the Czar will resort to this means; with what result, remains to be seen. We have not spoken of Prussia—she is likely to go, finally, with the West against Russia, though perhaps only after some storms which nobody can foresee. At all events, until some national movement takes place, her troops are not likely to play a very important part, and, therefore, we may for the present take very little account of her.

Written about February 20, 1855

First published in the *New-York Daily Tribune*, No. 4332, March 8, 1855, reprinted in the *New-York Semi-Weekly Tribune*, No. 1022, March 13, 1855; an abridged German version was first published in the *Neue Oder-Zeitung*, No. 93, February 24, 1855

Marked with the sign ×

Reproduced from the *New-York Daily Tribune*

[a] Here ends the text reproduced by Marx in his report "Condition of the Armies" in the *Neue Oder-Zeitung*.—*Ed.*

Karl Marx and Frederick Engels

PARLIAMENTARY AND MILITARY AFFAIRS

London, February 20. Although the House of Commons sat yesterday from 4 p. m. to 2 a. m. and voted away some £7.5 million sterling for the army, the debates lacked anything interesting enough to report. Therefore, we shall only note that Palmerston disconcerted his liberal opponents both by the deliberate triviality of his replies and by the provocatively confident insolence with which he delivered these trivialities.[a] Having declaimed about the battle of Balaklava[37] in the manner of Astley's Amphitheatre, he attacked Layard for "vulgar declamation against the aristocracy", for it was not the aristocracy that was dug-in in the Commissariat, in Transport and in the Medical department. He forgot that its lackeys are dug-in there. Layard rightly emphasised that the commissions invented by Palmerston are good for nothing but stirring up conflicts of competence in the expeditionary army. "What!" cried Palmerston (he saw himself again in the place of Richard II and Parliament in the role of Wat Tyler's mob). "You want to set up a parliamentary committee good for nothing but producing Blue Books,[38] and you take exception to my commissions, which 'have to work'!" Palmerston treated Parliament with such superciliousness that for once he even found it superfluous to make his own jokes. He borrowed them from the ministerial morning papers which the Members of Parliament had in front of them on the table. They were spared neither the "Committee of Public Safety" of *The Morning*

[a] An account of Palmerston's speech was published in *The Times*, No. 21982, February 20, 1855.—*Ed.*

Chronicle[a] nor the jibe of *The Morning Post* about transporting the inquisitorious Members to the Crimea—and leaving them there. Only a parliament constituted like this one could have stood for this.

So, while in Parliament Palmerston out-Aberdeens Old Aberdeen, he lets it be known—not directly, through his own papers, but through the gullible newspaper of the united victuallers,[b] that he is not a free agent but bound in chains by the Court, etc.

As a peace congress[39] is soon to meet in Vienna, it is time to speak of the war and to estimate the military forces at the disposal of the powers which have so far appeared—more or less—on the battlefield. This is not a question only of the numerical strength of the armies, but of that part of them which can be used in offensive operations. We shall give details only of the infantry, as the other arms must be proportionate.[c]

England possesses, in all, 99 regiments, or 106 battalions of infantry. Of these, at least 35 battalions are on Colonial service. Of the remainder, the first five divisions sent to the Crimea took up 40 battalions more; and at least eight battalions have been sent since as reinforcements. There remain about 23 battalions, hardly one of which could be spared for service abroad. The militia, embodied to the number of over 50,000, are allowed to volunteer for foreign service. They are to occupy Gibraltar, Malta, Corfu, and thus to relieve about twelve battalions, which then may be sent to the Crimea. A foreign legion, as Palmerston stated in the House of Commons yesterday, will not be set up. Finally, on the 13th February, orders were issued to create second battalions for 93 regiments—43 of 1,000 men and 50 of 1,200 men each. This would give an addition of 103,000 men, besides about 17,000 more men for the cavalry and artillery. But not one of these 120,000 men has as yet been enlisted, and afterwards they have to be drilled and officered.

The admirable organisation existing at present has contrived to employ almost the whole of the infantry—with the exception of depot companies and a few depot battalions—between the Crimea and the colonies, and moreover not only the men but, though this

[a] *The Morning Chronicle*, No. 27504, February 19, 1855.—*Ed.*

[b] *The Morning Advertiser*, which had published the articles "A Minister must be ambitious..." (No. 19863, February 17, 1855) and "Faithful are the wounds of a friend...", No. 19864, February 19, 1855.—*Ed.*

[c] The following paragraphs are largely based on Engels' article "The War That Looms on Europe", which was published in the *New-York Daily Tribune*, No. 4332, March 8, 1855 (see this volume, pp. 32-39).—*Ed.*

seems incredible, the cadres as well. Now, there are plenty of half-pay generals, colonels and majors on the British army list and they can be employed for this new force. But there are hardly any captains on half-pay, and no lieutenants and non-commissioned officers at all. But it is well known that the non-commissioned officers form the cornerstone of every army. According to General Sir William Napier, the historian of the Peninsular war,[a] the best authority in this field, it takes fully three years to drill the "tag-rag" and "bobtail"[b] (the lumpenproletariat) of Old England into "the best blood of England", "the first soldiers of the world". If that is the case when the cadres are at hand and need only to be replenished, how long will it therefore take to manufacture heroes out of these 120,000 men? During the next twelvemonth, the utmost the British Government can do is to keep up a "heroic little band" of fifty thousand men before the enemy. That number could be exceeded for short periods, but only at the cost of considerably upsetting all preparation for future reinforcements.

The departure of the mail compels us to break off at this point.

Written on February 20, 1855

First published in the *Neue Oder-Zeitung*, No. 91, February 23, 1855

Marked with the sign ×

Printed according to the newspaper

Published in English for the first time

[a] This refers to W. F. P. Napier's *History of the War in the Peninsula and in the South of France from the Year 1807 to the Year 1814*, Vols. I-VI.—*Ed.*

[b] The words in quotation marks are given in English in the original.—*Ed.*

Karl Marx

ON THE NEW MINISTERIAL CRISIS

London, February 24. Yesterday, the House of Commons was packed, as ministerial statements on the breaking up of the *first* Palmerston administration had been announced.[40] The closely-crowded Members waited impatiently for the arrival of the noble Viscount, who at last appeared, an hour after the House had opened, received with laughter by one side, with cheers[a] by the other. The Ministers who had broken away—Graham, Gladstone and Herbert—took their seats on the benches of the so-called Radicals (the Manchester School[41]), where Mr. Bright seemed to welcome them. One bench in front of them Cardwell, who had also resigned, sat enthroned. Lord Palmerston rose to move that the Roebuck Committee should be considered immediately. Sir James Graham then opened the ministers' case[b] and was still on the threshold of his rhetorical phantasy building when Palmerston began to accompany him with unmistakable signs of healthy sleep.

Graham's polemic against the Committee of Inquiry was mainly confined to the claim that it represented an intrusion into the royal prerogatives by the House of Commons. As everyone knows, for a century and a half it has been the custom of English ministries to talk about the privileges of the House *vis-à-vis* the Crown and about the prerogatives of the Crown *vis-à-vis* the House. In fact Graham spoke threateningly about danger to the Anglo-French alliance in consequence of the Committee's investig-

[a] Marx uses the English word.—*Ed.*

[b] The speeches of Graham and the others were reported in *The Times*, No. 21986, February 24, 1855.—*Ed.*

ations. What was this but an insinuation that the French ally would prove to have been the main cause of the deplorable mishaps! As to his own resignation from the Ministry, the Ministry had regarded Roebuck's motion from the beginning simply as a disguised vote of no confidence. Aberdeen and Newcastle had therefore been sacrificed and the old Ministry dissolved. The new Ministry consisted of the old personnel with the exception of Canning and Panmure; how then should Roebuck's motion suddenly be capable of a new interpretation? Not he, but Lord Palmerston had changed his views from Friday to Tuesday. Not he, but his noble friend, was a deserter. In addition—and this was a naive admission—Graham gave as reason for his resignation from the renewed Ministry that he had become convinced

> "that the present Administration [...] does not [...] possess in a greater degree the confidence of the House than that Administration which only a few weeks since retired".

During his statement Graham said *inter alia:*

> "When the new Administration was formed I wished to know from my noble Lord" (Palmerston), "whether there was to be any change in the foreign policy of Lord Aberdeen's Administration [...]; and also whether [...] there was any alteration with respect to the stipulated peace terms. Lord Palmerston gave me the fullest assurance that in these respects everything will remain as before."

(These words are quoted here as they were *spoken* in the House of Commons, not as they were *printed* in more circumscribed form in the newspapers.)[42]

Bright at once took up this pronouncement by Graham, stating that he did not wish the Palmerston Government to be overthrown, that he had no personal animosity against the noble Lord, that rather he was convinced Palmerston and Russell possessed everything the unjustly persecuted Aberdeen had lacked, namely sufficient popularity to make peace on the basis of the four points.[43]

Sidney Herbert: Roebuck's motion consisted of two quite different parts. First, he proposed to investigate the state of the army at Sevastopol; second, to investigate the conduct of the Government departments specifically in charge of the maintenance of the army. The House was entitled to do the second, but not the first. Presumably it was for that very reason that he, Herbert, had opposed the "second" on 26 January[a] as violently as he now,

[a] Herbert's speech in the House of Commons on January 26, 1855. *The Times*, No. 21962, January 27, 1855.—*Ed.*

on 23 February, opposed the "first"? When he (Herbert) took his position in the present Ministry, Lord Palmerston, in line with his speech of last Friday,[a] had declared the Committee unconstitutional, abolished with the resignation of Aberdeen and Newcastle. Palmerston had not even doubted that the House would now reject Roebuck's motion without a debate. The Committee, in so far as its object was not a charge against the Government but an investigation of the state of the army, would prove an immense sham. Lord Palmerston, since he did not have the courage of his repeatedly expressed conviction, was weakening the Government. What was the use of a strong man if he pursued a weak policy?

Gladstone in fact added nothing to the statements of his colleagues except the kind of argumentation which, on the occasion of Gladstone's resignation from Peel's administration—it was then a question of the Maynooth college[44]—moved the late Peel to declare that he believed he understood the reasons for his friend's resignation before his friend undertook to lay them before Parliament in a two-hour speech.

Palmerston considered it superfluous to enter into the explanations of his ex-colleagues. He regretted their resignations, but would be able to console himself. In his view the Committee did not intend any reproof but an investigation of the state of the army. He had opposed the setting up of the Committee but had become convinced that the decision of the House could not be rescinded. The country could not be without a government, hence he would remain the Government with or without the Committee. To Bright's question he replied that the peace negotiations were meant seriously and that Russell's instructions had been drafted on the basis of the four points. He told the House nothing of the position in his own Ministry.

It is incontestable, that in spite of the sudden breaking up of his first administration, Palmerston has already won some victories, if not in public opinion, then in the Ministry and in Parliament. By Russell's mission to Vienna he has got rid of a troublesome, temperamental rival. By his compromise with Roebuck he has transformed the Parliamentary Committee of Inquiry into a Government Commission which counts only as the fourth after the three appointed by himself. As Sidney Herbert says, he has put "immense sham" in place of a real thing. The resignation of the Peelites has enabled him to form a ministry consisting of nothing

[a] February 16, 1855.—*Ed.*

but ciphers with himself as the only figure. It is beyond question, however, that the formation of such a real Palmerston Ministry will have to struggle with almost insuperable obstacles.

Written on February 24, 1855

First published in the *Neue Oder-Zeitung*, No. 97, February 27, 1855

Marked with the sign ×

Printed according to the newspaper

Published in English for the first time

Karl Marx

[JOSEPH] HUME

London, February 24. With Hume, the veteran of the House of Commons has died. His long parliamentary life was an accurate barometer of the radical bourgeois party which reached its highest point in 1831. In the initial period of the reformed House[45] a kind of parliamentary Warwick or Member-maker, eight years later he figured with Daniel O'Connell and Feargus O'Connor as one of the originators of the People's Charter,[46] which to this day forms the political programme of the Chartists and basically contains only the demand for a *universal franchise* together with the conditions which would make it a reality in England.

The break between the workers and the bourgeois agitators which soon followed found Hume on the side of the latter. At the time of the Russell Ministry he drafted the "Little Charter", which was adopted by the so-called "parliamentary and financial reformers"[47] as their programme. Instead of the six points of the People's Charter it contains three points and replaces the "universal" franchise by a more or less "enlarged" franchise.[a] Finally, in 1852, Hume proclaimed a new programme in which he even abandoned his "Little Charter" and demanded only *one* point: elections by ballot.[b] For the rest, Hume was the classical representative of the so-called "independent" opposition, which Cobbett aptly and exhaustively described as the "safety-valve" of the old system. In his last days the habit of proposing motions and

[a] Hume's speech in the House of Commons on June 20, 1848. *Hansard's Parliamentary Debates*, third series, Vol. XCIX, London, 1848.—*Ed.*

[b] Hume's speech in the House of Commons on March 25, 1852. *Hansard's Parliamentary Debates*, third series, Vol. CXX, London, 1852.—*Ed.*

then, just before the closure, at the nod of a minister, withdrawing them again, became a veritable mania with him. His flirting with "economising public funds" had become proverbial. Each Ministry allowed him to fight and reduce minor items so as to get the big ones the more safely through the House.

Written on February 24, 1855

First published in the *Neue Oder-Zeitung*, No. 98, February 28, 1855

Marked with the sign ×

Printed according to the newspaper

Published in English for the first time

Karl Marx

PALMERSTON[48]

London, February 27. The outcry against the aristocracy has been answered ironically by Palmerston with a ministry of ten lords and four baronets—ten lords, moreover, of whom eight sit in the House of Lords. He has met the dissatisfaction occasioned by the compromise between the various factions of the oligarchy with a compromise between various families within the Whig group. For the Grey clan, the ducal Sutherland family and, finally, the Clarendon family have received indemnification in his ministry. Sir George Grey, the Home Secretary, is a cousin of Earl Grey, whose brother-in-law is Sir Charles Wood, First Lord of the Admiralty. Earl Granville and the Duke of Argyll represent the Sutherland family. Sir George Cornewall Lewis, Chancellor of the Exchequer, is a brother-in-law of the Earl of Clarendon, the Foreign Secretary. India alone has been allotted to a man without a title, Vernon Smith; but at any rate he married into one of the Whig families. "A kingdom for a horse!" shouted Richard III.[a] "A horse for a kingdom!" shouts Palmerston, aping Caligula, and makes Vernon Smith Grand Mogul of India.[49]

"Lord Palmerston has given us not only the most aristocratic Administration of which we have any example in the history of the country", complains *The Morning Advertiser,* "but he has constructed his Government of the very worst aristocratic materials he could have selected."

The worthy *Advertiser,* however, finds comfort in the fact that

"Palmerston is not a free agent. [...] He is still in fetters and bonds".[b]

---

[a] Shakespeare, *Richard III,* Act V, Scene 4.—*Ed.*

[b] "The Ministry of Titles", *The Morning Advertiser,* No. 19872, February 28, 1855.—*Ed.*

As we predicted,[a] Lord Palmerston has formed a cabinet of ciphers, he himself being the only figure in it. Lord John Russell, who in 1851 had tumbled him undiplomatically out of the Whig cabinet, has been sent by him diplomatically on a journey.[50] Palmerston has made use of the Peelites to enter upon Aberdeen's heritage. As soon as he was sure of the premiership he dropped the Aberdeenites[b] and filched from Russell, as Disraeli says, not only the clothes of the Whigs but the Whigs themselves.[c] Despite the great similarity, almost identity, of the present government and Russell's Whig administration of 1846-1852, nothing could be more erroneous than to confuse them. This time we have not a cabinet at all but Lord Palmerston in lieu of a cabinet. Although its members are largely the same as before, the posts have been distributed among them in such a way, its following in the House of Commons is so different and it is making its appearance under such completely changed circumstances that whereas before it was a weak Whig ministry it is now the strong dictatorship of a single man, provided Palmerston is not a spurious Pitt, Bonaparte not a spurious Napoleon, and Lord John Russell continues to travel. Though the English bourgeois has been annoyed by the unexpected turn of events he is at present amused by the unconscionable adroitness with which Palmerston has duped and cheated both friend and foe. Palmerston, says the merchant of the City, has once more proved himself "clever".[d] But "clever" is an untranslatable qualification, full of ambiguity and rich in connotations. It comprises all the attributes of a man who knows how to blow his own trumpet, and understands what profits him and what brings harm to others. Virtuous and respectable as the English bourgeois is, he nevertheless admires most the man who is "clever", who does not bother about morals, who is not disconcerted by respect, who regards principles as snares in which to catch his fellows. If Palmerston is so "clever" will he not outwit the Russians just as he outwitted Russell? Thus speaks the politician of the English upper middle-class.

As for the Tories, they believe the good old times are back again, the evil coalition spell has been broken and the traditional Whig and Tory governmental seesaw has been restored. A real change, not confined to mere passive dissolution, could in fact

---

[a] See this volume, p. 45.—*Ed.*

[b] Graham, Gladstone and Herbert.—*Ed.*

[c] Disraeli's speech in the House of Commons on February 28, 1845. *Hansard's Parliamentary Debates*, third series, Vol. LXXVIII, London, 1845.—*Ed.*

[d] Marx uses the English word.—*Ed.*

only come about under a Tory government. Only when the Tories are at the helm is tremendous pressure from without[a] exerted and the inevitable transformations are put into effect. For example, the emancipation of the Catholics during Wellington's ministry; the repeal of the Corn Laws during Peel's ministry; and the same was true if not of the Reform Bill then at least of the reform agitation, which was more important than its result.[51]

When the English asked a Dutchman to come specially across the sea to become their King[b] it was for the purpose of ushering in with the new dynasty a new epoch—the epoch of the association of the landed aristocracy with the financial aristocracy. Ever since then we find privilege bestowed by blood and privilege bestowed by gold in constitutional equilibrium. Blood, for instance, decides in the case of certain army posts, whose incumbents hold them by virtue of family connections, nepotism or favouritism; but gold gets its due since all army commissions can be bought and sold for cash. It has been calculated that the officers now serving in the various regiments have invested an amount of £6 million in their posts. In order not to forfeit the rights they have acquired during their service and not to be ousted from their jobs by some young money-bags, the poorer officers borrow money to secure their advancement and thus become encumbered with mortgages.

In the church as in the army, family connections and ready cash are the two factors that count. While part of the ecclesiastical offices is allotted to the younger sons of the aristocracy, the other part belongs to the highest bidder. Trade in the "souls" of the English people—in so far as they belong to the Established Church—is no less usual than the slave trade in Virginia. In this trade there exist not only buyers and sellers but also brokers. One such "clerical" broker, named Simpson, appeared yesterday before the Court of Queen's Bench[c 52] to demand the fee due to him from a certain Lamb, who, he claimed, had contracted to procure him the right to have the rector Josiah Rodwell presented for the West-Hackney parish benefice. Simpson had stipulated 5 per cent from both buyer and seller, besides some minor charges. Lamb, he said, had not fulfilled his obligations. The circumstances were as follows: Lamb is the son of a seventy-year-old rector holding two benefices in Sussex whose market price is estimated at £16,000.

---

[a] Marx uses the English words "pressure from without" and gives the German translation.—*Ed.*

[b] William of Orange.—*Ed.*

[c] "Court of Queen's Bench. Guildhall, Feb. 26", *The Times*, No. 21988, February 27, 1855. Marx gives the name of the court in English.—*Ed.*

The price is naturally in direct proportion to the income from the parish and in inverse proportion to the age of the incumbent. Lamb junior is the patron of the livings held by Lamb senior and is also the brother of a still younger Lamb, the owner of the living and rector of West-Hackney. Since West-Hackney's rector is still very young, the market price of the next presentation to his sinecure is relatively low. Though it provides an annual income of £550 as well as a rectory, its owner has agreed to sell the right to the next appointment for only £1,000. His brother has promised him the Sussex parishes upon the death of their father, but wants to sell his thus vacated living in West-Hackney through Simpson to Josiah Rodwell for £3,000, thus pocketing a net profit of £2,000, and his brother obtaining a better benefice. The broker would have received a commission of 5 per cent., i.e., £300. It did not transpire why the deal did not go through. The court awarded the broker Simpson £50 in compensation "for work done".

Written on February 27, 1855

First published in the *Neue Oder-Zeitung*, No. 105, March 3, 1855

Marked with the sign ×

Printed according to the newspaper

Karl Marx

THE BRITISH CONSTITUTION[53]

London, March 2. While in every particular the British Constitution has failed at every point where the war has put it to the test, the coalition Ministry at home, the most constitutional of all ministries in the history of England, has broken up. Forty thousand British soldiers have died on the shores of the Black Sea—victims of the British Constitution! Officers, General Staff, Commissariat, Medical Department, Transport Service, Admiralty, Horse Guards,[a] Ordnance Office, Army and Navy, all have broken down and have discredited themselves in the esteem of the world; yet all have had the satisfaction of knowing that they have simply done their duty in the eyes of the British Constitution! *The Times* spoke more truly than it surmised when it exclaimed with reference to this universal bankruptcy: "It is the British Constitution that is under trial."[b] It has been tried and found guilty.

But what is the British Constitution? Does it essentially consist of a representative system and a limitation of the executive power? These features distinguish it neither from the Constitution of the United States of North America nor from the constitutions of the innumerable British joint-stock companies which understand "their business". The British Constitution is indeed nothing but an antiquated, obsolete, out-of-date compromise between the bourgeoisie, which *rules not officially* but in fact in all decisive spheres of civil society, and the landed aristocracy, which *governs officially.* Originally, after the "glorious" revolution of 1688, only a

[a] Marx uses the English term.—*Ed.*

[b] "Among all the political changes...", *The Times,* No. 21979, February 16, 1855.—*Ed.*

section of the bourgeoisie, the *aristocracy of finance,*[54] was included in the compromise. The Reform Bill of 1831 admitted another section, the *millocracy*[a] as the English call it, i.e. the high dignitaries of the *industrial* bourgeoisie.[55] The history of legislation since 1831 is the history of the concessions which have been made to the industrial bourgeoisie, from the new Poor Law to the repeal of the Corn Laws[56] and from the repeal of the Corn Laws to the death duties on landed property.

Even if the bourgeoisie—which is only the highest stratum of the middle classes—was on the whole acknowledged also *politically* as the *ruling class,* this was only on condition that the entire system of government in all its detail, even the executive department of the legislative power, i.e. the actual making of laws in both Houses of Parliament, remained safely in the hands of the landed aristocracy. [About] 1830 the bourgeoisie preferred the renewal of the compromise with the landed aristocracy to a compromise with the mass of the English people. Now the aristocracy, which, subject to certain principles laid down by the bourgeoisie, rules supreme in the Cabinet, in Parliament, in the administration, in the army and the navy—this section of the British nation, relatively the most important section, has just now been compelled to sign its own death warrant and to admit under the eyes of all the world that it no longer has the calling to govern Britain. One need only observe the attempts to galvanise its corpse! Ministry upon ministry is formed merely to go into dissolution after a regime of a few weeks. The crisis is permanent, the government only provisional. All political action is suspended, and everybody admits that his only aim is to keep the political machinery oiled sufficiently to prevent it from seizing up completely. The House of Commons does not even recognise itself in ministries created in its own image.

In the midst of this general helplessness not only has war to be waged, but an enemy even more dangerous than the Emperor Nicholas has to be fought. This enemy is the *crisis in trade* and *industry* which since last September is growing more violent and universal every day. Its iron hand immediately closed the mouths of the superficial apostles of free trade who preached for years that glutted markets and social crises had been banished forever into the shadowy realm of the past since the repeal of the Corn Laws. The glutted markets are there, but now nobody cries more loudly about the lack of prudence which prevented the manufac-

---

[a] Marx uses the English term.—*Ed.*

turers from limiting production than the selfsame economists who five months ago still taught—with the infallibility of dogmatism—that too much could never be produced.

This disease had already revealed itself in chronic form at the time of the strike in Preston.[57] Shortly afterwards the glut in the American market led to the outbreak of the crisis in the United States. India and China, though overstocked, as well as California and Australia, continued to form outlet channels for overproduction. As the English manufacturers could no longer sell their commodities in the home market without depressing prices, they resorted to the dangerous expedient of sending their commodities abroad on consignment, particularly to India, China, Australia and California. This makeshift enabled trade to proceed for a while with less disturbance than if the goods had been thrown on the market all at once. But no sooner did these shipments arrive at their destinations, than they determined prices there, and by the end of September the effect was felt here in England.

The crisis then changed its chronic character for an acute one. The first houses to collapse were the cotton printers, among them old established firms in and around Manchester. Then came the turn of the shipowners and the Australia and California merchants, then the Chinese houses, and finally the Indian. All took their turn, most of them suffered heavily, many had to suspend business, and the danger is not over for any of these branches of trade. On the contrary, it is constantly growing. The silk manufacturers were also hit; their industry is at the moment reduced to almost nothing, and the localities where it is carried on are experiencing the greatest distress. Now it will be the turn of the cotton spinners and manufacturers. Some of them have already succumbed and many more will yet have to share their fate. As we have seen earlier,[a] the fine-yarn spinners are working only short-time, and the coarse-yarn spinners will soon have to resort to the same remedy. A section of them are already working a few days a week only. How long will they be able to stand it?

A few more months, and the crisis in the factory districts will reach the depth of 1842, if it does not exceed it. But no sooner will its effects be generally felt among the working classes, than the political movement which has more or less been dormant among these classes over the past six years, leaving behind only the cadres for a new agitation, will spring up again. The conflict

---

[a] See this volume, p. 23.—*Ed.*

between the industrial proletariat and the bourgeoisie will flare up again at the same time that the conflict between the bourgeoisie and the aristocracy reaches its climax. Then the mask which has so far hidden the real features of Britain's political physiognomy from foreigners, will drop. Nevertheless, only those unfamiliar with the wealth of this country in human and material resources will doubt that it will emerge victorious and freshly rejuvenated from the impending great crisis.

Written on March 2, 1855

First published in the *Neue Oder-Zeitung*, No. 109, March 6, 1855

Marked with the sign ×

Printed according to the newspaper

Karl Marx

LAYARD

London, March 2. Layard, the great Nineveh scholar, in a speech to his constituents of Aylesbury the day before yesterday, made an interesting chapter public characterising the way in which the oligarchy distributes the most important state posts on the one hand, and the highly ambiguous attitude of the so-called liberal and independent Members of Parliament to this oligarchy on the other.

Layard told us that Lord Granville appointed him Under-Secretary of State in the Foreign Office, where he served for three months, when Russell's Ministry was overthrown and the Derby Cabinet was being formed. Derby proposed to him that he should stay in his post until the successor appointed for him, Lord Stanley (Derby's son), returned from India. Then he would entrust him (Layard) with a diplomatic mission abroad.

"All my political friends," Layard said, "thought I ought to have accepted that offer. Lord J. Russell alone expressed a contrary opinion, which I unhesitatingly accepted."[a]

So Layard rejected Derby's offer. Well! Lord Russell is Minister again and Layard is not forgotten. Russell now invites him to a ministerial banquet where he is to take his seat as Under-Secretary of the "Board of Control",[b] i. e. the Ministry for India. Layard agrees. Suddenly, however, Russell remembers that an elderly Whig gentleman, by the name of Sir Thomas Redington, who in the past had been in charge of Irish, though

[a] "Mr. Layard and His Constituents", *The Times,* No. 21990, March 1, 1855.—*Ed.*

[b] Marx uses the English term.—*Ed.*

never of Asiatic affairs, "is still unprovided for" (literally). He therefore gives Layard to understand that he should not stand in the way of the accommodation of the elderly gentleman. Layard resigns again. Russell, encouraged by the self-sacrificing modesty of the scholar, conveys to him that he should get right out of the way and accept a consular post in Egypt. This time Layard is infuriated, he refuses and becomes conspicuous in Parliament by making important speeches against the oriental policy of the Ministry.

Palmerston has no sooner formed his Cabinet than he seeks to compensate him by offering him the post of Secretary in the Ordnance Office. Layard rejects this, as he knows nothing at all about artillery, etc. How naive! As though the retiring Secretary—Mr. Monsell, one of the brokers of the Irish Brigade[58]—had ever been able to tell an ordinary musket from a needle gun! Palmerston now offers him the Under-Secretaryship in the War Ministry. Layard accepts, but the next morning Palmerston has discovered that Frederick Peel—that bureaucratic nonentity—can at this moment not be spared from the War Ministry, of whose functions Peel notoriously understands nothing. As a substitute he finally offers Layard the Under-Secretaryship in the Colonial Office, in Russell's name. Layard considers that the present situation is too difficult to engage in the study of fifty colonies with which he has never before been concerned. He refuses, and there this edifying story ends.

The only moral which the ministerial papers draw from it is: that Layard is still very inexperienced in the way of the world and has iniquitously forfeited his Assyrian fame.

Written on March 2, 1855

First published in the *Neue Oder-Zeitung*, No. 107, March 5, 1855

Marked with the sign ×

Printed according to the newspaper

Published in English for the first time

New-York Weekly Tribune.
Vol. XIV......No. 707. NEW-YORK, SATURDAY, MARCH 31, 1855 TWO DOLLARS A YEAR.

Karl Marx

THE CRISIS IN ENGLAND

Of course, the most interesting feature of the news from Europe by the *Atlantic*[59] must be the death of the Czar[a] and the influence of that event on the pending complications. But important as may be the intelligence on this subject, or on other continental affairs, in its interest for the thoughtful observer it can hardly surpass the gradual indications and developments of that momentous political crisis in which, without any will of their own, the British nation are now involved at home. The last attempt to maintain that antiquated compromise called the British Constitution—a compromise between the class that rule officially and the class that rule non-officially—has signally failed. The coalition ministry, the most constitutional of all, has not only broken down in England but the constitution itself has broken down in detail at every point where it has been tested by the war. Forty thousand British soldiers have died on the shores of the Black Sea, victims to the British Constitution. Officers, Staff, Commissariat, Medical Department, Transport Service, Admiralty, Horse Guards, Ordnance, Army and Navy, all and every one have broken down, have ruined themselves in the estimation of the world; but all and every one have failed with the satisfaction of knowing that they had but done their duty in the eyes of the British Constitution. The London *Times* spoke more truly than it knew, when it said, with respect to this universal failure, that it was the British Constitution itself which was on its trial[b]!

[a] Nicholas I died on March 2, 1855.—*Ed.*

[b] "Among all the political changes...", *The Times*, No. 21979, February 16, 1855.—*Ed.*

It has been tried, and found guilty. This British constitution, what is it but a superannuated compromise, by which the general governing power is abandoned to some sections of the middle class, on condition that the whole of the real Government, the Executive in all its details, even to the executive department of the legislative power—or that is the actual law-making in the two Houses of Parliament—is secured to the landed aristocracy? This aristocracy which, subject to general principles laid down by the middle class, rules supreme in the Cabinet, the Parliament, the Administration, the Army and the Navy—this very important half of the British constitution has now been obliged to sign its own death-warrant. It has been compelled to confess its incapacity any longer to govern England. Ministry after Ministry is formed, only to dissolve itself after a few weeks' reign. The crisis is permanent; the Government is but provisional. All political action is suspended; nobody professes to do more than to keep the political machine greased well enough to prevent it from stopping. That pride of the constitutional Englishman, the House of Commons itself, is brought to a dead stand. It knows itself no longer, since it is split up in numberless fractions, attempting all the arithmetical combinations and variations, of which a given number of units is capable. It can no longer recognize itself in the various Cabinets, which it makes in its own image, for no other purpose than to unmake them again. The bankruptcy is complete.

And not only has the war had to be carried on in the midst of this national helplessness, which, breaking out like a pestilence in the Crimea, has gradually seized all the branches of the body politic, but there is an opponent to contend with far more dangerous than Russia—an opponent more than a match for all the Gladstones, Cardwells, Russells and Palmerstons of past, present and future Cabinets put together. That opponent is the commercial and industrial crisis which, since September last, has set in with a severity, a universality, and a violence, not to be mistaken. Its stern, iron hand at once shut up the mouths of those shallow Free Traders who for years had gone on preaching, that since the repeal of the Corn Laws glutted markets were impossible. There the glut is, with all its consequences, and in its most acute form; and in view of it nobody is more eager to accuse the improvidence of manufacturers, in not reducing production, than those very economists, who told them only a few months before that they never could produce too much. We long since called attention to the existence of this disease in a chronic form. It has been aggravated, of course, by the late difficulties in

America, and the crisis that depressed our trade. India and China, glutted though they were, continued to be used as outlets—as also California and Australia. When the English manufacturers could no longer sell their goods at home, or would not do so rather than depress prices, they resorted to the absurd expedient of consigning them abroad, especially to India, China, Australia and California. This expedient enabled trade to go on for a while with less embarrassment than if the goods had been thrown at once upon the home market; but when they arrived at their destinations they produced embarrassment at once, and about the end of September last the effect began to be felt in England.

Then the crisis exchanged its chronic form for an acute one. The first houses that felt it were the calico printers; a number of them, including very old established houses in Manchester and that vicinity, broke down. Then came the turn of the shipowners and the Australian and Californian merchants; next came the China traders, and finally the Indian houses. All of them have had their turn; most of them losing severely, while many had to suspend; and for none of them has the danger passed away. On the contrary it is still increasing. The silk manufacturers were equally affected; their trade has been reduced to almost nothing, and the localities where it is carried on have suffered, and still suffer, the greatest distress. Then came the turn of the cotton-spinners and manufacturers. Some of them had already succumbed at our last advices, and a great many more must do so. The spinners of fine yarns, as we also learn, had begun to work only four days a week, and the coarse spinners would shortly have to do the same. But how many of them will be able to stand this for any length of time?

A few months more and the crisis will be at a hight which it has not reached in England since 1846, perhaps not since 1842. When its effects begin to be fully felt among the working classes, then will that political movement begin again, which has been dormant for six years. Then will the working-men of England rise anew, menacing the middle classes at the very time that the middle classes are finally driving the aristocracy from power. Then will the mask be torn off which has hitherto hid the real political features of Great Britain. Then will the two real contending parties in that country stand face to face—the middle class and the working classes, the Bourgeoisie and the Proletariat—and England will at last be compelled to share in the general social evolutions of European society. When England entered into the French Alliance she finally abandoned that isolated character which her insular position had created for her, but which the commerce of the world, and the increasing facilities for intercourse, had long since undermined. Henceforth she can hardly help undergoing the great internal movements of the other European nations.

It is also a striking fact that the last moments of the British Constitution are as prolific in evidences of a corrupt social state as the last moments of Louis Philippe's monarchy. We have before referred to the Parliamentary and Government scandals, to the Stonor, the Sadleir, the Lawley[a] scandals; but, to crown all, came the Handcock and De Burgh revelations, with Lord Clanricarde, a peer of the realm, as a principal though indirect party to a most revolting deed.[60] No wonder that this should seem to complete the parallel, and that people, on reading the damning details, should involuntarily exclaim "The Duc de Praslin! The Duc de Praslin!" England has arrived at her 1847; who knows when and what will be her 1848?

Written on March 2, 1855

First published in the *New-York Daily Tribune*, No. 4346, March 24, 1855, reprinted in the *New-York Semi-Weekly Tribune*, No. 1027, March 30, 1855 and the *New-York Weekly Tribune*, No. 707, March 31, 1855 as a leading article

Reproduced from the *New-York Daily Tribune*

[a] See the article "The Late British Government" by Marx and Engels (present edition, Vol. 13, pp. 620-26).—*Ed.*

Karl Marx

THE BUYING OF COMMISSIONS.— NEWS FROM AUSTRALIA

London, March 3. At the sitting the day before yesterday the House of Commons, as everybody knows, rejected Lord Goderich's motion allowing non-commissioned officers to reach the rank of captain. Palmerston used the old dilemma: a partial reform is impossible because one part of the old system depends upon the other.[a] Individual practical reforms are thus impossible because they are theoretically impossible. The total reform of the system is impossible because that is not reform but revolution. Theoretical reform therefore is impossible because it is not practical. This House of Commons—a House which takes to heart the principle *principiis obsta*[b] was eager to be convinced, or rather it did not need convincing as it had passed sentence before the trial.

Palmerston argued on this occasion that the system of selling officers' commissions was old, and he was right there. As we indicated earlier,[c] it began with the "glorious" revolution of 1688,[61] with the introduction of the National Debt, banknotes, and the Dutch succession. Already in the Mutiny Act of 1694[62] the necessity is stated of forestalling

"the great mischief of buying and selling Military Employment in his Majesties Armies", and it is enacted that "every commissioned officer" (only non-commissioned officers have *no* commissions) should swear that he has not bought his commission.

---

[a] Palmerston's speech was reported in *The Times*, No. 21991, March 2, 1855.—*Ed.*

[b] Resist temptation (Ovidius, *Remedia amoris*, 91).—*Ed.*

[c] See Marx's article "Parliamentary News" (present edition, Vol. 13, pp. 605-08).—*Ed.*

This restriction was, however, not carried into effect; on the contrary, in 1702 Sir Nathan Wright, the Lord Keeper,[a] decided in the opposite sense. On May 1, 1711, a statute of Queen Anne expressly recognised the system by decreeing

"that commissions shall no longer be sold without royal confirmation and that no officer may buy himself off unless he has served 20 years or has become incapacitated in the service, etc."

From this official recognition of the trade in military commissions it was but one step to officially regulating the market price of commissions. Accordingly, in 1719-20 market prices were fixed for the first time. The prices of officers' commissions were renewed in 1766, 1772, 1773, 1783, and finally in 1821, when the present prices were fixed. As early as 1766 War Minister Barrington published a letter which states:

"The consequence of this trade in officers' commissions frequently is that men who enter the army with the most ardent desire to serve, who have distinguished themselves at every opportunity, are kept for their whole lives in the lowest rank because they are poor. These deserving officers suffer the most cruel humiliation of being under the command of youths from wealthy families who entered the service much later but whose fortune enabled them to find entertainment outside the service, while the others, who are constantly at service quarters, carry out the duties of these gentlemen and have learnt their own."

It is true that England's common law declares it illegal to give a present or a "broker's fee" for any public office, just as the Rules of the Established Church place a ban on simony.[63] Historical development, however, shows that the law does not determine practice nor does practice remove a contradictory law.

The latest news from Australia adds a new element to the general discomfort, unrest and insecurity. We must distinguish between the riot in Ballarat (near Melbourne) and the general revolutionary movement in the State of Victoria.[64] The former will by this time have been suppressed; the latter can only be suppressed by far-reaching concessions. The former is merely a symptom and an incidental outbreak of the latter. Concerning the Ballarat riot, the facts are simply these: A certain Bentley, owner of the Eureka Hotel at the Ballarat goldfields, had got into all sorts of conflicts with the gold diggers. A murder which occurred at his house increased the hatred of him. At the coroner's inquest Bentley was discharged as innocent. Ten of the twelve jurymen, who functioned at the inquest, however, published a protest

[a] Marx uses the English expression.—*Ed.*

against the partiality of the coroner,[a] who had attempted to suppress witnesses' evidence disadvantageous to the prisoner. At the demand of the people a second inquest was held. Bentley was again discharged despite very suspicious evidence by some witnesses. It became known, however, that one of the judges had financial interests in the hotel. Many earlier and later complaints show the dubious character of the government officials of the Ballarat district. On the day Bentley was discharged for the second time, the gold diggers held a tremendous demonstration, set his hotel on fire and then withdrew. Three of the ringleaders were arrested on a warrant issued by Sir Charles Hotham, the Governor-General of Victoria State. On November 27 a deputation of gold diggers demanded their release. Hotham rejected the demand. The gold diggers held a monster meeting. The Governor sent police and troops from Melbourne. It came to a clash, several dead remained on the scene, and according to the latest news, up to December 1, the gold diggers have hoisted the flag of independence.

Even this story, which is in the main taken from a government paper, does not put the English judges and government officials in a favourable light. It shows the prevailing distrust. There are actually two big issues around which the revolutionary movement in Victoria State is revolving. The gold diggers are demanding the abolition of the gold digging licences, i.e. of a tax directly imposed on labour; secondly, they demand the abolition of the property qualification for Members of the Chamber of Representatives, in order themselves to obtain control over taxes and legislation. Here we see, in essence, motives similar to those which led to the Declaration of Independence of the United States,[65] except that in Australia the conflict is initiated by the workers against the monopolists linked with the colonial bureaucracy. In the Melbourne *Argus* we read of big reform meetings and, on the other hand, of large-scale military preparations on the part of the Government. It says among other things:

> "At a meeting of 4,000 persons it was decided that the [...] license-fee is an imposition and an unjustifiable tax on free labour. This meeting therefore pledges itself to take immediate steps to abolish the same, by at once burning all their licenses. That in the event of any party being arrested for having no licenses, [...] the united people will [...] defend and protect them".[b]

---

[a] Marx uses the English term, with the German equivalent in brackets.— *Ed.*

[b] "Ballaarat. Wednesday, November 29th, 1854", *The Argus* (Melbourne), No. 2359, December 1, 1854.— *Ed.*

On 30 November Commissioners Rede and Johnson appeared with cavalry and police at Ballarat and demanded with drawn swords and fixed bayonets that the gold diggers show their licences. These, mostly armed, held a mass meeting and resolved to resist the collection of the hated tax to the utmost. They refused to show their licences; they declared they had burnt them; the Riot Act[66] was read, and so the revolt was complete.

To describe the joint actions of the monopolists lording it in the local legislatures and the colonial bureaucracy in league with them, it is sufficient to mention that in 1854 government expenditures in Victoria amounted to £3,564,258 sterling, including a deficit of £1,085,896, that is of more than one-third of the total income. And in face of the present crisis, of the general bankruptcy, Sir Charles Hotham demands for the year 1855 a sum of £4,801,292 sterling. Victoria has barely 300,000 inhabitants, and of the above sum £1,860,830 sterling, that is £6 sterling per head, are intended for public works, namely roads, docks, quays, barracks, government buildings, customs offices, botanical gardens, government stables, etc. At this rate of £6 per head, the population of Great Britain would have to pay £168,000,000 sterling annually for public works alone, i.e. three times as much as their total tax. It is understandable that the working population is indignant at this supertaxation. It is likewise evident what good business the bureaucracy and the monopolists between them must make with such extensive public works defrayed at other people's expense.

Written on March 3, 1855

First published in the *Neue Oder-Zeitung*, No. 111, March 7, 1855

Marked with the sign ×

Printed according to the newspaper

Published in English for the first time

Karl Marx

THE ENGLISH PRESS ON THE LATE TSAR

[*Neue Oder-Zeitung*, No. 109, March 6, 1855]

London, March 3. Today's entire daily and weekly press carries, of course, leading articles on the death of the Emperor of Russia[a]—but all, without exception, commonplace and dull. *The Times* has at least attempted to inflate its style to the heights of Timur Tamburlaine[b] by exaggerated grandiloquence. We shall single out only two passages, both of them compliments for Lord Palmerston. The strain which had hastened the Emperor's death had been exacerbated by the appointment as Prime Minister of Palmerston, the "worst enemy of the Czar". Between 1830 and 1840 (the first decade of Palmerston's foreign policy), the Tsar had abandoned his policy of encroachment and world domination. The former assertion is as much worth as the latter.

The Morning Advertiser, on the other hand, distinguishes itself by the discovery that Michael is the Emperor's eldest son and thus the legitimate heir to the throne.[c] *The Morning Post*, Palmerston's private *Moniteur*, in its funeral oration, reveals to the English public that

> "The Conference at Vienna will, of course, be delayed for a short time, and will be renewed under new auspices;" and that "this very afternoon [...] Lord Clarendon will have an interview with the Emperor Napoléon, at Boulogne, in which [...] the ideas of the two Governments, with reference to this sudden and momentous event, will be interchanged and discussed".[d]

---

[a] Nicholas I.—*Ed.*

[b] This refers to the items "Scarcely had the intelligence..." and "The Emperor of Russia is dead...." in *The Times*, No. 21992, March 3, 1855.—*Ed.*

[c] "No event of greater importance...", *The Morning Advertiser*, No. 19875, March 3, 1855. Actually, the eldest son of Nicholas I was Alexander.—*Ed.*

[d] "Nicholas Paulovitch, Emperor and Autocrat of All the Russias...", *The Morning Post*, No. 25325, March 3, 1855.—*Ed.*

The Daily News does not believe in the peaceful consequences of this "sudden event" for the Western powers could not withdraw *before* the fall of Sevastopol and Russia could not withdraw *after* it.[a]

[*Neue Oder-Zeitung*, No. 116, March 10, 1855][b]

London, March 6. The death of Emperor Nicholas has been the occasion for strange claims in the press here. Dr. Granville is surpassed by Mr. James Lee, who has made no medical observations.[67]

In today's *Morning Advertiser* he writes: "On the 6th of February I sent a letter [...] to you, in which I said, that the Emperor of Russia would be a corpse at the expiration of three weeks, dating the time from my letter."

In a postscript, the editor of *The Morning Advertiser* states that his paper had in fact received Lee's letter, but consigned it to the wastepaper basket as the figment of a sick brain. Lee goes even further. He offers to prophesy to the *Advertiser* the early demise of another potentate, on the one condition that his communication be published. Lee's predictions seem to be cheaper than the books of the Sibyl.

Similarly, the Emperor's death has led *Urquhart* who, as Highland Scot, possesses the gift of second sight, to make several Pythian utterances,[68] of which the following is the most characteristic and also the most intelligible:

"There was blood between him [Nicholas] and the Poles, who could not be left behind to be watched, and whose five hundred thousand warriors were required. And it was well understood that the restoration of the white double-headed eagle—the symbol of that reunion of the Slavonic races announced in the Cathedral of Moscow by his predecessor, Alexander, was not to take place in his day."[c]

Urquhart thinks that now the moment has come when Russia will be absorbed by Slavdom, as the Muscovite empire had earlier been absorbed by Russia.

Written on March 3 and 6, 1855

First published in the *Neue Oder-Zeitung*, Nos. 109 and 116, March 6 and 10, 1855

Marked with the sign ×

Printed according to the newspaper

Published in English for the first time

---

[a] "The Death of the Czar. (Communicated)", *The Daily News*, No. 2742, March 3, 1855.—*Ed.*

[b] The second instalment was published without a heading.—*Ed.*

[c] D. Urquhart, "On the Death of the Emperor Nicholas. To the Editor of *The Morning Advertiser*", *The Morning Advertiser*, No. 19877, March 6, 1855. Instead of "reunion of Slavonic races" "reunion of Slavonic faces" is printed in Urquhart's article.—*Ed.*

Karl Marx

ON THE HISTORY OF THE FRENCH ALLIANCE

London, March 6. Today's *Morning Herald* has surprised London by the following announcement:

"We have excellent authority for stating that the French Emperor has remonstrated against the committee for inquiring into the conduct of the war, and that he has said, that, in the event of its continuing to sit, the armies of the two nations cannot act together, although they may act for the same object. In order [...] to satisfy Louis Napoleon, without affronting the English people, a dissolution of Parliament will [...] take place[a] as soon as possible."

Without attributing too much importance to this paragraph in the *Herald*, we record it as one of the many symptoms which indicate that *secret forces on both sides of the Channel are working to bring about a dissolution of the Anglo-French alliance.*

In this context the statements made by ex-minister *Sir James Graham* should be recalled[b]: under pressure from the Committee of Inquiry our Admiral[c] would be forced to reveal all the considerations which led to the postponement of the blockade, and the inquiry would include our relations with our great and powerful ally at a time when it is of the utmost importance that there should not be the least misunderstanding.

Sidney Herbert: He challenged the Committee to get to the bottom of the affair without taking the risk of insulting our army in the Crimea and possibly shaking the confidence of our allies. Unless one of its members were able to check the Committee when

[a] "England and France. Probable Dissolution of Parliament", *The Morning Herald*, No. 22372, March 6, 1855.—*Ed.*

[b] The speeches of Graham, Herbert and Gladstone in the House of Commons on February 23 were reported in *The Times*, No. 21986, February 24, 1855.—*Ed.*

[c] J. W. D. Dundas.—*Ed.*

it stepped on dangerous ground, great injustice would be done, and even the officers summoned by it might perhaps be sacrificed, since incriminating questions might be put to them, while they would not be permitted to answer because in so doing they might have to make dangerous and delicate revelations. He for one thought it his duty to prevent officers of the British army being placed in a position where they would be made the object of accusations while their hands were tied and they were unable to defend themselves.

Gladstone: Among other things, a committee would have to examine why a road from Balaklava had not been constructed earlier! If the Committee did not investigate this, it would achieve nothing. If however it investigated this question, the reply would be: shortage of labour. If it then asked what caused this shortage of labour, the reply would be that the men were digging trenches and that these *were extensive owing to the proportion in which the lines had been distributed between the French and the English.* I further declare that an investigation would be empty pretence unless you probed the question of the roads, and, if you probed that, the defence of the accused parties would directly disturb the most intimate relations between England and France.

Understandably these ministerial statements have forced the widely scattered seeds of distrust into abundant growth. National pride had already been severely wounded by the relegation of the British army in the Crimea to guard duty at Balaklava. Then came the semi-official article in the *Moniteur* with its "imperatorial" remarks on the British Constitution.[a] It called forth caustic replies in the weekly press here. Then came the publication of the Brussels *Mémoire,* in which Louis Bonaparte is represented as the originator of the Crimean expedition on the one hand, and of the concessions to Austria on the other.[b] By their ruthlessness, the comments on this *Mémoire*—as, for instance, that in *The Morning Advertiser*—remind one of the "Letters of an Englishman" on the *coup d'état* of December 2.[c] The following extract from the Chartist

---

[a] *Le Moniteur universel,* No. 48, February 17, 1855.—*Ed.*

[b] The reference is to the anonymous pamphlet *De la conduite de la guerre d'Orient...,* published in Brussels in 1855, which criticised the conduct of the Crimean campaign. The pamphlet was attributed, among other writers, to Prince Napoleon (Jérôme Bonaparte, Jr.).—*Ed.*

[c] The comparison is between the article "Secret History of the Crimean Expedition" (*The Morning Advertiser,* No. 19875, March 3, 1855) and the anonymous "Letters of an Englishman" by A. Richards, which were published in *The Times* between December 1851 and November 1852 and appeared in book form in 1852.—*Ed.*

organ, *The People's Paper*, will illustrate the repercussions of all this in the true popular press[a]:

"He [Bonaparte] it was that lured England to the Crimea. [...] Our army, once in that snare, was placed by him in such a position, that it broke the edge of Russia's strength before that strength could reach his own. [...] At Alma, at Balaklava, at Inkermann, at Sebastopol, the British were played into the post of danger. They had to bear the brunt—they had to suffer the chief loss; [...] England engaged to send only one-third as many men as France. That one-third had to fight nearly the whole of the battles. That one-third had to take more than half the lines before Sebastopol. Our army was destroyed, because they could not get the food and clothes which lay rotting at Balaklava. They could not get them because there was no road from Balaklava to Sebastopol, and there was no road from Balaklava to Sebastopol because Napoleon insisted that the British with less than one-third of the force [...] should do more than half the work in the trenches; and, therefore, they had no men to spare to make the road.[...] This is the secret at which Graham, Sidney Herbert, and Gladstone hinted.... Thus he, Napoleon, has deliberately murdered 44,000 of our soldiers, etc."

All these signs of suspicious vexation with the French ally gain importance because Lord Palmerston is at the head of the government—a man who on each occasion has reached his position by climbing up the ladder of the French alliance, then suddenly turned this alliance into almost unavoidable war between France and England. Thus it was in the Turko-Syrian affair of 1840, and the treaty of July 15 [69] with which he crowned his ten-year-old alliance with France. In reference to this, Sir Robert Peel remarked in 1842 that

"*he had never clearly understood* why the alliance with France of which the noble lord had always pretended to be so proud, had been broken."[b]

And thus, once again, in 1847, on the occasion of the Spanish marriages.[70] At the time, it was asserted by Palmerston—who, in 1846, was allowed to resume his post only after he had paid his respects to Louis Philippe, become reconciled to him with great ostentation, and flattered the Frenchman in a speech in the House of Commons—that it was Louis Philippe who had dissolved the alliance because the Treaty of Utrecht [71] had been violated (a treaty lapsed in 1793 and never renewed since that time) and because he had committed an "act of perfidy" against the English Crown. As to the "act of perfidy" it was really committed, but, as the documents

---

[a] The extract is from the speech delivered by Ernest Jones at St Martin's Hall on February 27, 1855. Marx quotes from a report published in *The People's Paper*, No. 148, March 3, 1855.—*Ed.*

[b] From Peel's speech in the House of Commons on August 10, 1842. *Hansard's Parliamentary Debates*, third series, Vol. LXV, col. 1281-82, London, 1842.—*Ed.*

subsequently published proved, Palmerston had manoeuvred the French Court into this act of perfidy in the most cunning manner so as to obtain a *pretext* for the break. While the wily Louis Philippe thought he was outwitting him, he simply fell into the carefully laid trap of the "facetious" viscount. The February revolution alone prevented the outbreak of war between England and France at that time.

Written on March 6, 1855

First published in the *Neue Oder-Zeitung*, No. 115, March 9, 1855

Marked with the sign ×

Printed according to the newspaper

Published in English for the first time

Karl Marx

THE COMMITTEE OF INQUIRY

London, March 7. The rumour of an impending dissolution of Parliament, on the pretext that the Committee of Inquiry was compromising the French alliance, seems to be correct. A correspondent of *The Morning Advertiser* remarks in this connection:

"But who made the committee an open one? Lord Palmerston, who, they say, will dissolve the House [...]. Mr. Roebuck had demanded and compelled an inquest, and he desired secrecy—Lord Palmerston had refused and had been driven to an inquest, and he was for publicity. [...] He compels the Committee to pursue the course most obnoxious to our French Ally. That obnoxiousness then is to enable the Minister to dissolve the House, extinguish the Inquiry, and laugh in his sleeve at both!"[a]

In a leading article on the same subject, *The Morning Herald* says, *inter alia*:

"When the allied armies took up their positions before Sebastopol the English contingent was the stronger of the two, and the subsequent destruction of our army was to be attributed entirely to the want of reserves in the Mediterranean and of an organised militia at home; from which causes it became impossible to supply the English army with those reinforcements [...]. The attempt to involve the name of our [...] allies in the discussion is an almost undisguised effort, on the part of desperate and unprincipled men, to screen themselves from that inquiry which they well know must be fatal to their future political existence. [...] Lord Clarendon has unconstitutionally sought an interview with the Emperor of the French, for the sole purpose of extracting from him some declaration of opinion which might be tortured and twisted into a disapproval of an inquiry [...]. Having obtained this, [...] it is the intention of these patriotic Ministers to attempt to intimidate

---

[a] "The Reported Dissolution", *The Morning Advertiser*, No. 19878, March 7, 1855.—*Ed.*

the House of Commons [...] by a threat of dissolution, and an appeal to the country upon a cry that '*the French alliance is in danger!*'."[a]

It is obvious that, if this pretext of the English Government serves to get rid of the Committee of Inquiry, it serves no less to jeopardise the French alliance and so to prepare for the very thing which it pretends to be preventing. The conviction that the Committee was being abandoned because it would unearth "delicate and dangerous" mysteries, compromising to the French ally, effectively compromises that ally. The suppression of the Committee would speak more loudly against him than could the Committee itself. Besides, the slightest acquaintance with the tides of public opinion in England must convince anyone that consciousness of so great a concession to a foreign state as suppressing a parliamentary committee, or dissolving Parliament at Bonaparte's alleged request, would lead at the next opportunity to a terrible reaction against French influence in an attempt to redress the balance.

We have compiled General Sir de Lacy Evans'[b] statements from reports on the first two sittings of the Committee of Inquiry. At Malta, whither a commissary had been sent some time before the army, he was surprised that no purchase of mules was made. No adequate preparation was made at Scutari for killing cattle or baking. Some of the Treasury regulations at this time proved very inconvenient. He firmly believed the war was commenced under the delusion that matters would be settled without any explosion of gunpowder, and that there was no necessity for any magazines at all. Though the Commissariat was under the control of the commander, yet it was closely connected also with the Treasury (and therefore with the Prime Minister), and the officers of the Commissariat must have been given to understand that it was extravagant to make the disbursements necessary for a real war. At Varna, hardly any preparations had been made for looking after the wounded. Evidently the predominant impression had been that this would be a war without wounds. Arrangements were not made to enable the army to take the field at once. When the Russians crossed the Danube Omer Pasha applied for assistance, and the answer was that the army had not the means of transport, which ought to have been provided long before. He

[a] "A more audacious and unconstitutional attempt...", *The Morning Herald*, No. 22373, March 7, 1855.—*Ed.*

[b] Published in *The Times*, No. 21994, March 6, and No. 21995, March 7, 1855.—*Ed.*

thought the Government was still waiting for notes and protocols from Vienna, and no great exertions were made to put the army in a condition to move; it was, of course, the Government, not the Commissariat, that was responsible for this sort of delay. The Russians were carrying on the siege of Silistria, and still the army was not in readiness to move. The two departments entrusted with the procurement of food supplies were the Commissariat and the Department of the Quartermaster General. Clashes with the Commissariat were the order of the day. Its officials might have been efficient clerks in the Treasury: in fact, they spent most of their time writing letters to the Treasury. In the field they proved useless. Even eighteen miles from Varna, there was the greatest difficulty in getting provisions. There the Commissariat proved to be so short of staff that he had to lend 100 non-commissioned officers for service in the department. Mortality among troops at Varna was due mainly to low morale, a consequence of their trying and prolonged inactivity.

As to the situation of the troops in the Crimea, de Lacy partly repeats what is already common knowledge—lack of food, of clothing, of wooden huts, etc., etc. As to detail, we merely quote the following statements:

"Filder, as old as the hills, in charge of the Commissariat as far back as the Pyrenean campaign and now Quartermaster General never consulted with him as to the wants of his [Evans'] division; it was his duty to do so; he [Evans] wanted him to do it, but Mr. Filder declined. Mr. Filder was under the direct orders of Lord Raglan, but, of course, he carried on a correspondence with the Treasury." "It was very inconvenient that the cavalry and artillery horses should have been employed for the transport of forage. The consequence was that his [Evans'] guns were latterly not more than half horsed." "The road from Balaklava harbour to the camp had been frightfully churned up and waterlogged. [...] The work of 1,000 men for ten days would have secured a road from Balaklava [...] but he believed that all the men who could be spared [...] were set to work in the trenches".

Finally, on the melting away of the British army before Sevastopol, Evans declares

"...his conviction that neither the deficiency in the supply of clothes, food, or fuel would have produced the shocking sickness and death in the army, had not the troops been overworked in the trenches. It was the fatigue of the men that was so injurious. From the first the work cut out for them was entirely beyond their numerical strength. The overwork during the nights was decidedly the main cause of the suffering of the army".

Written on March 7, 1855

First published in the *Neue Oder-Zeitung*, No. 117, March 10, 1855

Marked with the sign ×

Printed according to the newspaper

Published in English for the first time

Karl Marx

THE BRUSSELS *MEMOIRE*

London, March 7. Today *The Morning Post*, Palmerston's private *Moniteur*, prints the well-known Brussels *Mémoire*[a] in an English translation with a brief foreword according to which Prince Napoleon is supposed to be the pamphlet's author. Simultaneously the same paper prints a leading article full of vicious attacks on Napoleon Bonaparte, making the fulsomely often repeated point that "only a *Russian spy*" could be the author of the *Mémoire*.

Under the pretext of standing up for Louis Bonaparte against his cousin and of preserving the memory of the unsullied Achille Leroy, *alias* Florimond, *alias* de S[ain]t-Arnaud, the *Post* obviously only means to accumulate material for Anglo-French collisions. *Saint*-Arnaud was one of those *saints* who turn up in the calendar of French *chevaliers d'industrie* at any given period, e. g. Saint-Germain, Saint-Georges, etc. Credit is due to *The Morning Post* for having canonised them and transformed them into saints befitting their station. The assertion that the *Mémoire* made "military" revelations to the Russians is completely absurd. Neither in England nor in America or Germany have critics waited for the *Mémoire* to present the Crimean expedition as a failure. The *Mémoire* has added not one syllable to criticism made so far, although it does have the merit of supplying informal portraits of the mediocrities who were laying down the law at Sevastopol. It is

[a] The reference is to the anonymous pamphlet *De la conduite de la guerre d'Orient...* (see this volume, p. 70) which was published in English under the title "Memoir Addressed to the Government of H. M. the Emperor Napoleon III" in *The Morning Post*, No. 25328, March 7, 1855. The leading article mentioned below was printed in the same issue.—*Ed.*

only in the interest of the Russians to keep alive illusions about the Crimean expedition, and the grandiloquence with which the *Post* holds forth about Russian agents and Russian spies reminds one of Aeschines, who similarly boasted that he was the first to see through the king of Macedonia's plans, while reproaching Demosthenes with having been bribed by Philip. However, we are, of course, far from presenting Prince Napoleon Bonaparte as a Demosthenes.

Written on March 7, 1855

First published in the *Neue Oder-Zeitung*, No. 118, March 11, 1855

Marked with the sign ×

Printed according to the newspaper

Published in English for the first time

Karl Marx

IRELAND'S REVENGE[72]

London, March 13. Ireland has revenged herself upon England, *socially*—by bestowing an *Irish quarter* on every English industrial maritime or commercial town of any size, and *politically*—by presenting the English Parliament with an "Irish Brigade".[73] In 1833, Daniel O'Connell decried the Whigs as "base, bloody and brutal". In 1835, he became the most efficient tool of the Whigs; although the English majority was opposed to the Melbourne Administration, it remained in office from April 1835 to August 1841 because of the support it received from O'Connell and his Irish Brigade. What transformed the O'Connell of 1833 into the O'Connell of 1835? It was an agreement, known as the *Lichfield-House Contract*, according to which the Whig Cabinet granted government patronage in Ireland to O'Connell and O'Connell promised the Whig Cabinet the votes of the Irish Brigade in Parliament.[74] "King Dan's" Repeal[a] agitation[75] began immediately the Whigs were overthrown, but as soon as the Tories were defeated "King[b] Dan" sank again to the level of a common advocate. The influence of the Irish Brigade by no means came to an end with O'Connell's death. On the contrary, it became evident that this influence did not depend on the talent of one person, but was a result of the general state of affairs. The Tories and Whigs, the big traditional parties in the English Parliament, were more or less equally balanced. It is thus not surprising that the new, numerically small factions, the Manchester School[76] and the Irish Brigade, which took their seats in the reformed Parliament, should

---

[a] Marx uses the English word "Repeal" here and below.—*Ed.*
[b] Marx uses the English word here.—*Ed.*

play a decisive role and be able to turn the scale. Hence the importance of the "Irish quarter" in the English Parliament. After O'Connell left the scene it was no longer possible to stir the Irish masses with the "Repeal" slogan. The "Catholic" problem,[77] too, could be used only occasionally. Since the Catholic Emancipation it could no longer serve as a permanent propaganda theme. Thus the Irish politicians were compelled to do what O'Connell had always avoided and refused to do, that is, to explore the real cause of the Irish malady and to make landed property relations and their reform the election slogan, that is to say a slogan that would help them to get into the House of Commons. But having taken their seats in the House, they used the rights of the tenants, etc.—just as formerly the Repeal—as a means to conclude a new Lichfield-House Contract.

The Irish Brigade had overthrown the Derby ministry and had obtained a seat, even though a minor one, in the coalition government. How did it use its position? It helped the coalition to burke measures designed to reform landed ownership in Ireland. The Tories themselves, having taken the patriotism of the Irish Brigade for granted, had decided to propose these measures in order to gain the support of the Irish M.P.s. Palmerston, who is an Irishman by birth and knows his "Irish quarter", has renewed the Lichfield-House Contract of 1835 and has broadened its scope. He has appointed Keogh, the chief of the Brigade, Attorney-General[a] of Ireland, Fitzgerald, also a liberal Catholic M.P. for Ireland, has been made Solicitor-General, and a third member of the Brigade[b] has become legal counsel to the Lord Lieutenant of Ireland, so that the judicial general staff of the Irish government is now composed entirely of Catholics and Irishmen. Monsell, the Clerk of Ordnance in the coalition government, has been reappointed by Palmerston after some hesitation, although—as Muntz, deputy for Birmingham and an arms manufacturer, rightly observed—Monsell cannot distinguish a musket from a needle-gun. Palmerston has advised the lieutenants of the counties always to give preference to the protégés of Irish priests close to the Irish Brigade when nominating colonels and other high-ranking officers in the Irish militia. The fact that Sergeant *Shee* has gone over to the government side, and also that the Catholic Bishop of Athlone has pushed through the re-election of Keogh and that moreover

[a] Here and below Marx gives the titles in English: Attorney-General, Solicitor-General, Lord Lieutenant, Clerk of Ordnance, Sergeant.—*Ed.*

[b] G. W. F. Howard.—*Ed.*

the Catholic clergy has promoted the re-election of Fitzgerald shows that Palmerston's policy is already producing an effect. Wherever the lower ranks of the Catholic clergy have taken their "Irish patriotism" seriously and have stood up to those members of the Irish Brigade who deserted to the government, they have been rebuked by their bishops who are well aware of the diplomatic secret.

A protestant Tory newspaper[a] exclaims in distress: "It is perfectly understood between Lord Palmerston [...] and [...] the Irish priests, that if Lord Palmerston hands over Ireland to the priests, the priests will return members who will hand over England to Lord Palmerston".

The Whigs use the Irish Brigade to dominate the British Parliament and they toss posts and salaries to the Brigade; the Catholic clergy permits one side to buy and the other to sell on condition that both sides acknowledge the power of the clergy and help to extend and strengthen it. It is, however, a very remarkable phenomenon that in the same measure as the Irish influence in the *political* sphere grows in England, the Celtic influence in the *social* sphere decreases in Ireland. Both the "Irish quarter" in Parliament and the Irish clergy seem to be equally unaware of the fact that behind their back the Irish society is being radically transformed by an Anglo-Saxon revolution. In the course of this revolution the *Irish agricultural system is being replaced by the English system, the system of small tenures by big tenures,* and *the modern capitalist* is taking the place of the old landowner.

The chief factors which prepared the ground for this transformation are: 1847, the year of famine, which killed nearly one million Irishmen; emigration to America and Australia, which removed another million from the land and still carries off thousands; the unsuccessful insurrection of 1848, which finally destroyed Ireland's faith in herself; and lastly the Act of Parliament which exposed the estates of the debt-ridden old Irish aristocrats to the hammer of the auctioneer or bailiff, thus driving them from the land just as starvation swept away their small tenants, subtenants and cottagers.[78]

Written on March 13, 1855

First published in the *Neue Oder-Zeitung,* No. 127, March 16, 1855

Marked with the sign ×

Printed according to the newspaper

---

[a] *The Morning Herald,* No. 22378, March 13, 1855.—*Ed.*

Frederick Engels

THE RESULTS IN THE CRIMEA[79]

The illusions with which official incapacity and national self-love have surrounded the military operations in the Crimea,[a] now begin to melt away, along with the sheet of snow which has covered the scene of action through the winter months. The recent pamphlet of Napoleon Bonaparte[b] says distinctly, that while in the Crimea everything went wrong, the generals-in-chief

"must have been in possession of orders from their governments enjoining them to pass under silence and to dissimulate the obstacles which opposed themselves to the taking of Sevastopol".

This supposition is fully borne out by the reports of these generals,[c] and especially by the repeated reports which they caused to be sent, indirectly, from the camp,[d] as to the assault being fixed on such and such a day. Everybody recollects that from the 5th of November down to the beginning of March the European public was kept in constant expectation of this grand and final spectacle. Though continually postponed, every adjournment was to be for a short time only, and public curiosity was but increased by it. But

---

[a] The *Neue Oder-Zeitung* has: "with which official incapacity, English ministerial intrigues and self-interested Bonapartism have surrounded the military operations in the Crimea".—*Ed.*

[b] Thus in the *New-York Daily Tribune*—presumably a mistake; the version in the *Neue Oder-Zeitung* reads: "The pamphlet of Jérôme Bonaparte (Jr.)", the reference being to the anonymous pamphlet *De la conduite de la guerre d'Orient....*—*Ed.*

[c] Raglan and Canrobert.—*Ed.*

[d] Instead of the passage "the repeated reports which they caused to be sent, indirectly, from the camp", the *Neue Oder-Zeitung* has: "the rumours which they repeatedly spread".—*Ed.*

now matters begin to take a different turn,[a] and the length of the siege has at last called into existence a sort of public opinion in the camp, based upon the views publicly expressed by officers who know something about these matters, and the gentlemen of the staff are no longer able to whisper about the camp, with all the importance and oracularity inherent to their position, that on such and such a day the assault will take place and the town will be overwhelmed. Every private now knows better. The nature of the defenses, the superiority of the enemy's fire, the disproportion of the besieging forces to the task before them, and, above all, the decisive importance of the North Fort, are by this time too well understood to admit of such preposterous tales being successfully repeated.[b]

About the end of February, the Allies are said to have had before Sevastopol 58,000 French, 10,000 English, and 10,000 Turks—all together about 80,000 men, which agrees pretty nearly with our own computations at various epochs.[c] Supposing they had even 90,000 men, they would still be unable to maintain the siege with one portion, and to detach the other upon an offensive movement against the Russians at Bakshiserai; for this field army of the Allies could not arrive before Bakshiserai with more than 40,000 men, while the Russians could bring at least 60,000 against them in an open field, where the advantages of the position between Inkermann and Balaklava would not exist, and where, therefore, the moral superiority of the allied army would be considerably affected by maneuvers which could not be effectually employed by superior numbers of Russians either at Balaklava or at Inkermann.[d] Thus, the Allies must remain besieged on their Chersonese, until they are strong enough to advance beyond the Chernaya with something like 100,000 men. This shows the vicious circle in which they move: the more men they bring into this pestilential mouse-trap, the more they lose by sickness; and yet, the only way to get successfully out of it, is to send more men thither.

The other expedient they have hit upon to get out of the

---

[a] Part of this sentence and the preceding sentence do not occur in the *Neue Oder-Zeitung*.—*Ed.*

[b] The *Neue Oder-Zeitung* further has: "We have even had reports of letters by English officers which permit no doubt on this point."—*Ed.*

[c] The end of the sentence beginning with the words "which agrees..." does not occur in the *Neue Oder-Zeitung*.—*Ed.*

[d] The end of this sentence beginning with the words "and where, therefore the moral superiority..." does not occur in the *Neue Oder-Zeitung*.—*Ed.*

scrape—the Turkish Expedition to Eupatoria[80]—now turns out to be a perfect repetition of the original Crimean blunder. The Turks landed at Eupatoria are far too weak to advance into the interior. The intrenchments around the place appear to be so extensive that an army of some 20,000 men is required for their defense. The reports of the "battle" of February 17, before Eupatoria, lead to the conclusion that at least one-half of the 40,000 men assembled there found active employment in the defense.[a] The extent of an intrenched camp intended to shelter 40,000 men must, besides, be such that about one-half of the men will be required for active service in case of an attack. Thus the town will require about 20,000 men for its defense, and 20,000 only remain disposable for field operations. But 20,000 men cannot venture more than a few miles out of Eupatoria without exposing themselves to all sorts of flank and rear attacks from the Russians, and to the risk of having their communications with the town intercepted. Now the Russians, having a double line of retreat either toward Perekop or toward Sympheropol, and being, besides, in their own country, can always avoid a decisive action with the 20,000 Turks who may emerge from Eupatoria.

Thus, 10,000 Russians, placed at a day's march from the town, will always be able to keep in check the 40,000 Turks concentrated in it; if they retreat for another ten or twelve miles they will be a match for any number of Turks who can venture to advance to that distance from their base of operations. In other words, Eupatoria is another Kalafat; but with this difference, that Kalafat had the Danube in its rear, and not the Black Sea, and that Kalafat was a defensive position, while Eupatoria is an offensive one. If 30,000 men at Kalafat could maintain a successful defense, with occasional and equally successful offensive sallies, extending to a limited distance, 40,000 men at Eupatoria are far too many to defend a place which about 1,000 English and French held for five months; while they are far too few for any offensive operations. The consequence is, that a Russian brigade, or at the outside a Russian division will be abundantly sufficient to check the whole Turkish force at Eupatoria.

The so-called battle of Eupatoria was a mere reconnaissance on the part of the Russians. They advanced, 25,000 to 30,000 strong, against the place from the north-west, the only available side, as the south is sheltered by the sea, and the east by a marshy lake, called Sasik. The country to the north-west of the town is formed

---

[a] This sentence does not occur in the *Neue Oder-Zeitung*.—*Ed.*

by low, undulating ground, which, to judge from the maps and from the experience of this action, does not command the town within effective field-gun range. The Russians, with a force inferior by 10,000 men to the garrison, and exposed besides, on both flanks, and especially on the right one, to the fire from the men-of-war in the bay, could never have had any serious intention of taking the place by assault. They consequently confined themselves to an energetic reconnaissance, opening a cannonade on the whole of the line, at a distance which precluded the possibility of serious damage; they then advanced their batteries nearer and nearer, keeping their columns as much as possible out of range, and then moved up these columns as if for attack so as to force the Turks to show their strength, and made one attack at a point where the shelter afforded by the monuments and shrubbery of a burying-ground allowed of their approaching close to the defenses. Having ascertained the situation and strength of the intrenchments, as well as the approximative numbers of the garrison, they retired, as every other army, judiciously commanded, would have done. Their object was attained; that their losses would be greater than those of the Turks, they knew beforehand. This very simple affair has been magnified by the allied commanders into a glorious victory. People must be very much in want of something to boast of, if they attempt to impose upon the public in such a barefaced way.[a]

It certainly was a great mistake that the Russians allowed the Allies to maintain themselves in Eupatoria for five months, until the Turks came. A Russian brigade, with a sufficient number of twelve-pounders, might have driven them into the sea, and by a few slight earthworks on the shore, might even have kept the men-of-war at a respectful distance. If the allied fleets had detached an overwhelming force to Eupatoria, the place could have been burned down, and thus made valueless as a future base of operations for a landing force. But as it is, the Russians may be quite satisfied with having left Eupatoria in the possession of the Allies. Forty thousand Turks, the last remnant of the only respectable army Turkey ever possessed, blocked up in a narrow camp, where 10,000 Russians can keep them in check, and where they are exposed to all the diseases and sufferings of men crowded closely together—these forty thousand paralyzed Turks are a not inconsiderable deduction from the offensive forces of the Allies.

[a] Instead of this sentence the *Neue Oder-Zeitung* has: "What does this prove but the great demand for and the small supply of real victories?"—*Ed.*

The French and English, after having lost 50,000 to 60,000 men, are still besieged on the Heracleatic Chersonese, and the Turks are besieged at Eupatoria, while the Russians are in full communication with both the North and South sides of Sevastopol, whose defenses are much stronger than ever.[a] Such is the glorious result of five months' experimenting in the Crimea![b]

Written about March 16, 1855

First published in the *New-York Daily Tribune,* No. 4353, April 2, 1855, reprinted in the *New-York Semi-Weekly Tribune,* No. 1028, April 3, 1855 and the *New-York Weekly Tribune,* No. 708, April 7, 1855 as a leading article; the German version was first published in the *Neue Oder-Zeitung,* No. 131, March 19, 1855, marked with the sign ×

Reproduced from the *New-York Daily Tribune*

[a] In the *Neue Oder-Zeitung* the words "after having lost 50,000 to 60,000 men" and "whose defenses are much stronger than ever" do not occur.—*Ed.*

[b] The *Neue Oder-Zeitung* further has: "There are also military and political questions to be taken into account, which we shall consider in our next letter."—*Ed.*

Frederick Engels

FATE OF THE GREAT ADVENTURER[81]

We published the other day some interesting extracts from the pamphlet lately issued by Prince Napoleon, which, we doubt not, were duly considered by our readers. That pamphlet[a] reveals the striking and most important fact, that the Crimean Expedition was an original invention of Louis Bonaparte himself; that he elaborated it in all its details, without communicating with anybody; that he sent it in his own handwriting to Constantinople, in order to avoid the objections of Marshal Vaillant. Since all this is known, a great portion of the flagrant military blunders connected with this expedition is explained by the dynastic necessities of its author. In the council of war at Varna it had to be forced upon the Admirals and Generals present, by St. Arnaud, appealing, in the most direct manner, to the authority of the "Emperor," while that potentate, in return, publicly branded all opposing opinions as "timid counsels." Once in the Crimea, Raglan's really timid proposal to march to Balaklava was readily adopted by St. Arnaud, as it led directly, if not into, at least to somewhere near, the gates of Sevastopol. The frantic efforts to push the siege, though without sufficient means—the eagerness to open the fire, which made the French neglect the solidity of their works to such a degree that their batteries were silenced by the enemy in a couple of hours—the consequent overworking of the troops in the trenches, which is now proved to have done as much as anything else toward the destruction of the British army—the inconsiderate and useless cannonade from the 17th of October to the 5th of November—the neglect of all defensive works, and

[a] *De la conduite de la guerre d'Orient....*—*Ed.*

even of a sufficient occupation of the ridge toward the Chernaya, which ended in the losses of Balaklava and Inkermann[82]—all this is now as clearly explained as can be wished for. The Bonaparte dynasty was bound to take Sevastopol at any cost, and at the shortest notice; and the allied armies had to do it. Canrobert, if successful, would be made a Marshal of France, Count, Duke, Prince, whatever he liked, with unlimited powers to commit "irregularities" in financial matters; while if unlucky, he would be a traitor to the Emperor, and would have to go and join his former comrades, Lamoricière, Bedeau, and Changarnier, in their exile. And Raglan was just enough of an old woman to give way to his interested colleague.

All this, however, is but the least important feature of the consequences incumbent upon this Imperial plan of operations. Nine French divisions, equal to eighty-one battalions, have been engaged in this hopeless affair. The greatest efforts, the most lavish sacrifices have accomplished nothing; Sevastopol is stronger than ever; the French trenches are, as we now learn from authentic sources, still fully four hundred yards from the Russian works, while the British trenches are twice that distance; Gen. Niel, sent by Bonaparte to look into the siege works, declares that an assault is not to be thought of; he has changed the principal points of attack from the French to the British side, thereby not only causing delay in the siege, but directing the main attack toward a suburb which, even if taken, is still separated from the town by the Inner Harbor Creek. In short, device after device, dodge after dodge is resorted to, to keep up, not the hope, but the mere appearance of a hope of success. And when matters are come to this pitch, when a general war on the Continent is imminent, when a fresh expedition to the Baltic is preparing—an expedition which must do something this season, and therefore must be far stronger in land-troops than that of 1854—at this moment, obstinacy goads Louis Bonaparte to engage five more divisions of infantry in this Crimean slough, where men, and even whole regiments, vanish as by enchantment! And, as if that were not sufficient, he has made up his mind to go there himself, and to see the final assault carried out by his soldiers.

This is a situation to which the first strategic experiment of Louis Bonaparte has reduced France. The man who, with some sort of reason, thinks he is bound to be a great Captain, approaching, in some degree, the founder of his dynasty, turns out at the very beginning a mere presumptuous piece of incapacity. With very limited information, he forms the plan of the expedition at some 3,000 miles from the spot, works it out in its details, and sends it off secretly and without consulting anybody, to his General-in-Chief,[a] who, though but a few hundred miles from the point of attack, is yet equally ignorant as to the nature of the obstacles and the force of resistance likely to be encountered. The Expedition once commenced, disaster follows disaster; even victory is worse than sterile, and the only result obtained is the destruction of the expeditionary army itself. Napoleon, in his best days, would never have persisted in such an undertaking. In such a case, he used to find some fresh device, to lead his troops on a sudden to a fresh point of attack, and by a brilliant maneuver, crowned with success, make even temporary defeat appear as but contributive to final victory. What if he had resisted to the last at Aspern[83]? It was only in the time of his decline, when the thunderstroke of 1812 had shaken his confidence in himself, that his energy of will turned into blind obstinacy, that, as at Leipsic,[84] he clung to the last to positions which his military judgment must have told him were completely false. But here is just the difference between the two Emperors; what Napoleon ended with, Louis Napoleon begins with.

That Louis Bonaparte has the firm intention to go to the Crimea, and to take Sevastopol himself, is very likely. He may delay his departure, but nothing short of peace will shake his resolution. Indeed, his personal fate is bound up with this expedition, which is his first military effort. But, from the day he actually sets out, the fourth and greatest French revolution may be said to date its beginning. Everybody in Europe feels this. Everybody dissuades him. A shudder runs through the ranks of the French middle-class when this departure to the Crimea is mentioned. But, the hero of Strassburg[85] is inflexible. A gambler all his life, a gambler accustomed of late to the very heaviest of stakes, he stakes his all upon the one card of his "star," against the most fearful odds. Besides, he knows well enough that the hopes of the bourgeoisie, to escape the crisis by retaining him in Paris, are entirely hollow. Whether he be there or not, it is the fate of the French Empire, the fate of the existing social order of things, which is still approaching its decision in the trenches before Sevastopol. If successful there against hope, by his presence he will overstep the barrier between a highwayman and a hero, at least in the opinion of Europe; unsuccessful, his Empire is gone under all circumstances. That he calculates upon the possibility of such an

[a] Saint-Arnaud.—*Ed.*

event, is shown by his taking with him his rival and heir presumptive, the young Jérôme Bonaparte, in the livery of a Lieutenant-General.

For the moment, this Crimean Expedition serves nobody better than Austria. This slough which drains off by army-corps after army-corps the strength of both France and Russia, must, if the struggle before Sevastopol lasts a few months longer, leave Austria the main arbiter of the Continent, where her 600,000 bayonets remain disposable, in a compact mass, to be cast as an overwhelming weight into the scale. But, fortunately, there is a counterpoise against this Austrian supremacy. The moment France is launched again in the revolutionary career, this Austrian force dissolves itself into its discordant elements. Germans, Hungarians, Poles, Italians, Croats are loosened from the forced bond which ties them together, and instead of the undetermined and hap-hazard alliances and antagonisms of today, Europe will again be divided into two great camps with distinct banners and new issues. Then the struggle will be only between the Democratic Revolution on one side and the Monarchical Counter-Revolution on the other.

Written about March 16, 1855

First published in the *New-York Daily Tribune*, No. 4353, April 2, 1855, reprinted in the *New-York Semi-Weekly Tribune*, No. 1028, April 3, 1855 as a leading article

Reproduced from the *New-York Daily Tribune*

Karl Marx and Frederick Engels

CRITICISM OF THE FRENCH CONDUCT OF THE WAR

London, March 17. Now that the pamphlet of Jérôme Bonaparte (junior)[a] has revealed the fact that the Crimean expedition was an invention of Louis Napoleon himself, that he had worked it out in every detail without consulting others, that he had sent it to Constantinople in his own handwriting in order to avoid the objections of Marshal Vaillant—since all this has become known, a large proportion of the most flagrant military blunders of this expedition is explained by the dynastic needs of its author. In the war council at Varna it had to be forced upon the generals and admirals present by S[ain]t-Arnaud's direct appeal to the authority of the "Emperor", who, in turn, publicly branded the opposing views as "timid counsel". Once in the Crimea, Raglan's really "timid counsel"—to march to Balaklava—was eagerly adopted by St.-Arnaud, as it led, although not directly into Sevastopol, at least close to its gates. The frantic efforts to push the siege ahead, though without sufficient means; the eagerness to open fire which made the French neglect the solidity of their works to such a degree that their batteries were silenced by the enemy in a couple of hours; the over-exertion of the troops in the communication trenches which is now proved to have contributed as much towards the destruction of the British army as did the Commissariat, the Transport Service, the Medical Department, etc.; the rash and useless cannonade from October 17 to November 5; the neglect of all defensive works—all this has been sufficiently explained. The Bonaparte dynasty required the capture of Sevastopol, and in the shortest time; and the allied army was to

[a] *De la conduite de la guerre d'Orient....—Ed.*

carry it out. Canrobert, if successful, would be made Marshal of France, Count, Duke, Prince—whatever he desired, with unlimited powers in financial matters. If unsuccessful, his career was at an end. Raglan was enough of an old woman to give way to the self-interests of his colleague.

These, however, are not the most important consequences of the imperatorial plan of operation. Nine French divisions or 81 battalions have been engaged in this hopeless affair. It is recognised to be almost hopeless; the greatest efforts, the most lavish sacrifices have accomplished nothing; Sevastopol is stronger than ever; the French trenches, as we now know from an authentic source, are still fully four hundred yards from the Russian works, while the British trenches are twice as far away. General Niel, sent by Bonaparte to inspect the siege works, has declared that an assault is not to be thought of; he has shifted the principal point of attack from the French to the British side, thereby causing not only a delay in the siege, but directing the main attack toward a suburb which, even if taken, is still separated from the town by the inner harbour. In short, there is plan after plan, dodge after dodge, to keep up, not the hope of success, but the mere semblance of such a hope. And when things have come to this pass, when a general war on the continent is imminent, when a new expedition to the Baltic is being prepared—an expedition which, this time, must do something and therefore must dispose of far more landing troops than in 1854—at this moment Bonaparte is sending five fresh infantry divisions to the Crimean swamp where men vanish and regiments disappear as if by magic. Indeed, he is determined to go there himself, and go there he will, unless an improbable peace or significant events at the Polish border decide otherwise. That is the situation to which Bonaparte's first strategic experiment has reduced Bonaparte and "imperial" France. What drives him is not only obstinacy, but the fatalistic instinct that the destiny of the French empire will be decided in the trenches at Sevastopol. Up to now, there has been no Marengo to justify the second edition of the 18th Brumaire.[86]

It may be regarded as historical irony that, however meticulously the restored empire copies its model, it is forced everywhere to do the opposite of what Napoleon did. Napoleon attacked the very heart of the states on which he made war; present-day France has attacked Russia in a *cul-de-sac.* It did not aim at great military operations, but at a fortunate *coup de main,* a surprise attack, an adventure. In this change of purpose lies the whole difference between the first and the second French empire and their respective representatives. Napoleon used to enter the capitals of *modern* Europe as conqueror. His successor moved French garrisons into the capitals of *ancient* Europe, Rome, Constantinople and Athens under various pretexts—the protection of the Pope, the protection of the Sultan, the protection of the King of the Hellenes[a]—in fact, there has been no increase in power, but merely a dispersal of strength. Napoleon's art consisted in concentration, that of his successor in dispersal. When Napoleon was obliged to conduct a war in two different theatres, as in his wars against Austria, he concentrated by far the greater part of his fighting force along the decisive line of operation (in the wars with Austria this was the line between Strasbourg and Vienna), while leaving a comparatively minor fighting force in the secondary theatre of war (Italy), confident that, even if his troops should be defeated here, his own successes along the principal line would hinder the progress of the enemy army more certainly than any direct resistance. His successor, however, scatters the fighting force of France over many areas, concentrating a part in the very place where the least significant results—if any—must be achieved with the greatest sacrifices. Besides the troops in Rome, Athens, Constantinople and the Crimea, an auxiliary force is to be despatched to the Polish border in Austria, and another to the Baltic Sea. Thus the French army must be active in at least three theatres of war, separated from each other by at least a thousand miles. By this plan, the entire French fighting force would be as good as disposed of even *before* the war had seriously begun in Europe. Napoleon, if he found that an undertaking he had begun was not feasible (as at Aspern), would rather than persist in it, find some new turn, lead his troops in a surprise move to a fresh point of attack, and, by a brilliant manoeuvre crowned with success, make even temporary defeat appear to be but a contribution to final victory. It was only at the time of his decline, after 1812 had shaken his self-confidence, that the energy of his will turned into blind obstinacy which made him hold on to positions (as at Leipzig) which his military judgment must have rejected. His successor, however, is *forced* to begin where his predecessor ended. What with one was the result of unaccountable defeats, was the result of unaccountable good fortune with the other. For one his own genius became the star in which he believed; for the other, his belief in his star has to serve as a substitute for his lack of genius. One defeated a real revolution, because he was the only

[a] Pope Pius IX, Sultan Abdul Mejid and King Otto I.—*Ed.*

man to carry it through; the other defeated the newly revived recollection of a past revolutionary epoch, because he bore that unique man's name, and hence was himself a recollection. It would be easy to demonstrate that the pretentious mediocrity with which the Second Empire is conducting this war is reflected in its internal administration, that here, too, semblance has taken the place of essence, and that the "económic" campaigns were in no way more successful than the military ones.

Written on March 17, 1855

First published in the *Neue Oder-Zeitung*, No. 133, March 20, 1855

Marked with the sign ×

Printed according to the newspaper

Published in English for the first time

Karl Marx

AGITATION AGAINST PRUSSIA.—A DAY OF FASTING

London, March 19. To show the attitude of the press here towards Prussia, we have chosen two extracts, one from *The Morning Herald,* the Tory organ, the other from *The Morning Post,* Palmerston's organ. Referring to the speech made by Sir Robert Peel, newly appointed Junior Lord of the Admiralty, to his constituents at Portsmouth, *The Morning Herald* remarks:

"Sir Robert Peel has most truthfully represented the people of England's sentiments when he demanded that Prussia should be urged to adopt an unequivocally stated policy, or our second expedition to the Baltic will be as futile as the first one. We have had enough of protocoling and 'points'; it is now high time to cut off Russia from her resources and to bring about repercussions within Russia." [a]

The Morning Post has received the following report about General Wedell's mission from Paris:

"General Wedell has [...] communicated his new instructions to the Cabinet of Napoleon. And what are they? [...] General Wedell tells the Government of France—First: His Majesty the King of Prussia [b] is deeply afflicted at the death of cousin Nicholas [c]; [...] Secondly: [...] Prussia quite agrees with the Western Powers about the protocol of Dec. 28,[87] and is ready to subscribe to the same in any and every imaginable form! *Ergo,* Prussia must have a place at the Council board of Vienna.[88] [...] But it happens that the protocol of December 28 does not bind any one to anything—it is only a diplomatic sketch for an historical work. And as [...] Prussia refuses to countersign the *real* alliance treaty between England, France and Austria, Mr. Wedell's mission is, I suppose, closed". [d]

---

[a] "Portsmouth—Saturday", *The Morning Herald,* No. 22383, March 19, 1855.—*Ed.*

[b] Frederick William IV.—*Ed.*

[c] Nicholas I.—*Ed.*

[d] "Paris, Friday Evening", *The Morning Post,* No. 25338, March 19, 1855.—*Ed.*

It is well known that the rulers of Tyre and Carthage assuaged the wrath of the gods, not by sacrificing themselves, but by buying children from the poor to fling them into the fiery arms of Moloch. Official England orders the people to humble themselves before the Lord, to do penance and fast for the disgrace the misrule of their former government brought upon them, the millions of pounds which it extorted from them to no purpose, and the thousands of lives of which it unscrupulously robbed them. For the Privy Council has ordered a Day of Fasting and Prayer for next Wednesday,[a]

"to obtain pardon of our sins, and in the most devout and solemn manner send up our prayers and supplications to the Divine Majesty, imploring His blessing and assistance on our arms, for the restoration of peace to her Majesty and her dominions".[b]

Just like the Lord Chamberlain at Court ceremonies, the Archbishop of Canterbury[c] has published a "set of rules" for these religious ceremonies, rules which prescribe how the divine Majesty is to be addressed. On the occasion of this extraordinary competition of the English State Church with that of Russia, which has also entreated God's blessing for their arms, the latter obviously has the advantage over the former.

"Read by the Czar's countrymen," *The Leader* remarks, "the prayer prescribed by Canterbury is the prayer of cowards; read by Englishmen [...], it is the prayer of hypocrites. [...] Read by Dissenters, it is the prayer of one sect dictating to the rest; and read by the working people, it is the prayer of the rich who belong to that one sect, and who keep up these mummeries [...] through a belief that the mummeries are an indirect means of sustaining the monopolies of rank and office. The Archbishop's unctuous verbiage has aroused the working classes in several parts of the country. A day of fast and humiliation is to them a reality. To the other 'persuasions', besides those of poverty, it only means the addition of fish and egg sauce to the usual dinner, with a closing of their place of business, as if it were Sunday. To the working men a '*fast*' means stopped wages and the want of dinner."

In a previous despatch we stated:

"The conflict between the industrial proletariat and the bourgeoisie will flare up again at the same time that the conflict between the bourgeoisie and the aristocracy reaches its climax."[d]

At a large meeting which took place at the London Tavern last Friday,[e] this was manifestly demonstrated. We preface our report

---

[a] March 21, 1855.—*Ed.*

[b] "A Proclamation for a Day of Solemn Fast, Humiliation and Prayer. Victoria R.", *The Leader*, No. 260, March 17, 1855. Below Marx quotes another article from the same issue, headlined "Humiliation 'Ex-Officio'".—*Ed.*

[c] J. B. Sumner.—*Ed.*

[d] See this volume, pp. 55-56.—*Ed.*

[e] March 16, 1855.—*Ed.*

of this meeting with some particulars of the skirmishes which have recently taken place inside and outside Parliament between bourgeoisie and proletariat. A short time ago the manufacturers of Manchester held meetings where it was resolved to agitate for the removal of the official factory inspectors, since these inspectors not only presume to supervise the observance of working hours fixed by law, but even demand that the measures prescribed by Parliament to prevent damage to life and limb by machinery should actually be put into effect in the factories. The factory inspector for South Lancashire, the well-known Leonard Horner, has incurred their particular displeasure because, in his latest report,[a] he insisted on a legally prescribed appliance in spinning mills, the neglect of which, as one manufacturer—a member of the Peace Society,[89] of course—exclaimed naively, had "cost the lives of *only* five adult workers last year".

This was *extra parliamentary. Inside the House of Commons,* Sir Henry Halford's Bill, which declared the "stoppage of wages"[b] illegal, was thrown out during the second reading. "Stoppage of wages" means *deductions from the money wages,* partly as penalty for infringements of factory regulations framed by the employer, and partly, in branches of industry where the modern system has not yet been introduced, deduction of rents, etc., for looms, etc., lent to workers.

The latter system prevails particularly in the stocking factories of Nottingham, and Sir Henry Halford has proved[c] that, in many instances, instead of being paid by his employer, the worker has actually to pay his employer. For, under various pretexts, so many deductions are made from the money wages that the worker must give back an excess, which the capitalist notes down in the form of a debit. The worker is thus turned into his employer's debtor, and is forced by him to renew his contract under ever more unfavourable conditions until he has become a bondsman in the fullest sense, but unlike the bondsman, he does not receive even the guarantee of physical survival.

While the House of Commons rejected Sir Henry Halford's Bill, which was to put an end to this malpractice, at its second reading, it refused *even to consider* the Bill of Cobbett, son of the great

---

[a] "Report of Leonard Horner, Esq., Inspector of Factories, for the Half Year ended the 31st of October, 1854."—*Ed.*

[b] Marx uses the English phrase "stoppage of wages" here and below.—*Ed.*

[c] In his speech in the House of Commons on March 8, 1855. *The Times,* No. 21997, March 9, 1855.—*Ed.*

English pamphleteer. The aim of this Bill[a] was (1) to replace the ten-and-a-half hours law of 1850 by the "ten-hours law" of 1847[90]; (2) to make the legal restrictions of working hours in factories a "reality" by the compulsory shutting down of machinery at the end of each legal working day.

Tomorrow we shall revert to the meeting at the London Tavern.

Written on March 19, 1855

First published in the *Neue Oder-Zeitung*, No. 137, March 22, 1855

Marked with the sign ×

Printed according to the newspaper

Published in English for the first time

[a] Submitted on March 16, 1855.—*Ed.*

Karl Marx

A MEETING[91]

London, March 20. For several months *The Morning Advertiser* has endeavoured to set up a propaganda society under the name of National and Constitutional Association for the purpose of overthrowing the oligarchic regime. After many preparations, appeals, subscriptions, etc., a public meeting was at last called for last Friday at the London Tavern.[a] It was to be the birthday of the new, much advertised Association. Long before the meeting opened the great hall was crowded with working men, and the self-appointed leaders of the new movement, when they appeared at last, had difficulty in finding room on the platform. Mr. James Taylor, made chairman, read letters from Layard, Sir George de Lacy Evans, Wakley, Sir James Duke, Sir John Shelley, and others, who gave assurances of their sympathy for the aims of the Association, but at the same time under various pretexts declined the invitation to appear in person. Then an "Address to the People" was read. In it, the conduct of the war in the East and the ministerial crisis were spotlighted and then followed the declaration that

> "there were 'practical men of every class, *and especially the middle class*, with all the attributes for governing the country'".

This clumsy allusion to the special claims of the middle class was received with loud hisses.

---

[a] A detailed account of this meeting, held on March 16, 1855, was published in *The Morning Advertiser*, No. 19887, March 17, 1855. Reports based on it appeared in other newspapers. Below Marx quotes from a report printed in *The Morning Post*, No. 25338, March 19, 1855.—*Ed.*

"The chief object of this Association," continues the address, "will be to destroy the aristocratical monopoly of power and place, which has proved fatal to the best interests of the country. Among its collateral objects will be included *the abolition of the system of secret diplomacy* [...]. It will be the peculiar mission of this Association to address itself to the constituencies of the United Kingdom, warning and exhorting them to be careful into whose hands they entrust the liberties and resources of the country and to shrink from bestowing their votes any longer on the mere nonentities of Aristocracy and Wealth, and their nominees...."

Thereupon Mr. *Beale* rose and seconded the first motion in a lengthy speech:

"...The perilous state of public affairs, and the manifest hopelessness of improvement under the present oligarchical system, which has usurped the functions of Government, monopolised place and privilege, and brought disgrace and disaster upon the country, makes it incumbent on the people to unite, in order to prevent a continuation of the existing [...] system.... That an Association be therefore now formed; and be called '*The National and Constitutional Association*'."

Mr. *Nicolay*, one of the Marylebone luminaries, supported the motion. So did *Apsley Pellatt*, M.P., saying the people would

"go about their work of reforming the Government with determination, temperance, steadiness, and the resolution of *the Ironsides*[a] *of Cromwell*. [...] The electors of England had it in their own hands to rectify every abuse, if they determined to send honest men to Parliament *free of expense*; but they could never expect to be honestly represented whilst a man like Lord Ebrington only got returned to Parliament for Marylebone at an expense of £5,000, and the unsuccessful candidate[b] had to spend upwards of £3,000".

Mr. *Murrough*, M.P., now rose, but after considerable opposition was forced to give way to George Harrison (a worker and Chartist from Nottingham).

"This movement," Harrison said, "was an attempt of the middle classes to get the government into their own hands, to divide amongst themselves the places and the pensions, and establish a worse oligarchy than that now in existence."

He then read an *amendement*[c] in which he denounced equally the landed aristocracy and monied aristocracy as enemies of the people and declared that the only way to regenerate the nation was to introduce the *People's Charter*[92] with its five points: universal suffrage, vote by ballot, equal constituencies, annual parliaments and abolition of the property qualification.

---

[a] Marx uses the English word. Ironsides was the name given to Oliver Cromwell's soldiers in the English bourgeois revolution after Cromwell was referred to as "Old Ironsides" following the Battle of Marston Moor in 1644.—*Ed.*

[b] J. Bell.—*Ed.*

[c] Marx uses the French spelling.—*Ed.*

Ernest Jones (the Chartist leader, member of an aristocratic family) speaking in support of the *amendement* said among other things:

"The people would be destroying their own position were they to support this movement of the middle classes to get into their own hands place and power. There were no doubt many hungry prime ministers on the platform"—cheers[a]—"many expectant placemen." (Cheers.) "The people must not, however, ally themselves to the Cobdens, the Brights, and the moneyed interests. It was not the landed aristocracy, [...] it was the moneyed interest that opposed a humane Factory Act and turned down the Bill against the stoppage of wages,[b] that had prevented the passing of a good partnership law—and it was the moneyed and manufacturing interest that always endeavoured to keep down and degrade the people. He had no objection to join at any moment in an endeavour to upset the influence of the Duke of Devonshire, et al., but he would not do so to establish in its stead that of the Duke of Devil's Dust or a Lord of Shoddy" (cheers and laughter). "It had been said the workers' movement, the Chartist movement, was dead. He declared to the reforming gentlemen of the middle class that the working class was sufficiently alive to kill any movement. It would not allow the middle class to move unless it decided to include the People's Charter and its five points in its programme. It had better not deceive itself. A repetition of the old deception was out of the question."

After some further discussion, amid considerable commotion, the chairman attempted to get rid of the *amendement*, by declaring that it was not an *amendement*, but he found himself compelled to change his mind. The *amendement* was put to the vote and passed with a majority of at least ten to one, with loud acclamation and waving of hats. After declaring the *amendement* passed, the chairman stated amid loud laughter that he still believed the majority of the people present was in favour of founding the Constitutional and National Association. They would therefore proceed with its organisation and later address another appeal to the public; he intimated, though covertly, that only persons with membership cards would be admitted in future to avoid opposition. The Chartists in high spirits complimented the chairman with a vote of thanks, and the meeting broke up.

It cannot be denied that logic was on the side of the Chartists, even from the standpoint of the publicly proclaimed principles of the Association. It wants to overthrow the oligarchy by an appeal from the Ministry to Parliament. But what is the Ministry? The creation of the parliamentary majority. Or it wants to overthrow Parliament by appealing to the electors. But what is Parliament? The freely elected representation of the electors. Hence there

---

[a] Marx uses the English word.—*Ed.*
[b] Marx uses the English phrase "stoppage of wages".—*Ed.*

remains only: extension of the franchise. Those who refuse to broaden the franchise to cover the whole of the people by adopting the People's Charter are admitting that they wish to replace the old aristocracy by a new one. *Vis-à-vis* the existing oligarchy they wish to speak *in the name of the people*, but at the same time they would like to prevent the people from appearing in person when they call it.

Written on March 20, 1855

First published in the *Neue Oder-Zeitung*, No. 141, March 24, 1855

Marked with the sign ×

Printed according to the newspaper

Karl Marx

REPORTS FROM THE ENGLISH PRESS

London, March 20. The Duke of Newcastle has ordered the recall of Lord Lucan; Lord Panmure has published Raglan's letter attacking him, and Lord Hardinge, the fabulous Lord High Constable of the British Army, has refused him an investigation and a military tribunal. In spite of the opposition of two ministries, of the Commander-in-Chief in the Crimea and of the Commander of the Horse Guards[a] in London, Lord Lucan proved in a detailed speech in the House of Lords yesterday that not he, but Raglan alone was responsible for the sacrifice of the Light Brigade at Balaklava[93] and that the Aberdeen and Palmerston Ministries had sacrificed Lord Lucan to the displeased public in order to save the obedient, feeble-minded and tractable Commander in the Crimea. The public monster had to be satisfied. A half-completed letter found on the body of General Cathcart addressed to his wife and dated November 2, three days before the battle of Inkerman[94] and a week after the charge of the Light Brigade at Balaklava, is decisive on this question. This letter says word for word:

> "Neither Lord Lucan nor Lord Cardigan was to blame, but on the contrary, for they obeyed orders."[b]

In an article on the Vienna Conference,[95] *The Times* today makes the characteristic comment that should the Congress become a reality, the main difficulties were [to be] expected from the Turkish side.[c] Within the framework of the four points the main

---

[a] Marx uses the English expression "Horse Guards". The designation "Commander of the Horse Guards" referred to the Commander-in-Chief of the British army (see footnote on p. 24 of this volume).— *Ed.*

[b] Cathcart's letter was quoted by Lucan in the House of Lords on March 19, 1855. *The Times*, No. 22006, March 20, 1855.— *Ed.*

[c] "The Conferences at Vienna were opened in due form...", *The Times*, No. 22006, March 20, 1855.— *Ed.*

concessions would have to be extorted from the Sultan, not from the Tsar.[a]

Yesterday *The Times* mystified its public yet again with the "authentic" announcement that the great bombardment and final storming of Sevastopol had undoubtedly taken place before March 19.[b] Whence this sudden turn from desperate hopelessness to sanguine superstition? *The Times* began its Crimean campaign against the overthrown coalition and its "*ceterum censeo*"[c] that a Committee of Inquiry was necessary at the very moment that Gladstone threatened its monopoly by the proposal to abolish the stamp duty and to limit the weight of newspapers that can be sent for one penny by post to four ounces—less than the weight of one copy of *The Times*. No sooner was Gladstone overthrown, than his successor, Sir George Cornewall Lewis withdrew the Bill, and *The Times*, hoping that everything would remain as before, suddenly transformed its bilious view of the Crimea into a mobile panorama, radiant with hope of success, in which even the army, whose obituary it published three months ago, has become active again. Today its view is again darkened, because yesterday Sir George Cornewall Lewis, against all expectations, himself brought in a Bill to abolish the newspaper stamp duty. The animosity of a writer of retrospective reviews to fresh news! *The Times* ejaculates. Lewis as everybody knows was editor of *The Edinburgh Review*.

We shall return to the Bill as soon as the details are laid before the House of Commons, but meanwhile note that it is a concession to the *Manchester School*[96] which retains the merit of having untiringly agitated for the introduction of free competition in the field of the press. The concession of the Palmerston Ministry to the *Manchester School* is a *captatio benevolentiae*[d] in case of the dissolution of the Lower House and new elections.

Written on March 20, 1855

First published in the *Neue Oder-Zeitung*, No. 139, March 23, 1855

Marked with the sign ×

Printed according to the newspaper

Published in English for the first time

---

[a] Abdul Mejid, Alexander II.—*Ed.*
[b] *The Times*, No. 22005, March 19, 1855.—*Ed.*
[c] Something constantly repeated. The phrase derives from the famous dictum with which, after 157 B.C., Cato the Elder concluded every speech: "Ceterum censeo Carthaginem esse delendam" (For the rest I take the view that Carthage must be destroyed).—*Ed.*
[d] An attempt to curry favour.—*Ed.*

Karl Marx

FROM PARLIAMENT

London, March 21. At yesterday's sitting of the House of Lords, Lord Lyndhurst, the old colleague of Liverpool and Castlereagh, brought in his long-expected motion "on the position of Prussia with reference to the Vienna Conference". Two circumstances, he said, had lately imparted new interest to this question: The message of the dying Emperor of Russia[a] to the Prussian Court, and the manifesto of Alexander II, in which he promises to consummate the policies of Peter, Catherine, Alexander, and his father. How Russia herself regarded Prussian policies can be seen from the following excerpt from a secret despatch which Pozzo di Borgo sent to Nesselrode shortly before the outbreak of the war of 1828-29. It reads in part:

"Suppose then that Russia should undertake alone to put in execution those coersive means against Turkey, there is every reason to believe that Prussia would not in any manner oppose Russia. But, on the contrary, her attitude at once unfettered and friendly, would operate as a powerful check on other States and bring them to submit to results suited to the dignity and interests of Russia. It will be necessary to let the Cabinet of Berlin, to a certain extent, into our confidence, and to convince it that the part we assign to Prussia will contribute to increase the happy intimacy between the two Sovereigns and the two Courts."[b]

Was it possible, Lord Lyndhurst exclaimed, to anticipate in a more prophetic spirit the line which the Prussian Court has taken in the past six or twelve months? It was true that Prussia had joined in signing the protocols of December 5, January 13 and April 9.[97] The purpose of these protocols had been to bring about

---

[a] Nicholas I.—*Ed.*

[b] The despatch was quoted by Lyndhurst in the House of Lords on March 20, 1855. The speeches by Lyndhurst and Clarendon quoted in this article were reported in *The Times*, No. 22007, March 21, 1855.—*Ed.*

the evacuation of the Danubian principalities and to obtain guarantees for the protection of the Sultan's independence and the integrity of Turkey. Had the Prussian Court acted in this spirit? On the occasion of the loan of 30 million taler for military operations Baron Manteuffel had declared that in these protocols Prussia had expressed her view on Russia's policy, namely that a great injustice had been committed; but she did not consider herself obliged to go further and take an active part. Was this the language of a great nation? And was Prussia not expressly committed to the protection of Turkey by the Agreements of 1840 and 1841[98]? Baron Manteuffel had added that Germany's independence and German interests were not involved in the dispute and Prussia was therefore not obliged to make any sacrifices.[a] Baron Manteuffel himself had, however, stated the opposite in another document.[b] Besides, once the Tsar seized Constantinople, it would be superfluous to talk any more of German independence and German interests. They would then succumb to an overwhelming power. After Lord Lyndhurst had alluded to the dismissal of War Minister Bonin, to the recall of Ambassador Bunsen from London and to the rejection of an address of the Prussian Chambers in reply to a speech from the throne,[c] he came to the "second act of this political drama". After a considerable time had elapsed Austria had deemed it proper to demand of Russia that she evacuate the Danubian principalities. This demand was drafted and sent to Berlin for signature. Counter-proposals were sent from Berlin to Vienna, which were completely inadequate but caused delay in as much as they had to be communicated to the Allies for examination. In the meantime Russia had evacuated the principalities, but retained one part under occupation for military reasons, declaring that she wished to keep entirely on the defensive. Prussia had thereupon withdrawn from the confederation, because Russia had satisfied all reasonable claims. From this moment on Prussia had made every effort to thwart Austria's plans. For this purpose she had, to a great extent with success, made proposals to the Federal Diet and to the individual German states. At the same time Russia had publicly thanked two German states for their refusal to join the Allies. He (Lyndhurst) was now coming to the third and last act of the drama. The Allies had arranged for a conference to be

[a] This refers to Manteuffel's speech in the Credit Committee of the First Chamber on April 22, 1854.—*Ed.*

[b] In his speech in the First Chamber on April 25, 1854, Manteuffel said: "Si vis pacem, para bellum..." (If you desire to maintain peace, be prepared for war).—*Ed.*

[c] Frederick William IV's speech of November 30, 1854.—*Ed.*

held on August 8 in Vienna to decide what should be demanded of Russia as a basis for any provisional negotiations. Prussia had been informed of the meeting in the usual manner and repeatedly. Prussia had not expressly refused to attend, but in fact did not appear at the conference. In consequence of her absence the Allies, instead of drafting a Protocol, had signed a Note laying down the four points[99] as a basis for future negotiations. The four points had then been submitted to Russia for her acceptance, but she had refused to accept them. Prussia for her part published and circulated a document in which she raised objections to the four points. She also continued to hinder, both at the Federal Diet and at the individual German courts, the adhesion of the small German states to the Allies. After the conclusion of the Agreement of December 2[100] Prussia was informed that room had been left for her accession. She refused to accede but declared that she was ready to conclude similar agreements with France and England separately. From the moment that these latter accepted this proposal, Prussia had in various negotiations and divers proposals demanded innumerable modifications, which France and England would certainly have to reject. When he (Lyndhurst) was speaking of Prussia, he was referring to the *official* Prussia. He knew that the vast majority of the Prussian nation was anti-Russian. It was incomprehensible that Prussia, after refusing to accede to the Agreement of December 2, could demand to be invited to the Vienna negotiations. He hoped the Allied Powers would not admit a Prussian envoy on any pretext: for if they did, Russia would have two votes at the Vienna Congress instead of one. Prussian diplomacy had not changed since Frederick the Great. He recalled 1794, the time just before and after the battle of Austerlitz, etc.

Lord *Clarendon*: He would confine himself to filling in a few gaps in respect of the communications which had taken place between England and Prussia. After the Russian Government had rejected the conditions of the Allies a conference of the respective plenipotentiaries had been called, which, however, could not be held since the representative of the Prussian Government would not attend. It was true that later the Prussian Ambassador in London[a] had informed him [Clarendon] that his Government would give the requested permission to its plenipotentiary in Vienna.[b] He (Clarendon) had declared, however: "It was too late."

---

[a] A. Bernstorff.— *Ed.*
[b] H. F. Arnim-Heinrichsdorf-Werbelow.— *Ed.*

The correspondence between Prussia and Austria had helped Russia. Before the signing of the Agreement of December 2 Prussia had already been invited to accede, but in vain. Prussia had demanded to be admitted unconditionally to the new conference because it was a continuation of the earlier conference, which had not yet been concluded and from which she had by no means withdrawn. With respect to the latter, the British Government referred to the fact that at an earlier occasion no conference could be held because Prussia would not attend, although repeatedly asked. Moreover, the new conference was not at all a continuation of the old one, for, when in October and November Austria requested France and England to resume it, she received the reply that the time for protocols and conferences had passed, but that if Austria would enter into a military commitment with them, they would see whether peace was realisable. This had led to the Agreement of December 2. Later, they had been prepared to enter into special treaties with Prussia.

"But, to admit Prussia to claim all the privileges without incurring any of the risks—to admit her unconditionally to a conference that might end in peace, but which might lead to war on a more extended sphere—without her telling us what were her intentions or her policy—without entering into any engagement with us, either immediate or prospective—without knowing whether she entered on the conference as a neutral, as a foe, or as a friend—was utterly impossible."

The special missions sent later by Prussia had been received with equal friendliness in London and Paris, but so far had not led to anything. He did not, however, regard the negotiations as broken off. Only three days ago new proposals had been made. Unfortunately, the Vienna conferences had opened, however, while Prussia remained excluded by her own action. A great power like Prussia should not restrict itself to the narrow German confines. They had repeatedly remonstrated against this attitude. The constant reply was that Prussia's policy was peace. In fact her policy was neither "European nor German nor Russian", more likely to thwart Austria than to keep Russia in check. In spite of all this Prussia could not long remain in isolation when important European interests were at stake. She could not side with Russia in opposition to national feeling in Prussia and Germany. She knew well that on Russia's side against Austria she would become dependent on the former. She did not want to take Austria's side. On the contrary, she had taken an unfriendly attitude to Austria.

"I say, therefore, that Prussia is in an insular and in a false position [...]. This may be satisfactory to her enemies, but it is deeply regretted by her allies, and by the noble-minded and patriotic of her own population."

He declared finally that every effort would be made to win Prussia's co-operation.

In the Lower House *Lord William Graham* asked the Prime Minister

"whether the Austrian Ambassador[a] had called upon Lord Clarendon for any explanation of the words [...] used by Sir Robert Peel, when he was re-elected that no settlement of the Eastern question would be satisfactory unless Hungary and Poland were restored?"[b]

Lord Palmerston, instead of giving some reply to this question, began by congratulating himself on Sir Robert Peel's having accepted a post in his administration. Concerning Hungary, Austria had long known that England would regard its separation from the imperial state as a great calamity for Europe, since the imperial state as a totality in the centre of Europe was an essential element in the balance of powers. Concerning Poland (considerable laughter was here caused by a little pause in Palmerston's reply and the peculiar manner in which he resumed his speech) it was his opinion that the Kingdom of Poland, as now constituted and as now possessed, was a constant threat to Germany. Nevertheless, stipulations concerning a re-organisation of Poland formed no part of the points now being negotiated in Vienna. England and France had, however, reserved the right, according to circumstances and the events of war, to add to the four points, on the basis of which the negotiations were now being conducted, further stipulations which appeared to them essential for the future security of Europe.

Written on March 21, 1855

First published in the *Neue Oder-Zeitung*, No. 141, March 24, 1855

Marked with the sign ×

Printed according to the newspaper

Published in English for the first time

---

[a] F. de Paula Colloredo-Wallsee.—*Ed.*

[b] Graham's question in the House of Commons on March 20, 1855, and Palmerston's reply were reported in *The Times*, No. 22007, March 21, 1855.—*Ed.*

Frederick Engels

NAPOLEON'S LAST DODGE [101]

"If Croesus does pass the Halys, he will destroy a great empire." This answer, given to the Lydian King by the oracle of Delphi,[a] might, with equal aptness, now be sent to Louis Bonaparte on his Crimean excursion. It is not the Russian Empire which this journey is calculated to destroy, but his own.

An extraordinary, anomalous position creates anomalous necessities. Every other man, in his place, would be considered a fool if he undertook this trip, whose unfavorable chances are to the favorable as ten to one. Louis Bonaparte must be quite aware of that fact, and nevertheless he must go. He is the originator of the whole expedition; he has got the allied armies into their present unenviable position, and is bound, before all Europe, to get them out of it again. It is his first military feat, and upon its issue will depend, for some time at least, his reputation as a general. He answers for its success with no less a pledge than his crown.

There are, besides, minor reasons, which equally contribute to make this hazardous journey a matter of State necessity. The soldiers in the East have shown, on more than one occasion, that their expectations of the military glories of the new Empire have been sadly disappointed. At Varna and Bazardshik, the paladins of the mock Charlemagne were saluted by their own troops with the title of "apes." "*A bas les singes!*[102] *Vive Lamoricière!*" was the cry of the Zouaves when St. Arnaud and Espinasse had sent them into the Bulgarian desert, to die of cholera and fever. Now it is no longer the banished generals alone whose fame and popularity are opposed to the commanders of doubtful reputation, now leading the French army. The singular conduct of Napoleon Jérôme junior, while in the East,[103] has recalled to the mind of the old

---

[a] Herodotus, *History*, I, 53.—*Ed.*

Algerian soldiers the far different behavior of the Orleans Princes in Africa, who, whatever else may be said against them, were always at the head of the troops and did their duty as soldiers. The contrast between young Aumale and young Napoleon was certainly strong enough to make the soldiers say: If the Orleans were still in power, the Princes would be with us in the trenches, sharing our dangers and fatigues; and yet, their name was not Napoleon! Thus the soldiers *do* speak, and what is to be done to stop them? The man who "is permitted to wear the uniform of a General of Division," has managed to throw a stain upon the military traditions of the name of Napoleon; the remainder of the family are all very quiet civilians, naturalists, priests, or else unmitigated adventurers; old Jérôme cannot go on account of his age, and because his warlike feats of old throw no great halo of glory around his head; so Louis Napoleon cannot but go himself. Then the rumor of the Crimean journey has been made known in the remotest hamlets of France, and has been hailed with enthusiasm by the peasantry; and the peasantry it was that made Louis Napoleon Emperor. The peasantry are convinced that an Emperor of their own make, and who bears the name of Napoleon, must actually be a *Napoleon redivivus*[a]; his place is, in their eyes, at the head of the troops, who, led by him, will rival the legions of the great Army.[b] If Sevastopol is not taken, it is only because the Emperor has not yet gone there; let him but once be on the spot, and the ramparts of the Russian fortress will crumble into dust like the walls of Jericho. Thus, if ever he wished to retract his promise to go, he cannot now do so, since the report has once gone forth.

Accordingly, everything is being prepared.[c] The ten divisions now in the Crimea are to be followed by four new ones, two of which are to form, in the beginning of the campaign, an army of reserve at Constantinople. One of these divisions is to consist of the Imperial Guard, another of the combined élite companies, or the Grenadiers and Voltigeurs of the army of Paris; the two other divisions (11th and 12th) are already getting embarked or concentrated at Toulon and Algiers. This fresh reenforcement

[a] Napoleon risen from the dead.—*Ed.*

[b] The army of Napoleon I which invaded Russia in 1812.—*Ed.*

[c] Here begins the text of the German version of Engels' articles "Napoleon's Last Dodge" and "A Battle at Sevastopol", which was published in the *Neue Oder-Zeitung*, No. 143, March 26, 1855 under the title "On the Latest Events in the Crimea". The opening sentence in it reads as follows: "While the peace talks continue in Vienna, the war preparations are being stepped up in France."—*Ed.*

would bring the French troops in the Crimea to some 100,000 or 110,000 men, while, by the end of April, the 15,000 Piedmontese troops, and numerous British reenforcements will be arriving.[a] But yet, it can hardly be expected that the Allies can well be in a position to open the campaign in May, with an army of 150,000 men. The state of the Heracleatic Chersonese, which has been turned into one great and wretchedly managed burial-ground, is such that with the return of hot and damp weather, the whole must form one hotbed of pestilence of all kinds; and whatever portion of the troops will have to stop in it, will be exposed to losses by sickness and death far more terrific than at any previous time. There is no chance for the Allies to break forth with an active army from their present position, before all their reenforcements are up; and that will be somewhere about the middle of May, when the sickness must have already broken out.

In the best event the Allies must leave 40,000 men before the south side of Sevastopol, and will have from 90,000 to 100,000 men at liberty for an expedition against the Russian army in the field. Unless they maneuver very well and the Russians commit great blunders, this army, on debouching from the Chersonese, will have first to defeat the Russians, and drive them back from Sympheropol, before it can effect its junction with the Turks at Eupatoria. We will, however, suppose the junction to be effected without difficulty; the utmost reenforcement which the Turks will bring to this motley body of French, English and Piedmontese, will be 20,000 men not very well adapted for a battle in the open field. Altogether this would make an army of some 120,000 men. How such an army is expected to live in a country exhausted by the Russians themselves, poor in corn, and whose main resource, the cattle, the Russians will take very good care to drive off toward Perekop, it is not very easy to see. The least advance would

[a] The further text in the version of the *Neue Oder-Zeitung* up to the end of the article is abridged and changed: "Apart from all difficulties of a purely local character, there remains the principal objection to this mode of campaigning in the Crimea, viz., that it consigns a whole quarter of France's disposable forces to a secondary theatre of war, where even the greatest success decides nothing. The fictitious value that has been attributed to the successes and defeats in the Crimea rebounds with redoubled force upon the originator of the scheme. Sevastopol is far from being Russia for Alexander II, but it has become France for Bonaparte.—As for the local difficulties, it is clear that Chersonese, at present the burial-ground of thousands of people and animals, will with the first ray of sun turn into a hothouse of pestilential diseases. Assuming that the Allies will bring up their army to 150,000 men, keeping them supplied with provisions in a Crimea already grazed down by the Russians and poor in corn will be the harder for the fact that the Russians will not fail to drive off the cattle in good time before their own retreat."—*Ed.*

necessitate extensive foraging and numerous detachments to secure the flanks and the communications with the sea. The Russian irregular cavalry, which has hitherto had no chance to act, will then commence its harassing operations. In the meantime, the Russians will also have received their reenforcements; the publicity with which the French armaments have been carried on for the last six weeks, has enabled them to take their measures in time. There can be no doubt that at this present moment two or three Russian divisions, either from the army of Volhynia and Bessarabia, or from the new-formed reserves, will be on the march so as to maintain the balance of power there.

The greatest detachment to be made from the allied army, must, however, be the force which has to inclose Sevastopol on the north side. For this purpose, 20,000 men will have to be set aside, and whether the remainder of their forces will then be sufficient, fettered as they must be by difficulties of sustenance, embarrassed with trains of carriages for stores and provisions, to drive the Russian field army out of the Crimea, is very doubtful.

So much is certain, that the laurels by which Louis Bonaparte intends to earn the name of a Napoleon in the Crimea are hung up rather high, and will not be so very easily plucked. All the difficulties, however, which have been hitherto mentioned, are of a merely local character. The great objection to this mode of campaigning in the Crimea is, after all, that it transfers one-fourth of the disposable forces of France to a minor theater of war, where even the greatest success decides nothing. It is this absurd obstinacy about Sevastopol, degenerating into a sort of superstition, and giving to successes, but also to reverses, fictitious values, which forms the great fundamental mistake of the whole plan. And it is this fictitious value given to events in the Crimea which rebounds with redoubled force upon the unfortunate originator of the scheme. For Alexander, Sevastopol is not Russia, far from it; but for Louis Bonaparte, the impossibility of taking Sevastopol is the loss of France.

Written about March 23, 1855

First published in the *New-York Daily Tribune,* No. 4358, April 7, 1855, reprinted in the *New-York Semi-Weekly Tribune,* No. 1030, April 10, 1855 as a leading article; an abridged German version was published in the *Neue Oder-Zeitung,* No. 143, March 26, 1855, marked with the sign ×

Reproduced from the *New-York Daily Tribune*

Frederick Engels

A BATTLE AT SEVASTOPOL[104]

Our columns, this morning, contain the official French, English, and Russian reports of a contest between the antagonists at Sevastopol. It was sufficiently important to require, in addition to the official documents, some words of explanation and comment from us.

About a month ago, from the generally-successful sorties of the Russians, we came to the conclusion that the trenches had been pushed forward to a point at which the force of the besieged was equal to that of the besiegers[a]; in other words, that the proximity of the trenches was such as to enable the Russians to bring, in a sally, to any portion of the trenches, a force at least equal to what the Allies could bring up during the first hour or two hours. As an hour or two are quite sufficient to destroy the rivetings, and to spike the guns of a battery, the natural consequence was, that beyond this point the Allies could not push their approaches. Since then the siege came to a stand, until the arrival[b] of three French brigades (one of the Eighth, and two of the Ninth Division) allowed them to relieve part of the English infantry, and to establish stronger trench-guards. At the same time, the arrival

---

[a] See this volume, pp. 5-7.—*Ed.*

[b] Here follows the continuation of the German version of Engels' articles "Napoleon's Last Dodge" and "A Battle at Sevastopol", published in the *Neue Oder-Zeitung*, No. 143, March 26, 1855 under the title "On the Latest Events in the Crimea". Instead of the preceding text this paragraph has: "As regards the obstacles created to the siege of Sevastopol, in particular by Russian engineers (partly Frenchmen), *the affair of Malakhov* provides an instructive illustration. As is generally known, about a month ago the siege came to a stand, but the arrival...".—*Ed.*

of Generals Niel and Jones, of the Engineers, gave fresh activity to the siege operations, and remedied mistakes caused, principally, by the obstinacy of the French General Bizot, and by the numeric weakness of the British infantry. New approaches were now pushed forward, especially on the English side, where a parallel was opened at about 300 yards from the Russian works on the hill of Malakoff. Some of the batteries now erected were so far toward the Inkermann side that they would have taken part of the Russian batteries in the rear, or enfiladed them, as soon as their fire could be opened. Against these new lines the Russians have just taken a step which has been carried out with uncommon skill and boldness.[a]

The Russian lines, as every plan shows, extend in a semicircular arch round the town, from the head of the Quarantine Bay to that of the inner war harbor, and thence to the head of the Careening Bay. This latter bay is a small creek, formed by the extremity of a deep ravine, extending from the great harbor or Bay of Sevastopol far up the plateau on which the Allies are encamped.[a] On the western side of this ravine extends a range of hights forming the Russian lines; the most considerable of these elevations is the hill of Malakoff, forming, by its commanding position, the key of the whole Russian right. On the eastern side of the ravine and the Careening Bay, another elevation is situated, which, being completely under the fire both of the Russian batteries and of their men-of-war, remained out of the reach of the Allies as long as they could not completely interrupt the communication of Sevastopol with Inkermann, which was protected by the fire of the forts and batteries on the north side of the harbor. But since the Allies had found positions to the east and south-east of Malakoff, for batteries to take in the Russian lines, flank and rear, this neutral hill had become important. Accordingly, on the night of February 21, the Russians sent a party of workmen to erect on it a redoubt, planned beforehand by their engineers.[b] In the morning the long trench and a beginning of parapets behind it, were visible to the Allies. They appear to have been entirely unable to understand the meaning of this; accordingly, they were content to let well alone. Next morning, however, the redoubt was all but complete, at least in its outline, for the sequel showed that the profile, that is, the depth of the ditch and strength of the parapet, was still very weak. By this time

[a] This sentence does not occur in the *Neue Oder-Zeitung*.—*Ed.*

[b] The Selenghinsk redoubt; in the *Neue Oder-Zeitung* the end of this sentence beginning with the words "planned beforehand" does not occur.—*Ed.*

the Allies began to find out that this work was admirably situated to enfilade their own enfilading batteries, and thus to make them all but useless. The engineers protested that this work must be taken at any cost. Accordingly, Canrobert organized with the greatest secrecy, a storming column, consisting of about 1,600 Zouaves and 3,000 Marines. The orders having to be given at a late hour, and all on a sudden, some delay occurred in collecting the troops at the rendezvous, and it was 2 o'clock on the morning of the 24th before they could start for the assault, the Zouaves leading. A short march brought them up to twenty yards from the ditch. As usual in assaults, not a shot was to be fired; the soldiers were made to take off the percussion-caps from their guns to prevent their being entangled in useless and dilatory firing. All at once, a few Russian words of command were heard; a strong body of Russians in the interior of the redoubt, rose from the ground, leveled their guns over the top of the parapet, and poured a volley into the advancing column. From the darkness and the well known inveterate habit of soldiers in intrenchments to fire always straight across the parapet, this volley can have had but little effect upon the narrow head of the column.[a] The Zouaves, hardly detained by the sloping sides of the incomplete ditch and rampart, in a moment were in the redoubt, and rushed at their opponents with the bayonet. A terrible hand-to-hand struggle took place. After some time the Zouaves possessed themselves of one-half of the redoubt, and, at a later period, the Russians entirely abandoned it to them. In the mean time, the marines, following the Zouaves at a short distance, either lost their way, or from some other reason, stopped on the brink of the hill. Here they were assailed in each flank by a Russian column, which, after a desperate resistance, drove them down the hill. During or shortly after this struggle, daylight must have dawned, for the Russians speedily retired from the hill—leaving the redoubt in the possession of the Zouaves—upon whom now opened all the Russian artillery which could be brought to bear on the spot. The Zouaves lay down for a moment, while some rifle volunteers, who had accompanied them, crept up to the Malakoff works, trying to fire at the Russian gunners through the embrasures. But the fire was too heavy; and, before long, the Zouaves had to retreat on the side toward Inkermann, which sheltered them against most of the batteries. They profess to have carried all their wounded with them.

This little affair was carried out with great bravery by the

[a] This sentence does not occur in the *Neue Oder-Zeitung*.—*Ed.*

Zouaves and a Gen. Monet, and with great skill combined with their usual tenacity by the Russians. They consisted of the two regiments of Selenghinsk and Volhynia, the strength of which, after several campaigns, cannot have exceeded 500 men per battalion, or 4,000 men in all. Gen. Kroushoff commanded them.[a] Their arrangements were so admirable that the French declare that the whole plan of attack must have been known to them. The attack upon the marines was completely and almost instantaneously successful, while their retreat out of the incomplete redoubt had the effect of exposing the unfortunate and unsupported Zouaves to an overwhelming fire, which must have remained silent as long as the struggle within the redoubt was going on.

Gen. Canrobert found that this defeat had a very great effect on his troops. Their impatience which had made itself remarkable on various occasions, now broke out with full force. The assault upon the town was demanded by the soldiers. The word of treason, that everlasting excuse for a defeat suffered by the French, was loudly pronounced, and Gen. Forey, without any apparent reason, was even nominally pointed out as the party who betrayed to the enemy the secret resolutions of the French Council of War. So confused was Canrobert, that in one breath he wrote an order of the day representing the whole affair as a brilliant though relative success, and a note to Lord Raglan proposing an immediate assault, a proposal which Lord Raglan, of course, declined.[b]

The Russians, on their part, maintained their new redoubt, and have since been busy completing it. This position is of great importance. It secures the communication with Inkermann and the arrival of supplies from that direction. It menaces the whole right of the allied siege-works,[c] by taking them in flank, and necessitating fresh approaches to paralyze it. Above all, it shows the capability, in the Russians, not only to hold their ground, but even to advance beyond it. In the latter part of February they pushed trenches of counter-approach toward the allied works from their new redoubt. The reports do not, however, state the exact direction of these works. At all events, the presence of the two regiments of the line in Sevastopol proves that the garrison,

[a] The last two sentences do not occur in the *Neue Oder-Zeitung*.—*Ed.*

[b] Instead of this paragraph the *Neue Oder-Zeitung* has: "General Forey was loudly accused in the French camp of having communicated the secret decisions of the Council of War to the enemy."—*Ed.*

[c] The identical text of the English and German versions ends here. In the *Neue Oder-Zeitung* the article closes as follows: "Lastly, with its capture the Russians have taken the offensive."—*Ed.*

hitherto consisting of marines and sailors only, has been considerably reenforced, and is strong enough for any eventuality.

It is now reported that by the 10th or 11th of March, the Allies would be in a position to open their batteries upon the Russian defenses, but, with the resources of the Russians and the difficulties of the Allies, how is it to be expected that the first condition will be fulfilled, namely: That the besiegers' fire will be superior to that of the besieged, and so far superior, too, as to silence the Russian batteries before the English and French have exhausted their stores of ammunition? But let us suppose even this result is obtained. Suppose even that at this decisive moment the Russians in the field should neglect attacking the positions of Inkermann and Balaklava. Suppose the assaults attempted upon the first Russian line, and suppose that line even carried: What then? Fresh defenses, fresh batteries, strong buildings converted into small citadels requiring a new set of batteries to bring them down, are before the storming columns; a hail of grape and musketry drives them back, and it is as much as they can do if they hold the first Russian line.

Then follows the siege of the second, then that of the third line—not to mention the numerous minor obstacles which the Russian engineers, as we now have learned to know them, cannot have failed to accumulate in the interior of the space intrusted to their care. And during this time, wet and heat, and heat and wet alternately, on a ground impregnated with the animal decay of thousands of men and horses, will create diseases unknown and unheard of. The pestilence, it is true, will reign within the town as well as without; but which party will have to give in to it first?

Spring will carry along with it terrible things on this little peninsula of five miles by ten, where three of the greatest nations of Europe are fighting an obstinate struggle; and Louis Bonaparte will have plenty of reason to congratulate himself when his great expedition comes to develop its full fruit.

Written about March 23, 1855

First published in the *New-York Daily Tribune*, No. 4358, April 7, 1855, reprinted in the *New-York Semi-Weekly Tribune*, No. 1030, April 10, 1855 as a leading article; an abridged German version was published in the *Neue Oder-Zeitung*, No. 143, March 26, 1855, marked with the sign ×

Reproduced from the *New-York Daily Tribune*

Karl Marx

SOME OBSERVATIONS ON THE HISTORY OF THE FRENCH ALLIANCE

London, March 24. *The Press*, the organ of Disraeli, last week raised a storm in a teacup by maintaining that "Emperor Louis" was the only obstacle to the conclusion of peace and had tied Austria to himself by a secret "agreement" of which Austria was endeavouring to rid itself. Until now the Tories had maintained that the Anglo-French alliance was their own handiwork. Had not their Lord Malmesbury sealed the union with Bonaparte[105]? Had not Disraeli in Parliament showered sarcasms on Graham and Wood, who had wickedly calumniated the coup of December 2 before their electors? Had not the Tories for two years, in speeches and in the press, been the loudest heralds of war? And now, suddenly, without transition, entirely without any mitigating circumstances, insinuations are made against the French Alliance, and caustic remarks about "Emperor Louis" and the homily on peace? *The Morning Herald*, the senile organ of the High Tories, uninitiated into the secret of the Party leaders, shook its head doubtfully, and murmured violent protests against the, to it, incomprehensible hallucinations of *The Press*.[a] The latter nevertheless returns today to the fateful subject. The following announcement appears in bold letters at its top:

"Important circumstances have transpired. When we last wrote there was a prospect of the Congress breaking up '*re infecta*',[b] and of Lord John Russell returning abruptly to England. [...] The altered tone adopted to Russia by Austria since the death of the Emperor Nicholas [...] and especially the declaration of the

[a] This refers to an item published in *The Morning Herald*, No. 22385, March 21, 1855, in reply to the statement of *The Press* cited above.— *Ed.*

[b] Without achieving its purpose.— *Ed.*

Austrian Emperor[a] to Alexander II, have doubtless mainly contributed to this result. We have reason to believe that the Emperor of the French has removed the obstacles which existed to a general pacification, and that France will consent to the complete evacuation of the Crimea without any conditions as to the demolition or diminution of any of the fortresses of that province."[b]

To elucidate the meaning of the oracle *The Press* refers to the "authentic details of its leading article". Oddly enough, these very details refute the conclusion allegedly based on them and stated beforehand.

According to the leading article "...the situation of affairs in Vienna is becoming every hour less rational and satisfactory; and it is of importance that enlightened opinion on both sides of the Channel should exercise its influence to prevent results which may become alike mortifying and deplorable. [...] Had the Anglo-French alliance been sincere on the part of our Ministers in 1853, we should, probably, never have had occasion to embark in war; but, had such an appeal proved necessary, its conduct, in all probability, would have been triumphant and effective. Instead of acting cordially with France [...] a year was wasted by the British Government in obtaining what they styled '*the adhesion of the great German Powers*' [...]. Nothing could justify a war with Russia but a determination, on the part of the Western Powers, materially to reduce its empire in the South. This is the only solution of the Eastern question. The occasion in 1853 was favourable, it has been lost. Time, treasure, armies, reputation, have been alike squandered. Had we acted cordially with France in 1853 the German Powers must have followed in our wake. What has now happened? The Emperor of Austria has assured the Emperor Alexander of Russia, 'That Austria seeks neither to diminish the limit of his empire, nor to inflict on his territory any dishonor'. There is only one meaning which can be attributed to these words. With reference to an allusion, which we made earlier, to the secret engagements entered into between France and Austria, we are assured, on high authority, that 'while those engagements [...] indicate a [...] probably permanent union between the two empires there is nothing in those engagements that would necessarily lead to an invasion of Russia on the part of Austria'. [...] The Emperor of Russia is prepared to submit to terms of peace, which, though they offer no solution of 'the Eastern question', are, unquestionably, an admission of baffled aggression, and, in some degree, an atonement for the outrage. We believe that the opportunity for the higher policy has been lost, and that the combination of circumstances which [...] might have secured the independence of Europe, will not speedily recur; but a peace, on the whole, advantageous to Europe, beneficial to Turkey, and not discreditable to the Western Powers, may still be obtained. [...] We have reason to fear that such a peace will not be negotiated. What is the obstacle? The Emperor of the French. If the Emperor of the French, notwithstanding the [...] adverse circumstances [...], were still of opinion that the solution of the Eastern question ought to be attempted, we are not prepared to say that England should falter, but it reaches us that the views of his Imperial Majesty are of a very different order [...]. Between the reduction of the Russian limits and the negotiation of the projected peace, the Emperor of the French has devised a *mezzo termine*,[c] which is perilous, and may be fatal. There is to be a campaign of brilliant achievement,

[a] Francis Joseph I.—*Ed.*

[b] Quoted from *The Press*, No. 99, March 24, 1855. The long quotation below is from the leading article in the same issue.—*Ed.*

[c] Middle road.—*Ed.*

which is to restore the *prestige*, and then conclude with a peace, which will not affect the present territorial arrangement of Europe or Asia one whit more than the Austro-Russian propositions to which [...] her Majesty's Plenipotentiary Extraordinary at Vienna[a] was prepared to accede. We will not dwell on that part of this scheme which would sacrifice many thousands of human lives to the mere restoration of *prestige*.... We hold that the impolicy of this project is as flagrant as its immorality. Suppose the campaign of *prestige* do not succeed? In addition to the obstacles presented by the Russian army in the Crimea pestilence is as likely to be at hand as war. [...] If the campaign of *prestige* fail, where will be France and England? On whose side will then be arrayed the great German Powers? The vista is no less than the decline and fall of Europe. Even if the odds were not against us, are we justified in running such a chance—not even in favour of a policy, but of a demonstration? It may be mortifying to the ruler of France that a great opportunity has been lost: [...] it is not less mortifying to the people of England. But statesmen must deal with the circumstances before them. Neither France, nor England, nor Russia, in 1855, are in the position they respectively occupied in the year 1853. Woe to the men who have betrayed the highest interests of Europe! May they meet the doom they deserve! The ruler of France and the Queen of England[b] are guiltless; but they must not, like bewildered gamesters, persist in backing their ill luck in a frenzy of disappointment, or in a paroxysm of despair".

The same paper refers to Girardin's pamphlet *La Paix*, in which the simultaneous disarming of Sevastopol and Gibraltar is extolled as the true solution for peace.

"Remember," *The Press* exclaims, "this pamphlet, or rather its sale, is authorised by the French Government, and its author is the dear and intimate friend, adviser and companion, of the heir presumptive to the Throne Imperial."[c]

Here we shall only allude to the fact that the Derbyites, whose organ *The Press* is, are working for a coalition with the (peaceable) Manchester School and that the Ministry for its part is also trying to win round the Manchester School by the newspaper stamp Bill (to which we shall return[d]). The idea of a campaign designed to be a mere display of force, of a European war not to endanger the hostile power but to save one's own *prestige*, of a war resembling a spectacular show, must certainly disconcert every sober Englishman. Query: is this not one of the *idées napoléoniennes*[e] as understood and bound to be understood by the restored empire?

Written on March 24, 1855

First published in the *Neue Oder-Zeitung*, No. 145, March 27, 1855

Marked with the sign ×

Printed according to the newspaper

Published in English for the first time

---

[a] Lord John Russell.—*Ed.*

[b] Victoria.—*Ed.*

[c] Prince Jérôme Bonaparte, Jr.—*Ed.*

[d] See this volume, 121-23.—*Ed.*

[e] An allusion to Louis Bonaparte's book *Des idées napoléoniennes* published in 1839.—*Ed.*

Karl Marx

NAPOLEON AND BARBÈS.—THE NEWSPAPER STAMP

London, March 27. We learn from the best source that Bonaparte's visit to St. James's Palace[106]—expected on April 16—will occasion a great *counter-demonstration*. For the Chartists have invited the French refugee *Armand Barbès* also to visit London on April 16, when he is to be received with a public procession and a big meeting. There is, however, some question whether his state of health will permit a sea voyage.

The Bill to abolish the newspaper stamp passed its second reading in the House of Commons yesterday. The main articles of this Bill are as follows: 1. The compulsory newspaper stamp is abolished; 2. Periodicals printed on stamped paper will continue to enjoy the privilege of free distribution through the post. A third clause concerns thc size of printed matter distributed through the post, and another decrees that stamped newspapers will have to furnish security in case of any action for libel. The old newspaper duty system is sufficiently characterised by two facts. The publication of a daily paper in London requires a capital of at least £50,000 to £60,000. The whole English press, with very few exceptions, raises a shameless and disgraceful opposition to the new Bill. Is further proof needed that the old system was a protective tariff system for the established press and a system prohibiting free mental production? Press freedom in England up to now has been the exclusive privilege of capital. The few weekly journals which represent the interests of the working class—daily papers were, of course, out of the question—manage to survive thanks to the weekly contributions of the workers, who in England are making very different sacrifices for public purposes than those on the Continent. The tragicomic, blustering rhetoric with which the Leviathan of the English press—*The Times*—fights *pro aris et focis*,[a] i. e., for the newspaper monopoly, now modestly comparing itself with the Delphic oracle, now affirming that England possesses only one single institution worth preserving, namely *The Times*; now claiming absolute rule over world journalism, and, without any Treaty of Kuchuk-Kainardji,[107] a protectorate over all European journalists.

All this cant[b] by *The Times* was properly disposed of in yesterday's sitting of the Lower House by the whimsical *Drummond*:

"Nowadays the press was a mercantile speculation, and nothing else.... Why Messrs. Walter", the principal shareholders of *The Times*, "should not set up a manufactory of gossip just as well as Mr. Bright should set up a manufactory of calico?... *The Times* seemed to him to carry on their business [...] better than their rivals [...]. The Walter family have always found a convenient man [...]—a seven years' barrister or some one of that stamp, who was ready to take up anything. [...] There was Barnes, Alsager, Sterling, Delane, Morris, Lowe and Dasent. [...] These gentlemen were all of different opinions. Now, the foolish papers who did not understand the matter, like *The Morning Chronicle*, for instance, took up with some particular party. One was a Peelite[108]; another a Derbyite, etc. When the Peelite party was thriving the paper throve too, but when the Peelites went down, down went the paper. It was quite clear these were not men of business. The thing was to get a set of gentlemen of different opinions"—and *The Times* is a master of this—"and to set them writing. Of course, you could accuse no one man of inconsistency; he might always have held the same opinions; and so individually these were most consistent, while, collectively, nothing in the world could be more inconsistent. It seemed to him that the very perfection of journalism was—individual honesty, and collective profligacy, political and literary. There was [...] a great advantage in this, and *The Times* newspaper always put him very much in mind of one of his farmers. When he suggested draining a bit of bog the farmer [...] replied, 'No, no! don't drain it. In wet weather there's something for the cow, and if there's nothing for the cow there's something for the pig, and if there's nothing for the pig, there's something for the goose.' [...] As to the bribery of newspapers there was positive proof respecting *The Times* of which Napoleon said, 'You have sent me *The Times*,—that infamous *Times*, the journal of the Bourbons'—and it was stated in a work by Mr. O'Meara[c] that the Bourbons paid *The Times* 6,000 f. [...] a month. He had found the receipt for the money, signed by the editor. Mr. O'Meara also stated that before he was exiled to Elba Napoleon received several offers [...] from the editors of newspapers, and among them offers from *The Times*, to write for them. Napoleon declined to accept the offers made to him, but afterwards regretted the course he took."[d]

---

[a] For hearth and home. The reference is to an article on the Bill to lift stamp duty, published in *The Times*, No. 22011, March 26, 1855.—*Ed.*

[b] Marx uses the English word.—*Ed.*

[c] O'Meara's diary *Napoleon in Exile, or A Voice from St. Helena*, published in 1822.—*Ed.*

[d] Drummond made this speech in the House of Commons on March 26, 1855. *The Times*, No. 22012, March 27, 1855.—*Ed.*

In this context we merely observe that in 1815 *The Times* urged that Napoleon, whom it presented as the centre of European demagogy[109] should be shot under martial law. In 1816 this same paper wanted to bring the United States of North America, "this disastrous example of successful insurrection", back under English despotism.

Written on March 27, 1855

First published in the *Neue Oder-Zeitung*, No. 151, March 30, 1855

Marked with the sign ×

Printed according to the newspaper

Published in English for the first time

Karl Marx

THE COMMITTEE OF INQUIRY

London, March 28. The Committee of Inquiry of the Commons has now held more than a dozen meetings, and the results of its findings are in great part available to the public. Witnesses from the most divers walks of life have been heard, from the Duke of Cambridge to Mr. Macdonald of *The Times*, and rarely has a hearing of witnesses been distinguished by so much agreement of the testimony. The various branches of the administration have been reviewed and all have been found to be not only deficient but in an appallingly shocking state. The Army Staff, the Medical Department, the Board of Ordnance, the Commissariat, the Transport Service, the Hospital Administration, the Health Inspection, and the Harbour Police of Balaklava and Constantinople have all been condemned without any opposition. But bad as every department was shown to be on its own, the full glory of the system was displayed only in their contact and collaboration with each other. The regulations were so beautifully arranged that as soon as they came into force nobody knew where his authority began and ended, or to whom to turn. Read the descriptions of the condition of the hospitals, of the infamous brutalities committed through neglect or indolence on the sick and wounded in the transport ships and on arrival at their destination. Nothing more horrible occurred on the retreat from Moscow.[a] And these things happened in Scutari, opposite Constantinople, a big city with multifarious resources, not during a hasty retreat with Cossacks on the heels of the fleeing soldiers, cutting off their supplies but as a result of an up-till-then successful campaign, in a place secure from all hostile attack, in the big central depot where

[a] The retreat of Napoleon's army in 1812.—*Ed.*

Great Britain stores its supplies for the army. And those who caused all these horrors were no barbarians but gentlemen belonging to the "Upper Ten Thousand", mild men in their way. *Fiat* the regulations, *pereat* the army[a]! "Turn to another department, the matter is not our responsibility." "But to whom should we turn?" "It is no part of our responsibility to know which department is responsible, and even if it was, we would not be authorised to tell you." "But the sick need shirts, soap, bedding, housing, medicines, arrowroot,[b] port. They are dying in their hundreds." "I am indeed very sorry to hear that the best blood of England is so rapidly ebbing away, but we are unable to help. We cannot provide anything, even if we have it, without the necessary requisitions, signed by half a dozen persons, of whom two-thirds are absent in the Crimea or elsewhere." And like Tantalus, the soldiers had to die in the face, even within smelling distance of the comforts which could have saved their lives. Not a single man there possessed the energy to break through the network of routine, to act on his own responsibility, as the needs of the moment demanded, and in defiance of the regulations. Only one person dared to do that, and that was a *woman*, Miss *Nightingale*. Once she had made sure that the things required were there, she chose a number of sturdy fellows and committed what amounted to burglary of Her Majesty's stores. She told the horror-stricken suppliers:

"Now I have got what I needed. Now go and report at home what you have seen. I take it all upon myself."

The old wives in authority in Constantinople and Scutari, far from being capable of such a bold enterprise, were cowards to a degree which would seem incredible if we did not have their own candid admissions. One of them, a certain *Dr. Andrew Smith*, for example, for a time chief of the hospitals, was asked by the Committee of Inquiry whether there were no funds available in Constantinople for purchases and no markets where the necessary commodities could be procured?

"Oh yes," he replied. "But after forty years of routine and drudgery at home I assure you that it was months before I could convince myself that such a power to spend money was vested in me."[c]

---

[a] Let there be regulations, though the army perish—a paraphrase of the Latin saying, *Fiat justitia—pereat mundus* (Let justice be done though the world perish).—*Ed.*

[b] Marx uses the English word.—*Ed.*

[c] "The State of the Army before Sebastopol", *The Times*, No 22007, March 21, 1855.—*Ed.*

And it was to such old wives that the British Army was entrusted! Indeed, the most eloquent descriptions in the press and in Parliament seem colourless compared with the reality as it unfolds in the witnesses' evidence. And what shall we say of the Herberts, the Gladstones, the Newcastles and *tutti quanti*,[a] of Peel's fashionable clerks[b] who in Parliament repeatedly denied all the facts that have now been proved, rejecting them with a passionate bitterness with which these "eminent" gentlemen had not hitherto been credited! These dandies of Exeter Hall, the elegant Puseyites, for whom the difference between "*transubstantiation*" and "*real presence*" is a life-and-death question,[110] with their characteristically modest arrogance, undertook the conduct of the war and were so successful with the "transubstantiation" of the British Army that its "real presence" was nowhere. "Yes, it is somewhere," Gladstone replied. "On January 1 the British Army in the Crimea amounted to 32,000 men." Unfortunately, we have the evidence of the Duke of Cambridge that on November 6, after the battle of Inkerman,[111] the British Army did not number 13,000 bayonets, and we know that since November and December it has lost about 3,000 men.

In the meantime the news of the uproar in the Commons against the Ministers, of Roebuck's Committee and of the popular indignation in England, has reached the Crimea. Welcomed by the soldiers with jubilation, it struck the generals and department heads with horror. A week later the news arrived that commissioners were on their way with authority to investigate and to negotiate. This had the effect of a galvanic battery on paralytics. Meanwhile the railway workers set to work unfettered by precedence, regulations or office habits. They secured a landing place, set shovels in motion, erected wharves, huts, dams, and before the quaint old gentlemen had any idea the first rail had been laid. Insignificant as the railway probably is for the siege—all its advantages could be obtained more cheaply and simply—it proved of the greatest use by the mere example, by the live contrast of modern industrial England to the helpless England of routine. The "Forward" operations of the railwaymen broke the spell which had held the whole British Army paralysed, the spell generated by an illusion of phantastic impossibilities which had brought British officers and men close to the stolid fatalism of the Turks, and induced them calmly to watch certain ruin as if it were

[a] The whole lot.—*Ed.*
[b] Marx uses the English word.—*Ed.*

an inescapable fate. With the railway workers the adage *Aide-toi et le ciel t'aidera*[a] revived in the army. Within six weeks everything took on a new look. Raglan and his staff, divisional and brigade generals are daily in the trenches, inspecting and giving orders. The Commissariat has discovered horses, carts and drivers, and the troops have found means of bringing their sick under cover, and some of the troops as well. The medical staff has removed the most flagrant horrors from the hospital tents and barracks. Ammunition, clothing, even fresh meat and vegetables are beginning to be available. A certain degree of order has begun to prevail, and though a great deal of the old trouble still remains, the improvement in the conditions is indisputable and amazing.

Written on March 28, 1855

First published in the *Neue Oder-Zeitung*, No. 153, March 31, 1855

Marked with the sign ×

Printed according to the newspaper

Published in English for the first time

[a] "God helps those who help themselves."—*Ed.*

Karl Marx

THE BRITISH ARMY[112]

We have now before us the report of some dozen sittings of the famous Committee appointed by the House of Commons to investigate the condition of the British army in the Crimea. Witnesses have been examined of every rank and station, from the Duke of Cambridge down, and their testimony is surprisingly unanimous. All departments of the administration have been passed in review, and all have been found to be not only deficient, but scandalously so. The staff, the medical department, the purveyor's department, the commissariat, the transport service, the hospital administration, the sanitary and disciplinary police, the harbor police of Balaklava, have one and all been condemned without an opposing voice.

Bad as every department was in itself, the full glories of the system were, however, developed only by the contact and cooperation of all. The regulations were so beautifully arranged that as soon as they came to be put in force, when the troops first landed in Turkey, nobody knew where his authority began nor where it ended, nor to whom to apply for anything; and thus, from a wholesome fear of responsibility, everybody shifted everything from his own shoulders to those of somebody else. Under this system, the hospitals were scenes of infamous brutality. Indolent neglect did its worst upon the sick and wounded on board the transports and after their arrival. The facts revealed are incredible; indeed, there was nothing more horrible in the retreat from Moscow.[a] And yet, they actually happened at Scutari, within sight of Constantinople, a large city, with all its resources in labor and material comforts. They happened, not on a hasty retreat,

[a] Of Napoleon's army in 1812.—*Ed.*

with the Cossacks at the heels of the fugitives and cutting off their supplies, but in the course of a partially successful campaign, at a place sheltered from all hostile attack, at the great central depot where Great Britain had heaped up her stores for the army. And the authors of all these horrors and abominations are no hard-hearted barbarians. They are, every one of them, British gentlemen of good extraction, well-educated, and of mild, philanthropic and religious dispositions. In their individual capacity, they no doubt were ready and willing to do anything; in their official capacity, their duty was to look coolly and with folded arms upon all these infamies, conscious that the case was not provided for in any part of her Majesty's regulations affecting themselves. Perish a thousand armies sooner than infringe upon her Majesty's regulations! And Tantalus-like, the soldiers had to die within sight, almost within reach of the comforts which would have saved their lives.

Not a man on the spot had the energy to break through the net-work of routine, to act upon his own responsibility as the necessities of the case demanded, and in the teeth of the regulations. The only party who has dared to do this is a woman, Miss Nightingale. Having once ascertained that the things wanted were in store, she is reported to have taken a handful of stout fellows and to have actually committed a burglary upon the Queen's store-houses! The old women in authority at Constantinople and Scutari, far from being capable of such daring, were cowards to a degree we could scarcely credit, were it not openly admitted by themselves. One of them, Dr. Andrew Smith, for a time chief of the hospitals, was asked if there were in Constantinople no funds to buy, and no market to supply, many of the things wanted?

"Oh, yes," he replied, "*but after forty years' routine and drudgery at home, I assure you I could hardly for some months realize the idea that I actually had funds placed at my command!*"[a]

The very blackest descriptions of the state of matters which had been given in both newspapers and Parliamentary speeches, are far outdone by the reality, as it now is brought before us. Some of the most glaring features had been broached, but even these now receive a gloomier coloring. Although the picture is as yet far from complete, we can see enough of it to judge of the whole. Excepting the female nurses sent out, there is not one redeeming feature in it. One group is as bad and as stupid as the other, and

[a] "The State of the Army before Sebastopol", *The Times*, No. 22007, March 21, 1855.—*Ed.*

if the Committee, in their report, have the courage to speak out according to evidence, they will be embarrassed to find in the English language words strong enough to express their condemnation.

In view of these disclosures it is impossible to repress a strong glow of indignation and contempt not only for the immediate actors, but above all for the Government which arranged the expedition, and which, with the facts staring it in the face, had the impudence to declare they were mere fictions. Where, now, is that great Coalition of All the Talents,[113] that galaxy of statesmen with whose advent the Golden Age was to dawn upon England? Between Whigs and Peelites, Russellites and Palmerstonians, Irishmen and Englishmen, Liberal Conservatives and Conservative Liberals, they have been huckstering and bargaining among themselves, and every man they have put into place turns out to be an old woman or an unmitigated fool. These statesmen were so sure the machine they had been managing for thirty years would work admirably, that they did not even send out a person invested with extraordinary powers for unforeseen circumstances; unforeseen circumstances, of course, could never occur under a well-regulated Government! Subalterns by nature and by habit, these British ministers, suddenly placed in a position of command, have achieved the utter disgrace of England. There is old Raglan, all his life a head-office-clerk to Wellington; a man that never was permitted to act upon his own responsibility; a man bred to do just as he was bid, up to his 65th year; and this man is all of a sudden appointed to lead an army against the enemy, and to decide everything at once and for himself! And a pretty mess he has made of it. Vacillation, timidity, total absence of self-confidence, firmness and the initiative, mark every one of his steps. We know now how feebly he behaved in the council of war where the Crimean expedition was resolved upon. To be taken in tow by a blustering blackguard like St. Arnaud, whom old Wellington would have silenced forever with one dry, ironical word! Then his timid march to Balaklava, his helplessness at the siege[a] and during the sufferings of the winter, when he found nothing better to do than to hide himself. Then there is Lord Hardinge, equally subaltern in character, who commands the army at home. An old campaigner as he is, one would judge from his administration, and the way he defends it in the Lords, that he had never been out of his barracks or his office. To say he is

[a] Of Sevastopol.— *Ed.*

totally ignorant of the very first requisites of an army in the field, or too lazy to recollect them, is the most favorable aspect that can be given to his case. Then come Peel's clerks—Cardwell, Gladstone, Newcastle, Herbert, and *tutti quanti*. They are well-bred, good-looking young gentlemen, whose elegance of manners and refinement of feeling do not permit them to handle a thing roughly, or to act with even a show of decision in the matters of this world. "Consideration" is their word. They take everything into consideration; they keep everything under consideration; they hold everybody in consideration; in consideration of which they expect to be held in consideration by everybody. Everything with them must be round and smooth. Nothing is so objectionable as the angular forms which mark strength and energy.

Whatever reports came from the army as to its being ruined by mismanagement were impudently denied by these mild, veracious and pious gentlemen, who being *a priori* convinced of the perfection of their Government, had the best authority for such denials; and when the subject was persevered in, and even the official reports from the seat of war compelled them to admit part of these statements, their denials were still made with a degree of acrimony and passion. Their opposition to Roebuck's motion for an inquiry is the most scandalous instance on record of public perseverance in untruth. The London *Times,* Layard, Stafford, and even their own colleague, Russell, gave them the lie,[a] but they persevered. The whole House of Commons, by a majority of two out of three, gave them the lie, and they still persevered. Now they stand convicted before Roebuck's Committee; but, for aught we know, they are persevering still. But their perseverance has now become a matter of small account. With the truth disclosed to the world in all its horrible reality, it is impossible that there should not be a reform in the system and administration of the British Army.

Written on March 28, 1855

First published in the *New-York Daily Tribune,* No. 4364, April 14, 1855, reprinted in the *New-York Semi-Weekly Tribune,* No. 1032, April 17, 1855 as a leading article

Reproduced from the *New-York Daily Tribune*

---

[a] This refers to the speeches made by Layard, Stafford and Russell in the House of Commons on January 26 and 29, 1855 during the discussion of Roebuck's motion for setting up a committee to inquire into the condition of the army at Sevastopol. *The Times,* Nos. 21962 and 21964, January 27 and 30, 1855.—*Ed.*

Frederick Engels

PROGRESS OF THE WAR

While the diplomats assembled at Vienna are discussing the fate of Sevastopol, and the Allies are trying to make peace on the best terms they can, the Russians in the Crimea, profiting by the blunders of their opponents, as well as by their own central position in the country, are again taking the offensive on every point. It is a curious state of things, considering the boasts with which the Allies began their invasion, and looks like a vast satire on human presumption and folly. But though it thus has its comic side, the drama is deeply tragic, after all; and we once more invite our readers to a serious examination of the facts, as they are disclosed by our latest advices received here on Sunday morning by the *America*'s mails.[114]

At Eupatoria, Omer Pasha is now actually hemmed in on the land side. Their superiority in cavalry permits the Russians to place their picquets and videttes close to the town, to scour the country by patrols, intercepting supplies, and in case of a serious sally, to fall back upon their infantry. Thus they are doing what we predicted they would do—holding the superior force of Turks in check by a body perhaps not more than one-fourth or one-third their number.[a] Accordingly Omer Pasha is waiting for additional cavalry to come up, and in the meantime has been to the Anglo-French camp to inform his allies that for the present he can do nothing, and that a reenforcement of some 10,000 French troops would be very desirable. No doubt it would; but no less desirable to Canrobert himself, who, by this time, must have found out that he has both too many troops, and too few—too many for the mere carrying on of the siege, such as it is, and for the

[a] See this volume, pp. 82-85.—*Ed.*

defense of the Chernaya; but not enough to debouch from the Chernaya, drive the Russians into the interior, and invest the North Fort. To send 10,000 men to Eupatoria, would not enable the Turks to take the field with success; while their absence would cripple the French army at the time when, with the reenforcements arriving in spring, it is expected to take the field.

The siege is now becoming a very sorry affair, indeed. The night attack of the Zouaves on Feb. 24, was even more disastrous in its results than we stated a week ago.[a] It appears from Canrobert's own dispatch that he did not know what he was about when he ordered this attack. He says:

"The purpose of the attack being now attained, our troops retired, as nobody ever could think of our establishing ourselves on a point so completely commanded by the fire of the enemy."[b]

But what was the purpose thus attained? What was there to do if the point could not be held? Nothing whatever. The destruction of the redoubt was not accomplished, and could not have been accomplished under the enemy's fire, even if the Zouaves, as the first report pretended, had for a moment exclusive possession of the work. But that they never had; the Russian report denies it most positively, and Canrobert does not pretend to anything of the kind. What, then, was meant by this attack? Why, plainly this: that Canrobert, seeing the Russians establishing themselves in a position very embarrassing and equally humiliating to the besiegers, without any reflection, without giving himself the trouble of examining the probable issue of the affair, sent his troops to the charge. It was a downright, useless butchery, and will leave a serious stain upon Canrobert's military reputation. If any excuse can be found, it is only in the supposition that the French troops having become impatient for the assault, the General intended giving them a slight foretaste of what the assault would be. But this excuse is quite as discreditable to Canrobert as the charge itself.

By the affair of Malakoff the Russians ascertained their superiority on the ground immediately in front of their defenses. The work situated on the crest of the hill, and vainly attacked by the Zouaves, is called by them the Selenghinsk redoubt, from the regiment which defended it. They at once proceeded to follow up their advantage and act upon the certitude thus obtained. Selenghinsk was enlarged and strengthened, guns were brought

---

[a] See this volume, pp. 115-16.—*Ed.*

[b] Canrobert's dispatch of February 27, 1855 was published in *The Times*, No. 22008, March 22, 1855.—*Ed.*

up to it, though they must have passed under the heaviest fire of the besiegers, and counter-approaches were made from it, probably with a view to erect one or two minor works in its front. On another spot, too, in front of the Korniloff bastion, a series of new redoubts was also thrown up 300 yards in advance of the old Russian works. From former British reports, the possibility of such a step seems astonishing, for we were always told the Allies had thrown up their own trenches at less than that distance from the Russian lines. But as we were enabled to state, upon first-rate professional authority about a month since, the French lines were still some 400 yards from the Russian outworks, and the British even twice that distance. Now, at last, *The Times*' correspondent's[a] letter of March 16 confesses that even up to that date the British trenches were still 600 to 800 yards off, and that, in fact, *the batteries about to open upon the enemy were but the same which opened their fire on the 17th of October last!*[b] This, then, is that great progress in the siege—that pushing forward the trenches, which cost two-thirds of the British army their lives!

Under such circumstances, there was plenty of room for erecting these new Russian works in the intermediate space between the two lines of batteries; but it nevertheless remains a most unparalleled act, the boldest and most skilful thing that was ever undertaken by a besieged garrison. It amounts to nothing less than opening a fresh parallel against the Allies, at from 300 to 400 yards from their works; to a counter-approach on the grandest scale against the besiegers, who thereby are at once thrown back into a defensive state, while the very first essential condition of a siege is that the besiegers shall hold the besieged in the defensive. Thus the tables are completely turned, and the Russians are strongly in the ascendant.

Whatever blunders and fantastical experiments the Russian engineers may have made under Schilder, at Silistria,[115] the Allies have, here at Sevastopol, evidently a different set of men to deal with. The justness and rapidity of glance—the promptness, boldness, and faultlessness of execution, which the Russian engineers have shown in throwing up their lines around Sevastopol—the indefatigable attention with which every weak point was protected as soon as discovered by the enemy—the excellent arrangement of the line of fire, so as to concentrate a force, superior to that of the besiegers, upon any given point of the ground in front—the preparation of a second, third and fourth

[a] W. H. Russell.—*Ed.*
[b] *The Times*, No. 22014, March 29, 1855.—*Ed.*

line of fortifications in rear of the first—in short, the whole conduct of this defense has been classic. The late offensive advances on Malakoff hill and to the front of the Korniloff bastion are unparalleled in the history of sieges, and stamp their originators as first-rate men in their line. It is but just to add that the Chief Engineer at Sevastopol is Col. Totleben, a comparatively obscure man in the Russian service. But we must not take the defense of Sevastopol as a fair specimen of Russian engineering. The average between Silistria and Sevastopol is nearer the reality.

People in the Crimea, as well as in England and France, now begin to discover, though very gradually, that there is no chance of Sevastopol being taken by assault. In this perplexity the London *Times* has applied to "high professional authority," and has been informed that the proper thing to do is to act on the offensive, either by passing the Chernaya, and effecting a junction with Omer Pasha's Turks, before or after a battle against the Russian Army of Observation, or by a diversion against Kaffa, which would force the Russians to divide themselves.[a] As the allied army is now supposed to number from 110,000 to 120,000 men, such movements should be in their power. Now, nobody knows better than Canrobert and Raglan that an advance beyond the Chernaya and a union with Omer Pasha's army would be most desirable; but, unfortunately, as we have proved over and over again,[b] the 110,000 to 120,000 Allies on the hights before Sevastopol do not exist, and have never existed. On the 1st of March they did not number above 90,000 men fit for duty. As to an expedition to Kaffa, the Russians could wish for nothing better than to see the allied troops dispersed over three different points, from 60 to 150 miles distant from the center one, while at neither of the two points which they now hold have they sufficient strength to perform the task before them! Surely, the "high professional authority" must have been hoaxing *The Times* in seriously advising it to advocate a repetition of the Eupatoria expedition!

Written about March 30, 1855

First published in the *New-York Daily Tribune*, No. 4366, April 17, 1855 and in the *New-York Semi-Weekly Tribune*, No. 1032, April 17, 1855 as a leading article

Reproduced from the *New-York Daily Tribune*

[a] See "The last accounts from the Crimea...", *The Times*, No. 22012, March 27, 1855.—*Ed.*

[b] See, e.g., this volume, pp. 32-33.—*Ed.*

Frederick Engels

THE SITUATION IN THE CRIMEA[116]

London, March 30. The reports on the progress of the peace negotiations fluctuate wildly from one day to the next. Today peace is certain, tomorrow war. Palmerston's article in the *Post* bristles with swords and cannon—evidence that he would like to make peace as soon as possible.[a] Napoleon orders his press to write hymns of peace—the surest proof that he intends to continue the war. The course of events in the Crimea by no means indicates that the fall of Sevastopol is imminent. Omer Pasha is now in fact firmly trapped at Eupatoria, on the land-side. The superiority of their cavalry allows the Russians to station their pickets and mounted sentinels quite close to the town, to despatch patrols into the surrounding territory to cut off supplies and, in the event of a serious attack, to fall back on the infantry stationed further off. As we assumed earlier,[b] they are succeeding in keeping a superior Turkish force in check with a quarter or a third of their number. The attack made by the Turkish cavalry under Iskander Bey (the Pole Iliński, who earned himself such a glorious reputation at Kalafat[117]) was repulsed by a simultaneous charge by three Russian detachments which attacked from three different points. Like all cavalry which is badly trained and lacking in confidence the Turks, instead of charging headlong at the Russians with sabres drawn, halted at a respectful distance and began firing their carbines. This clear sign of indecision drove the Russians onto the offensive. Iskander Bey attempted an attack with one squadron but was left in the lurch by everybody except the *bashi-bazouks*[118] and had to force his retreat right through the

---

[a] "The discussion upon the Third Point...", *The Morning Post*, No. 25348, March 30, 1855.—*Ed.*

[b] A reference to the German version of Engels' article "The Results in the Crimea" (see the English version in this volume, pp. 81-85).—*Ed.*

ranks of the Russians. Omer Pasha awaits the arrival of cavalry reinforcements and has been in the meantime to the Anglo-French camp to inform the allies that for the moment he can do nothing, and that reinforcements of some 10,000 French troops would be very desirable. No doubt, but it is no less desirable for Canrobert himself, who has already discovered that he has at one and the same time too many and too few troops at his disposal. Too many to besiege Sevastopol in the old way and to defend the Chernaya; not enough to sally forth from the Chernaya, to drive the Russians into the interior and surround the northern fortress.[a] Detaching 10,000 men to Eupatoria would not enable the Turks to enter the battle successfully, but would weaken the French army for operations in open country. The *siege* is daily becoming a more critical affair for the besiegers.

We have seen that, on February 24 the Russians held the redoubt on the Sapun hill (in front of the Malakhov fortifications).[b] They have now extended and strengthened this redoubt, mounted cannon on it, and have made counter-approaches from it. Similarly a series of new redoubts have been constructed in front of the Kornilov bastion, 300 yards beyond the old Russian fortifications. The reader of *The Times* must find this inexplicable, for according to that newspaper the allies had long since thrown up their own trenches at less than that distance from the Russian lines. Now at last, e. g. in his letter of March 16, the *Times* correspondent[c] admits that even at the time of his latest reports the British trenches were still 600-800 yards away, and that the *batteries on the point of firing on the enemy are the same ones that opened fire on October 17 last year.*[d] This then is the great progress, made in the siege, these are the advances made with the building of trenches, which cost two-thirds of the English army their lives or their health. Under these circumstances there was sufficient space between the two lines of batteries to construct the new Russian fortifications. This can be regarded as the opening-up of a new parallel against the besiegers at a distance of 300-400 yards from their fortifications, as a counter-approach on the largest scale against the besieging army. Thus the besiegers are forced onto the defensive, whereas the first and most essential condition for a siege is that the besiegers should force the besieged onto the defensive.

---

[a] In the *Neue Oder-Zeitung*: the "town side".—*Ed.*

[b] A reference to the German version of Engels' article "A Battle at Sevastopol" (see the English version in this volume, pp. 113-17).—*Ed.*

[c] W. H. Russell.—*Ed.*

[d] *The Times,* No. 22014, March 29, 1855.—*Ed.*

Just as in the camp at Sevastopol people in England are now beginning to discover that there is no likelihood of taking Sevastopol by storm. In this awkward situation *The Times* has sought the aid of a "high military authority" and learned that it is necessary to take the offensive, either by crossing the Chernaya and effecting a link-up with the Turks under Omer Pasha, whether it be before or after a battle with the Russian observation army, or by means of a diversion towards Kaffa which would force the Russians to split up. As the allied army now numbers 110,000-120,000 men movements of this kind must be within its capabilities. Thus says *The Times*.[a]

Now no one knows better than Raglan and Canrobert that a link-up with Omer Pasha's army is highly desirable, but unfortunately the allies do [not] as yet have 110,000-120,000 men at their disposal on the heights above Sevastopol, but at the outside 80,000-90,000 men fit for service. As for an expedition to Kaffa the Russians could not wish for anything better: the allied troops dispersed in three different locations, 60-150 miles from the central point, whilst not being strong enough at either of the two positions they are holding to carry out the task before them! It would appear that *The Times* has taken its advice from "Russian" military experts.

Since at least some of the men of the 11th and 12th French divisions are on their way and the rest as well as the 13th and 14th divisions and the two Piedmontese divisions are about to follow, the allied army will by the end of May be brought up to a strength which will both enable it and force it to advance from its defensive position on the Chernaya. The troops will be concentrated at Constantinople and probably shipped together, so that they will have to spend as little time as possible on the ill-starred Chersonese. This measure will cause some delay but will bring great advantages. The reinforcements, which up to now were sent to the Crimea in small detachments—although when taken together they form a whole army—never strengthened the expeditionary forces sufficiently to enable them to launch offensive operations.

Written on March 30, 1855

First published in the *Neue Oder-Zeitung*, No. 155, April 2, 1855

Marked with the sign ×

Printed according to the newspaper

Published in English for the first time

[a] "The last accounts from the Crimea...", *The Times*, No. 22012, March 27, 1855.—*Ed.*

Karl Marx

A SCANDAL IN THE FRENCH LEGISLATURE.— DROUYN DE LHUYS' INFLUENCE.— THE STATE OF THE MILITIA

London, April 3. We are informed by a correspondent in Paris:

"In the Bonapartist *corps legislatif* there occurred a *scene*, which has failed to get into the English press. During the debate on the *Replacement* Law[119] *Granier de Cassagnac* jumped up—after *Montalembert*'s speech—and in his fury he let the cat out of the bag. Only when this law comes into force, he said, will the army become what it ought to be, dedicated to law and order and the Emperor, and we shall never again witness the shameful sight of soldiers turning their muskets round" (*soldats à baionnettes renversées*). "The conclusion of this speech, in which the janissary system was openly preached as an ideal for the army, provoked loud protests even in *this* assembly, and Granier was obliged to sit down. Another member of the legislature jumped to his feet and made a scathing attack on Granier. The scandal was so great that even Morny had to challenge Cassagnac" (it is well known that he was called *le roi des drôles*[a] by Guizot when he was still editing his little rag, the *Globe*) "to explain himself. Granier made a *formal apology* with the greatest meekness, and personally moved that the incident be passed over in silence in the *Moniteur*. The sitting was as stormy as in the finest days of Louis Philippe's Chamber of Deputies."

"The British public," writes *The Morning Chronicle* today,[b] "have come to the conclusion that M. Drouyn de Lhuys is gone to Vienna to act as a kind of prompter or fly-flapper to Lord John Russell whose proceedings hitherto have not given satisfaction either to his own compatriots or to our Allies. [...] The noble lord is famous for his fits and starts of patriotism and liberalism; for his extreme public spirit while in Opposition, or when in need of political capital, and his sudden collapses when the immediate necessity is over. Something of this kind seems to have happened to him on the present occasion; and the people are beginning to grumble. Since M. Drouyn de Lhuys has come to London a more decided tone is perceptible in high quarters. It has even transpired that his mission has so far been successful, that the peaceful aspirations of Lord John Russell have been officially frustrated, and that *our 'man of vigour'*" (Palmerston) "has

---

[a] King of the rascals.—*Ed.*
[b] April 3, 1855.—*Ed.*

reluctantly assented to an ultimatum which Russia [...] is likely to reject with disdain."

The English Army has vanished, and the English militia is in the process of vanishing. The militia, which was created by Act of Parliament in 1852 under Lord Derby, should by law not be called up for more than 28 days each year under normal circumstances. In the case of a war of invasion, however, or for any other important and urgent reason, it could be incorporated into the army for permanent service. But by an Act of Parliament of 1854 all men recruited after May 12, 1854 were obliged to serve for the duration of the war. The question has now been raised what the obligations were of those recruited under the Act of 1852. The Crown lawyers declared that they considered this category also to be liable for permanent service during the war. But a few weeks ago Lord Panmure in contradiction with this juridical decision, issued an order permitting all those recruited before the Act of 1854 to leave but granting them a cash-payment of £1 if they re-enlist for a further five years. As at present the cash-payment for recruits enlisting for two years in the regular army is £7 for the infantry and £10 for the cavalry, a payment of £1 for five years' service in the militia was the most infallible means of dissolving it. Lord Palmerston, who hesitated to call up the militia for almost a year, seems to want to be rid of it again as soon as possible. Accordingly we learn that in the last fortnight one militia regiment after the other has lost from $^2/_3$ to $^5/_8$ of its strength. Thus in the First Regiment of the Somerset Militia 414 men out of 500 have left, in the North Durham Militia 770 out of 800, in the Leicester Militia 340 out of 460, in the Suffolk Artillery 90 out of 130, etc.

Written on April 3, 1855

First published in the *Neue Oder-Zeitung*, No. 163, April 7, 1855

Marked with the sign ×

Printed according to the newspaper

Published in English for the first time

Karl Marx

PROSPECT IN FRANCE AND ENGLAND[120]

London, Tuesday, April 10, 1855

Allow me once more to resume my long-interrupted correspondence with the *Tribune.* Yesterday and to-day will most likely be the first two decisive days in the Vienna Conferences,[121] as they were to open on the 9th in the presence of Mr. Drouyn de Lhuys, and as, at the same time, the Russian Embassador[a] was expected to have received his instructions relative to the Third and Fourth Points. The journey of Drouyn de Lhuys was at first puffed up on every Stock Exchange as a certain symptom of peace; for such an eminent diplomatist, it was said, surely would not go to take personal part in these debates unless he were sure of success. As to the "eminence" of this diplomatist, it is of a very mythical cast, and exists principally in the paid newspaper articles by which he magnifies himself into a second Talleyrand, as though his long career under Louis Philippe had not long since established his "eminent" mediocrity. But the real reason of his journey is this: Lord John Russell has managed within a few weeks, through his notorious ignorance of the French language, to embroil the Allies in concessions which he never intended to make, and which it will take extraordinary efforts to retrieve. Lord John's French is of the real John Bull species, such as "Milord" speaks in *Fra Diavolo,*[b] and other theatrical pieces formerly popular in France; it begins with "Monsieur l'Aubergiste,"[c] and ends with "Très bien;" and if he understands but one-half of what is said to him, he is revenged in the consciousness that other people understand still less of what

[a] A. M. Gorchakov.— *Ed.*

[b] Lord Cokbourg, a character in a comic opera by the French composer D. F. E. Auber (libretto by A. E. Scribe).— *Ed.*

[c] "Mr. Innkeeper".— *Ed.*

he utters. It was for this very reason that his friend and rival, Lord Palmerston, sent him to Vienna, considering that a couple of blunders on that stage would be sufficient finally to demolish poor little John. And so it has turned out. Half the time he could not make out what was going on, and a quick and unexpected interpolation from Gorchakoff or Buol was sure to draw an embarrassed "Très bien" from the unfortunate diplomatic débutant. In this way Russia, and to some degree Austria, lay claim that several points are settled, at least so far as England is concerned, which poor Lord John never intended to concede. Palmerston, of course, would have no objection to this, as long as the blame falls exclusively upon his hapless colleague. But Louis Bonaparte cannot afford to be cheated into peace that way. To put a stop to this sort of diplomacy, the French Government at once resolved to bring matters to an issue. They fixed upon an ultimatum, with which Drouyn de Lhuys went to London, got the adhesion of the British Government, and then took it with him to Vienna. Thus, at present, he may be considered the joint representative of France and England, and there is no doubt that he will use his position to the best interest of his master. And as the only, the exclusive interest of Louis Bonaparte is *not* to conclude peace until he has reaped fresh glory and fresh advantages for France, and until the war has served to the full its purpose, as a "moyen de gouvernement,"[a] Drouyn's mission, far from being peaceful, will turn out, on the contrary, to have for its object to secure a continuance of the war under the most decent pretext available.

With the middle-classes both of France and England this war is decidedly unpopular. With the French bourgeoisie it was so from the beginning, because this class was ever since the 2d of December[b] in full opposition against the government of the "savior of society." In England, the middle-class was divided. The great bulk had transferred their national hatred from the French to the Russians; and although John Bull can do a little annexation business himself now and then in India, he has no idea of allowing other people to do the same in other neighborhoods in an uncomfortable proximity to himself or his possessions. Russia was the country which in this respect had long since attracted his anxious notice. The enormously increasing British trade to the Levant, and through Trebizond to Inner Asia, makes the free navigation of the Dardanelles a point of the highest importance to

[a] "Means of government".— *Ed.*

[b] December 2, 1851, the date of Louis Bonaparte's *coup d'état* in France.— *Ed.*

England. The growing value of the Danubian countries as granaries forbids England to allow their gradual absorption into Russia, and the closing of the navigation of the Danube by the same power. Russian grain forms already a too important item in British consumption, and an annexation of the corn-producing frontier-countries by Russia would make Great Britain entirely dependent upon her and the United States, while it would establish these two countries as the regulators of the corn-market of the world. Besides, there are always some vague and alarming rumors afloat about Russian progress in Central Asia, got up by interested Indian politicians or terrified visionaries, and credited by the general geographical ignorance of the British public. Thus, when Russia began her aggression upon Turkey, the national hatred broke forth in a blaze, and never, perhaps, was a war as popular as this. The peace-party was for a moment interdicted from speaking; even the mass of its own members went along with the popular current. Whoever knew the character of the English must have felt certain that this warlike enthusiasm could be but of short duration, at least so far as the middle-class was concerned; as soon as the effects of the war should become taxable upon their pockets, mercantile sense was sure to overcome national pride, and the loss of immediate individual profits was sure to outweigh the certainty of losing, gradually, great national advantages. The Peelites,[122] adverse to the war, not so much out of a real love of peace, as from a narrowness and timidity of mind which holds in horror all great crises and all decisive action, did their best to hasten the great moment when every British merchant and manufacturer could calculate to a farthing what the war would cost him, individually, per annum. Mr. Gladstone, scorning the vulgar idea of a loan, at once doubled the income-tax and stopped financial reform. The result came to light at once. The peace-party raised their heads again. John Bright dared popular feeling with his own well-known spirit and tenacity, until he succeeded in bringing the manufacturing districts round to him. In London the feeling is still more in favor of the war, but the progress of the peace-party is visible, even here; besides, it must be recollected that the peace-society[123] never, at any time, commanded any mentionable influence in the capital. Its agitation, however, is increasing in all parts of the country, and another year of doubled taxation, with a loan—for this is now considered to be unavoidable—will break down whatever is left of warlike spirit among the manufacturing and trading classes.

With the mass of the people in both countries, the case is

entirely different. The peasantry in France have, ever since 1789, been the great supporters of war and warlike glory. They are sure, this time, not to feel much of the pressure of the war; for the conscription, in a country where the land is infinitesimally subdivided among small proprietors, not only frees the agricultural districts from surplus labor, but also gives to some 20,000 young men, every year, the opportunity of earning a round sum of money, by engaging to serve as substitutes. A protracted war only would be severely felt. As to war-taxes, the Emperor cannot impose them upon the peasantry, without risking his crown and his life. His only means of maintaining Bonapartism among them, is to buy them up by freedom from war-taxation; and thus, for some years to come, they may be exempted from this sort of pressure. In England, the case is similar. Agricultural labor is generally over-supplied, and furnishes the mass of the soldiery, which only at a later period of the war receives a strong admixture of the rowdy-class from the towns. Trade being tolerably good, and a good many agricultural improvements being carried out, when the war began, the quota of agricultural recruits was, in this instance, supplied more sparingly than before, and the town-element is decidedly preponderant in the present militia. But even what has been withdrawn has kept wages up, and the sympathy of the villagers is always accompanying soldiers who came from among them, and who are now transformed into heroes. Taxation, in its direct shape, does not touch the small farmers and laborers, and until an increase of indirect imposts can reach them, sensibly, several years of war must have passed. Among these people, the war-enthusiasm is as strong as ever, and there is not a village where is not to be found some new beer-shop with the sign of "The Heroes of the Alma," or some such motto, and where are not, in almost every house, wonderful prints of Alma, Inkermann, the charge at Balaklava,[124] portraits of Lord Raglan and others, to adorn the walls. But if in France, the great preponderance of the small farmers (four-fifths of the population), and their peculiar relation to Louis Napoleon, give to their opinions a great deal of importance, in England the one-third of the population forming the countrypeople has scarcely any influence, except as a tail and chorus to the aristocratic landed proprietors.

The industrial working population has, in both countries, almost the same peculiar position with regard to this war. Both British and French proletarians are filled with an honorable national spirit, though they are more or less free from the antiquated national prejudices common, in either country, to the peasantry.

They have little immediate interest in the war, save that if the victories of their countrymen flatter their national pride, the conduct of the war, foolhardy and presumptuous as regards France, timid and stupid as regards England, offers them a fair opportunity of agitating against the existing governments and governing classes. But the main point, with them, is this: that this war, coinciding with a commercial crisis, only the first developments of which have, as yet, been seen, conducted by hands and heads unequal to the task, gaining at the same time European dimensions, will and must bring about events which will enable the proletarian class to resume that position which they lost, in France, by the battle of June, 1848,[125] and that not only as far as France is concerned, but for all Central Europe, England included.

In France, indeed, there can be no doubt that every fresh revolutionary storm must bring, sooner or later, the working-class to power; in England, things are fast approaching a similar state. There is an aristocracy willing to carry on the war, but unfit to do so, and completely put to the blush by last winter's mismanagement. There is a middle class, unwilling to carry on that war which cannot be put a stop to, sacrificing everything to peace, and thereby proclaiming their own incapacity to govern England. If events turn out the one, with its different fractions, and do not admit the other, there remain but two classes on which power can devolve: the petty Bourgeoisie, the small trading class, whose want of energy and decision has shown itself on every occasion when it was called upon to come from words to deeds—and the working-class, which has been constantly reproached with showing far too much energy and decision when proceeding to action as a class.

Which of these classes will be the one to carry England through the present struggle, and the complications about to arise from it?

Written on April 10, 1855

First published in the *New-York Daily Tribune*, No. 4375, April 27, 1855, reprinted in the *New-York Semi-Weekly Tribune*, No. 1036, May 1, 1855

Signed: *Karl Marx*

Reproduced from the *New-York Daily Tribune*

Frederick Engels

NAPOLEON'S APOLOGY [126]

Napoleon III, in his quality as chief editor of the *Moniteur*, has published a long leading article on the Crimean Expedition,[a] the important portions of which we have duly published. The purpose of this manifesto is evidently to console the French nation for the failure of the enterprise, to shift the responsibility of it from the Imperial shoulders, and at the same time to reply to the famous pamphlet lately issued by Prince Napoleon.[b] In that half familiar, half dignified style, characteristic of the man who writes at the same time for French peasants and for European Cabinets, a sort of history of the campaign is given, with the alleged reasons for each step. Some of these reasons merit a special examination.[c]

The Imperial adventurer informs us[d] that the allied troops were brought up to Gallipoli, because otherwise the Russians might have crossed the Danube at Rustchuk, and turning the lines of Varna and Shumla, passed the Balkan and marched upon Constantinople. This reason is the worst ever given for the landing

[a] See "Paris, le 10 avril. Expédition d'Orient", *Le Moniteur universel*, No. 101, April 11, 1855. In the *Neue Oder-Zeitung* this passage is preceded by the following words: "The public, even in France, seems to have uncovered the mysteries surrounding the siege of Sevastopol. Therefore Louis Bonaparte...".— *Ed.*

[b] *De la conduite de la guerre d'Orient....* (see this volume, pp. 76-77).— *Ed.*

[c] Instead of this sentence the *Neue Oder-Zeitung* has: "The document is in the highest degree unpolitical because it is exceedingly feeble and inadequate. Yet the 'pressure from without' must have been dangerously strong if Bonaparte has had to come forward in this way and defend himself." The phrase "pressure from without" is in English in the original.— *Ed.*

[d] In the *Neue Oder-Zeitung* this sentence begins as follows: "After a ponderous introduction he recounts part of the instructions received by St. Arnaud at the beginning of the campaign and explains...".— *Ed.*

at Gallipoli. In the first place Rustchuk is a *fortress*, and not an open town, as the illustrious editor of the *Moniteur* seems to fancy.[a] As to the danger of such a flank march of the Russians, it is well to recollect that an army of 60,000 Turks, firmly established between four strong fortresses, could not safely be passed without leaving a strong corps to observe them; that such a flank march would have exposed the Russians, in the ravines of the Balkan, to the fate of Dupont at Baylen, and of Vandamme at Culm[128]; that in the most favorable case they could not bring more than 25,000 men to Adrianople; and that whoever thinks such an army dangerous to the Turkish metropolis, may have his opinions corrected by reading Major Moltke's well-known observations on the campaign of 1829 lately republished in English at London.[b]

In case there should be no danger to Constantinople, the Allies were, as we learn from the *Moniteur*, to push some divisions to Varna, and to end any attempt at besieging Silistria. This done, two other operations would offer themselves—a landing near Odessa, or the seizure of the Crimea. Both were to be discussed by the allied Generals on the spot. Such were the instructions to St. Arnaud, which wound up with some sound military advice in the form of maxims and apothegms:—

> Always know what your enemy is doing; keep your troops together, divide them on no account; or if you must divide them, manage so that you can reunite them on a given point in twenty-four hours—and so forth.

Very valuable rules of conduct, no doubt, but so trite and common place, that the reader must at once conclude St. Arnaud to have been, in the eyes of his master, the greatest dunce and ignoramus in the world. After this, the instructions wind up with:

> "You have my entire confidence, Marshal. Go, for I am certain that, under your experienced leadership, the French eagles will earn new glory!"

As to the main point, the Crimean Expedition, Mr. Bonaparte confesses that it was certainly a favorite idea with him, and that at a later period he sent another batch of instructions to St. Arnaud

---

[a] The *Neue Oder-Zeitung* further has the following sentence, which does not occur in the *New-York Daily Tribune*: "This recalls the historical howler made by the *Moniteur* in its obituary for Emperor Nicholas [*Le Moniteur universel*, No. 86, March 27, 1855] in which, in particular, the Treaty of Adrianople was confounded with the Treaty of Kuchuk-Kainardji."[127]—*Ed.*

[b] H. K. B. Moltke, *Der russisch-türkische Feldzug in der europäischen Türkei 1828 und 1829.* The English translation appeared in London in 1854 under the title *The Russians in Bulgaria and Rumelia....* There is no reference to it in the *Neue Oder-Zeitung.*—*Ed.*

respecting it. But he denies having elaborated the plan in its details, and sent it to headquarters; according to him the Generals still had the choice of landing near Odessa. As a proof of this, a passage from his fresh instructions is given. In it he proposes a landing at Theodosia (Kaffa), on account of its offering a safe and capacious anchorage to the fleets, which must form the base of operations of the army. What a base of operations is he had explained to St. Arnaud in his first instructions, in terms which leave no doubt that the illustrious Marshal was supposed never to have read any standard work whatever upon his profession. From this point—Kaffa—the army was to march upon Sympheropol, drive the Russians into Sevastopol, before the walls of which a battle would probably be fought, and, finally, to besiege Sevastopol. "Unfortunately" this "plan was not followed up by the allied generals"—a circumstance very fortunate for the Emperor, as it allows of his shuffling off the responsibility of the whole affair, and leaving it on the shoulders of the generals.

The plan of landing 60,000 men at Kaffa and marching thence upon Sevastopol is indeed original. Taking as a general rule that the offensive strength of an army in an enemy's country decreases in the same ratio as its distance from its base of operations increases, how many men would the Allies have brought to Sevastopol after a march of more than 120 miles? How many men were to be left at Kaffa? How many to hold and fortify intermediate points? How many to protect convoys, and to scour the country? Not 20,000 men could have been collected under the walls of a fortress requiring three times that number barely to invest it. If Louis Napoleon ever goes to the war himself, and conducts it upon this principle, he may as well order quarters at Mivart's Hotel,[129] London, at once, for he will never see Paris again.[a]

As to the safety of the anchorage at Kaffa, every mariner in the Black Sea knows, and every chart shows that it is an open roadstead, with shelter against northerly and westerly winds alone, while the most dangerous storms in the Black Sea are from the south and south-west. Of this the storm of the 14th of November is an instance. Had the fleets then been at Kaffa they would have been driven upon a lee-shore.[b] In this way our hero clears himself

[a] In the *Neue Oder-Zeitung* the end of this sentence reads as follows: "and conducts it upon this principle, then one and the same family will certainly represent the most astounding contrast in the history of wars."—*Ed.*

[b] The *Neue Oder-Zeitung* further has a sentence which does not occur in the *New-York Daily Tribune*: "Now comes the most ticklish part of the article."—*Ed.*

from the responsibility thrown upon him by his cousin[a]; but it would never do to sacrifice Raglan and Canrobert. Accordingly, to show the cleverness of the said Generals, a very decent sketch is given of siege-operations according to Vauban—a sketch which, from the total ignorance of the subject it supposes in the reader, might have been written for the benefit of Marshal St. Arnaud.[b] This sketch, however, but serves to show how Sevastopol was *not* to be taken, for it winds up with the assertion that all these rules were inapplicable to Sevastopol. For instance,

> "in a common siege where one front is attacked, the length of the last parallel would be about 300 yards, and the whole length of trenches would not exceed 8,000 yards; here the extent of parallel is 3,000 yards, and the whole linear length of all the trenches is 41,000 yards."

This is all true enough, but the question here is why has this enormous extent of attack been adopted, when every circumstance called for the greatest possible concentration of fire upon one or two determined points? The answer is:

> "Sevastopol is not like any other fortress. It has but a shallow ditch, no masonry scarps, and these defenses are replaced by abattis and palisades; thus our fire could make but little impression on the earth breastwork."

If this was not written for St. Arnaud, it is surely written for the French peasantry alone. Every sub-lieutenant in the French army must laugh at such nonsense. Palisades, unless at the bottom of a ditch, or at least out of the sight of the enemy, are very soon knocked over by shot and shell. Abattis may be set on fire, and must be at the foot of the glacis, about 60 or 80 yards from the breastwork, else they would obstruct the fire of the guns. Moreover, these abattis must be large trees laid on the ground, the pointed branches toward the enemy, and the whole firmly connected together; but where such trees could have come from, in a woodless country like the Crimea, the *Moniteur* does not say. The absence of masonry scarps has nothing to do with the protracted siege, for according to the description in the *Moniteur* itself, they only come into play when the breaching batteries have been established on the top of the glacis—a position from which the Allies are yet far distant.[c] That palisades are an improvement upon masonry scarps, is certainly new; for these wooden ramparts

[a] Prince Napoleon (Jérôme Bonaparte, Jr.), the presumed author of the pamphlet *De la conduite de la guerre d'Orient....*—*Ed.*

[b] In the *Neue Oder-Zeitung* the end of this sentence beginning with the words "according to Vauban" does not occur.—*Ed.*

[c] This sentence does not occur in the *Neue Oder-Zeitung*.—*Ed.*

can be very easily destroyed by enfilading fire, even at the bottom of the ditch; and thus they allow of an assault as soon as the defending guns are silenced.

In conclusion, we are told by this new military authority, that all the facts show that the allied generals have done what they could—have done more than, under the circumstances, could have been expected from them—and have, indeed, covered themselves with glory.[a] If they could not properly invest Sevastopol—if they could not drive away the Russian army of observation—if they are not yet in the place—why, it is because they are not strong enough. This is also true: but who is responsible for this greatest of all faults? Who but Louis Bonaparte! Such is the final conclusion which the whole French public must inevitably draw from this wordy, round-about, shuffling, and ridiculous explanation of their Emperor.[b]

Written about April 14, 1855

First published in the *New-York Daily Tribune*, No. 4377, April 30, 1855, reprinted in the *New-York Semi-Weekly Tribune*, No. 1036, May 1, 1855 and the *New-York Weekly Tribune*, No. 712, May 5, 1855 as a leading article; the German version was first published in the *Neue Oder-Zeitung*, No. 177, April 27, 1855, marked with the sign ×

Reproduced from the *New-York Daily Tribune*

---

[a] The *Neue Oder-Zeitung* further has: "Dubious glory if it needs to be *proved*, and is proved in *this* manner!"—*Ed.*

[b] Instead of this last sentence the article in the *Neue Oder-Zeitung* has the following concluding passage: "That is the inevitable conclusion following from the leading article in the *Moniteur*. What impression it produced in Paris is shown by the following passage from the letter of the otherwise servile Paris correspondent of *The Times*: 'There are persons [...] who [...] consider it as [...] preliminary to the abandonment of the Crimea altogether [...] and in some Legitimist circles [...] these words have been made use of:—"We were led to expect a *war à la Napoleon*; but it seems we are now to have a *peace à la Louis Philippe*." On the other hand [...] an impression of a similar kind'" prevails "'in the minds of the working classes of the Faubourg St. Antoine.'" They "'interpret it as an avowal of weakness [...]'." (*The Times*, No. 22028, April 14, 1855.)—*Ed.*

Frederick Engels

THE SIEGE OF SEVASTOPOL[130]

The siege of Sevastopol continues to drag on its weary course, barren of events and decisions, scarcely enlivened, now and then, by some resultless encounter or desultory attack, every one of which looks exactly like all its predecessors and successors. Always excepting the superiority evinced by the defense in the engineering department, it is certain that very few campaigns have been carried on for an equal length of time with such a degree of mediocrity in the commanding officers as has now been developed. The whole affair is becoming a public nuisance to the world in general, and to those, in particular, who have to expose, in the Press, the different phases assumed by this eminently stationary operation.[a]

The French and English reports of the affair of March 23 we published some days ago; a Russian detailed report we have not yet received. As usual, the dispatches of the Allied Generals are conceived in so obscure a style that we cannot learn anything distinct from them. With the help of private letters published in Europe and the reports of newspaper-correspondents, of which we now have several at hand, we are enabled to make out the following summary view of the facts.

The "right attack" of the Allies, directed against the south-eastern fronts of Sevastopol, from the head of the inner harbor to that of the Careening Bay, has been carried forward to the distance of some 600 yards from the first Russian line, by three lines of approaches or zig-zags, connected with each other at their

[a] This sentence does not occur in the *Neue Oder-Zeitung*.—*Ed.*

ends by what is called the second parallel. Beyond this, the three zig-zags are still being pushed forward, though irregularly and slowly, and it is intended to unite them by a third parallel, and to form, on the central approach, a *place d'armes*, or covered rallying-ground, spacious enough to hold a reserve force. Of these three approaches, the middle one is in the hands of the English, and the right and left are occupied by the French. These two flank approaches have been pushed on rather quicker than the central one, so that the French trenches here are, perhaps, fifty yards nearer to the place than the position occupied by the English.

Before daybreak of the 23d of March, a considerable Russian force, amounting to about twelve battalions, advanced from the town upon the siege-works. Well aware that the trenches had been constructed with an utter neglect of the habitual and prescribed precautions, that their flanks were neither thrown back sufficiently nor defended by redoubts, that consequently a bold dash upon the extreme flanks of the parallel must lead the assailants into the trenches, the Russians began their attack by a sudden and rapid movement, by which the eastern and western extremities of the parallel were turned. A front attack occupied the trench-guard and their reserves, while the outflanking columns, gallantly but vainly resisted by the French, descended into the works and swept the trench until they came upon the central position defended by the British. The British lines being secure from serious annoyance in front, were not molested until the fusillade going on to the right and left had brought up part of their reserves; and even then, the front attack was of no great vehemence, as the strength of the sortie was concentrated in the turning columns. But these too, from the great extent of trench they had overrun, had already spent their first ardor, and when they came upon the British, their officers had to bear constantly in mind the chance of ultimate retreat. Accordingly, the struggle very soon came to a point where each party held its ground, and that is the moment when a sallying detachment should look out for a safe retreat. This the Russians did. Without attempting seriously to dislodge the British, they maintained the fight until most of their troops had got a fair start homeward, and then the rearguard, heavily pressed, by this time, by the French and British reserves, made the best of its way toward Sevastopol.

The Russians must have expected to find many guns and a deal of ammunition and other material in the second parallel, for to destroy such could have been the only purpose of this sortie. But there was very little of the sort, and thus the only advantage they gained by the attack was the certainty that at this distance from their own lines they might still, in the first hour or two of a sortie, and before the enemies' reserves could come up, show the strongest front. This is worth something, but hardly worth the losses of such an attempt. The material damage done to the siege-works was repaired in a day or two, and the moral effect gained by this sortie was null. For, as every sortie must necessarily end in a retreat, the besiegers will always believe that they have been the victors; and unless the losses of the besieged are disproportionately small compared with those of the besiegers, the moral effect is generally more encouraging to the latter than otherwise. In this instance, when Raglan and Canrobert were more than ever in want of an apparent success, this sally, with its comparatively worthless fruits, and its final precipitate retreat, was a real godsend for them. The French troops give themselves enormous credit for having followed up the enemy to the very lines of Sevastopol—which in such a case is not so difficult, as the guns of the place cannot play for fear of hitting their own troops; while the British, passing over in silence their exceptional retired position, which gave them the character of a reserve more than that of a body of troops in the front line of battle, are again, with less cause than ever, blustering about their own invincibility and that unflinching courage which forbids the British soldier ever to give way a single inch. The few British officers in the hands of the Russians, taken in the midst of these unflinching soldiers and carried off safely into Sevastopol,[a] must know what all these big words mean.

In the meantime, the great strategists of the British press have gone on declaring, with considerable emphasis, that before the storming of Sevastopol could be thought of, the new outworks erected by the Russians must needs be taken; and that they hoped they would be taken shortly. This assertion is certainly as true as it is common-place; but the question is, How are they to be taken, if the Allies could not prevent their being completed under their very batteries? The attack upon the Selenghinsk redoubt[b] showed clearly enough that, with great sacrifice of life, such a work can be taken for a moment; but of what use that is to be, when it cannot even be held for the time necessary to destroy it, it is not easy to

---

[a] The words "Colonel Kelley and others" are added in commas in the *Neue Oder-Zeitung*.—*Ed.*

[b] The *Neue Oder-Zeitung* further has: "(on Mount Sapun)".—*Ed.*

see. The fact is, that these new Russian works,[a] being flanked and commanded in the rear by their main line, cannot be taken unless the same means are put into operation against them as against the main line. Approaches will have to be made up to a convenient distance, covered parallels with *places d'armes* will have to be completed, and batteries to engage the Russian main line will have to be erected and armed, before an assault of, and lodgment in, these outworks can be seriously thought of. The London *Times,* which was foremost in its outcry for the capture of these works, has not attempted to specify the new method by which this very desirable but very difficult object was to be accomplished "within the very few hours" within which it expected, the other day, to hear of the feat having been performed. But unfortunately, hardly had that journal uttered this fond hope,[b] when a letter arrived from its Crimean correspondent stating that the new Russian outworks not only appeared quite untakable, but that they were evidently the first landmarks only of an intended further advance of Russian counter-approaches.[c] The rifle-pits in front of the Mamelon redoubt[d] have been connected with each other by a regular trench, thus forming a new line of defense. Between the Mamelon redoubt and Mount Sapun, or the Selenghinsk redoubt, a rather curiously-shaped trench has been dug out, forming three sides of a square and enfilading part of the French approaches, by which, in part, it is said again to be enfiladed. The situation and line of this new work are, however, so incompletely described that neither its exact position nor its intended use can be as yet clearly made out.[e] Thus much is certain, that a complete system of advanced works is contemplated by the Russians, covering Malakoff on both sides and in front, and aiming, perhaps, even at an ultimate attempt at a lodgment in the allied trenches, which, if obtained, would of course be tantamount to a breaking through of the siege lines on that side. If during six months the Allies have barely held their ground, and rather strengthened than advanced their batteries, the Russians have in one single month advanced

---

[a] The *Neue Oder-Zeitung* further has: "which form an integral part of the Russian defences".—*Ed.*

[b] *The Times,* No. 22028, April 14, 1855.—*Ed.*

[c] This refers to a report by W. H. Russell published anonymously in *The Times,* No. 22028 (second edition), April 14, 1855.—*Ed.*

[d] The *Neue Oder-Zeitung* further has: "(called Kamchatka by the Russians)".—*Ed.*

[e] This sentence and the end of the preceding one beginning with the words "by which, in part" do not occur in the *Neue Oder-Zeitung.*—*Ed.*

considerably upon them and are still advancing. Surely, if many a defense has been quite as glorious as that of Sevastopol, not a single siege can be shown in the annals of war, since that of Troy, carried on with such a degree of incoherence and stupidity.

Written about April 15, 1855

First published in the *New-York Daily Tribune*, No. 4377, April 30, 1855, reprinted in the *New-York Semi-Weekly Tribune*, No. 1036, May 1, 1855 as a leading article; the German version was first published in the *Neue Oder-Zeitung*, No. 179, April 18, 1855, marked with the sign ×

Reproduced from the *New-York Daily Tribune*

Frederick Engels

GERMANY AND PAN-SLAVISM[131]

I

[*Neue Oder-Zeitung*, No. 185, April 21, 1855]

We are assured by the best of sources that the *present* Tsar of Russia has sent certain courts a dispatch saying, among other things:

"The moment Austria irrevocably allies itself with the West, or commits any openly hostile act against Russia, *Alexander II will place himself at the head of the Pan-Slav movement* and transform his present title, *Tsar of all the Russians*, into that of *Tsar of all the Slavs.*" (?)

This declaration by Alexander, if authentic, is the first straight word since the outbreak of war. It is the first step towards giving the war the European character which until now has been lurking behind all manner of pretexts and allegations, protocols and treaties, sections from Vattel and citations from Pufendorf.[a] The independence, even the existence of Turkey has thereby been pushed into the background. The question is no longer who is to govern in Constantinople, but who is to rule the whole of Europe. The Slav race, long divided by internal disputes, pushed back towards the East by the Germans, subjugated, partly, by Germans, Turks and Hungarians, quietly reuniting its branches after 1815, by the gradual growth of Pan-Slavism, now for the first time asserts its unity and thus declares war to the death on the Roman-Celtic and German races, which have hitherto dominated Europe. Pan-Slavism is not merely a movement for national independence, it is a movement that strives to undo what the history of a thousand years has created, which cannot attain its ends without sweeping Turkey, Hungary and half Germany off

[a] E. Vattel, *Le Droit des gens...* and S. Pufendorf, *De jure naturae et gentium.—Ed.*

the map of Europe, a movement which—should it achieve this result—cannot ensure its future existence except by subjugating Europe. Pan-Slavism has now developed from a creed into a political programme, with 800,000 bayonets at its service. It leaves Europe with only one alternative: subjugation by the Slavs, or the permanent destruction of the centre of their offensive force—Russia.

The next question we have to answer is: how is Austria affected by Pan-Slavism which has been uniformed by Russia? Of the 70 million Slavs who live east of the Bohemian forest and the Carinthian Alps, approximately 15 million are subject to the Austrian sceptre, including representatives of almost every variety of the Slavonic language. The Bohemian or Czech branch (6 million) falls entirely under Austrian sovereignty, the Polish is represented by about 3 million Galicians; the Russian by 3 million Malorussians (Red Russians, Ruthenians) [132] in Galicia and North-East Hungary—the only Russian branch outside the borders of the Russian Empire; the South Slav branch by approximately 3 million Slovenians (Carinthians and Croats) [133] and Serbs, including scattered Bulgars. The Austrian Slavs thus fall into two categories: one part consists of the remnants of nationalities whose own history belongs to the past and whose present historical development is bound up with that of nations of different race and language. To crown their sorry national plight these sad remains of former grandeur do not even possess a national organisation within Austria, but rather they are divided between different provinces. The Slovenians, although scarcely 1,500,000 in number, are scattered through the various provinces of Carniola, Carinthia, Styria, Croatia and Southwest Hungary. The Bohemians, although the most numerous branch of the Austrian Slavs, are partly settled in Bohemia, partly in Moravia and partly (the Slovak line) in Northwest Hungary. Therefore these nationalities, though living exclusively on Austrian territory, are in no way recognised as constituting distinct nations. They are regarded as appendages of either the German or the Hungarian nation, and in fact they are no more than that. The second group of the Austrian Slavs consists of fragments of different tribes which in the course of history have been separated from the main body of their nation, with their focal points therefore lying outside Austria. Thus the Austrian Poles have their natural centre of gravity in Russian Poland, the Ruthenians in the other Malorussian provinces united with Russia, and the Serbs in Turkish Serbia. It goes without saying that these fragments detached from their respective nationalities gravitate towards their natural centres, and this tendency becomes more conspicuous as civilisation and hence the need for national-historical activity becomes increasingly widespread amongst them. In both cases the Austrian Slavs are merely *disjecta membra*,[a] striving for re-unification, either amongst themselves or with the main body of their particular nationalities. This is the reason why *Pan-Slavism is not a Russian invention but an Austrian one.* In order to achieve the restoration of each particular Slav nationality the various Slavonic tribes in Austria are beginning to work for a link-up of all the Slavonic tribes in Europe. Russia, strong in itself, Poland, conscious of the indomitable tenacity of its national life and furthermore openly hostile to Slavonic Russia—clearly neither of these two nations were apt to invent Pan-Slavism. The Serbs and Bulgars of Turkey, on the other hand, were too barbaric to grasp such an idea; the Bulgars quietly submitted to the Turks, while the Serbs had enough on their hands with the struggle for their own independence.

II

[*Neue Oder-Zeitung,* No. 189, April 24, 1855]

The first form of Pan-Slavism was purely literary. *Dobrovský,* a Bohemian, the founder of the scientific philology of the Slavonic dialects, and *Kollár,* a Slovak poet from the Hungarian Carpathians, were its inventors. Dobrovský was motivated by the enthusiasm of the scientific discoverer, in Kollár political ideas soon predominated. But Pan-Slavism was still finding its satisfaction in elegies; the splendour of the past, the ignominy, the misfortune and the foreign oppression of the present were the main themes of its poetry. "Is there then, O God, no man on earth who will give the Slavs justice?" The dreams of a Pan-Slav empire, dictating laws to Europe, were as yet hardly even alluded to. But the period of lamenting soon passed, and with it the call for mere "justice for the Slavs". Historical research, embracing the political, literary and linguistic development of the Slav race, made huge progress in Austria. *Šafařík, Kopitar* and *Miklosich* as linguists, *Palacký* as an historian placed themselves at the head, followed by a swarm of others with less scientific talent, or none whatsoever, such as *Hanka, Gaj,* etc. The glorious epochs of Bohemian and Serbian history were depicted in glowing colours,

[a] Separated members. Paraphrase of Horace's expression, *disjecti membra poetae*—"the limbs of the dismembered poet" (*Satirae,* liber I, IV, 62).—*Ed.*

in contrast to the downtrodden and broken-spirited present of these nationalities; and just as politics and theology were subjected to criticism under the cloak of "philosophy" in the rest of Germany, so in Austria, before the very eyes of Metternich, philology was employed by the Pan-Slavists to preach the doctrine of Slav unity and to create a political party whose unmistakable goal was to transform the conditions of all the nationalities in Austria and to turn it into a great Slavonic empire.

The linguistic confusion prevailing east of Bohemia and Carinthia to the Black Sea is truly astonishing. The process of de-nationalisation among the Slavs bordering on Germany, the slow but continuous advance of the Germans, the invasion of the Hungarians, which separated the North and South Slavs with a compact mass of 7 million people of Finnish race, the interposition of Turks, Tartars and Wallachians in the midst of the Slavonic tribes, have produced a linguistic Babel. The language varies from village to village, almost from farm to farm. Bohemia itself counts among its 5 million inhabitants 2 million Germans alongside 3 million Slavs, and is furthermore surrounded on three sides by Germans. This is also the case with the Austrian Slavonic tribes. The restitution of all originally Slavonic territory to the Slavs, the transformation of Austria except for the Tyrol and Lombardy into a Slavonic empire, which was the goal of the Pan-Slavists, amounted to declaring the historical development of the last thousand years null and void, cutting off a third of Germany and all Hungary and turning Vienna and Budapest into Slav cities—a procedure with which the Germans and Hungarians in possession of these districts could hardly be expected to sympathise. In addition, the differences between the Slavonic dialects are so great that with few exceptions they are mutually incomprehensible. This was amusingly demonstrated at the Slav Congress at Prague in 1848,[134] where after various fruitless attempts to find a language intelligible to all the delegates, they finally had to speak the tongue most hated by them all—*German.*

So we see that Austrian Pan-Slavism lacked the most vital elements of success: mass and unity. *Mass,* because the Pan-Slavist party, limited to a section of the educated classes, exerted no influence on the people and therefore did not have the power to offer resistance simultaneously to the Austrian government and to the German and Hungarian nationalities which it was challenging. *Unity,* because its principle of unity was purely an ideal which collapsed on its first attempt at realisation on account of the fact of linguistic diversity. As long as Pan-Slavism remained a purely

Austrian movement it constituted no great danger, but the centre of mass and unity which it needed was very soon found for it.

The national movement of the Turkish Serbs at the beginning of the century[135] soon drew the attention of the *Russian government* to the fact that in Turkey some 7 million Slavs were living whose language resembled Russian more than any other Slavonic dialect, whose religion and *holy* language—Old or Church Slavonic—was completely identical to that of the Russians. It was among these Serbs and Bulgars that Russia first began a Pan-Slavist agitation, helped by its position as head and protector of the Greek Church. When the Pan-Slavist movement had gained some ground in Austria, Russia soon extended the ramifications of its agencies into the area of its ally. Where it encountered Roman Catholic Slavs, the religious aspect of the issue was dropped and Russia simply depicted as the centre of gravity of the Slav race, as the kernel around which the regenerated Slavonic tribes were to crystallise, as the strong and united people, destined to make a reality of the great Slavonic empire from the Elbe to China, from the Adriatic Sea to the Arctic Ocean. Here, then, they had found the unity and mass that had been lacking! Pan-Slavism immediately fell into the trap. It thus pronounced its own sentence. In order to re-assert imaginary nationalities the Pan-Slavists declared their readiness to sacrifice 800 years of actual participation in civilisation to Russian-Mongolian barbarism. Was not this the natural result of a movement that began with a determined reaction against the course of European civilisation and sought to turn back world history?

Metternich, in the best years of his power, recognised the danger and saw through the Russian intrigues. He suppressed the movement with all the means at his disposal. All his means, however, could be summarised in *one* word: *repression.* The only appropriate means, free development of the German and Hungarian spirit, more than sufficient to scare off the Slavonic spectre, had no place in the system of his petty politics. Consequently, after Metternich's fall in 1848, the Slav movement broke out stronger than ever and embracing wider strata of the population than ever before. But at this point its thoroughly reactionary character straightway emerged into the open. While the German and Hungarian movements in Austria were decidedly progressive, it was the Slavs who saved the old system from destruction, and enabled Radetzky to march on the Mincio and Windischgrätz to conquer Vienna. In order to complete the dependence of Austria on the Slav race, the great *Slav reserve,* the Russian Army, had to descend on Hungary in 1849 and there dictate peace to her.

But if the adhesion of the Pan-Slav movement to Russia was its self-condemnation, Austria likewise acknowledged its lack of viability by accepting, indeed by asking for this Slav aid against the only three nations among its possessions which have and demonstrate historical vitality: Germans, Italians and Hungarians. After 1848 this debt to Pan-Slavism constantly weighed on Austria, and her awareness of it was the mainspring of Austrian policies.

The first thing Austria did was to act against the Slavs on its own ground, and that was only possible with a policy that was at least partly progressive. The privileges of all the provinces were abolished, a centralised administration supplanted a federal one; and instead of the different nationalities an *artificial* one, the *Austrian,* was to be the only one recognised. Although these innovations were partly aimed at the German, Italian and Hungarian elements too, their greatest weight fell on the less compact Slavonic tribes, giving the German element a position of considerable ascendancy. If the dependence on the Slavs inside Austria had thus been eliminated, there remained the dependence on Russia, and the necessity of breaking this direct and humiliating dependence, at least temporarily and to some extent. This was the real reason for Austria's anti-Russian policy in the Eastern question, a policy which although vacillating was at least publicly proclaimed. On the other hand Pan-Slavism has not disappeared; it is deeply offended, resentful, silent and, since the Hungarian intervention, regards the Tsar of Russia as its predestined Messiah. It is not our purpose here to inquire whether Austria—should Russia emerge openly as the head of Pan-Slavism—can reply with concessions to Hungary and Poland, without jeopardising its existence. This much is certain: it is no longer Russia alone, it is the Pan-Slavist conspiracy that threatens to found its empire on the ruins of Europe. The union of all Slavs, because of the undeniable strength which it possesses and may yet acquire, will soon force the side confronting it to appear in an entirely new form. In this context we have not spoken of the Poles—most of whom are to their credit definitely hostile to Pan-Slavism—nor of the allegedly democratic and socialist form of Pan-Slavism, which ultimately differs from the common, honest Russian Pan-Slavism solely in its phraseology and its hypocrisy. Neither have we discussed the German speculation, which from lofty ignorance has sunk to being an organ of Russian conspiracy.[a] We shall deal in detail with these and other questions relating to Pan-Slavism later.

Written about April 17, 1855

First published in the *Neue Oder-Zeitung*, Nos. 185 and 189, April 21 and 24, 1855

Marked with the sign ×

Printed according to the newspaper

Published in English for the first time

[a] An allusion to Bruno Bauer, who propounded Pan-Slavist ideas in his pamphlets *Russland und das Germanenthum* (1853), *Deutschland und das Russenthum* (1854), *Die jetzige Stellung Russlands* (1854), *Russland und England* (1854) and others.— *Ed.*

Frederick Engels

THE EUROPEAN STRUGGLE[136]

The all-absorbing facts in the news brought by the *Atlantic*, are the breaking off of the Vienna Conferences,[137] and the partial if not total separation of Austria from the Allies. For both of these events we were not unprepared. The rejection by Russia of any plan of settlement which should not substantially admit all she claimed before the war, was, in the present state of that war, a matter of course. The return of Austria to her old expectant, wavery policy was also the result of certain circumstances of great importance, which we proceed to explain.

The French Government discovered some time since, and the fact could not be denied by the British Cabinet, that Lord John Russell had committed a great blunder at Vienna[a] in allowing those of the points before the Conference in which Austria was directly interested to be first disposed of. These points were the freedom of the Danube and the question of the Principalities. From this moment Austria appeared satisfied. Expecting, as she does, to share sooner or later in the partition of Turkey—Servia, Bosnia, and Albania are provinces which she cannot allow to fall into any other hands than her own. It is her interest to keep the question respecting the Christians in Turkey an open one. And as she can never expect to cope with Russia's naval power in the Black Sea, she has but little interest in humiliating her in that quarter. From this point of view, then, Austria has every reason to be satisfied with what she has obtained, and to turn the weight of her seemingly impartial arbitration against England and France. But this diplomatic success has very little to do with her present

[a] On Russell's role at the Conference of Vienna see this volume, pp. 141-45.— *Ed.*

wavering. The cause of this is of a far more overpowering nature.

Some six months ago we alluded to the private and confidential dispatch by which Nicholas informed both Austria and Prussia, that in case they allied themselves with the West against him he would reply to such a treaty of alliance by a proclamation of Hungarian independence and Polish restoration.[a] At that time, and whenever we have considered the chances of a war in Poland and Volhynia, we have always taken into consideration the great military advantage which such a proclamation might give to Russia, if put forth after the conquest of Galicia and from the hights of the Carpathians, with Hungary open to her victorious armies. On that account, especially, we have always pointed out the fact that Austria could not undertake a war against Russia unless she was in a state at once to take the offensive and to parry, by successful battles and an advance upon Russia, the effects of such a proclamation.[b] So long, therefore, as the Austrian army in Galicia and the Principalities was strong enough to march upon Warsaw or Kiev there was little immediate danger from such a step.

This dispatch of Nicholas has, however, as we now learn, lately been followed up by another from his successor, which contains quite different and far more serious menaces. The moment Austria shall irrevocably ally herself to the West, it says, or commit any overt act of hostility against Russia, Alexander II *will place himself at the head of the Panslavist movement*, and change his title of Emperor of all the Russians into that of *Emperor of all the Slavonians.*

At last! Let Alexander take such a step, and the struggle concerning the Christians in Turkey, the independence of the Porte, Sevastopol, the Principalities, and other such local trifles, may now be considered at an end. This declaration of Alexander's is the first plain-spoken word since the war began; it is the first step toward placing the war upon the continental theater, and giving it, frankly and openly, that European character which has hitherto been lurking behind all sorts of pretexts and pretenses, protocols and treaties, Vattel phrases and Pufendorf quotations.[c] Turkey—her independence and existence—is thrown into the back-ground. Who is to rule in Constantinople? would then no

[a] The reference is presumably to the article "Progress of the War" by Marx and Engels (see present edition, Vol. 13, pp. 546-52).—*Ed.*

[b] See this volume, pp. 37-39.—*Ed.*

[c] E. Vattel, *Le Droit des gens*... and S. Pufendorf, *De jure naturae et gentium*.—*Ed.*

longer be the question—but who is to command all Europe? The Slavonic race, long divided by internal contests; repelled toward the East by Germans; subjugated, in part, by Turks, Germans, Hungarians; quickly reuniting its branches, after 1815, by the gradual rise of Panslavism, would then for the first time assert its unity, and, in doing so, declare war to the knife against the Romano-Celtic and Germanic races which have hitherto ruled the Continent. Panslavism is not a movement which merely strives after national independence; it is a movement which, thus acting upon Europe, would tend to undo what a thousand years of history have created; which could not realize itself without sweeping from the map Hungary, Turkey and a large part of Germany. Moreover, it must subjugate Europe in order to secure the stability of these results, if they are ever obtained. Panslavism is now, from a creed, turned into a political programme, or rather a vast political menace, with 800,000 bayonets to support it.

Nor are these 800,000 soldiers all the forces it could command. A word from the Russian Emperor at the head of an army, marching upon the Carpathians, and nine or ten millions of Slavonians in Austria would be agitated as in 1848; a victory over the Austrians, and they would be in full insurrection; while Hungary and Italy would be hardly less plowed by revolutionary agitation. Here is a danger which might well make Francis Joseph pause; for unless he could at once defeat the great Slavonian army on his frontiers and carry the war into the enemy's country, he might as well give up the contest before entering the lists.

Written about April 17, 1855

First published in the *New-York Daily Tribune*, No. 4382, May 5, 1855, reprinted in the *New-York Semi-Weekly Tribune*, No. 1038, May 8, 1855 and in the *New-York Weekly Tribune*, No. 713, May 12, 1855 as a leading article

Reproduced from the *New-York Daily Tribune*

Karl Marx

ON THE HISTORY OF POLITICAL AGITATION

London, May 7. In times of major political agitation in England the City of London has never been able to put itself in the vanguard. Up to now the fact that it joined a campaign merely indicated that the purpose of the agitation had been achieved and become a *fait accompli.* So it was with the *Reform Movement,* in which Birmingham took the initiative. So it was with the *Anti-Corn Law Movement,* which was led from Manchester. The Bank Restriction Act of 1797 [138] was an exception. The meetings of the bankers and merchants of the City of London made it easier for Pitt at that time to *prohibit* the Bank of England from continuing cash-payments—*after* the directors of the Bank had informed him a few weeks earlier that the Bank was tottering on the brink of bankruptcy and could only be saved by a *coup d'état,* by a fixed rate of exchange for bank-notes. Circumstances at the time required just as much resignation on the part of the Bank of England to letting itself be *prohibited* from making cash-payments, as on the part of the city merchants, whose credit stood or fell with the Bank, to supporting Pitt's prohibition and recommending it to the country man.* The salvation of the Bank of England was the

* It is incredible that even in the most recent histories of political economy the conduct of the City at that time is cited as evidence of English patriotism. It is even more incredible that in his work on Russia (3rd vol., 1852) Herr von Haxthausen is gullible enough to maintain that by suspending the cash-payments of the Bank, Pitt was preventing the money from going abroad.[a] What may a man who is so credulous have swallowed in Russia? And what indeed are we to think of the Berlin criticism who believe implicitly in Herr von Haxthausen, and by way of proof *plagiarize* him?

---

[a] A. Haxthausen, *Studien über die innern Zustände, das Volksleben und insbesondere die ländlichen Einrichtungen Russlands,* Dritter Theil.—*Ed.*

salvation of the City. Hence their "patriotic" meetings and their "agitational" initiative. The initiative taken by the City at present with the meetings held last Saturday[a] in the London Tavern and the Guildhall, and the founding of an *"Association for Administrative Reform"*,[139] has the merit of novelty, the merit, rare in England, of having no precedent. Moreover, there was no eating or drinking at these meetings, which is also a new feature in the annals of the City, whose "turtle-soup patriotism" has been immortalised by Cobbett. Finally another novelty was the fact that the meetings of the City merchants in the London Tavern and the Guildhall were held in business hours, in broad daylight. The current stagnation in business may have something to do with this phenomenon, as indeed it may altogether form a leaven in the fermentation of the City mind, and a considerable leaven too. For all that, the importance of this City movement cannot be denied, however hard the West End may try to laugh it off. The bourgeois reform papers—*The Daily News, The Morning Advertiser,* and *The Morning Chronicle* (the last having belonged to this category for some time now)—seek to demonstrate to their adversaries the "great future" of the City Association. They overlook the more obvious aspects. They have failed to realise that very vital, very decisive points have already been decided by the mere fact of these meetings: 1. The breach between the ruling class *outside* Parliament and the governing class *within* it; 2. a dislocation of those elements of the bourgeoisie that have hitherto set the tone in politics; 3. the disenchantment with Palmerston.

As we know, *Layard* has announced that he intends to table his reform proposals in the House of Commons tonight. As we know, about a week ago he was shouted down, hissed and booed in the House of Commons. The princes of the English merchant world in the City replied at their meetings with frantic cheers for Layard. He was the hero of the day at the London Tavern and the Guildhall. The *cheers* of the City are a provocative retort to the *groans*[b] of the Commons. If the House of Commons proves tonight to have been intimidated, its authority is lost, it abdicates. If it repeats its groans, the cheers of its opponents will resound all the more loudly. And from the tale of the *Abderiten*[c] we know to what happenings the rivalry between cheers and groans may lead.[140] The City meetings were a blatant challenge to the House of Commons,

---

[a] May 5, 1855.—*Ed.*
[b] Here and below Marx uses the English words "cheers" and "groans".—*Ed.*
[c] Ch. M. Wieland, *Die Abderiten, eine sehr wahrscheinliche Geschichte.*—*Ed.*

similar to Westminster's election of Sir Francis Burdett in the first decade of this century.[141]

Until now, of course, the *Manchester School* with its Brights and Cobdens has stood at the head of the movement of the English bourgeoisie. The manufacturers of Manchester have now been ousted by the merchants of the City. Their orthodox opposition to the war convinced the bourgeoisie, which in England can never remain static for a moment, that they have at least temporarily lost their vocation to lead it. At present the Manchester gentry can only maintain their "hegemony" by outbidding the City gentlemen. This rivalry between the two most important factions of the bourgeoisie actually demonstrated by the City meetings, from which the Brights and Cobdens were excluded and from which they excluded themselves, augurs well for the popular movement. In evidence of this we can already cite the fact that the secretary of the City committee[a] has addressed a letter to the Chartists in London requesting them to appoint a member to its standing committee. Ernest Jones has been delegated by the Chartists to this committee. The merchants do not, of course, stand in such *direct* opposition to the workers as do the manufacturers, the millocracy,[b] and thus they are able, at least initially, to take *joint* action, which the Chartists and the Manchester men could not do.

Palmerston—this is the last major fact emerging from the City meetings—has, for the first time, been booed and hissed by the most important constituency in the country. The magic of his name has been dispelled forever. What brought him into discredit in the City was not his Russian policy, which is older than the Thirty Years' War.[142] It was the careless disdain, the pretentious cynicism, and above all the "bad jokes" with which he affected to cure the most terrible crisis England has ever known. This outraged the bourgeois conscience, however well it may go down in the corrupt House of "Commons".[c]

Administrative reform *with* a Parliament such as now constituted: everyone recognises the illogical nature of these pious wishes at first glance. But our century has seen reforming popes.[143] We have seen reform banquets headed by Odilon Barrot.[144] No wonder,

---

[a] J. Acland. His letter to the Chartists mentioned below and their reply to it are quoted in the article "London Organisation Committee" published in *The People's Paper*, No. 157, May 5, 1855.—*Ed.*

[b] Marx uses the English term. For its meaning see Note 55.—*Ed.*

[c] A pun in the original: *Haus der Gemeinen* can mean both "House of Commons" and "House of base, or vulgar fellows".—*Ed.*

then, that the avalanche that will sweep away Olde England appears at the outset as a snowball in the hand of the reforming City merchants.

Written on May 7, 1855

First published in the *Neue Oder-Zeitung*, No. 215, May 10, 1855

Marked with the sign ×

Printed according to the newspaper

Published in English for the first time

Frederick Engels

FROM SEVASTOPOL[145]

The mails of the *America*, received here on Saturday evening, once more enable us to lay before our readers some clear account of the state of the war in the Crimea, though still the contradictory and indefinite nature of the official reports as well as of the newspaper letters renders our task no easy one. It is manifest that the failure of Vienna was attended by greater alertness and activity in the allied camp at Sevastopol, and that though the bombardment may be said to have been given up on April 24, yet the fortnight succeeding was not wholly unimproved. Still it is very difficult to say what advantages have been gained; indeed one writer pretends that the Russian advanced works, Selenghinsk, Volhynsk and Kamtchatka, as well as the rifle trenches in front of the whole line, have been abandoned by the defense.[146] As this is certainly the very utmost advantage obtained by the Allies we will for the present assume it to be true. Some correspondents report that the Flagstaff bastion itself had been stormed by the French and a lodgment effected therein,[a] but this deserves no credit. It is a mere ignorant exaggeration of the affair of April 21, when the French, by blowing up mines, formed an advanced trench in front of that bastion.[b]

---

[a] Reports on the bombardment of the Flagstaff bastion by the Allies appeared in *The Times*, Nos. 22043-22045, May 2-4, 1855.—*Ed.*

[b] Instead of this opening paragraph the version published in the *Neue Oder-Zeitung* has: "As far as the public is concerned, the opening of telegraphic communication from Balaklava to London and Paris has so far only served to make the information offered to it more confused.

"The British Government publishes nothing at all or at most vague assurances about successes achieved; the French Government publishes dispatches under the

We will then assume it to be correct that the Russians are thrown back upon their original line of defense, although it is very remarkable that no reports of the occupation of Mount Sapun and the Mamelon by the Allies have yet been received. But even if the redoubts on these hills are no longer in the hands of the Russians, nobody can dispute the great advantages they have drawn from them. They have held Sapun from Feb. 23, and the Mamelon Kamtschatka redoubt from March 12 to the end of April, during which time the allied trenches were either enfiladed or taken under close front fire by them, while the key of the whole position—Malakoff—was completely sheltered by them during the fifteen days' cannonade. After having turned them to such good use, the Russians could afford to lose them.

The various night attacks by which the Allies made themselves masters of the Russian rifle-trenches and counter-approaches, need not be described here, no more than the sally undertaken by the Russians to recover them. Such operations possess no tactical interest except for such as know the ground from personal inspection, being mainly decided by the intelligence, the dash and tenacity of the subaltern officers and soldiers. In these qualities the Anglo-French are superior to the Russians, and consequently they have made good their footing in some places close to the Russian works.[a] The distance between the combatants has been reduced, here and there, to the range of hand-grenades, that is to some twenty or thirty yards from the Russian covered way, or from forty to sixty yards from the main rampart. The Russians say

---

name of Canrobert, but cut and distorted to such an extent that it is almost impossible to glean anything from them. For example, the bastion against which the main French attack is directed was hitherto invariably called the *Flagstaff Bastion* or *Bastion du Mât.* Now we learn that great advantages have been gained in action against the Central Bastion, and then against Bastion No. 4. A careful collation of these dispatches with earlier reports, particularly Russian ones, has shown that what is meant is still our old acquaintance, the Bastion du Mât, but it is given different names and appellations. This kind of mystification is thoroughly tendentious and therefore, to a certain extent, also 'providential'.

"But if the telegraph holds no benefits for the public, it has indisputably brought some life to the allied camp. Beyond doubt the first dispatches received by Canrobert contained strict orders to act more resolutely and achieve some sort of success at any cost. An unofficial report asserts that the Russians have evacuated *all* advanced works, Selenghinsk, Volhynsk and Kamchatka, as well as the rifle trenches in front of their whole line."—*Ed.*

[a] In the *Neue Oder-Zeitung* the passage beginning with the words "After having turned them to such good use" and ending with the words "close to the Russian works" does not occur. The next sentence begins: "Through the Allies' latest successes the distance between the combatants...:"—*Ed.*

the besiegers are at thirty sagenes[a] or sixty yards from it.[b] This is the case especially in front of the Flagstaff bastion, the Middle bastion and the Redan, where the ground forms dead angles, with hollows so situated that the Russian guns cannot be sufficiently depressed to plunge their shot into them. As the Russian artillery is anything but silenced, the communications with these hollows and the turning them into a complete system of trenches is a matter of great difficulty, and the flanking fire of the Russians will be very sorely felt by the Allies.[c] Indeed, so long as the allied batteries are about four or five hundred yards to the rear of the advanced trenches, it is not to be explained how they expect to hold such exposed positions against sallies undertaken on a sudden and with a sufficient force; and after the acknowledged failure of the bombardment it will be some time before new and more advanced batteries can be brought into play.

This sudden advance of the Allies to the very foot of the Russian ramparts, different as it looks from their previous sloth and indecision, is yet quite of a piece with it. There never was either system or steady consistency in the conduct of this siege; and as a siege is essentially a systematic operation in which every step gained must be at once turned to some fresh advantage, under penalty of proving fruitless, it is plain that the Allies have conducted this upon the worst possible plan. Notwithstanding the disappointment in the minds of the allied generals when they first beheld the place, notwithstanding the errors committed last Autumn, during what we may call the first siege, they might yet have made greater progress. We leave the north side of the town entirely out of the question, as the allied generals did so themselves. They had once for all made up their minds to attack the south side separately and to run the risk of getting into a place commanded by a fortress to them inaccessible. But here an alternative arises: either the allied generals felt themselves strong enough to take the south side, and then they must now admit that they were unpardonably mistaken; or they felt themselves too weak, and then why did they not procure reenforcements? The fact is now beyond denial that blunder has succeeded blunder in this "memorable and unparalleled" siege. The hardships of the Winter-quarters appear to have imparted a spirit of unconquera-

---

[a] An old Russian unit of length equal to 2.1336 metres.—*Ed.*

[b] This sentence does not occur in the *Neue Oder-Zeitung*.—*Ed.*

[c] This sentence and the end of the preceding one beginning with the words "where the ground forms dead angles" do not occur in the *Neue Oder-Zeitung*.—*Ed.*

ble drowsiness, apathy and languor to both army and generals. When the Russians, in February, boldly came out of their lines and formed fresh ones in advance, it should have been a sufficient incentive to them to muster up their energies; yet Canrobert could use this very serious admonition to no other purpose than to cool the zeal of the Zouaves by an attack which he knew beforehand could lead to no good. The work in the trenches was resumed, but more in order to form covered roads for storming columns than to push the batteries nearer to the enemy. Even after six months spent before the place, every act shows that no definite plan had been settled, no point of chief attack singled out, nay, that the old fixed idea of taking Sevastopol by a *coup de main*[a] still reigned supreme in the heads of the Allies, crossing every sensible proposal, frustrating every attempt at systematic progress. And what little was done was executed with three times the slowness of regular siege operations, while the inconsistency and want of plan characterizing the whole, did not even impart to it the certainty of success inherent in such regular operations.[b]

But everything was expected from the late opening of the fire. That was the great excuse for all delays and do-nothingisms. Though it is difficult to say what was expected from this grand event—from batteries at from 600 to 1,000 yards from their object, at last the fire did open. About 150 rounds per gun the first two or three days, then 120 rounds, then 80, then 50, finally 30 were fired; after which the cannonade was suspended. The effect was hardly visible, except in the used-up guns and emptied magazines of the Allies. Five days cannonading with full force would have done more harm to the Russians and opened more chances of advantage to the Allies than fifteen days of a fire beginning with great fury and slackening down as fast as it was

---

[a] Sudden attack.—*Ed.*

[b] Instead of this paragraph the *Neue Oder-Zeitung* has: "Even this sudden advance of the Allies is only another in the series of desultory moves characteristic of this siege, in which systematic blockade, assault in force and wishful *coups de main* go together in utter confusion. The very first bombardment of October 17 to November 5 was preceded by the Allies' decision to leave the north side of the town entirely out of account and attack the south side separately, thus running the risk of getting into a position commanded by a fortress impregnable to them. Moreover, in that first bombardment the fire, instead of being concentrated upon one or two points, was dispersed over an enormous front. The five months between the first and the second bombardment were not used to single out main points of attack, but merely to work out in detail, and with maximum sluggishness, the plan for a simultaneous attack on all points of a huge semicircle, which meant a repetition of the original error."—*Ed.*

begun. But with their ammunition spent and their guns rendered unserviceable, would the Allies have been in a position to seize these favorable chances? Quite as much as now, while the Russians, from witnessing the slackening of the fire and from being spared the infliction of a hail of 50,000 projectiles per day during five successive days, are in a far better position than they would have been.[a] This prolongation of the cannonade, by reducing its intensity is so great and unaccountable a deviation from all military rules, that political reasons must be at the bottom of it. When the first and second days' fire had disappointed the expectations of the Allies, the necessity of keeping up a semblance of a cannonade during the Vienna Conferences must have led to this useless waste of ammunition.

The cannonade ends, the Vienna Conferences are suspended, the telegraph is completed. At once the scene changes. Orders arrive from Paris to act promptly and decisively. The old system of attack is given up; partial assaults, lodgments by mining explosions, a struggle of rifles and bayonets, succeed the resultless roar of artillery. Advanced points are gained and even maintained against a first sally of the besieged. But unless it is found practicable to construct batteries within short distances from the Russian lines, and to make these lines too hot for the besieged, nothing is gained. The advanced points cannot be held without great and daily repeated losses, and without regularly recurring combats of doubtful and wavering issue. And supposing even that these batteries of the second and third parallel are to be constructed, and that it was necessary for their opening first to dislodge the Russians from their rifle-trenches—how long will it be before these fresh batteries will have guns enough to reply successfully to that Russian fire which in two cannonades has proved equal to that of the Allies? The nearer the batteries are placed to the enemy's works, the more destructive a crossfire can be concentrated upon them, and the more confined becomes the space for placing guns; in other words, the more equal becomes the fire of the attack to that of the defense, unless the latter has been previously subdued by the more distant batteries, which here is not the case.[b]

How, then, has it been possible for the Russians so successfully to withstand the attacks of the Allies? First, by the mistakes and vacillations of the Allies themselves; secondly, by the bravery of

[a] The last two sentences do not occur in the *Neue Oder-Zeitung*.—*Ed.*

[b] The German version of this article, published in the *Neue Oder-Zeitung*, ends here.—*Ed.*

the garrison and the skill of the directing engineer, Col. Todtleben; thirdly, by the natural strength of the position. For it must be admitted that the position is a strong one. The bad maps which up to a very recent period have alone been accessible represented Sevastopol as situated at the lower end of a slope and commanded by the hights in the rear; but the latest and best maps prove that the town stands on several rounded, isolated hills, separated by ravines from the slope of the plateau, and actually commanding quite as much of it as has any command over the town. This disposition of the ground seems fully to justify the hesitation to assault the place in September last; though it has appeared much too imposing to the allied generals, who did not even attempt to make the enemy show what strength he could muster for the defense. The Russian engineer has turned these natural advantages to the greatest possible use. Wherever Sevastopol presents a slope toward the plateau, two and even three rows of batteries have been constructed on its sides, one above the other, doubling and trebling the strength of the defense. Such batteries have been constructed in other fortifications (for instance on the slope of Mont Valérien at Paris), but they are not generally approved of by engineers, who call them shell-traps. It is true that they offer a larger object of aim to the besieger, whose shot may hit the battery above or below, if they miss the one they are fired at, and they will always cause greater losses to the defense on this account; but where a fortress is not even invested, like Sevastopol, such a drawback counts for nothing against the enormous strength they impart to the defending fire. After this siege of Sevastopol, we fancy we shall have very few complaints about these shell-traps. For fortresses of the first order, containing plenty of material and difficult to invest, they can be most advantageously used where the ground favors them. Beside these shell-traps, the Russians have deviated in another point from the usual engineering routine. According to the old-fashioned systems of bastioned fortifications, fifteen or seventeen bastions would have been insufficient to encircle the place and would have defended it very badly. Instead of this, there are only six bastions on projecting hights, while the curtains connecting them are broken in such angular lines as to give a flanking fire independent of that of the bastions, and heavy guns from these salient points sweep the ground in front. These curtains are armed with guns for nearly their whole extent, which again is an innovation, as the curtains in regular bastioned fortresses are generally armed with one or two guns only for special purposes, and the whole of the defense by fire is intrusted to the bastions and demi-lunes. Without entering into further technical details, it will be seen from the above that the Russians have made the most of their means, and that if ever the Allies should come into possession of the Flagstaff or Malakoff bastions, they may be sure to find a second and a third line of defense before them which they will have to put all their wits together to reduce.

Written about May 8, 1855

First published in the *New-York Daily Tribune,* No. 4401, May 28, 1855, reprinted in the *New-York Semi-Weekly Tribune,* No. 1045, June 1, 1855 and the *New-York Weekly Tribune,* No. 716, June 2, 1855 as a leading article; an abridged German version was published in the *Neue Oder-Zeitung,* No. 217, May 11, 1855, marked with the sign ×

Reproduced from the *New-York Daily Tribune*

Karl Marx

PIANORI.—DISSATISFACTION WITH AUSTRIA

London, May 9. *The Morning Chronicle, Advertiser, The Daily News*, etc., all end their philippics against the assassin Pianori[147] with more or less timid criticisms of the issue of the *Moniteur*,[a] which published the indictment of Pianori at the same time as the decree ordering to pay the Napoleonic legacy of 10,000 francs to the former French N.C.O. Cantillon, now on the shelf in Brussels, as the reward for his attempted assassination of Wellington. Especially amusing are the twists and turns of the *Chronicle*, a paper that is serious by profession. Napoleon III, it says, must be ignorant of this strange, and at the present moment so tactless tribute to Napoleon I. The name "Cantillon" must have strayed into the morally spotless columns of the *Moniteur* by a *lapsus pennae*.[b] Or some officious junior civil servant must have endowed Cantillon with the 10,000 francs off his own bat, etc.[c] The worthy *Chronicle* seems to imagine that the French bureaucracy is formed on the English pattern, where it is indeed possible, as we have seen from the last hearing of the parliamentary Committee of Inquiry, for a junior civil servant of the *Board of Ordnance*[d] to place an order for a certain type of rocket, involving thousands of pounds, of his own accord and without informing his superiors or, as Palmerston has told the House of Commons, for diplomatic documents to be withheld from Parliament for weeks because the "person" in the Foreign Office entrusted with the translation of

[a] *Le Moniteur universel*, No. 126, May 6, 1855.—*Ed.*
[b] Slip of the pen.—*Ed.*
[c] "The trial of the assassin...", *The Morning Chronicle*, No. 27571, May 9, 1855.—*Ed.*
[d] Marx uses the English term.—*Ed.*

the said documents happens to be suffering from a cold or from rheumatism.

For the last few days the London press has been trying to edge away from its admiration for Austria and prepare its readership for an abrupt transition into an opposite key. As usual it is left to "our own correspondents"[a] to break the ice. Thus *The Morning Chronicle* carries the following report from Berlin:

"No positive act of deception or formal breach of promise can be laid to the charge of the Prussian Cabinet [...].

"If Western Cabinets have been deceived, it has been their own fault, or those whose business it is to open their eyes. But can the same be said of Austria? Has her conduct been as undisguised [...] as that of Prussia? The latter has done all the mischief in her power to the West openly and undisguisedly. She defies and laughs at us without mask or restraint. The former has dallied with England and France during twenty months; laughed at us [...] in her sleeve; held out hopes officially as well as privately; lured us on from concession to concession[b]; given assurances of the most formal character; and, as long since predicted by those who were not blinded by overweening confidence, is now on the eve, it appears, of leaving us in the lurch if we do not assent to conditions of peace, [...] upon terms the most advantageous to Russia, and utterly [...] detrimental to France and England [...]. So, in fact, Austria after having served as a shield to Russia on the Pruth, and enabled Gorchakoff to detach nearly the whole of his force from Bessarabia to the Crimea, is to step forward and insist on a peace, which shall 'leave things as they are' [...]. If this be all we have to expect from Austrian friendship, then the sooner the mask is thrown aside the better."[c]

On the other hand, *The Times* carries this report from Vienna[d]:

"...Baron Hess, the Commander-in-Chief of the 3rd and 4th armies, has recently drawn up and presented to his Imperial master[e] a memorial, in which it is demonstrated that it would not, under present circumstances, be advisable for Austria to declare war against Russia. A cry will probably be raised against me for thus publicly touching on such a delicate matter, but in my opinion it is a service rendered to the British and French nations to tell them that they must depend on their own resources, and that Austria is not likely to come to their assistance. If she could have persuaded Prussia and the Bund to cover her left flank with an army of 100,000 men, she would probably, in spite of numerous impediments [...] long since have pledged herself to assume the offensive against Russia. It is not positively known what arguments Baron Hess employed in his memorial, but the Austro-Russians, who [...] are always best informed on such matters, say that it contained matter something like the following: The Western Powers, having proved to demonstration that they require all their own resources and those of Turkey in order to make head against the Russians in

---

[a] Marx uses the English words "our own correspondents".—*Ed.*

[b] The *Neue Oder-Zeitung* has "from commission to commission". Presumably a misprint.—*Ed.*

[c] "Banks of the Spree, May 6", *The Morning Chronicle*, No. 27571, May 9, 1855.—*Ed.*

[d] From its own correspondent Bird T. O'M. The report was dated May 4 and published in *The Times*, No. 22049, May 9, 1855.—*Ed.*

[e] Francis Joseph I.—*Ed.*

the Crimea, it would be highly imprudent for Austria, unless she can induce her federal allies to support her, to engage in a war with Russia. It is acknowledged [...] that the latter has an army of 250,000 men, including the Guard and Grenadier Corps, in Poland; and, as it is posted within the rayon of seven of the strongest fortresses in the empire, no force that was not at least twice as large could hope to obtain any advantage over it. It is also said that mention is made of the disordered state of the finances, of the inability of France to place a hundred thousand men at Austria's disposal, of the helplessness displayed by the British Government, and of the little reliance that can be placed on Prussia. Since Sunday last another argument has been added to the foregoing, [...] on the mutability of things in general, [...] the uncertainty of the life of man, and [...] the dilemma Austria would be in should anything happen to Louis Napoleon while she was engaged in a war with Russia."

Written on May 9, 1855

First published in the *Neue Oder-Zeitung*, No. 219, May 12, 1855

Marked with the sign ×

Printed according to the newspaper

Published in English for the first time

Frederick Engels

THE NEW MOVE IN THE CRIMEA[148]

The letter of our Paris correspondent published yesterday gave the outlines of the plan which, according to the best sources of information at Paris, the Allies propose to follow in the Summer campaign in the Crimea; and a scheme substantially the same having been divulged by Gen. Canrobert in the camp, we may fairly conclude that in this respect at least the truth is now known. It is simply that 25,000 men of the French reserves now distributed at Maslak, Gallipoli and Adrianople, are to be brought to the Crimea, to be followed by from 30,000 to 40,000 additional troops—Piedmontese and French. As soon as the reserves arrive, and without waiting for the additional reenforcements, the French army will proceed to cross the Chernaya, flog the Russians on the field if it can penetrate to Sympheropol and then with the coming reenforcements to help out the operation, go on to clear the peninsula of Russians, and to occupy and fortify Perekop; after which the main army will return and finish the siege of Sevastopol at leisure.[a] In the mean time the steamers of the fleets are to attack Kaffa and Kertch, and if they succeed in reducing those

---

[a] Instead of the preceding text, the version published in the *Neue Oder-Zeitung* has: "*London*, May 11. The impatience of the French army has forced Canrobert to divulge the Allies' plan of operations. The 25,000 men of the reserve army are to be brought to the Crimea, to be followed by another 30,000 to 40,000 men—French and Piedmontese. As soon as the reserve army arrives the French

places, to occupy them as possible pivots or points of retreat for the active army in the field.

This is certainly the only thing to be done by the Allies if they expect ever to bring the operations in the Crimea to a satisfactory conclusion. But thus to act in the field requires that the balance of forces should be considerably in their favor; otherwise they cannot expect to obtain any important advantage over the Russian army of observation. How, then, does the balance of strength stand at present?

The French have in the Crimea nine divisions of infantry and one brigade of cavalry (Chasseurs d'Afrique[a]). At 7,000 men to a division, this gives a force of 63,000 infantry and 1,500 cavalry. The English have five divisions of infantry amounting at a very high estimate to 6,000 men each, and a division of say 2,000 horse. Then there are the remains of the Turkish force originally sent to the Crimea, which cannot possibly exceed 6,000 infantry. Add to these the troops which Omer Pasha can withdraw from Eupatoria, where he must leave at least 15,000 men to garrison the extensive works erected there, and we shall increase the number of the allied army by say 20,000 infantry and perhaps 3,000 or 4,000 cavalry. These troops, as we learn from our correspondent at London, have already been transported to the Chersonese and are encamped at Kadikoi, back of Balaklava, ready for the expected field movements. This is a much more judicious disposition than to attempt to effect a junction by a separate inland movement of both the Anglo-French and Turkish armies, exposing them to be separately attacked by a superior Russian force. Our correspondent states the number of men Omer has brought to Kadikoi at a higher figure than we have estimated it, but he allots a corresponding English force to make up the garrison at Eupatoria, so that on the whole his estimates do not vary from ours.[b] With these forces we must take into our account 20,000 men of the French army of reserve who may be expected to arrive by the time Canrobert intends to take the field, and the 4,000 Piedmontese landed on the 9th of May. The allied strength in the Chersonese will then be as follows:

---

will take the field, cross the Chernaya, attack the Russians wherever they encounter them, try to link up with Omer Pasha's troops somewhere near the Alma and Kacha and then act according to circumstances."—*Ed.*

[a] African riflemen.—*Ed.*

[b] In the *Neue Oder-Zeitung* the text beginning with the words "Add to these the troops" and ending with the words "do not vary from ours" does not occur.—*Ed.*

French Infantry and Artillery	83,000	Cavalry	1,500
English " "	30,000	"	2,000
Turks " "	26,000	"	4,000
Piedmontese " "	4,000		
Totals	143,000		7,500[a]

Whether the French reserves have any cavalry with them we do not know, or if they have, whether it will arrive in season for the commencement of operations is uncertain; however, to make as liberal a calculation as possible for the Allies, let us add 2,000 horse to the above figures, which would give a total cavalry force of 9,500.[b]

A part of the plan is to continue to carry on the siege, and for this at least as many troops will be required as are now engaged in that service—that is to say:

Four French divisions at	7,000	each	28,000 men
Three English divisions at	6,000	each	18,000 men
		Total	46,000 men

To this number must be added the sailors and the troops intrusted with guarding Balaklava and the line of intrenchments to Inkermann, and who at the same time serve as an army of reserve to the besieging corps. We put these down at a low estimate at 12,000. Estimating the sailors and marines at 4,000, we shall therefore have to deduct 56,000 men from the above 143,000, leaving available for field operations 87,000 infantry and artillery and 9,500 cavalry, or altogether about 96,500 men.[c] And this, as we have said, is a very liberal computation.

---

[a] The *Neue Oder-Zeitung* gives the following figures:

"French infantry	83,000	Cavalry	1,500
English "	30,000		2,000
Turkish "	6,000	"	
Total: Infantry	119,000	cavalry	3,500."—*Ed.*

[b] In the *Neue Oder-Zeitung*: "5,500".—*Ed.*

[c] The *Neue Oder-Zeitung* gives the following calculation: "Estimating the sailors and marines at 4,000, we shall have to deduct 54,000 from the total of 119,000, leaving available for field operations 65,000 infantry and 5,500 cavalry, altogether somewhat more than 70,000."

The *Neue Oder-Zeitung* further has: "One should also take into account Omer Pasha's corps at Eupatoria, roughly 35,000 infantry and 3,000 or 4,000 cavalry. Of these, 15,000 must stay back for garrison duty, so that Omer Pasha will probably take the field with 20,000 infantry and 4,000 cavalry, 24,000 all told.

Now, according to a Russian military correspondent of the *Augsburg Gazette,* who has always put down the Russian forces at very low estimates, the Russians have now in the Crimea, of

Regular Infantry	93,000	Regular and irregular Cavalry	20,000
Sailors, Marines, &c.	8,000		
Chornomorski[a] Cossacks ...	6,000		
Artillery, Engineers, &c. ..	13,000		
Total Infantry	120,000	Total Cavalry.......	20,000[b]

The distribution of this force may be approximatively stated as follows:

For the defense of the south side of Sevastopol (infantry, artillery, &c.), men	26,000
As Garrison to the North Fort and Intrenched Camp	24,000
Total..........	50,000[c]

This leaves as available for the field, 70,000 infantry and artillery and 20,000 cavalry.

In point of infantry the Allies will thus have a striking superiority, their numbers exceeding those of their antagonists by 26,500 men.[d] As to the relative strength in artillery we are in the dark; but from the difficulty the Allies have always found in procuring horses, and from the large proportion of guns accompanying every Russian army, it is probable that the Russians will be superior to their opponents. In cavalry they will certainly have the advantage. Even if from their 20,000 horse we must subtract 8,000 Cossacks, who would at all events come in for patrolling, outpost and orderly duties, they still retain 12,000 cavalry intact from detachment service, against 9,500 of the Allies,

"Hence we have the following sum total of allied troops for *field operations* in two separate corps:

	Infantry	Cavalry	Total
Army at Sevastopol	65,000	5,500	70,500
Army at Eupatoria	20,000	4,000	24,000
	85,000	9,500	94,500."—*Ed.*

[a] Black Sea.—*Ed.*

[b] The source in question—the Augsburg *Allgemeine Zeitung,* No. 125 (supplement), May 5, 1855—gives the following figures: infantry, 90,000; artillery, 15,000.—*Ed.*

[c] Instead of the two preceding paragraphs the *Neue Oder-Zeitung* has: "At the lowest estimate, the one the *Russians* themselves give of their present forces in the Crimea, we get 120,000 infantry and 20,000 cavalry. One must deduct 50,000 of these for the defence of Sevastopol—26,000 for the south side and 24,000 as garrison for the North Fort and the entrenched camp."—*Ed.*

[d] This sentence does not occur in the *Neue Oder-Zeitung.*—*Ed.*

of which number, on a day of battle, no more than 7,000 can be brought forward in line.[a]

The advance of the Allies toward the interior can hardly be made otherwise than on the road toward Mackenzie's farm and the space between this road and the head of Sevastopol Bay or Inkermann; because east of Mackenzie's farm the steep ridge encircling the Baidar Valley extends south-eastward until it joins the southern ridge of the Crimea near Yalta, forming a rocky barrier impassable for cavalry and artillery, and practicable for infantry by a few footpaths only. From Yalta there is indeed a road crossing the hills, but this can be defended by a very few troops, and has no doubt been fortified by the Russians long since, as well as the footpath passes. Besides, the direction of this road, the distance of Yalta from Balaklava, and the chance it offers to the Russians to cut off any corps operating on this line, will hardly admit of its being used by the Allies as their main line of operations.[b]

The road by Mackenzie's farm to the Alma and Sympheropol is defended by a double row of intrenchments; first on the ridge overhanging the Chernaya, and secondly on the north side of a ravine running down from the edge of the rocky range, near Mackenzie's farm, to the head of Sevastopol Bay. This second and main line of defense, which is not more than two English miles in extent, is said to be very strongly intrenched, and here the first decisive action will have to be fought—an action deciding whether the Allies are to continue imprisoned on the Heracleatic Chersonese or to gain the interior of the country. This position will cost a harder struggle to carry than the Alma, for the forces will be more equally balanced, unless the Russians commit the mistake of dispersing their troops. They can easily concentrate 75,000 men

---

[a] Instead of the last sentence the *Neue Oder-Zeitung* has: "As regards infantry, the Allies' *joint* forces are superior to the Russians', but separately each of their two fighting corps is weaker. The Russians' greatest advantage, however, is their position. Deployed over the triangle between the Alma, Sevastopol and Simferopol, they hold a consolidated position against Omer Pasha along that river in the North, which can be maintained with 15,000 infantry along the front, while a flanking movement of the Russian cavalry threatens to cut off the Turks from Eupatoria. If therefore Omer Pasha himself advanced up to the Alma, he would never be able to cross it until the English and the French had thrown the Russians back to Simferopol and thus forced them to give up the Alma. In this case the two corps could link up. An advance of the Anglo-French army is therefore the basic condition of any success."—*Ed.*

[b] The text beginning with the words "and the space between this road" to the end of the paragraph does not occur in the *Neue Oder-Zeitung*.—*Ed.*

for the defense of these intrenchments, and if the Allies attack with from 80,000 to 90,000 men, this superiority will in a great measure be made up by the intrenchments, and by the narrow front on which the Allies must necessarily act. If the Russians behave as they should, they must here check the advance of the Allies at once and force them back into their stronghold on the Chersonese.[a] But if the Russians are defeated and the position carried, there remains nothing for them but to retire upon the Belbek and attempt to hold that line.[b] In this case the garrison of the north side of Sevastopol would have to be observed by the Allies, whose army in the field would thereby be weakened by some 8,000 or 10,000 men; and if even then the Russians suffered a second defeat, their superiority in cavalry would secure them a safe retreat, although their line of retreat would lie in the prolongation of their left wing—a very unfavorable position unless made up for by some countervailing advantage.

These are a few of the considerations offering themselves on this new turn of affairs in the Crimea. They are far from exhausting the subject, to which we shall therefore soon return.[c]

Written about May 11, 1855

First published in the *New-York Daily Tribune*, No. 4402, May 29, 1855; reprinted in the *New-York Semi-Weekly Tribune*, No. 1045, June 1, 1855 as a leading article; the German version was first published in the *Neue Oder-Zeitung*, No. 221, May 14, 1855, marked with the sign ×

Reproduced from the *New-York Daily Tribune*

---

[a] Instead of the text beginning with the words "This position will cost" and ending with the words "their stronghold on the Chersonese", the *Neue Oder-Zeitung* has: "The narrow front on which the Allies must act here is to the Russians' advantage."—*Ed.*

[b] The *Neue Oder-Zeitung* further has: "while a detached corps keeps the Turks in check on the Alma".—*Ed.*

[c] In the *Neue Oder-Zeitung* the article ends as follows: "Even if the Russians were defeated here, their superiority in cavalry and the Allies' inadequate transport facilities making it impossible for the latter to take up positions far from the coast, would enable the Russians to retreat from the area controlled by the Allies. Their line of retreat would lie in the prolongation of their left wing, which is of course a very unfavourable route. However, it is probable that the Russians will *try* from the beginning to keep the Allies busy on the Chernaya and throw the bulk of their forces against Omer Pasha in order to encircle and crush him with their cavalry and then turn their total forces against the Anglo-French troops."—*Ed.*

Karl Marx

THE MORNING POST VERSUS PRUSSIA. —THE CHARACTER OF THE WHIGS AND TORIES [149]

London, May 14. Palmerston's private organ, *The Morning Post*, today carries a threatening article against *Prussia*,[a] which includes the following:

"It was in the month of April, 1854, that permission was given, by an Order in Council, to import Russian produce into the United Kingdom in neutral bottoms, and of this permission we find that Prussia availed herself with astonishing rapidity. The following returns" (taken from official tables presented to Parliament) "will show the comparative amount of our imports of tallow, hemp, and flax, from the last-named country, during the years 1853 and 1854; the difference clearly indicating the quantity of Russian produce which has found its way through Memel and Danzig to the British market, notwithstanding our strict blockade of the Russian ports[b] in the Baltic:

"Imported from Prussia into the United Kingdom

	1853	1854
Tallow	54 cwts	253,955 cwts
Hemp	3,447 "	366,220 "
Flax	242,383 "	667,879 "
Flax- and linseed	57,848 qrs	116,267 qrs

"These figures sufficiently indicate the value of this new traffic to Prussia [...]. The result is that in spite of our blockade Russia is enabled to sell her produce as freely as in time of peace, while we have to pay some 50 per cent more for it, in the shape of dues and profits to the Prussian trader [...].We admit that our present policy is grossly inconsistent, but the remedy is to be sought not by raising the blockade of the enemy's ports, but by stopping to the utmost of our power the overland traffic through the Prussian dominions."

---

[a] *The Morning Post*, No. 25386, May 14, 1855.—*Ed.*
[b] *The Morning Post* has: "the enemy's ports".—*Ed.*

The *anti-aristocratic* movement in England can only have one *immediate* result: *to bring* the *Tories,* i. e. the *specifically aristocratic party, to the helm.* If not, it must necessarily subside at first into a few Whig platitudes, a few administrative mock-reforms not worth mentioning. Layard's announcement of his motion on the "state of the nation"[a] and the reception that announcement received in the House of Commons, produced the City meetings. But close on the heels of the City meetings followed Ellenborough's motion[150] in the House of Lords,[b] whereby the Tories appropriate the new reform agitation, and transform it into a ladder to office. Layard himself has altered the words "*aristocratic influence*" in his motion to "*family influence*"—a concession to the Tories. Every movement outside the House assumes, *inside* the House, the form of the squabble between the two factions of the governing class. In the hands of the Whigs the Anti-Corn Law League became a means of bringing down the Tories.[151] In the hands of the Tories, the Administrative Reform Association[152] became a means of bringing down the Whigs. Only one must not forget that in this way one base of the old regime after another was sacrificed alternately by the two factions—and the regime itself remained intact, we may add. We have already stated our view that only the Tories are forced to make major concessions, because only under them does the pressure from without assume a threatening, indeed revolutionising character.[c] The Whigs represent the real oligarchy in England, the domination of a few great families such as the Sutherlands, Bedfords, Carlisles, Devonshires, etc.; the Tories represent the squireocracy,[d] they are the *Junker* party, if you will, although broad demarcation lines must be drawn between the English squire and the North German *Junker.* The Tories are therefore the receptacles of all the old English prejudices regarding Church and State, protection and anti-Catholicism. The Whigs, the oligarchs, are *enlightened,* and have never hesitated to discard prejudices standing in the way of their hereditary tenancy of the offices of state. By their friendship the Whigs have constantly prevented the middle classes from moving; by their friendship the Tories have always thrown the masses into the arms of the middle classes, who put them at the disposal of the Whigs...

---

[a] A. H. Layard's speech in the House of Commons on April 27, 1855. *The Times,* No. 22040, April 28, 1855.—*Ed.*

[b] E. L. Ellenborough's speech in the House of Lords on May 14, 1855. *The Times,* No. 22054, May 15, 1855.—*Ed.*

[c] See this volume, pp. 50-51.—*Ed.*

[d] Marx uses the English word.—*Ed.*

At the present moment there is no longer any difference between Whigs and Tories except that the latter represent the plebs of the aristocracy and the former its *haute-volée*.[a] The old aristocratic phrase is on the side of the aristocratic plebs; the liberal phrase on the side of the aristocratic *haute-volée*. In fact, however, since the High Tories (Lord Bolingbroke, etc.) quit the scene the Tory Party has always been ruled by parvenus such as Pitt, Addington, Perceval, Canning, Peel and Disraeli. The *homines novi*[b] were always to be found in the ranks of the Tories. When Derby (himself a renegade Whig) formed his ministry, it contained, apart from himself, perhaps two other old names. All the others were plain squires plus one man of letters. On the other hand, the Whigs, who never hesitated for a moment to trim their sails and their views to the wind and who apparently forever renewed and metamorphosed themselves, needed no new men. They were able to perpetuate the family names. If one surveys English history since the "glorious" revolution of 1688, one finds that all the laws directed against the mass of the people have been initiated by the Whigs, from the Act for a Seven-Year Parliament to the latest Workhouse[153] and Factory legislation. But the Whig reaction has always taken place in agreement with the middle classes. The Tory reaction has been directed even more against the middle class than against the masses. Hence the Whigs' reputation for liberality.

Written on May 14, 1855

First published in the *Neue Oder-Zeitung*, No. 227, May 18, 1855

Marked with the sign ×

Printed according to the newspaper

Published in English in full for the first time

---

[a] Upper crust.—*Ed.*
[b] New men.—*Ed.*

Karl Marx

A SITTING OF THE HOUSE OF LORDS

London, May 15. The galleries of the House of Lords were packed full yesterday afternoon before the sitting even commenced. A sensational show had been announced—Lord Ellenborough's motion, and a regular battle between the *Ins* and *Outs*.[a] In addition to this, it was piquant to see with one's own eyes the hereditary legislators playing the part of crusaders *against* the aristocracy. The performance was a poor one. The actors kept forgetting what parts they were playing. The play began as drama and ended in farce. During the mock-battle not even the illusion, the artistic illusion, was maintained. It was evident at first glance that the noble warriors were trying reciprocally to preserve not only themselves but even their weapons unscathed.

Insofar as the debate revolved around the criticism of the conduct of the war up to now it failed to rise to the level of any run-of-the mill *debating club*[b] in London, and it would be sheer waste of time to dwell on it for a moment. We will attempt, however, to indicate in a few strokes how the noble lords conducted themselves as the champions of administrative reform, as the opponents of the aristocratic monopoly of government and as an echo of the City meetings. The right man in the right place, cried Lord Ellenborough.[c] And as proof that honour falls to merit, and merit alone, he cited the fact that *he* (Ellenborough) and Lord

---

[a] Marx uses the English words "Ins" and "Outs" (referring to the party in the government and the opposition).—*Ed.*

[b] Here and below Marx uses the English words "debating club".—*Ed.*

[c] The debate in the House of Lords on May 14, 1855 was reported in *The Times*, No. 22054, May 15, 1855.—*Ed.*

Hardwicke sat in the Lords because *their fathers* had worked their way into the House of Lords by their own merit. This seems, on the contrary, to be precisely an instance of how men can benefit from the merits of *others*, namely their fathers, to secure not merely a post for life but the dignity of a legislator of England. And what were the *merits* by which the *Lord Chief Justice of the Queen's Bench*,[a] Ellenborough senior, and Mr. Charles Yorke, Lord Hardwicke's father, made their way into the House of Lords? The story is an instructive one. The late Ellenborough, an English lawyer and subsequently judge, managed to earn himself the reputation of a *Jeffreys en miniature* in the press trials, conspiracy trials and police-spy trials that were constantly taking place under Pitt and his successors. Under Ellenborough's leadership the special jury[b] attained a reputation in England that even the "*jurés probes et libres*"[c] of Louis Philippe never possessed. That was the *merit* of Ellenborough senior, and that paved his way into the House of Lords. As for Mr. *Charles Yorke*, the ancestor of Lord Hardwicke, he has even outdone old Ellenborough in the matter of *merit*. This Charles Yorke, the Member for Cambridge for twenty years, was one of the chosen band entrusted by Pitt, Perceval and Liverpool "to do the dirty work for them".[d] Each of the "loyal" terror measures of that time found its Pindar in him. In every petition against the openly practised sale of seats in the House of Commons, he discerned "Jacobin machinations". Every motion opposing the shameless system of sinecures, at a time when pauperism was coming into being in England, was denounced by Charles Yorke as an attack on the "blessed comforts of our sacred religion". And on what occasion did this Charles Yorke celebrate his Ascension to the House of Lords? In 1810 the Walcheren expedition[154] had produced similar effects in England as the Crimean expedition did in 1855. Lord Porchester tabled a motion in the House of Commons to set up a committee of investigation. Charles Yorke opposed it violently, he spoke of plots, the stirring up of discontent, etc. Nevertheless, Porchester's motion was carried. But then Yorke decided to withhold the inquiry findings from the public, insisting, on the basis of an old and absurd parliamentary privilege, that the public galleries be cleared of listeners and reporters. This was done. A Mr. Gale Jones, the

---

[a] Marx uses the English term.—*Ed.*
[b] Marx uses the English words "special jury".—*Ed.*
[c] "Honest and free juries."—*Ed.*
[d] Marx uses the English phrase.—*Ed.*

chairman of a London debating club, then published an advertisement announcing that the subject to be discussed at the next meeting of the club would be the infringement of the freedom of the press and Charles Yorke's gross insult to public opinion. Charles Yorke promptly had Gale Jones summoned before the House of Commons for libel of a Member and breach of "parliamentary privilege", whence, in contravention of all English laws, he was immediately dispatched to Newgate Prison, without inquiry or reference to a judge, "to be confined there *as long as* it should please the Commons". While performing these heroic deeds, Charles Yorke assumed great airs of independence. He claimed to be acting only as an upright "country squire", as a "friend of the King", as a "loyal anti-Jacobin". Not three weeks had elapsed since his closing of the gallery before it became known that meanwhile he had presented his account to the Perceval ministry and obtained a lifetime sinecure as *Teller of the Exchequer*[a] (similar to "The Guardian of the Green Wax"), i. e. a life emolument of £2,700 per annum. On accepting this sinecure Charles Yorke had to submit himself to his constituents in Cambridge for re-election. At the election meeting he was greeted by booes and hisses, rotten apples and eggs, and was forced to run for it. As compensation for this indignity Perceval elevated him to the peerage. Thus it was that Charles Yorke was transformed into a lord, and thus, Lord Ellenborough informs Lord Palmerston, merit must be able to make its way in a well-ordered economy. Discounting this extremely naive and characteristic *lapsus linguae*,[b] Ellenborough—who bears an unmistakable likeness to the Knight of the Doleful Countenance[c]—adhered more to the phraseology of the City meetings.

His friend Derby strove to restrict even the purely rhetorical concession. He rejected the rumour that he had allied himself with Layard. He whose entire talent consists of discretion, accused Layard of indiscretion. There was, he said, a lot of truth in the views of the City men, but they had proceeded to draw extravagant (!!) conclusions. A minister had to seek his colleagues in Parliament, and not merely in Parliament but in the party to which he belongs, and not merely in this party but within the circle of men in his party possessing parliamentary influence.

---

[a] Marx uses the English term.—*Ed.*
[b] Slip of the tongue.—*Ed.*
[c] Don Quixote.—*Ed.*

Within this circle ability should, of course, be decisive, and this had hitherto often been neglected. The fault, Derby claimed, lay in the parliamentary reform of 1831. The "rotten places", "the rotten boroughs",[a] had been expunged, and it was precisely these rotten boroughs[155] that had furnished the sound statesmen of England. They had enabled influential men to introduce talented but impecunious young people into Parliament and thence into the service of the state. Thus even according to Lord Derby no administrative reform is possible without parliamentary reform—but, a parliamentary reform in the opposite sense, restoration of the "rotten boroughs". Derby's complaint does not seem entirely justified if one considers that 85 seats in the House of Commons still belong to some 60 little "rotten boroughs" (in England alone), none of which have more than 500 inhabitants, with some electing two members.

Lord Panmure, on behalf of the ministry, brought the Lords debate back to the real point. You want, he stuttered, to exploit the cry outside the walls of Parliament in order to declaim us out of office and put yourselves in. Why did Derby not form a ministry three months ago when charged to do so by the Queen? Ah, replied Derby with a smirk, three months ago! Things have changed in the last three months. Three months ago Lord Palmerston was *l'homme à la mode*,[b] the great and indispensable statesman. Palmerston has discredited himself, and now it's our turn.

The debate in the House of Lords has shown that neither side possesses the stuff that men are made of. As to the House of Commons, Ellenborough rightly observed that it has become insipid, that it has lost its credit and that political influence is no longer to be sought *within* the House, but *outside* it.

The debates in the Lords clearly showed the *mala fides*[c] of the aristocratic opposition, which intends to conjure away the bourgeois movement and simultaneously to use it as a battering-ram against the ministry. In a subsequent letter we shall have the opportunity of similarly demonstrating the *mala fides* of the City reformers towards the working class, with whom they intend to play just as the aristocratic opposition does with them. From this one may draw the conclusion that the present movement in

---

[a] Here and below Marx uses the English phrase.—*Ed.*
[b] A popular man.—*Ed.*
[c] Insincerity.—*Ed.*

England is extremely complex and, as we have indicated earlier,[a] simultaneously contains two antithetical and hostile movements.

Written on May 15, 1855

First published in the *Neue Oder-Zeitung*, No. 228, May 19, 1855

Marked with the sign ×

Printed according to the newspaper

Published in English for the first time

[a] See this volume, pp. 186-88.—*Ed.*

Karl Marx

THE AGITATION OUTSIDE PARLIAMENT

London, May 16. The resentment of the bourgeois opposition caused by the vote in the House of Lords on the occasion of Ellenborough's motion is a symptom of weakness. On the contrary, they ought to celebrate the rejection of the motion as a victory. To force the House of Lords, the supreme council of the aristocracy, in solemn public debate to declare its satisfaction with the way the war has hitherto been conducted, loudly to acknowledge Palmerston as their champion and representative, and definitely to reject mere pious wishes for administrative reform, for any kind of reform—what more favourable results could the *enemies of the aristocracy* expect from Ellenborough's motion? Above all they had to seek to discredit the House of Lords, the last bastion of the English aristocracy. But they complain that the House of Lords disdains fleeting popularity at the cost not of its privileges but of the existing cabinet. It is in the order of things for *The Morning Herald* to complain, being the Tory organ, the organ of all the prejudices of "our incomparable constitution".[a] For *The Morning Herald* it was a comforting prospect, after the Whig oligarchy performing as the friends of the bourgeoisie and of "liberal progress" for a century and a half, to see the roles change and the *Tories* now entrusted for another century and a half with the role of "aristocratic" representatives of the bourgeoisie and of "liberal progress". *The Morning Herald* has a right to complain, a good, solid right. But the bourgeois opposition? Did it perhaps imagine that a moderate demonstration of City merchants would be

[a] This refers to an article on the debate in the House of Lords on May 14, 1855, published by *The Morning Herald*, No. 22432, May 16, 1855.—*Ed.*

enough to force the aristocracy into committing suicide, into abdicating? The truth, however, is that the bourgeoisie desires a compromise, that it expects flexibility from the other side to enable it too to be flexible; that it would like, if possible, to avoid a real struggle. As soon as the struggle becomes a real one, the "million", as they call the "lower" classes, too, will rush into the arena, not just as spectators, not just as referees, but as a party. And the bourgeoisie would like to avoid this at all costs. It was a similar reason that kept the Whigs out of the Cabinet from 1808-1830. They wanted to throw out their opponents at any price except the price of real concessions to the bourgeoisie, without whose aid the Tories could not be thrown out, except the price of a parliamentary reform. We have seen the ambiguous, off-hand way and the aloof, ironically non-committal manner in which Ellenborough and Derby set themselves up as supporters of the bourgeois administrative reform, while doing everything to ward off their supposed allies. We now see, on the other hand, how timidly and perfidiously the reforming businessmen of the City first tried to forestall any opposition from the Chartists and temporarily secure their silence, so as to juggle them out of the positions they had voluntarily granted them. In the case of the City merchants no less than in that of the Tories, fear and dislike of the supposed ally outweighs hostility towards the supposed enemy. The course of events was briefly this.

The "Administrative Reform Association" feared opposition from the Chartists, who, as the reader will remember, had got the better of the "National and Constitutional Association" at two large meetings in St. Martins Hall and Southwark, forcing it to retreat from the territory it had chosen itself.[a] On April 26 they sent Mr. James Acland (a former Anti-Corn Law lecturer[b]) to the rooms of Ernest Jones, where he announced himself as an "envoy" of the Administrative Reform Association, which was counting on the support of the Chartists, it being its wish to abolish the "class legislation" and install a popular government. He invited Ernest Jones to a meeting the next day with the *committee* of the said administration.[c] Jones declared that he was not entitled to reply in the name of the Chartist party. He had to decline to attend the meeting until he had consulted the London

---

[a] Probably a reference to Marx's article "A Meeting" (see this volume, pp. 98-100).—*Ed.*

[b] Marx uses the English words "Anti-Corn Law lecturer".—*Ed.*

[c] See this volume, pp. 166-69.—*Ed.*

executive committee of the Chartists,[156] which was to meet the following Sunday.

On Sunday evening, April 29, Jones informed the Chartist committee of the whole affair. He was authorised to proceed with the negotiations. The following morning Jones had a meeting with Mr. Ingraham Travers, the leader of the City movement, who personally accredited Mr. James Acland as the authorised agent and representative of his party. Mr. I. Travers assured Jones that their intention was to form a popular government. The resolutions as printed in *The Times*[a] were only *provisional*; the means of achieving their goal had to be decided first by the executive committee to be elected at the London Tavern meeting. As evidence of their sympathy for the cause of administrative reform the Chartists should appoint a speaker to represent them at the meeting. He would be called upon by the chairman to support one of the resolutions. Further, the Chartists should appoint a representative who, at the suggestion of the provisional committee of the City merchants, would be appointed a permanent member of the executive committee of the Reform Association at the Tavern meeting. Finally it was agreed that, admittance being by ticket only, the Chartists would receive their due share of these tickets. Jones declined to let the matter be left to a purely verbal agreement and informed Mr. Ingraham [Travers] that he would have to put forward all the points mentioned in a letter to the Chartists' executive committee.

This was done. The letter arrived, overflowing with assurances. However, when the time came for the delivery of the admission tickets, only 12 tickets arrived. When the Chartist committee complained about this breach of promise, the others apologised saying there were no more tickets left. However, if the Chartist committee would station two of its members at the door of the Tavern, they would be authorised to admit whoever they pleased, even without a ticket. Messrs. Slocombe and Workman were elected by the Chartists for this purpose and received Mr. Travers's authorisation. To eliminate all suspicion the Administrative Reform Association sent a special messenger with a letter for Jones on the day of the meeting,[b] a few hours before its commencement, to remind him that the chairman would request him to speak in favour of resolution 4, and that he would be proposed to the meeting as a member of the executive committee, in his status as representative of the Chartists.

[a] "Administrative Reform", *The Times*, No. 22040, April 28, 1855.—*Ed.*
[b] May 5, 1855.—*Ed.*

About an hour before the meeting large numbers of Chartists assembled outside the Tavern. As soon as the doors were opened, Messrs. Slocombe and Workman were forbidden to admit anyone without a ticket. Eight tickets were reluctantly distributed in order *to gain time* at a moment when the pressure from outside seemed to be getting serious. This time was used to bring along a unit of police waiting in readiness in a sidestreet. From this moment on nobody else was admitted except "well-known merchants and bankers". Indeed, people in *working-class dress,* in the familiar corduroy jackets, were turned away even if they had entrance tickets. To deceive the crowd of workers waiting in the street, the doors were suddenly locked and notices put up saying, "The hall is full. Nobody else will be admitted". At the time, however, the hall was not even half full, and "gentlemen" arriving in their carriages were admitted through the windows and by way of a back-door through the kitchen. The crowd of workers dispersed calmly, since they did not suspect any treachery. Although Ernest Jones showed his "platform ticket" at the meeting, he was not allowed up on the platform, much less permitted to speak of course. The Association had achieved two aims—to prevent any opposition from the Chartists, and to be able to point to the crowd in the street as *their supporters.* But these were only supposed to appear as extras in the street.

Ernest Jones, in an appeal to the workers of England, relates this comedy of intrigues and on behalf of the Chartists throws down the gauntlet to the Administrative Reform Association.[a]

Written on May 16, 1855

First published in the *Neue Oder-Zeitung,* No. 229, May 19, 1855

Marked with the sign ×

Printed according to the newspaper

Published in English for the first time

[a] E. Jones, "Political Felony. Infamous Chicanery and Fraud of Administrative Reform Association", *The People's Paper,* No. 158, May 12, 1855.—*Ed.*

Karl Marx

QUESTIONS OF FINANCE

London, May 19. According to the optimists of the press here the economic crisis in England has now ended, and commerce and industry are once again taking an upward course. They draw this consoling conclusion from the fact that there has been an *easing of the money market*. For on the one hand there has been an increase in the *gold reserve* in the vaults of the Bank of England, and on the other the bank has lowered its *rate of interest*. Whilst on January 20, 1855, the value of the gold holdings was only £12,162,000, on May 12, 1855, it had risen to £16,045,000—an increase of £3,883,000. The rate of interest, which stood at 5 per cent on January 20, 1855, was lowered by the Bank to $4^1/_2$ per cent on March 31, and to 4 per cent on April 28. However, those gentlemen have overlooked the fact that an accumulation of gold in the vaults of the Bank and a fall in its rate of interest can be caused by something other than an economic boom—namely the very *opposite*: stagnation of business and, linked with that, a *falling-off in the demand for capital*. That the latter is really the cause on this occasion is shown by the tables published every week by the Bank of England. Only one should not, like those optimists, look exclusively at two columns contained in the tables, gold holdings and rate of interest. One has to compare two other columns—those showing *reserve bank-notes* and *discounted bills*. As is generally known, the Bank of England is split into two different departments, the Issue Department[a] and the Banking Department. We can describe the former as the *mint* of the Bank of England. It is engaged solely in manufacturing bank-notes. Robert Peel's Act

[a] Here and below Marx uses the English terms.—*Ed.*

of 1844 laid down legal limitations on the issue of bank-notes. That is to say, above the sum of £14 million, which is the amount of capital it is owed by the state, the Bank can issue no more bank-notes than there is gold in its vaults. If then, for example, the Bank issues bank-notes to the value of £20 million there has to be gold worth £6 million in its vaults. The Issue Department of the Bank is engaged solely in manufacturing and issuing bank-notes in accordance with the restrictions described. It transfers all the bank-notes it manufactures in this way to the Banking Department, the actual Bank, which does business with the public like any other deposit and discount bank, and which puts bank-notes into circulation by discounting bills, advancing money on interest-bearing papers, paying dividends to state creditors, paying off deposits it holds, etc. Robert Peel cleverly devised both this division of the Bank of England into two self-contained departments and this method of regulating the amount of notes to be issued, because he fancied this would make it possible to guard against any future monetary crisis arising, and to adjust the amount of paper currency to that of metallic currency by means of an automatic and mechanical law. What the celebrated statesman overlooked was the not insignificant fact that his restriction only regulated circulation between the Issue Department and the Banking Department, between two offices of the Bank of England, but by no means determined circulation between the Banking Department and the outside world. The Issue Department of the Bank transfers to the Banking Department as many bank-notes as it is allowed by law to manufacture, for example £20 million if there are £6 million gold in its coffers. However, what proportion of these £20 million actually goes into circulation depends on the state of business, and on the requirements and demand in the world of commerce. The remainder, which the Bank cannot dispose of and which is thus left in the coffers of the Banking Department, appears in the accounts rendered by the Bank under the heading of *reserve bank-notes*.

Seeing, as we have, that, from January 20, 1855, to May 12, 1855, the gold holdings of the Bank increased by £3,883,000, we also find that during the same period the quantity of bank-notes held in reserve rose from £5,463,000 to £9,417,000, i. e. by £3,954,000. The greater the quantity of reserve bank-notes, i. e. the notes left in the coffers of the Banking Department, the smaller is the quantity of notes actually circulating amongst the public. However, from the figure just quoted it follows that the accumulation of gold in the vaults of the Bank has been accompanied by a decline in the quantity of bank-notes circulating amongst the public. What is the reason for this contraction in circulation? Simply a decline in trade and a fall in business transactions. Any doubt as to the accuracy of this view will be dispelled when one sees from the same accounts rendered by the Bank that the value of bills discounted by the Bank was £25,282,000 on January 20, 1855, whereas on May 12, 1855 it had fallen to £23,007,000—a decrease of £2,275,000. But the value of bills discounted by the Bank is the most reliable gauge of the quantity of business transacted between the Bank and the world of commerce. The evidence is even more conclusive if one considers that the Bank lowered its rate of interest to 4 per cent on April 28, and thus offered its commodity—capital—20 per cent cheaper than in the previous January. And from April 28, when the Bank lowered its rate of interest, to May 12 the quantity of bank-notes spent on discounting bills fell instead of rising—proof that under the present state of the economy capital is still too expensive at 4 per cent to find even the demand it found at the beginning of January at 5 per cent; proof that the fall in the rate of interest cannot be ascribed to a greater influx of capital but rather to a reduced demand on the part of commercial and industrial enterprises; proof, finally, that the increase in the metal held in the vaults of the Bank is only an increase in idle capital which, at this moment, cannot be utilised.

Written on May 19, 1855

First published in the *Neue Oder-Zeitung*, No. 233, May 22, 1855

Marked with the sign ×

Printed according to the newspaper

Published in English for the first time

Frederick Engels

THE CRIMEAN WAR

As we write, the field operations in the Crimea, to which we alluded some days since as in preparation,[a] must have commenced. With these operations, the war, so far as it is confined to the peninsula, enters into a new and probably decisive stage of development. The rapid arrival of the Piedmontese and French reserves, and particularly the sudden change by which Canrobert left his command for that of a single corps, while Pélissier takes the command in chief, are sure indications that the time for a change in the tactics of the Allies is at hand.

For a general description of the ground to which the theater of operations is to be transferred and a general statement of the forces about to be engaged we refer to our former article. It will be recollected that the Russian army of observation in communication with the north side of Sevastopol has its main position on the plateau between Inkermann and the point where the road from Balaklava to Sympheropol crosses the mountain-ridge, separating the valleys of the Chernaya and the Belbek. This position, of great natural strength, has been completely intrenched by the Russians. It extends for about four miles between the head of the bay of Sevastopol and the impassable range of mountains, and the Russians will be able to concentrate there at least 50,000 or 60,000 men, of infantry and artillery, which number is fully sufficient for the defense.

To attack this position in front would require a great numerical superiority and involve terrible sacrifices, while the Allies cannot

[a] Here and below Engels refers to his article "The New Move in the Crimea" (see this volume, pp. 180-85).—*Ed.*

afford either. Even if they succeeded in carrying the intrenchments, their losses would be so severe as to disable them from an energetic continuance of the campaign. They must therefore attempt to draw a number of Russians away from it and to find means to turn it. For this purpose the mysterious expedition to Kertch was sent out. About 15,000 allied troops embarked, were seen by the Russians to pass Yalta, sailed to Kertch, and returned again. Why they did not attempt a landing is sought to be explained by a telegraphic order from Paris. At all events, this mere apology for a demonstration must be pronounced an utter failure; no General in his senses would be induced to divide his troops by an expedition which does not venture to show even a semblance of fight. An attempt on Kaffa, if even it was under contemplation at headquarters, seems also to have been finally abandoned. To transport troops to Eupatoria and sally forth from that place cannot be under consideration, else the Piedmontese and French reserves would have been sent thither at once. And, as there is no other harbor or good roadstead on the coast between Balaklava and Kaffa, nor between Sevastopol and Eupatoria, the idea of turning the Russians by sea seems to have been finally given up, and nothing remains but to turn them by land, which, as we have already stated, must prove an exceedingly difficult operation.

There is, beside the road occupied by the Russians above Inkermann, but one other high road leading from Balaklava to Sympheropol. It runs along the south coast as far as Alushta, where it turns to the interior, passes the mountains east of Chatyr Dagh or Tent Mountain, the highest in the Crimea, at a point 2,800 feet above the sea and descends to Sympheropol by the valley of the Salghir, the main river of the Crimea. From Balaklava to Alushta there are four marches, from Alushta to Sympheropol three—together about 95 English miles. But as no side-roads exist allowing the troops to march in several parallel columns, the whole army would have to advance on this one road in one enormously extended column, requiring them to march at least for four or five days in one continuous defile. Near Alushta and on the pass there are some old fortifications, and we may be sure that the pass itself will be found strongly intrenched. Instead of seven days the army would perhaps require twelve before even the pass of Chatyr Dagh could be crossed—time enough for the Russians to make an attempt on the corps remaining to protect the siege, or to march with the greater part of their forces against the enemy and meet him with superior numbers on debouching from the hills, while light, movable columns sent along the foot-paths of the Upper Katsha and Alma would fall upon his flank and rear. The greatest fault of a flank movement by way of Alushta would, however, be its utter want of a base of operations. The open roadstead of Alushta forbids the idea of turning that place even into a temporary base; so that even before Alushta is passed, Russian light infantry descending by the foot-paths across the hills, may interrupt the communication with Balaklava quite effectually.

The march by Alushta, therefore, can hardly be undertaken. Its risks far outweigh its possible advantages. There is, however, another way of turning the Russians. If in the march by Alushta all the advantages offered to the Allies by the high road are far outweighed by the means of attack given to the Russians by the foot-paths, cannot these same foot-paths be turned to the same advantage by the Allies? This would imply an entirely different operation. In this case the Allies would place the main body of their field-troops, including the corps destined to invest the north side of Sevastopol, directly opposite the Russian camp above Inkermann, forcing their opponents thereby to keep the great body of their troops concentrated in the intrenchments. Meantime, Zouaves, Chasseurs, Light Infantry, British Rifles, and even the mounted Chasseurs d'Afrique, and what can be got together of mountain-artillery, would be formed into as many columns as there are foot-paths leading from the valley of Baidar and from the South Coast near Alupka, 30 miles from Balaklava, into the valleys of the Belbek and Katsha. A night march would conveniently bring the troops destined to turn the extreme Russian left across the valley of Baidar to the South Coast, where the enemy could no longer perceive them. Another march would bring them to Alupka. Above Alupka is the steep range of the Yaila mountains, forming on their northern slope an elevated plain about 2,000 feet above the sea, affording good pasturage for sheep, and descending by rocky precipices into the glens of the rivulets Biuk Uzen and Uzen Bash, which by their junction form the Belbek river. Three foot-paths lead up to this plain near Alupka, and pass into the glens of the two Uzens. All this ground is perfectly practicable for infantry such as the Zouaves and Chasseurs, who in Africa have got accustomed to mountain warfare of a far more difficult character. Then, from the valley of the Upper Chernaya, better known as the Baidar Valley, at least two foot-paths lead to the valley of the Upper Belbek, and finally one branches off from the Balaklava and Sympheropol road just before the mountain pass, and traverses the ridge three miles south-east of Mackenzie's farm, leading immediately to the left of the Russian intrenched position. Now if these paths be ever so difficult they must be practicable for the French light troops from Africa. "Where a goat passes, a man can pass; where a man, a whole battalion; where a battalion, a horse or so may get through with a little trouble; and finally, you will perhaps manage even to pass a field-gun."[a] In fact we should not be at all astonished if these sheep-tracks and foot-paths marked on the maps, should even turn out to be country roads, bad enough, but quite practicable for a flanking movement, in which even artillery might accompany the columns. In that case the turning should be carried out with as large a force as possible, and then the Russians will soon have to give up their intrenchments, even without a serious front attack. But if these paths should be impracticable for field-guns (rockets and mountain howitzers can go anywhere), the turning parties will take the character of mere movable columns, drive back the Russian troops as far as they can from the upper valleys of the Belbek, pass into that of the Katsha, menace the Russian rear, intercept their communications, destroy their convoys, collect trustworthy information, reconnoiter the country, draw upon themselves as many Russian detachments as possible, until that road which offers the least difficulties is made so far practicable as to admit of the passage of artillery. Then a strong force may be sent after them, and the Russian rear be so seriously menaced as to force an evacuation of the intrenchments. That an advance of mere infantry and light cavalry across these mountains on the left flank and rear of the Russians can have that effect we do not believe, as they could not seriously menace the Russian communications without descending into a country where artillery regains its full effect, and thereby secures the advantage to the party possessed of it. But there is no doubt that with a little ingenuity artillery can be made to follow the turning columns. At Jena,[157] Napoleon exhibited what can be done with a simple foot-path winding up a steep hill; in five hours the road was wide enough for guns, the Prussians were taken in flank, and the next day's victory secured. And where a Crimean araba can pass, a field-gun can pass too; some of the pathways in question, particularly those from the Chernaya to the Belbek, appear to be such old araba country roads.

But to carry out such a movement the possession of sufficient

[a] A free rendering of one of Napoleon I's principles of mountain warfare.— *Ed.*

forces is the first condition. The Russians will certainly have the advantage of numbers and of the better knowledge of the ground. The first may be done away with by a bold advance of Omer Pasha from Eupatoria to the Alma. Though the Russian superiority in cavalry will not allow him to move fast or far, yet by good maneuvering and well-secured communications he may force Prince Gorchakoff to detach more infantry against him. But for the Allies to depend upon any such collateral operation would be a matter of great uncertainty. In order to carry out, therefore, the advance from Balaklava, the best thing for them would be to transfer (as they were some time since reported to have done[a]), a day or two before the actual attack, some 20,000 Turks to the Chersonese, where they would be worth twice their number in Eupatoria. This would allow them to attack the Russians with nearly 110,000 men, including about 6,000 cavalry, to which force the Russians could oppose about 65,000 or 75,000 infantry (including 15,000 to 20,000 men from the garrison of the north side) and 10,000 cavalry. But as soon as the turning corps should begin to tell upon the left flank and rear of the Russians, the force to be opposed to it would be comparatively weak, as the drafts from the north side could not expose themselves to be cut off from their intrenched camp around the citadel; and therefore the Allies, being enabled to employ the whole of their available field-army wherever they like, would have a great superiority. In this case then they might with certainty count upon success; but if they attack the Russians single-handed, and the numerical proportions of both armies as stated by the most trustworthy authorities be correct, they stand but little chance. Their flanking corps would be too weak, and might be entirely neglected by the Russians, who by a bold sally from their lines could drive the weakened Allies down the precipices into the Chernaya.

Another movement on the part of the Allies has been suggested—an immediate assault on the south side of Sevastopol. We are even told that a peremptory order to undertake this assault had been telegraphed from Paris, and that Canrobert resigned because he did not feel warranted in executing a movement which in his opinion would imply a loss of 40,000 men. Now, from what we have seen of the military notions of Louis Bonaparte as displayed in his interference with the present campaign, it is not at all incredible that such an order should have

---

[a] The words in parenthesis were probably added by the editors of the *New-York Daily Tribune*.—*Ed.*

been given. But what is less probable is that even a reckless *sabreur*[a] like Pélissier should lend himself to execute such an order. The last month must have given the French soldiers a pretty good idea of what the resistance is like which they are to meet with on storming. And an operation which cannot be carried out without the loss of some 40,000 men—above one-third of the whole army available for the assault—has certainly very few favorable chances of success. Pélissier may eagerly wish to pick up the Marshal's baton which has slipped from the hands of Canrobert, but we very much doubt whether he is enough of a Bonapartist to stake his fortune and reputation against such odds. For supposing even that the assault was successful; that not only the first line of defense but also the second line was taken; that even the barricades, crenellated houses and defensive barracks forbidding the approach to the shore forts—that these shore forts too were carried and the whole of the south side in the hands of the Allies, at a loss we will say of only 30,000 to a Russian loss of 20,000—what then? The Allies would have lost 10,000 men more than the Russians, the place would instantly have to be abandoned; and the campaign in the field would become even more difficult than before.

But there is one fact which at once precludes the idea of an immediate general assault. From some half-official reports we were induced in a former article on the siege[b] to admit, merely for argument's sake, that the Russians had been driven out of their new outworks in front of the place. We stated at the same time that we had every reason to doubt the correctness of such reports, as any such advantage gained would have been loudly and distinctly announced by the Allies. Now we are indeed positively informed by the Russians that the Kamtschatka (the Mamelon), Selenghinsk and Volhynsk redoubts are still in their possession, while evidence from the allied camp not only goes to confirm this, but also acknowledges that further outworks have been thrown up by the besieged. Thus the advantage gained by the Allies in pushing their advanced approaches nearer to the fortress has been fully made up for by the counter-approaches of the Russians, and the line where both parties can meet each other in equal strength is very distant yet from the main ditch. Now, an assault becomes advisable only when the line, where the force of the attack for common siege operations is equal to that of the defense, lies in the main ditch itself; otherwise it is clear that the

[a] War-horse.—*Ed.*
[b] See this volume, p. 170.—*Ed.*

storming columns would be broken down and shattered before they could reach the top of the breastwork. Thus as long as the Russians cannot be driven back across the main ditch, it will be impossible to assault the main rampart situated behind this main ditch. As to carrying the second line constructed behind that ditch, it is entirely out of the question at the present time.

There may be a chance for partial assaults on the left or town side from the Quarantine to the Flagstaff Bastion where the main French attack is carried on. But here the policy of the French Government keeps us in utter darkness as to the extent and strength of the Russian outworks, and the recent Russian dispatches, of late being all telegraphic, contain no definite and detailed description. On the Flagstaff Bastion, however, it is acknowledged by the Russians themselves that the French works are close to the main rampart and that a mine has been sprung under it, though without any considerable results. Here, then, a local assault might be successful but from the salient position of this bastion and the commanding ground behind (the Russian Jasonovsky Redoubt[a]) it is very doubtful whether anything would be gained by the conquest of the bastion, which must have been isolated from the remainder of the works by one or two cross-ramparts in its rear, thereby preventing the storming columns from establishing themselves in it or at least from penetrating any further.

Thus whether the assault is attempted, or field operations are undertaken, the Allies will have to struggle with considorable difficulties. But at any rate the drowsy style of warfare pursued since the arrival of the Allies before Sevastopol is drawing to a close; and more stirring events and operations of real military interest may now be looked for.

Written about May 21, 1855

First published in the *New-York Daily Tribune*, No. 4411, June 8, 1855; reprinted in the *New-York Weekly Tribune*, No. 718, June 16, 1855 as a leading article

Reproduced from the *New-York Daily Tribune*

---

[a] The *New-York Daily Tribune* has: "the Russian Garden Battery".—*Ed.*

Karl Marx

ON THE REFORM MOVEMENT[158]

London, May 21. Today all the London newspapers publish an address from the City reformers, or rather their executive committee, to the "People of England".[a] The style of the document is dry, businesslike, not quite as lofty as that of the trade circulars that periodically emanate from the same source, offering for sale coffee, tea, sugar, spices and other products of the tropical countries in a more or less tastefully arranged fabric of phrases. The Association[b] promises to provide the material for a veritable physiology of the various government departments and to disclose all the mysteries of Downing Street,[c] Downing Street which is full of hereditary wisdom. This is what it promises. For its own part, it demands that the electoral districts of England send to Parliament candidates freely chosen according to their hearts' desire and recommended solely by merit, instead of, as hitherto, imposed on them by the aristocratic clubs. It thus recognises the existing privileged electoral districts as normal, the selfsame districts which, in their corruptibility, their reliance on a few clubs, their lack of independence, it admits to being the birthplace of the present House of Commons, and thus of the present government. It does not want to dissolve these exclusive districts, nor to extend them, but simply to moralise. Why not then appeal directly to the conscience of the oligarchy itself, instead of threatening it with the abolition of its privileges? It should at any rate be an easier job to convert the oligarchical heads than the oligarchical electoral

[a] Excerpts from this address were later published in *The People's Paper*, No. 160, May 26, 1855.—*Ed.*

[b] The Administrative Reform Association (see this volume, pp. 166-69).—*Ed.*

[c] 10 Downing Street is the British Prime Minister's official residence.—*Ed.*

districts. The City Association would obviously like to bring into existence an anti-aristocratic movement, but a movement *within* the limits of the *legal* (as Guizot called it), the official England. And how do they intend to rouse the stagnant bog of electoral districts? How to drive them into emancipating themselves from interests and customs which make them the vassals of a few select clubs and the pillars of the governing oligarchy? With a physiology of Downing Street? Not entirely. Also by means of *pressure from without*, by mass meetings and the like. And how are they going to set the non-official, non-enfranchised masses in motion so as to influence the privileged circle of electoral districts? By inviting them to renounce the People's Charter (which basically contains nothing but the demand for *universal suffrage* and the conditions under which alone it can become a reality in England), and to acknowledge the privileges of these electoral districts which, by the admission of the City reformers themselves, are in the process of decay. The City Association must be aware of the example of the "financial and parliamentary reformers". It knows that this movement, headed by Hume, Bright, Cobden, Walmsley and Thompson, failed because it sought to replace the People's Charter by the so-called Little Charter,[159] because it merely wanted to make concessions to the masses, merely to reach a compromise with them. Do they imagine that *without* concessions they can achieve what the others could not achieve *despite* their concessions? Or do they deduce from the Anti-Corn Law movement that it is possible to set the English people in motion for partial reforms? But the object of that movement was very general, very popular, very tangible. The symbol of the Anti-Corn Law League was, as is well known, a big thick loaf of bread in contrast to the diminutive loaf of the Protectionists. A loaf of bread, particularly in the famine year 1846, naturally speaks quite a different popular dialect from a "physiology of Downing Street". We need not recall a well-known booklet, *The Physiology of the City*.[a] There it is demonstrated with the greatest precision that however well the gentlemen may run their own businesses, in the management of *common* enterprises, for example the various *insurance companies*, they more or less faithfully follow the official pattern of Downing Street. Their management of the *railways*, with the glaring frauds, swindles and total neglect of safety

[a] The reference is to D. M. Evans' pamphlet *The City; or, the Physiology of London Business*, published anonymously. Marx quotes a passage from it in Volume III of *Capital*.— *Ed.*

precautions, is so notorious that the question has been raised more than once in the press, in Parliament and outside Parliament whether the railways should not be placed under direct state control and taken out of the hands of the private capitalists! The physiology of Downing Street, then, will accomplish nothing—as the English say, "This will not do, sir!"[a]

Written on May 21, 1855

First published in the *Neue Oder-Zeitung*, No. 237, May 24, 1855

Marked with the sign ×

Printed according to the newspaper

[a] Marx uses the English phrase.—*Ed.*

Karl Marx

A CRITIQUE OF THE CRIMEAN AFFAIR.— FROM PARLIAMENT

London, May 23. The menacing discontent in the allied Army and Navy outside Sevastopol caused by the recall of the Kerch expedition has found an echo, if only a weak, faint one, in the London press. People are beginning to fear that the unity and artistic course of the war drama in the Crimea are threatened less by the Russians than by the presumptuous and capricious intervention of a *deus ex machina*,[a] the military genius of Napoleon III. The exhibition of this genius in the well-known strategic didactical "essay" in the *Moniteur*[b] is in fact anything but soothing and reassuring. Until now, however, the distance between the theatre of war and the Tuileries has provided a kind of guarantee against actual interference by the military dilettantism of Paris. Now submarine telegraph has eliminated the distances, and with the distances the guarantee, and John Bull, who is wont to call himself "the most thinking people of the world",[c] is beginning to reflect, to grumble and complain that the British Army and Navy are expected to furnish the *corpus vile*[d] for the inherited and providentially existing "military genius", to perform his experiments on.

---

[a] Literally "a god from a machine" (in the ancient Greek and Roman theatre, actors playing gods appeared on the stage with the help of machinery); in a figurative sense, a person or event that appears suddenly and solves a difficult situation.— *Ed.*

[b] This refers to the leading article "Paris, le 10 avril. Expédition d'Orient", published in *Le Moniteur universel*, No. 101, April 11, 1855. The article contained Napoleon III's instructions to Marshal Saint-Arnaud. For a critique of it see this volume, pp. 146-50.— *Ed.*

[c] Marx uses the English words.— *Ed.*

[d] Literally "worthless body".— *Ed.*

Today's *Morning Herald*[a] asserts positively that the expedition has been recalled because Bonaparte has revived his dangerous idea of storming Sevastopol from the south side. We do not doubt for a moment that the military genius of the Tuileries is obsessed by this *idée fixe*, but we cannot persuade ourselves that even a simple *sabreur*[b] such as Pélissier is capable of carrying out such a senselessly ruinous plan. Hence we believe that it has been decided to attempt a mass crossing of the Chernaya and that it was deemed inadvisable to split the main force by detaching a corps of 12,000 men. In fact, instead of detaching these 12,000 men, just before the army sets out, 15,000-20,000 Turks ought to be embarked in Eupatoria and incorporated into the main army, only leaving behind a garrison of sufficient size to hold the place. As stated in an earlier letter,[c] the entire success of the campaign depends on the strength of the army that crosses the Chernaya. However that may be, the recall of the Kerch expedition is fresh evidence of the uncertainty and vacillation and the shilly-shallying bungling that are nowadays passed off as "idées napoléoniennes".[d]

Meanwhile the heroes improvised for the purpose of the *coup d'état* wear out with incredible rapidity. The array was headed by Espinasse, who after his ignominious campaign in the Dobrudja[160] was forced by the Zouaves to retreat head over heels to Paris. This *Espinasse* is the same man who, after being entrusted with guarding the building of the National Assembly, handed it over to its enemies.[161] The second in the line of descent was *Leroy*, alias *Saint-Arnaud*, the War Minister of December 2. He was followed by *Forey*, so bold in the persecution of the unfortunate peasants of south-east France, and so considerately humane towards the Muscovites. The army's suspicion that he was revealing the secrets of the French Council of War to the Russians made it necessary to remove him from the Crimea to Africa. Finally *Canrobert* was demoted on account of notorious incompetence. The irony of history has appointed *Pélissier* as his successor, and thus more or less commander-in-chief of the Anglo-French army—the same Pélissier of whom in 1841 it was asserted over and over again in Parliament, in London officers' clubs and at country-meetings,[e] in *The Times* and in *Punch*, that *no* honourable English officer could

---

[a] "Siege of Sebastopol", *The Morning Herald*, No. 22438, May 23, 1855.—*Ed.*
[b] War-horse.—*Ed.*
[c] See this volume, p. 137.—*Ed.*
[d] An allusion to Louis Bonaparte's book *Des idées napoléoniennes* published in Paris in 1839.—*Ed.*
[e] Marx uses the English words "country-meetings".—*Ed.*

ever serve alongside "that ferocious *monster*".[a] And now the British Army is not only serving *alongside* him, but *under* him—the entire British Army! Just after the Whigs and their Foreign Secretary Palmerston had been defeated by the Tories, Palmerston called a meeting of his constituents in Tiverton and proved his right to break the Anglo-French alliance and unite with Russia by the fact that the French government, that Louis Philippe was employing such a "*monster*" as Pélissier in his service. It must be admitted that while the French Army is paying dearly for its revolt in December, things are not all "roses" for England either, in its alliance with the restored empire.

The Ministry suffered a defeat in the Commons yesterday, which proves nothing except that Parliament occasionally avenges itself on the Ministers for the scorn it enjoys "out of doors".[b] A certain Mr. *Wise* tabled the motion, that

> "it is the opinion of this House that complete revision of our diplomatic establishments recommended in the report of the Select Committee of 1850 on Official Salaries should be carried into effect".[c]

Mr. Wise is a friend of Palmerston. His motion has been drifting about on the agenda of the House for about two years without coming up for discussion. Chance yesterday cast it before the discontented Commons. Wise made his speech, thinking that, after a few remarks by Palmerston, he would be able to play the usual game and withdraw his motion. But in contravention of the agreement Mr. Baillie picked up the motion that Wise had dropped and it was carried, despite Wise and Palmerston, by a majority of 112 to 57. This defeat did not in the least worry an old experienced tactician like Palmerston for he knows that in order to preserve an appearance of independence the House must occasionally condemn a ministerial motion to death and promote an anti-ministerial motion to life. Disraeli's motion, on the other hand, had the effect of an electric shock on the ministerial benches.[162] Palmerston himself, a master at parliamentary play-acting, congratulated "the writers and actors of this unforgettable scene". This was not irony. It was the involuntary tribute of an artist to his rival when the latter beats him at his own game. In the Monday sitting[d] Palmerston had toyed so skilfully with Milner

---

[a] Marx uses the English phrase.—*Ed.*
[b] Marx uses the English words.—*Ed.*
[c] Wise's motion in the House of Commons and the following debate were reported in *The Times*, No. 22061, May 23, 1855.—*Ed.*
[d] May 21, 1855.—*Ed.*

Gibson and Gladstone and Herbert and Bright and Lord Vane that it seemed certain that all debates on foreign policy would be postponed until after Whitsun, the Ministry and House being obliged to proceed in a particular manner, and that the noble Viscount could be sure of a dictatorship of several weeks' duration. The only day still available for debate, Thursday,[a] was reserved for Layard's reform motion. So no one could prevent Palmerston from concluding peace over Whitsun and, as he has done more than once, surprising the House when it re-assembled with one of his notorious treaties. The House, for its own part, might not have been unwilling to submit to this fate of surprise. Peace made *behind its back*, even peace *à tout prix*, was acceptable with a few *post festum* gestures of protest for decency's sake. But the moment the House and the Ministry were obliged to declare their views *before* the adjournment, the latter could no longer spring any surprises, nor the former let itself be taken unawares. Hence the consternation when Disraeli got up and tabled his motion and Layard relinquished *his* day to Disraeli. This "conspiracy between Layard and Disraeli", as the *Post* called the affair, thus brought to naught all the skilful manoeuvring since the "end" of the Vienna Conference, which has not yet been concluded.[163]

Written on May 23, 1855

First published in the *Neue Oder-Zeitung*, No. 241, May 26, 1855

Marked with the sign ×

Printed according to the newspaper

Published in English for the first time

[a] May 24, 1855.—*Ed.*

Frederick Engels

THE NEW FRENCH COMMANDER [164]

It is certain that Gen. Canrobert's resignation of the command of the French army in the Crimea did not take place a moment too soon. The *morale* of the army was already in a very unsatisfactory and doubtful state. After they had been made to undergo the hardships and dangers of an unparalleled Winter campaign, the soldiers had been kept in something like order and good spirits by the return of Spring and by ever-repeated promises of a speedy and glorious termination of the siege. But day after day passed away without making any progress, while the Russians actually advanced out of their lines and constructed redoubts on the disputed ground between the two parties. This roused the spirit of the French soldiers, the Zouaves mutinied, and the consequence was that on February 23 they were led to the butchery on Mount Sapun. A little more bustling—it can hardly be called activity—was then shown on the part of the allied commanders; but there was evidently no distinct aim, and no definite plan was followed up consistently.

Again, the spirit of mutiny among the French was kept down by the continued sallies of the Russians and by the opening of the second bombardment which was—positively for the last time—to end in the grand spectacle of the assault. But the fire went on, slackened, and slackened still more, and at last ceased without any attempt at an assault. Then came engineering operations, slow, difficult and barren of those results which keep up the spirits of soldiers. Soon they got tired again of nightly trench-fighting, where hundreds fell to no visible purpose. Again the assault was demanded, and again Canrobert had to make promises which he knew he could not fulfill. Then Pélissier saved him from a renewal of disorderly scenes by the night attack of the lst of May; it is stated that not only did Pélissier plan this attack, but even execute it in spite of a counter-order from Canrobert arriving the moment the troops were put in motion. This affair is said to have revived the courage of the soldiers.

Meantime the reserve and the Piedmontese arrived. The Chersonese became crowded. The soldiers considered that these reenforcements enabled them to do anything. Why was nothing done? The expedition to Kertch was resolved upon, and sailed. But before it had reached the offing of that town a dispatch from Paris induced Canrobert to recall it. Raglan of course gave in at once. Brown and Lyons, the commanders of the British land and sea forces on this expedition, besought their French colleagues to attack the place in disobedience to the order; in vain—the expedition had to sail back, and it is even stated that Canrobert had in his hurry misread the order, which was merely conditional. Now the exasperation of the troops was no longer to be mastered. Even the English spoke in unmistakable terms; the French were in a state bordering on mutiny. Accordingly there was nothing left for Canrobert but to resign the command of an army over which he had lost all control and influence. The only possible successor was Pélissier. The soldiers were sick of these young generals, advanced to the highest honors in the quick hotbed of Bonapartism. They had all the while been clamoring for a leader of long standing of the old African school—a man who had held a responsible command in the Algerian wars, and held it with credit. Pélissier was almost the only man of the sort at the command of the Emperor; he had been sent there with the evident intention of being, sooner or later, made the successor of Canrobert. Whatever else his qualifications might be, he had the confidence of the troops, and that is a great deal.

But he takes his command under difficult circumstances. He must act, and speedily too, before the men lose the freshness of the enthusiasm which the certainty of immediate action must have inspired them with. The assault being impossible, nothing remains but to take the field, and that can be done only by turning the Russian position in the manner we have previously described.[a] Indeed, we find our views on this subject confirmed by a British officer in the London *Morning Herald*, who says that it is the general opinion among competent men that there is no other way to take the field with success.

---

[a] See this volume, pp. 201-07.—*Ed.*

There is however one very serious difficulty in carrying out this plan. The French with all their army have no more means of transport than will supply 30,000 men for a very short distance from the coast. As to the English, their means of transport would be exhausted if they had to supply one single division no further off than Chorgun on the Chernaya. How then is the field to be taken, in case of success the north side of Sevastopol invested, the enemy pursued to Bakshiserai and a junction effected with Omer Pasha? Of course the Russians will take very good care to leave nothing but ruins behind them, and a supply of carts, horses or camels can only be obtained after the Allies have completely routed their enemy. We shall see how Pélissier will extricate himself from this difficulty.

Written about May 24, 1855

First published in the *New-York Daily Tribune,* No. 4414, June 12, 1855, reprinted in the *New-York Semi-Weekly Tribune,* No. 1049, June 15, 1855 as a leading article

Reproduced from the *New-York Daily Tribune*

Karl Marx and Frederick Engels

PROLOGUE AT LORD PALMERSTON'S.—COURSE OF THE LATEST EVENTS IN THE CRIMEA [165]

London, May 24. No sooner had Disraeli's motion [166] presented the prospect of a regular battle between the *Ins* and *Outs*[a] in the House of Commons than Palmerston sounded the alarm and, a few hours before the commencement of the sitting, he asked his ministerial retinue along with Peelites, Manchester School and so-called Independents to come to his official residence in Downing Street.[b] Two hundred and three M.P.s turned up, including Mr. *Layard* who felt incapable of resisting the ministerial siren-call. Palmerston played the diplomat, the penitent, the apologist, the appeaser, the wheedler. Smilingly he bore with the censorious rebukes of Messrs Bright, Lowe and Layard. He left it to Lord Robert Grosvenor and Sir James Graham to mediate with the "agitated". From the moment he saw the malcontents clustering about him in his official residence, mingling with his faithful followers, he knew he had them in his pocket. They were disgruntled but anxious for reconciliation. Thus the result of the sitting in the Commons was anticipated; nothing more remained but the parliamentary performance of the comedy before the public. The crisis was over. We shall be sending a brief account of this comedy as soon as the final act has been played out.

The types of illness peculiar to the spring and summer season in the Crimea have been reactivated by the return of warm, humid weather. Cholera and ague have again made their appearance in

[a] Marx uses the English words "Ins" and "Outs" (the reference is to the supporters and opponents of the government).—*Ed.*

[b] 10 Downing Street is the official residence of the British Prime Minister. These details are contained in "The Ministry and Its Supporters" published in *The Times*, No. 22063, May 25, 1855.—*Ed.*

the allied camp, not as yet in particularly virulent form but sufficiently so to provide a warning for the future. Also in evidence is the miasma given off by the mass of putrefying animal matter that is buried only a few inches below ground throughout the entire extent of the Chersonese. The *morale* of the besieging army is also in a very unsatisfactory state. After they had undergone the hardships and dangers of an unparalleled Winter campaign, the soldiers had been kept in something like order and good spirits by the return of Spring and by ever-repeated promises of a speedy and glorious termination of the siege. But day after day passed away without making any progress, while the Russians actually advanced out of their lines and constructed redoubts on the disputed ground between the two parties. The Zouaves became unruly and were consequently led to the slaughter on Mount Sapun on February 23. A little more bustling—it can hardly be called activity—was then shown on the part of the allied commanders; but there was evidently no distinct aim, and no definite plan was followed up consistently.

Again, the spirit of mutiny among the French was kept down by the continued sallies of the Russians which kept them occupied and by the opening of the second bombardment which was this time definitely to end in the grand spectacle of the assault. A deplorable fiasco ensued. Then came engineering operations, slow, difficult and barren of those results which keep up the spirits of soldiers. Soon they got tired again of nightly trench-fighting, where hundreds fell to no visible purpose. Again the assault was demanded, and again Canrobert was compelled to make promises which he knew he could not fulfil. Then Pélissier saved him from a renewal of disorderly scenes by the night attack of the 1st of May; it is stated that Pélissier executed it in spite of a counter-order from Canrobert arriving the moment the troops were put in motion. The success of this affair is said to have revived the courage of the soldiers. Meantime the Piedmontese reserve arrived; the Chersonese became crowded. The soldiers considered that these reinforcements enabled them to go into action immediately. Something *had* to be done. The expedition to Kerch was resolved upon, and sailed. But before it had reached the offing of that town a dispatch from *Paris* induced Canrobert to *recall* it. Raglan of course gave in at once. Brown, and Lyons, the commanders of the British land and sea forces on this expedition, besought their French colleagues to attack the place *in spite* of the countermand; in vain—the expedition had to sail back. Now the exasperation of the troops was no longer to be mastered. Even the

English spoke in unmistakable terms; the French were in a state bordering on mutiny. Accordingly there was nothing left for Canrobert but to resign the command of an army over which he had lost all control and influence.

Pélissier was the only possible successor, since the soldiers, long sick of generals who had shot up in the forcing-house of Bonapartism, *had been repeatedly calling for a leader of the old African school.* Pélissier enjoys the confidence of the soldiers but he is taking command under difficult circumstances. He must act, and act quickly. Since an assault is impossible, there is no other choice than to move into the field against the Russians, not, however, in the manner we have previously described when the entire army would have to march along *one single* road that had, moreover, been heavily barricaded by the Russians, but by distributing the army over the numerous small upland paths and tracks mostly used only by shepherds and their flocks, which would make it possible to outflank the Russian position. One difficulty arises here. The French have only sufficient means of transport to supply about 30,000 men for a very short distance from the coast. The means of transport of the English would be exhausted if they had to convey a single division no further than Chorgun on the Chernaya. Given this lack of transport it is difficult to see how then is the field to be taken, in case of success the north side of Sevastopol invested, the enemy pursued to Bakshiserai and a junction effected with *Omer Pasha*? Especially since the Russians in accordance with their custom will take good care to leave nothing but ruins behind them, so that a supply of carts, horses, camels, etc., can only be obtained after the Allies have completely routed their enemy. We shall see how Pélissier will extricate himself from this difficulty.

We have previously drawn attention to a number of peculiar circumstances connected with Pélissier's appointment.[a] However there is a further aspect to be considered here. When the war began, that Bonapartist general *par excellence*, S[ain]t-Arnaud, was entrusted with the supreme command. He did his emperor the service of promptly dying. Not one of the Bonapartists of the first rank was appointed in his place, neither Magnan, nor Castellane, nor Roguet, nor Baraguay d'Hilliers. Recourse was had to Canrobert, a man tarred neither so heavily nor so long with the Bonapartist brush, but having greater African experience. Now, with another change of command, the Bonapartists *du lendemain*[b]

[a] See this volume, pp. 212-13.—*Ed.*
[b] Of tomorrow.—*Ed.*

have been passed over in the same way as those *de la veille*,[a] and the post awarded to a simple African general of no pronounced political complexion, but with many years of service and a name in the army. Must not this descending line inevitably lead to *Changarnier, Lamoricière* or *Cavaignac*, i.e. away from Bonapartism?

"Unfitness for peace no less than for war—such is our situation!" observed a day or two ago a French statesman for whom everything is at stake with the imperial régime. Every action of the restored empire, right up to the appointment of *Pélissier*, proves that he was right.

Written on May 24, 1855

First published in the *Neue Oder-Zeitung*, No. 243, May 29, 1855

Marked with the sign ×

The English version was published in the *New-York Daily Tribune*, No. 4414, June 12, 1855 and reprinted in the *New-York Semi-Weekly Tribune*, No. 1049, June 15, 1855 as a leading article

Printed according to the newspaper

Published in English for the first time

[a] Of the day before.—*Ed.*

Karl Marx

PARLIAMENTARY REFORM.—THE BREAK-OFF AND CONTINUATION OF THE VIENNA CONFERENCE. —THE SO-CALLED WAR OF ANNIHILATION

London, May 26. Further details have become known regarding the *Comité du Salut Ministériel*[a] called by Lord Palmerston the day before yesterday before the opening of the House of Commons, characteristic of the parliamentary mechanism and the position of the various factions which have provided the Ministry with a majority of 100 votes. Right at the outset Palmerston threatened *resignation* if Disraeli's motion[167] were carried. He threatened the prospect of a *Tory Ministry*.[b] The so-called radical parliamentarians, poor fellows,[c] have enjoyed the privilege of having this great and ultimate threat suspended over them since 1830, whenever they break out in mutiny. It never fails to recall them to a sense of discipline. And why? Because they fear the mass movement that is inevitable under a Tory Ministry. How literally correct this view is may be gathered from the confession of a radical who is himself a minister at the moment, if only Minister responsible for the Crown Forests, Sir William Molesworth. This job is well suited for a man who has all along possessed the talent of not being able to see the wood for the trees. M.P. for Southwark, a part of London, he received an invitation from his constituents to attend a public meeting for Southwark held last Wednesday.[d] (N.B. At this meeting, as at the majority of those hitherto held in the provinces, a resolution was passed that administrative

[a] Committee of Ministerial Safety. (See this volume, p. 218).—*Ed.*

[b] In his speech in the House of Commons on May 25, 1855, a report on which was published in *The Times*, No. 22064, May 26, 1855.—*Ed.*

[c] Marx uses the English words "poor fellows".—*Ed.*

[d] May 23, 1855.—*Ed.*

reform without prior parliamentary reform is *sham* and *humbug*.[a] Molesworth did not appear but sent a letter and in this letter the radical and Cabinet minister declared: "If Mr. Disraeli's motion is carried the need for administrative reform will become more evident." Which "evidently" means: If the Tories take over the government the reform movement will become serious. The threat of resignation, though, was not the biggest gun that Palmerston fired off. He alluded to the *dissolution of Parliament* and to the fate of the many unfortunates who scarcely three years ago had bought their way into the "honourable House" at tremendous sacrifice. This argument was irresistible. It was no longer just a question of *his* resignation. It was a question of *their* resignation.

Although Palmerston thus secured a majority of 100 votes against Disraeli's motion, by threatening some with *his* resignation, and others with *their* ejection from the House of Commons, presenting some with the prospect of peace and others with the prospect of war—the newly founded coalition immediately collapsed again, this happening during the public performance of the agreed farce. The statements which the ministers were induced to make during the debate neutralised the statements they had made *en petit comité*.[b] The mortar which loosely held together the reluctant groupings crumbled away, not in a hurricane but in the parliamentary wind. For in yesterday's sitting Roebuck put a question to the Prime Minister about the rumoured re-opening of the Vienna Conferences. He demanded to know whether the British ambassador in Vienna[c] was instructed to take part in these conferences. Ever since the return of Russell, that hapless diplomat, from Vienna, Palmerston, as is common knowledge, had rejected all debates on war or diplomacy on the pretext of not jeopardising the "admittedly interrupted but by no means concluded Vienna Conferences". Milner Gibson had withdrawn or postponed his motion[168] last Monday[d] because according to a statement by the noble Lord "the conferences were still pending". On that occasion Palmerston had expressly emphasised that the British government was leaving it to *Austria*, "our ally within certain limits", to devise new starting-points for peace negotiations. The continued existence of the Vienna Conference was, he said, beyond all doubt. Though Russell had left Vienna, Westmorland was continuing to reside in Vienna, where, moreover,

[a] Marx uses the English words "sham" and "humbug".—*Ed.*
[b] In a small circle.—*Ed.*
[c] J. F. Westmorland.—*Ed.*
[d] May 21, 1855.—*Ed.*

the plenipotentiaries of all the great powers were engaged in consultations; in other words, all the elements of a permanent conference were present.[a]

Since Monday, the day Palmerston favoured Parliament with these revelations, a major change had occurred in the situation. Disraeli's motion and a day spent debating it[b] separated the Palmerston of Monday from the Palmerston of Friday, and Disraeli had motivated his motion with the misgiving that the government might "drift into a shameful peace" during the recess, just as it had "drifted" into a shameful war under Aberdeen's auspices. Thus the outcome of the vote hung on Palmerston's answer to Roebuck's question. This time he could not call up the ghost of the Vienna Conference and inform the House that in Vienna they were deciding, while in the Halls of St. Stephen's[c] they were debating: that here they were proposing but there they were disposing. This was all the more impossible as only the previous evening Russell had disowned Austria and the peace projects and the Vienna Conference. Accordingly he replied to Roebuck: the Vienna Conference had *not* been resumed, and the British envoy had *no* permission to attend a new conference without special instructions from Downing Street. Then Milner Gibson got up in a state of moral indignation. A few days ago, he said, the noble Lord had declared that the Conference was merely *suspended*, and that Westmorland possessed *absolute authority* to negotiate at it. Had he been deprived of this authority, if so, when?—Authority! replied Palmerston, his authority is as complete as ever, but he has not the power to use it. To possess authority and to be permitted to use it are two different things. This answer to Roebuck's question broke the ties between the Ministry and the peace-at-any-price party augmented by the Peelites. But this was neither the only nor the most important "misunderstanding". The day before yesterday Russell was stretched on the rack by Disraeli and tortured and pricked with red-hot pins for hours. With one hand Disraeli displayed the rhetorical lionskin in which the Whig Aztec likes to parade; with the other, the diminutive gutta-percha manikin hiding beneath the

---

[a] Palmerston's speech in the House of Commons on May 21, 1855. *The Times*, No. 22060, May 22, 1855.—*Ed.*

[b] May 24, 1855. Below Marx quotes a passage from Disraeli's speech and mentions the speeches of Gladstone and Russell at that sitting. *The Times*, No. 22063, May 25, 1855.—*Ed.*

[c] The House of Commons met in St. Stephen's Chapel, Westminster Palace, since 1547.—*Ed.*

skin. Although Russell is armed against harsh words by his long parliamentary experience and adventures like the invulnerable Siegfried against wounds, he was unable to remain composed in the face of this ruthless, naked exposure of his true self. He pulled faces while Disraeli spoke. He twisted and turned in his seat uneasily and incessantly while Gladstone followed with his sermon. When Gladstone made a rhetorical pause Russell got up and was only reminded by the laughter of the House that his turn had not yet come. At last Gladstone fell silent for good. At last Russell could unburden his oppressed heart. He now told the House everything that he had wisely concealed from Prince Gorchakov and Herr von Titov. Russia, whose "*honour and dignity*" he supported at the Vienna Conference, now seemed to him to be a power unscrupulously striving for mastery of the world, making treaties as pretexts for wars of conquest, making wars so as to spread poison with treaties. Not only England but all Europe seemed to him to be threatened, nothing short of a war of annihilation would do. He alluded to Poland too. In short, the Vienna diplomat was suddenly transformed into a "street demagogue" (one of his favourite expressions). In a cunningly calculating way Disraeli had launched him into this odic style.

But immediately *after the division* Sir James Graham, the Peelite, rose to speak.[a] Was he to believe his ears? Russell had declared a "new war" on Russia, a crusade, a war to the death, a war of the nationalities. The matter was too serious for the debate to be concluded now. The House was even more in the dark about the intentions of the ministers than before. Russell thought that *after* the vote he could cast off the lionskin in his usual way. He therefore did not beat about the bush. Graham had "*misunderstood*" him. He only sought "security for Turkey". There you are! cried Disraeli, you who have acquitted the Ministry of the charge of "ambiguous language" by rejecting my motion, you now hear how honest he is! This Russell retracts *after* the vote the whole of the speech that he made *before* the vote! I congratulate you on your voting!

The House could not resist this *demonstratio ad oculos*[b]; the debate was adjourned until after the Whitsun recess; the victory won by the Ministry had been lost again in a moment. The comedy was only supposed to consist of two acts, and to end with the division. Now it has had an epilogue added to it that threatens

---

[a] Graham's speech in the House of Commons on May 25, 1855.—*Ed.*
[b] Visual proof.—*Ed.*

9—3754

to be more serious than the grand historical drama. In the meanwhile the parliamentary recess will enable us to analyse the first two acts more closely. It remains unprecedented in the annals of Parliament that the debate should only start in earnest *after* the vote. Hitherto, parliamentary battles have usually ended with the vote just as romantic novels end with the wedding.

Written on May 26, 1855

First published in the *Neue Oder-Zeitung*, No. 245, May 30, 1855

Marked with the sign ×

Printed according to the newspaper

Published in English for the first time

Karl Marx

DISRAELI'S MOTION

London, May 28. The Commons were offered a "rich menu", as the elegant Gladstone put it, in the choice between Disraeli's motion and Baring's amendment to Disraeli's motion, between Sir William Heathcote's sub-amendment to Baring's amendment and Mr. Lowe's counter-sub-amendment against Disraeli, Baring and Sir William Heathcote.[a] Disraeli's motion contains a censure of the ministers and an address on the war to the Crown, the former definite and the latter flexible, both connected by a link accessible to the parliamentary thought process. The feeble form in which the war address was wrapped was soon explained. Disraeli had to apprehend mutiny in his own camp. One Tory, the Marquis of Granby, spoke *against* it, another, Lord Stanley, spoke *for* it, but both in a spirit of peace. Baring's amendment was a *ministerial* one. It suppresses the vote of censure against the Cabinet, and adopts the bellicose part of the motion with Disraeli's own terminology, only prefacing it with the words that the House "has seen with regret that the Conferences of Vienna have not led to a termination of hostilities". He is blowing hot and cold in the same breath. The "regret" for the peace lobby, the "continuation of the war" for the war lobby, no definite obligation on the part of the Cabinet to either lobby—a *shell-trap*[b] for votes, black and white, a part for the flute and a part for the trumpet. Heathcote's sub-amendment rounds off Baring's two-tongued amendment in a thoroughly idyllic turn of phrase by adding the words: "that the

[a] Disraeli's motion and the amendments to it, and his speech in the House of Commons on May 24, 1855, were reported in *The Times*, No. 22063, May 25, 1855; the amendments and the speech by Lowe in the Commons on May 25, 1855 were published in *The Times*, No. 22064, May 26, 1855.—*Ed.*

[b] Marx uses the English expression.—*Ed.*

House is still cherishing the hope" ("cherishing"[a] is a thoroughly cosy expression) "that the communications in progress may arrive at a successful issue". Lowe's amendment, on the other hand, declares the peace negotiations closed with the rejection of the Third Point[169] by Russia and thus motivates the war address to the Crown. It can be seen that the eclectic amendment of the Ministry has both sides, which it sought to hush up and neutralise, independently and peacefully confronting each other. Continuation of the Vienna Conferences! cries Heathcote. No Vienna Conference! retorts Lowe. Vienna Conference and warfare! whispers Baring. We shall hear the themes of this terzetto performed in a week's time, and for the moment return to the debate on Disraeli's motion, on whose first night[b] only three principal political personages appeared, *Disraeli*, *Gladstone* and *Russell*, the first pungent and drastic, the second smooth and casuistic, the third banal and blustering.

We do not agree with the objection that in his personal attack on Russell, Disraeli lost sight of the "actual issue". The secrets of the Anglo-Russian war are not to be found on the battlefield but in Downing Street.[c] Russell, Foreign Secretary at the time of the Petersburg Cabinet's secret communications, Russell, envoy extraordinary at the time of the last Vienna Conference, Russell, at the same time Leader[a] of the House of Commons; he is Downing Street personified, he is its secret *revealed*. Not because he is the soul of the Ministry but because he is its mouth-piece.

Towards the end of 1854, relates Disraeli, Russell gave a blast on the trumpet of war, and among loud cheers[a] told a full House:

> "England could not lay down arms until *material guarantees* are obtained, which, reducing Russia's power to *proportions* innocuous for Europe, will afford perfect security for the future."

This man was a member of a Cabinet that approved the Vienna Protocol of December 5, 1853, in which the English and French plenipotentiaries stipulated that the war should not lead to a reduction or alteration of the "material conditions" of the Russian Empire.[170] Clarendon, questioned by Lyndhurst about this protocol, declared on behalf of the Ministry:

> "It might be the will of Austria and of Prussia, but it was not the will of England and France that a reduction of Russian power in Europe should be brought about."

---

[a] Marx uses the English word.—*Ed.*
[b] May 24, 1855.—*Ed.*
[c] The Prime Minister's official residence.—*Ed.*

To the House Russell denounced the conduct of Emperor Nicholas as "false and fraudulent". In July 1854 he flippantly announced the invasion of the Crimea, declaring that the destruction of Sevastopol was a matter of European necessity. He finally brought about the fall of Aberdeen for, in his opinion, conducting the war too feebly. So much for the lionskin, now for the lion. Russell was Foreign Secretary for two or three months in 1853, at the time when England received the "*secret and confidential correspondence*" from Petersburg in which Nicholas openly demanded the partition of Turkey, to be attained chiefly through his pretended protection of the Christian subjects of Turkey, a protection which, as Nesselrode admits in his last despatch, has never existed. What did Russell do? He addressed a despatch to the British ambassador in Petersburg,[a] which literally says:

"The more the Turkish Government adopts the rules of impartial law and equal administration, the less will the Emperor of Russia find it necessary to apply that exceptional '*protection*' which he has found so burdensome and inconvenient, though, no doubt, prescribed by duty and sanctified by treaty."

Thus Russell concedes the point at issue from the start. He not only declares the protection legal but obligatory. He traces it back to the Treaty of Kainardji.[171] And what does the "Fourth Point" of the Vienna Conference[b] state? That "the erroneous interpretation of the Treaty of Kuchuk-Kainardji was the principal cause of the present war". If we see Russell at the outbreak of war as the advocate of Russian *rights*—now renounced even by Nesselrode—at the end of the first stage of the war, at the Vienna Conference, we observe him as the champion of Russia's *honour*. As soon as the real business, the discussion of the Third Point,[172] began on March 26, the Russian-eater Russell rose and solemnly declared:

"In the eyes of England and of her allies, the best and *only admissible* conditions of peace would be those which, being the most in harmony with the honour and dignity of Russia, should at the same time be sufficient for the security of Europe, etc."

On April 17 the Russian envoys therefore refused to take the initiative in making proposals for the Third Point, being convinced after Russell's statement that the conditions offered by the allied envoys would be conceived more in the Russian spirit than any that Russia herself could devise. But was the limitation of Russian naval forces "most in harmony with Russia's honour"? In his latest

[a] G. H. Seymour.—*Ed.*
[b] In this paragraph the *Neue Oder-Zeitung* has "Vienna Congress" instead of "Vienna Conference".—*Ed.*

circular Nesselrode therefore adhered firmly to Russell's concessions of March 26. He quotes Russell. He asks him whether the proposals of April 19 are "the best and only admissible ones". Russell appears as the patron of Russia on the threshold of war. He appears as her patron at the end of the first stage of the war, at the green table in Count Buol's palace.

Thus far Disraeli against Russell. He then traced both the disasters at the front and the discord in the country itself back to the contradictory actions of the Ministry, which is working for war in the Crimea and peace in Vienna, combining warlike diplomacy with diplomatic warfare.

Disraeli exclaimed:

"I deny that all you have to do to make war is to levy taxes and to fit out expeditions. [...] You must keep up the spirit of the people. You cannot do this if you are perpetually impressing on the country that peace is impending and [...] that the point of difference between ourselves and our opponents is, [...] after all, [...] comparatively speaking, of a very petty character. Men will endure great sacrifices if they think they are encountering an enemy of colossal power [...]. A nation will not count the sacrifices which it makes if it supposes that it is engaged in a struggle for its fame, its existence, and its power; but when you come to a doubled and tripled income tax, when you come to draw men away from their homes for military service, when you darken the hearts[a] of England with ensanguined calamities—when you do all this, men must not be told that this is merely a question of whether [...] Russia shall have four frigates or eight in the Black Sea.... If you would carry on war, it is necessary not merely to keep up the spirit of the nation, but also to keep up the spirit of foreign Powers; but you may rest assured that so long as you appeal to a foreign Power as a mediator that foreign Power will never be your ally.... Lord Palmerston told us that he was not going to make an ignominious peace [...]. The noble lord is witness for himself, but who will be witness for the noble lord?...

"...You cannot, however, extricate yourselves from these difficulties by conferences at Vienna. You will only increase your difficulties and augment your dangers if you trust to diplomacy. Your position is one that is entirely deceptive; and you never can carry on war with success unless [...] you are supported by an enthusiastic people, and unless [...] you can count upon allies [...] who know that you are determined to support them.

"...I want this House by its decision tonight to put an end to that vicious double system by which we have so long carried on [...] war and diplomacy. I want it to say openly and in distinct language that the time for negotiations has passed. No man, I think, will be inclined to deny that proposition who has read Nesselrode's circular."

Written on May 28, 1855

First published in the *Neue Oder-Zeitung*, No. 247, May 31, 1855

Marked with the sign ×

Printed according to the newspaper

Published in English for the first time

[a] In Disraeli's speech: "hearths".—*Ed.*

Karl Marx

FROM PARLIAMENT

London, May 29. *Gladstone*'s kind of eloquence has never been given more complete and exhaustive expression than in his "speech"[a] on Thursday evening.[b] Polished blandness, empty profundity, unction not without poisonous ingredients, the velvet paw not without the claws, scholastic distinctions both grandiose and petty, *quaestiones* and *quaestiunculae*,[c] the entire arsenal of probabilism[173] with its casuistic scruples and unscrupulous reservations, its unhesitating motives and motivated hesitation, its humble pretensions of superiority, virtuous intrigue, intricate simplicity, Byzantium and Liverpool. Gladstone's speech revolved not so much around the question of war or peace between England and Russia as the examination of why Gladstone, who until a short while ago had been a member of a Ministry engaged in war, had now become the Gladstone of the peace-at-any-price party. He analysed, he scrutinised the limits of his own conscience in all directions with all manner of subtleties, and with characteristic modesty demanded that the British Empire move within the limits of the Gladstonian conscience. His speech thus had a diplomatic-cum-psychological colouring which may have brought conscience into diplomacy, but even more definitely brought diplomacy into conscience.

The war against Russia was originally a just one, but we have now reached the point where its continuation would be sinful.

---

[a] Marx uses the English word.—*Ed.*

[b] The speeches of Gladstone and Russell in the debate on Disraeli's motion in the House of Commons on May 24, 1855 were published in *The Times*, No. 22063, May 25, 1855.—*Ed.*

[c] Minor questions.—*Ed.*

Since the start of the Eastern troubles we have gradually raised our demands. We have followed an ascending line with our conditions, while Russia has been moving down from the heights of her intransigence. At first Russia claimed not only a spiritual, but also a temporal protection over the Greek Christians of Turkey. She was unwilling to give up any of the old treaties, and would agree to evacuate the Danubian provinces only under certain conditions. She refused to attend any congress of the powers at Vienna, and summoned the Turkish ambassador to St. Petersburg or to the Russian headquarters. That was Russia's language up to February 2, 1854. What a distance between the demands of the Western powers at that time, and the Four Points[174]! And as late as August 26, 1854, Russia declared that she would never accept the Four Points except after a long, desperate and calamitous struggle. Again, what a distance between Russia's language in August 1854 and her language of December 1854, when she promised to accept the Four Points "unreservedly"! These Four Points are the nodal point to which our demands can rise, and Russia's concessions descend. Whatever lies beyond the Four Points lies outside the pale of Christian morality. Well! Russia has accepted the 1st point; she has accepted the 2nd point, and has not rejected the 4th point, for it has not been discussed. That only leaves the 3rd point, i.e. only a quarter, and not even the whole of the 3rd point but only a half of it, thus a difference of only one-eighth. For the 3rd point consists of two parts: No. 1, the guarantee of Turkish territory; No. 2, the reduction of Russian power in the Black Sea. Russia has stated that she is more or less willing to accept No. 1. So that only leaves the second half of the 3rd point. And even here Russia has not said that she objects to the limitation of her superiority at sea; she has merely declared her opposition to *our methods* of carrying it out. The Western powers have suggested one method, while Russia suggests not merely one but two alternative methods, thus here again she is ahead of the Western powers. As regards the method proposed by the Western powers, it is an affront to the honour of the Russian Empire. But one must not affront the honour of an empire without reducing its power. On the other hand, one must not reduce its power because one is thereby affronting its honour. These are different views on "method", a difference of one-eighth of a point, and as it is a matter of "method" it can be regarded as 1/32 of a point—and for that another half a million men is to be sacrificed? On the contrary, it must be stated that we have attained the aims of the war. Should we therefore continue it for pure *prestige*, for military glory? Our soldiers have covered themselves with glory. If England has nevertheless fallen into discredit on the Continent,

"For God's sake," cried the honourable gentleman, "don't let us seek to avenge that discredit—don't let us wipe it out by human blood, but rather by sending abroad more correct information".

And, indeed, why not "correct" the foreign newspapers? Further successes on the part of the allied forces—where do they lead to? They force Russia to resist more stubbornly. Allied defeats? They make the Londoners and Parisians excited and force them to make bolder attacks. What is the result of waging war for war's sake? Originally Prussia, Austria, France and England were *united* in their demands on Russia. Prussia has already withdrawn. If we go on, Austria, too, will withdraw. England would be isolated except for France.

If England continues the war for reasons shared by no other power but France, "the moral authority of its position is greatly weakened and undermined". But on the other hand a peace with Russia, if it forfeits the *prestige* that is of this world, will strengthen its "moral authority", which neither moth nor rust doth corrupt.[a] Moreover, what do the people want who do not accept Russia's method of carrying out the second half of the 3rd point? Do they intend to dismember the Russian Empire? Impossible without provoking a "war of the nationalities". *Will* Austria, *can* France support a war of the nationalities? If England undertakes a "war of nationalities" it must undertake it *alone*, i.e. "it will not undertake it at all". So nothing is possible except to demand nothing that Russia has not already conceded.

That was Gladstone's speech in spirit, if not in letter. Russia has changed her *language*: proof that she has backed down in *substance*. For the honourable Puseyite[175] the language is the only issue. He too has changed his language. He is now uttering jeremiads over the war; he is overwhelmed by the suffering of all mankind. He uttered apologias when he inveighed against the Committee of Inquiry and found it quite in order to abandon an English army to all the sufferings of death from starvation and the plague. Of course! Then the army was being sacrificed for *peace*. The sin begins when it is sacrificed for *war*. He is, however, fortunate in demonstrating that the British government was never in earnest in the war against Russia, fortunate in demonstrating that neither the present British government nor the present

[a] Matthew 6:20.—*Ed.*

French government would be able or willing to wage serious war on Russia, fortunate in demonstrating that the *pretexts* for the war are not worth a single bullet. But he forgets that these "pretexts" belong to him and his former colleagues, the "war" itself however was forced on them by the British people. The leadership of the war was for them simply a pretext for paralysing it and maintaining their positions. And from the history and metamorphoses of the false pretexts under which they waged war he successfully concludes that they could make peace under equally false pretexts. He finds himself at variance with his old colleagues only on one point. He is Out, they are In.[a] A false pretext good enough for the ex-minister is not a false pretext good enough for the minister, although what's sauce for the goose is sauce for the gander.

Gladstone's terrible confusion of ideas gave *Russell* the long-awaited signal. He got up and painted Russia black where Gladstone had painted her white. But Gladstone was "Out" and Russell was "In". After blustering forth all the familiar, and despite their triviality, true platitudes about Russia's plans for world conquest, he came to the point, to Russell's point. Never, he declared, had such a great national issue been so totally degraded as this had been by Disraeli. True enough: can one degrade a national issue, indeed a matter of world history, further than by identifying it with little[b] *Johnny,* with *Johnny Russell*? But it was in fact not Disraeli's fault that *Europe* versus *Russia* at the beginning and end of this first stage of the war appeared as *Russell* versus *Nesselrode.* The little man performed some odd contortions when he came to the Four Points. On the one hand, he had to show that his peace terms were related to the Russian horrors he had just exposed. On the other hand, he had to show that true to his voluntary, unprovoked promise to Titov and Gorchakov, he had proposed terms "which harmonised best with the honour of Russia". Hence he proved, on the one hand, that Russia exists only *nominally* as a naval power, and so can well afford a limitation of this merely imaginary power. On the other hand, he proved that the navy, scuttled by Russia herself, is a terrible thing for Turkey and hence for European equilibrium, i.e. "the second half of the 3rd point" formed one great whole. Many a man is caught by his opponent between the two horns of a dilemma. Russell impaled himself on

[a] Marx uses the English words "Out" and "In" (the reference is to the opposition and the government).—*Ed.*

[b] Marx uses the English word.—*Ed.*

both horns. He gave new samples of his *diplomatic talent.* Nothing could be expected of Austria's active alliance *because* a battle lost would bring the Russians to Vienna. *This* is the way he encourages an ally.

"We say," he continued, "that Russia intends to get possession of Constantinople, and to rule there, as *Turkey is obviously in a state of decay;* and I do not doubt that Russia harbours the same opinion of the intentions of England and France in the case of the break-up of that country."

All that was lacking was for him to add: "She is wrong, however. Not England and France, but England alone must take possession of Constantinople." In this way the great diplomat encouraged Austria to take sides; thus he betrayed to Turkey the "obvious" opinion of her *saviours* and supporters. He has, however, improved as a parliamentary tactician on one count. In July 1854, when he was bragging about the seizure of the Crimea, he let himself be so startled by Disraeli that he ate his heroic words *before* the House divided. *This time* he postponed this process of self-consumption—the retraction of his proclaimed world struggle against Russia—until *after* the vote had been taken. A great improvement!

His speech also contained two historical illustrations, his extremely comical account of the negotiations with Emperor Nicholas over the Treaty of Kainardji,[176] and a sketch of *German* conditions. Both deserve a mention in extract. As the reader will remember, *Russell* had conceded Russia's protection at the outset, based on the Treaty of Kainardji. The British ambassador in Petersburg, Sir Hamilton Seymour, turned out to be more awkward and more sceptical. He made inquiries of the Russian government, the story of which Russell is naive enough to recount as follows:

"Sir Hamilton Seymour asked the late Emperor of Russia to have the goodness to point out the part of the Treaty [...] upon which the right he claimed was founded. His Imperial Majesty said [...] 'I would not point out to you the particular article in the treaty on which my claim " (to protection) "is based. You may go to Count Nesselrode and he will show you the article.' Hamilton Seymour did go to Count Nesselrode [...]. Count Nesselrode replied he was not very conversant with the articles of the treaty and told Hamilton to go to Baron Brunnow or refer his government to him and the Baron would tell him what part of the treaty it is which gives the Emperor the right he claims.' I believe Baron Brunnow never attempted to point out any such article in the treaty."

About Germany the noble Lord related:

"In Germany she [Russia] is connected with many of the smaller Princes by marriage. Many of the Princes of Germany, I am sorry to say, live in great fear of what they think the revolutionary disposition of their subjects, and rely on their armed forces for protection. But what are those armed forces? The officers of those forces are seduced and corrupted by the Russian Court. That Court distributes rewards, orders and distinctions among them, and in some cases Russia regularly supplies them with money to pay their debts so that Germany which ought to be in a state of independence—Germany which should stand forward for the protection of Europe against Russian domination—has for years been corrupted, and has been undermined in its vital strength and independence, by Russian arts and Russian means."

And in order to precede Germany like a column of fire and rouse it to the "categorical imperative",[177] *duty*, Russell declared himself at the Vienna Conference the champion of the "honour and dignity of Russia" and let Germany hear the proud language of the free and independent Englishman.

Written on May 29, 1855

First published in the *Neue Oder-Zeitung*, No. 249, June 1, 1855

Marked with the sign ×

Printed according to the newspaper

Published in English for the first time

Karl Marx

A CRITIQUE OF PALMERSTON'S LATEST SPEECH

London, June 1. If Gladstone deceives by his air of profundity, Palmerston deceives by his air of superficiality. He knows how to conceal his real intention with true artistry beneath loosely connected phrases meant for effect and commonplace concessions to the opinion of the day. His Cabinet speech has now lain before the public for a week.[a] The daily and weekly press has ventilated, scrutinised and criticised it. His enemies say that after keeping to the language of old Aberdeen for many months he has now found it appropriate to speak the language of old Palmerston again for an evening. They say: the noble lord is witness for himself, but who will be witness for the noble lord[b]? They regard his speech as a clever feat since he manages to avoid giving any definite account of his policies, and adopts such an elastic, airy form that it is impossible to pin him down anywhere. His friends, on the other hand, do not hesitate to hail the wind he expended on his rhetorical organ-playing as the music itself. From the beginning he correctly grasped the situation in which he had to present himself to the House and to the country. Who confronts me?

"...There are those who think, on the one hand, that we have not been sufficiently vigorous in the prosecution of the war while there are those who wish, on the other hand, to drive the country to a peace upon ignominious terms; on the one hand, there are those who reproach us for having opened negotiations with Austria that are pointless and only paralyse the war, but, on the other, those

---

[a] A report on Palmerston's, Disraeli's, and Layard's speeches in the House of Commons on May 25, 1855 was published in *The Times*, No. 22064, May 26, 1855.—*Ed.*

[b] A quotation from Disraeli's speech in the House of Commons on May 24, 1855 (see this volume, p. 230).—*Ed.*

who think that we have not gone far enough in these negotiations and have wrecked them by making extravagant demands."

Thus he took up the stance of a man of the true centre. He repulsed the attacks of the war men by referring them to the peace men and the attacks of the peace men by referring them back to the war men. The about-turn against the committed peace men then gave him the opportunity to indulge in well-calculated outbursts of patriotic fervour, loud protestation of energy and all the brave words which he has so often used to bamboozle the *ninnies*. He flattered national pride by listing the great resources that England has at its disposal—his sole reply to the accusation that he is incapable of handling large resources.

"The noble lord," said Disraeli, "reminds me [...] of that *parvenu* who used to recommend himself to his mistress's good graces by enumerating his possessions. 'I have a house in the country, a house in town, a gallery of pictures, a fine cellar of wines.'"

Thus England has a Baltic fleet and a fleet in the Black Sea, and an annual national income of £80 million, etc. However, among all the rhetorical trivialities in which Palmerston's speech petered out, he succeeded in throwing in one *definite statement*, to which he can return later at a suitable opportunity and which he can proclaim as the principle of his policy, sanctioned by the House. No English newspaper has *emphasised* it, but the art of Palmerstonian oratory has always consisted of concealing its own point and sweeping it away from the memory of his listeners in the smooth, shallow flow of his phraseology. But as it is not simply a question of momentary success for Palmerston, as it is for Russell, because he plans ahead, he does not merely content himself with the oratorical expedients of the moment but carefully lays the foundation for his subsequent operations. The statement mentioned above says literally:

"We are engaged in a great operation in the Black Sea. We trust and hope that we shall be *successful* in that operation. We *think success in that operation will lead to the obtaining those conditions which* [...] *we have thought, in the present state of the conflict, Britain, France and Austria have a right to demand.*"

In other words, however protracted the operations in the Black Sea may be, the diplomatic basis of the war remains the same. However great the military success may be, final success is determined in advance, and limited to what are called the Four Points.[178] And Palmerston makes this declaration when only a few hours earlier Layard had stripped the Four Points of their Russophile mask. But Palmerston diverted attention from Layard's criticism, he avoided dealing with the real question, the value of the ostensible aims and objectives of the war, by defending the second half of the 3rd point[a] against Gladstone and advancing this *half* of the point as the *entire thing*.

Palmerston's speech was interrupted by an incident that is worthy of mention. An English bigot by the name of Lord Robert Grosvenor preached a penitential sermon at him because he had discussed military successes and the chances of war without taking into account the grace and favour of the Almighty, without even "mentioning the name of God". So he called down divine judgment on his nation. Palmerston immediately did penance, beating his breast and proving that if necessary he, too, can preach and roll his eyes just as well as Lord Robert Grosvenor. But the parliamentary episode received a popular sequel. The citizens of Marylebone (a part of London) had called a large meeting in the School Room, Cowper Street, to protest against the "Bill for the Suppression of Trade on Sundays". As their constituents were involved here, Lord Ebrington and Lord Robert Grosvenor appeared to defend the Bill, which they themselves had tabled in Parliament. Instead of relying on the protection and grace of God, however, they had taken pains to place a dozen paid clappers and trouble-makers at various spots in the meeting. The secret was soon discovered, and the hired agents of bigotry were immediately seized by the good citizens and thrown out into the street. Incapable of facing the hissing, booing and whistling that now broke out, the "noble lords" resumed their seats in a state of embarrassment. As soon as they left the meeting, an "unpaid" mob followed their carriage with unmistakable manifestations of sinful scorn and hardness of heart.

Written on June 1, 1855

First published in the *Neue Oder-Zeitung*, No. 253, June 4, 1855

Marked with the sign ×

Printed according to the newspaper

Published in English for the first time

[a] See this volume, pp. 232-33.—*Ed.*

Karl Marx

THE ASSOCIATION FOR ADMINISTRATIVE REFORM. [—PEOPLE'S CHARTER] [179]

London, June 5. The Association for Administrative Reform [180] has gained a victory in Bath. Its candidate, Mr. Tite, has been elected a Member of Parliament by a large majority against the Tory candidate.[a] This victory, gained on the territory of its "legal" country, is being celebrated as a great event by today's Liberal papers. Bulletins about the poll[b] are being published with no less ostentation than those about the bloodless successes on the Sea of Azov. Bath and Kerch! is the motto of the day. But the press—pro-reform and anti-reform, Ministerial, Opposition, Tory, Whig and Radical papers alike—says nothing about the defeats and disappointments which the Association for Administrative Reform has suffered in the last few days in London, Birmingham and Worcester. To be sure, this time the battle was not fought on the well defined territory of a privileged electoral body. Nor were its results such as to draw cries of triumph from the opponents of the City reformers.

The first truly *public* meeting (i.e., one *without* admission tickets) which the Reform Association held in *London* took place in Marylebone last Wednesday.[c] One of the Chartists[d] countered the resolutions of the City reformers by moving the amendment

"that the money aristocracy represented by the City men is as bad as the landed aristocracy; that, under the pretext of reform, it merely wants to climb, on the shoulders of the people, into Downing Street, and there to share offices, salaries

[a] Q. C. Whateley.—*Ed.*
[b] Marx uses the English word.—*Ed.*
[c] May 30, 1855. A report on the meeting was published in *The People's Paper*, No. 161, June 2, 1855.—*Ed.*
[d] M'Dickey.—*Ed.*

and ranks with the oligarchs; that the Charter with its five points is the only programme of the people's movement".

The chairman of the meeting,[a] one of the City illuminati, voiced a number of misgivings, first, whether he should put the amendment to the vote at all, then, whether he should first take a vote on the resolution or on the amendment, and lastly, *how* he should take the vote. The audience, being tired of his indecision, tactical considerations and troublesome manoeuvres, declared him incapable of presiding further, called on Ernest Jones to replace him in the chair, and voted by a vast majority against the resolution and for the amendment. In *Birmingham*, the City Association called a public meeting in the Town Hall with the Mayor in the chair.[b] The resolution proposed by the Association was countered by an amendment similar to that moved in London. The Mayor, however, flatly refused to put the amendment to the vote unless the word "Charter" was replaced by a less objectionable one. If not, he would withdraw from the chair, he said. The word "*Charter*" was therefore replaced by "*universal suffrage* and voting by ballot". Thus edited, the amendment was passed by a majority of 10 votes. In *Worcester*, where the City reformers held a public meeting, the victory of the Chartists and the defeat of the Administrative Reformers were even more complete. There the *Charter* was proclaimed without more ado.[c]

The extremely embarrassing success of these large meetings in London, Birmingham and Worcester decided the Administrative Reformers to circulate in all the bigger and more populous towns petitions to be signed by people holding similar views, rather than to make public appeals to the *vox populi*. The City notables' manifold links with businessmen in the United Kingdom, and the influence these gentlemen exert upon their clerks, warehousemen[d] and "minor" commercial friends will no doubt enable them to fill the petitions with names very quietly, behind the back of the public, and then to send them to the "Honourable House" with the label, *Voice of the People of England*. But they are mistaken if they think they can intimidate the Government with signatures collected by cadging, intrigue and stealth. The Government observed with ironical self-satisfaction that the Administrative

---

[a] H. Farrer.—*Ed.*

[b] The meeting was held on May 21, 1855. A report on it was published in *The People's Paper*, No. 160, May 26, 1855.—*Ed.*

[c] The meeting was held at the end of May. A report on it appeared in *The People's Paper*, No. 161, June 2, 1855.—*Ed.*

[d] Marx uses the English word.—*Ed.*

Reformers were hissed out of the *theatrum mundi*. Its organs are silent for the time being, partly because they would otherwise have to register the successes of Chartism, and partly because the ruling class is already toying with the idea of putting itself at the head of the Administrative Reformers should the people's movement become importunate. They keep a "misunderstanding" in reserve should this danger set in: a misunderstanding allowing them sometime in the future to regard the Administrative Reformers as the spokesmen of the masses. Such misunderstandings are an essential element of England's "historical" development, and no one is more familiar with handling them than the free-thinking Whigs.

The *Charter* is a very laconic document; besides the demand for *universal suffrage*, it contains only the following five points, which are all prerequisites for exercising it: 1) vote by ballot; 2) *no* property qualifications for Members of Parliament; 3) payment of Members of Parliament; 4) annual Parliaments; 5) equal electoral districts. After the experiments which undermined *universal suffrage* in France in 1848,[181] the continentals are prone to underrate the importance and meaning of the English *Charter*. They overlook the fact that two-thirds of the population of France are peasants and over one-third townspeople, whereas in England more than two-thirds live in towns and less than one-third in the countryside. Hence the results of universal suffrage in England must likewise be in *inverse* proportion to the results in France, just as town and country are in the two states. This explains the diametrically opposite character which the demand for universal suffrage has assumed in France and England. In France the political ideologists put forward this demand, which every "educated" person could support to a greater or lesser extent, depending on his convictions. In England it is a distinguishing feature roughly separating the aristocracy and bourgeoisie on the one hand, and the people, on the other. There it is regarded as a political question and here, as a social one. In England agitation for universal suffrage had gone through a period of historical development before it became the slogan of the masses. In France, it was *first* introduced and *then* started on its historical path. In France it was the practice of universal suffrage that failed, whereas in England it was its ideology. In the early decades of this century, universal suffrage as propounded by Sir Francis Burdett, Major Cartwright and Cobbett was still a very vague and idealistic concept, so that it could become the pious wish of all sections of the population that did not belong directly to the ruling classes.

For the bourgeoisie, it was in fact simply an eccentric, generalised expression of what it had attained through the parliamentary reform of 1831. In England the demand for universal suffrage did not assume its concrete, specific character even after 1838. Proof: Hume and O'Connell were among those who signed the Charter. The last illusions disappeared in 1842. At that time Lovett made a last but futile attempt to formulate universal suffrage as a *common* demand of what are known as Radicals and the masses of the people.[182] Since that day there has no longer been any doubt about the meaning of universal suffrage. Nor about its name. It is the *Charter* of the people and implies the assumption of political power as a means of satisfying their social needs. Universal suffrage, which was regarded as the motto of universal brotherhood in the France of 1848, has become a battle cry in England. There universal suffrage was the direct content of the revolution; here, revolution is the direct content of universal suffrage. An examination of the history of universal suffrage in England will show that it casts off its idealistic features at the same rate as modern society with its immense contradictions develops in this country, contradictions that are produced by industrial progress.

Alongside the official and semi-official parties, as well as alongside the Chartists, there is another clique of "wise men" emerging in England, who are discontented with the Government and the ruling classes as much as with the Chartists. What do the Chartists want? they exclaim. They want to increase and extend the omnipotence of Parliament by elevating it to democratic power. They are not breaking up parliamentarism but are raising it to a higher power. The right thing to do is to break up the representative system! A wise man from the East, *David Urquhart*, heads that clique. He wants to revert to England's Common Law. He wants to squeeze Statute Law[a] back into its bounds. He wants to localise rather than centralise. He wants to unearth "the true old legal sources of Anglo-Saxon times" from the rubbish. Then they will gush forth of themselves and will water and fertilise the surrounding country. But David is at least consistent. He also wants to reduce modern division of labour and concentration of capital to the old Anglo-Saxon level or, preferably, to that of the Orient. A Highlander by birth, an adoptive Circassian and a Turk by free choice, he is able to condemn civilisation with all its evils,

[a] Marx uses the English terms "Common Law" and "Statute Law" and explains their meaning in German in brackets.—*Ed.*

and even to evaluate it from time to time. But he is not trite like the men with lofty ideas who separate the modern political forms from modern society, and who prattle about local autonomy combined with concentration of capital, and about the uniqueness of the individual combined with the anti-individualising division of labour. David is a prophet who looks backwards, and is in an old-fashioned way enraptured by old England. He must therefore consider it quite all right that new England passes him by and leaves him behind, however urgent and persuasive he may be exclaiming: "David Urquhart is the only man who can save you!" As he did only a few days ago, at a meeting in Stafford.

Written on June 5, 1855

First published in the *Neue Oder-Zeitung*, No. 261, June 8, 1855

Marked with the sign ×

Printed according to the newspaper

Karl Marx

PARLIAMENTARY

London, June 6. Palmerston has again given proof of his old mastery at handling diplomacy by means of Parliament and Parliament by means of diplomacy. The policy of the ministry was to be discussed on the basis of the amendments of Baring, Heathcote and Lowe.[a] The amendments were all based on the Vienna Conference.[183] During Whitsun week Palmerston conjured away the Vienna Conference, by referring in his dealings with Austria to the past parliamentary debate; and in his dealings with the newly re-opened Parliament[b] he conjured away the debate, by referring to the *past* Conference, which, allegedly, now existed only as a myth. With the Vienna Conference are thrown overboard the amendments which presuppose it; with the amendments, the discussion of the ministry's policy ceases, and with this discussion, disappears the need for the ministry to make any statement about the *tendency, aim and object of the "new" war.* We are assured by *David Urquhart*, alias *David Bey*, that this aim is nothing less than to acquaint the allied troops with the summer diseases of the Crimea, now that they have sampled the winter diseases of the Crimea. And though Urquhart does not know everything, he knows his Palmerston. But he is mistaken about the power that secret design has over public history. Thus Palmerston informs the reassembled Parliament that there is no longer any subject for debate, and that the House could now do nothing better than send a war address to the Crown, i.e. give the ministry

[a] Amendments to Disraeli's motion of May 24, 1855 (see this volume, pp. 227-28).—*Ed.*

[b] Parliament re-opened on June 4, 1855.—*Ed.*

a *vote of confidence.* For the time being he is thwarted by the stubbornness of the parliamentarians, who have prepared long speeches on the amendments and are resolved to dispose of their goods. By the mere act of disbanding the Conference he has broken the point off these speeches and the *horror vacui,* boredom, will drive Parliament into accepting his address. To save itself from the speeches it will seize on the address.

With the change in the situation, Lowe's amendment has changed its meaning. Originally it meant the break-up of the Vienna Conference. Now it means sanctioning the Vienna Conference and ministerial diplomacy, insofar as it raises Russell's formula for the reduction of Russian maritime power in the Euxinus[a] to the *ultimate aim,* to the real *object* of the war. It is a stumbling block for the peace party insofar as it demands too much, for the war party insofar as it demands too little, and a stumbling block for the ministry insofar as it demands any object, that is any admitted object, for the war. Hence the phenomenon of pro-peace men and Tories being *for* the continuation of the *debate* on Lowe's amendment and the ministry *against* it; hence Palmerston's attempt to jettison it. The attempt failed. He therefore adjourned the debate until Thursday evening. A day's respite gained. In the meantime the final protocol of the Vienna Conference is printed. It is presented to the House. A new and secondary question is raised, and with his "dissolving views"[b] Palmerston can hope to remove the real issue from the focus of the debate.

The two-day parliamentary discussion[c] was as boring, tedious and confused as can only be expected of speeches whose point has been broken off in advance. It offered, however, a characteristic spectacle: whereas before the vote on Disraeli's motion the peace men flirted with the ministry, they now flirted with the Opposition, by which we mean the professional Opposition. Further, it revealed the *entente cordiale* between the Peelites and the Manchester School.[184] The Peelites obviously flatter themselves that they will rule England *after* the war, at the head of the industrial bourgeoisie. Thus, after their long wanderings, the Peelites would at last have a real party behind them, and the industrialists at last have found professional statesmen. If the peace men have thus won Gladstone, Graham and Co., they have lost the "radical" *Sir William Molesworth,* a friend of more than twenty years' standing.

---

[a] Ancient Greek name for the Black Sea.—*Ed.*

[b] Marx uses the English expression.—*Ed.*

[c] An account of the debate in the House of Commons on June 4 and 5 was published in *The Times,* Nos. 22072 and 22073, June 5 and 6, 1855.—*Ed.*

Molesworth must have read in Hobbes, whom he published,[185] that "intelligence comes through the ears". He therefore appealed not to the intelligence but to the ears. He did what Hamlet forbids the actors to do.[a] He out-tyrannised the tyrant and was more Russell than Russell himself. He had also read in his Hobbes that all men are equal, because each can take the life of the other. As he is now concerned with prolonging his ministerial life he spoke in the spirit of the men who can take it from him. It was indeed a curious thing to see this adding-machine indulging in dithyrambs. Not even *Babbage* in his "Philosophy of Machines"[b] would have imagined it. *Milner Gibson,* the baronet from the Manchester area, was monotonous, soporific, desiccated and desiccating. He has obviously learnt from the nearby metropolis of British industry how to deliver as much as possible while keeping production costs as low as possible. He is a man whose whole appearance proclaims that he is bored. Why should he seek to amuse his fellow-men? Do as you would be done by! Moreover, he clearly counts spirit, wit and life among the *faux frais de production,*[c] and it is the first law of the economic school to which he belongs to avoid "false costs". *Bulwer* hovered between the heroic mood of his "king-maker" and the contemplative one of his "Eugene Aram".[d] In the former he threw down the gauntlet to Russia, in the latter he wove a myrtle wreath around Metternich's brow.

Milner Gibson, Molesworth and Bulwer were the *coryphaei* of the first evening, *Cobden, Graham and Russell* of the second. Cobden's speech alone deserves an analysis which space and time do not permit at present. Let us only remark that he claims Bonaparte was prepared to accept the last Austrian proposals. The late Sir Robert Peel's dirty boy, who has recently taken to "sentiments",[e] "broken hearts" and "love of truth", gave a self-apology on behalf of his neighbour, namely Sir James Graham. He had forbidden Napier to act in the Baltic Sea until the time of year when any action is ruinous for the British Navy. He had forbidden Dundas to shell Odessa. He had thus neutralised the British Navy both in

---

[a] The reference is to Hamlet's warning against overacting (Shakespeare, *Hamlet,* Act III, Scene 2).—*Ed.*

[b] Ch. Babbage, *On the Economy of Machinery and Manufactures.*—*Ed.*

[c] False costs of production.—*Ed.*

[d] "King-maker" was the nickname of Richard Neville, Earl of Warwick, described in Bulwer-Lytton's novel *The Last of the Barons,* the action of which takes place during the Wars of the Roses; Eugene Aram is the title character of another of Lytton's novels.—*Ed.*

[e] Marx uses the English words "dirty boy" and "sentiments".—*Ed.*

the Baltic and in the Black Sea. He justifies himself with the size of the fleets which he had equipped. The mere existence of these fleets was proof of British power. Their action was therefore superfluous. A few days ago Napier addressed a laconic letter to a friend of Urquhart, which Urquhart read out at the Stafford meeting. This letter says literally:

"Sir! I hold Sir James Graham capable of any base act. *Charles Napier*."

Russell has finally excelled himself. At the beginning of his speech he declared that the big question confronting the House was the following:

"If you are determined to have peace, upon what conditions can you obtain it? If you mean to carry on the war, for what objects is that war to be carried on?"

As to the first question, his answer could be found in the Vienna protocols. As to the second, the object of the war, his answer had to be a *very general* one, in other words, no answer at all. If one were to accept the phrase "security for Turkey" as an answer, he would not mind. One interpretation of this "security" was given in the *Vienna Note*; another in the *Four Points*[186]; finding a third was not Russell's business but the *war's*. It was Napoleon's principle that war must cover its own costs; it is Russell's principle that war must find its own *object*.

Written on June 6, 1855

First published in the *Neue Oder-Zeitung*, No. 263, June 9, 1855

Marked with the sign ×

Printed according to the newspaper

Published in English for the first time

Frederick Engels

FROM THE CRIMEA [187]

The arrival of the *Asia*'s mail at a late hour on Thursday night enabled us yesterday to publish the dispatch of Gen. Pélissier concerning the fight which took place before Sevastopol on the night of May 22, as well as an authentic account of the allied advance upon Chorgun, which was accomplished on the 25th of that month. Some 25,000 men under Canrobert crossed the Chernaya and occupied the line of that streamlet, expelling the Russian outposts from their positions on the hights immediately overhanging the right bank. The Russians fell back as a matter of course, this not being their proper field of battle, in order to concentrate all their forces on the strong line between Inkermann and the range of cliffs to the east of that place. By this advance the Allies have nearly doubled the extent of ground occupied by them—giving them room of which their increased forces stood greatly in need—and managed an opening into the valley of Baidar which may prove very useful. The first step toward a resumption of field operations has been accomplished with success, and should be followed by actions of greater importance.

As for the affair of May 22, the scene of the struggle was between the Quarantine Bay and the Central Bastion—No. 5 of the Russians. It was a very hard-contested and sanguinary conflict. The Russians, as we now learn from Pélissier's report, have occupied all the ground from the head of the Quarantine Bay to the Cemetery, and thence to the Central Bastion by detached works and rifle trenches, though the official British Admiralty plan of the siege-works shows that there are trench-works all over this important ground. But the truth now appears to be that as soon as the Flagstaff and Central Bastions were seriously menaced and the outworks protecting them taken by the French, this piece of ground was turned by the Russians into one vast works. In a couple of nights long lines of connecting breastworks were thrown up inclosing the whole ground, and thus forming a large *place d'armes* or protected space where troops could safely be concentrated in order to act upon the flanks of any French attack, or even to attempt strong sorties on the flanks of the advanced French works. Pélissier knew by experience the rapidity with which the Russians proceed in structures of the sort, and the tenacity with which they defend their works when once completed. He fell upon them at once. On the night of May 22 an attack in two columns was made. The left column established itself in the Russian trenches at the head of Quarantine Bay, and effected a lodgment; the right column also got possession of the advanced trenches, but being unable to work under the heavy fire of the enemy, had to withdraw at daybreak. On the following night the attempt was renewed with stronger columns and with complete success. The entire work was carried and turned against the Russians by transplanting the gabions from one side of the trench to the opposite one. In this action the French appear to have fought with the greatest gallantry—with some sort of revival of that old *furia francese* which made them so celebrated in former times, although it must be confessed that the statements of Gen. Pélissier as to the odds they had to contend against have some little show of brag about them.

With regard to the third bombardment of the city, which our Halifax dispatch reported as having commenced on the 6th, followed by the storm and capture of the Mamelon and White Tower[a] on the 7th, the *Asia*'s mail furnishes no new information, and enables us to add nothing to our remarks of Wednesday last. We learn however that 25,000 men had been transported to the Chersonese from Omer Pasha's army at Eupatoria, with a view evidently to operations in the field, since if another bombardment and an assault were contemplated, these Turks had better have been left in their former quarters. But it also appears that the allied army was very insufficiently furnished with means of transport and supplies for a campaign in the interior; and the probability is that while waiting for them to be provided, Pélissier has occupied the troops with this active renewal of the siege operations, not with the intention of really undertaking to storm the place at present, but to keep up the *morale* of the men.

[a] The Selenghinsk and Volhynsk redoubts.—*Ed.*

From the conduct of Pélissier since taking the command, it seems certain that he is determined to be guided by his own judgment only and to take no notice of whatever plans and projects the imagination of Louis Bonaparte may be inclined to hatch. Plan-making for Crimean campaigns seems now to be a fashionable occupation at Paris; even old Marshal Vaillant has sent one or two; but Pélissier at once telegraphed that if Vaillant thought his plans so good he had better come to the Crimea to carry them out himself. How this energetic but obstinate and brutal Commander will go on we shall see very shortly; at all events, if it be true, as we see it intimated, that he has ventured to forward "orders" to the British, Turkish and Sardinian Chiefs of the Staff without even taking the trouble to inform the respective Commanders of their contents, he will very soon get up a pretty squabble in the allied camp, where hitherto no single General, but the Council of War, composed of all the Commanders, has been considered supreme. Imagine old Field Marshal Lord Raglan under the command of a single French Lieutenant-General!

Meantime the Russians are not idle. The "expectant" position into which Austria has relapsed and the arrival of reserves and new levies from the interior have enabled Russia to send fresh troops to the Crimea. The 3d, 4th, 5th and 6th Infantry Corps are there already, beside several Cavalry Divisions. Now the 2d Infantry Corps, which was said to be in the Crimea six weeks ago, has actually left Volhynia for the seat of war, followed by the 7th Light Cavalry Division, attached to the Grenadier Corps. This is a pretty sure sign that the infantry and artillery of the Grenadier Corps are next on the list to march to the Crimea; and indeed they are already moving to Volhynia and Podolia to take the place of the 2d Corps. This latter body, commanded by Gen. Paniutin, who in Hungary[a] commanded the Russian Division attached to Haynau's army, will bring to the Crimea 49 battalions of Infantry, beside Artillery and Light Cavalry—in all, about 50,000 or 60,000 men—for there can be no doubt that these corps, which have not yet been engaged, have been raised to the full war-complement. The troops of the 2d Corps will successively arrive on the seat of war from June 15 to July 15, at a time when decisive operations will very likely be taking place, and thus they may take a very important part in the coming Crimean campaign.

The month of June must bring some decision into this Crimean

[a] In 1849.—*Ed.*

warfare. Before June, or at the outside July, has elapsed, either the Russian field-army will have had to leave the Crimea, or the Allies will have to prepare for their own retreat.

Written about June 8, 1855

First published in the *New-York Daily Tribune,* No. 4424, June 23, 1855; reprinted in the *New-York Semi-Weekly Tribune,* No. 1052, June 26, 1855 and the *New-York Weekly Tribune,* No. 720, June 30, 1855 as a leading article

Reproduced from the *New-York Daily Tribune*

Frederick Engels

A CRITIQUE OF THE EVENTS IN THE CRIMEA [188]

London, June 8. The arrival of three French reserve divisions in addition to the two Sardinian divisions makes it impossible for the allies to remain spellbound within the narrow confines of the Heracleatic Chersonese. So, on May 25, shortly after General Pélissier assumed command, they sent 20,000-25,000 men to the Chernaya, occupied the line of this river and expelled the Russian outposts from their positions on the heights overhanging the river's right bank. It will be remembered that more than a month ago we pointed out [a] that this, the Russians' advanced line of defence, was not their true battlefield and that consequently, instead of holding their ground and accepting battle along this line, they would probably give it up at the first serious assault so as to concentrate all their forces on the strong line between Inkerman and the range of hills to the east of that place. This has now happened. By this advance the allies have nearly doubled the extent of the area occupied by them, and opened a gateway to the fertile valley of Baidar, which may become very useful in the future. Up to now, however, the advantage gained has not been swiftly and vigorously followed up. The first movement was immediately followed again by stagnation. Lack of transport facilities may have made this inevitable. Disunity between the allied commanders is cited as one cause. The shelling of Sevastopol, resumed on June 6, shelling No. 3, arouses the suspicion that it may be intended to return after an interlude to the old routine. The shelling may, however, be combined with operations in the field. At any rate, one necessary measure (cf. No. 241 of the *N.O-Z.*) [b] has at last been taken—the transportation of

[a] See this volume, pp. 184-85.—*Ed.*
[b] Ibid., p. 212.—*Ed.*

some 20,000 Turks under the personal command of Omer Pasha from Eupatoria to Chersonese. The allied army has thus increased to a full 200,000 men. With a fighting force of this size active operations can certainly be begun as soon as the organisation of supplies and transport facilities permits the army to take the field. But here there seem to be great difficulties to be overcome.

The second affair to be mentioned in the story of the main army is the battle between the Quarantine Harbour and the Central Bastion (No. 5 of the Russians). It was stubborn and bloody. As we can now see from General Pélissier's report, the Russians held all the ground from the head of the Quarantine Harbour to the churchyard, and from there to the Central Bastion by means of detached earthworks and trenches, although even the official British Admiralty map of the siege-works indulges in the fantasy of placing French fortifications over the whole of this important area. As soon as the Flagstaff and Central bastions were seriously threatened, and the outer works protecting them were taken by the French, the Russians turned this extensive stretch into one great fortification. In a few nights long lines were connected with one another, ramparts thrown up intended to enclose the whole area and form a spacious *place d'armes*, i.e. a fortified place where the troops could be gathered in safety in order to act against the flanks of any French attack or to undertake strong assaults on the flanks of the advanced French fortifications. To deprive the Russians of the time to carry out their plan, Pélissier decided to fall on them immediately, while their earthworks were still incomplete. On the evening of May 22 an attack was made in two columns. The left column established itself in the Russian trenches at the head of the Quarantine Harbour and managed to dig itself in; the right column also captured the advance trenches but was forced to retire again at daybreak by the heavy fire of the enemy. On the following evening the attempt was renewed with stronger columns and complete success. The entire fortification was captured and turned against the Russians by removing the gabions from one side of the trench to the opposite side. In this action the French seem to have fought again with the famous *furia francese,* although it has to be admitted that the manner in which Pélissier describes the difficulties to be overcome is not free from a tinge of boasting.

It is generally known that the expedition to the Sea of Azov was rewarded with total success. A flotilla consisting chiefly of the light warships of the two fleets, manned by 15,000 British, French and

Turks, seized Kerch, Yenikale and the straits leading to the Sea of Azov without encountering resistance. Advancing into this lake, the ships appeared off Berdyansk, Genichesk and Arabat, destroying or compelling the Russians to destroy large supplies of corn and munitions, a number of steamships and nearly 200 transport boats. At Kerch they succeeded in capturing Gorchakov's letters to the commander of the place. The Russian commander-in-chief complains about the lack of provisions in Sevastopol and urges the rapid despatch of fresh supplies. Now it turns out that throughout the campaign the Sea of Azov was the main channel along which the Russians in the Crimea had been receiving their supplies and that 500 *sailing-boats* had been used to transport them. As the allies have up to now only found and destroyed 200 such boats, the remaining 300 must be further up near Taganrog or Azov. A squadron of steamships has therefore been sent out in search of them. The success of the allies is all the more important as it forces the Russians to send all supplies along a slow and less safe land-route via Perekop or via the interior of the Sivash Sea[a] and to set up their main depots at Kherson or Berislav on the Dnieper, in positions far more exposed than those at the head of the Sea of Azov. The almost uncontested success of this expedition is the greatest reproach to the allies' conduct of the war. If such results can now be achieved in four days, why was the expedition not sent out in September or October last year, at a time when similar breaches in the Russians' line of communication might have entailed the retreat of their army and the surrender of Sevastopol?

The land forces accompanying this expedition are intended to protect the steamers if necessary, to supply the captured places with garrisons and to go into action against the Russian communications. Their main corps seems intended to act in the field as a simple flying corps, making sorties whenever there is a chance of dealing a swift blow, retiring behind its fortifications under cover of the ships' guns, and, if the worst comes to the worst, embarking again when threatened by a greatly superior enemy force. If this is its purpose it can perform important duties, and 15,000 are not too many for this. If on the other hand it is intended to act as an independent corps with its own base of operations, undertaking a serious flanking movement against the Russians and attempting to pose a serious threat to the interior of the Crimea, then 15,000 men, weakened by detachments, are far too few for such an operation and run a considerable risk of being

[a] Most western part of the Sea of Azov.—*Ed.*

cut off, surrounded by superior forces and annihilated. At present we only know that they have landed at Kerch and are engaged in preparing it for defence against the interior. The Russians having voluntarily evacuated Sudjouk Kale, Anapa remains the only fortress in their hands on the Circassian coast. It is a natural stronghold that is now moreover well fortified. We doubt that the allies will attack it at the moment. Should they do so they will be making a big mistake, if not positive of rapid success. They would be dispersing troops that need the utmost concentration and wasting their energies by attacking new targets before the old ones are secured.

Written about June 8, 1855

First published in the *Neue Oder-Zeitung*, No. 265, June 11, 1855

Marked with the sign ×

Printed according to the newspaper

Published in English for the first time

Karl Marx

THE GREAT PARLIAMENTARY DEBATE

London, June 9. The great parliamentary debate has ended, or rather perished because of hypersalivation. Baring's motion[a] was carried without opposition "*amidst the general laughter of the House*". The motion, insipid as it is, concludes with a war address to the Crown. Did the House declare the war "une guerre pour rire"[b]? Or did it declare itself "une parlement pour rire"[c]? At any rate, the real conclusion of the two-week debate did not lie in the acceptance of Baring's motion—a mere formality—but in the general laughter, the spontaneous muscular spasm contravening the regulations, the indiscreet cry of nature beneath which the "honourable House" buried motions and counter-motions, amendments and sub-amendments, ministry and opposition, speeches, counter-speeches, sermons, deductions, shrill sarcasm and pathetic entreaty, prayers for peace and war-cries, tactics and tactlessness, itself and its vote. The House saved itself from the laughable situation by laughing at itself. Thus it confessed that world-historical seriousness in this parliamentary medium first becomes contorted into conventional seriousness, and this contrived seriousness then turns into natural jesting.

Every attempt to get Palmerston to formulate ministerial policy, to make any statement about the object, tendency or purpose of the war failed completely. He flatly declared that

> "*it was impossible* to question a minister, or indeed any friend, about the object of the war."[d]

---

[a] Baring's amendment to Disraeli's motion of May 24, 1855 (see this volume, pp. 227-28). The amendment was passed by the House of Commons on June 8, 1855.—*Ed.*

[b] A war for laughter.—*Ed.*

[c] A parliament for laughter.—*Ed.*

[d] Palmerston's speech in the House of Commons on June 8, 1855, published in *The Times*, No. 22076, June 9, 1855.—*Ed.*

It was the peace men that helped him most of all. Do you wish to know why we are waging war? There is Richard Cobden who wants peace at any price. Do you not prefer war without any price to peace at any price? Aim your blows at Richard Cobden! In this way he continually thrust Cobden or Bright or Graham or Gladstone between himself and his antagonists.

The cotton heroes did not merely serve him as padding to line his battle-dress with. More than that. He manufactured gunpowder out of their cotton. It also appeared during the debate that in Russell, just as formerly in Aberdeen, Palmerston possesses a lightning-conductor for his sacrosanct person, a lightning-conductor belonging to the Cabinet itself. It was for this purpose that he sent Russell to Vienna, for the purpose of turning him into his lightning-conductor. And Roebuck is now declaring Russell responsible for the "shortcomings"[a] of the heroic Palmerston just as Layard and Co. formerly did with Aberdeen. The "wingbeats" of his "free soul"[b] are now impeded by the Russellites just as they used to be by the Peelites. He has these weights hanging from him not in order to work, like Black Forest clocks, but so as to strike the hour wrongly.

All the cliques of the House of Commons have emerged the worse for wear from the conventional mock battle. The *Peelites* have at last admitted that they have hitherto been officers without armies. They have given up the pretension of forming a grouping of their own and have openly joined the Manchester School. As they were entrusted with the leadership of the army and navy during the first year of the war they have, by professing their belief in eternal peace, foolishly denounced themselves as the *traitors* within the coalition, to the happy surprise of Palmerston-Russell. They have made themselves impossible.

The *Manchester School* actually want peace in order to wage industrial war at home and abroad. They want to establish the mastery of the English bourgeoisie on the world market, where fighting is only to be permitted with their weapons—cotton-bales—and in England itself, where the aristocrat is to be pushed aside as superfluous in modern production, and the proletarian, as the mere instrument of this production, is to be subjugated, while they themselves, as the leaders of production, are to head the state and take over the offices of government. And now Cobden denounces a clergyman, Dr. Griffiths, for declaring at a public

[a] Marx uses the English word.—*Ed.*

[b] From Georg Herwegh's poem "Aus den Bergen" (*Gedichte eines Lebendigen*).—*Ed.*

meeting that the House of Lords is superfluous. And Bright weeps over the fate of the *royal* children, who will be obliged by the ruin consequent on the war to wash their own shirts. Both denounce popular agitation.[a] Are these the heroes of the Anti-Corn Law League,[189] who, carried to the top on the waves of popular agitation, used to denounce the "barbaric splendour of the Crown", Lords, landed aristocracy, etc., as "false production costs"? Their whole point consisted of the struggle against the aristocracy, not excepting the peace homily. And now they are denouncing the masses to the aristocracy! *Et propter vitam vivendi perdere causas.*[b] In this debate the Manchester School have renounced their *raison d'être.*

As for the Tories, they have discovered a peace party in their own bosom and proved that they have preserved their tradition as the representatives of English nationalism as little as their hatred for the "Bonapartes".

Finally, the ministerial side? Nothing characterises them better than their frantic efforts to cling to a motion which Palmerston himself had to turn down only a week before, which the proposer wished to drop, but which was accepted by Walpole in the name of the Tories, by Gladstone in the name of the peace men, and by the House in the name of "general merriment".

The Morning Herald has received the following communication from the Gulf of Finland:

"16 miles off Cronstadt, May 28. The *Orion* has been in to reconnoiter, and reports that the Russian fleet in Cronstadt consists of six line-of-battle ships, ready for sea; six nearly dismantled ones, thirteen apparently fitted as floating batteries, and eight steamers of a large size, besides gun-boats, which could not be counted."

"Visited Bomarsund [...] found things exactly the same as they were left, the Russians had done nothing to repair the fortifications, we saw neither man, woman, or child ... the inhabitants fight rather shy of us, in consequence of the Russians having punished a number of them for having traded with the allied squadrons last year...".[c]

Written on June 9, 1855

First published in the *Neue Oder-Zeitung,* No. 267, June 12, 1855

Marked with the sign ×

Printed according to the newspaper

Published in English for the first time

[a] The reference is to the speeches delivered in the House of Commons by Cobden on June 5, 1855, and by Bright on June 7, 1855. *The Times,* Nos. 22073 and 22075, June 6 and 8.—*Ed.*

[b] And for the sake of life to sacrifice life's only end (Juvenalis, *Satirae,* VIII, 85).—*Ed.*

[c] Quoted from two reports published in *The Morning Herald,* No. 22450, June 6, 1855—"Gulf of Finland, 16 Miles off Cronstadt" and "Visit to Bomarsund".—*Ed.*

Frederick Engels

SEVASTOPOL[190]

The mails of the *Baltic* have put us in possession of the official documents in regard to the late events at Sevastopol. The dispatches of Gen. Pélissier and Lord Raglan we published yesterday; and we now proceed to set forth the facts as they are established by this and other testimony:

On the 6th of June, the allied batteries on the right attack again opened their fire upon the town. This time, however, it was no general bombardment; it was a cannonade concentrated upon certain points with a view to reduce them at once.[a] The outworks constructed by the Russians on the 23d February and 12th March on this front of defense, the Selenghinsk, Volhynsk and Kamtschatka redoubts, had hitherto kept the besiegers and their batteries at a distance. On the Western front, the allied left attack, there were no such outworks, and the French being by this time established almost on the brink of the ditch or of the covered way (if there is one) of the defenses, the progress made on that side had by far left behind the slower advance of the right attack. As in the siege-plan of the Allies the two great divisions of the lines—the town west of the inner harbor[b] and the suburb of Karabelnaya, on its eastern side—are considered as two separate

[a] Instead of the preceding text the *Neue Oder-Zeitung* version begins: "The telegraphic dispatch announcing that the bombardment of Sevastopol had been resumed on June 6 was inaccurate. There was only a cannonade concentrated upon certain points which were to be captured at once."—*Ed.*

[b] The southern harbour.—*Ed.*

fortresses which must be attacked at the same time, the right attack had to be pushed with greater energy and the outworks to be forced so as to bring the Allies on this side up into line with their advanced parallels on the left attack. In order to accomplish this, the above redoubts and some minor intrenchments in a quarry flanking the Mamelon (Kamtchatka[a]) on its right, had to be taken. Accordingly, after 36 hours' cannonading, on the evening of the 7th of June the French advanced upon the two redoubts Selenghinsk and Volhynsk over the Careening Bay and upon the Mamelon, while the British assaulted the quarry. After an hour's sharp struggle the Allies were in possession of the works. A number of guns were taken as well as 400 prisoners, among them 13 officers. The loss on both sides was very heavy.[b]

Thus affairs on that side are nearly in the same state now as they were before the 22d February. Of the redoubts carried by the Allies, that of the Mamelon (called by the Russians the Kamtschatka redoubt) was the most important. It was constructed on the 12th of March and the following days. At that time we at once pointed out the great importance of this work and the considerable part it would play in the struggle.[c] The event has fully justified our views. This hastily constructed fieldwork has arrested the progress of the besiegers on one-half of the whole line of attack for eighty-eight days, or for a period which in ordinary sieges is considered more than sufficient to take a good-sized fortress twice over. We will now explain this astonishing phenomenon, which has but two parallels in the history of sieges: one in the defense of Colberg, 1807, by the Prussians; the other in the defense of Dantzic by the French in 1813-14.[191]

With the increase of armies in the field, the old and generally small fortifications of the time of Vauban lost their significance. They were safely passed by the hosts of the victor and scarcely observed by his flying corps, until the reserves of his army came up and found time to take them. But when these considerable armies on their march fell in with large fortresses they were

---

[a] The Kamchatka demi-lune.—*Ed.*

[b] The end of this paragraph beginning with the words "After an hour's sharp struggle" does not occur in the *Neue Oder-Zeitung*.—*Ed.*

[c] See this volume, pp. 151-55. This and the following sentence do not occur in the *Neue Oder-Zeitung*.—*Ed.*

invariably arrested. This was the case with Napoleon at Mantua in 1797, and at Dantzic in 1807.[192] The reason is evident.[a] When an army of 150,000 men advanced into a hostile country the small fry of fortresses offered no danger in the rear: all their garrisons put together were not strong enough to meet the reenforcements and reserves which were dispatched from the depots to keep up the active army to its full strength. Such small garrisons, besides, could not detach any strong bodies of troops to scour the field and to interrupt the communications of the hostile army. But when a fortress of considerable extent was met with, garrisoned by 15,000 to 25,000 men, the case was different. Such a fortress was the nucleus of defense for a whole province; it could detach in any direction, and to a considerable distance, a strong body of troops capable of acting in the field and always sure, in case of superior attack, of a safe retreat to the stronghold. To observe such a fortress was nearly as troublesome as to take it; therefore, it had to be taken at once.

Now the old fortresses of the Vauban and Cormontaigne sort concentrated all their means of defense around the main rampart and in the main ditch. All their tenailles, demi-lunes, counter-guards, tower-reduits were accumulated so as to form with all but one line of defense, which, when once broken into, was pierced altogether in a few days; and a breach once made through these defenses, the place was taken. It is evident that such a system was totally unadapted to the large fortresses which alone could check the advance of large invading armies; it would have amounted to sacrificing the garrison; the breach once effected the fort became defenseless.[b] Another system had to be resorted to—that of advanced works. The French General Montalembert, the teacher of Carnot, was the first who boldly stood up, in spite of the prejudices of his profession, for detached forts; but the method of constructing large fortresses with detached forts so as to form a complete system of defense was elaborated to its present perfection in Germany, particularly by the Prussian General Aster. The splendid defenses of Cologne, Coblentz, Posen, Königsberg, and partly of Mayence are his work, and they mark a new era in the history of fortifications. The French at last acknowledged the necessity of coming round to this system and constructed the

---

[a] The following two sentences do not occur in the *Neue Oder-Zeitung.—Ed.*

[b] The end of this sentence beginning with the words "it would have amounted to" does not occur in the *Neue Oder-Zeitung.—Ed.*

defenses of Paris with detached works planned and executed in first-rate style.[a]

The system of detached forts at once necessitated a new mode of defense. The garrisons of large fortresses had to be increased to such numbers that there was no necessity of keeping up a merely passive defense, until the enemy, advancing to the glacis, came within reach of sallies. A garrison of 20,000 or 25,000 men was strong enough to attack the enemy on his own ground. The fortress and the space around it, so far as it was protected by the detached forts, took the nature of an intrenched camp, or of a base for the field operations of the garrison, which itself was converted into a small army. The hitherto passive defense became active; it took on an offensive character. So necessary was this that when the French in 1807 besieged Dantzic, the Prussian garrison, which numbered about 20,000, constructed those very detached forts which were not in existence, but which were immediately found to be required in order to apply the resources of this large garrison to a proper defense of the place. When the French defended Dantzic in 1813-14 against the Allies they carried out the same principle with still greater success.[b]

A siege, which since Vauban had ever been an operation of short duration, and the end of which could almost with certainty be attained in a given number of days, unless the proceedings were interrupted from without—a siege now becomes an operation subject to as many chances as a war in the open field. The artillery on the ramparts at once became of secondary importance; field artillery almost took precedence over it even in the defense of a place. The skill of the engineer was no longer applied merely to the repairs of the damage done during the siege; it had, as in the field, to choose and to fortify positions situated in advance of the forts themselves; to meet trench by trench; to take in flank the enemy's works by counter-works; to change suddenly the front of defense, and thus to force the enemy to change his front of attack.

---

[a] The end of this paragraph beginning with the words "The splendid defenses of Cologne" does not occur in the *Neue Oder-Zeitung*.—*Ed.*

[b] The *Neue Oder-Zeitung* gives this paragraph in abridged form: "The system of detached forts changed the mode of defence of fortresses. The garrisons of big fortresses swelled to the size of small armies; the fortress and the space around it, so far as it was controlled by the detached forts, assumed the nature of an entrenched camp or of a base for the field operations of the garrison; the hitherto passive defense became active and took on an offensive character."—*Ed.*

Infantry became the main stay in the war of sieges as in the field, and cavalry was made a very necessary ingredient of almost every garrison. There was no longer any means to fix the probable duration of a siege, and the rules of Vauban for the attack of a place, retaining most of their correctness as far as the details of the artillery attack were concerned, became utterly inapplicable to the *ensemble* of a siege.

The Russians at Sevastopol had no time[a] to construct detached works. They were compelled to act upon the old method of fortifying a place. They erected a main rampart as a first defense; it was indeed the thing most required for the moment. Behind this they made a second and a third line of defense, and all the while went on strengthening the first. Then gradually feeling their superiority, even at a certain distance from the main wall, they advanced, constructed the Selenghinsk and Volhynsk redoubts, and finally the work on the Mamelon, and a long line of rifle pits, while on the western front, where the main body of the French was placed, they could merely construct a few lunettes close to the main ditch, and a series of rifle trenches not much further in advance. Thus from the moment the Mamelon was fortified by the Russians, the eastern front was comparatively safe; while on the western front, where such protecting outworks did not exist, the besiegers gradually advanced to the very brink of the main ditch.[b] To approach on the right attack the commanding and decisive position of Malakoff bastion the besiegers had therefore first to take the Mamelon; but the Mamelon while it defended the Malakoff was again defended by all the works in its own rear; and how they defended it, was shown in the second bombardment, when Canrobert dared not seriously assault it. Even now there can be no doubt that the loss of the French in carrying this work must have been very great.[b]

The reopening of the fire by the Allies and the energy with which General Pélissier, heedless of the lives of his soldiers, follows up every favorable chance to gain on the defense, are accompanied by a complete stagnation of operations on the Chernaya. This mode of proceeding at once gives us an insight into the character of Pélissier confirmatory of his former reputation for tenacity, obstinacy and recklessness. There were two ways open to him; to take the field, inclose Sevastopol on the north side also,

---

[a] The *Neue Oder-Zeitung* has here: "after the notorious flanking march".—*Ed.*
[b] This sentence does not occur in the *Neue Oder-Zeitung*.—*Ed.*

and then take up the siege again with redoubled energy and a quadrupled chance of a speedy success,[a] or else to go on in the faulty way of the last eight months; to cling doggedly to the south side, destroy every stone of it and drive the Russians out of a place which after all, if reduced, could not be occupied by his own troops on account of the batteries on the north side.

There is not a military man of sense in either hemisphere who, on the news of Pélissier's nomination to the command, and of the great reenforcements received by the Allies, did not expect that he would at once take the first course. Most particularly when Omer Pasha with 25,000 Turks came round to Balaklava, there was no doubt that the Allies were strong enough to carry on the siege, to send 15,000 men to Kertch and still to advance into the field with more men than the Russians could spare to oppose them. Why have they not done so? Are they still in want of means of transport? Have they no confidence in their ability to carry on a campaign in the Crimea? We do not know. But this is certain: unless Pélissier has *very cogent* reasons to abstain from taking the field, he is pursuing, out of sheer obstinacy and self-will, an extremely faulty course; for with a loss equal to that he is now continually subjecting his army to, in assaults, he might obtain results in the field of far greater magnitude, and of a far more decisive effect. To take the south side without having even invested the north side, which completely commands it, is to proceed in utter defiance of all rules of warfare, and if Pélissier is bent upon that, he may yet ruin the great army he commands.

We will, however, give the new commander the benefit of every doubtful circumstance. It may be that the struggles on the left attack were inevitable and provoked by the counter-approaches of the Russians. It may be that it was necessary to confine the Russians to the limits of their original lines—to convince them, by a few hard, irresistible blows, of the superiority of the besiegers—before a separation of the army into a siege-corps and a field-corps could be ventured on. But allowing even this, we now must say that the utmost limit has been reached, and that any further serious attempt upon the body of the place will be a downright blunder, unless the strength of the Russian army in the

---

[a] The following text is added here in the *Neue Oder-Zeitung*: "This was all the more to be expected after not only the reinforcements but also Omer Pasha had arrived in Balaklava with 25,000 Turks."—*Ed.*

field has been first tried with all the forces that can be made available for the purpose.[a]

Written about June 12, 1855

First published in the *New-York Daily Tribune,* No. 4429, June 29, 1855; reprinted in the *New-York Semi-Weekly Tribune,* No. 1054, July 3, 1855 and the *New-York Weekly Tribune,* No. 721, July 7, 1855; as a leading article; the German version was first published in the *Neue Oder-Zeitung,* No. 273, June 15, 1855, marked with the sign ×

Reproduced from the *New-York Daily Tribune*

[a] Instead of the last two paragraphs the *Neue Oder-Zeitung* has the following concluding passage: "With the same losses, to which Pélissier now continuously exposes his army with his assaults, he could obtain results of far greater magnitude, and of a far more decisive nature in the field. To try to take the south side without having even invested the north side which commands it, is an incomprehensible procedure. Pélissier may still be lacking means of transport for field operations. Or the counter-approaches of the Russians may have made it necessary to push them back to their original lines and show them the superiority of the besiegers *before* proceeding to field operations. However that may be, with the seizure of Malakhov no excuses are left. Should Pélissier be stubborn enough to *persist* in serious attempts upon the main body of the enemy instead of trying to break the strength of the Russians in the field with all the forces that can be made available, the *destruction of the army he commands is not at all improbable,* especially since the area in which such vast numbers of people are confined is one big graveyard whose deadly miasmas will be let loose by the first heat of the summer."—*Ed.*

Frederick Engels

NAPOLEON'S WAR PLANS[193]

The French Government has thought proper again to give to the world through the columns of the Paris *Constitutionnel* another intimation respecting the manner in which the war is to be carried on for the next couple of months.[a] These exposés are now becoming not only fashionable but periodical, and although they are apt to be inconsistent with each other, they afford for the time a pretty good idea of what favorable chances are open to the French Government. Take them all in all, they form a collection of all Louis Bonaparte's possible plans of campaign against Russia. As such they deserve some attention, for they involve the destiny of the second Empire and the possibility of French national resurrection.

It seems then that there is to be no "*grande guerre*" with 500,000 Austrians and 100,000 French on the Vistula and Dnieper. Nor is there to be a general rising of those "oppressed nationalities" which are constantly looking toward the West. No Hungarian, Italian, Polish armies are to appear at the magic call of the man who put down the Roman Republic.[194] All that belongs to the past. Austria has done her duty to the West. So has Prussia. So has all the world. Everybody is satisfied with everybody. This war is no grand war at all. It is not destined to renew the glory of the old struggles of the French with the Russians, though Pélissier accidentally says as much in one of his dispatches. The French troops are not sent to the Crimea to reap a harvest of glory; they are simply there to do police duty. The question pending is a

[a] This refers to A. de Cesena's article on the aims and prospects of the Crimean war published in the semi-official *Constitutionnel*, No. 169, June 18, 1855.—*Ed.*

mere local one: the supremacy of the Black Sea—and it will be settled on the very locality concerned. To give the war any larger dimensions would be folly. "Respectfully but firmly" will the Allies knock down every attempt at resistance by the Russians in the Black Sea and on its coasts; and when they have done that—why then of course they or Russia, or both of them will make peace.

Thus another of the Bonapartist self-delusions has been put aside. The dreams of the Rhine as the boundary of France, of the acquisition of Belgium and Savoy, have vanished, and a sober modesty of no common degree has taken their place. We are not fighting to restore France to the position which is due to her in Europe. Far from it. Not even are we fighting for civilization, as we used to say a short time ago. We are too modest to pretend to anything of such magnitude. What we are fighting for is—why, nothing more than the interpretation of the Third Point[195] of the Vienna protocol! Such is the language now held by his Imperial Majesty Napoleon III, by the grace of the army and the toleration of Europe, Emperor of the French.

And what does this all amount to? We are told the war is being carried on for a purely local object, and can be brought to a successful termination by purely local means. Take the actual supremacy of the Black Sea out of the hands of Russia, and the end will be accomplished. Once masters of the Black Sea and its shores, hold what you have got, and Russia will very soon give in. Such is the most recent of all the many plans óf campaign issued from headquarters at Paris. We proceed to look at it a little more closely.

We will take matters as they stand at present. From Constantinople to the Danube on the one side, and round by the Circassian coast, Anapa, Kertch, Balaklava, to Eupatoria, the whole coast is taken out of the hands of the Russians. Kaffa and Sevastopol are the only points that hold out, the one hard pressed, the other so situated that it must be abandoned as soon as it is seriously menaced. More than that, the allied fleets sweep the inland sea of Azoff; their light vessels have been up as far as Taganrog, and every place of importance has been assailed by them. No portion of the coast can be said to remain in the hands of the Russians, except the tract from Perekop to the Danube, or about one-fifteenth part of their possessions on that coast. Now we will even suppose that Kaffa and Sevastopol have fallen, and that the Crimea is in the hands of the Allies. What then? That Russia will not make peace in that situation, she has already loudly proclaimed. She would be mad if she did. It would be giving up the battle after your advanced guard has been thrown back, at the very moment your main body is coming up. What then can the Allies do, after having secured these advantages at an immense cost?

They can, we are told, destroy Odessa, Cherson, Nikolaieff; they can even land a strong army at Odessa, fortify themselves there so as to hold out against any number of Russians, and then act according to circumstances. They can, besides, detach troops to the Caucasus and all but destroy the Russian army which, under General Muravieff, now holds Georgia and the other trans-Caucasian countries. But suppose all these things to be accomplished: and again we ask, what then, if Russia, as she certainly will do, refuse to make peace under these circumstances? Let it not be forgotten that Russia is not placed in the same position as France or England. England can afford to conclude a shabby peace. In fact, as soon as John Bull has had enough of excitement and war-taxes, he will be but too eager to creep out of the mess and leave his dear allies to shift for themselves. England's real power and source of strength do not exactly lie in that direction. Louis Bonaparte may, too, find himself placed in a position where an unseemly peace will be preferable, for him, to a war to the knife; for it must not be forgotten that with such an adventurer, in a desperate case, the chance of prolonging his dominion for another six months outweighs every other consideration. Turkey and Sardinia are sure to be left to their own puny resources in the decisive moment. So much, at least, is certain. But Russia *cannot* make peace, any more than ancient Rome could, while the enemy is on her territory. Russia, for a hundred and fifty years past, has never made a peace by which she lost ground. Even Tilsit[196] gave her an increase of territory, and Tilsit was concluded before a single Frenchman had put his foot on Russian soil. To make peace while a large and advancing army is on Russian soil, a peace involving a sacrifice of territory, or at least a restriction of the Czar's sovereignty in his own dominions, would be to break at once with the traditions of a century and a half. Such a step could not be thought of by a Czar new to the throne,[a] new to the people, and anxiously watched by a powerful national party. Such a peace could not be concluded until all the resources offensive and (above all) *defensive* of Russia had been brought into play and found wanting. That day will doubtless come, and the necessity of minding her own business will be imposed upon Russia, but by

[a] Alexander II.—*Ed.*

other enemies than Louis Bonaparte and Palmerston, and after struggles far more decisive than the "local" execution put in force on her Black Sea dominions. But let us suppose the Crimea conquered and garrisoned by 50,000 Allies—the Caucasus and everything to the South of it cleared of Russian troops, and an allied army checking the Russians on the Kuban and Terek—Odessa taken, and converted into an intrenched camp, holding say 100,000 Anglo-French troops; Nikolaieff, Cherson, Ismail, destroyed or occupied by the Allies. We will even suppose that beside these "local" exploits, something of some importance may have been accomplished in the Baltic, although with the information at our command it is hard to say what that may be. What then?

Will the Allies confine themselves to holding their positions and tiring out the Russians? Their men in the Crimea and the Caucasus will vanish faster under the effects of disease than they can be replaced. Their main army, say at Odessa, will have to be fed by the fleets, for the country for hundreds of miles around Odessa produces nothing. The Russian army, surrounded by Cossack scouts—nowhere more useful than in these steppes—will harass them whenever they show themselves out of their intrenchments, if it cannot take up a permanent position somewhere in the neighborhood of the town. It is impossible under such circumstances to force the Russians to give battle; their great advantage will always be to draw the Allies into the interior of the country. To every advance of the Allies, they will respond by a slow retreat. Yet a large army cannot be confined for any length of time in an intrenched camp without giving it something to do. The gradual progress of disorder and demoralization would force the Allies to some decided movement. Sickness, too, would make the place too hot for them. In a word, to occupy the principal points on the coast and there to await the moment when Russia finds it necessary to give in is a game that will never do at all. There are three chances to one that the Allies would be tired of it first, and that the graves of their soldiers on the shores of the Black Sea would soon be counted by hundreds of thousands.

It would be a military blunder, too. To command a coast, it is not sufficient to possess its principal points. It is the possession of the inner country which alone gives the possession of the coast. As we have seen, the very circumstances arising from an establishment on the coast of South Russia would all but force the Allies to march into the interior. And here it is that the difficulties begin. Up to the frontiers of the Governments of Podolia, Kieff, Poltava, Charkoff, the country is an almost uncultivated plain, very scantily watered, furnishing nothing but grass, and not even that after the heats of Summer. Supposing Odessa, Nikolaieff, Cherson to be taken for a base of operations, where would be the object against which the Allies could direct their efforts? The towns are few and far between, and there are none of sufficient importance to give, if occupied, a decisive character to the operation. There is no decisive point nearer than Moscow, and that is 700 miles off! Five hundred thousand men would be required for a march on Moscow, and where are they to come from? Surely, the case is such that in this way the "local" war can never lead to any decisive result; and we defy Louis Bonaparte with all his exuberance of strategic imagination to find another.

All this, however, presupposes not only the strict neutrality but even the moral support of Austria. And where is that power at the present moment? Austria and Prussia have declared they would consider an advance of the Russian army towards the Balkan, in 1854, as a *casus belli* against Russia.[197] Where is the guarantee that in 1856 they will not consider a French advance on Moscow or even Charkoff as a cause of war against the Western Powers? We need not forget that every army advancing from the Black Sea toward the interior of Russia as much offers its flank to Austria as a Russian army advancing into Turkey from the Danube; and at a given distance, therefore, its communication with its base of operations, that is to say its very existence, is at the mercy of Austria. To keep Austria quiet, even for a time, she will have to be bought off by the surrender of Bessarabia to her troops. Once on the Dniester, her army commands Odessa as completely as if that town were garrisoned by Austrians. And under such circumstances could an allied army venture on a wild-goose chase after the Russians into the interior of the country? Nonsense! But this nonsense, let us remember, is the logical consequence of Louis Bonaparte's latest plan of "local warfare."

The first plan for the campaign was the "grande guerre," by means of the Austrian alliance. It would have placed the French army in the same numerical inferiority and virtual dependence with respect to the Austrian army as the English army is now with regard to the French. It would have given the revolutionary initiative to Russia. Louis Bonaparte could do neither. Austria refused to act; the subject dropped. The second was the "war of nationalities." This would have roused a storm between the Germans, Italians, Hungarians on one hand, and the Slavonian insurrection on the other, which must have reacted upon France at once and overturned Louis Bonaparte's Lower Empire[198] in less time than it took to set it up. The counterfeit "iron man," passing himself off as a Napoleon, shrunk back. The third and most modest of all is the "local war for local objects." It reduces itself at once to an absurdity. We are again obliged to ask: What next? After all, it is far easier to be made Emperor of the French, with every circumstance to favor the design, than to act as such, even when long study before the looking-glass has made his Majesty perfectly familiar with all the theatrical portion of the business.

Written about June 15, 1855

First published in the *New-York Daily Tribune,* No. 4431, July 2, 1855; reprinted in the *New-York Semi-Weekly Tribune,* No. 1054, July 3, 1855; an abridged and altered German version was first published as part of Marx's report in the *Neue Oder-Zeitung,* Nos. 279 and 287, June 19 and 23, 1855, marked with the sign ×

Reproduced from the *New-York Daily Tribune*

Karl Marx

NAPIER'S LETTERS.—ROEBUCK'S COMMITTEE

London, June 15. Sir *Charles Napier* has published a series of letters about the Baltic Fleet,[a] the following being No. 1:

"People ask why our squadron in the Baltic, which did nothing to signify last year, is likely to do nothing this? The question is easily answered, viz., *because* Sir James Graham did not attend to the plans I sent him last June, and which he pretended to know nothing about; and because the Admiralty did not attend to the plans I sent them last September. Had Admiral Dundas been furnished with the appliances I pointed out, Sweaborg might have been bombarded, and probably destroyed. Instead of doing that, they spent about [...] a million of money in building iron floating batteries, which will hardly swim, and if sent to the Baltic will probably never return; and this, after it was proved, at Portsmouth, that 68-pounders would destroy them at 400 yards; and at 800 yards everybody knows they could do no harm to granite walls. Had the same money been spent in mortar vessels, something might have been expected, or had half the money been laid out in putting Lord Dundonald's plans (which he communicated to me) in execution, I have no doubt they would have been successfully employed, both in the Baltic and Black Sea. My time will come, and before long, when I shall be able to expose all Sir James Graham's conduct to me. He has been shown to have opened private letters" (in the Bandiera affair [199]) "by Mr. Duncombe. He endeavoured to throw the blame of poor Captain Christie's death on Mr. Layard, and I have accused him of perverting my letters, which I am prevented from proving, by the pretence that the publication would afford information to the enemy. That pretence will soon cease, and the country shall know what means the Right Hon. Baronet used to induce Admiral Berkeley and Admiral Richards to sign instructions, which, if carried out, would have lost the Queen's fleet. The country shall know whether the First Lord of the Admiralty has the power to turn an officer's private letters into public ones, and prevent him doing the same with the First Lord's.

Sir *Charles Napier*."[b]

---

[a] Published in *The Morning Advertiser*.—*Ed.*

[b] *The Morning Advertiser*, No. 19964, June 15, 1855.—*Ed.*

Roebuck's Committee met again yesterday, for the 49th time, to reach a decision about the report to be submitted to the House of Commons. After a four hours' debate its members were just as incapable of reconciling their views as in earlier sessions. They adjourned again until Monday in the "hope" that they will finally be able to announce the conclusion of their proceedings.

The "Administrative Reform Association"[200] held a large meeting yesterday in the Drury Lane Theatre; not, be it noted, a *public* meeting but a *ticket-meeting*,[a] a meeting to which only those favoured with tickets were admitted. The gentlemen were thus completely at their ease, *au sein de leur famille*.[b] They were avowedly meeting to give "public opinion" an airing. But to shield public opinion from draughts from outside half a company of constables were posted at the doors of the Drury Lane. What a fragile public opinion that only dares to be made public with the protection of constables and tickets of admission! The meeting was, above all, a demonstration in support of Layard, who is at last due to present his reform bill to the House tonight.

At a public meeting held in Newcastle-upon-Tyne the day before yesterday David Urquhart denounced "the treacherous Ministry and the feeble-minded Parliament".

About the meetings now being prepared by the Chartists in the provinces, another time.[201]

While thus the status quo is coming in for criticism from various quarters and different points of view, *Prince Albert*, at a dinner in *Trinity House*,[c] has seized the opportunity of stating the position of the *Court* with regard to the general ferment.[d] He too has a panacea for the crisis. It is: *"patriotic,* [...] *self-denying confidence in the Cabinet!"* According to Prince Albert only the despotism of the Cabinet can enable constitutional England to stand up to Russia and wage war against the despotism of the North. The comparison he made between England and Russia was neither striking nor felicitous. For example: The Queen[e] had no power to levy troops nor had she any troops at her command but such as offered their

---

[a] Marx uses the English expression. The meeting was held on June 13, 1855.—*Ed.*

[b] In the bosom of the family.—*Ed.*

[c] The headquarters of the British mariners' corporation, which received its first charter from Henry VIII in 1514. Trinity House is at Tower Hill.—*Ed.*

[d] Prince Albert's address at Trinity House on June 9, 1855, and Palmerston's reply were reported in *The Times*, No. 22080, June 14, 1855 ("Prince Albert on Public Affairs").—*Ed.*

[e] Victoria.—*Ed.*

services voluntarily! Prince Albert forgets that the Queen has approximately £30 million at her disposal to *buy* troops with. Since when has *forced labour* been more productive than *wage-labour*? What would be said of a Manchester manufacturer who deplored the competition of the Muscovite manufacturers on the grounds that he only had at his disposal workers "offering their services voluntarily"? Instead of emphasising that the Emperor of Russia[a] has had the purpose of his "holy" war clearly and firmly proclaimed to his people from the pulpit, whereas for two years England has been waging a war of which the Prime Minister[b] has said in Parliament that "nobody can state its *object*", Prince Albert deplores the fact that

"Her Majesty's Government can take *no measure* for the prosecution of the war which it has not beforehand to explain in Parliament"!

As though Roebuck's committee had not been set up only *after* two-thirds of the British army had been sacrificed! As though the debate on the Vienna Conferences had not been held *after* they were over! In actual fact there was not a single explanation of any war measure in Parliament apart from Russell's blustering, unprovoked announcement of the Sevastopol expedition, whose only aim evidently was to give the Petersburg Cabinet timely warning! And if the blockade was debated it was not because the Ministry took this step but because it proclaimed it without taking it. Instead of deploring that in a war against Russia the Crown was compelled by parliamentary intrigues to submit to the dictatorship of an avowedly Russophile and notoriously peaceful Cabinet, Prince Albert complains, on the contrary, that an unfavourable vote in Parliament "forced the Queen to dismiss her confidential servants". Instead of rightly complaining that blunders, foibles and acts of villainy which, in Russia, would render generals, ministers and diplomats liable for Siberia, in England are followed at most by a little half-hearted gossip in the press and in Parliament, Prince Albert complains, on the contrary, that

"no mistake, however trifling, can occur, no want or weakness exist, which is not at once denounced, and even sometimes exaggerated, with morbid satisfaction".

Prince Albert inserted these morbidly irritated expectorations in a toast to his long-standing enemy Lord Palmerston. But Palmerston is not given to magnanimity. He at once used the false

---

[a] Nicholas I.—*Ed.*
[b] Palmerston.—*Ed.*

position taken by the Prince in order to beat his own breast in front of him, protesting loudly:

"I am bound to say that the English people have given us the most generous support."

He went further. He declared outright that he possessed "the confidence" of the English people. He spurned the Prince's obtrusive exhortations to the people. He paid court to the people after the Prince had paid court to him. He did not even think it worth the trouble to reply with a compliment to the Crown. Prince Albert had sought to set himself up as the protector of the Ministry, hence proclaiming the Cabinet's "*independence*" of Parliament and the people; Palmerston replied by pointing out the Crown's "*dependence*" on the Cabinet.

Written on June 14 and 15, 1855

First published in the *Neue Oder-Zeitung*, No. 277, June 18, 1855

Marked with the sign ×

Printed according to the newspaper

Published in English for the first time

Karl Marx and Frederick Engels

THE DEBATE ON LAYARD'S MOTION.— THE WAR IN THE CRIMEA[202]

London, June 16. The debate on Layard's motion[203] was not concluded yesterday but adjourned until Monday evening. So we shall also adjourn our account of it for the time being.

One incident in the Commons sitting deserves mention.[a] During the talks about the Vienna Conference Palmerston had intimated that the Peelites had made the stipulation of certain peace terms a condition for their entry into his Cabinet. Russell defended these same terms in Vienna. Yesterday *Otway* called on Palmerston to state whether he was adhering to peace terms that had originated from the Peelites, in other words from a party confessedly acting in the interests of Russia. Gladstone rose and demanded that the speaker accusing him and his friends of *treason* should be called to order. The call to order was made. Otway, however, repeated his description of the Peelites and his question to Palmerston. As is his custom, Palmerston refused to reply. The peace terms were naturally dependent on the events of the war. As regards the Peelites, they had in particular stipulated that a "certain" condition, which he could not name, would not be made a *conditio sine qua non* of peace. In his reply to Palmerston, Gladstone for his part denied ever having had talks with Palmerston about the peace terms. It might be otherwise with his friend Graham. Moreover, he protested against Palmerston's system of affected official reserve on the one side, and the concealed hint, ambiguous

[a] The debate in the House of Commons on June 15, 1855 was reported in *The Times*, No. 22082, June 16, 1855.—*Ed.*

allusion and quasi-statement on the other. Let the ministry speak out frankly or be silent. Gladstone administered this lesson to Palmerston with sanctimonious bitterness.

The French government has issued in the *Constitutionnel* a new *exposé* of the conduct of the war in the coming months.[a] These *exposés* have now become not only fashionable but also regular. Although in profound contradiction with themselves, they are valuable as revelations of "various" plans of campaign devised against Russia by Louis Bonaparte. They are valuable insofar as they document the disappearance of one Bonapartist illusion after the other. The first plan was that of "*grand war*" by means of the Austrian alliance, with 500,000 Austrians and 100,000 Frenchmen on the Vistula and the Dnieper. The plan would have assigned to the French Army the same numerically subordinate relationship to the Austrians as the English have to the French in the Crimea. It would have conceded the revolutionary initiative to Russia. Austria refused to act. The plan was dropped. The second plan was the "war of nationalities", a general rising of the "oppressed, who are constantly looking to the West". It would have provoked a storm between the Germans, Italians and Hungarians on the one side, and the Slav insurrection on the other. Recoiling on France, it would have threatened the "second" Empire with its end. The imitation "man of iron" shrank back from it. The plan was dropped. All this is now over and done with. Austria has done its duty, Prussia has done its duty, the whole world has done its duty, and Bonaparte has come to the third and most modest plan. "*Local war for local aims.*" The French troops in the Crimea are not fighting for glory, they are merely there on police duty. The question to be settled is a purely local one: *predominance in the Black Sea*, and it must be cleared up there, on the spot. It would be foolishness to give the war wider dimensions. "Respectfully but firmly" the allies will crush any Russian attempt to resist them in the Black Sea, and then they or the Russians or both will make peace. Nothing is left of the high-sounding phrases, not even the phrase about civilisation, nothing but the fight for the 3rd point[204] of the Vienna Protocol. *War with a purely local aim*, remarks the imperial oracle, *can only be waged with local means.* Deprive the Russians simply of their predominance in the Black Sea! In our next letter we shall show[b] that Bonaparte has descended from

---

[a] A. de Cesena's article on the aims and prospects of the Crimean war published in the semi-official *Constitutionnel*, No. 169, June 18, 1855.—*Ed.*

[b] See this volume, pp. 287-89.—*Ed.*

"grand war" to the "war of the nationalities", and from the "war of nationalities" to "local war serving local purposes and waged with local means", and this final war becomes "*preposterous*".

Written on June 16, 1855

First published in the *Neue Oder-Zeitung*, No. 279, June 19, 1855

Marked with the sign ×

Printed according to the newspaper

Published in English for the first time

Karl Marx

PRINCE ALBERT'S TOAST.— THE STAMP DUTY ON NEWSPAPERS

London, June 18. There were several curious circumstances connected with the publication of Prince Albert's speech and Palmerston's reply. The speeches were made at Trinity House[a] on Saturday, June 9. The following Monday the daily newspapers only mentioned the annual dinner of the Trinity Brotherhood in passing, without dwelling on Prince Albert's toast. Not until Wednesday, June 13, did *The Daily News* print the toast and the speech of thanks, followed by *The Times* on Thursday, June 14. It has turned out that their publication was a trick of Lord Palmerston's to restore his own popularity at the expense of his royal wellwisher. Prince Albert has now discovered at his own expense where "self-sacrificing confidence" in the noble viscount leads, the sort of confidence that he recommended so eagerly to the country. The following extract from *Reynolds' Weekly* will show how Prince Albert's toast was received by the majority of the weekly press. *Reynolds' Weekly,*[b] it should be noted, has a circulation of 2,496,256 copies. After detailed criticism it goes on to say:

"The royal censor maintains that no want or weakness exist, which is not at once denounced, and even sometimes exaggerated with a kind of *morbid satisfaction.* The patience of the English people is proverbial; [...] like Issachar, they may be compared to an ass crouched down between two burdens—usury and land monopoly; but this taunt of the Prince-Consort is the most insolent and deadly insult with which even Englishmen have borne. "Morbid satisfaction!" That is, the English people have a

[a] The headquarters of the British mariners' corporation in London (for the speeches of Prince Albert and Palmerston see this volume, pp. 273-76).—*Ed.*

[b] *Reynolds' Weekly Newspaper.—Ed.*

'morbid satisfaction' in contemplating the horrible sufferings to which [...] treason and aristocratic imbecility have exposed our heroic soldiers—morbid satisfaction at having been made the dupes of Austria—morbid satisfaction at having squandered 40,000,000*l.* of treasure and lost 40,000 of the bravest human lives—morbid satisfaction at having excited the distrust of the ally whom we profess to help, and the contempt of the foe whom we wish to chastise. But the charge is not only insolent and insulting, it is also false and calumnious in the highest degree. Whatever may be the faults of the English people—and heaven knows they are many—they have no *satisfaction* in the miseries and disasters of their soldiers and sailors, nor in the disgrace that have been entailed on the national character [...] with the exception of royal Germans, aristocratic traitors and their abominable and disgusting parasites.... At the same time, we are prepared to admit that it is very difficult for an obese and lazy Sybarite and feather-bed soldier to conceive of the sufferings and trials of real soldiers and sailors.... There is one thing in which we agree with the royal warrior. Constitutionalism is an enormous sham—a most clumsy, bungling, incongruous, and mischievous form of government. But the Prince is silly in supposing that there is no other alternative than despotism. We beg to remind him that there is such a thing as republicanism—an alternative to which it is possible for this nation to have recourse, and in the direction of which, we think, the current of public opinion is tending, rather than to the unlimited despotism which the martial Prince covets."

Thus writes *Reynolds' [Weekly Newspaper]*.[a]

The new Act for the *abolition of stamp duty on newspapers* received the royal assent last Sunday and will come into force on June 30. Thereafter, stamp duty is only required on copies to be sent *free* by post. Of the London dailies, *The Morning Herald* is the only one to announce that it will reduce its price from 5d. to 4d. A large number of weeklies, on the other hand, such as *Lloyd's*,[b] *Reynolds'*, *The People's Paper*, etc., have already announced a reduction from 3d. to 2d. A new London daily, the *Courier and Telegraph*, in the same format as *The Times*, is announced, price 2d. As for *new* weekly papers at 2d., the following have appeared in London to date: *The Pilot* (Catholic magazine); the *Illustrated Times* and Mr. *Charles Knight*'s *Town and Country Paper*. Finally Messrs. Willet and Ledger have given notice of a new weekly London penny paper.[c] What is more significant, though, is the revolution in the provincial press caused by the abolition of stamp duty. In Glasgow alone four new daily penny papers are to appear. In Liverpool and Manchester the papers that have hitherto only appeared weekly or twice weekly are to turn into dailies at 3d., 2d., and 1d. The emancipation from London of the provincial press, the

---

[a] *Reynolds' Newspaper*, No. 253, June 17, 1815.—*Ed.*
[b] *Lloyd's Weekly Newspaper*.—*Ed.*
[c] *The Penny Times*. Marx uses the English expression "penny paper" here and below.—*Ed.*

decentralisation of journalism was, in fact, the main aim of the Manchester School in their fierce and protracted campaign against stamp duty.

Written on June 18, 1855

First published in the *Neue Oder-Zeitung,* No. 283, June 21, 1855

Marked with the sign ×

Printed according to the newspaper

Published in English for the first time

Karl Marx

ECCENTRICITIES OF POLITICS

In his book on the *Congrès de Vienne* the Abbé de Pradt justly accuses that dancing Congress, as it was called by the Prince de Ligne, of having laid the foundation of Russian supremacy in Europe and given its sanction thereto.[205]

> "Thus," he exclaims, "it happens that the European war of independence against France terminates with the subjection of Europe to Russia. It was not worth while to fatigue oneself so much for such a result."[a]

The war against France being at the same time a war against the Revolution, an Anti-Jacobin war, naturally led to a transfer of influence from the West to the East, from France to Russia. The Vienna Congress was the natural offspring of the Anti-Jacobin War, the Treaty of Vienna the legitimate product of the Vienna Congress, and Russian supremacy the natural child of the Treaty of Vienna. The crowd of English, French and German writers cannot therefore be allowed to throw all the blame upon Prussia, because Frederick William III, by his blind devotion to the Emperor Alexander and the categorical orders he gave his Embassadors to side with Russia in all important questions, thwarted that infamous triumvirate, Castlereagh, Metternich and Talleyrand, in their deep-laid schemes to erect safe territorial barriers against Russian encroachments[206] and thus ward off the unpleasant but inevitable consequences of the system they had so zealously imposed upon the Continent. Even to such an unscrupulous conclave it was not given to falsify the logic of events.

---

[a] Dominique Dufour de Pradt, *Du Congrès de Vienne*, t. I, p. 262.— *Ed.*

Russia's preponderance in Europe being inseparable from the Treaty of Vienna, any war against that power not proclaiming at the outset the abolition of the Treaty, cannot but prove a mere tissue of shams, delusions and collusions. Now, the present war is undertaken with a view not to supersede but rather to consolidate the Treaty of Vienna by the introduction, in a supplementary way, of Turkey into the protocols of 1815. Then it is expected the conservative millennium will dawn and the aggregate force of the Governments be allowed to direct itself exclusively to the "tranquilization" of the European mind. From the following remarkable passages translated from the Prussian Marshal Knesebeck's pamphlet "relating to the equilibrium of Europe, composed at the meeting of the Vienna Congress,"[a] it will be seen that even at the epoch of that Congress, the principal actors were fully aware of the maintenance of Turkey being as much interwoven with "the system" as the partition of Poland.[207]

"The Turks in Europe! What harm have the Turks done to you? They are a powerful and honest people; quiet for centuries among themselves, if you leave them undisturbed, confidence may be placed in them. Have they ever deceived you? Are they not sincere and frank in their policy? Brave and warlike indeed; but this is wholesome and good for more reasons than one. They are the best bulwark against the encroachment of the Asiatic surplus population, and just because they have a footing in Europe they ward off every encroachment. If they were driven away, they themselves would encroach. Just imagine them away. What would happen? Either Russia or Austria would get possession of those entire countries, or a separate Greek State would be founded there. Do you wish to make Russia still more powerful? to draw down on this side also the colossus on your own heads? Are you not yet content that it has advanced its stride from the Volga to the Niemen, from the Niemen to the Vistula, and will now probably extend it as far as the Wartha? And if this be not the case, do you wish to turn the power of Austria in the direction of Asia, and to make it by that means weak or indifferent to the maintenance of its central position to the encroachments from the West? Recall to yourselves the position of the past times of John Sobieski, of Eugène of Savoy, and of Montecucculi. In what way did France at first gain dominion in Germany, but because the power of Austria was of necessity constantly engaged in opposing the encroachments of Asia? Do you wish to restore this state of things, and to increase it still more by bringing it nearer Asia?

"A separate Grecian" or Byzantine "State is, therefore, to be founded! Would this ameliorate the condition of Europe? In the state of torpidity into which that people" (the Greeks) "have sunk, would not Europe, on the contrary, be obliged to be continually under arms to protect itself against the returning Turks? Would not Greece become merely a Russian colony, in consequence of the influence which Russia would possess over this State through religion, commerce and interest? Rather let the Turks alone where they are, and do not arouse the restless power

---

[a] K. F. Knesebeck, *Denkschrift, betreffend die Gleichgewichts-Lage Europa's, beim Zusammentritte des Wiener Congresses verfasst.* The excerpts quoted below (with omissions and explanatory addenda) are from pp. 11-14.—*Ed.*

while it reposes. 'But,' exclaims a well-meaning philanthropist, 'men are maltreated there. The most beautiful part of the world, including the ancient Athens and Sparta, is inhabited by barbarians!'

"It may be all true, my friend: men there are at present, or until lately were, strangled; but they are bastinadoed, beaten, scourged, and sold in other parts. Before you change anything, think whether you could also better at the same moment; whether the bastinado and the rod, with Greek perfidy, would be easier to bear than the silk cord and a firman" with the Turks. "Do away first with those things, and with the slave trade in Europe, and console yourself about the uncivilization of the Turk; his uncivilization has power, his faith gives courage, and we require strength and courage to be able to watch tranquilly the Muscovite pushing himself on as far as the Wartha.

"The Turks are then to be maintained, but the Poles as a nation are to sink! Yes, it cannot be otherwise.

"Whatever has strength to stand, endures; where all is rotten, it must perish. And so it is. Let any one ask himself what would be the result if the Polish nation were maintained independent in its natural character. Drunkenness, gluttony, servility, contempt for all that is better and for every other people, contemptuous derision of all order and custom, extravagance, dissoluteness, venality, cunning, treachery, immorality from the palace to the cottage; that is the element in which the Pole exists. For this he sings his songs, plays on his fiddle and guitar, kisses his mistress and drinks out of her shoe, draws his sword, strokes his moustaches, mounts his horse, marches to battle with Dumouriez and Bonaparte or anybody else on earth, delights in excessive brandy and punch, fights with friend and foe, ill-treats his wife and his serf, sells his property, goes abroad, disturbs half the world, and swears by Kościuszko and Poniatowski Poland shall not die as sure as he is a Pole.

"Here you behold what you would support when you say Poland shall be restored.

"Is such a nation worthy to exist? Is such a people fit for a Constitution? A Constitution presupposes an idea of order, [...] for it does nothing but regulate, and points out to each member of the community the place to which he belongs, for which reason it determines the ranks of which the State is to be composed, and to each rank its place, condition, order, rights and duties, as well as the course of the State machine and the principal traits of its government. What! Rule a people when no one will have order? A Polish King (Stefan Batory) once exclaimed: 'Poles—not order—you know none; not government—you respect none; to a mere chance you owe your continued existence!'

"And thus it is still. Disorder, immorality, is the Poles' element. No; let this people undergo the bastinado. Providence wills it. Heaven knows what is profitable for mankind.

"For the present, therefore, no more Poles!"

Old Marshal Knesebeck's views are then to be realized by the present war—a war undertaken for the extension and consolidation of the Vienna Treaty of 1815. During the whole period of the Restoration and the Monarchy of July there was the delusion afloat in France that Napoleonism meant the abolition of the Treaty of Vienna, which had placed Europe under the official tutelage of Russia, and France under the *"surveillance publique"* of Europe. Now the present imitator of his uncle, haunted by the inexorable irony of his fatal position, is proving to the world that Napoleonism means war, not to emancipate France *from*, but to subject Turkey *to*, the Treaty of Vienna. War in the interest of the Treaty of Vienna and under the pretext of checking the power of Russia!

This is the true "Idée Napoléonienne,"[a] as interpreted by the resurrection-man at Paris. The English being the proud allies of the second Napoleon, feel themselves, of course, authorized to deal with the sayings of the old Napoleon as his nephew does with his ideas. We are then not to be astonished at reading in a recent English author (Dunlop)[b] that Napoleon foretold that the next struggle with Russia would involve the great question of whether Europe should be "Constitutional or Cossack." Before the days of the Lower Empire[208] Napoleon was supposed to have said "Republican or Cossack."[c] However, the world lives and learns.

—And it is for failing to appreciate the glories of the Treaty of Vienna and of the European "system" based upon it, that the *Tribune* is charged with infidelity to the cause of human rights and of Freedom![209]

Written on June 19, 1855

First published in the *New-York Daily Tribune*, No. 4437, July 10, 1855 as a leading article

Reproduced from the newspaper

---

[a] An allusion to Louis Bonaparte's book *Des idées napoléoniennes*, published in Paris in 1839.—*Ed.*

[b] This presumably refers to A. G. Dunlop's book *Cossack Rule, and Russian Influence in Europe, and over Germany*.—*Ed.*

[c] A reference to Napoleon's statement on St. Helena that Europe was bound to become "Republican or Cossack" (quoted by E. Las Cases in his *Mémorial de Sainte-Hélène...*, t. 3, p. 111).—*Ed.*

Karl Marx and Frederick Engels

THE LOCAL WAR.— DEBATE ON ADMINISTRATIVE REFORM.— REPORT OF THE ROEBUCK COMMITTEE, ETC.[210]

London, June 20. The *local war* proclaimed by Bonaparte in the *Constitutionnel*[a] is a war in the Black Sea, and its purpose is the destruction of the alleged Russian supremacy in the Black Sea—a supremacy, moreover, that has never stood the test at sea, not even against the Turks. What is the state of affairs at the moment? The whole coast, from Constantinople to the Danube on one side and right round the Circassian shores to Balaklava and Eupatoria, has been snatched out of the hands of the Russians. Only Kaffa and Sevastopol are still holding out, with the former hard-pressed and the latter so situated that it will have to surrender as soon as it is seriously threatened. And more. The fleets are carrying out mopping-up operations in the inland sea of Azov, their light ships penetrate as far as Taganrog and every important place is bombarded by them. No part of the coast remains in Russian hands except the stretch from Perekop to the Danube, approximately $^{1}/_{15}$ of their possessions on this coast. Supposing Kaffa and Sevastopol also fall, and the Crimea is under the control of the allies, then what? Russia will not conclude peace, as it has already proclaimed. It would be madness. It would be tantamount to giving up a battle after the vanguard has been repulsed, at the very moment that the main force is entering the battlefield. What remains for the allies to do? We are told they can destroy Odessa, Kherson, Nikolayev. They can go ahead and land a strong army at Odessa, fortifying it against any number of Russians and then

---

[a] A reference to A. de Cesena's article on the aims and prospects of the Crimean war published in the semi-official *Constitutionnel*, No. 169, June 18, 1855.—*Ed.*

acting according to circumstances. In addition, they can send a detachment of troops to the Caucasus, wiping out the Russian army in Georgia and the other trans-Caucasian possessions (under General Muraviev) and cutting off the Russian Empire from its south Asian possessions. And if Russia still refuses to make peace? Russia cannot make peace as long as the enemy remains on its soil. It has not lost through any peace it has concluded in the last 150 years. Even at Tilsit[211] it acquired additional territory, and that peace was made before a single Frenchman had set foot on Russian soil. Having only recently succeeded to the throne, Alexander II dare not even attempt something that would have been perilous even for Nicholas. He cannot suddenly break with the imperial tradition. Supposing the Crimea has been captured and garrisoned with 50,000 allied troops; that the Caucasus and all the possessions in the south have been cleared of Russians; that an allied army is holding the Russians in check at the Kuban and the Terek; that Odessa has been taken and turned into a fortified camp with an army of 100,000 men; that Nikolayev, Kherson and Ismail have been destroyed or occupied by the allies—will the allies then limit themselves to maintaining their positions and count on wearing out the Russians? Their troops in the Crimea and the Caucasus will dwindle from disease faster than they can be replaced. Their main army at Odessa would have to be supplied by the fleets, as the land produces nothing for hundreds of miles around Odessa. Wherever they dared emerge from the camp they would be exposed to the harassment of the Russians, particularly the Cossacks. To force the latter to stand and fight would be impossible. It would always be to their advantage to entice the allies into the interior of the country. They would respond to all allied advances with a slow retreat. Moreover, large armies cannot be kept idle in a fortified camp for long. Disease and the gradual breakdown of discipline and morale would compel the allies to take a decisive step. It is therefore not feasible to occupy the main points of the coast and wait until the Russians find themselves constrained to give in. It would also be a military blunder. To control a coast it is not sufficient to hold the main points. Only possession of the country's interior guarantees possession of the coast. With the allied forces established on the south coast of Russia, conditions would arise which would compel them to advance into the interior. But this is where the difficulties begin. All the way to the borders of the gubernias of Podolia, Kiev, Poltava and Kharkov the terrain is mostly uncultivated steppe, very poorly watered and yielding nothing but grass, and not even that when the heat of the sun has dried it out. Taking Odessa, Nikolayev and Kherson as their base of operations, where is the *object* at which the allies are supposed to direct their efforts? There appears to be none except Moscow, 700 miles away and requiring 500,000 men to march on it. But all this presupposes not merely the strict neutrality of Austria but even her moral support. And where is it? In 1854 Prussia and Austria declared the advance of the Russians across the Balkans to be a *casus belli.* Why not, then, a French advance on Moscow or even Kharkov in 1856? One must never for a moment forget that any army marching from the Black Sea towards the interior of Russia exposes its flank to Austria just as much as a Russian army advancing from the Danube into Turkey, and therefore, at a given distance, renders its lines of communication and its base of operations, i.e. its very existence, dependent on Austria. Should the allied armies pursue the Russians on a wild goose chase into the interior under these circumstances? It is nonsense, sheer nonsense, but it is the inevitable consequence of Bonaparte's latest plan of "local warfare". On all counts an inexorable dialectic drives the "local war" beyond the appointed local boundaries, turning it into a "grand" war, but without the prerequisites, conditions and resources of a grand war. Nevertheless, Bonaparte's latest "plan" remains important. It constitutes an admission that other powers must step on to the stage to continue the war against Russia, and that the restored Empire finds itself condemned to the impotence of waging war on Russia on a local scale when it can only be done on a European scale. All the grotesque metamorphoses undergone by the *"idées napoléoniennes"*[a] under the restored Empire have been surpassed by the transformation of the Napoleonic war against Russia into a "local war".

In the *debate on administrative reform,* to be resumed this evening, the amendment moved by Bulwer on behalf of the Tories gave the government the opportunity of defeating the "administratives" by a majority of 7 to 1.[212] What characterised the whole debate was its *junior civil-servant nature,* which it failed to transcend for a moment. Details of favouritism and nepotism, investigations as to the "best type of examination", resentment at merit neglected—everything was petty and pusillanimous. One seemed to be listening to a written complaint from an assistant gamekeeper to a

[a] An allusion to Louis Bonaparte's book *Des idées napoléoniennes,* which was published in Paris in 1839.—*Ed.*

government board. Aberdeen, too, had a reform of the bureaucracy *in petto*,[a] Gladstone asserted. Derby too, asserted Disraeli. Not less my Ministry, asserted Palmerston.[b] So the city gentlemen need not swing into action to reform, inform and re-organise our Departments. Too kind!

In their earlier agitation the English bourgeoisie took the ruling caste by surprise and drew the masses behind them as a chorus, by vastly overstating their real purpose in their programme. This time the programme does not even venture to rise to the height of the real purpose. One after the other you assure us that you do not seek the fall of the aristocracy but simply want to patch up the government machine in friendship with us! Very well![c] Friendship for friendship! We are willing to reform the administration for you—within its traditional limits, of course. "Administrative reform" is not a matter of conflict between the classes as you assert. It is simply a question of the "issue", of "well-intentioned" reforms. As initial evidence of your good intentions we ask you to leave the details to us, and it is only a matter of details. We ourselves must know best how far we can go without jeopardising our class, without administrative reform inadvertently becoming a matter of conflict between the classes and forfeiting its philanthropic character. The reforming bourgeoisie are obliged to acquiesce in this ironic language of aristocratic *bonhomie* because they themselves speak a fraudulent language to the masses. The aristocracy, ministry and opposition, Whigs and Tories were never mistaken about the relationship of the Administrative Reformers to the masses. They knew that the agitation had failed before it had even had a chance to be produced in Parliament. And how could they have been mistaken? Although the Reform Association admitted selected guests only to its Drury Lane meeting, although its audience was sifted twice and thrice, their fear of a popular motion, or even simply an unorthodox speech, was so excessive that the chairman[d] declared at the opening of the meeting that the audience was only there to "listen to the addresses of the speakers announced in the programme", no "resolutions" would be put to the vote, therefore "no amendments could be moved", and "no addition could be made to the list of set speakers". Agitation

---

[a] Up his sleeve.—*Ed.*

[b] Gladstone's speech was made on June 15, 1855 and the speeches by Disraeli and Palmerston on June 18. *The Times*, Nos. 22082 and 22084, June 16 and 19, 1855.—*Ed.*

[c] Marx uses the English phrase.—*Ed.*

[d] S. Morley. For a description of the meeting see this volume, p. 274.—*Ed.*

like this is definitely not suitable to impress the tough English oligarchy and wring concessions from it.

The *report of the Roebuck committee* which was read out in the Commons the day before yesterday envelops its points in a broad, feeble gush of words.[a] It contains timidly formulated criticism of the various departments, such as Ordnance, the Commissariat, the Medical Department, etc. It condemns Palmerston for his management of the militia, and the entire coalition ministry for the heedless frivolity with which it undertook the Sevastopol expedition. As during the examination of witnesses the committee scrupulously avoided inquiring into the fundamental reasons for the stupendous calamities, it is only natural that in the report, too, it is obliged to keep the balance between quite general criticism of the political heads and petty, detailed faulting of the administrative machinery. On the whole the committee has fulfilled its purpose of acting as a safety-valve for the pressure of public passions.

The daily papers have let out a cry of indignation at the "dastardly murders" by the Russians at Hangö.[213] The fact that ships sailing under flags of truce have been misused by the British for taking soundings with a plummet and spying out Russian positions, e.g. at Sevastopol and Odessa, is, however, admitted by *The Morning Chronicle*.[b]

Written on June 20, 1855

First published in the *Neue Oder-Zeitung*, No. 287, June 23, 1855

Marked with the sign ×

Printed according to the newspaper

Published in English for the first time

---

[a] "State of the Army before Sebastopol", *The Times*, No. 22084, June 19, 1855.—*Ed.*

[b] This refers to a Letter to the Editor signed R.G.A. published in *The Morning Chronicle*, No. 27607, June 20, 1855.—*Ed.*

Karl Marx

ANNOUNCEMENT CONCERNING THE TAKING OF SEVASTOPOL.—FROM THE PARIS BOURSE.—ON THE MASSACRE AT HANGÖ IN THE HOUSE OF LORDS[214]

[*Neue Oder-Zeitung*, No. 289, June 25, 1855]

London, June 22. The second act of *La Sonnambula*[a] had just finished, and the curtain of the Drury Lane Theatre was coming down when suddenly a mighty drum-roll summoned the audience back into the auditorium just as they were thronging out for refreshments. The curtain went up again, the manager stepped forward and, with great melodramatic effect, made the following announcement:

"Ladies and gentlemen! I am very happy to be able to announce a great event to you. *The allies have taken Sevastopol*."

There were enthusiastic shouts of triumph, people cheered and applauded, bouquets were flying everywhere. The orchestra played and the audience sang "God save the Queen", "Rule Britannia" and "Partant pour la Syrie".[b] A voice from the upper regions shouted "La Marseillaise!", but it died away without an echo. The manager's improvised speech was based on a telegraphic message which did not, however, report the taking of Sevastopol, but on the contrary that the French in their storming of the Malakhov, and the English in their storming of the Redan, on June 18, had been *repulsed, suffering considerable losses*.[215] That play actor yesterday evening on the stage at Drury Lane copied another manager who almost a year ago, in the middle of a military spectacular,[216] improvised the following unexpected and unforgettable words: "Messieurs, Sevastopol est pris!"[c]

---

[a] Opera by the Italian composer Vincenzo Bellini.—*Ed.*

[b] "Leaving for Syria", a song frequently performed at official festivities during the Second Empire in France. The titles of the English songs are given in English in the original.—*Ed.*

[c] "Gentlemen, Sevastopol has been taken!"—*Ed.*

[*Neue Oder-Zeitung*, No. 290, June 26, 1855]

The reason for the incomprehensible obduracy with which Pélissier continues to exhaust the forces of the allied army in one-sided assaults on the southern flank is said to be not *military* but *financial*. It is well known that Bonaparte has already drawn bills of exchange for thousands of millions on the prospect of taking Sevastopol and had them discounted by the French nation. He is on the point of drawing bills for another 800 millions or thereabouts.[217] It therefore seemed essential to make an advance payment on the bills already circulating, and if crossing the Chernaya brings *real results* an assault on the southern flank of Sevastopol promises to produce a *dazzling illusion of success*. "The fall of Sevastopol" would look well in the prospectus for the new loan, and if a loan can be made for the war, why not a war for the loan? Confronted with that point of view, all the criticism based on military science will have to be silent. There is anyway quite a mysterious link between the war in the Crimea and the Bourse at Paris. It is well known that, just as all roads lead to Rome, so all electric wires converge in the Tuileries, where they end in a "secret closet". It has been noticed that the most important telegrams are published in Paris hours later than in London. During those hours a certain Corsican by the name of *Orsi* is said to be extremely busy at the Paris Bourse. It is generally known in London that this fellow Orsi was previously the "providential" agent on the London Stock Exchange[a] of the man in exile at the time.[b]

If the dispatches from Admiral Dundas, which have been published by the English Cabinet, did not already prove that there was no abuse of a flag of truce on the part of the officers and crew of the boat dispatched by the *Cossack*, which could serve as a pretext for the Russian *massacre at Hangö*,[218] then the story told by the *Invalide Russe* would dispel any doubt on this point.[c] Evidently the Russians did not suspect that a sailor, John Brown, had escaped with his life and would testify against them. The *Invalide* therefore considered it superfluous to accuse the English boat of espionage, or of taking soundings, etc., and concocted its tale on the spur of the moment, following Abbé Sieyès in the conviction that "dead men tell no tales".[d] The matter was raised in the

[a] Marx uses the English term.—*Ed.*

[b] Louis Bonaparte.—*Ed.*

[c] Marx refers to the reports on the Hangö events published in *Russky Invalid*, No. 118, June 1, 1855, and *The Times*, No. 22086, June 21, 1855.—*Ed.*

[d] "La mort sans phrase"—words allegedly uttered by Sieyès when voting in the French Convention on January 17, 1793 for Louis XVI's execution.—*Ed.*

House of Lords yesterday. We cannot, however, agree with *The Times* that this assembly, otherwise "cold and unimpassioned by habit and by policy", was on this occasion trembling with the unadulterated expression of true passion.[a] We find affected indignation in the choice of phrase, but in fact affectionate concern for "Russian honour" and an anxious warding off of national revenge. The Tories' spokesman for Foreign Affairs, the Earl of Malmesbury, rose yesterday, set forth the facts briefly and then exclaimed:

"I have ransacked English history, and I cannot find an instance of a similar atrocious act [...]. What course does the Government mean to take under the circumstances? [...] It is a matter of the greatest importance to every officer and every army in Europe that the matter should be noticed and that condign punishment should be meted out to the perpetrators [...]."

Clarendon, the Whigs' Foreign Secretary, declared that he shared the "indignation" of his colleague. It is an outrage so horrible and unparalleled, so utterly at variance with the usages and the customs of civilised nations, that we are compelled to believe that the perpetrators of it cannot have acted upon the instructions or with the permission of their superiors. It was possible that the person in command of the 500 Russians had not been a commissioned officer[b] (every English officer down to the rank of lieutenant has a commission, not sergeants and other non-commissioned officers, however). It is therefore quite plausible that the Russian Government disapproved of this act. He had therefore instructed the English Envoy at Copenhagen[c] to request the Danish Envoy at St. Petersburg[d] to state to the Russian Government that the British Cabinet waited with extreme anxiety to learn what steps the Russian Government had taken or intended to take to establish their attitude to an act which might possibly have happened in some one of the savage islands of the South Sea without exciting any degree of surprise, but which was not to be expected in civilised Europe, and which, if not severely and appropriately punished by the Russian Government, would deserve the severest of reprisals. Clarendon closed by saying that the British Government was awaiting the Russian statement before determining what course to adopt.

---

[a] *The Times*, No. 22087, June 22, 1855. The debate in the House of Lords on June 21, 1855, was reported in the same issue of *The Times*.—*Ed.*

[b] Marx uses the English words "commissioned officer" and, below, "commission".—*Ed.*

[c] A. Buchanan.—*Ed.*

[d] O. Plessen.—*Ed.*

Lord *Colchester* believes that

> "in any such case as this it was the duty of the officer commanding [...] immediately to communicate by a flag of truce with the highest Russian authority he could find, mentioning the circumstances, and demanding that the atrocity should be disclaimed".

The Earl of *Malmesbury* rises again and declares that on the whole he has no fault to find with the course taken by the Government, but shudders to have heard Clarendon use the word "reprisal". England must not sink to the level of the Russians in this matter. She must take *moral* revenge on the Tsar,[a] have every Court in Europe protest at the St. Petersburg court and thus pronounce an international judgment on Russia. Anything like "revenge" would only serve to increase public "disgust". The nominal president of the English Cabinet,[b] Earl *Granville*, avidly seizes upon the Tory's words and recites like a good Christian: "No retaliation!"

Now, what does this outburst of passion in the Lords, as *The Times* calls it, show us? Full of moral indignation the Tory asks a question. The Whig outdoes him in indignation, but himself surreptitiously provides the Russian Government with an excuse and shows them the way to get out of the situation, by repudiating and sacrificing a subaltern. He covers his retreat by muttering something about reprisals "as a possibility". Lord Colchester seeks to chastise the Russians for having murderously attacked intermediaries bearing a flag of truce by sending another intermediary under a flag of truce. The Tory rises again and invokes a moral solution rather than reprisals. The Whig, glad to be rid of reprisals, even only as a possibility, joins in the call for "No retaliation!"[c] Pure farce. The House of Lords places itself between the passions of the people and Russia in order to protect Russia. The only peer who did not act the part was *Brougham*. "If ever the land called for blood," he said, "it is now." As far as English sensitivity to "reprisals" and "jus talionis"[d] is concerned, the Earl of Malmesbury has ransacked English history without finding an Irish page, or an Indian or North American. When was the English oligarchy ever squeamish except in the case of Russia!

In the report of the Roebuck committee, which was read to the House, oddly enough the final paragraph has been suppressed, a

---

[a] Alexander II.—*Ed.*
[b] Marx refers here to the Lord President of the Council.—*Ed.*
[c] Marx uses the English phrase.—*Ed.*
[d] Right of retaliation.—*Ed.*

paragraph which Roebuck proposed and which was accepted by the committee after a vote. It runs as follows:

"What was planned and undertaken without sufficient information, was conducted without sufficient care or forethought. This conduct on the part of the Administration was the first and chief cause of the calamities which befell our army in the Crimea."[a]

Written on June 22, 1855

First published in the *Neue Oder-Zeitung*, Nos. 289 and 290, June 25 and 26, 1855

Marked with the sign ×

Printed according to the newspaper

Published in English for the first time

[a] The report, headlined "State of the Army before Sebastopol", was published in *The Times*, No. 22084, June 19, 1855; the omitted paragraph is quoted here from the article "The Sebastopol Committee", *The Times*, No. 22087, June 22, 1855.—*Ed.*

Karl Marx

THE MISHAP OF JUNE 18.—REINFORCEMENTS

London, June 23. June 18, the anniversary of the battle of Waterloo,[219] was of course not celebrated in London this year. It was to be celebrated in the Crimea with a victory, not *over* the French but *alongside* the French. The event seemed all the more piquant since Raglan, Wellington's famulus, was carrying out his command more or less under the orders of a General of Napoleon III.[a] The inscription was ready, only the event that it was to immortalise failed to happen. It will not escape people's notice that in the history of the restored Empire there is a fatalistic predilection for resurrecting its great dates, affirming successes and disavowing misfortunes, in a second and improved edition. This glorious resurrection of Napoleonic dates, successful so far with respect to blows against the Republic, is failing with respect to blows against the enemy abroad. And the Empire without the victories of the Empire reminds one of the adaptation of Shakespeare's *Hamlet* which not only lacks the melancholy of the Prince of Denmark but also the Prince himself.[b] Paris had arranged for a great feat of arms in the Crimea on December 2, 1854.[c] It came to grief thanks to a surplus of rain and a shortage of ammunition. On June 18, 1855 an improved version of the battle, with a different result, was to be performed at Sevastopol. Instead, the Franco-English army suffered *its first serious defeat.*

London is in sombre mood; the stocks have fallen, and in one day Palmerston has forfeited what it took him months of the most

---

[a] Pélissier.—*Ed.*
[b] An allusion to the English saying: "It's *Hamlet* without the Prince."—*Ed.*
[c] The third anniversary of the Bonapartist coup in France.—*Ed.*

subtle tactical manoeuvrings to secure. The defeats occurred on June 18; the telegraphed dispatch was not published until June 22. Last Thursday the official *Globe*[a] announced on Palmerston's behest that "nothing serious had happened". In the Commons' night sitting of the same date Palmerston solemnly repeated the same statement.[b] And now it has been established that he received the telegram as early as 4 p.m. on Wednesday, June 20. *The Leader* asserts that this happened at the urgent request of Paris, where the misfortune in the field had been turned into good fortune at the stock exchange.[c] However that may be, the cockneys[d] are seriously annoyed with Palmerston. Being beaten is bad enough. But to let oneself be carried away at Drury Lane and Covent Garden by the Ministers' tricks into ludicrous ovations at the capture of Sevastopol—this is too bad, Sir[e]!

We prepared our readers sufficiently for the fact that Pélissier's stubborn persistence in attacking the southern flank heralded disaster for the allied armies. Immediately he assumed command we drew attention to the mitigating circumstance that lack of transport would place great obstacles in his way when it came to operations in the open field.[f] Both points have now been confirmed by the English press. For instance, today's *Morning Herald* says:

> "The army *cannot* take the field—as, according to all rules of strategy, it ought to do, beat the relieving army at Simpheropol [...]. That it cannot do because the 'Government grave-diggers', Neglect and Delay, have been at their murderous work again, and of 20,000 baggage cattle, which we ought to have, we have not above 4,000 or 5,000; and this while disease is once more becoming rampant in a camp which contains every possible incitement to fever, cholera, and plague. This incapacity of moving them, the same as it was at Varna and in the Valley of Death, is the cause why, day after day, our generals are compelled to waste the lives of our soldiers in desperate attacks upon almost impregnable earthworks, while the noble army that should take the field is lying on the Chernaya, without cavalry or means of transport."[g]

The ingenious negligence with which, from the outset of the war, the Cabinet administered the resources at its disposal has

---

[a] *The Globe and Traveller.* Marx refers to the issue of June 21, 1855.—*Ed.*

[b] Palmerston made that statement on Friday, June 22. *The Times*, No. 22088, June 23, 1855.—*Ed.*

[c] *The Leader*, No. 274, June 23, 1855.—*Ed.*

[d] Marx uses the English word.—*Ed.*

[e] Marx uses the English words "this is too bad, Sir!"—*Ed.*

[f] This refers to the German version of the article "Sevastopol" (see this volume, pp. 260-66) and to other articles in the *Neue Oder-Zeitung*.—*Ed.*

[g] *The Morning Herald*, No. 22465, June 23, 1855.—*Ed.*

been shown anew by financial reports which have just been published. According to this official report the balance in hand on January 1, 1854 of the money allocated for the army was £1,835,882 and the amount expended on the army on April 1, 1854 was only £2,270,000, so that less than three-quarters of the money voted by Parliament for raising troops was used. And what was it that, according to the report of the Roebuck Committee,[a] ruined the army? Overwork. And what is the reason of this overwork? Lack of numbers. But this lack of numbers, as the financial report shows, was the result of a Cabinet intrigue. And Prince Albert complains that the Queen[b] has no troops at her disposal! And that the Cabinet's hands are tied! The Layard debate revealed that the self-same Cabinet, whilst complaining about lack of transport, sent troopships to Portsmouth via Newcastle-upon-Tyne to collect coal, or from the Clyde to Liverpool and from Deptford to Woolwich to be inspected by the Surveyor.[c]

The misfortunes of June 18 have made immediate *reinforcements* necessary. Accordingly orders were issued yesterday for immediate embarkation: the 15th Infantry Regiment, which has recently returned from Ceylon; the King's 51st Light Infantry Regiment, the 80th and 94th Infantry Regiments, all the India detachments from the various depot companies, and 1,200 men of the cavalry are to leave immediately for the theatre of war. Orders have been telegraphed to Marseilles for special steamships to be sent from there to the Governors of Malta and Gibraltar and to the Lord High Commissioner[c] of the Ionian Islands with the task of transporting all the men who are fit for service not only from the garrisons but also from the reserve of the Household Brigade and all the reserve battalions that can be spared *before* the arrival of the relieving regiments and militia. Sailing at once are: the 13th Light Infantry Regiment of Gibraltar, the 31st Infantry Regiment from the Ionian Islands, the 48th from Corfu, the 54th from Gibraltar, the 66th from Gibraltar, and the 92nd Scottish Highland Regiment from Gibraltar. British forces in the Crimea will thus be increased by more than 13,000 men. To this must be added four field batteries, a troop of mounted artillery and reinforcements for the siege train, all of which are ready and are

---

[a] "State of the Army before Sebastopol", *The Times,* No. 22084, June 19, 1855.—*Ed.*

[b] Victoria. For an account of Prince Albert's speech see this volume, pp. 273-76.—*Ed.*

[c] Marx uses the English term.—*Ed.*

only waiting for ships. Incidentally, England is in the same position as in 1854. No reserve army. And even worse. In 1854, as the Roebuck report admits, Palmerston prevented and delayed the formation of the militia; but in 1855 he succeeded in practically dissolving the militia which was already formed. As one can see from the above list, the reinforcements absorb not only the bulk of the army, but they also swallow up the depot battalions and break up the cadres. Thus England resembles Montesquieu's savage who fells the tree in order to get hold of the fruit.[a] The economical country *par excellence* is spending its military capital instead of the interest. This is the result of the manoeuvrings of the Cabinet in which Prince Albert demands that one have implicit confidence! Nothing could be less accurate than the view held on the Continent that England has too small a population to be able to raise armies. In 1815, after 22 years of war, England had more than 350,000 men mobilised! But the Cabinet purposely ignores both remedies: raising the bounty for the standing army, and balloting for the militia. What else can one expect from the Prime Minister, whose debts Princess Lieven paid in 1827, and whom she appointed Foreign Secretary in 1830, a man who procured for Russia eight years of dictatorship over Turkey by means of the Treaty of Unkiar-Skelessi, and eight days before the treaty expired, renewed it in the Dardanelles treaty[220]?

Yesterday in the Commons Roebuck gave notice that on July 3 (Tuesday week) he would table the following motion:

> "That this House, deeply lamenting the sufferings of our army during the winter campaign in the Crimea, and coinciding with the resolution of their committee that the conduct of the Administration was the first and chief cause of these misfortunes, hereby visits with its severe reprehension *every member of the Cabinet* whose counsels led to such disastrous results."[b]

Roebuck's motion therefore deliberately includes: Palmerston, Russell, Clarendon, Granville and Lansdowne, at one and the same time members of the present Cabinet and the previous one. The small, venomous, Thersites-like but crafty barrister, the perfect master of parliamentary tactics, saw himself forced into tabling this motion, as his constituents at Sheffield threatened to subject him to a vote of no confidence at a public meeting, because he had denounced Palmerston on Tuesday and expressed his confidence in the same Palmerston on Thursday. Prince Albert's unfortunate interference in matters between the Cabinet

---

[a] Ch. Montesquieu, *L'Esprit des Lois,* V, XIII.—*Ed.*

[b] *The Times,* No. 22088, June 23, 1855.—*Ed.*

and Parliament, and his challenging of the authority of Parliament was a further reason for this motion, which threatens to rob the Queen once more of "her confidential servants".

We shall report on the latest activities and fortunes of the *Administrative Reformers*, and the machinations of the clerics next time.

Written on June 23, 1855

First published in the *Neue Oder-Zeitung*, No. 291, June 26, 1855

Marked with the sign ×

Printed according to the newspaper

Published in English for the first time

Karl Marx

ANTI-CHURCH MOVEMENT.[—DEMONSTRATION IN HYDE PARK][221]

London, June 25. It is an old and historically established maxim that obsolete social forces which are still nominally in possession of all the attributes of power and continue to vegetate long after the basis of their existence has rotted away, because the heirs are quarrelling among themselves over the inheritance even before the obituary notice has been printed and the testament read, such forces, when they face their final death struggle, will once more muster all their strength, pass from the defensive to the offensive, become defiant instead of evasive and seek to draw extreme conclusions from premises which have not only been put in question but already found wanting. This is the case today with the English oligarchy and the *Church*, its twin sister. Countless attempts at reorganisation have been made within the Established Church, both the High and the Low Church, attempts to come to an understanding with the Dissenters[222] and thus to set up a compact force to oppose the impious mass of the nation. There has been a rapid succession of religious coercive measures. The pious Earl of Shaftesbury, formerly known as Lord Ashley, mournfully announced in the House of Lords that in England alone five million had become wholly alienated not only from the Church but from Christianity.[a] *"Compelle intrare"*,[b] is the reply of the Established Church. It leaves it to Lord Ashley and similar dissenting, sectarian and overwrought pietists to pull the chestnuts out of the fire for it.

---

[a] Shaftesbury's speech on June 12, 1855. *The Times*, No. 22079, June 13, 1855.—*Ed.*

[b] "Compel them to come in, that my house may be filled" (Luke, 14:23).—*Ed.*

The first measure of religious coercion was the Beer Bill,[a] which shut down all places of public entertainment on Sundays, except between 6 and 10 p.m. This Bill was smuggled through the House at the end of a sparsely attended sitting, after the pious men had bought the support of the big public-house owners of London by assuring them that the licensing system would continue, that is, that big capital would retain its monopoly. Then came the Sunday Trading Bill, the third reading of which has now taken place in the Commons and separate clauses of which have just been debated in the Committee of the Whole House.[223] This new coercive measure too was sure to receive the votes of big capital, because only small shopkeepers keep open on Sunday and the proprietors of the big stores are quite willing to do away with the Sunday competition of the small fry by parliamentary means. In both cases there is a conspiracy of the Church with the monopoly of capital, but in both cases religious penal laws are to be imposed on the lower classes to set the conscience of the privileged classes at rest. Just as the *Beer Bill* did not hurt the aristocratic clubs so the *Sunday Trading Bill* does not interfere with the Sunday occupations of genteel society. The workers get their wages late on Saturday: it is for them alone that trade is carried on on Sundays. They are the only ones compelled to make their purchases, small as they are, on Sundays. The new bill is therefore directed against them alone. The French aristocracy said in the eighteenth century: For us, Voltaire; for the people, the mass and the tithes. The English aristocracy says in the nineteenth century: For us, sanctimonious phrases; for the people, Christian practice. The classical saints of Christianity mortified *their* body for the salvation of the souls of the masses; the modern, educated saints mortify *the bodies of the masses* for the salvation of their own souls.

This alliance between a dissipated, degenerating and pleasure-seeking aristocracy and the Church, an alliance based on squalid profiteering on the part of beer magnates and monopolistic wholesalers, occasioned yesterday a *mass demonstration* in Hyde Park, the like of which London has not seen since the death of George IV, "the first gentleman of Europe". We saw it from beginning to end and do not think it is an exaggeration to say that the *English Revolution began in Hyde Park yesterday.* The latest news from the Crimea acted as an effective ferment upon this *"unparliamentary"*, *"extraparliamentary"*, and *"anti-parliamentary"* demonstration.

---

[a] Marx uses the English terms "Beer Bill" and, below, "Sunday Trading Bill".—*Ed.*

When someone objected that the Sunday Trading Bill was directed exclusively against the poor and not at all against the rich, Lord *Robert Grosvenor*, who initiated the Bill, retorted that

"the aristocracy was largely refraining from employing its servants and horses on Sundays".[a]

The following wall poster, issued *by the Chartists*, which could be seen throughout London at the end of last week announced in huge letters:

"*New Sunday Bill* prohibiting newspapers, shaving, smoking, eating and drinking and all kinds of recreation and nourishment, both corporal and spiritual, which the *poor people* still enjoy at the present time. *An open-air meeting* of artisans, workers and '*the lower orders*' generally of the capital will take place in Hyde Park on Sunday afternoon to see how religiously the aristocracy is observing the Sabbath and how anxious it is not to employ its servants and horses on that day, as Lord Robert Grosvenor said in his speech. The meeting is called for three o'clock on the right bank of the Serpentine (a small river in Hyde Park) on the side towards Kensington Gardens. Come and bring your wives and children in order that they may profit by the example their '*betters*' set them!"

It should be borne in mind, of course, that what *Longchamps*[b] means to the Parisians, the riding track along the Serpentine in Hyde Park means to the English *haute volée*[c]—the place where in the afternoon, particularly on Sunday, they parade their magnificent carriages and their finery and exercise their horses, followed by swarms of lackeys. It will be realised from the above poster that the struggle against clericalism assumes the same character as every serious struggle in England—that of a *class struggle* waged by the poor against the rich, the people against the aristocracy, the "lower orders" against their "betters".

Approximately 50,000 people had gathered at the place announced on the immense lawn on the right bank of the Serpentine in Hyde Park at about 3 o'clock. Gradually the assembled multitude swelled to a total of at least 200,000 due to additions from the other bank. One could see that small groups of people were made to move from one spot to another. The police, who were present in force, were obviously endeavouring to deprive the organisers of the meeting of what Archimedes had asked for to move the earth, namely, one firm spot to stand upon. Finally a fairly large crowd made a firm stand and *Bligh* the Chartist constituted himself chairman on a small eminence in the midst of the throng. No sooner had he begun his harangue than

---

[a] From Grosvenor's speech in the House of Commons on June 13, 1855. *The Times*, No. 22080, June 14, 1855.—*Ed.*

[b] A hippodrome on the outskirts of Paris.—*Ed.*

[c] The upper crust.—*Ed.*

Police Inspector Banks at the head of 40 truncheon-swinging constables explained to him that the Park was the private property of the *Crown* and that meetings could not be held there. After some *negotiations* in which Bligh sought to demonstrate to him that parks were public property and in which Banks rejoined he had strict orders to arrest him if he should insist on carrying out his intention. Bligh shouted amidst the bellowing of the masses surrounding him:

> "Her Majesty's police declare that Hyde Park is private property of the Crown and that Her Majesty[a] is unwilling to let her land be used by the people for their meetings. So let's move to Oxford Market."

With the ironical cry: "God save the Queen!"[b] the throng broke up to walk to Oxford Market. But meanwhile *Finlen*, a member of the Chartist Executive,[224] rushed to a tree some distance away followed by a crowd who in a twinkle formed so close and compact a circle around him that the police abandoned their attempt to get at him.

> "Six days a week," he said, "we are treated like slaves and now Parliament wants to rob us of the bit of freedom we still have on the seventh. These oligarchs and capitalists allied with sanctimonious parsons wish to do *penance* by mortifying us instead of themselves for the unconscionable murder in the Crimea of the sons of the people."

We left this group to approach another where a speaker stretched out on the ground addressed his audience from this horizontal position. Suddenly, shouts could be heard on all sides: "Let's go to the Row, to the carriages!" The heaping of insults upon riders and occupants of carriages had already begun. The constables, who constantly received reinforcements from the city, drove the promenading pedestrians off the road. They thus helped to form a thick throng of people on either side of Rotten-Row, from Apsley House along the Serpentine as far as Kensington Gardens—a distance of more than a quarter of an hour walk. The spectators consisted of about two-thirds workers and one-third members of the middle class, all with women and children. The involuntary actors comprising elegant ladies and gentlemen, "commoners and lords", in their high coaches-and-four with liveried lackeys in front and behind, joined by a few elderly gentlemen on horseback slightly under the weather from the effects of wine—were not showing off this time but were made to run the gauntlet. A babel of jeering, taunting, discordant ejaculations, in which no language is as rich as English, enveloped

[a] Victoria.—*Ed.*
[b] Marx uses the English words.—*Ed.*

them from both sides. As it was an improvised concert, instruments were lacking. The chorus therefore had to use its own organs and was compelled to confine itself to vocal music. And what a diabolical concert it was: a cacophony of grunting, hissing, whistling, squeaking, snarling, growling, croaking, shrieking, groaning, rattling, howling, gnashing sounds! A music that could drive men mad and move a stone. To this must be added outbursts of genuine old-English humour peculiarly mixed with long-contained seething wrath. "Go to church!"[a] were the only articulate sounds that could be distinguished. One lady soothingly offered a prayer book in conventional binding from her carriage. "Give it to read to your horses!"[b] came the thunderous reply, shouted by a thousand voices. When the horses started to take fright and began to rear, buck and finally run away, jeopardising the lives of their genteel burdens, the derisive shouting grew louder, more menacing and more ruthless. Some of the noble lords and ladies, among them Lady Granville, the wife of a minister and President of the Privy Council, were forced to alight and use their own legs. When some elderly gentlemen rode past whose apparel and especially their broad-brimmed hats betrayed their special claim to perfectitude in matters of belief, the cries of fury as if by command were drowned by irrepressible laughter. One of these gentlemen lost his patience. Like Mephistopheles he made an impolite gesture, sticking out his tongue at the enemy.[c] "He is a word-catcher, a parliamentary man! He fights with his own weapons!"[d] someone shouted on one side of the road. "He is a saint! He is psalm singing!" was the antistrophe from the opposite side. Meanwhile the metropolitan electric telegraph had informed all police stations that a riot was about to break out in Hyde Park and the police were ordered to the theatre of military operations. Soon one detachment after another marched at short intervals through the double file of people, from Apsley House to Kensington Gardens, each received with the popular ditty:

"Where are gone the geese?
Ask the police!"[e]

---

[a] Marx uses the English words "Go to church!" followed by a German translation in brackets.— *Ed.*

[b] Marx uses the English words "prayer book" and "Give it to read to your horses!" followed by a German translation in brackets.— *Ed.*

[c] Cf. Goethe, *Faust*, Der Tragödie erster Teil. Hexenküche.— *Ed.*

[d] Marx gives these and the following exclamations in English and translates them in brackets.— *Ed.*

[e] Marx quotes in English and gives the German translation in brackets.— *Ed.*

This was an allusion to a notorious theft of geese which a constable had perpetrated in Clerkenwell a short time ago. The spectacle lasted three hours. Only English lungs could perform such a feat. During the performance opinions such as "This is only the beginning!" "That is the first step!" "We hate them!" and the like were voiced by various groups. While rage was inscribed on the faces of the workers, such smiles of blissful self-satisfaction covered the physiognomies of the middle classes as we had never seen there before. Shortly before the end the demonstration increased in violence. Canes were menacingly raised at the carriages and the cry of "you rascals!" could be heard through the welter of discordant noises.[a] During the three hours zealous Chartists, men and women, made their way through the throng distributing leaflets which stated in big type:

"*Reorganisation of Chartism!*

"A big public meeting will take place next Tuesday, June 26th, in the Literary and Scientific Institute in Friar Street, Doctors' Commons, to elect delegates to a conference for the reorganisation of Chartism in the capital. Admission free."

Most of the London papers carry today only a brief account of the events in Hyde Park. No leading articles have appeared as yet, except in Lord Palmerston's *Morning Post.* It writes that

"a scene in the highest degree disgraceful and dangerous was enacted yesterday in Hyde Park", an "outrage on law and decency. [...] It was distinctly illegal to interfere, by physical force, with the free action of the Legislature [...]. We must have no repetition of violence on Sunday next, as has been threatened".[b]

At the same time, however, it declares that the "fanatical" Lord Grosvenor is solely "responsible" for this mischief, and that he has provoked the "just indignation of the people"! As though Parliament had not passed Lord Grosvenor's Bill in three readings! Or perhaps he too brought his influence to bear "by physical force on the free action of the Legislature"?

Written on June 25, 1855

First published in the *Neue Oder-Zeitung,* No. 295, June 28, 1855

Marked with the sign ×

Printed according to the newspaper

---

[a] Marx uses the English words followed by a German translation in parenthesis.—*Ed.*

[b] *The Morning Post,* No. 25422, June 25, 1855.—*Ed.*

Karl Marx

MISCELLANEOUS REPORTS

London, June 26. During yesterday's sitting in the Commons[a] Mr. Otway rose and asked whether Lord Palmerston

"intended to take any measures to induce Lord Grosvenor to withdraw the *Sunday Trading Bill*." (*General cheering.*[b])

Lord Palmerston replied:

"If my noble friend" (Grosvenor) "hears that cheer I think he will be disposed to attend to it." (*Cheers.*)

As one can see the mass demonstration in Hyde Park has intimidated the Commons. They are dropping the Bill and make *bonne mine à mauvais jeu.*[c] *The Times* describes the scene on Sunday in Hyde Park as a "great act of retributive justice", and calls the Bill a product of "class legislation", "a measure of organised hypocrisy" and pokes fun at this display of "parliamentary theology".[d]

On the question of the *Hangö massacre*[225] the First Lord of the Admiralty, Sir Charles *Wood*, announces that today he has received dispatches from Admiral Dundas. According to them five seamen and the Finnish captain had been killed by the fire of the Russians, four seamen and two Finns had been wounded and

---

[a] The speeches by Otway, Palmerston, Wood, Duncombe and Malins were published in *The Times*, No. 22090, June 26, 1855.—*Ed.*

[b] Marx uses the English terms "Sunday Trading Bill" and "cheers".—*Ed.*

[c] Make the best of a bad job.—*Ed.*

[d] *The Times*, No. 22090, June 26, 1855.—*Ed.*

taken prisoner, and three officers, four seamen and two Finns had been taken prisoner without being wounded. Admiral Dundas had written a letter to the Governor of Helsingfors[a] stating what had happened and remonstrating most strongly against the atrocious act of firing on a boat under a flag of truce. He had received an answer in which the Governor excused and to a certain extent *justified* the act. He declared that the officers and soldiers said they had *not seen* the flag of truce. They had been irritated because on some *other occasions* vessels had hoisted the Russian flag and it had been reported in the newspapers that English vessels had *elsewhere* hoisted the flag of truce to take soundings. The whole justification can be reduced to the short-sightedness of the Russian soldiers and officers. At any rate it is a sign of civilisation that Russian soldiers should read newspapers and be "irritated" by newspaper reports.

The *Administrative Reformers*[226] have announced another meeting for tomorrow in the Drury Lane [Theatre]. As before: a meeting with tickets of admission and speakers by previous arrangement. Pontius Pilate asked: What is truth? Palmerston asked: What is *worthiness*? The Administrative Reformers have replied: worthiness is equivalent to a man's annual earnings.[b] Accordingly those reformers have undertaken a change in their internal organisation. Previously the members of the general committee—in reality electing themselves—had to go through the motions of an election in the form of a general vote taken within the association. Now anyone who pays £50 and above in annual subscriptions becomes a member of the general committee as a matter of course. Previously the ten-guinea and the one-guinea rule were considered sufficient for protecting the "movement" from plebeian importunity. Now the ten-guinea gentlemen are no longer considered sufficiently "respectable" and the one-guinea people are actually regarded as the mob. The posters advertising the meeting say literally:

> "Admission only by ticket, which can be obtained by members. Anyone subscribing £50 and above is a member of the general committee, anyone subscribing ten guineas or one guinea is a member of the association."

The rights of members within the association are therefore calculated according to a sliding scale of guineas. The naked,

[a] J. M. Nordenstam.—*Ed.*

[b] In the original a pun on the word "Verdienst" which can mean either "merit", "deserts", "worthiness" or "earnings", "income".—*Ed.*

undisguised dominion of guineas is brutally proclaimed. The City reformers have let their secret out. What agitators! Moreover, circumstances were not very favourable for them lately. Drummond openly accused them in Parliament of "systematic immorality" and "corruption".[a] And what fine examples of the purity of their class have followed each other in rapid succession, as if on command! Firstly *The Lancet* (medical journal) furnishes proof that the adulteration and contamination of all goods and foodstuffs is a practice by no means confined to the retail traders, but is done in the wholesale trade as a matter of principle. Then it transpires that "respectable" City firms have been circulating false dock warrants.[b] Finally, the great fraudulent bankruptcy, directly connected with the theft of deposited securities, of the private bank of Strahan, Sir Jones Paul and Bates. In this last instance the aristocracy has learned to do homage to the "administrative" talent of the City gentlemen, for the bank "administered" mainly aristocratic guineas. Palmerston is amongst those to suffer, as is the Marquess of Clanricarde, and Admiral Napier has lost almost all his wealth. The *Church* has also been deprived of a good deal of worldly goods, since Messrs Strahan, Paul and Bates enjoyed a particular odour of sanctity, occasionally chaired meetings for the "conversion of heathens" at Exeter Hall, were amongst the first subscribers to the society for "the Dissemination of the Bible" and were on the committee of the "Association for the Reform of Criminals". Their faith had secured them credit. They were the favourite bank of clerical gentlemen and independent foundations. But their "administrative" talent spared nothing and no one from widows' and orphans' allowances down to the small savings of sailors. Why not let them administer the "public funds" which they are now reaching out for?

"There are symptoms at this moment among ourselves," ruefully exclaims *The Daily News*, the organ *par excellence* of the City reformers, "which indicate that no time is to be lost in averting a dangerous lapse from a high and severe tone of morality among our industrial classes."

The crisis of Messrs Strahan and Co. has of course given rise to a run[c] by the public on the counters of the City's private banks,

[a] Marx refers to Drummond's speech in the House of Commons on June 18, 1855. *The Times*, No. 22084, June 19, 1855.—*Ed.*

[b] Marx uses the English words "dock warrants".—*Ed.*

[c] Marx uses the English word.—*Ed.*

which up to then had been regarded as far more respectable than the joint stock banks. Already the big private bankers are obliged "publicly" to invite each other periodically to examine their holdings of securities deposited with them, and also to request their customers through *The Times* to inspect for themselves the effects entrusted to them. Another circumstance which arises at a very inopportune moment for the reforming City gentlemen is the following: As is well known, one of their kings, *Rothschild*, is standing as their elected representative at the threshold of the Commons, but is not being allowed to enter that Holy of Holies because *he* will not swear "on the true oath of a Christian" and because Lord *John Russell*, his colleague, will not "realise" the Jewish Bill.[227] And yesterday *Duncombe* rose to his feet having found out that, under an Act of Parliament of 1782, any member entering into a delivery contract with the government *after* he has been elected loses his seat in the House of Commons, and that Rothschild had stood security for the most recent loan of £16,000,000. Having discovered this he gave notice that tomorrow evening he would move that a writ be issued for a by-election in the City of London. And there is more. Malins followed in Duncombe's wake and gave notice of a similar motion against *Lindsay*, who had been directly charged by Sir Charles Wood in the reform debate with having negotiated contracts with the government for the supplying of ships, while he was and still is a member of Parliament. The incident is not only important because of the people who have been compromised, a City magnate and a City reform magnate! It is important because it reminds the public that it was amongst the high dignitaries of the City, those people entering into contracts for loans and supplies with the government both inside and outside Parliament, that Pitt, Perceval and Liverpool, who ignored the act of 1782, found their main support. The financial aristocracy—at that time more corrupt than under Louis Philippe—was the moving-force of the anti-Jacobin war. Whilst they plucked the golden apples of the Hesperides, they demonstrated to the nation in notorious City meetings that

> "it must sacrifice money and blood in order to preserve the blessed comforts of our holy religion from the desecrating French, and to preserve itself from the mournful desperation of atheism".

Thus the nation is reminded, at the most inopportune time, that the City, which is rebelling against the oligarchy, was the forcing house in which that same oligarchy grew and put forth its most luxuriant blooms.

Written on June 26, 1855

First published in the *Neue Oder-Zeitung*, No. 297, June 29, 1855

Marked with the sign ×

Printed according to the newspaper

Published in English for the first time

Frederick Engels

FROM SEVASTOPOL[228]

Contrary to public expectation the mail of the *Pacific*, which arrived yesterday morning, brings no detailed account of the repulse of the Allies at Sevastopol on the 18th of June. We have, it is true, some bare statements respecting the number of killed and wounded in that affair, on which we briefly comment below. But instead of the expected dispatches, we have at last Gen. Pélissier's detailed account of the capture of the Mamelon and Quarries. Even this however is not of a nature to distinctly show the drift of the military policy of the man who now virtually commands the 200,000 allied troops in the Crimea. We have to trust to negative rather than positive evidence if we desire to come to a conclusion on that subject. To guess what Pélissier intends to do, we must look not so much at what he does as at what he refrains from doing. But let us look again at the capture of the Mamelon; it has some features that repay examination.[a]

The 6th and 7th of June were devoted to a cannonade on the whole line of the allied batteries. But while on the left attack (the Flagstaff to the Quarantine Bastion) this cannonade was a mere demonstration, on the right attack (Redan to Mount Sapun) it was in good earnest. Here the Russian outworks were particularly subjected to a heavy fire. Their fire appearing to be sufficiently silenced and their defenders sufficiently weakened, on the evening of the 7th the assault was ordered. The French had two distinct positions to carry, forming two plateaux, separated from each other by a ravine; the English one plateau, with a ravine on either

[a] Instead of this paragraph the *Neue Oder-Zeitung* has: "Detailed and official dispatches about the events of June 6, 7 and 8 arrived only a few days ago."—*Ed.*

side. The mode in which the two armies prepared for the assault was characteristic of their peculiar qualities and traditions. The French set apart four divisions, two for each separate attack. Thus, against the Mamelon Vert (Kamtchatka redoubt) two divisions were collected, and two more against Mount Sapun; each attack having two brigades, in distinct columns, in front for the charge, and two brigades in reserve. Thus eighteen battalions were to charge and eighteen to support—in all at least 28,000 to 30,000 men. This disposition was perfectly in accordance with the regulations and traditions of the French army, which in grand charges always attacks in columns, and sometimes in rather too unwieldy ones. The English, if formed in the same way, would have required two divisions for their part of the business; two brigades for the attack and two for the reserve. True to their own system, however, they told off for the charge about 1,000 men, or about two battalions—hardly equal to half a French brigade. They had strong reserves no doubt; but, nevertheless, where the French would have employed three men they employed only one. This is a consequence partly of the British system of attacking in line instead of in column, and partly of the great tenacity of the British soldier in defensive positions. These 1,000 British soldiers were not even let loose all at once; at first 200 charged and carried the Russian works; then 200 more were sent as a reenforcement; the remainder followed in the same way; and then 1,000 British soldiers, once established in the Russian position, held it against six successive attacks, and under the continuous front and enfilading fire of the Russian works.[a] When the morning dawned, of their number above one-half were dead or wounded; but the place was theirs, and some of them had even now and then followed the Russians into the Redan. This was an exploit which no 1,000 Frenchmen could have achieved. But the passive endurance of the British soldier under fire knows hardly any bounds; and when, as in that night, the hand-to-hand combat takes the form of his favorite amusement, the street-row, then he is in his own element, and will fight six to one with all the reckless delight in the world.

As to the French attack, Gen. Pélissier gives us a long account of the brigades and regiments engaged, and has a complimentary

[a] Instead of this sentence the German version has: "These 1,000 British soldiers were not even let loose all at once; at first 200 charged and carried the Russian works; the remainder followed in the same way, and these British soldiers, once established in the Russian position, held it against successive attacks, and under the continuous front and enfilading fire of the Russian works."—*Ed.*

word for each of them; but his statements as to the respective positions and lines of attack of each column are very indistinct, while his narrative of the development of the action is almost incomprehensible, and an indication of the losses is entirely wanting. By comparing this official bulletin with other accounts, we are enabled to make out that the French took the Mamelon in the first onset, followed the retiring Russians up to the Malakoff bastion, entered it here and there, were repulsed by the Russians, again lost the Mamelon, drew up in a semi-circle behind it, and by another advance finally took possession of it. On the other side of the Careening Bay ravine the Volhynsk redoubt was taken with little loss; the struggle at the Selenghinsk redoubt, which is situated to its rear, was more severe, but nothing like that at the Mamelon. Owing to the exaggerated number of troops which Pélissier brought to bear upon the points attacked, and to the unwieldy columns they must have formed, the French loss must have been very great. The fact that no official statement of it has been made, is sufficient to prove this. We should say from 1,500 to 2,000 would not be exaggerated.[a]

As to the Russians, they were placed in peculiar circumstances. They could not garrison these outworks with great numbers of men, as this would have been to expose them to certain destruction by the enemy's artillery, even before the assault was attempted. Thus, they could only keep a minimum of defenders in these redoubts, and had to trust to the commanding fire of their artillery in the Malakoff and the Redan, as well as to the action of their reserves in the place. They had two battalions—about 800 men—in the Mamelon. But the redoubts once taken, they never got into them again so as to establish themselves properly. They discovered that a besieged army may very quickly lose a position, but cannot easily regain it.[b] Beside this, the Mamelon redoubt was so complicated in its construction, by traverses and blindages, forming a sort of impromptu casemates, that although exceedingly well covered against artillery, its garrison was almost helpless against an assault—each compartment being scarcely capable of holding a gun and the men to serve it. As soon, therefore, as the guns were dismounted, the infantry who had to defend the work against an assault, had no space for a position from which they could act upon the assaulting columns by simultaneous fire in masses. Broken up into small detachments they succumbed to the

---

[a] This sentence does not occur in the *Neue Oder-Zeitung*.—*Ed.*
[b] The last two sentences do not occur in the *Neue Oder-Zeitung*.—*Ed.*

impetuosity of the assailants, and again proved that where they cannot fight in large masses, the Russian infantry neither equals the intelligence and quickness of glance of the French, nor the desperate bull-dog valor of the English.

The engagement of the 7th was followed by a ten days' repose, during which trenches were finished and connected, batteries traced, and guns and ammunition brought up. At the same time two reconnaissances were pushed into the interior of the country. The first, to Baidar, 12 miles from Balaklava, on the road which leads down to the south coast, was merely preliminary; the second, toward Aïtodor, six miles beyond Chorgun, on the Chernaya, was made in the right direction. Aïtodor is situated on the high ground leading toward the valley of the Upper Belbek, by which alone, as we have stated long ago,[a] the Russian position at Inkermann can be effectually turned. But then, to send a reconnoitering column thither, and not to follow it up by occupying the ground in force and commencing operations at once, is nothing but putting the enemy on his guard by pointing out to him from which side he is menaced. Now, it may be that the country about Aïtodor was found impracticable, but we doubt it; and even in that case, the intention of a flank march to turn the enemy is too plainly indicated in this maneuver.[b] If this flank march could be used as a mere feint, well and good; but we are convinced that it must be made the chief movement, and therefore it should not be hinted at before the Allies really mean to undertake it.

Instead, however, of following up these weak demonstrations in the field, General Pélissier attempted something very different. The 18th of June, Waterloo day,[229] saw the English and French troops marching abreast to storm the Russian lines on the right attack. The English attacked the Redan, the French Malakoff. Waterloo was to be thus avenged; but unfortunately the affair went wrong. They were both repulsed with terrific slaughter. The official lists state their loss at about 5,000, but from the known want of veracity in the French accounts we are induced to calculate it about 50 per cent higher. As no particulars have been received, the tactical features of this battle must be left entirely

---

[a] See this volume, pp. 201-04.—*Ed.*

[b] Instead of this sentence the *Neue Oder-Zeitung* has: "The intention of a flanking march to bypass the enemy was too plainly indicated in this manoeuvre to be misunderstood by the Russians." The rest of this paragraph does not occur in the *Neue Oder-Zeitung*.—*Ed.*

aside for the present. What we can take into consideration now is its strategical and political nature.

Pélissier is held up by the entire press of Europe as a man who will not be commanded by telegraph from Paris, but who acts unflinchingly by his own judgment. We have had reasons to doubt this peculiar sort of obstinacy, and the fact of his attempt to avenge Waterloo "nobly," that is by a common victory of the French and English, fully confirms our doubt. The idea of such a feat could only come from his Majesty, the Emperor of the French—the great believer in anniversaries, the man who cannot let the 2d of December[a] pass by in any year without attempting some extraordinary trick; the man who, before the Chamber of Peers,[b] said that his special vocation was to avenge Waterloo. That Pélissier had the strictest orders to celebrate the Battle of Waterloo by a splendid anniversary there can be no doubt. The way in which he did it is the only part of the business for which he is responsible.[c]

The assault upon the lines of the redoubt of Karabelnaya must, as we are more than ever convinced, be considered a blunder. But until we know the man thoroughly, we will continue to give Pélissier the benefit of every circumstance which at this distance from the spot may appear to involve a doubt. Now, it may be that the sanitary state of the Heracleatic Chersonese—a subject to which we long since called attention[d]—is such that a speedy termination of the operations in that small space of ground is highly desirable. The exhalations from the decomposing bodies of 25,000 men and 10,000 horses are such as to seriously affect the health of the army during Summer. Of the other abominations accumulated there we will not speak. Pélissier may think that it is

---

[a] I.e., the anniversary of the Bonapartist coup in France, which took place on December 2, 1851.—*Ed.*

[b] The Senate.—*Ed.*

[c] Instead of the preceding two paragraphs the *Neue Oder-Zeitung* has: "Instead of following up these weak demonstrations in the field Pélissier undertook the abortive assault of June 18. He did this on the orders of the man who had declared before the Chamber of Peers that 'his special vocation was to avenge Waterloo'. Pélissier is only responsible for the way he carried out his instructions. As no detailed reports have been forthcoming so far, the tactical features of this battle cannot be judged for the present. As regards strategy, every child realises now that the nearest road to Sevastopol leads through Inkerman and the Russian army defending it." The passage that follows, up to the words "The necessity of reenforcing her force in the Crimea...", does not occur in the *Neue Oder-Zeitung*.—*Ed.*

[d] See this volume, pp. 109-12, 113-17, 215-17.—*Ed.*

possible in a short time to drive the Russians from the south side, to destroy the place completely, to leave but a few men to guard it, and then to take the field with a strong army. We make this supposition because we prefer to see at least some rational motive in the actions of an old soldier. But if this is the case he mistook the strength of the place. We said at the time, that any attempt to follow up the successes of the 7th against the town itself would be defeated[a]; our opinion is confirmed by events. We said the key to Sevastopol lay north of Inkermann[b]; the engagement of the 18th seems to prove it.

Thus we are ready to admit that Gen. Pélissier was led by perfectly logical considerations to prefer an assault on Karabelnaya to an advance into the field; but at the same time we must equally admit that people on the spot are very apt to take minor facts for the premises of their conclusions, and that Pélissier, by the repulse of the 18th, appears to be convicted of having given in to this weakness; for if it shows strength of character to stick obstinately to the business in hand, it equally shows weakness of intellect to follow up that business in a roundabout way, because it has once been entered upon. Pélissier would be right in attempting to take Sevastopol at all hazards; but he is evidently wrong in not seeing that the nearest road into Sevastopol leads through Inkermann and the Russian army defending that position.

Unless the allied armies take good care to profit without delay by their superiority, they will before long find themselves in a very awkward position. The necessity of reenforcing her force in the Crimea has long been recognized by Russia. The completion of the reserve battalions of the regular army, and the levy and organization of the militia in 200 battalions, but more especially the reduction of the Austrian army of observation to 180,000 men—the rest being either dismissed on furlough or stationed in the interior of the empire—now offer an opportunity to do this.[c] In consequence a reserve army has been formed at Odessa, about 25,000 men of which are said to be stationed at Nikolaieff, some twelve to fifteen days' march from Sevastopol. Two divisions of grenadiers are also said to be on the march from Volhynia. By the middle of July therefore, and perhaps sooner, the Russians may again have recovered the superiority of numbers, unless decisive

---

[a] See this volume, pp. 264-66.—*Ed.*

[b] See this volume, p. 249.—*Ed.*

[c] In the *Neue Oder-Zeitung* the words between the dashes do not occur.—*Ed.*

defeats of the troops now opposing the Allies occur in the mean time. We are, indeed, informed that 50,000 more Frenchmen are marching to Toulon and Marseilles for embarkation; but they will certainly be too late, and can hardly do more than fill up the gaps which battle and sickness (now reappearing in the allied camp) have made in the ranks.[a]

The operations in the Sea of Azoff have destroyed one source of supply for the Russians; but as the Dnieper is far more than the Don the natural outlet of the Russian corn districts, there is no doubt that great quantities of it are at Kherson—more than the Russians in the Crimea require to feed them. Thence the transport to Sympheropol is so not very difficult. Whoever expects from the Azoff expedition a serious and immediate effect on the provisioning of Sevastopol, labors under a great error.

The scales, though for some time past turned in favor of the Allies, may yet be balanced again, or even be turned against them. The Crimean campaign is far from being decided, if the Russians act promptly.

Written about June 29, 1855

First published in the *New-York Daily Tribune*, No. 4439, July 12, 1855, reprinted in the *New-York Semi-Weekly Tribune*, No. 1057, July 13, 1855 and the *New-York Weekly Tribune*, No. 772, July 14, 1855 as a leading article; an abridged and altered German version was first published in the *Neue Oder-Zeitung*, No. 301, July 2, 1855, marked with the sign ×

Reproduced from the *New-York Daily Tribune*

[a] The German version ends here.—*Ed.*

Karl Marx

MISCELLANEOUS REPORTS

London, June 30. As Lord Grosvenor refuses to withdraw his *Sunday Trading Bill*[a] voluntarily, posters have appeared in London's busiest streets today inviting people to attend another monster demonstration in Hyde Park tomorrow afternoon. When Grosvenor asked whether the sudden change in opinion of the majority was inspired by the mob in Hyde Park, the House was childish enough to reply with a vigorous No! No![b]

In passing, replying to the question of a Tory peer, Panmure mentioned that the Ministers had issued a proclamation to the army in the *name of the Queen*, according to which certain corps and certain regiments, those at present in the theatre of war, are to receive (not only for the duration of their present service but also back-dated for several months) a significant increase in pay and an increase in their pensions.[c] This announcement has, for the time being, been made in the name of the Queen,[d] while the House of Commons was in session and without the Ministers giving the House any information. Thus the Ministers are arrogating to themselves a right which constitutionally is the exclusive prerogative of the House of Commons, that *of fixing the pay of the army*. However, they have to go before the House in a few weeks' or days' time to have their promised increases passed.

[a] Marx uses the English name.—*Ed.*

[b] Marx uses the English words "No! No!". It was on June 26, 1855 that Grosvenor asked a question in the House of Commons about the demonstration in Hyde Park on June 24 (see this volume, pp. 303-04).—*Ed.*

[c] Panmure's speech in the House of Lords on June 28, 1855, in reply to a question by Richmond. *The Times*, No. 22093, June 29, 1855.—*Ed.*

[d] Victoria.—*Ed.*

But the proclamation anticipated the vote of the House. If the House were to reject the demand it would come into conflict with the army. This is the answer to the finding of the Roebuck Committee to the effect that the Ministry was responsible for the misfortunes endured by the army. A step in the direction pointed by Prince Albert.[a]

Bouverie's Bill, which had its second reading in the House of Commons yesterday,[b] is significant as far as English commercial law is concerned. In England up to now anyone receiving a definite share of the profits of a business was regarded as a partner and as such was liable with the *whole of his possessions* for the commercial commitments of that business. Bouverie's Bill, tabled in the name of the Ministry, aims to abolish this legal obligation. Even more important is his Bill concerning *joint-stock companies*. Up to now every member of a company of this kind was *liable not only for the sum of his own share* but also *to the full extent of his possessions for all the obligations of the company*. According to one of the Bills the liability of the individual shareholder is to be limited to the amount of the shares he holds but this applies only to companies whose total capital amounts to at least £20,000, the articles of association of which are signed by shareholders whose shares total at least £15,000, and where at least 20 per cent of the total capital has been paid up. The mere necessity of a law of this kind proves how much the legislature has been in the hands of high finance until now, which has succeeded, in this the first trading nation in the world, in subjecting commercial contracts to the most absurd and arbitrary legal restrictions. The new Bill claims that it is its principle "to place labour and small capitalists on an equal footing (in terms of commercial law) with big capital." And how is this to be done? By excluding share-capital amounting to *less* than £20,000 from the benefits of this law and allowing it to remain subject to the old restrictions. Nothing proves more conclusively than the English legislation on joint-stock companies and commercial companies in general that big capital, not content with the superior economic weapons with which it fights the competition from the small capitalists, in England also resorts to legal privileges and exceptional laws. Until a few years ago, for example, a bank was not allowed to comprise more than six partners. It was a long time before joint-stock companies acquired the right to take legal action in the name of their boards

[a] For an account of Prince Albert's speech see this volume, pp. 273-76.—*Ed.*
[b] June 29, 1855. *The Times*, No. 22094, June 30, 1855.—*Ed.*

of directors or have actions brought against them. In order, however, to enjoy this privilege they must be registered or incorporated, and a law dating from 1837 declares that the Crown has the right to incorporate only on the basis of a report from the Board of Trade,[a] so that whether a company is incorporated or not depends on the grace and favour of the Board of Trade. Banks, benevolent and mutual aid societies, etc., are completely excluded from the effects of the new Bill.

One of the newspapers today publishes the following *parliamentary statistics*: there are 327 constituencies.[b] A number of these constituencies are controlled by electoral magnates. One magnate controls 9 constituencies, 4 magnates control each 8, 1 magnate controls 7, 3 magnates control 6, 8 magnates control 5, 26 magnates control 4, 29 control 3, so that 72 magnates control 297 constituencies. There remain 30 so-called "independent" constituencies. The House of Commons comprises 654 members, 594 of whom are elected by the 297 dependent constituencies. These 594 include 274 people who are directly related to peers or belong to the aristocracy.

Written on June 30, 1855

First published in the *Neue Oder-Zeitung*, No. 303, July 3, 1855

Marked with the sign ×

Printed according to the newspaper

Published in English for the first time

[a] Marx uses the English term.—*Ed.*
[b] This figure does not include the 72 constituencies in Ireland.—*Ed.*

Karl Marx

AGITATION OVER THE TIGHTENING-UP OF SUNDAY OBSERVANCE[230]

London, July 2. Yesterday there was a repeat of the demonstration against the Sunday Bill in Hyde Park,[a] but this time on a larger scale, under more ominous auspices and with more serious consequences. The general mood of gloomy agitation in London today is witness to that.

The posters which called on people to hold a second meeting also invited them to assemble in front of the house of the pious Lord Grosvenor on Sunday at 10 a.m., and to accompany him on his way to church. But the pious gentleman had already left London on Saturday in a private carriage—in order to travel incognito. That he is more inclined by nature to make martyrs of other people rather than become a martyr himself has already been proved by his circular letter which appeared in all the London newspapers, in which on the one hand he sticks to his bill whilst on the other hand he is at pains to show that it is meaningless, pointless and insignificant.[b] His house was occupied all Sunday, not by psalm-singers but by constables, 200 in number. Also the house of his brother, the Marquis of Westminster, famous for his wealth.

On Saturday Sir Richard Mayne, chief of the London police, had pasted notices on the walls of London not only "*forbidding*" a meeting in Hyde Park but also "*forbidding*" people to assemble there in "large numbers" and to exhibit any signs of approval or

[a] For an account of the first demonstration, held on June 24, see this volume, pp. 302-07.—*Ed.*

[b] R. Grosvenor, "The Sunday Trading Bill. To the Editor of *The Times*", *The Times*, No. 22093, June 28, 1855.—*Ed.*

disapproval. The result of these ukases was, even according to the report in the police circular, that as early as 2.30 p.m. 150,000 people from *all* classes and of all ages, were surging to and fro, and that gradually the crowd in the park swelled to dimensions which were immensely large and astonishing even by London standards. Not only did London appear *en masse*; people again lined both sides of the road along the Serpentine, only this time the crowds were more closely packed and deeper than on the previous Sunday. The people who did not, however, appear were the upper crust. All in all perhaps 20 carriages appeared, the majority of which were small gigs and phaetons which were allowed to pass unmolested, whereas their more portly, larger bellied, and taller brothers, trimmed with more braid, were greeted with the same calls as previously and with the same babel of sounds, the waves of which made the air vibrate for about a mile around. The police ukases were rebutted by the mass meeting and the exercising of thousands of pairs of lungs. The upper crust had avoided the scene of action and by its absence recognised the sovereignty of the *vox populi*.

It was 4 o'clock and the demonstration seemed to be fizzling out into a harmless Sunday diversion from lack of anything to keep it going. But that did not suit the police. Were they to retire a general laughing-stock, casting melancholy parting glances at their own notices, which people could read at the main gate of the park in huge letters? What is more, their high dignitaries were present, Sir Richard Mayne and superintendents Gibbs and Walker on horseback, and inspectors Banks, Darkin and Brennan on foot. Eight hundred constables were strategically positioned, mainly hidden in buildings and ambuscades. Stronger detachments had been positioned at intervals nearby as reinforcements. The home of the chief park attendant, the powder magazine and the premises of the rescue services, all situated at a point where the road along the Serpentine turns into a path leading to Kensington Gardens, had been converted into improvised block houses manned by large forces of police and prepared for the accommodation of prisoners and casualties. Hackney cabs were put in position outside Vine Street police station at Piccadilly ready to go to the scene of action and to escort the vanquished safely back. In short, the police had planned a far more "vigorous" campaign, as *The Times* puts it, "than any of which we have yet had notice in the Crimea".[a] The police needed bloody heads

[a] *The Times*, No. 22095, July 2, 1855.—*Ed.*

and arrests so as not to go plunging directly from the sublime to the ridiculous. As soon as the two lines of people had begun to thin out more and the crowds had dispersed in various groups over the huge area of the park further away from the road, the police chiefs took up positions in the middle of the road between the two lines of people, and from their horses began issuing pompous-sounding orders right and left. Supposedly for the protection of passing carriages and riders. As, however, neither carriages nor riders appeared and there was thus nothing for them to protect, they began to pick individuals out of the crowd "under false pretences" and to have them arrested, the pretext being that they were *pickpockets*.[a] When these experiments became more numerous and the pretext no longer held good, a single cry ran through the crowds, and the hidden corps of constables rushed out of their ambuscades, quickly drew their truncheons, rained blows upon people's heads until they bled, here and there pulled an individual out of the crowd (a total of 104 people were arrested in this manner), and dragged them off to the improvised block houses. The left-hand side of the road is only separated from the water of the Serpentine by a narrow strip of land. By a manoeuvre a police officer and his troop managed to drive the onlookers up to the very edge of the liquid element and were threatening to give them a cold bath. In an attempt to escape the police truncheons, one individual swam across the Serpentine to the opposite bank; however, a policeman set off after him in a boat, caught him and brought him back in triumph.

How greatly had the character of the scene changed since last Sunday! Instead of the state carriages, dirty hackney cabs which drove to and fro from the police station at Vine Street to the improvised prisons in Hyde Park and from there to the police station. Instead of footmen up on the box a constable seated next to the drunken cab-driver. Instead of the elegant ladies and gentlemen inside the coaches there were prisoners with bloody heads, tousled hair, hatless, their clothes torn, guarded by shifty-looking characters recruited from among the Irish lumpen-proletariat and pressed into the London police. Instead of the swishing of fans the whizzing of the constables' leather truncheons.[b] Last Sunday the ruling classes had shown their fashionable physiognomy, now they showed their political physiognomy.

---

[a] Marx uses the English word and gives the German translation in brackets.—*Ed.*

[b] Here and below Marx uses the English word.—*Ed.*

Behind the kindly grinning old gentlemen, the fashionable dandies, the genteel and frail widows, the fragrant beauties in cashmere and ostrich feathers, adorned with garlands of diamonds and flowers—was the constable with his water-proof coat, greasy oilskin hat and *truncheon.* It was the reverse side of the coin. Last Sunday the crowd was confronted with the ruling class in its individual form. This time it appeared as political power, the law, the truncheon. This time to resist was to commit insurrection, and the English have to be heated up slowly and for a long time before they are prepared for insurrection. Thus the counter-demonstration was on the whole limited to cat-calling and hooting and whistling at the police vehicles, to isolated and weak attempts at freeing the prisoners, and above all to passive resistance and a phlegmatic determination to remain at the scene of action.

Characteristic was the role played in this drama by the soldiers—partly from the Guards and partly from the 66th Regiment. They were present in large numbers. Twelve of them, Guards, some decorated with medals from the Crimea, were in the middle of a group of men, women and children who were the targets for police truncheons. One old man fell to the ground after receiving a blow. "The London *stiffstaffs*[a]" (name of abuse for the police) "are worse than the Russians were at Inkerman,"[231] cried one of the heroes from the Crimea. The police grabbed him. He was immediately released to loud shouts from the crowd of "Three cheers[b] for the army!" The police considered it advisable to retire. In the meantime a number of grenadiers had joined the crowd, the soldiers formed a troop and, surrounded by the crowd and accompanied by the cry of "Long live the army, down with the police, down with the Sunday Bill!", they strutted up and down the park. The police were standing there not knowing quite what to do, when a sergeant from the guards appeared who loudly took them to task for their brutality, attempted to calm the soldiers and persuaded some of them to follow him to their barracks so as to avoid more serious collisions. The majority of the soldiers, however, stayed behind and, amongst the crowd, gave vent to their indignation against the police in impassioned terms. The antagonism between the police and the army in England goes back a long way. The present moment, when the army is the *pet child*[c] of the masses, is certainly not suited to diminish that in any way.

[a] Marx uses the English word.—*Ed.*
[b] Marx uses the English word.—*Ed.*
[c] Marx uses the English expression.—*Ed.*

An old man by the name of Russell is reported to have died today as a result of the injuries he received; half a dozen injured people are in St. George's Hospital. During the demonstration various attempts were again made to hold separate meetings. At one such meeting, at Albert Gate, outside that part of the park originally occupied by the police, one anonymous speaker harangued his public in roughly the following manner:

"Men of Old England! Awake, rise from your slumbers, or be for ever fallen! Oppose the Government, the 'send-us-to-Church' Bill, every succeeding Sunday, as you have done today. [...] Don't fear to demand your just rights [...] but throw off the shackles of oligarchical oppression and misrule. If you do not [...] you will be irretrievably oppressed and ruined. Is it not a pity that the inhabitants of this great metropolis—the greatest in the civilised world—should have their liberties placed in the hands of my Lord Robert Grosvenor or such a man as Lord Ebrington? His Lordship wants to drive us to church and make us religious by act of Parliament; but it won't do [...]. What are we, and what are they! Look at the present war; is it not carried on at the expense and the sacrifice of blood of the productive classes? And what are the unproductive classes doing? They are bungling it."[a]

The speaker and the meeting were of course interrupted by the police.

At Greenwich, near the observatory, Londoners held a similar meeting attended by 10,000-15,000 people. It was also cut short by the police.

Written on July 2, 1855

First published in the *Neue Oder-Zeitung*, No. 307, July 5, 1855

Marked with the sign ×

Printed according to the newspaper

---

[a] The text of this speech was given in the report on the demonstration published in *The Times*, No. 22095, July 2, 1855.—*Ed.*

Frederick Engels

THE LATE REPULSE OF THE ALLIES[232]

The mail of the *Canada* reached us last evening from Boston, with Gen. Pélissier's report on the repulse of the Allies on the 18th of June (which will be found in our columns today) and with other documents which complete the history of that disastrous affair. Having thus before us all necessary sources of information, we proceed to give our readers an exact and impartial analysis of the entire operation. With regard to its general character it is enough to say that of the many blundering affairs we have had to notice in this Eastern war, this is by far the most perfect piece of bungling.

The French advanced trenches were from 400 to 500, and the English from 500 to 700 yards from the Russian batteries.[a] These distances mark the lengths of road which the respective columns of attack had to pass over without cover from the Russian fire, and unsupported by the fire of their own artillery; with sharp running, then, such as would destroy every vestige of order, they would be exposed to a fire of grape and musketry during from three to five minutes, a time quite sufficient to completely disorganize them. This single fact is characteristic of the whole plan. Unless the enemy's fire were completely silenced, and the accumulation of large masses of troops in the hostile works effectively prevented by incessant vertical shell firing, there was not the slightest chance of success.

The Russians appear to have judged well of the plans of the Allies, if they were not, as Pélissier supposes, fully acquainted with

[a] Marx included this and the following two paragraphs in his report "Clashes between the Police and the People.—The Events in the Crimea" published in the *Neue Oder-Zeitung* (see this volume, pp. 333-36).—*Ed.*

them. They but feebly replied to the besieging fire on the 17th, withdrew their guns behind the parapets during the day, and blinded the embrasures, so that scarcely any were disabled for the next day's work. This was decidedly the best plan, as their object could not be to extinguish the enemy's fire at that time. During the night the guns were brought back into their positions, the columns and reserves told off for the defense were stationed, and thus they were in a condition to meet any assault that could be made upon their position.

The plan agreed upon between Pélissier and Raglan was to reopen their fire at daybreak on the 18th with all the vigor they could give to it for a couple of hours, and then on a sudden to launch simultaneously seven storming columns—one French against the bastion close to the Careening Bay, two French against the Malakoff bastion, three English against the Redan bastion and one English against the cluster of houses and the cemetery situated between the Redan and the head of the inner harbor. This plan was sensible enough if there was to be an assault at all; its execution would subdue the Russian fire and disperse the Russian masses concentrated for the defense before the actual attack took place. On the other hand, the allied troops would have to suffer from the Russian fire while crowding the trenches, and the defenders would very probably soon perceive the presence of columns destined to attack their position with the bayonet. But this was by far the lesser evil. The original plan therefore was the best that could be devised under the circumstances.

However, we are informed that[a] very late in the evening Pélissier learned that the Russians intended again to attack the Mamelon in force on the 18th. This should have been considered a godsend, for the defense of the Mamelon against any force the Russians could bring against it must have been safe, or else how could the Mamelon[b] serve as a base of operations for the assault upon the Malakoff? Thus the Russians, defeated in their assault upon the Mamelon, would have been in a sad plight to fight a second battle for the Malakoff, and it would almost appear that under these circumstances the success of the operation against the latter position must have been

---

[a] The German version of this article, published in the *Neue Oder-Zeitung* under the title "The Assault of the 18th [June]", begins here. It is introduced as follows: "London, July 7. Yesterday we examined the Allies' original plan for the assault on June 18."—*Ed.*

[b] The version published in the *Neue Oder-Zeitung* has here: "(now christened the *Brancion* redoubt)".—*Ed.*

certain. Pélissier appears to have thought differently. He countermanded, late at night, the cannonade, and ordered the assault for 3 o'clock in the morning, the signal to be given by three rockets. The English were informed of this change of disposition.

This proceeding ended, as it was sure to do, in the way Napoleon used to say of bungling Generals: *Ordre, contre-ordre, désordre.*[a] Half an hour before the appointed time, the extreme right French column somehow or other got engaged with the enemy. Whether the Russians drew them out by a false sally, or whether, as Pélissier says, the General[b] mistook a French shell for the signal rockets, is not quite clear. At all events, Pélissier had to hurry his signal, and the columns, still engaged in finding their proper places in the trenches, had to start in half confusion, and in part from different starting points from those assigned to them. The middle French column, intended to turn the flank of the Malakoff, effected its purpose and got into the Russian works; but the other two columns could make no headway in the hail-storm of case-shot and musketry which assailed them. Each column consisted of a brigade of four battalions; the second brigade of each division was in second line, while the Guard formed the general reserve. Thus nearly four divisions, or 20,000 men, were at hand for the purpose. The second line was brought up to the support of the first attack, but in vain; the Guards were sent forward, and they were arrested and then thrown back as well. Two battalions only remained disposable. It was now half-past eight. The brigade of the middle column, which had penetrated into the works, was ejected; on every point the French had been repulsed with great loss and no fresh troops were at hand. The English had not succeeded either. Pélissier gave the order for the retreat, which he says was effected with "dignity."

On the English side the columns of attack were told off with that parsimoniousness characteristic of the British Army. The leading columns counted but 1,800 men each, or 1,000 men less than the French columns.[c] Of these 1,800, but 1,000 were intended

---

[a] In the *Neue Oder-Zeitung* this passage reads as follows: "The operation ended as it was bound to end, in the manner in which Napoleon, the real Napoleon, describes the fate of wavering and bungling generals: 'Ordre, contre-ordre, désordre'."—*Ed.*

[b] J. D. N. Mayran.—*Ed.*

[c] Instead of the preceding two sentences the *Neue Oder-Zeitung* has: "On the *English* side each of the leading columns comprised only 1,800 men, 1,000 men less than the French."—*Ed.*

for fighting—the rest for working parties. In second line, the remainder of the brigade from which the force was taken, say 1,200 to 1,400 men, were behind each column. In third line, the second brigade of each division was behind its first brigade. Finally, the Guards and Highlanders (first division) formed the general reserve. Thus, of the whole English infantry assembled on the ground, but 7,200 men were to be launched in the first onset, and of these but 4,000 were actual combatants. This weakness in the first columns was caused, first, by the traditions of the British service, and, secondly, by their habit of attacking in line; for all reports lead to the conclusion that even in this instance they attacked in line, and thus offered a gratuitously large aim to the grape of the enemy. The complication caused by the arrangement of four different lines one behind another, in narrow and irregular trenches, created great disorder and mischief from the beginning, and would have created utter confusion had the struggle become anything like serious.

The first and third columns (from right to left) were to turn the flanks of the Redan, while the second was to attack its salient angle as soon as they had succeeded. The fourth or extreme left column, as stated, had to attack the head of the inner harbor. When the signal was given, as was the case with the French, the columns were still in movement toward their respective positions. The first column, however, jumped over the parapet of the trenches and was instantly saluted with a murderous fire of case-shot. The troops, disordered by the climbing, could not form. Col. Yea, who commanded, was already shouting for a bugler to sound the retreat; no bugler was found, and on they went in great disorder. Some penetrated to the abattis surrounding the Redan, but in vain. The mass of the column fell back at once and sought the shelter of the trenches. The third column advanced a minute or two later. It missed its road, and assailed the face of the Redan near the apex, instead of the flank. It staggered forward under a tremendous hail of projectiles, but was broken and retreated in complete disorder in a very few minutes. The whole affair lasted less than fifteen minutes.[a] Thus ended the attack upon the Redan, before any of the complicated reserves of Lord Raglan had time to come up to its support. The second column was so startled by this sudden breakdown of its flanking bodies that it did not even stir out of the trenches.

[a] This sentence does not occur in the *Neue Oder-Zeitung*.—*Ed.*

The fourth column, commanded by Maj. Gen. Eyre, whose report we publish,[a] alone succeeded in establishing itself in the cemetery and the houses surrounding. Here about 1,800 men held out during the day. They could not retreat, for the ground behind them was open and under the cross fire of the Russians. Thus they fought as well as they could till 9 o'clock at night, when they effected their retreat during the darkness. Their losses amounted to more than one-third of their number.

Thus ended Pélissier's grand attack upon the Karabelnaya suburb. It was hastily determined upon, more hastily changed in its main features at a late period, and carried out with extreme blundering. The Russian was right who said to an English officer during the armistice of the 19th "Your Generals must have been drunk yesterday when they ordered the assault."

A newspaper correspondent writing from the scene describes it as "an infantry Balaklava."[233] This is perfectly just, and sums up in the briefest manner the criticisms which all intelligent military men must make upon this calamitous repulse.[b]

Written about July 6, 1855

First published in the *New-York Daily Tribune*, No. 4447, July 21, 1855, reprinted in the *New-York Semi-Weekly Tribune*, No. 1060, July 24, 1855 and the *New-York Weekly Tribune*, No. 724, July 28, 1855 as a leading article; the German version was published in the *Neue Oder-Zeitung*, partly in Marx's report printed in No. 313 on July 9, and as a separate article in No. 317 on July 11, 1855, marked with the sign ×

Reproduced from the *New-York Daily Tribune*

---

[a] The German version makes no mention of Eyre or his report.—*Ed.*

[b] The last paragraph does not occur in the *Neue Oder-Zeitung*.—*Ed.*

Karl Marx and Frederick Engels

CLASHES BETWEEN THE POLICE AND THE PEOPLE.— THE EVENTS IN THE CRIMEA[234]

London, July 6. London witnessed a continuous series of clashes, lasting from Monday to yesterday evening, between the police and the "mob"; the former with their truncheons behaved provocatively, the latter reciprocated by throwing stones. We saw scenes in Marlborough Street and the nearby streets which were strongly reminiscent of Paris. Duncombe asked Parliament yesterday evening to investigate the "base and brutal" conduct of the police last Sunday.[a] The masses intend to visit the clubs in Pall Mall[b] the day after tomorrow. The Chartists are planning an *armed* procession—armed not with sabres and muskets but with tools and sticks—to move from Blackfriars Bridge to Hyde Park carrying banners with the inscription "No Mayne Law".[c] (This is deliberately ambiguous. *Maine* Law, as everybody knows, is the name of the puritanical American law prohibiting alcoholic drinks.[235] *Mayne* is the name of the chief of the London police.) It will have been obvious from our previous reports[d] that the demonstrations in Hyde Park were improvised events brought about by the instinct of the masses. The unrest was afterwards increased and heightened by the provocative brutality of the police, whose chief, Sir Richard Mayne, proved worthy of the decoration he had received from Paris. It is however even now possible to discern several distinct parties which seek to accelerate, guide and utilise the mass movement for their own more far-reaching ends. These parties are:

---

[a] July 1, 1855.—*Ed.*

[b] Street in London.—*Ed.*

[c] "No Mayne Law" and "Maine Law" are given in English in the article together with a German translation.—*Ed.*

[d] See this volume, pp. 297-307, 323-27.—*Ed.*

First the Government itself. During Bonaparte's stay in London,[236] all wall posters directed against him disappeared as if by magic. Now even the most virulent posters are not removed by the police. Everything indicates a hidden purpose: the constables' *enjoined* brutality, the provocative language of government counsel at the Court[a] in Marlborough Street, the *unlawful* employment of the arrested persons on the treadmill,[a] the insulting manner of the official newspapers, and the Cabinet's vacillating behaviour in Parliament. Does Palmerston need a small *coup d'état* to maintain his Government, or does he require widespread internal disturbances to divert attention from the Crimea? If we understand correctly this reckless statesman, who hides his profound and ruthless calculations under the cloak of frivolous superficiality, we can say of him, as Voltaire says of Habakuk, that he is "*capable de tout*".[b][237]

Secondly the advocates of Administrative Reform.[238] They try to use the mass movement to intimidate the aristocracy on the one hand, and as a means of winning popularity for themselves on the other hand. It is for this reason that in *their* name and for *their* account, the case of those arrested last Sunday was conducted by *Ballantine* before the police-court[a] in Marlborough Street. This is why they ransomed all those sentenced yesterday by depositing their fines. This is why *their* newspapers defend the "mob" (as the ministerial *Globe* calls the people) and attack the police and the Ministry.

Thirdly the *Chartists*, whose aims are self-evident.

Official and private reports on the unfortunate attack of June 18 have at last appeared. The publication of the official dispatches was put off for several days, and there was certainly good reason for the delay. This is undoubtedly a most perfect example of the blunders made in the Eastern affair.

The French advanced trenches were from 400 to 500, and the English from 500 to 700 yards from the Russian batteries.[c] These distances mark the lengths of road which the respective columns of attack had to pass over without cover from the Russian fire, and unsupported by the fire of their own artillery; with sharp running, then, such as would destroy every vestige of order, would expose them defencelessly to musket fire during three to five

[a] Marx and Engels use the English term.—*Ed.*

[b] Capable of anything.—*Ed.*

[c] This and the following two paragraphs largely correspond to the second, third and fourth paragraphs of Engels' article "The Late Repulse of the Allies" (see this volume, pp. 328-32).—*Ed.*

minutes, a time quite sufficient to completely disorganise them. This single fact is characteristic of the whole plan. Unless the enemy's fire were *completely* silenced, and the accumulation of large masses of troops in the hostile works *effectively* prevented by incessant vertical shell firing, there was not the slightest chance of success.

The Russians appear to have judged well of the plans of the Allies, if they were not, as Pélissier supposes, fully acquainted with them. They but feebly replied to the fire of the Allies on the 17th, withdrew their guns behind the parapets during the day, and in general made such arrangements that scarcely any other preparations were required for the next day's work. During the night the guns were brought back into their positions, the columns and reserves told off for the defence were stationed.

The plan originally agreed upon between Pélissier and Raglan was to reopen their fire at daybreak on the 18th with all the vigour they could give to it for a couple of hours, and then on a sudden to launch simultaneously seven storming columns—one French against the bastion close to the Careening Bay, two French against the Malakoff bastion, three English against the Redan bastion and one English against the cluster of houses and the cemetery situated between the Redan and the head of the inner harbour. This plan was sensible enough if there was to be an assault at all; its execution would subdue the Russian fire and disperse the Russian masses concentrated for the defence before the actual attack took place. On the other hand, the Allied troops would have to suffer from the Russian fire while crowding the trenches, and the defenders would very probably soon perceive the presence of columns destined to attack their position with the bayonet. But this was by far the lesser evil. The original plan with all its shortcomings was still the best that could be devised under the circumstances. How the plan was failed, how Pélissier's premature laurel wreath withered away and how under the protective eagles of the restored Empire, the Allied armies suffered an "*infantry Balaklava*"[239]—all this we shall discuss tomorrow.

This summer seems to have severe tribulations in store for the "*saints*". The foremost bill broker of London, and apparently the chief of the Quakers,[240] *Gurney* (one of whose daughters is married to Bunsen's son), Gurney, who is as rich as he is pious, seems to be badly compromised by the fraudulent Strand bankruptcy. He discounted bills of exchange amounting to £37,000 for Strahan and Co. though he knew that they were bankrupt, thus enabling them to defraud the public for a few months longer. He himself managed to extricate himself without incurring any loss. The mundane press delights in making malicious remarks about the iniquities committed even by the select.

Written about July 6, 1855

First published in the *Neue Oder-Zeitung*, No. 313, July 9, 1855

Marked with the sign ×

The English version of part of the text was published in the *New-York Daily Tribune*, No. 4447, July 21, 1855, reprinted in the *New-York Semi-Weekly Tribune*, No. 1060, July 24, 1855 and in the *New-York Weekly Tribune*, No. 724, July 28, 1855 as a leading article

Printed according to the newspaper

Published in English in full for the first time

Karl Marx

FROM PARLIAMENT. [—ROEBUCK'S AND BULWER'S MOTIONS]

London, July 11. As is generally known, Roebuck's motion censuring *all* the members of the old Coalition Cabinet[a] has been put down for next Tuesday. Whilst numerous meetings supporting his motion are being held at Birmingham, Sheffield, Newcastle, etc., and at the same time public petitions are being signed in support of it in every corner of London, members of Parliament are decamping to Paris, Naples and their country homes, in order to avoid the division. In an attempt to prevent this exodus, supported by Palmerston in every respect, Roebuck yesterday moved for power to call over the Commons next Tuesday. The "Call"[b] is an old parliamentary practice which had sunk into oblivion since the time of the debate on Catholic Emancipation.[241] At the opening of the sitting the name of every single Member of Parliament is called out. Those who are absent are subject to arrest by the parliamentary serjeant-at-arms,[c] a public apology before the assembled House and the payment of certain fines. By a majority of 133 to 108, however, the Commons refused Roebuck the right to coerce members by means of a Call. Nothing could be more characteristic of the British Parliament and its press organs than their attitude towards Roebuck's motion. The motion does not emanate from any member of the "official" opposition. That is its first blemish. It is directed not only against members of the present Cabinet but also against members of the dissolved Cabinet.

---

[a] Roebuck first gave notice of his motion in the House of Commons on June 22, 1855. See this volume, pp. 297-301.—*Ed.*

[b] Here and below Marx uses the English word.—*Ed.*

[c] Marx uses the English term.—*Ed.*

It is not, therefore, a purely party manoeuvre. It declares that the sins of the old Ministry are not expiated by the forming of a new Ministry. It opens the way for a motion calling for impeachment. That is the other great blemish of this motion. For the official opposition is of course only willing to wage the parliamentary war "*within the limits of a change of Ministers*". It is far removed from waging war against ministerial responsibility. The clique of *Outs* is no less anxious about maintaining ministerial omnipotence than the clique of *Ins*.[a] The skill in conducting parliamentary battles consists of course precisely in ensuring that during the fight it is never the office that is hit but always the person holding the office at a given time, and even he only to an extent that will permit him after being brought down as a *Minister* immediately to come forward as a *candidate for the Ministry*. The oligarchy does not perpetuate itself by retaining power permanently *in the same* hand, but by dropping it with one hand in order to catch it again with the other, and so on. The Tories are therefore just as dissatisfied with Roebuck's motion as the Whigs are.

As to the *press*, the reaction of *The Times* is crucial. Was there a newspaper that clamoured louder for the Roebuck Committee to be set up, as long as its purpose was, on the one hand, to bring about a change of Ministers and, on the other, to provide an outlet for the public passion? However, from the moment that Roebuck comes forward and, supported by the findings of his Committee, threatens to lay *all* the members of the coalition open to explicit censure by Parliament, is there a newspaper which observes a more stubborn silence than *The Times*? As far as *The Times* is concerned, Roebuck's motion does not exist; yesterday's incident in Parliament concerning the "Call" does not exist; the meetings at Birmingham, Sheffield, etc., do not exist in its columns. Roebuck himself is, of course, no Brutus. On the one hand, he has seen how miserably the Whigs have rewarded him for the services he has rendered over many years. On the other hand, he has his constituents behind him. He represents a large body of constituents whom he has to pay in popularity as he cannot pay them in cash. And finally, the role of a modern Warwick, the parliamentary King-Maker, can hardly be displeasing to this ambitious but so far scarcely successful barrister. The Tories who form the opposition cannot, of course, oppose Roebuck's motion in the same way as the Whigs can. They are therefore seeking to forestall it. This is the

[a] Marx uses the English words "Outs" and "Ins" (i.e. members of the opposition on the one hand and the ruling party on the other).—*Ed.*

secret behind *Bulwer*'s motion calling for a *vote of no confidence* in the Ministry,[a] based on Lord John Russell's strange revelations about the Vienna conferences.[b] Bulwer's motion remains entirely "within" the limits of a government reshuffle. It takes the fate of the Ministry out of Roebuck's hands. If it succeeds then it will be the Tories who have toppled the Whigs, and once holding the Ministry, conventional "*magnanimity*" would forbid them to pursue their victory and to continue supporting Roebuck. But the artfulness of the Tories at the same time enables Palmerston to employ old parliamentary tricks. The dismissal of *Russell,* whether voluntary or imposed, will serve to parry Bulwer's motion just as Bulwer has parried Roebuck's motion. Russell's departure would be certain to bring Palmerston's Cabinet down were it not to occur shortly before the end of the session. Now, however, it may on the contrary prolong the life of his Cabinet. If so, then no English Minister before Palmerston has managed with such skill and good fortune to use the people's clamouring in order to force himself upon the parliamentary parties on the one hand, and, on the other, to use the petty parliamentary interests, groupings and formalities that exist to force himself upon the people. He is like the old man of the sea whom Sindbad the Sailor found impossible to shake off once he had allowed him to climb onto his shoulders.

Written on July 11, 1855

First published in the *Neue Oder-Zeitung,* No. 323, July 14, 1855

Marked with the sign ×

Printed according to the newspaper

Published in English for the first time

[a] The motion was tabled in the House of Commons on July 10, 1855. *The Times,* No. 22103, July 11, 1855.—*Ed.*

[b] See this volume, pp. 222-26.—*Ed.*

Karl Marx

FROM THE HOUSES OF PARLIAMENT. [—BULWER'S MOTION.—THE IRISH QUESTION][242]

London, July 13. It is difficult for those not initiated into the mysteries of jurisprudence to understand why it should be that, in the most straightforward lawsuits, unexpected legal problems arise which owe their existence, not to the nature of the lawsuit, but to the rules and formalities of legal procedure. It is the handling of these legal ceremonies that makes your lawyer, just as it is the handling of ecclesiastical ceremonies that makes your Brahmin. Just as in the course of development of religion, so in the course of development of law too, form becomes content. But what legal procedure is to courts of law, the agenda and standing orders are to legislative bodies. The history of agrarian law proves that the old Roman oligarchs, the originators of chicanery in legal proceedings, were also the first to introduce procedural chicanery into legislation. In both respects they have been outdone by England. The technical difficulties involved in tabling a motion, the various metamorphoses that a bill has to go through before it can become law; the formalities which permit the opponent of a motion or a bill to prevent the former from entering the House and the latter from leaving it—all this provides an inexhaustible arsenal of parliamentary chicanery, pettifogging and tactics. But no English Minister before Palmerston has so thoroughly lent the House of Commons[243] the appearance, tone and character of a *Court of Chancery*.[a] Where diplomacy does not suffice, he has recourse to chicanery. Under his guidance every debate on an objectionable motion is turned into a preliminary debate about the day when the debate shall actually take place and the case be put.

[a] Marx uses the English term.—*Ed.*

So it was with Milner Gibson's motion, so it was with Layard's motion and so it is now with Bulwer's motion.[a] So overloaded were the orders of the day at the close of the session that Bulwer was only able to bring in his motion on a day when the House went into a *Committee of Supply*,[b] i.e. when the Government puts its financial requirements before the House of Commons.[244] Friday is generally set aside for this business. However, it depends, of course, on the Government *when* it asks the Commons for supplies and hence when the House goes into a Committee of Supply. Palmerston promptly told Bulwer that he would not, to use the technical term, go into Supply that Friday, but proceed with the Bill on the limited liability of trading companies, and that Bulwer might "fix a day for himself".[c] Last Tuesday, therefore, Disraeli gave notice that he would appeal to the House the following Thursday (yesterday) to set aside this piece of chicanery. Palmerston forestalled him. He rose during yesterday's sitting and declared amidst the general laughter of the House that it was certainly not his intention either to delay the debate on Bulwer's vote of no-confidence or, by placing technical difficulties in the way, to prevent the honourable House from forming an opinion. But, he went on, despite every effort, the supplementary documents relating to the Vienna Conference could not have been laid upon the table of the House of Commons before the following day, and how could the House form an opinion without having seen the documents of the case? He was, he said, prepared to set aside Monday for a discussion of Bulwer's motion.[d] Disraeli pointed out that "the supplementary documents" bore no relation whatever to Bulwer's motion; the Bill on the limited liability of trading companies was quite important in its own way, but what the nation presently wanted to know was:

> "whether the Cabinet is collectively liable for its actions or whether the principle of limited liability is also applicable here. Above all, it wanted to know the conditions under which the partners of the firm in Downing Street[e] conducted their business."

---

[a] For the motions of Layard (tabled April 27), Gibson (May 11) and Bulwer (July 10) see this volume, pp. 167, 187, 223, 338-39.—*Ed.*

[b] Marx uses the English name here and below.—*Ed.*

[c] Palmerston's speech in the House of Commons on July 10, 1855. *The Times*, No. 22103, July 11, 1855.—*Ed.*

[d] The speeches by Palmerston, Disraeli, Bulwer, Russell and Shee in the House of Commons on July 12, 1855, were published in *The Times*, No. 22104, July 13, 1855.—*Ed.*

[e] 10 Downing Street is the residence of the British Prime Minister. Here the reference is to the government as a whole.—*Ed.*

Bulwer said he would accept Monday as the day for the debate. Russell, for his part, took advantage of this incident to attempt to tone down and distort the meaning of the statement he made last Friday.[a] But in vain; the second, amended version arrived too late, as is patently evident from today's *Times*. Indeed, for several days *The Times* has been using every artifice to save Palmerston's Cabinet at Russell's expense, wherein it is steadfastly supported by the simple-minded *Morning Advertiser*, which regains its whole-hearted faith in Palmerston each time Parliament shows signs of losing it. Meanwhile Palmerston has gained a few days' respite in which to do some manoeuvring. How he exploited each of those days is evident from the Irish *row*[b] which occurred yesterday in the House of Commons.

For two years, as everyone knows, three bills have been drifting through Parliament, their purpose being to regulate the relations between Irish landlords and tenants. One of these bills lays down how much compensation the tenant is entitled to claim on improvements effected on the land, in the event of his landlord giving him notice to quit. Hitherto the improvements effected by Irish tenants (virtually all of whom hold a one-year lease) only served to enable the landlord to demand a higher rent on expiration of the lease. Thus the tenant, should he not wish to renew the agreement on less favourable terms, either loses the farm and, with the farm, the capital he has laid out on improvements, or he is compelled to pay the landlord interest, over and above the original rent, for improvements effected with *his* (the tenant's) capital. Support for the above-mentioned bills was one of the conditions with which the coalition Cabinet bought the vote of the Irish Brigade.[245] Hence, in 1854, they were passed by the Commons, but deferred by the Lords, with the connivance of the Ministers, until the following session (1855), when they suffered such drastic revision that all their teeth were drawn, and in this mutilated form were returned to the Commons. There, last Thursday, the main clause of the Compensation Bill was sacrificed on the altar of landed property and the Irish were astonished to discover that the scales had been tipped against them, partly by the votes of members of the Government, partly by the votes of its immediate allies. Serjeant Shee's furious onslaught upon Palmerston portended a riot[c] in Parliament's

---

[a] July 6, 1855.—*Ed.*
[b] Marx uses the English word.—*Ed.*
[c] Marx uses the English words "serjeant" and "riot".—*Ed.*

"Irish Quarter", something which might, at this particular juncture, have serious consequences. Palmerston therefore, through the medium of Sadleir, ex-member of the coalition and broker to the Irish Brigade, arranged for a deputation of eighteen Irish Members of Parliament to wait upon him the day before yesterday with the request that he use his influence to have the parliamentary vote rescinded and to carry the clause through the House in another division. He, of course, declared that he was ready to do anything so as to secure the Irish votes against the motion of no-confidence. The premature exploding of this intrigue in the House of Commons gave rise to one of the rowdy scenes typical of the decline of an oligarchic Parliament. The Irish dispose of 105 votes. However, it transpired that the majority had not given a mandate to the eighteen-strong deputation. For that matter, Palmerston can no longer make quite the same use of the Irish in Ministerial crises as he was wont to do in O'Connell's day. With the disintegration of all the old parliamentary factions, the Irish Quarter too has split up and become fragmented. At all events, the incident demonstrates how Palmerston is exploiting the respite he gained to manipulate the various coteries. At the same time he is awaiting favourable news of some kind from the theatre of war, a minor event of some kind capable of parliamentary—if not military—exploitation. The submarine telegraph has taken the conduct of the war out of the hands of the generals and subjected it to the amateurish astrological whims of Bonaparte and to parliamentary and diplomatic intrigue. Hence the inexplicable and completely unprecedented character of the second Crimean campaign.

Written on July 13, 1855

First published in the *Neue Oder-Zeitung*, No. 325, July 16, 1855

Marked with the sign ×

Printed according to the newspaper

Published in English for the first time

Frederick Engels

THE GREAT CRIMEAN BLUNDER[246]

If "time is money" in trade, time is victory in war. To let the favorable moment slip away, to miss the opportunity when your own superior strength should be brought to bear upon your opponent, is as great a fault as can be committed before an enemy. The fault is doubled if you commit it when acting on the offensive; for while merely defending a position the consequences of your neglect may be remedied, but when you are in an enemy's country, on an errand of invasion, then such inattention may involve the ruin of your army. All this is very trite, and there is not a lieutenant or cornet in the world but would treat it as a matter of course. Yet there is no rule of strategy or tactics sinned against oftener than this; and it would appear as if Gen. Pélissier, the impetuous man of action, the "Marshal Forward"[247] of the Crimean army, were the very man doomed to exemplify in his own person this common neglect of commonplace things.

The road into Sevastopol leads round by Inkermann to the north side of the fortress, as we have said over and over again.[a] It is not to be supposed that Pélissier and his staff do not know this as well as we do. But to go to the north side the allied army must take the field with its main strength and defeat the Russians, afterward investing the north side, and detaching a corps to keep the Russian field-army at a distance. The moment to do this was when the Sardinian corps had arrived, and the Turks, under Omer Pasha, were at Kamiesh. At that time the Allies must have been considerably stronger than the Russians. But nothing of the sort was done. The expedition to Kertch and the Sea of Azoff was

[a] See this volume, pp. 203, 318.—*Ed.*

undertaken, and assault after assault was attempted. The field operations were confined to reconnaissances and to an extension of the camping ground to the entrance of Baidar Valley. Now, at last, we learn what is the professed reason for this inactivity: the means of transport are not forthcoming, and after fifteen months campaigning the Allies are as much tied to the sea, to Kamiesh and Balaklava harbors, as ever!

This is really intolerable. The Crimea is not a desert island somewhere about the North Pole. It is a country the resources of which may certainly be exhausted as to food, but which is still able to furnish plenty of provender, draught animals, carts and beasts of burden, to anybody who has the boldness to take them. Cautious and slow movements, forward and backward within a few miles of the Chernaya, are of course not the means to get hold of these useful articles; but even if we leave the camels, ponies and arbas of the Crimea entirely out of the question, there is plenty of means of transport to be had on the Asiatic and European shores of the Black Sea, within two days' steaming from Balaklava. Why are they not impressed into the allied service? We say impressed, for impressment, commonly called requisition, is the proper way to make them available. To employ Spanish muleteers and Bulgarian laborers at a high price will never do; and in a country like Turkey even less than anywhere else. A regiment of cavalry scouring the shores of Anatolia would very soon bring hundreds of conveyances and thousands of animals together, along with the forage required. The war is prosecuted on behalf of the Turks, and to furnish means of transport is the least that can be expected of them. In every continental war the country in which armies operate is expected to do the same. To be more delicate with Turks is doubly absurd; if the Turks have not to work for their Allies, they will have to work for their Pashas, who will treat them much worse. They may not like it, but neither do they like to toil for their Pashas; and if they will not yield to discipline and order, a little application of martial law will soon break them in, as the Pashas always keep them under a similar sort of law. It is perfectly ridiculous that, with such resources within reach, the allied Generals should still complain of inability to move for want of transports.

The Russians, indeed, have given them lessons enough how they should act. The 3d, 4th, and 5th army-corps, beside several divisions of the reserves, were transported into the Crimea at a time when the Allies could not bring up food from Balaklava to the trenches. The troops were partly carried across the steppes in wagons, and they always had plenty of food. And yet the country within a semicircle of 200 miles around Perekop is but very thinly inhabited. But the resources of the more distant provinces were put under contribution; and surely, to bring the wagons of Ekaterinoslav, Poltava and Charkoff, to assist the Russians in the Crimea, is more difficult than to get the conveyances of Anatolia and Roumelia to work there for the Allies.

Nevertheless, under the pretext of want of transports, the opportunity to conquer the Crimea as far as Sympheropol has been allowed to slip by. Now the situation is different. The Russians have formed a reserve army for the Crimea between Odessa and Cherson. What this army consists of we can judge by the simple fact that from the Western army the whole of the second army-corps and two divisions of grenadiers have been detached toward the formation of this new force. The advanced guard of this reenforcement must already have passed Cherson. These troops consist in all of five divisions or eighty-two battalions of infantry; one division or thirty-two squadrons of cavalry; and from fifty to eighty guns. To these we must add a number of reserves, and also a division at least of the reserve cavalry; and as the above eighty-eight battalions belong to the troops which have been chiefly under the eye of the Emperor,[a] they must have their full war numbers. Allowing, therefore, for the loss on the march, the whole force assembled between Odessa and Perekop, and intended for the Crimea, may safely be estimated at something like 70,000 to 80,000 men. The heads of their columns must be past Cherson, perhaps past Perekop, by this time; and before July is out they will begin to tell upon the Allies.

Now, what have the Allies to oppose to these reenforcements? Their ranks are again thinned by cholera and fever, no less than by the slaughter of the different assaults. The British reenforcements are slow in arriving, and very few regiments indeed are being sent off. The French Government state that they do not intend to send out fresh divisions, but merely detachments from the depots to fill up the gaps made in the ranks of the various regiments at the seat of war. If these reenforcements arrive in time they will hardly suffice to bring up the allied army to the strength it had in the beginning of June; that is to say, 210,000 men at the outside, including Turks and Sardinians. The probability is it will never exceed 180,000 men at any time; to which force the Russians, by the beginning of August, will be able

---

[a] Alexander II.—*Ed.*

to oppose at least 200,000 men in good positions, in command of the country at their rear, and in possession of the south side of Sevastopol as a bridgehead.

Then the chances are that the Allies will be driven back upon the plateau behind the Chernaya, unable to move forward or backward, and with an army now so numerous that it must change this narrow piece of ground into one hotbed of disease. And then Pélissier will repent his want of energy and resolution as regards the advance into the field, and his excess of energy as regards the storming of the place. Still, there is yet time for a move in the field. The best moment has passed, but for all that, a bold advance might secure even now a wider range of ground to the Allies. But it does not look as if they were going to avail themselves of this chance.

It must, however, be stated, in fairness to Pélissier, that public opinion in Paris, and in Europe generally, lays the principal fault at the door of Louis Bonaparte. That unfortunate would-be general is said to meddle in everything. The matter is not quite clear yet, but in a short time the nature of the interference of this ambitious adventurer in the Crimean military operations must be cleared up, and we shall then know where the blame of these enormous blunders is to be placed.

Written about July 14, 1855

First published in the *New-York Daily Tribune*, No. 4452, July 27, 1855, reprinted in the *New-York Semi-Weekly Tribune*, No. 1061, July 27, 1855 and the *New-York Weekly Tribune*, No. 725, August 4, 1855 as a leading article; an abridged German version was included in the report by Marx and Engels published in the *Neue Oder-Zeitung*, No. 327, July 17, 1855, marked with the sign ×

Reproduced from the *New-York Daily Tribune*

Karl Marx and Frederick Engels

RUSSELL'S RESIGNATION.—THE EVENTS IN THE CRIMEA[248]

London, July 14. Our last report but one[a] treated *Lord John Russell's resignation*, whether voluntary or under duress, as a *fait accompli*. It took place yesterday afternoon, and it is in fact a *composite* resignation, both voluntary and under duress. For the section of the Whigs most eager to obtain posts, headed by Bouverie, were driven by Palmerston into a minor revolt. They stated that they would be obliged to vote for Bulwer's motion[b] unless Lord John resigned. No resistance could be offered to this. Not satisfied with their grand deed, the disloyal Whig mob collected signatures in the lobby of the House of Commons for a petition requesting Palmerston to induce the Queen to accept Russell's resignation which had already been submitted. At any rate Russell may have gained one satisfaction from these base manoeuvres, namely that of having created a party in his own image.

The resignation of a man who, as Urquhart says, is in the habit of clasping his hands behind his back to give himself moral support, would hardly have affected the continued existence of the Cabinet had not the majority of the House of Commons been eager to use any pretext allowing it to postpone the fateful dissolution. And dissolution of the House is the inevitable consequence of passing Bulwer's motion. If Palmerston were to retain his post despite the vote of no-confidence, he would have to

[a] See this volume, p. 339.—*Ed.*

[b] For further details of Bulwer's motion, tabled on July 10, 1855, see this volume, pp. 337-43.—*Ed.*

dissolve the House, and if he were succeeded by Derby, the latter would likewise have to dissolve it. The House seems hardly inclined to sacrifice itself on the altar of patriotism.

Sir George Grey has set up a commission to investigate the police brutalities. It consists of the Recorders[a] of London, Liverpool and Manchester and will meet next Tuesday.

If in commerce time is money, in warfare time is victory. The greatest blunder that can be committed in warfare is to miss the favourable moment, the moment when superior forces can be hurled against the enemy. The blunder is magnified if it is committed not during defensive operations, when the consequences of neglect can be repaired, but during offensive operations, in a war of invasion, where such carelessness can cause the loss of an army. These are truisms which, as every cadet knows, are self-evident. And yet no other rule of strategy or tactics is transgressed as frequently as this one, and General Pélissier, the impetuous man of action, the "Marshal Forward"[249] of the Crimean army, seems to be destined by his action to illustrate the common disregard of these commonplace rules.

The road to Sevastopol leads through Inkerman to the northern side of the fortress. No one knows this better than Pélissier and his staff. But in order to conquer the northern side, the Allied armies have to take the field with their main forces, beat the Russians, encircle the north side and detach a corps to keep the Russian field army at a distance. The favourable moment to do this came when the Sardinian corps and the Turks under Omer Pasha arrived. The Allies were then considerably stronger than the Russians. But nothing of the sort was undertaken. The expedition to Kerch and the Sea of Azov was launched and one assault after another attempted. Field operations were restricted to reconnoitring and extending the camp up to the entrance to the valley of Baidar. The alleged reason for this inactivity is now at last revealed. *Means of transport are said to be lacking,* and after a campaign of fifteen months the Allies are just as much confined to the Sea, Kamysh and Balaklava as ever. This is indeed unsurpassable. The Crimea is not a desolate island somewhere near the South pole. It is a country whose food supplies are undoubtedly not inexhaustible, but which is capable of providing large quantities of fodder, draught-animals and carts if one has sufficient skill and daring to take them. Timorous and slow forward and backward movements within a circle of a few English miles around the

[a] Marx and Engels use the English term.—*Ed.*

Chernaya are of course not a suitable means to get hold of them. But even if we leave the camels, ponies and arbas of the Crimea completely out of account, there still remain ample means of transport on the European and Asian shores of the Black Sea which steamers can reach within two days. Why are they not commandeered for use by the Allies? The Russians have certainly given them enough lessons demonstrating how they ought to act. The 3rd, 4th and 5th army corps and several reserve divisions were transported to the Crimea at a time when the Allies had despaired of bringing provisions from Balaklava to the trenches. Some of the troops were moved in carts across the steppe, and they seem to have suffered acutely from lack of food. And yet the country within a radius of 200 miles from Perekop is only thinly populated. But the resources of the more distant provinces were requisitioned, and it is certainly more difficult for the Russians to send carts from Yekaterinoslav, Poltava, Kharkov, etc., to the Crimea, than for the Allies in the Crimea to procure means of transport in Anatolia and Rumelia. In any case, under the pretext of lack of transport, the Allies let the chance to conquer the Crimea up to Simferopol slip. Now the position has changed. The Russians have formed a reserve army for the Crimea located between Odessa and Cherson. The strength of this army can only be estimated by us on the basis of the detachments made from the western army; these consist of the entire 2nd army corps and two infantry divisions. Together this amounts to five infantry divisions (82 battalions), one cavalry division (32 squadrons) and 80 cannon. Infantry and cavalry reserves have to be added to this. Taking into account the losses it suffered during the march, the army destined for the Crimea and assembled between Odessa and Perekop can therefore be assessed at approximately 70,000 to 80,000 men. The vanguard of their columns must by now have already passed through Perekop, and their weight will be felt by the Allies before the end of July.

What can the Allies set against these reinforcements? Their ranks are being thinned again by cholera and fever just as much as by the various attempted assaults. British reinforcements are rather slow in arriving—very few regiments have in fact sailed. The 13,000 men reported by us[a] to have left some time ago have proved to be a government bluff. The French government for its part declares that it does not intend to send fresh divisions but merely detachments from the depots to make good the losses

---

[a] See this volume, p. 299.—*Ed.*

incurred at the theatre of war. These reinforcements, provided they arrive in time, will hardly be sufficient to bring the Allied army up to the strength it had in June, i.e. 200,000 men, including Turks and Sardinians. It will probably amount to no more than 180,000 men, who at the beginning of August will be opposed by at least 200,000 Russians in good positions, in command of the country in their rear and holding the south side of Sevastopol as a bridgehead. If under these circumstances the allied army were again squeezed into the narrow plateau behind the Chernaya, these human masses would by their momentum turn the restricted space into a graveyard.

There is still time to take the offensive. True the most favourable moment has been missed, but nevertheless a bold advance by the allied army would even now ensure an extension of their living space. But there is no indication that they intend to use this opportunity.

Finally, in justification of Pélissier one might mention that public opinion here and in Paris has sought and found the cause of the wretched state of the second Crimean campaign in the intervention of Louis Bonaparte, the general from afar.

Written on July 14, 1855

First published in the *Neue Oder-Zeitung*, No. 327, July 17, 1855

Marked with the sign ×

The English version was first published in the *New-York Daily Tribune*, No. 4452, July 27, 1855, reprinted in the *New-York Semi-Weekly Tribune*, No. 1061, July 27, 1855 and the *New-York Weekly Tribune*, No. 725, August 4, 1855 as a leading article

Printed according to the *Neue Oder-Zeitung*

Published in English in full for the first time

Karl Marx

RUSSELL'S DISMISSAL

London, July 17. Whether voluntary or under duress, Russell's dismissal has served to parry Bulwer's motion[a] just as Bulwer parried Roebuck's motion. This view, which we expressed in our report of July 11,[a] was confirmed beyond any shadow of doubt by yesterday's sitting in the Commons.[b] It is an old Whig axiom that "parties are like snails—the tails move the heads". The present Whig Cabinet, however, seems to be polypoid; it appears to thrive on amputation. It survives the loss of its limbs, its head, anything except its tail. Although Russell was not the head of the Cabinet, he was the brains of the party which forms the Cabinet and which is represented by it. Bouverie, the Vice-President of the Board of Trade,[c] represents the tail of the Whig polyp. He discovered that the Whig body would have to be decapitated to keep the Whig rump alive, and he made this discovery known to Palmerston in the name of and on behalf of the Whig tail. Russell yesterday assured that tail of his "contempt". Disraeli tormented Bouverie with a "physiology of friendship" and a biological description of the various types in which the species being known as *"friend"* is distinguishable. Finally, Bouverie's attempt to justify the action by saying that he and the tail had discarded Russell in order to save him, completes the genre picture of this party of office-hunters.

The natural head of the Whig party being amputated in this way, its usurped head, Lord Palmerston, has become all the more

[a] See this volume, pp. 337-39.—*Ed.*
[b] A report of the House of Commons debate of July 16, 1855 was published in *The Times*, No. 22108, July 17, 1855.—*Ed.*
[c] Marx uses the English term.—*Ed.*

firmly attached to the rump. After the fall of Aberdeen and Newcastle he used Gladstone, Graham and Herbert to take possession of the inheritance of the Coalition Cabinet. After the departure of Gladstone, Graham and Herbert he used Lord John Russell to help him form a purely Whig Cabinet. Finally he used the Whig tail to whisk Russell away and thus to become sole ruler in the Cabinet. All those metamorphoses were just so many steps on the way to the formation of a purely Palmerston Cabinet. Russell's statements show that he repeatedly tendered Palmerston his resignation, but was persuaded each time by him to withdraw it. In exactly the same way Palmerston persuaded Aberdeen's Cabinet to resist Roebuck's Committee of Inquiry to the utmost. On both occasions with the same degree of success and to the same end.

He linked Bulwer's motion so closely to Russell that it fell through of its own accord as soon as the *corpus delicti*, Russell, vanished from the Cabinet. Bulwer was therefore obliged to declare that he was withdrawing his motion. However, he could not resist the temptation of actually delivering the speech which was to have supported his motion. He forgot that the motion on which his speech was based no longer existed. Palmerston exploited this unfortunate situation. He immediately assumed the pose of a gladiator after the battle had been called off. He was rude, blustering and boastful, but in this way he incurred chastisement at the hands of Disraeli, which, as the expression on his face revealed, caused even this accomplished play-actor to lose his usual cynical composure. However, the most important part of Disraeli's reply was the following statement:

"I have reason to believe that the views which Lord Russell brought from Vienna[250] were favourably received, not merely by a majority, but by the *whole of his colleagues*, and that nothing but *circumstances which they did not anticipate* [...] prevented the plan of the noble Lord being cordially and unanimously accepted. I do not make that statement without due authority. I make it with the same conviction that I spoke six weeks ago of the ambiguous language and uncertain conduct of the Government, the truth of which subsequent events have already justified. I make it with the conviction that, even before this Session of Parliament terminates, evidence confirming that statement will be in the possession of the House."

The "circumstances" to which Disraeli refers were, as he explains in the course of his speech, "the difficulties presented by the French". Disraeli indicates that Clarendon's correspondence, which was intended for use in Parliament, contradicts the secret instructions issued by the Ministry. He concluded his speech with the following words:

"A belief exists in the land that there is guilt in the management of our affairs. A foreign document appears" (Buol's circular), "the people are agitated, they think, they talk, their representatives in this House ask questions. What happens? The foremost of our statesmen dare not meet the controversy which such questions bring forward. He mysteriously disappears. [...] But who dares meet with it? The First Minister of the Crown, who has addressed this House tonight in accents and in language utterly unworthy of his position, and utterly unworthy of the occasion, which have convinced me that if the honour and interests of the country be any longer intrusted to his care, the first will be degraded, and the latter, [...] will be *betrayed.*"

Roebuck surpassed Disraeli in the intensity of his language. "*I want to know who are the traitors who are now in the Cabinet?*" First Aberdeen and Newcastle. Then Graham and Gladstone and Herbert. Then Russell. Who is next?

In the meantime the position of the man who secretly ruled over the coalition, as he now officially rules the Ministry, is quite secure. If another vote of no-confidence were to take place before the end of the session, which is not likely, he will dissolve Parliament. At all events he has six months before him in which to conduct Britain's foreign policy without restriction, not even disturbed by the noise and mock battles of the Commons.

Written on July 17, 1855

First published in the *Neue Oder-Zeitung*, No. 333, July 20, 1855

Marked with the sign ×

Printed according to the newspaper

Published in English for the first time

Karl Marx

FROM PARLIAMENT

London, July 18. The turbulent, uproarious and noisy night sitting of the Commons of July 16 was inevitably followed by a reaction of languor, fatigue, and enervation. The Ministry, well versed in the secrets of parliamentary pathology, was counting on this general mood of dejection as a means of preventing any division on Roebuck's motion,[a] and not only the division but the debate itself. Not a single member of the Ministry spoke before midnight, shortly before the close of the sitting, although for a moment there was a lull in the proceedings in the House which invited statements from Ministers, and despite repeated demands from all sides of the House. The Cabinet persisted in stoic silence and left it to the representatives of the Marquess of Exeter, the representative of Lord Ward, and similar peers' representatives in the Commons to bury the honourable House in that tedious mire which Dante, in his "Inferno", makes the eternal residence of the indolent.[b] Two amendments to Roebuck's motion had been tabled, one from General Peel and the other from Colonel Adair, both proposed by military men and both lapsing into flanking marches.[c] Peel's amendment demands that the House vote on the "previous question",[251] i.e. neither for nor against the main motion, declining to answer Roebuck's question. Colonel Adair demands approval of the "policy which decided upon the expedition to Sevastopol" and that "this policy be persevered in". Roebuck's censure in respect of the bad execution of the Crimean expedition

[a] For Marx's discussion of Roebuck's motion see this volume, pp. 337-38.—*Ed.*
[b] Dante, *Divina commedia.* Part I, "Inferno", Canto III.—*Ed.*
[c] The debate was reported in *The Times*, No. 22109, July 18, 1855.—*Ed.*

is thus countered by him with praise for its good origin.

The Cabinet refrained from making any statement as to which of the amendments it intended to adopt as the Ministerial amendment. It seemed to want to feel the pulse of the House, in order to seek refuge either in General Peel's question without an answer or in Colonel Adair's answer without a question. At last the House seemed to have sunk into that semi-sleep that Palmerston was waiting for. Then he sent forward the most insignificant member of the Cabinet, Sir Charles Wood, to declare that the Ministry was backing Peel's amendment. Supported by cries of "Divide! Divide!" from the benches of his allies, Palmerston rose and "hoped the House would come to a decision tonight". He thought he had managed to burke[a] Roebuck and even to rob him of the honour of a "great debate", a parliamentary tournament. But Disraeli was not the only one to oppose the division. *Bright*, with his characteristic massive earnestness, rose to his feet:

> "The Government had evidently wished to shirk this question, and had abstained until midnight from declaring what course they intended to take. The question was the most important one ever to come before the House. The debate, he thought, might last a whole week to the advantage of the country."

Thus obliged to accept the *adjournment* of the debate Palmerston had to abandon his original plan of campaign. He suffered a defeat.

Roebuck's speech possessed the great merit of brevity. With simplicity and clarity he summed up the reasons for his verdict, not as a barrister but as a judge, a manner befitting him as chairman of the Committee of Inquiry. He evidently had to contend with the same obstacles which are preventing the allied fleet from entering the harbour of Sevastopol—namely the *sunken ships*, the Aberdeens, Herberts, Gladstones, Grahams, etc. It was only by manoeuvring his way past them that he could reach Palmerston and the other *surviving* members of the Coalition Cabinet. They were barring the way to the present Cabinet. Roebuck tried to dispose of them by means of compliments. Newcastle and Herbert had to be praised for the conscientious way they had discharged their official duties, and Graham too. The other sins which they had committed from lack of insight had been punished with their exclusion from Downing Street.[b] All that

---

[a] Marx uses the English verb "to burke" in the corresponding German grammatical form (*geburkt*).—*Ed.*

[b] 10 Downing Street is the British Prime Minister's residence. Here the reference is to the government as a whole.—*Ed.*

remains is to deal with the wrongdoers who have not yet been punished. This, he said, was the real purpose of his motion. He attacked Palmerston especially not only as an accomplice, but in particular as the person in charge of the militia. In order to keep his motion within the traditional limits set by Parliament Roebuck evidently took the point out of it. The arguments produced by the ministerial seconds were so feeble that the soporific form in which they were developed actually had a soothing effect. The evidence given by the witnesses is incomplete, called some. You are threatening to ostracise us, cried others. The whole affair happened so long ago, said Lord Cecil. Why not condemn Sir Robert Peel belatedly for what he did? Every member of the Cabinet is in a general manner responsible for the acts of the Cabinet, but no one in particular. That was the view of the "liberal" Phillimore. You are endangering the French alliance and setting yourselves up as a jury over the Emperor of the French.[a] That was the view expressed by Lowe (of *The Times*) followed by Sir James Graham. Graham, the man of clear conscience, states that he himself is dissatisfied with General Peel's pure negative. He insists that the House should decide "Guilty" or "Not guilty". He will not be satisfied with a verdict of "not proven"[b] such as the Scottish courts use to dismiss doubtful criminal cases. Do you really want to reintroduce the antiquated and unparliamentary procedure of impeachment[c 252]? The press, public opinion is to blame for everything. It forced the Ministers to undertake the expedition, at an inopportune time and with inadequate means. If you condemn the Ministry then you ought to condemn the House of Commons, which gave its backing! And finally Sir Charles Wood's attempt at a justification. If Roebuck exonerates even Newcastle and Herbert and Graham, how can he accuse *us*? We were *nothing*, and we are responsible for *nothing*. Thus Wood with his "feeling which penetrates nothing".[d]

Written on July 18, 1855

First published in the *Neue Oder-Zeitung*, No. 335, July 21, 1855

Marked with the sign ×

Printed according to the newspaper

Published in English for the first time

---

[a] Napoleon III.—*Ed.*

[b] Marx uses the English term and gives the German translation in brackets.—*Ed.*

[c] Marx gives the English term in brackets.—*Ed.*

[d] An expression used by the Duke of Alba in Schiller's *Don Carlos* (Act II, Scene 5).—*Ed.*

Frederick Engels

WAR PROSPECTS[253]

At our last advices there was a lull in the warlike operations in the Crimea. No more assaults had taken place; the guns were all but silent; and but for the rifle-firing carried on constantly between the two lines of intrenchments, for the sapping and mining by which the Allies were pushing on toward the Malakoff hill, and for an occasional sortie by the Russians, we might suppose that hostilities had been suspended. But this can be nothing but the calm that precedes the storm; and ere this, that storm must have burst. There is every probability that a struggle more savage than Inkermann, the Mamelon Vert, or the assault of June 18,[254] has already been consummated at Sevastopol.

In fact the month of August must to a certain degree decide the result of the campaign. By this time the great part, if not all of the Russian reenforcements must have arrived, while the ranks of the Allies cannot but be thinned by sickness. If they hold their ground on the plateau of the Chersonesus it will be as much as they can do. That they will not take the south side of Sevastopol this year is a notion abandoned now even by the British press. They are reduced to the hope of knocking the place to pieces bit by bit, and if they manage to proceed at the speed they have hitherto exhibited, the siege will equal in duration that of Troy. There is no reason to expect that they will do their work with increased rapidity, for we are now all but officially informed that the vicious system hitherto followed is to be obstinately continued. The Crimean correspondent of the *Constitutionnel* of Paris, a man of high rank in the French army, and believed to be Gen. Regnault de St. Jean d'Angély, Commander of the Guards, has announced the fact, that the public may spare themselves the trouble of making speculations as to a field campaign and eventual investment of the north side of Sevastopol. Under present circumstances, he says, this could not be done without raising the siege and abandoning to the Russians the entire plateau; and therefore it has been decided to knock away as hard as possible at the position already attacked, until it is completely destroyed.[a] Now, the announcements of this letter may be relied on, as there is every reason to believe that the French Emperor[b] not only approves, but even revises every letter from this source before it is printed, and as Regnault is one of his special pets.

What is to be the consequence of all this we can easily discover. The Russian army at and about Sevastopol now consists of the third and fourth corps, two divisions of the fifth and one of the sixth corps, beside marines, sailors, local troops, Cossacks and cavalry—presenting a force under arms of 180 battalions, or 90,000 infantry, with 30,000 artillery and cavalry, beside about 40,000 sick and wounded. Even the French *Moniteur* estimates their effective strength under arms at 110,000 men.[c] Now the whole of the second corps (50 battalions, 32 squadrons, 96 guns) and two divisions of grenadiers, with one division of cavalry (24 battalions, 32 squadrons, 72 guns), are on the march or already at Sevastopol, representing an additional force of 55,000 infantry, 10,000 cavalry and Cossacks, and 5,000 artillery. The Russians thus will shortly have concentrated a force of at least 175,000 men or considerably more than the Allies can have left after their recent losses by combats and disease. That with these the Russians should be able at least to hold their own, particularly as they can constantly relieve the garrison by fresh troops after the old ones are exhausted by fatigue, is certainly the least that is to be expected from them.

The Allies, on the other hand, have no chance of receiving similar reenforcements. They now number 21 divisions of infantry (12 French, 4 English, 3 Turkish, 2 Piedmontese), or about 190 battalions; 3 divisions of cavalry (1 French, 1 English, 1 Turkish), or about 60 squadrons; and a corresponding number of guns. But as their battalions, and especially their squadrons, are very much thinned by the losses of the campaign, the whole force will not

[a] "Devant Sébastopol, 26 juin", *Le Constitutionnel*, No. 192, July 11, 1855.—*Ed.*
[b] Napoleon III.—*Ed.*
[c] *Le Moniteur universel*, No. 198, July 17, 1855.—*Ed.*

exceed 110,000 infantry, 7,500 cavalry, and 20,000 to 25,000[a] artillery, train, and non-combatants fit for duty. Now if the forces of the two contending parties were so nicely balanced before the arrival of the Russian reenforcements, the scale must evidently turn against the Allies as soon as they arrive. All the allied reenforcements arrived and now being sent out are merely detachments from the depots to keep up the battalions and squadrons engaged; and they are not very strong if we are to believe the statements of the Press. However, three divisions are said to be on the march to Marseilles and Toulon, where steamers are concentrating; while, in England, the regiments intended for the Crimea are ordered to be ready for immediate embarkation. They will perhaps amount to another division of infantry and one of cavalry. Thus about 33,000 infantry, with perhaps 2,500 cavalry and artillery may be gradually arriving in the Crimea during August and September; but all this depends very much upon the celerity with which they are got off. At all events, the Allies will find themselves once more in a numerical inferiority, and may again be locked up on the plateau where they spent the last dreary Winter. Whether the Russians can now succeed in driving them off that stronghold we will not undertake to say. But to hold their own is evidently the only thing the Allies can expect, until they receive reenforcements on a gigantic scale. Thus the war promises to be reduced to a series of resultless and bloody encounters, in which each party will send forth fresh bodies of troops, day after day, to meet the enemy in hand-to-hand struggles, whether on the ramparts of the town, on the parapets of the trenches, or on the escarped hights around Inkermann and Balaklava. No position of hostile armies can be imagined in which the shedding of more blood can lead to results less important than we must expect from such fights.

There is, however, one chance of something decisive occurring. If the Russians, beside the troops they have sent, can afford to send another 50,000 men, so as to insure to their army an incontestable superiority, serious defeats may be incurred by the Allies, so as to force them to reembark. To judge of this possibility we must look at the force the Russians have under arms on the whole extent of their frontier. The Crimean army, including the reenforcements mentioned above, we set down at about 175,000 men. In the Caucasus, where, beside the local troops and Cossacks,

[a] Marx and Engels give other figures—30,000 to 35,000—in their article "From Parliament.—From the Theatre of War" (see this volume, pp. 363-66).—*Ed.*

the 16th and 17th divisions are engaged, they may have about 60,000 men. In Bessarabia they are said to have 60,000 men under Lüders—mostly combined battalions and reserves, as we should say, since only one division of the infantry of the fifth corps is there, and nothing has ever been stated about troops of the first or second corps having marched in that direction. In Poland and Volhynia there would remain two divisions of guards, one of grenadiers, three of the first army-corps, and various reserves—amounting to about 160,000 men. The greater portion of the reserves and part of the guards are concentrated on the Baltic in the following manner: 50,000 men under Sievers in the German Baltic Provinces, 30,000 in Finland under Berg, and 50,000 men in and about St. Petersburg, as an army of reserve under Rüdiger; in all about 585,000 men. The remainder of the Russian forces, about 65,000 men, are in the interior; and thus the total armed force would make up 650,000 men. Considering the enormous levies made by Russia, this number does not appear at all exaggerated.

Now, it is clear that at this advanced season of the year no serious danger of a landing on the Baltic coast is to be apprehended, and a general shifting toward the south of the various detachments placed there might be effected so as to liberate say 30,000 men, to be replaced by the militia or other troops from the interior. These 30,000 men marching toward Poland, would liberate in that country an equal number, and by the time the Austrians have reduced their army on the frontier to the harmless number of 70,000 or 80,000 men, which must soon be the case, another 30,000 to 40,000 men from the Polish army might be spared. Thus the troops might be found for such a reenforcement as would preclude all possibility of the Allies ever mastering the Crimea singlehanded, and they might be brought to the scene of war by the middle of October. But the question arises whether it will be possible for the Government to feed such a large number of troops during the Winter, especially since the Sea of Azoff has been cleared of Russian vessels. As to this we have not sufficient data to venture an opinion; but if that can be done, and the measure be adopted, the Allies might as well batter away at the rocks that surround Balaklava harbor as at the ramparts of Sevastopol defended directly and indirectly by a force of 250,000 men.

Russia has hitherto been held in check by 300,000 Austrians on the flank of her line of communication with the Crimea. Let her once get rid of that trammel, and the Allies will soon see what a power they have to deal with. They have allowed the time to slip away when, aided indirectly by Austria, they might have taken Sevastopol. Now, that Russia begins to be safe on that side, and has only the Allies to deal with, it is too late.

Written about July 20, 1855

First published in the *New-York Daily Tribune,* No. 4459, August 4, 1855, reprinted in the *New-York Semi-Weekly Tribune,* No. 1064, August 7, 1855 and the *New-York Weekly Tribune,* No. 726, August 11, 1855 as a leading article; an abridged German version was included in the report by Marx and Engels published in the *Neue Oder-Zeitung,* No. 337, July 23, 1855, marked with the sign ×

Reproduced from the *New-York Daily Tribune*

Karl Marx and Frederick Engels

FROM PARLIAMENT.—FROM THE THEATRE OF WAR[255]

London, July 20. The debate on Roebuck's motion[a] did not turn out in the way the Ministry was fond of thinking. Even yesterday morning it was prophesying in its semi-official organs that Roebuck's motion would be defeated by five votes to one. Last night it considered itself fortunate in obtaining 289 votes to 182 for the previous question,[b 256] i.e. the refusal of the House to decide on the motion at all. The same House that forced Aberdeen to resign because he refused to set up a Committee of Inquiry, saved Palmerston by refusing to come to a conclusion on the verdict of its own Committee. The adjournment of Parliament adjourns the fate of Palmerston's Cabinet until the new session. That is when its lease of life will end. We shall return later to the sitting itself.

At present there is a lull in the war operations in the Crimea. No more attempted assaults, the cannon are almost silenced; and if it were not for the constant exchange of rifle fire between the two lines of trenches, if the allies were not advancing their position up the Malakhov hill by mining and sapping, and if the Russians did not make the occasional sorties, one might think that all hostilities had been suspended.

That is the calm before the storm. In two or three weeks a battle will begin, man against man, much fiercer than at Inkerman, the Green Mamelon or the assault of June 18.[257] The month of August ought to be decisive up to a certain point: the Russian forces which are now on their way will have arrived,and the allied

---

[a] See this volume, pp. 337-38, 356-57.—*Ed.*
[b] The authors use the English words "previous question".—*Ed.*

forces will have been reduced by sickness. The life-and-death battle will then begin, and the allies will have enough to do maintaining their ground on the plateau.

Even the English press has now given up the idea of the south side of Sevastopol being taken this year. They are now reduced to the hope of subduing Sevastopol bit by bit; and if they manage to proceed with the same speed as they have up to now the siege will last as long as that of Troy. There is absolutely no reason to believe that they will speed up their task, for we have been as good as told officially that the deficient system adopted so far will be stubbornly continued. The Crimea correspondent of the *Constitutionnel*, a man of high rank in the French army (it is said to be General Regnault de Saint-Jean-d'Angély, commander of the guards), has announced to the public that it can spare itself the effort of indulging in speculation about a campaign in the open and the possible blockade of the northside of Sevastopol. He maintains that under the present circumstances this could not happen without first abandoning the siege and surrendering the whole of the plateau to the Russians. It has therefore been decided to hammer away as fiercely as possible at the position which has already been attacked until it has been completely destroyed.[a] The announcements contained in this letter can be regarded as semi-official, as there is every reason to believe that Bonaparte not only approves of them but that he also checks every report from this source before it goes to print. Regnault is one of his special favourites—the Minister of War who, at the time of the Legislative Assembly, gave his signature to the dismissal of Changarnier.[258]

The consequences of all this are not hard to predict. The Russian army in and around Sevastopol consisted of the 3rd and 4th Corps, two divisions of the 5th and one of the 6th Corps, apart from marines, sailors, local troops, Cossacks and cavalry, all in all an army of 180 battalions or 90,000 infantry with 30,000 men of the artillery, cavalry, etc., plus about 40,000 sick and wounded. Even the French *Moniteur* estimates their effective force under arms to be 110,000 men.[b] Now, the whole of the 2nd Corps (50 battalions, 32 squadrons and 96 cannon) and two divisions of infantry with a division of cavalry (24 battalions, 32 squadrons, 72 cannon) are marching towards or are already near Sevastopol. They represent an additional force of 55,000 infant-

[a] "Devant Sébastopol, 26 juin", *Le Constitutionnel*, No. 192, July 11, 1855.—*Ed.*
[b] *Le Moniteur universel*, No. 198, July 17, 1855.—*Ed.*

ry, 10,000 cavalry and Cossacks and 5,000 artillery. Thus the Russians will soon have concentrated an army of at least 175,000 men, considerably more than the allies can have after their most recent losses in the sorties and from sickness. It is all the more to be expected that the Russians will be capable of at least holding the territory they have held so far, since they are able constantly to relieve with fresh forces the garrison troops exhausted by their efforts.

The allies on the other hand have no chance of receiving similar reinforcements. They now number 21 divisions of infantry (12 French, 4 English, 3 Turkish, 2 Piedmontese), or approximately 190 battalions, 3 divisions of cavalry (1 French, 1 English, 1 Turkish), or approximately 60 squadrons and a corresponding number of cannon but, since their battalions and particularly their squadrons have been substantially thinned by the losses in the campaign, their total strength will not exceed 110,000 infantry, 7,500 cavalry and 30,000-35,000 artillery, vehicle train and those unfit for active service. If the forces of the two opposing parties were thus almost equally balanced before the arrival of the Russian reinforcements, the scale must clearly tip to the disadvantage of the allies as soon as those reinforcements arrive. What has been sent so far have merely been detachments from the depots, who were to make up the losses suffered by the battalions and squadrons engaged in combat, and they cannot be many in number, if the press reports are reliable. In the meantime it is reported that 3 divisions are marching to Marseilles and Toulon where steamships are being concentrated, whilst in England regiments intended for the Crimea have received orders to be ready for immediate embarkation. They will comprise approximately one division of infantry and one division of cavalry. Thus approximately 33,000 infantry with perhaps 2,500 cavalry and artillery might arrive little by little in the Crimea in August and September. This, however, depends entirely on how quickly they embark. At all events the allies will again find themselves numerically inferior and can be wedged in on the plateau once more, where they were brought to ruin during last year's sad winter.

Whether the Russians will succeed this time in driving them from that fortified hiding-place we dare not say. But it is clear that all the allies can expect to do is to maintain their own ground, unless they were to receive reinforcements on a gigantic scale. Thus the war could be reduced to a series of encounters and hand-to-hand fights, as fruitless as they are bloody, with each side sending forward fresh troops daily to meet the enemy in hand-to-hand fighting, whether it be on the ramparts of the city, on the parapets of the trenches, or on the escarpments round Inkerman and Balaklava. Of all the possibilities it is most likely that matters will take that course. No situation involving two enemy armies could be devised where greater spilling of blood will lead to results of less significance than can be expected from engagements of this kind. And this has been brought about by the mediocrity of the commanders-in-chief on both sides, by impotent dilettantism at Paris and deliberate treachery in London.

Written on July 20, 1855

First published in the *Neue Oder-Zeitung*, No. 337, July 23, 1855

Marked with the sign ×

The English version of part of the text was published in the *New-York Daily Tribune*, No. 4459, August 4, 1855, and reprinted in the *New-York Semi-Weekly Tribune*, No. 1064, August 7, 1855 and the *New-York Weekly Tribune*, No. 726, August 11, 1855

Printed according to the newspaper

Published in English in full for the first time

Karl Marx

PALMERSTON.—THE PHYSIOLOGY OF THE RULING CLASS OF GREAT BRITAIN

London, July 23. If the guarantee of the Turkish loan[259] should run into the same opposition this evening as it did last Friday, then Palmerston will immediately *dissolve* the House of Commons. To the adroit all circumstances are favourable. Dissolving the Commons as a result of Bulwer's motion, or dissolving it on account of Roebuck's motion[a]—both methods are equally risky. The diplomatic activity at the Vienna conferences,[260] the administration organising the winter campaign—neither position is suitable for appealing to the electorate from Parliament. But the "*guarantee of the Turkish loan*"! Scenery, situation and motive are transformed as if by a stroke of magic. It is no longer Parliament that condemns the Cabinet on the grounds of treachery or incompetence. It is the Cabinet which accuses Parliament of hindering the conduct of the war, of jeopardising the French alliance and of abandoning Turkey. The Cabinet no longer appeals to the country to absolve it from Parliament's condemnation. It appeals to the country to condemn Parliament. In fact the loan is so formulated that Turkey receives no money directly, but, under the most humiliating conditions for a nation, she is put under guardianship and has to allow the sum allegedly loaned to her to be administered and dispensed by English commissioners. The English administration has stood the test so brilliantly during the Eastern war that it must indeed be tempted to extend its blessings to foreign realms. The Western Powers have taken possession of the Ministry of Foreign Affairs in Constantinople, and not just the Ministry of Foreign Affairs but the Ministry

[a] For a description of the Bulwer-Lytton and Roebuck motions and their discussion in the House of Commons see this volume, pp. 337-43, 353-57.—*Ed.*

of Home Affairs too. Since Omer Pasha was transplanted from Bulgaria to the Crimea, Turkey has ceased to exercise authority over her own army. The Western Powers are now trying to seize the Turkish finances. For the first time the Ottoman Empire is contracting public debts without receiving a loan. It finds itself in the position of an estate owner who does not only raise an advance on a mortgage but also binds himself to relinquish to his creditor the administration of the sum advanced. The one remaining step is to relinquish the estate itself. Palmerston has demoralised Greece and paralysed Spain by means of a similar system of loans. But *appearances* are on his side. The participation of the peace party in the opposition to the loan adds strength to these appearances. Thanks to a nimble somersault he again stands as the representative of war against the whole opposition as the representatives of peace. We know *which* war he intends to conduct. Chaining Finland more securely to Russia in the Baltic by means of useless and unproductive acts of murder and arson. Perpetuating in the Crimea a series of butcheries in which defeat alone, not victory, can produce a decision. Following his old habit he casts foreign alliances into the parliamentary scales. Bonaparte has already had the loan sanctioned by his so-called "legislative corps". The English Parliament must condescend to becoming the echo of the "legislative corps"—the echo of an echo, or the alliance will be jeopardised. Using the French alliance as a shield to ward off all blows from himself, Palmerston at the same time has the satisfaction of seeing it receive a pummelling. As a proof that he can send "the right man to fill the right place"[a] Palmerston has promoted Sir W[illiam] Molesworth to Colonial Secretary, and Sir B[enjamin] Hall to Commissioner of Forests and Land Revenues[b] in place of Molesworth. Molesworth belongs to *Wakefield*'s school of colonisation.[261] Its principle is to make land in the colonies artificially dear and labour artificially cheap in order to engender the "necessary combination of productive forces". The experimental use of this theory in Canada drove immigrants away from that country to the United States and Australia.

In London there are three committees of inquiry in session at the moment, one appointed by the Cabinet, the other two by

[a] From Layard's speech in the House of Commons on June 15, 1855. *The Times*, No. 22082, June 16, 1855.—*Ed.*

[b] Marx calls it *Minister der Waldungen und Domänen*. The actual title was up to 1857 Commissioner of Woods, Forests and Land Revenues and in that year was changed to Commissioner of Works and Public Buildings.—*Ed.*

Parliament. The first, composed of the Recorders[a] of London, Manchester and Liverpool, investigating the *events in Hyde Park*,[b] finds itself flooded daily with evidence not only that the constables used unprecedented brutality, but also that this brutality was intentional and used *on orders*. If it were uncompromising the inquiry would have to begin with Sir George Grey and the Cabinet as the principal offenders. The second committee, under *Berkeley*'s chairmanship, dealing with the effects of the Act on the "sale of spirits on Sundays", shows the sanctimonious superficiality of sabbatarian experiments for the improvement of society. Instead of decreasing, the number of excesses from drunkenness has increased. The only difference is their partial displacement from Sundays to Mondays. The third committee, chaired by *Scholefield*, is concerned with the adulteration of food and drink and of all commodities contributing to the maintenance of life.[262] Adulteration seems to be the *rule*, purity the *exception*. For the most part the substances added to impart colour, odour and taste to worthless materials are poisonous, and all of them are detrimental to health. Trade appears here as a vast laboratory of fraud, the list of commodities as a diabolical catalogue of phantoms, free competition as the freedom to poison and be poisoned.

The *Report of the Inspectors of Factories* for the half-year ending April 30[c] has been laid before both Houses of Parliament—an invaluable contribution to the characterisation of the *Manchester* men of peace and the class disputing the aristocracy's monopoly of government. In the report the "accidents arising from machinery" are classified under the headings:

> 1. "Causing death", 2. "Loss[d] of right hand or arm. Loss of part of right hand. Loss of left hand or arm. Loss of part of left hand. [...] Fracture of hand or foot. Injuries to head and face" and 3. "Lacerations, contusions and other injuries not enumerated above."[e]

We read of a young woman "who lost her right hand", of a child who "had the nasal bones crushed in and the sight of both eyes destroyed by this machine", of a man whose "left leg was cut off, [...] right arm broken in three or four places", whose head

---

[a] Marx uses the English word.—*Ed.*

[b] See this volume, pp. 323-27.—*Ed.*

[c] *Reports of the Inspectors of Factories to Her Majesty's Principal Secretary of State for the Home Department, for the Half Year Ending 30th April 1855.*—*Ed.*

[d] Here and in the rest of this passage the *Report* has "Amputation of" where Marx writes "Loss of".—*Ed.*

[e] Marx paraphrased the extract.—*Ed.*

was cut and "mutilated in a shocking manner"; of a youth who had his "left arm torn out at the shoulder joint", among other injuries, and of another man who had "both arms torn out of the shoulder joints, his abdomen lacerated, the intestines protruded, both legs broken, head contused", etc., etc. The industrial bulletin of the factory inspectors is more terrible and more appalling than any of the war bulletins from the Crimea. Women and children provide a regular and sizeable contingent in the list of the wounded and killed. Deaths and injuries are no more praiseworthy than the colours marked on the body of a Negro by the plantation owner's whip. They are almost exclusively caused by the absence of the legally prescribed *protective guards* around the machines. It will be recalled that the manufacturers of Manchester—this metropolis of the party of peace at any price—assailed the Cabinet with deputations and protests against the Act ordering certain safety precautions in the use of machinery. Since they were unable to change the law at present, they attempted by intrigues to get rid of the Factory Inspector L[eonard] Horner, and to manoeuvre a more pliant guardian of the law into his place. So far without success. They claimed that the introduction of the safety equipment would eat up their profit. Horner has now proved that there are few factories in his district which could not be made safe for £10. The total number of accidents arising from machinery during the six months covered by the report is 1,788, among these 18 *fatal* accidents. The sum total of money fines imposed on the manufacturers, of compensation for injuries paid by them, etc., is £298 for the same period. To make up this sum fines for "permitting work during illegal hours", for "employing children under 8 years of age", etc., are included in it, so that the fines imposed for the 18 deaths and the 1,770 mutilations fall far short of £298. £298! This is less than the cost of a third-class racehorse![263]

The Roebuck committee and the British oligarchy! Scholefield's committee and the British commercial class! The report of the Factory Inspectors and the British factory owners—these three headings provide a graphic idea of the physiology of the classes now ruling in Great Britain.

Written on July 23, 1855

First published in the *Neue Oder-Zeitung*, No. 343, July 26, 1855

Marked with the sign ×

Printed according to the newspaper

Published in English for the first time

Karl Marx

LORD JOHN RUSSELL[264]

Written July 25-August 12, 1855

First published in the *Neue Oder-Zeitung*, Nos. 347, 359, 363, 365, 369 and 377, July 28, August 4, 7, 8, 10 and 15, 1855

Marked with the sign ×

An abridged English version was published in the *New-York Daily Tribune*, No. 4479, August 28, 1855

Printed according to the *Neue Oder-Zeitung*

Published in English in full for the first time

[I]

[*Neue Oder-Zeitung*, No. 347, July 28, 1855]

London, July 25. Lord *John Russell* was fond of quoting an old Whig axiom that "parties were like snails, for with them it is the tail that moves the head". He hardly could have surmised that to save itself the tail will strike off the head. If not the head of the "*last Whig cabinets*", he was indisputably the head of the *Whig Party*. Burke said once that

"the number of estates, country-houses, castles, forest lands and the like which the *Russells* had wrested away from the English people was *quite incredible*".[a]

The great repute in which Lord John Russell has been held and the prominent role which he has dared to play for over a quarter of a century would be even more incredible if the "number of estates" which his family has usurped did not furnish the clue to the puzzle.

Lord John seems to have spent his whole life simply chasing after *posts* and holding on so stubbornly to the posts he captured that he forfeited all claim to *power*. So it was in 1836-1841 when he was given the post of leader of the House of Commons. So in 1846-1852 when he could call himself Prime Minister. The semblance of power that enveloped him as the leader of an opposition assaulting the exchequer always disappeared the day he came to power. As soon as he changed from an Out to an In[b] he

[a] "A Letter from the Right Honourable Edmund Burke to a Noble Lord, on the Attacks Made upon him and his Pension, in the House of Lords, by the Duke of Bedford...", p. 37. Marx gives the English words "quite incredible" in brackets after the corresponding German words.—*Ed.*

[b] Marx uses the English words "Out" (member of the opposition) and "In" (member of the Government).—*Ed.*

was *done for.* With no other English statesman did power so abruptly change into powerlessness. But, on the other hand, no other knew so well as he how to transform powerlessness into power.

The sham power Lord John Russell periodically wielded was not only sustained by the influence exerted by the family of the Duke of Bedford, whose younger son he was, but also by the absence of all the qualities which generally fit a person to rule over others. His Lilliputian views on everything spread to others like a contagion and contributed more to confuse the judgment of his hearers than the most ingenious misrepresentation could have done. His real talent consists in his capacity to reduce everything that he touches to his own dwarfish dimensions, to diminish the external world to an infinitesimal size and to transform it into a vulgar microcosm of his own invention. His instinct to belittle the magnificent is excelled only by the skill with which he can make the petty appear great.

Lord John Russell's entire life has been lived on false pretences: the false pretences of parliamentary reform, the false pretences of religious freedom, the false pretences of Free Trade. So sincere was his belief in the sufficiency of false pretences that he considered it quite feasible to become, not only a British statesman on the basis of false pretences, but also a poet, thinker and historian. Only this can account for the existence of such balderdash as his tragedy *Don Carlos, or, Persecution,* or his *Essay on the History of the English Government and Constitution, from the Reign of Henry VII to the Present Time,* or his *Memoirs of the Affairs of Europe from the Peace of Utrecht.*[265] To his egoistic narrow-mindedness every object is nothing but a *tabula rasa* on which he is at liberty to write his own name. His opinions have never depended upon the actual facts; on the contrary, he regards facts as dependent on the way he arranges them in his rhetorical efforts. As a speaker he has not produced a single idea worth mentioning, not one profound maxim, no penetrating observation, no impressive description, no beautiful thought, no poignant allusion, no humorous portrait, no true emotion. Russell's "*most docile mediocrity*", as Roebuck admits in his history of the reform ministry,[a] surprised his audience even when performing the greatest deed of his public life: when he tabled his so-called Reform Bill[266] in the House of Commons. He has a peculiar

---

[a] J. A. Roebuck, *History of the Whig Ministry of 1830, to the Passing of the Reform Bill,* Vol. II, p. 67.—*Ed.*

manner of combining his dry, drawling and monotonous delivery resembling that of an auctioneer with schoolboy illustrations from history and a certain solemn gibberish on "the beauty of the constitution", the "universal liberties of this country", "civilisation" and "progress". He gets really heated only when personally provoked or goaded by his opponents into abandoning his pose of affected arrogance and self-satisfaction and displaying all the symptoms of extreme helplessness. In England it is generally agreed that his numerous failures are due to a certain natural rashness. This rashness, too, is really merely a false pretence. It is brought about by the subterfuges and expedients intended only for the given moment necessarily coming into conflict with the adverse circumstances of the next moment. Russell does not act instinctively but calculatingly; but his calculations are petty like the man himself—they are always merely makeshifts intended for the next hour. Hence his constant wavering and dodging, his rapid advances and disgraceful retreats, his insolent words prudently retracted, pledges proudly made and wretchedly redeemed, and, if nothing else was of any avail, there were sobs and tears to move the world to pity. His whole life can be viewed, therefore, either as a systematic sham[a] or as an uninterrupted blunder.

It may seem astonishing that a public figure should have survived such a host of stillborn measures, crushed projects and abortive schemes. But just as a polyp thrives on amputation, so Lord John Russell on abortion. Most of his plans were advanced solely for the purpose of placating his discontented allies, the so-called Radicals, while an understanding with his adversaries, the Conservatives, ensured the "*burking*" of these plans. Who can say that since the days of the reformed Parliament he ever staked the fate of his Cabinet on a single one of his "comprehensive and liberal measures", or of his "great reforms presented by instalments". On the contrary. The proposal of measures to satisfy the Liberals and their withdrawal to satisfy the Conservatives contributed more than anything else to maintain and prolong his Ministry. There were times when Peel deliberately kept him at the helm in order not to be compelled to *do* things which he knew Russell would only *prattle* about. In such periods of secret understanding with the official opponent Russell exhibited impudence *vis-à-vis* his official allies. He became bold—on false pretences.

---

[a] Marx uses the English word.—*Ed.*

We shall cast a retrospective glance on his performance from 1830 until the present day. This *commonplace genius* has deserved it.

[II]

[*Neue Oder-Zeitung*, No. 359, August 4, 1855]

London, August 1.[267]

"If I was a painter," said Cobbett, "there would I place the old oak (the British Constitution), corroded at the root, his top dead, his trunk hollow, loosened at his base, rocking with every blast, and there would I place Lord John Russell, in the person of a tom-tit, endeavoring to put all right by picking at a nest of animalculae seated in the half-rotten bark of one of the meanest branches. There are some who even think that he is eating the buds while he pretends to clear the tree of injurious insects."

So minute were Lord John Russell's reform efforts during his antediluvian career from 1813 to 1830; but minute as they were, they were not even sincere, and he never hesitated to repudiate them as soon as he perceived merely the scent of a ministerial post.

Since 1807 the Whigs had pined in vain for a share in the proceeds of taxation, when in 1827 the formation of Canning's cabinet, with whom they pretended to agree on the subject of commerce and of foreign policy, seemed to afford them the long-sought-for opportunity. Russell, at that time, had given notice of one of his tom-tit Parliamentary reform motions. But upon Canning's stern declaration that he should oppose Parliamentary reform to the end of his life, up rose Lord John and withdrew his motion. He said

"Parliamentary reform was a question on which there was a great diversity of opinion among those who advocated it, and to which the leaders of the Whigs were always unwilling to be pledged as to a party question. It was now for *the last time* that he brought forward this question."[a]

He concluded his speech with the insolent statement that "the people no longer wished for Parliamentary reform". He, who had always made a show of his noisy opposition to Castlereagh's six infamous gagging acts of 1819,[268] now refrained from voting on

[a] Russell's speech in the House of Commons on May 3, 1827. Quotations from and references to Parliamentary speeches are as a rule based on *Hansard's Parliamentary Debates.—Ed.*

Mr. Hume's motion[a] for the repeal of one of those acts which made a man liable to transportation for life for uttering in print anything which had even a *tendency* to bring either house of Parliament into contempt.

Thus, at the conclusion of the first period of his Parliamentary life, we find Lord John Russell disavowing his support of Reform, to which he paid lip service for more than ten years, and fully concurring with the opinion of that Whig prototype, Horace Walpole, who remarked to Conway that[b]

"popular Bills are never really proposed but as an engine of party, and not as a pledge for the realisation of any such extravagant ideas".

It was, then, by no means Russell's fault that instead of bringing forward the motion for reform for the *last time* in 1827, he had to table it again four years later, on March 1, 1831, in the shape of the famous Reform Bill. He was not even the author of this Bill, which he still exhibits as his great claim to the admiration of the world in general, and England in particular.[c] In its principal features—the breaking up of the greater part of the nomination boroughs, the addition of county members, the enfranchisement of copyholders, lease-holders,[d] [269] and twenty four of the chief commercial and industrial towns of England—it was copied from the Bill which Lord Grey (the chief of the Reform Ministry in 1830) had moved in the House of Commons in 1797, when heading the Opposition, and which he had wisely forgotten about when he was a member of the Cabinet in 1806. It was the identical Bill, slightly modified. The ejection of Wellington from the Cabinet, because he had declared against Parliamentary Reform; the July Revolution in France; the threatening great political unions formed by the middle and working classes at Birmingham, Manchester, London, and elsewhere; the rural war in the agricultural counties[270]; the "bonfires" in the most fertile regions of England[e]—all these circumstances compelled the Whigs to propose some measure of Reform. They gave way grudgingly,

---

[a] Tabled in the House of Commons on May 31, 1827.—*Ed.*

[b] The *New-York Daily Tribune* has: "we find him fully concurring with the opinion of that Whig prototype, Horace Walpole, that".—*Ed.*

[c] Instead of the words "and England in particular" the *New-York Daily Tribune* has "and the gratitude of the English nation in particular".—*Ed.*

[d] Marx uses the English words "boroughs", "copyholders", "lease-holders" and, below, "freeholders".—*Ed.*

[e] The *New-York Daily Tribune* further has: "('Out of the fires came the Reform,' says a celebrated writer)".—*Ed.*

slowly, and after vainly reiterated efforts to keep their places by a compromise with the Tories.[a] They were prevented by the formidable attitude of the people, and also by the uncompromising intransigence of the Tories. Hardly, however, had the Reform Bill become law, and begun to work, when, to quote Mr. Bright's words (spoken on June 5, 1849), the people "began to feel that they had been cheated".[b]

Never, perhaps, had a mighty, and, to all appearances, successful popular movement been turned into such a mock result. Not only were the working classes altogether excluded from any political influence, but the middle classes themselves soon discovered that Lord Althorp, the soul of the Reform cabinet, had not used a rhetorical figure when telling his Tory adversaries that

> "the Reform Bill was the most aristocratic act ever offered to the nation".

The new country representation was far larger than the increase in votes granted to the towns. The franchise given to the tenants-at-will rendered[c] the counties, still more efficiently than before, the tools of the aristocracy. The substitution of the £10 householders for the payers of scot and lot, actually disfranchised a great number of former town voters. The granting or withdrawal of the franchise was, on the whole, calculated not to increase middle-class influence, but to exclude Tory patronage and promote Whig patronage. By a series of the most extraordinary tricks, frauds, and juggles, the inequality of the electoral districts was maintained, the monstrous disproportion between the number of representatives, on the one hand, and the size of the population and the importance of the constituencies, on the other, restored. If some fifty-six rotten boroughs, each with a handful of inhabitants, were extinguished, whole counties and populous towns were transformed into rotten boroughs. John Russell himself confesses, in a letter to his electors in Stroud, on the principles of the Reform Act (1839), that

> "the £10 franchise was fettered by regulation, and the annual registration was made a source of vexation and expense".

---

[a] The *New-York Daily Tribune* has: "It was their only means of rushing into office. They gave way grudgingly, slowly, and after vainly reiterated efforts at one time to shuffle out of the only liberal clauses of their own measure, and again to abandon it altogether, and to keep their places by a compromise with the Tories."—*Ed.*

[b] John Bright's speech in the House of Commons.—*Ed.*

[c] The *New-York Daily Tribune* has: "tenants-at-will[271] occupying at an annual value of £50, rendered".—*Ed.*

Intimidation and patronage, where they could not be perpetuated, were replaced by bribery, which, from the passage of the Reform Bill, became the main prop of the British Constitution. Such was the Reform Bill of which Russell was the mouthpiece, but not the author. The only clauses since proved to be due to his invention are that which compels all *freeholders*,[272] except parsons, to have had a year of possession, and the other clause preserving the privileges of Tavistock, the family "rotten borough" of the Russells.

Russell was but a subordinate member of the Reform Ministry, without a vote in the Cabinet, *viz.*: Paymaster of the Forces, from 1830 to November 1834. He was, perhaps, the most insignificant man among his colleagues, but he was nevertheless the youngest son of the influential Duke of Bedford. Hence it was decided to grant him the privilege of introducing the Reform Bill in the House of Commons. One obstacle stood in the way of this family arrangement. During the Reform movement, before 1830, Russell had always figured as "Henry Brougham's little man".[a] Russell could not be entrusted with bringing in the Reform Bill as long as Brougham sat beside him in the Lower House. The obstacle was removed by throwing the conceited plebeian on the woolsack in the House of Lords.[273] Because very soon the more prominent members of the original Reform cabinet either became members of the House of Lords (e.g. Althorp in 1834), died, or went over to the Tories, not only the entire inheritance of the Reform Ministry devolved upon Russell but soon he was regarded as the father of the child whose godfather he had been. He thrived on the false pretence of being the author of a Reform Bill which was itself a falsification and a piece of juggling. Apart from this he distinguished himself in the years 1830 to 1834 only by the irritable acrimony with which he opposed all inquiry into the pension-list.[b]

---

[a] Marx uses the English words "little man" and gives the German translation in brackets.—*Ed.*

[b] Instead of the passage beginning with the words "One obstacle stood in the way of this family arrangement" and ending with the words "inquiry into the pension-list" the *New-York Daily Tribune* has: "Beside the Reform-Bill discussion, Lord John distinguished himself by the acrimony and virulence with which he opposed all inquiry into the pension-list. Some years later, when all the prominent members of the original Reform cabinet, having been removed to the Lords, died out, or separated from the Whigs, Lord John not only entered upon their inheritance, but soon passed in the eyes of the country as the natural father of the bill of which he had been but the godfather by courtesy."—*Ed.*

[III]

[*Neue Oder-Zeitung*, No. 363, August 7, 1855]

London, August 3. Let us return to our *character sketch of Russell*. He is worth dealing with at greater length, first because he is *the classical representative of modern Whiggery*, and second because his story, at least from one aspect, comprises *the history of the reformed Parliament* up to the present day.

In introducing the Reform Bill Russell made the following statement with regard to the *ballot*[a] and *short parliaments* (the Whigs, of course, had prolonged the annual parliaments of England to three years in 1694 and to seven years in 1717)[b]:

"There can be no doubt that the *ballot* has much to recommend it; the arguments which I have heard advanced in its favour are as ingenious as any that I ever heard on any subject. But the House must beware of arriving at a hasty decision.... The question of *short parliaments*, is one of the utmost importance, which I shall leave to be brought before the House by some other member at a future time, in order not to embarrass the great subject with details."

On June 6, 1833 he claimed to have

"refrained from bringing forward those two *measures* in order to avoid a collision with the Lords, although *opinions* (!) deeply seated in his heart. He was convinced of their being most essential to the happiness, prosperity and welfare of this country."

(At the same time we have here an example of his species of rhetoric.)[c]

On account of this "deeply seated conviction" he proved to be a constant and relentless enemy of the ballot and short parliaments throughout his entire ministerial career. At the time these statements were made they served as a twofold expedient. They mollified the distrustful democrats of the House of Commons, and they intimidated the intractable aristocrats of the House of Lords. Yet as soon as Russell had secured the support of the new court of Queen Victoria (see *Brougham*'s reply to Russell's letter to the electors of Stroud, 1839)[d], thus imagining himself to

[a] Marx uses the English word here and below.—*Ed.*

[b] The preceding two paragraphs do not occur in the *New-York Daily Tribune*. The quotation from Russell's speech in the House of Commons on March 1, 1831, which follows immediately is shorter and is introduced with the words: "On bringing in the Reform Bill, he said:".—*Ed.*

[c] The sentence in brackets does not occur in the *New-York Daily Tribune*.—*Ed.*

[d] "Lord Brougham's Reply to Lord John Russell's Letter to the Electors of Stroud...", *The Times*, No. 17041, May 14, 1839. The words in brackets do not occur in the *New-York Daily Tribune*.—*Ed.*

be an immortal office-holder, out he comes with his statement of November 1837, justifying "the extreme length to which the Reform Bill had gone" by the fact that it ruled out the possibility of ever proceeding any further.

"The object of the Reform Bill," he stated, "was *to increase the preponderance of the landed interest*, and it was intended as a *permanent settlement* of a great constitutional question."

In short, he made the finality statement that earned him the title of "Finality John".[a] But this finality, this standing still, was no more seriously meant than the talk of proceeding further.[b] It is true, he opposed Hume's parliamentary reform motion in 1848. With the combined might of the Whigs, Tories and Peelites[274] he again defeated Hume over a similar motion in 1849 by a majority of 268 to 82. Emboldened by his conservative reserves he spoke out provocatively:

"In framing and proposing the Reform Bill, what we wished was to *adapt* the representation of this House to the other powers of the State, and keep it in harmony with the Constitution. Mr. Bright and those who agree with him are so *exceedingly narrow-minded*, they have intellect and understanding bound up in such a narrow round that it is quite impossible to get them to understand the great principles on which our ancestors founded the Constitution of the country, and which we, their successors, humbly admire and endeavour to follow. The House of Commons, in the 17 years that have elapsed since the Reform Bill, has satisfied all reasonable expectations. The existing system, although somewhat anomalous, works well: the better for its anomalies."[c]

However, as in 1851 Russell was defeated over Locke King's motion for extending the county franchise to £10 occupiers—and as he was even compelled to resign for a few days—his "broad" mind suddenly grasped the necessity for a *new reform bill*. He gave the House his pledge that he would introduce it. He did not say what his "measure" was but he drew a bill of exchange on it, *payable during the next session of Parliament*.

The *Westminster Review*, the organ of the so-called Radicals allied to Russell, wrote at the time,

"the pretence of the present ministry to office had become a byword of scorn and reproach; and at length, when its exclusion and party annihilation seemed imminent, forth comes Lord John with the promise of a new Reform Bill for 1852. Keep me in

---

[a] Russell's speeches in the House of Commons on November 20 and 21, 1837. Marx gives the nickname in English, and also "finality" in the next sentence.—*Ed.*

[b] Instead of this sentence the *New-York Daily Tribune* has: "But this finality was as false a pretence as his reform itself."—*Ed.*

[c] Russell's speech in the House of Commons on June 5, 1849. The last sentence but one is omitted in the *New-York Daily Tribune*.—*Ed.*

office, he says, till that time, and I will satisfy your longings for a large and liberal measure of reform."[a]

In 1852 he indeed proposed a Reform Bill, this time of his very own invention, but of such astonishingly Lilliputian proportions that neither the Conservatives considered it worth attacking, nor the Liberals worth defending. Still, the aborted reform afforded the little man the pretext, when he was eventually forced out of the Ministry, for hurling a Scythian arrow as he fled at the victorious Lord Derby, who succeeded him. He made his exit with the pompous threat that he "would *insist on the extension of the suffrage*".[b] The extension of the suffrage had now become a "matter of the heart" for him.[c] Scarcely had he been thrown out of the Cabinet when this child of expediency, now called by his own supporters Foul-Weather Jack,[d] invited to his private residence at Chesham Place the various factions whose marriage brought into being the sickly monster of the coalition. He did not forget to send for the "exceedingly narrow-minded" Brights and Cobdens, begging their forgiveness at this solemn meeting for his own broad-mindedness and giving them a new promissory note for a "larger" amount of reform. As a member of the coalition Cabinet in 1854 he amused the Commons with yet another reform project, which he knew was destined to become another Iphigenia to be sacrificed by himself, another Agamemnon, for the sake of another Trojan War. He performed the sacrifice in the melodramatic style of Metastasio, his eyes filled with tears, which however dried up as soon as the "unpaid" seat which he occupied in the Cabinet was exchanged for the Presidency of the Cabinet at a salary of £2,000 as a result of a miserable intrigue against Mr. Strutt, a member of his own party.[e]

[a] In the *New-York Daily Tribune* one more sentence of this passage is quoted: "The Reformers of the House of Commons yielded to that reasoning."—*Ed.*

[b] From Russell's speech in the House of Commons on February 23, 1852.—*Ed.*

[c] This sentence does not occur in the *New-York Daily Tribune.*—*Ed.*

[d] Marx uses the English nickname and gives a German translation in brackets.—*Ed.*

[e] The next paragraph is omitted in the *New-York Daily Tribune* and the end of this paragraph reads as follows: "Hardly out of office, this child of expediency, now emphatically called by his own followers Foul-Weather Jack, summoned to his private residence at Chesham-place the different sections of the Liberal party to make solemn asseverations of his own large-mindedness, and to hand to them another promissory bill of a larger amount of reform. When a member of the Coalition cabinet, he amused the House with a Reform bill which he knew would prove another Iphigenia, to be sacrificed by himself, another Agamemnon, for the benefit of another Trojan war. He performed the sacrifice indeed in true melodramatic style, his eyes filled with tears, but these soon passed away."—*Ed.*

The second reform plan was supposed to shore up his falling Cabinet, the third to bring down the Tory Cabinet. The second was a subterfuge, the third a piece of chicanery. He arranged the second so that no one would accept it; he presented the third at a moment when no one could accept it. With both he demonstrated that if fate had made him a Minister, nature had made him a tinker, just like Christopher Sly.[a] Even of the first Reform Bill, the only one put into effect, he grasped only the oligarchical knack and not the historical tack.

[IV]

[*Neue Oder-Zeitung*, No. 365, August 8, 1855]

London, August 4.[b] On the outbreak of the Anti-Jacobin War the influence of the Whigs in *England* entered a period of decline, and continued to sink lower and lower. On account of this they turned their eyes on *Ireland*, resolving to use it to tip the balance, and inscribed on their party banners *Irish Emancipation*. When they came into office for an instant in 1806 they did, in fact, bring a minor Irish Emancipation Bill before the House of Commons, carrying it through its second reading, only to withdraw it voluntarily in order to flatter the bigot idiocy of George III. In 1812 they attempted to foist themselves on the Prince Regent (later George IV) as the only possible instruments of reconciliation with Ireland, albeit in vain.[c] Before and during the reform agitation they fawned on O'Connell, and the "hopes of Ireland" served as powerful engines of war on their behalf. Yet the first act of the Reform Ministry at the first sitting of the first reformed Parliament was a declaration of war against Ireland with the "brutal and bloody" measure of the "Coercion Bill",[275] subjecting Ireland to martial law.[d] The Whigs fulfilled their old pledges "with

[a] Character in Shakespeare's *The Taming of the Shrew*.—*Ed.*

[b] The date is omitted in the *New-York Daily Tribune* and the article begins with the following sentence: "Another of the false pretenses on which he sought a niche in the temple of fame was his efforts on behalf of Ireland."—*Ed.*

[c] This sentence does not occur in the *New-York Daily Tribune*.—*Ed.*

[d] In the *New-York Daily Tribune* this sentence reads: "...a declaration of civil war against Ireland, a 'brutal and bloody measure', the Irish Coercion 'Red-Coat Tribunal bill', according to which men were to be tried in Ireland by military officers, instead of by Judges and Juries". (The phrase "brutal and bloody measure" was used by Daniel O'Connell in the House of Commons on February 5, 1833.)—*Ed.*

fire, imprisonment, transportation and even death". O'Connell was persecuted and convicted of sedition. The Whigs, however, had only introduced and carried the Coercion Bill against Ireland by expressly committing themselves to present another bill, a bill concerning the *Church of England in Ireland*. Furthermore, they had also promised that this bill should contain a clause placing certain *surplus funds* from the revenues of the Established Church in Ireland at the disposal of Parliament. Parliament, in its turn, was to employ them in the interests of Ireland. The importance of this clause lay in the recognition of the principle that Parliament possessed the power to expropriate the Established Church—a principle of which Lord John Russell ought to have been convinced all the more firmly as the entire immense fortune of his family consists of former Church estates. The Whigs promised to stand or fall by the Church Bill. But as soon as the Coercion Bill had been passed they withdrew the above clause, the only one of any value in the Church Bill, on the pretext of avoiding a collision with the House of Lords. They voted against and defeated their own motion. This occurred in 1834. Towards the end of that year, however, an electric shock seemed to have revived the Irish sympathies of the Whigs. The fact of the matter is that they had to relinquish the Cabinet in the autumn of 1834 to Sir Robert Peel. They had been hurled back into the Opposition benches. And straightaway we find our John Russell eagerly engaged in his work of reconciliation with Ireland.[a] He was the main agent in negotiating the *Lichfield House compact*,[276] which was concluded in January 1835. The Whigs hereby left patronage (the allocation of offices, etc.) in Ireland to O'Connell, while O'Connell secured them the Irish vote both inside and outside Parliament. But a *pretext* was needed to drive the Tories out of Downing Street.[b] With characteristic "impudence", Russell chose the *Church revenues* of Ireland as his battlefield, and as his battlecry the very same *clause*—notorious under the name of the *Appropriation Clause*—which he and his colleagues in the Reform Ministry had *themselves* withdrawn and abandoned shortly before. Peel was indeed beaten with the slogan of the "Appropriation Clause". The Melbourne Cabinet was formed and Lord John Russell installed himself as Home Secretary and Leader of the House of Commons.[c] Now he

[a] The last two sentences do not occur in the *New-York Daily Tribune*.—*Ed.*

[b] 10 Downing Street is the official residence of the British Prime Minister.—*Ed.*

[c] The *New-York Daily Tribune* has: "... and Lord Russell became leader in the House of Commons."—*Ed.*

began to sing his own praises: on the one hand for his intellectual constancy, because although now in office he continued to adhere to his *opinions* about the Appropriation Clause; on the other hand for his moral moderation in refraining to *act* on these opinions. He never translated them from words into action. When he was Prime Minister, in 1846, his moral moderation triumphed so emphatically over his intellectual constancy that he even repudiated his "opinion". He knew of no measures more fatal, he exclaimed, than those threatening the Established Church in its fundamental root, its revenues.[a]

In February 1833 John Russell, in the name of the Reform Ministry, denounced the Irish *Repeal agitation.*[277]

"Its real object," he exclaimed to the Commons, "is to overturn at once the United Parliament, and to establish, in place of King, Lords and Commons of the United Kingdom, some parliament of which Mr O'Connell was to be the leader and the chief."[b]

In February 1834 the Repeal agitation was again denounced in the Speech from the Throne, and the Reform Ministry proposed an address

"to record in the most solemn manner the fixed determination of Parliament to maintain unimpaired and undisturbed the legislative union of the three realms".[c]

But hardly had John Russell been cast up on the Opposition sandbanks when he declared:

"with respect to the *repeal of the union*, the subject was open to amendment or question, just as any other act of the Legislature",

that is no more and no less than any beer Bill.[d]

In March 1846 John Russell brought down Peel's administration by means of a coalition with the Tories, who were burning with desire to punish their leader for his disloyalty over the Corn Laws. Peel's Irish "*Arms Bill*"[278] served as a pretext, and Russell, full of moral outrage, lodged an unconditional protest against it. He becomes Prime Minister. His first act is to move the very same "Arms

[a] The *New-York Daily Tribune* has: "he could not conceive a more fatal measure than the disestablishment of the Church, and he declined to take any further notice of the project of 1835".—*Ed.*

[b] Russell's speech in the House of Commons on February 6, 1833.—*Ed.*

[c] "Address in Answer to the King's Speech", House of Commons, February 4, 1834.—*Ed.*

[d] The words "i.e. no more and no less than any beer Bill" do not occur in the *New-York Daily Tribune.*—*Ed.*

Bill".[a] However, he made a fool of himself to no avail. O'Connell had just been calling monster meetings against Peel's Bill, he had organised petitions with 50,000 signatures; he was in Dublin, whence he was manipulating all the springs of agitation. King Dan (the popular nickname of Daniel O'Connell)[b] would have lost all if he had appeared to be Russell's accomplice at this juncture. He therefore served notice on the little man in threatening terms to withdraw his Arms Bill at once. Russell withdrew it. O'Connell, despite his secret dealings with the Whigs, then heaped humiliation on top of defeat, an art he has brought to perfection. So as to leave no doubt *at whose behest* the retreat had been sounded, he announced the withdrawal of the Arms Bill to the repealers in Conciliation Hall in Dublin on August 17, the *same* day John Russell announced it to the Commons. In 1844 Russell charged Sir Robert Peel with "having filled Ireland with troops, and with not governing but militarily occupying that country".[c] In 1848 Russell occupied Ireland militarily, imposed the felony acts, proclaimed the suspension of the Habeas Corpus Acts[279] and boasted of the "energetic measures" of Clarendon.[d] This energy, too, was a false pretence. In Ireland there were on the one hand the O'Connellites and the priests, in secret agreement with the Whigs; on the other, Smith O'Brien and his supporters. The latter were simply dupes[e] who took the repeal game seriously and thus came to a comical end. The "energetic measures" taken by the Russell government and the brutalities they committed were thus not called for by circumstances. Their object was not the maintenance of English supremacy in Ireland, but rather the prolongation of the Whig regime in England.

[V]

[*Neue Oder-Zeitung*, No. 369, August 10, 1855]

London, August 6. The *Corn Laws*[280] were introduced in England in 1815, the Tories and the Whigs having agreed to raise their

---

[a] The following text up to the words "In 1844 Russell charged Sir Robert Peel..." does not occur in the *New-York Daily Tribune*.—*Ed.*

[b] Marx uses the English nickname and gives a German translation in brackets.—*Ed.*

[c] Russell's speech in the House of Commons on February 13, 1844.—*Ed.*

[d] The rest of the paragraph does not occur in the *New-York Daily Tribune*.—*Ed.*

[e] Marx uses the English word.—*Ed.*

rent of land by means of a tax on the nation. This object was attained not only because the Corn Laws—laws against the import of corn from abroad—artificially raised the price of grain in some years. Taking the period 1815-1846 as a whole, what was perhaps even more important was the illusion of the tenant-farmers that the Corn Laws were able to maintain the price of corn at an *a priori* determined level in all circumstances. This illusion had an effect on leases. We find that in order to revive this illusion time and again, Parliament was constantly occupied with new, improved versions of the Corn Laws of 1815. If corn prices proved unruly, and fell despite the dictates of the Corn Laws, parliamentary committees were appointed to investigate the reasons for "agricultural distress".[a] In so far as it was the object of these parliamentary investigations, "agricultural distress" was in reality limited to the disproportion between the prices paid by the tenant to the landowner for his land and the prices at which he sold the products of his land to the public—*the disproportion between rent of land and grain prices.* The problem therefore could be solved by simply reducing rent, the landed aristocracy's source of income. Instead of this, the latter naturally preferred to "reduce" corn prices by legislative means; one Corn Law was succeeded by another, slightly modified; failure was blamed on insignificant details which could be corrected by a new Act of Parliament. Though the price of corn was thus kept above the natural level under certain conditions, *rent* was kept above its natural level under all conditions. As this was a matter of the "holiest interests" of the landed aristocracy, of their cash income, both their factions, Tories and Whigs, were equally ready to revere the Corn Laws as a lodestar elevated *above* their party struggles. The Whigs even withstood the temptation of entertaining liberal "views" on this matter—especially as at that time there seemed little prospect of covering any losses on land tenure by winning back their hereditary tenure of government posts. In order to secure the vote of the finance aristocracy both factions voted for the Bank Act of 1819, whereby the interest on national debts contracted in depreciated money should be paid at full value. Having borrowed, say, £50, the nation had to repay £100. In this way the assent of the finance aristocracy to the Corn Laws was obtained. A fraudulent increase of the national interest rates in return for a fraudulent increase of rent—this was the gist of the agreement between finance

[a] Here and below Marx uses the English expression In the first case he gives a German translation in brackets.—*Ed.*

aristocracy and landed aristocracy.[a] It is not then surprising that Lord *John Russell* branded any *Corn Law reform* as mischievous, absurd, impracticable and unnecessary in the parliamentary elections of 1835 and 1837. From the start of his ministerial career he rejected every such proposal, at first politely, then passionately. In his defence of high corn duties he was a long way ahead of Sir Robert Peel. The prospect of famine in 1838 and 1839 did not succeed in shaking either him, or the other members of the Melbourne Cabinet. What the distress of the nation could not do, the distress of the Cabinet could.[b] A deficit in the exchequer of £7,500,000 and Palmerston's foreign policy, which threatened to cause a war with France, led the House of Commons to pass a vote of no confidence in the Melbourne Cabinet proposed by Peel. This occurred on June 4, 1841. The Whigs, always as eager to chase posts as unable to fill them and reluctant to give them up, attempted in vain to sidestep fate by dissolving Parliament. Then there awoke in John Russell's profound soul the idea of conjuring away the Anti-Corn-Law agitation just as he had helped to conjure away the reform movement. So he suddenly advocated a "moderate fixed duty" instead of the sliding tariff[c][281]—friend that he is of "moderate" political chastity and "moderate" reforms. He had the audacity to parade through the streets of London in a procession of government candidates accompanied by banner-bearers with two loaves impaled on their poles in blatant contrast to each other, one being a two-penny loaf with the inscription "*Peel loaf*", the other a shilling loaf inscribed "*Russell loaf*". The nation, however, refused to be misled this time. It knew from experience that the Whigs promised bread and paid out stones. Despite Russell's ridiculous carnival capers the general election left the Whigs with a minority of 76. They were at last forced to decamp. Russell avenged himself for the disservice which the moderate fixed duty of 1841 had done him by calmly letting Peel's "sliding scale" crystallise into law in 1842. He now despised the "moderate fixed duty"; he turned his back on it; he dropped it without expending a single word on it.[d]

---

[a] Instead of the preceding text of instalment [V] the *New-York Daily Tribune* has: "Let us now look at his Free-trade pretenses. The Corn Laws had been enacted in 1815, by the concurrence of Tories and Whigs."—*Ed.*

[b] Instead of the preceding two sentences the *New-York Daily Tribune* has: "During the prospect of dearth (1838-1839) he and Melbourne did not contemplate any alteration in the existing duties."—*Ed.*

[c] Russell's speech in the House of Commons on June 7, 1841.—*Ed.*

[d] The last two sentences do not occur in the *New-York Daily Tribune.*—*Ed.*

During the years 1841-45 the *Anti-Corn-Law League*[282] grew to colossal dimensions. The old alliance between landed aristocracy and finance aristocracy could no longer safeguard the Corn Laws, for the industrial bourgeoisie had increasingly supplanted the finance aristocracy as the chief element of the middle class. For the industrial bourgeoisie, however, the abolition of the Corn Laws was a matter of survival. Repeal of the Corn Laws meant for the industrial bourgeoisie reduced production costs, expansion of foreign trade, increase in profits, a reduction of the main source of revenue, and hence of the power, of the landed aristocracy, and the enhancement of their own political power. In the autumn of 1845 they found fearsome allies in the potato blight in Ireland, the high corn prices in England and the failure of the harvest in most of Europe.[a] Intimidated by the menacing economic outlook, Sir Robert Peel therefore held a series of Cabinet meetings at the end of October and the first weeks of November 1845 at which he proposed the suspension of the Corn Laws and even hinted at the necessity of a definitive repeal. There was a delay in the decisions of the Cabinet owing to the stubborn resistance of his colleague Stanley (now Lord Derby).

At that time, during the Parliamentary recess, John Russell was on holiday in Edinburgh, where he got wind of the proceedings in Peel's Cabinet. He decided to exploit the delay caused by Stanley and forestall Peel in this popular position, giving himself the appearance of having forced Peel's hand[b] and thus robbing any prospective moves by him of their moral weight. Accordingly, on November 22, 1845 he addressed a letter from Edinburgh to his City voters full of angry and malicious references to Peel, on the pretext that the ministers were delaying too long coming to a decision about the emergency in Ireland. The periodical famines in Ireland in 1831, '35, '37 and '39 had never been able to shake the faith of Russell and his colleagues in the Corn Laws. But now he was all fire. Even such an appalling disaster as the famine of two nations conjured up before the eyes of the little man nothing but visions of mousetraps for his rival "in office". In his letter he

---

[a] In the *New-York Daily Tribune* the preceding part of this paragraph is condensed as follows: "During the years 1841-45, the Anti-Corn-Law League became formidable. In the autumn of 1845, it found new and terrible allies in the famine in Ireland, the corn-dearth in England, and the failure of the harvest all over Europe."—*Ed.*

[b] Instead of the words "the appearance of having forced Peel's hand" the *New-York Daily Tribune* has: "the appearance of having forced Free trade upon Peel".—*Ed.*

tried to conceal the real motive for his sudden conversion to Free Trade with the following wretched confession:

"I confess that on the general subject my views have, in the course of twenty years, undergone a great alteration. I used to be of opinion that corn was an exception to the general rules of political economy; but observation and experience have convinced me that we ought to abstain from *all interference* with the supply of food."[a]

In the *same* letter he reproached Peel for *not* yet having interfered with the supply of food to Ireland.[b] Peel caught the little man in his own trap. He resigned, leaving a note with the Queen[c] pledging Russell his support should he undertake to carry out the abolition of the Corn Laws. The Queen summoned Russell and asked him to form a new Cabinet. He came, saw—and declared that he was *unable* to do so, even *with* the support of his rival. That was not what he had intended. For him it was merely a *false pretence*, and they were threatening to take him at his word! Peel stepped in again and repealed the Corn Laws. As a result of his act the Tory party collapsed and disintegrated. Russell allied himself with it in order to defeat Peel. So much for his claim to the title of "Free Trade Minister" of which he was still boasting in Parliament only a few days ago.

[VI]

[*Neue Oder-Zeitung*, No. 377, August 15, 1855]

London, August 12. Let us return once again to *Lord John Russell* so as to conclude his character sketch.[d] At the outset of his career he acquired a sort of reputation on the plea of his tolerance and at the end of his career on the plea of his bigotry, on the first occasion by his motion for the *repeal of the "Test and Corporation Acts"*,[283] on the second occasion by his "Ecclesiastical Titles Bill".[e] The Test and Corporation Acts prevented dissenters from holding

[a] "Lord John Russell to the Electors of the City of London. Edinburgh, Nov. 22", *The Times*, No. 19092, November 27, 1845.—*Ed.*

[b] The rest of this paragraph does not occur in the *New-York Daily Tribune*.—*Ed.*

[c] Victoria.—*Ed.*

[d] This sentence does not occur in the *New-York Daily Tribune*.—*Ed.*

[e] Here and below Marx uses the English word "repeal" and gives the names of the acts in English or in a Germanised English form. He gives the German translation of the name of the second act in brackets.—*Ed.*

civil service posts. They had long been a dead letter when Russell moved his famous repeal motion in 1827. He defended it on the ground that he was convinced that "the repeal will enhance the security of the Church of England".[a] A contemporary writer informs us: "No one was more astonished that the motion was carried than the mover himself." The solution to the riddle is obvious if one notes that the *Tory Ministry* itself moved the Catholic Emancipation Bill[284] the following year (1829), and hence must have been only too glad to get rid of the "Test and Corporation Acts" in the meantime. Apart from this the dissenters have never received anything from Lord John except promises whenever he was in opposition. While in office he even opposed the abolition of church rates.[b]

His *anti-Popery cry*[c] is, however, even more characteristic of the shallowness of the man and the pettiness of his motives. We have seen that in 1848 and 1849 he defeated the reform motions of his own allies by an alliance of the Whigs with the Peelites and Tories. Being so dependent on the conservative opposition his Ministry had grown very weak and shaky by 1850 when the Papal Bull establishing a Roman Catholic hierarchy in England and the appointment of Cardinal Wiseman Archbishop of Westminster provoked some surface agitation amongst the most hypocritical and fatuous sections of the English people. Russell, at any rate, was not caught unawares by the Pope's measures. His father-in-law, Lord Minto, was in Rome when the *Roman Gazette*[d] announced the appointment of Wiseman in 1848. In fact, we know from Cardinal Wiseman's Letter to the English People that the Pope had informed Lord Minto of the Bull establishing the hierarchy in England as early as 1848.[e] Russell himself took some preparatory steps by having the titles of the Catholic clergy in Ireland and the colonies officially recognised by Clarendon and Grey. But now, in view of the weakness of his Cabinet, perturbed by the historical recollection that the anti-Popery cry threw the Whigs out of the government in 1807, fearing that Stanley might imitate Perceval and forestall him, Russell, during the Parliamen-

---

[a] Russell's speech in the House of Commons on June 7, 1827. The *Neue Oder-Zeitung* gives 1828 as the date of Russell's motion—probably a misprint.—*Ed.*

[b] Marx gives the English term "church rates" in brackets after the German equivalent.—*Ed.*

[c] Russell's attacks on Pius IX.—*Ed.*

[d] *Gazzetta di Roma.*—*Ed.*

[e] "Cardinal Wiseman's Manifesto", *The Times*, No. 20651, November 20, 1855.—*Ed.*

tary recess, as he had tried to forestall Sir Robert Peel over the repeal of the Corn Laws—pursued by all these forebodings and phantoms, the little man turned a complete somersault into an unrestrained Protestant frenzy. On November 4, 1850[a] he published the notorious "Letter to the Bishop of Durham", in which he assured the Bishop:

"I agree with you in considering the late aggression of the Pope upon our Protestantism as insolent and insidious, and I therefore feel as indignant as you can do upon this subject."

He speaks of "the laborious endeavours which are now making to confine the intellect and enslave the soul". He calls the Catholic ceremonies "mummeries of superstition, upon which the great mass of the nation looks with contempt", and he finally promises the Bishop to see to it that new laws are passed against the Papal usurpation should the old ones be inadequate. The same Lord John had declared in 1845, though then admittedly out of office:

"I believe that we may repeal those disallowing clauses which prevent a Roman Catholic Bishop from assuming a title held by a Bishop of the Established Church. Nothing can be more absurd and puerile than to keep such distinctions."[b]

In 1851 he presented his Ecclesiastical Titles Bill[286] in order to maintain these "absurd and puerile" distinctions. But having been defeated during the year by a combination of the Irish Brigade with the Peelites, Manchester Men,[287] etc.—on the occasion of Locke King's motion for the extension of the suffrage—his Protestant zeal evaporated and he promised an alteration of the Bill, which in fact came into the world stillborn.[c]

As his anti-Popery zeal was a false pretence, so was his Jewish Emancipation zeal. All the world knows that his Jewish Disabilities Bill[d] is an annual farce—bait to catch the votes which the Austrian Baron Rothschild commands in the City. A false pretence, too, were his anti-slavery declarations.

"Your [...] opposition," Lord Brougham writes to him, "to all the motions in favour of the Negroes, and your resistance even to the attempts for stopping the newly established slave trade, widened the breach between you and the country [...]. The fancy that you, the opposers of all the motions against the slave trade in 1838, the

---

[a] The *New-York Daily Tribune* has: "just the day before the anniversary of Guy Fawkes"[285].—*Ed.*

[b] Russell's speech in the House of Commons on July 9, 1845.—*Ed.*

[c] This paragraph continues thus in the *New-York Daily Tribune*: "Some months later, being ejected from office, he fawned again on what he had called the Pope's minions."—*Ed.*

[d] Marx gives the name of the bill in English.—*Ed.*

enemies of every interference with the colonial Assemblies, which are composed of slave traders, should all of a sudden have become so enamoured of the Negro cause as almost to risk your tenure of place upon a bill for its furtherance in 1839, would argue a strange aptitude for being gulled [...]."[a]

False pretences, too, were his *legal reforms*. When Parliament passed a vote of no confidence on the Whig Cabinet in 1841, and with the imminent dissolution of the Commons boding little success, Russell attempted to rush a *Chancery Bill* through the House, in order to

"remedy one of the most urgent evils of our legal system, the delays in the Courts of Equity, by the creation of two new judges of equity" (judges whose guiding principle is not the letter of the law but equity, or fairness).[b]

Russell called this Bill of his "a large instalment of legal reform". His real intention was to smuggle two Whig sympathisers into the newly created posts, *before* the formation of a Tory Cabinet which was to be expected. Seeing through his game, Sir Edward Sugden (now Lord St. Leonards) moved an amendment that the Bill should not take effect until October 10 (that is *after* the opening of the newly elected Parliament).[c] Although not the slightest alteration had been made to the content of the Bill, regarded by Russell as so "urgent", he immediately withdrew it after the passing of the amendment. It had become a "farce" and had lost its point.[d]

Colonial reforms, educational schemes, the "liberties of the subject", public press and public meetings, enthusiasm for war and yearning for peace—all of them were but false pretences for Lord John Russell. The whole man is one false pretence, his whole life a lie, all his activity a continuous chain of petty intrigues for the achievement of shabby ends—the devouring of public money and the usurpation of the mere semblance of power. No one has ever illustrated more strikingly the truth of the biblical words that no man can add one cubit unto his stature.[e] Placed by birth, connections, and social accidents on a colossal pedestal, he always remained the same homunculus—a dwarf dancing on the tip of a pyramid. History has, perhaps, never exhibited any other man—so great in pettiness.

---

[a] "Lord Brougham's Reply to Lord John Russell's Letter to the Electors of Stroud...", *The Times*, No. 17041, May 14, 1839.—*Ed.*

[b] Marx uses the English terms "Chancery Bill", "Courts of Equity", "judges of equity".—*Ed.*

[c] The words in brackets do not occur in the *New-York Daily Tribune*.—*Ed.*

[d] The last sentence does not occur in the *New-York Daily Tribune*.—*Ed.*

[e] Matthew, 6:27.—*Ed.*

Karl Marx

THE LATE BIRMINGHAM CONFERENCE[288]

It is a great mistake to judge of the movement in England by the reports in the London press. Take, for instance, the late Birmingham Conference. The majority of the London newspapers did not even notice it, while the remainder contained only the meager intelligence of its having taken place. Yet what was this Conference? It was a public Congress composed of delegates from Birmingham, London, Huddersfield, Newcastle, Halifax, Sheffield, Leeds, Derby, Bradford, Nottingham and other places, convened to take the task of discussing the most important subject of the day—the foreign policy of England—out of the hands of an incapable and collapsing Parliament.

The movement, undoubtedly, had been instigated by the meetings addressed by Mr. Urquhart throughout the factory districts, and the distinguishing feature of the Conference just held at Birmingham was the harmonious working together of men from the middle and the laboring classes. The Conference divided itself into various Committees charged to report on the most prominent questions of British foreign policy. I have been favored with a detailed account of the proceedings and the documents connected therewith, of which I proceed to place the most characteristic before the readers of the *Tribune.* The first is a correspondence between the Secretary of the Conference and Lord Malmesbury, the Foreign Minister of Lord Derby, concerning the treaty on the Danish succession[289] of May 8, 1852. Lord Malmesbury writes[a]:

---

[a] Instead of the preceding text the *Neue Oder-Zeitung* has: "*London,* July 27. In contrast to the Administrative Reform Association, a *State Reform Association*[290] has been set up in London. It has included Ernest Jones and several other Chartist

"Sir: I have had the honor of receiving your invitation to attend the Birmingham Conference on the 17th, 18th and 19th July. It will not be in my power to do so. As you request me to furnish you with any useful information on the subject of the proposed subjects of inquiry, I do not hesitate to observe that your resolution passed on July 6, respecting the Danish treaty of 8th May, 1852, is founded on a totally erroneous view of the cases and facts. It is not true that the succession to Denmark, the Sound and Schleswig-Holstein, is secured to Russia by that treaty. Russia has obtained no right, present or prospective, that she did not possess before the treaty. There are now four male heirs to the crown of Denmark alive. The treaty prescribes that if their extinction should become universal, the high contracting parties—namely, Austria, Prussia, Russia, England, France and Sweden—shall engage to take into consideration any further proposition made to them by the King of Denmark[a] for securing the succession on the principle of the integrity of the Danish monarchy. Should this remote contingency occur, the contracting powers would therefore meet again to settle the Danish succession, and I leave you to judge whether the Five Powers who signed the treaty of 8th May with Russia are likely in such a case to determine that, as head of the house of Holstein-Gottorp, she should annex to her dominions the whole of the present Danish monarchy.

"I have the honor etc.

Malmesbury."[b]

The following is the answer of the Secretary to Lord Malmesbury's letter:

"My Lord: I am instructed by the Birmingham Conference to thank your lordship for your very important communication on the subject of the Danish Treaty. We gather from it that in the case of the expected failure of the four heirs

---

leaders in its Committee. At a public meeting which it held the day before yesterday it declared its principal aim to be a reform of Parliament on the basis of universal suffrage.

"The *Birmingham Conference* closed its deliberations on July 23. It was attended by delegates from Huddersfield, Newcastle-upon-Tyne, London, Halifax, Sheffield, Leeds, Derby, Bradford, Nottingham and Birmingham, who convened in Birmingham to form a *judgment* on the *foreign policy* of the ruling class and its representatives in Cabinet and Parliament. As the *Birmingham Daily Press* notes, the *Chartists* 'had refrained from involvement in any organised movement for years, but not in this. They took part in it heart and soul because they felt that it pursued no interest hostile or alien to them, indeed no class interest at all'.

"Urquhart's presence in the factory districts undoubtedly gave the impulse to this remarkable conference, whose sittings he attended to the very end. As lack of time prevented us from making use of the invitation to attend the conference, we are now presenting in extracts some interesting documents from the printed report of the Conference, which has been sent to us. The venal London press suppresses or distorts the facts. The following correspondence took place between the Earl of *Malmesbury* and the Secretary of the Committee appointed by the Conference:".—*Ed.*

[a] Frederick VII.—*Ed.*

[b] This and the following document are quoted from *Birmingham Conference. Report of Committee on the Danish Treaty.—Ed.*

to the United Monarchy of Denmark, England and Russia are pledged to interfere between the King of Denmark on the one hand, and the several States of Denmark, Schleswig and Holstein on the other. We are at a loss to know by what right such an interference can be justified, and we cannot but think the fact of war with Russia ought to be taken advantage of in order to enable us to abstain from so immoral and illegal action. You give us to understand that you think the character of the six Powers is a security against the admission of Russia to the whole succession in right, first, of Holstein-Gottorp, and secondly, of the principle of the integrity of the monarchy. We are most anxious to learn from your lordship who will come in for the whole if Russia does not, and, if England did not mean Russia to come in for the whole, why did she not make Russia's renunciation of Holstein-Gottorp a condition of the treaty? As your lordship signed the treaty in question, it is to be presumed either that these questions are unanswerable, or that your lordship will be the person of all others, best able to give to them a satisfactory answer. I am, therefore, instructed to request that your lordship will be so kind as to answer these questions, and thus relieve us from a source of great uneasiness. I have the honor to be, etc.,

"*Langford.*"

The correspondence stops here—Lord Malmesbury not having felt inclined to go on. His Lordship's inability to answer those questions is, however, not without an excuse—the noble lord having found all points concerning the Danish Succession so well settled by Lord Palmerston's Protocol of July 4, 1850,[a] that the Treaty required indeed his mere signature.

The second document is the report of the committee appointed by the Conference, on the famous *Four Points.*[b] [291] I quote as follows[c]:

"In endeavoring to ascertain the character of the Four Points as the basis of peace, your Committee have considered the development given to them by the Conference at Vienna, the amount of support or opposition that each proposal for such development has received from the respective Powers, the time and the manner in which the Points were first laid down by the Cabinets of England and France, the source from which they originally sprang, and their relevance to the avowed object of the War—viz., the Independence and Integrity of the Ottoman Empire. We find their *source* in the following proposition, laid down in the

[a] The final text of this Protocol was signed on August 2, 1850.—*Ed.*

[b] *Birmingham Conference. Report of Committee on the Proposed Bases of Pacification known as "The Four Points"*. The quotations that follow are taken from that publication.—*Ed.*

[c] Instead of the last two paragraphs the *Neue Oder-Zeitung* has: "The correspondence naturally stops here although his Lordship could have pointed out that his participation in this business was purely formal. Palmerston and Baron Brunnow had already signed the *Protocol* that laid down the clauses and principles of the future treaty.

"The Conference had formed various committees to inquire into and report on different matters. Most important of all is indisputably the *Memoir of the Committee on the Four Points,* from which we quote the most important passages:".—*Ed.*

dispatch of Count Nesselrode, of June 29, 1854, and headed, 'Consolidation of the Rights of the Christians in Turkey': 'Setting out from the idea that the civil rights to be obtained for all the Christian subjects of the Porte are inseparable from religious rights, as is stipulated by the Protocol—and would in fact become valueless to our co-religionists if, in acquiring new rights, they should lose their old ones—we have already declared, that, if this were the case, the demands made by the Emperor[a] on the Porte would be fulfilled, the cause of the dispute done away with, and his Majesty would be ready to give his concurrence to *a European guaranty for this privilege.*'

"This proposal, which is a proposal for the perpetual interference, not of one, but of five Powers, in the internal affairs of Turkey, was accepted on the part of England and France, in the shape of what is now known as the Fourth Point, couched in the following terms by Drouyn de Lhuys, in his dispatch of 22d of July, 1854, which was the reply to Count Nesselrode: 'That no Power shall claim the right to exercise any official protectorate over the subjects of the Sublime Porte, to whatever rights they may belong, but that France, Austria, Great Britain, Prussia and Russia, shall lend their mutual cooperation in order to obtain from the initiative of the Ottoman Government the consecration and observance of the religious privileges of the various Christian communities, and turn the generous intentions manifested by the Sultan[b] to the account of their various co-religionists, so that there shall not result therefrom any infringement of the dignity and independence of his crown.'

"The effect of the Fourth Point is to destroy the independence of the Ottoman Empire, which it is the avowed object of the war to defend, but its illegality consists in the fact that this proposed surrender has been made by England and France without the consent of Turkey, and persisted in by them in spite of Turkey's refusal to discuss the point at the Conference of Vienna. To use the words of Sidney Herbert, 'the matter is complicated by the fact that we are agreed with our enemy but not with our ally.'

"Had we been beaten in war by Russia and compelled to sue for peace we could not legally have made such a proposal on the part of another Power. In order to remove this illegality it would be necessary first for England and France to go over openly to Russia and to declare war against Turkey. As the Fourth Point is the surrender of the independence of Turkey, so the First Point is the surrender of her integrity; and, as in the Fourth Point, that surrender is made without the consent of the party concerned; such consent to the development of the First Point having been expressly reserved by the Turkish Plenipotentiary.

"We find that the separation of Wallachia, Moldavia and Servia from Turkey is concealed under the statement that they are still to be subject to the Porte.[...] The phrase, 'no exclusive protection shall in future be exercised over those provinces,' is developed in five succeeding articles, which put the Five Powers in the same condition with the Porte as Joint Suzerain, and receives its finishing stroke from the proposal made by France and England at the sixth meeting of the Conference, that Wallachia and Moldavia should be united in a single State, under a hereditary Prince chosen from one of the reigning families of Europe. But the infamy of this surrender, alike of the avowed purposes of England, and of the rights of our ally—Turkey—is enhanced by the fact that it was made at a time when the armies of Russia were compelled to evacuate the Turkish territory, without the smallest assistance from the forces of England and France. As the surrender of the integrity

---

[a] Nicholas I.—*Ed.*
[b] Abdul Mejid.—*Ed.*

and independence of the Ottoman Empire was thus made before the expedition to Sevastopol, it follows that this expedition must have been intended for the purpose of enforcing that surrender—enforcing it upon Turkey by exhausting her resources, enforcing it upon England by representing it as a triumph over Russia. We find this last view of the matter supported by Mr. Gladstone when he pointed out that Russia refused the Four Points before the expedition to Sevastopol, and accepted them afterward. [...]

"We cannot for a moment suppose that the English Cabinet was not aware that by substituting Austrian for Turkish soldiers in Wallachia and Moldavia they were setting free the Russian army to support Sevastopol, nor is the supposition that this was a concession to Austria, made for the purpose of obtaining her adherence to the Turkish cause, a tenable proposition in the face of the two facts that the nominal objects of our interference [...] were already on the one hand secured by the Turkish victories over the Russians, and on the other hand surrendered by the terms of peace already offered to Russia in the fourth and first points.[a]

"The second point was the free navigation of the Danube. The interruption of the navigation of the Danube dates from the cession by Turkey to Russia, at the Treaty of Adrianople in 1829, of the delta of the Danube—a cession which was contrary to the Treaty of London of July 6, 1827, which bound Russia to acquire no Turkish territory.[292] The acquiescence of England in this violation of public law was defended by her desire for peace—a pretense which is at all instances inconsistent with the existing state of war. The cession of the Danubian delta to Turkey was an indispensable demand in any real war of England against Russia. [...] It has, on the contrary, been made a means of injury to Austria. At the fourth meeting of the Vienna Conference, held March 21, 1855, Baron Prokesch, the Austrian Plenipotentiary, having proposed that Russia should admit the neutrality of the Danubian delta, the Russian Plenipotentiary[b] said 'that they would not consent to an arrangement which had the appearance of an indirect expropriation'. Lord J. Russell did not support the very moderate proposal of Austria, and the question was settled on the 23d of March in favor of the continued possession by Russia of the Danubian delta. [...][c]

---

[a] The passage beginning with the words "We find this last view" and ending with the words "in the fourth and first points" does not occur in the *Neue Oder-Zeitung*. The rest of the German version of this article was published in the next issue of the *Neue Oder-Zeitung*, on July 31, 1855. It was introduced by the following words: "With reference to the second point the *Birmingham document* goes on to say:".—*Ed.*

[b] A. M. Gorchakov.—*Ed.*

[c] In the *Neue Oder-Zeitung* there follows a passage from the same document which was omitted in the *New-York Daily Tribune*: "After fully conceding this point to Russia, Lord John writes on the 12th April to Lord Clarendon:—'Count Buol told us he had not pressed the neutrality of the islands at the mouth of the Danube, as he was sure if he had done so, the Russian Minister would have broken up the conference...' On the 16th April, Lord John Russell telegraphed to Lord Clarendon that 'Austria will not support any demand for cession of territory;' and having first neglected to support Austria in the half measure of neutrality of the Delta, having then ascertained that she will not support the whole measure, namely, the cession of the Delta to Turkey, which had been put out of court by Lord John Russell's submission to Russia on the 23rd March, he then proposes to Lord Clarendon to demand 'The cession to Turkey of the islands at the mouth of the Danube surrendered by the treaty of Adrianople.'"—*Ed.*

"The Third Point is as follows: That the treaty of 1841[293] shall be revised by the high contracting powers in the interest of the European equilibrium, and in the sense of a limitation of Russian power in the Black Sea.

"To give sincerity and reality to the Third Point, it is necessary to divide it into two, and then correct the false terms of the Second Point. These two Points should be: First, the limitation of the power of Russia; second, the restoration of the rights of Turkey in the Straits of the Dardanelles and of the Bosphorus. Russia has not a natural preponderance in the Black Sea: she is not able to descend from Sevastopol and take possession of Constantinople and of Turkey; had she possessed this power she would have used it. [...] She must, therefore, have been withheld in the past, and can only continue to be withheld for the future by the impracticability of the undertaking. As a preparation for such an undertaking, she has robbed Turkey by treaty, not of her fair share of power in the Black Sea, but of the exclusive control of the Straits which command her capital in the Bosphorus, and which secure it at the Dardanelles. [...][a] For the restoration of the Sultan's exclusive control of the Straits, no stipulation was necessary; it reverts to him on the abrogation by the fact of war of the treaties by which it has been temporarily placed in abeyance. This simple view of the case has, however, not even been suggested at the Conference of Vienna. If we read the dispatch of 14th June, 1853, of Lord Clarendon to the Austrian Government, we shall find the reason in the words: *the just claims of Russia.* If the claims of Russia were just, and if England intended to support them, England should have declared war against Turkey. [...]"[b]

"With regard to the limitation of the power of Russia, your Committee would direct attention to the following memorable words of the Austrian plenipotentiary, Count Buol, in his letter of 20th May, 1855: 'In our opinion the joint efforts of the Allies should be directed to limiting the political power of Russia to such a point as to render the abuse of its material resources if not impossible, at least in the highest degree difficult. The diminution, nay, even the total destruction of the Russian fleet in the Black Sea, would not of itself suffice to deprive Russia of the advantage which she derives from her geographical position with regard to Turkey.'

"Of all the delusions attempted by the English Government upon Parliament, the only one which has failed has been the proposal for limiting the naval power of Russia in the Black Sea. [...] Had the war been intended as announced—to protect the integrity and independence of the Ottoman Empire—the terms of peace offered to Russia would have been: 1. Cession to Turkey of the Danubian Delta, which *de jure* it still has; 2. indemnification by Russia of the expenses of the war. [...]"

The Committee wind up their report as follows:

"Your committee find it impossible to reconcile these facts with the innocence of the British Cabinet.[c] It would be a want of discernment to suppose that all the members of the Cabinet have been thoroughly cognizant of the nature of their conduct. One cannot however overlook the preeminence of the four Foreign Ministers, Lord Clarendon, Lord Aberdeen, Lord John Russell, and above all Lord Palmerston, whose aid in securing the recognition of the Treaty of Adrianople, the

---

[a] The passage beginning with the words "Russia has not a natural preponderance" and ending with the words "secure it at the Dardanelles" does not occur in the *Neue Oder-Zeitung.—Ed.*

[b] The last two sentences do not occur in the *Neue Oder-Zeitung.—Ed.*

[c] This sentence does not occur in the *Neue Oder-Zeitung.—Ed.*

payment to Russia, even in time of war, of the Russo-Dutch loan, the Treaty of Unkiar-Skelessi and of the Dardanelles, and the Treaty of Balta-Liman,[294] and whose perfidy toward Poland, Hungary, Sicily and Italy, no less than his treachery toward France, Persia, Spain, and Denmark, point him out as the implacable enemy—not only of Turkey, but of every nation of Europe, the willing tool of Russia, and the master in the English Cabinet of those whom he has reduced to the condition of accomplices, and compelled previously to assist in the crimes which at first they wanted the intellect to detect, the honesty to resist, the courage to punish. In such punishment dealt out by the highest tribunal in the land, and with all the solemnities with which the ancient law and custom surrounded those impeached of high treason, your committee place their only hope of rescuing the people from the conspirators who have betrayed them to a foreign power."

Written on July 27 and 28, 1855

First published in the *New-York Daily Tribune*, No. 4464, August 10, 1855 as a leading article; the German version was published in the *Neue Oder-Zeitung*, Nos. 349 and 351, July 30 and 31, 1855, marked with the sign ×

Reproduced from the *New-York Daily Tribune*

Frederick Engels

THE ARMIES OF EUROPE[295]

Written between late June and September 1855

First published in *Putnam's Monthly*, Nos. XXXII, XXXIII and XXXVI, August, September and December 1855

Reproduced from the journal

PUTNAM'S MONTHLY.

A Magazine of Literature, Science, and Art.

[FIRST ARTICLE]

[*Putnam's Monthly,* No. XXXII, August 1855]

The war raging on the shores of the Black Sea for the last two years, has called particular attention to the two millions of armed men kept in pay by Europe, even in the midst of peace, and destined, perhaps, to be very soon increased to twice that number; and if, as is all but certain, the war should continue, we may expect to see these four millions engaged in active operations, on a theater of war occupying, from sea to sea, the whole breadth of the European Continent.

For this reason, an account not only of the armies hitherto engaged in the Eastern conflict, but of the more important remaining armies of Europe as well, cannot be uninteresting to our readers, especially as, on this side of the Atlantic, nothing has fortunately ever been seen approaching, in any degree, the magnitude of even the second-rate armies of Europe; wherefore the organization of such bodies is but vaguely known to the non-professional public among us.

The jealousy which formerly surrounded the army of every power with mysterious secrecy, no longer exists.—Strange to say, even in countries the most adverse to publicity, where all departments of the civil administration remain, to the present day, enveloped in the darkness required by absolutism, the organization of the army is perfectly known to the public. Army lists are published, stating, not only the subdivision of the armed force in corps, divisions, brigades, regiments, battalions, and squadrons, but also the dislocations of these bodies, with the numbers and the names of the officers commanding them. Whenever great reviews take place, the presence of foreign officers is not only tolerated, but even courted, criticism is solicited, observations are exchanged, the distinctive institutions and contrivances of each army are sagely discussed, and a publicity is established, which but too strangely contrasts with many other features in the same government. The actual secrets which a European war-ministry can contrive to keep to itself, are a few recipes for chemical compositions, such as rockets or fuses; and even these are found out very soon, or are superseded by the progress of invention; as, for instance, the British congreve-rocket composition, by Mr. Hale's war-rockets, adopted in the U.S. army, and now in the British army also.

This publicity causes, in time of peace, the various war-ministries of the civilized world to form, as it were, one large military committee, for the purpose of discussing the merit of all proposed innovations, and allowing each member to profit by the experience of all the remainder. Thus it has been brought about that the arrangements, organization and general economy of almost all European armies are nearly the same, and in this sense it may be said that one army is about as good as any other. But national character, historical tradition, and, above all things, different degrees of civilization, create as many diversities, and give to each army its peculiar points of excellence and weakness. The Frenchman and the Hungarian, the Englishman and the Italian, the Russian and the German, under certain circumstances, may be equally good and efficient soldiers; but, in spite of a uniform system of drill, which appears to level all distinctions, every one will be good in his own way, by virtue of qualities different from those possessed by his rivals.

This brings us to a question but too often mooted between the military patriots of different nationalities: Which are the best soldiers? Of course, every people is jealous of its own fame; and, in the opinion of the general public, fed by narratives which, whatever they may lack in critical exactness, are amply adorned with high patriotic coloring,—one regiment of its own can "lick" any two or three of any other nation. Military history, as a science in which a correct appreciation of facts is the only paramount consideration, is but of very recent date, and boasts as yet of a very limited literature. It is, however, an established branch of science, and more and more every day scatters to the winds, like chaff, the unblushing and stupid bluster which too long has characterized works calling themselves historical because they made a trade of distorting every fact they recounted. The time is past when, in writing the history of a war, people can continue that war, so to say, on their own account, and safely cannonade the late enemy with dirt, after the conclusion of peace forbids them from cannonading him with iron.[296] And although many a minor point in military history remains still to be settled, yet thus much is certain, that there are none of the civilized nations which cannot boast of having, at some time or other, produced the best soldiers of their time. The German *Landsknechte* of the later middle ages, the Swiss soldiers of the sixteenth century, were for a period as invincible as the splendid Spanish soldiers, who succeeded them to the rank of "the first infantry of the world;" the French of Louis the Fourteenth, and the Austrians of Eugene disputed, for a while, with each other this post of honor, until the Prussians of Frederick the Great settled the question by defeating both of them; these, again, were hurled down into utter disrepute by a single blow at Jena,[297] and once more the French were universally acknowledged the first soldiers of Europe; at the same time, however, they could not prevent the English, in Spain, from proving themselves their superiors under certain circumstances and in certain moments of a battle.[298] No doubt, the legions which Napoleon led, in 1805, from the camp of Boulogne to Austerlitz,[299] were the finest troops of their time; no doubt Wellington knew what he said, when he called his soldiers at the conclusion of the Peninsular war "an army with which he could go any where, and do any thing;" and yet the flower of this Peninsular British army was defeated at New Orleans, by mere militia men and volunteers, without either drill or organization.[300]

The experience of all past campaigns, then, leads us to the same result; and every sensible old soldier, unbiassed by prejudice, will confirm it: that military qualities, both as regards bravery and aptitude for the work, are, upon the whole, pretty impartially distributed among the different nations of the world; that it is not so much the degree, as the special nature of the qualification, which distinguishes the soldiers of different nationalities; and that with the publicity established now-a-days in military matters, it is the assiduous application of thought, improvement, invention, to the military institutions and resources of a State, and the development of the military qualities specially distinguishing a nation, by which alone an army can be made, for a time, to rank foremost among its rivals. Thus we see, at once, what an advantage, in a military sense, a higher development of civilization gives to a country over its less advanced neighbors. As an example, we may mention that the Russian army, though distinguished by many soldier-like qualities of the first order, has never been able to establish a superiority over any army of civilized Europe. At even chances, the Russians would fight desperately; but up to the present war, at least, they were sure to be beat, whether their opponents were French, Prussians, Poles, or English.

Before we consider the different armies separately, a few general remarks respecting them all are requisite.

An army, especially a large one of from three hundred thousand to five hundred thousand and more men, with all its necessary subdivisions, its different arms, and its requirements in men, material, and organization, is itself so complicated a body that the highest possible simplification becomes indispensable. There are so many inevitable varieties, that it might be expected they would not be increased by factitious and unmeaning variegations. Nevertheless, habit and that spirit of show and parade which is the bane of old armies, has complicated matters in almost every European army to an incredible degree.

The differences in size, strength, and temperament which are found, both in men and horses, in every country, necessitate a separation of light infantry and cavalry from heavy infantry and cavalry. To attempt to completely obliterate this separation, would be to mix up in one body individuals whose military qualifications are opposite by nature, and would, therefore, to a certain degree neutralize each other; thereby lessening the efficiency of the whole. Thus, either arm is naturally divided into two separate bodies—the one comprising the heavier and clumsier men (and horses respectively), destined principally for the great decisive charges, and the fight in closed ranks; the other forming the lighter, more active men, specially adapted for skirmishing, outpost and advanced guard duty, rapid maneuvers, and the like. So far, the subdivision is perfectly legitimate. But, in addition to this natural distribution, in almost every army, each subdivision is again subdivided into branches distinguished by nothing but fanciful distinctions of dress and by theoretical quibbles which are constantly contradicted by practice and experience.

Thus, in every European army there exists a corps called Guards, pretending to be the *élite* of the army, but which in reality merely consists of the biggest monsters of men that can be got hold of. The Russian and the English Guards are most distinguished in this respect; though no proof exists that they exceed in bravery and effectiveness the other regiments in either service. Napoleon's Old Guard was a far different institution; it was the actual *élite* of the army; and bodily size had nothing to do with its formation. But even this guard weakened the rest of the army, by absorbing its best elements, and consideration for such an unrivaled corps led Napoleon, sometimes, into mistakes—as at Borodino,[301] where he did not bring the Guards forward at the decisive moment, and thereby missed the chance of preventing the Russian force from effecting their retreat in good order. The French have, beside their Imperial Guard, a sort of *élite* in every battalion, forming two companies—one of grenadiers, and the other of voltigeurs; thereby complicating the tactical evolutions of the battalion to an unnecessary degree. Other nations have similar corps. All these choice troops, beside their distinctive formation and dress, receive higher pay. It is said that such a system spurs the ambition of the private soldier, especially amongst excitable nations like the French and Italians; but the same object would be obtained, and perhaps more perfectly, if the men who had earned such distinctive marks should remain in the ranks of their respective companies, and were not made use of as a pretext for disturbing the tactical unity and symmetry of the battalion.

A still more striking humbug is practiced with regard to the cavalry. Here the distinction between light and heavy horse forms a pretext for subdivisions of all sorts—cuirassiers, dragoons, carabineers, lancers, chasseurs, hussars, and so on. All such subdivisions are not only useless, they are actually preposterous by the complications they cause. Hussars and lancers are imitated from the Hungarians and Poles; but in Hungary and Poland these arms have their sense—they were the national arms, and the dress of the troops carrying them was the national dress of the country. To imitate such peculiarities in other countries, where the national spirit is wanting that gave them life, is, to say the least of it, ridiculous; and well might, in 1814, the Hungarian hussar, when greeted with the title of "comrade" by a Russian hussar, reply, "No comrade—I hussar, you harlequin!" (*Nix camerad—ich husar, du hanswurst!*) Another such ridiculous institution, in almost all armies, is formed by the cuirassiers—men actually disabled, and disabling their horses, too, by the weight of their breast-plates (a French cuirass weighs twenty-two pounds), and, for all that, not protected by them from the effects of a rifle-ball fired at a hundred and fifty yards distance! The cuirass had been got rid of in almost all European armies, when Napoleon's love of show and of monarchical tradition re-introduced it among the French, and his example was soon followed by all the nations of Europe.

Beside our own little army, the Sardinian is the only one, among civilized nations, in which cavalry consists of plain light and heavy horse, without any further subdivision, and where the cuirass is completely done away with.

In the field artillery, a great complication of different calibers is found in every army. The English have the greatest diversity in theory, carrying eight calibers and twelve different models of guns; but in practice their enormous material allows them to reduce their artillery to great simplicity. In the Crimea, for instance, the nine-pounder and the twenty-four pound howitzer are almost the only calibers in use. The French have introduced, during the last few years, the greatest possible simplicity, by replacing their four different calibers by one, the light twelve-pound howitzer-gun, of which we shall speak in its place. In most other armies, from three to four calibers are still in existence, not counting the varieties of carriages, tumbrils, wheels, and the like.

The technical corps of the different armies, the engineers, and so on, to which we may add the staff, are organized in all armies upon a pretty similar footing, except that with the British, and to their great detriment, the staff does not form a separate corps at all. Other minor differences will be mentioned in their respective places.

We begin with that army which, from the organization it received during the revolution and under Napoleon, has served as a sort of model to all European armies since the beginning of this century.

I. THE FRENCH ARMY

France had, when the present war broke out, one hundred regiments of infantry of the line (the 76th to 100th were, up to a recent date, called "light infantry," but their drill and organization was in no way distinguished from the line regiments). Each regiment counts three battalions, two field-battalions, and the third as a reserve. In time of war, however, the third battalion can be very soon organized for field duty, and a fourth battalion, formed by the extra dépôt company of each of the three battalions, undertakes the duties of the dépôt. This was done during the wars of Napoleon, who even formed fifth, and, in some instances, sixth battalions. For the present, however, we can only count three battalions per regiment. Each battalion has eight service-companies (one of grenadiers, one of voltigeurs, and six center-companies); and each company, on the war footing, counts three officers and one hundred and fifteen non-commissioned officers and soldiers. A French battalion of the line, therefore, amounts, on the war footing, to about nine hundred and sixty men, one-eighth of whom (the voltigeur company) are especially set apart for light infantry duty.

The special corps destined for light infantry service consist of the *chasseurs-à-pied* and of the African corps. The chasseurs, before the war, only ten battalions, were, in 1853, raised to twenty battalions, so that nearly every infantry division of the army (four regiments) can, on its formation, receive one chasseur battalion. These battalions count ten companies, or nearly 1,300 men. The troops specially destined for African service consist of: three regiments, containing nine battalions of Zouaves; two regiments, or six battalions, of the Foreign Legion; six battalions of light infantry (of which, three battalions native chasseurs), together twenty-one battalions, or about 22,000 men.

The cavalry is divided into four distinct portions:—

1. Heavy or Reserve Cavalry, 12 regiments—2 of carabineers (cuirassier rifles), 10 of cuirassiers=72 squadrons.
2. Cavalry of the line, 20 regiments—12 of dragoons, 8 of lancers=120 squadrons.
3. Light Cavalry, 21 regiments—12 chasseurs-à-cheval, 9 hussars=126 squadrons.
4. African light cavalry, 7 regiments—4 *Chasseurs d'Afrique,* 3 spahis=42 squadrons.

The squadrons are of 190 men for the reserve and line cavalry, and 200 men for the light cavalry—on the war footing. In time of peace, there are scarcely four squadrons of 120 men fully equipped, so that, on every mobilization of the army, a great number of men on furlough have to be called in, and the horses for them to be found, which, in a country as poor in horses as France, can never be done without a large importation from abroad.

The artillery, as recently reorganized, is formed in seventeen regiments: five of foot-artillery, for garrison and siege duty; seven of the line (for service with the infantry divisions); four of horse-artillery, and one of pontoniers. The foot-artillery appear to be destined to act in the field on emergencies only. The artillery of the line have their gun-carriages and limbers constructed so that the gunners can ride on them during quick movements. The horse-artillery is organized as in other services. The line and horse-artillery count one hundred and thirty-seven batteries, of six guns each, to which sixty batteries of the foot-artillery may be added as a reserve, altogether, 1,182 guns.

Beside the above, the artillery comprises thirteen companies of workmen.

The special services of the army comprise:—A general staff of 560 officers; staffs for the fortresses, the artillery, and the engineers, of about 1,200 officers; three regiments of sappers and miners; five pack squadrons; five train squadrons; 1,187 medical officers, and so on. The total numbers are as follows:

Infantry

Line, 300 bat's and 300 dépôt comp's, ...	335,000
Chasseurs, 20 battalions, ...	26,000
African troops, 21 battalions, ...	22,000
	383,000

Cavalry

Reserve,	72	sq. and	12	dépôts,	16,300	
Line,	120	"	20	"	28,400	
Light,	126	"	21	"	31,300	
African,	42	"			10,000	86,000
Artil'y and special corps					1,200 guns and	70,000
					1,200 guns and	539,000

To these are to be added the newly formed Guard[302] in the strength of one division of infantry (two regiments of grenadiers, two of voltigeurs), one brigade of cavalry (one regiment of cuirassiers, one of guides), one battalion of chasseurs, and four or five batteries of artillery; as well as 25,000 men of the gendarmerie, 14,000 of whom are horse gendarmes. Two more regiments of infantry, the 101st and 102d, have recently been formed, and a new brigade of the foreign legion (Swiss) is in course of formation. Altogether, therefore, the French army, in its present organization, contains the cadres for about 600,000 men, and this will be a pretty correct estimate of its present strength.

The army is recruited by ballot, among all young men who have reached their twentieth year. It is presumed that about 140,000 men are annually available, of which number, however, in time of peace, from 60,000 to 80,000 only are taken for service. The remainder may be called in at any time during the eight years following their ballot. A great number of soldiers, besides, are dismissed on long furloughs during peace, so that the actual time of service, even of those called in, does not exceed from four to five years. This system, while it gives the troops actually serving a high degree of efficiency, does not prepare any drilled reserves for a case of emergency. A great continental war, in which France would have to act with two or three large armies, would force her, even in the second campaign, to bring into the field many raw levies, and would show, in the third campaign, a very sensible deterioration of the army. The French are, indeed, very handy at learning the trade of a soldier, but, in that case, why keep up the long period of service, which excludes the greater portion of the available young men from the benefit of a school of military instruction?

Wherever military service is both compulsory and of long duration, the necessity of European society has introduced the privilege, for the wealthier classes, of buying off by a money-payment, in some shape or other, the obligation to serve personally. Thus, in France, the system of finding substitutes is legally recognized,[303] and about eighty thousand of these are constantly serving in the French army. They are mostly recruited from what are called the "dangerous classes;" they are rather difficult to handle, but, when once broken in, form capital soldiers. They require a very strict discipline to keep them in good behavior; and their notions of order and subordination are sometimes rather extravagant. Wherever there are large numbers of them in a regiment, they are sure to cause difficulties in a garrison. For this reason, it is thought that the best place for them is before the enemy, and, thus, the light troops of Africa are especially recruited from them; for instance, the Zouaves, who almost all entered the army as "remplaçants." The Crimean campaign has fully shown that the Zouaves carry their African habits everywhere—their love of plunder, as well as their unruly conduct in adversity, and it is, perhaps, in this sense that a kindred genius, the late Marshal St. Arnaud, said, in his bulletin on the battle of the Alma,[304] "The Zouaves are, indeed, the first soldiers of the world!"[a]

The equipment of the French army is, upon the whole, first-rate. The arms are well constructed, and, especially the cavalry saber, of a very good model, though, perhaps, it is a little too long. The infantry are accoutred according to the new system which was introduced, at the same time, in France and Prussia; by

[a] A. de Saint-Arnaud, "Au quartier général à Alma. Champ de bataille d'Alma, le 21 septembre 1854", *Le Moniteur universel,* No. 280, October 7, 1854.—*Ed.*

it, the cross-belts, for pouch and sword, or bayonet, are done away with; both are worn on a belt round the waist, supported by two leather braces over the shoulders, while the knapsack is loosely worn over the shoulders by two straps, without the old-fashioned connecting strap across the chest. Thus, the chest is left entirely free, and the soldier becomes a different man altogether from the unfortunate being strapped and buckled up in the sort of leather cuirass in which the old system confined him. The dress is plain, but tasteful; it must, indeed, be admitted that, in military, as well as in civilian fashions, the French have showed more taste than any other nation. A blue tunic, or frock-coat, covering the thighs to the knees, with a low standing collar cut out in front, scarlet trowsers, moderately wide, a light *képi*, the most soldier-like headgear yet invented, shoes and gaiters, and a comfortable gray capote, form an outfit as simple and efficient as any known in European armies. In Africa, the head is protected from the rays of the sun by a white flannel capote, and flannel under-clothing is also served out to the troops. In the Crimea, heavy cloth capotes were worn during the last winter, covering the head, neck and shoulders. The *chasseurs-à-pied* are clothed all in gray, with green facings; the Zouaves have a sort of Turkish fancy costume, which appears well adapted to the climate and the duty they have to do. The Chasseurs, and some other African battalions, are armed with the Minié rifle, the remainder of the infantry, with plain percussion muskets. There appears to be, however, an intention to increase the proportion of the troops armed with rifled muskets.

The cavalry are a fine-looking class of men, lighter in weight than in many other armies, but none the worse for that. In the peace establishment, they are, upon the whole, passably well horsed by animals procured abroad, or from the horse-breeding establishments of the government, and the districts where they have succeeded in improving the native breed, which, until lately, was very poor. But, in case of war, when the number of horses has to be suddenly doubled, the resources of the country are altogether insufficient, and thousands of horses have to be bought abroad, many of which are scarcely fit for cavalry service. Thus, in any long war, the French cavalry will soon be deteriorated, unless the government can lay its hands on the resources of countries rich in horses, as it did in 1805, '6, and '7.

The artillery are now armed exclusively with the new light twelve-pound gun, the so-called invention of Louis Napoleon. But, as the light twelve pounder, adapted for a charge one quarter the weight of the ball, already existed in the English and Dutch armies, as the Belgians had already done away with the chamber in their howitzers, and as both Prussians and Austrians are in the habit, in certain cases, of firing shells from common twelve and twenty-four-pound guns, the pretended invention reduces itself to the adaptation of this light twelve pounder to the common French eight pounder carriage. However, the French artillery has evidently gained in simplicity and efficiency by the change; whether its mobility has not suffered, remains to be seen; as also, whether the twelve pounder will be found efficient enough for hollow shot. We have, at least, seen it stated that it has already been found necessary to forward howitzers of a heavier caliber to the army in the East.

The tactical regulations of the French army are a strange compound of soldierly sense and old-fashioned traditions. There is, perhaps, no language better adapted for the short, distinct, dictatorial military word of command, than the French; yet the command is generally given with an excessive prolixity of words—where two or three words would be sufficient, the officer has to shout out a whole sentence, or even two. The maneuvers are complicated, and the drill contains a good deal of old-fashioned nonsense, quite inapplicable to the present state of tactics. In skirmishing, that very function which appears innate to the Frenchman, the men are drilled with a pedantry hardly surpassed in Russia. The same is true in some of the cavalry and artillery maneuvers. But whenever the French have to go to war, the necessity of the case very soon dispenses with these antiquated and pedantic maneuvers; and new tactical methods, suited to new situations, are arranged and introduced by nobody so quickly as by the French.

Upon the whole, light troop duty is the *forte* of the French. They are literally the lightest troops in Europe. Nowhere is the average bodily size of the army so low as in France. In 1836, of about 80,000 men in the French army, only 743 were five feet eight inches or above; and only *seven* measured six feet; while full 38,000 measured from four feet ten and a half inches to five feet two inches! And yet these little men not only fight exceedingly well, but they also stand the heaviest fatigues, and beat, in agility, almost every other army. General Napier maintains that the British soldier is the heaviest laden fighting animal in the world; but he had never seen these French African campaigners carry, beside their arms and personal baggage, tents, firewood, provisions, heaped up on their backs to a hight far overtowering their shakos, and thus march thirty or forty miles in a day, under a tropical sun. And then compare the big, clumsy British soldier, who, in time of peace, measures five feet six inches, at least, with the puny, short-legged, tailor-like Frenchman, of four feet ten! And still, the little Frenchman, under all his load, remains a capital light-infantry-man; skirmishes, trots, gallops, lies down, jumps up, all the while loading, firing, advancing, retiring, dispersing, rallying, re-forming, and displays not only twice as much agility, but also twice as much intelligence as his bony competitor from the island of "rosbif." This light-infantry service has been brought to perfection in the twenty battalions of *chasseurs-à-pied.* These incomparable troops, incomparable for their peculiar service, are drilled to make every movement, when within range of the enemy, in a sort of easy trot, called *pas gymnastique,* in which they make between one hundred and sixty and one hundred and eighty paces per minute. But not only can they run, with short intervals, for half an hour and more, but creeping, jumping, climbing, swimming, every movement that can possibly be required, are equally familiar to them, while they are first-rate riflemen. Who, at even odds, can hold out, in skirmishing fights, against these dead shots, finding shelter behind the least inequality of ground?

As to the action of the French infantry in masses, their passionate character gives them great advantages with great disadvantages. Generally, their first charge will be business-like, rapid, determined, if not furious. If successful, nothing can resist them. If defeated, they will soon rally, and be in a position to be again brought forward; but, in an unfortunate or even chequered campaign, French infantry will soon lose its solidity. Success is a necessary element to all armies, but especially to those of the Romano-Celtic race. The Teutonic race has, in this respect, a decided superiority over them. The French, when Napoleon had once put them on the track, could, for fifteen years, overthrow everything before them, until reverses broke them down; but a seven years' war,[305] such as Frederick the Great carried through, a war where often enough he was on the brink of ruin, often defeated, and yet finally victorious—such a war could never be won with French troops. The war in Spain, 1809-14, affords a conclusive example on this head.

Under Napoleon, the French cavalry were, in contrast to the infantry, far more renowned for their action in masses than for their duty as light troops. They were deemed irresistible, and even Napier admits their superiority over the English cavalry of that day.[a] Wellington, to a certain degree, did the same. And strange to say, this irresistible cavalry consisted of such inferior horsemen, that all their charges were made in a trot, or, at the very outside, an easy canter! But they rode close together, and they were never launched except when the artillery, by a heavy fire, had prepared the way for them; and then in large masses only. Bravery and the flush of victory did the rest. The present French cavalry, especially the Algerian regiments, are very fine troops, good riders in general, and still better fencers; though, in horsemanship, they are still inferior to the British, Prussians, and, especially, the Austrians. But as the army, when placed on a war-footing, must double its cavalry, there is no doubt the quality will be deteriorated; it is, however, a fact, that the French possess, in a high degree, that essential quality of a horse-soldier which we call *dash,* and which makes up for a great many deficiencies. On the other hand, no soldiers are so careless of their horses as the French.

The French artillery has always ranked very high. Almost all improvements made in gunnery, during the last three or four centuries, have originated with the French. During the Napoleonic wars, the French artillery were especially formidable by their great skill in selecting positions for their guns, an art then but imperfectly understood in other armies. All testimony agrees that none equaled the French in placing their guns so that the ground in front, while covering them from the enemy's fire, was favorable to the effect of their own. The theoretical branch of artillery has also been constantly a favorite science with the French; their mathematical turn of mind favors this; and the precision of language, the scientific method, the soundness of views, which characterize their artilleristic literature, show how much this branch of science is adapted to the national genius.

Of the special corps, the engineers, staff, sanitary and transport corps, we can merely say that they are highly efficient. The military schools are models of their kind. The French officer is not required to have that general education which is expected in Prussia; but the schools he has to pass through furnish him with a first rate professional training, including a thorough knowledge of the auxiliary sciences, and a certain proficiency in at least one living language. There is, however, another class of officers in the French army, viz., that selected from old non-commissioned officers. These latter seldom advance higher than to a captaincy,

[a] W. F. P. Napier, *History of the War in the Peninsula...*, Vol. III, p. 272.—*Ed.*

so that the French often have young generals and old captains; and this system answers exceedingly well.

Upon the whole, the French army shows, in all its features, that it belongs to a warlike and spirited nation, that feels a pride in its defenders. That the discipline and the efficiency of this army have overcome the seductions laid out for it by Louis Bonaparte, and that the Pretorians of December, 1851,[a] could so soon be turned into the heroes of the Crimea, certainly speaks highly to their credit. Never was an army more flattered, more courted by a government, more openly solicited to all sorts of excesses than the French in the autumn of 1851; never were they allowed such license as during the civil war of December; yet they have returned to discipline and do their duty very well. The Pretorian element, it is true, has, several times, risen to the surface in the Crimea, but Canrobert always succeeded in quelling it.

II. THE ENGLISH ARMY[306]

The British army forms a complete contrast to the French. There are not two points of similarity between them. Where the French are strong, there the British are weak, and *vice versa*. Like old England herself, a mass of rampant abuses, the organization of the English army is rotten to the core. Everything seems to be arranged so as to prevent all possibility of the end aimed at ever being attained. By an inexplicable haphazard, the boldest improvements—though few, indeed—take their stand in the midst of a heap of superannuated imbecility; and yet, whenever the clumsy, creaking machine is set to work, it somehow or other manages to do its duty.

The organization of the British army is soon described. Of infantry there are three regiments of guards, eighty-five regiments of the line, thirteen regiments of light infantry, two regiments of rifles. During the present war, the guards, the rifles, and a few other regiments have three battalions, the remainder have two—a dépôt being formed by one company in each. The recruiting, however, is hardly sufficient to fill up the vacancies caused by the war, and so the second battalions can scarcely be said to be in existence. The present effective total of the infantry does certainly not exceed 120,000 men.

---

[a] I.e., the troops that took part in the Bonapartist *coup d'état* of December 2, 1851.—*Ed.*

Beside the regular troops, the militia form part of the infantry as a sort of reserve or nursery for the army. Their number, according to act of Parliament,[a] may come up to 80,000, but they cannot now number more than 60,000, although, in Lancashire alone, there are six battalions called out. As the law stands at present, the militia may volunteer to serve in the Colonies, but cannot be conducted to foreign theaters of war. They can, therefore, only serve to set free the line-soldiers who garrison Corfu, Malta and Gibraltar, or, perhaps, hereafter, some of the more distant settlements.

Of cavalry there are three regiments of guards (cuirassiers), six of dragoon guards (heavies), four of heavy dragoons, four of light dragoons, five of hussars, and four of lancers. Each regiment is to be raised, on the war-footing, to 1,000 sabers (four squadrons of two hundred and fifty men, beside a dépôt). Some regiments did go out with this strength, but the disasters of the Crimea in winter, the senseless charge at Balaklava,[307] and the dearth of recruits have re-established, on the whole, the old peace-footing. We do not think that the whole of the twenty-six regiments amount, at this moment, to 10,000 sabers, or 400 sabers per regiment, on an average.

The artillery consists of the regiment of foot-artillery (twelve battalions, with ninety-six batteries), and the brigade of horse artillery (seven batteries and one rocket-battery). Each battery has five guns and one howitzer; the calibers of the guns are three, six, nine, twelve, and eighteen pounders, those of the howitzers four and two-fifth inches, four and a half inches, five and a half inches, and eight inches. Each battery, also, has two models of guns, of almost every caliber, heavy and light ones. In reality, however, the light nine pounder and twelve pounder, with four and a half inch and five and a half inch howitzer, form the field-calibers, and, upon the whole, the nine pounder may now be said to be the universally adopted gun of the British artillery, with the four and a half inch (twelve pounder) howitzer as an auxiliary. Beside these, six pounder and twelve pounder rockets are in use.

As the English army, on its peace establishment, forms but a cadre for the war-footing, and as it is recruited entirely by voluntary enlistment, its real force, at a given moment, can never be precisely stated. We believe, however, we may estimate its present strength at about 120,000 infantry, 10,000 cavalry, and 12,000 artillery, with about 600 guns (of which, not one-fifth part

[a] The 1852 act of Parliament on the militia.—*Ed.*

are horsed). Of these 142,000 men, about 32,000 are in the Crimea, about 50,000 in India and the Colonies, and the remaining 60,000 (of whom one-half are raw recruits, the other half drilling them) at home. To these are to be added about 60,000 militia men. The pensioners, yeomanry cavalry, and other useless corps, not available for service abroad, we do not count at all.

The system of recruiting by voluntary enlistment, makes it very difficult, in time of war, to keep up the efficiency of the army, and this the English are now, again, experiencing. We see again, as under Wellington, that 30,000 or 40,000 men is the very outside of what they can concentrate and keep up on a given theater of war; and as, now, they have not Spaniards for their allies but French, the "heroic little band" of Britishers almost disappears in the midst of the allied army.

There is one institution in the British army which is perfectly sufficient to characterize the class from which the British soldier is recruited. It is the punishment of flogging. Corporal punishment does not exist in the French, the Prussian, and several of the minor armies. Even in Austria, where the greater part of the recruits consist of semi-barbarians, there is an evident desire to do away with it; thus the punishment of running the gauntlet has recently been struck out from the Austrian military code. In England, on the contrary, the cat-o'-nine-tails is maintained in its full efficiency—an instrument of torture fully equal to the Russian knout in its most palmy time. Strange to say, whenever a reform of the military code has been mooted in Parliament, the old martinets have stuck up for the cat, and nobody more zealously than old Wellington himself. To them, an unflogged soldier was a monstrously misplaced being. Bravery, discipline, and invincibility, in their eyes, were the exclusive qualities of men bearing the scars of at least fifty lashes on their backs.

The cat-o'-nine-tails, it must not be forgotten, is not only an instrument calculated to inflict pain; it leaves indelible scars, it marks a man for life, it brands him. Now, even in the British army, such corporal punishment, such branding, really amounts to an everlasting disgrace. The flogged man loses caste with his fellow soldiers. But, according to the British military code, punishment, before the enemy, consists almost exclusively in flogging; and thus, the very punishment which is said, by its advocates, to be the only means of keeping up discipline in cases of great urgency, is the means of ruining discipline by destroying the *morale* and the *point d'honneur* of the soldier.

This explains two very curious facts: first, the great number of English deserters before Sebastopol. In winter, when the British soldiers had to make superhuman exertions to guard the trenches, those who could not keep awake for forty-eight or sixty hours together, were flogged! The idea of flogging such heroes as the British soldiers had proved themselves in the trenches before Sebastopol, and in winning the day of Inkermann[308] in spite of their generals! But the articles of war left no choice. The best men in the army, when overpowered by fatigue, got flogged, and, dishonored as they were, they deserted to the Russians. Surely there can be no more powerful condemnation of the flogging system than this. In no former war have troops of any nation deserted in numbers to the Russians; they knew that they would be treated worse than at home. It was reserved to the British army to furnish the first strong contingent of such deserters, and, according to the testimony of the English themselves, it was flogging that made the men desert. The other fact is, the signal failure of the attempt to raise a foreign legion under the British military code. The Continentals are rather particular about their backs. The prospect of getting flogged has overcome the temptation of the high bounty, and good pay. Up to the end of June, not more than one thousand men had enlisted, where fifteen thousand were wanted; and this much is certain, if the authorities attempt to introduce flogging even among these one thousand reprobates, they will have to encounter a storm which will force them either to give way, or to dissolve the foreign legion at once.

The dress and equipments of the British soldiers are a model of what they should not be. Up to the present time, the dress in common wear is the same as armies used to wear as long ago as 1815. No improvement has been admitted. The old swallow-tail coatee, disfigured by ugly facings, still distinguishes the British from every other soldier. The trowsers are tight, and uncomfortable. The old cross-belt system for fixing bayonet-scabbard, pouch and knapsack, reigns supreme in almost all regiments. The cavalry wear a better fitting dress than the infantry, and far superior; but, for all that, it is much too tight and inconvenient. Besides, the English are the only nation who have maintained in their army the red coat, the "proud red coat" as Napier calls it. This coat, which makes their soldiers look like dressed-up monkeys, is supposed by its brilliancy to strike terror into the enemy. But alas, whoever has seen any of the brick-colored British infantry must confess that their coats, after four weeks' wear, inspire every looker-on with an incontrovertible idea, not of frightfulness, but of shabbiness, and that any other color would be far more terror-inspiring, if it only could stand dust, dirt, and wet. The Danes and Hanoverians used to wear the red coat, but they dropped it very soon. The first campaign in Schleswig proved to the Danes what a capital mark to the enemy is offered by a red coat and white cross-belts.

The new dress-regulation has brought forward a red coat of the cut of the Prussian coat. The infantry wear the Austrian shako, or the képi; the cavalry the Prussian helmet. The cross-belt accoutrements, the red color, the tight trowsers, are more or less maintained. Thus, the improvement amounts to nothing; and the British soldier will only look as strange as ever in the midst of the other European armies, dressed and accoutred, as they are, a little more in accordance with common sense.

Nevertheless, one improvement has been carried out in the British army, which far surpasses anything that has been done in other countries. This is, the arming of the whole of the infantry with the Minié rifle, as improved by Pritchett. How the old men, at the head of the army, men generally so obstinate in their prejudices, could come to so bold a resolution, it is difficult to imagine; but they did it, and thus doubled the efficiency of their infantry. At Inkermann, there is no doubt that the Minié rifle, by its deadly certainty of aim and great power, decided the day in favor of the English. Whenever an English line of infantry delivers its fire, the effect must be overpowering to any enemy armed with the common musket, for the English Minié rifle loads as quickly as any smoothbored gun.

The cavalry are fine men, well horsed, armed with swords of a very good model; and what they can do, they have shown at Balaklava. But, on the whole, the men are too heavy for their horses, and, therefore, a few months of active campaigning must reduce the British cavalry to nothing. The Crimea has given us a fresh example of this. If the standard for heavy cavalry was reduced to five feet six inches, and for light cavalry to five feet four or, even, two inches, as, we believe, it is now for the infantry, a body of men might be formed far more suitable for their actual field duties. But, as it is, the horses are too heavily loaded, and must break down before they can be used, with effect, against the enemy.

The artillery, too, is composed of taller men than it should be. The natural standard of size for an artilleryman is, that he should be big enough to unlimber a twelve pound gun, and five feet two to five feet six inches are ample for this purpose, as we know from abundant personal experience[309] and observation. In fact, men of about five feet five, or six, inches, if stoutly made, are, generally, the best handlers of guns. But the British want a crack corps, and their men, therefore, though tall and elegant to look at, lack that compactness of body which is so necessary to a really useful artilleryman. Their artillery material is first-rate. The guns are the best in Europe, the powder is acknowledged to be the strongest in the world, the shot and shell are of a smoothness of surface unknown anywhere else. But, for all that, no guns in the world have as much windage, and this shows by what sort of men they are commanded. There is hardly an artillery in Europe officered by men of so deficient professional education as the British. Their information very seldom goes beyond the mere elements of the science of artillery, and, in practice, the handling of field-guns is as much as they understand, and that but imperfectly. Two qualities, in both officers and men, distinguish the British artillery: uncommonly good eye-sight, and great calmness in action.[a]

---

[a] In the German version of this section, published in the *Neue Oder-Zeitung* of September 1, 1855 under the title "Dress and Equipments of the British Soldier", the text of the last five paragraphs is given in a condensed and altered form: "The dress and equipments of the British soldiers are a model of what they should not be. Up to the present time, the dress in common wear is the same as the army used to wear up to 1815, altered but superficially by a new dress-regulation which gave the red coat a Prussian cut, the infantry the Austrian shako, or the képi, and the cavalry the Prussian helmet. Britain alone has maintained in her army the red coat, the 'proud red coat' as Napier calls it. The Danes and Hanoverians used to wear the red coat. The first campaign in Schleswig proved to the Danes what a capital mark it offered to the enemy.

"Nevertheless, one improvement has been carried out in the British army, which far surpasses anything that has been done in other countries. This is, the arming of the whole of the infantry with the Minié rifle, as improved by Pritchett. There is no doubt that at Inkerman the Minié rifle, by its deadly certainty of aim, decided the day in favour of the English.

"The cavalry are fine men, well horsed, armed with swords of a very good model; and what they can do, they have shown at Balaklava. But, on the whole, the men are too heavy for their horses, and, therefore, a few months of active campaigning must reduce the British cavalry to nothing. As the horses are too heavily loaded, they must break down before they can be used, with effect, against the enemy. The Crimea has given us a fresh example of this.

"The artillery, too, is composed of taller men than it should be. The artillery material is first-rate. The guns are the best in Europe, the powder is acknowledged to be the strongest in the world, the shot and shell are of a smoothness of surface not to be found anywhere else. The artillery material is the product of modern, industrial England, whereas the artillery officers are the product of old England. The former, therefore, is just as much above the level of the European armies as the latter are below it. Their education in most cases does not go beyond the mere elements of the science of artillery, and, in practice, the handling of field-guns is as

Upon the whole, the efficiency of the British army is sorely impaired, by the ignorance, both theoretical and practical, of the officers. The examination which they are now expected to undergo, is actually ridiculous—a captain examined on the first three books of Euclid[a]! But the British army is mainly instituted for the stowing away, in respectable situations, of the younger sons of the aristocracy and gentry, and the standard of education for its officers must, therefore, be regulated, not by the requirements of the service, but by what little information is commonly expected in an English "gentleman." As to the practical military knowledge of the officer, it is equally insufficient. The British officer believes he has only one duty to perform: to lead his men, on the day of battle, straight against the enemy, and to give them an example of bravery. Skill in handling troops, seizing favorable opportunities, and the like, is not expected from him; and as to looking after his men and their wants, why, such a thing hardly ever enters his head. One half of the disasters of the British in the Crimea arose from this universal incapacity of the officers. They have, however, one quality which fits them for their functions: being, most of them, passionate huntsmen, they possess that instinctive and rapid appreciation of advantages of ground, which the practice of hunting is sure to impart.

The incompetence of the officers nowhere creates greater mischief than on the staff. As no regularly educated staff-corps exists, every general forms his own staff from regimental officers, ignorant of every part of their duty.[b] Such a staff is worse than none. Reconnoitering, especially, is always done in a slovenly manner, as it must be, when done by men who know little of what is expected from them.

The education of the other special corps is rather better, but far below the standard in other nations; and, in general, an English officer would pass as an ignoramus amongst men of his class in any other country. Witness the military literature of the British. Not a work hardly, but is full of blunders which would not be

---

much as they understand, and that but imperfectly. Two qualities, in both officers and men, distinguish the British artillery: uncommonly good eye-sight, and great calmness in action."—*Ed.*

[a] The reference is to Euclid's *Elements,* a work in 13 books which sets forth the fundamentals of ancient mathematics.—*Ed.*

[b] The *Neue Oder-Zeitung* has: "...every general forms his own staff from his relations and protégés among the regimental officers without the least regard for special knowledge".—*Ed.*

forgiven anywhere else, to a candidate for a lieutenancy. Every statement of facts is given in a slovenly, unbusiness-like, and unsoldier-like manner, leaving out the most important points, and showing, at once, that the writer does not know his business.[a] The consequence is, that the most ridiculous statements of foreign books are credited at once.* We must, however, not forget to state that there are some honorable exceptions, amongst which W. Napier's "Peninsular War," and Howard Douglas's "Naval Gunnery," rank foremost.[c]

The administrative, medical, commissariat, transport, and other accessory departments are in a deplorable state, and have experienced a thorough breakdown when put to the test in the Crimea.[d] Efforts are made to improve them, as, also, to centralize the administration, but little good can be expected while the civil administration, and, in fact, the entire governing power, remains altogether the same.

With all these enormous drawbacks, the British army manages to hobble through every campaign, if not with success, yet without disgrace. There is a loss of life, a deal of mismanagement, a compound of blunders which astonish us when compared with the state of other armies under the same circumstances; yet there is no loss of military honor, there is seldom a repulse, almost never a complete defeat. It is the great personal bravery and tenacity of the troops, their discipline and implicit obedience, which bring this about. Clumsy, unintelligent, and helpless as the British soldier is when thrown upon his own resources, or when called upon to do the duty of light troops, nobody surpasses him in a pitched battle where he acts in masses. His *forte* is the action in line. An English line of battle will do what has scarcely ever been done by other infantry: receive cavalry *in line*, keep their muskets charged to the last moment, and fire a volley when the enemy is at thirty yards,

* As an instance, we refer to the work on fire arms by Col. Chesney,[b] who is considered one of the best artillery officers in Great Britain.

---

[a] This sentence does not occur in the *Neue Oder-Zeitung*.—*Ed.*

[b] F. R. Chesney, *Observations on the Past and Present State of Fire-Arms*.... In the *Neue Oder-Zeitung* the words "now General" are added in brackets after "Col."—*Ed.*

[c] W. F. P. Napier, *History of the War in the Peninsula*...; H. Douglas, *A Treatise on Naval Gunnery*....—*Ed.*

[d] Instead of this sentence the *Neue Oder-Zeitung* has: "Earlier we repeatedly pointed to the lamentable state of the commissariat, transport and other accessory departments. They experienced a thorough breakdown during the Crimean campaign."—*Ed.*

and in almost every instance with perfect success. The fire of British infantry is delivered with such a coolness, even in the most critical position, that it surpasses, in effect, that of any other troops. Thus, the Highlanders, *in line*, repulsed the Russian cavalry at Balaklava. The indomitable tenacity of this infantry was never shown to greater advantage than at Inkermann, where the French, under the same circumstances, would certainly have been overwhelmed; but, on the other hand, the French would never have allowed themselves to be surprised, unguarded, in such a position. This solidity and tenacity in attack and defense, form the great redeeming quality of the British army, and have alone saved it from many a defeat, well-merited and all but intentionally prepared by the incapacity of its officers, the absurdity of its administration, and the clumsiness of its movements.

III. THE AUSTRIAN ARMY

Austria profited by the first moments of repose after her severe trials in 1848 and 1849, to reorganize her army upon a modern footing. Almost every department has been completely reformed, and the army is now far more efficient than ever.

First comes the infantry. The line consists of sixty-two regiments, beside which there are one regiment and twenty-five battalions of rifles, and fourteen regiments and one battalion of frontier-infantry. The latter, with the rifles, make up the light infantry.

An infantry regiment of the line consists of five field and one dépôt battalion—together thirty-two companies—of which the field companies count 220 men, and the dépôt companies 130 men. Thus, the field battalion numbers about 1,300 men, and the whole regiment nearly 6,000 men, or as many as a British division. The whole line, therefore, on the war-footing, is about 370,000 strong.

The frontier infantry have per regiment, two field and one dépôt battalion, together sixteen companies; in all, 3,850 men: the whole frontier infantry comprises 55,000 men.

The chasseurs, or rifles, count in all thirty-two battalions, of about 1,000 men each: total, 32,000 men.

In cavalry, the army has, of heavies: eight regiments of cuirassiers, and eight of dragoons; of light horse: twelve of hussars, and twelve of lancers (seven of which were formerly light dragoons, or *chevau-légers,* but have been, latterly, turned into lancers).

The heavy regiments count six squadrons, beside one dépôt—the light ones eight squadrons, and one dépôt squadron. The heavy regiments have 1,200 men, the light ones 1,600 men. The whole cavalry numbers about 67,000 men, on the war-footing.

Of artillery, there are twelve field regiments, each consisting of four six pounders, three twelve pounder foot batteries, six cavalry batteries, and one howitzer battery, on the war-footing: total, 1,344 guns; one coast regiment, and one rocket regiment, of twenty batteries, with one hundred and sixty tubes. Total, 1,500 guns and rocket tubes, and 53,000 men.

This gives a total effective number, on the war-footing, of 522,000 fighting men.

To these are to be added about 16,000 sappers, miners and pontoniers, 20,000 gens d'armes, the transport corps, and the like, raising the total to about 590,000 men.

By calling in the reserve, the army can be increased by from 100,000 to 120,000 men; and by draining the resources of the military frontier[310] to their utmost limit, another 100,000 to 120,000 men may be made available. But, as these forces could not be collected at a given moment, they would drop in gradually, and thus serve mainly to fill up the vacancies in the ranks. More than 650,000 men Austria could hardly bring together, at a time, under arms.

The army is divided into two quite distinct corps, the regular army and the frontier troops. For the first, the time of service is of eight years' duration—after which the men remain two more years in the reserve. Long furloughs, however, are granted—as in France—and five years may be nearer the actual time the men are kept with the colors.

The frontier troops are got together upon a quite different principle. They are the descendants of South-Slavonian (Croat or Serbian), Wallachian, and partly of German, settlers who hold their lands by military tenure under the crown, and were formerly employed to protect the frontier, from Dalmatia to Transylvania, against the inroads of the Turks. This service is now reduced to a mere formality, but the Austrian government, nevertheless, has shown no inclination to sacrifice this capital nursery of soldiers. It was the existence of the frontier organization, which in 1848 saved Radetzky's army in Italy, and which in 1849 made possible the first invasion of Hungary under Windischgrätz. Next to Russia, it is to the South-Slavonian frontier regiments that Francis Joseph owes his throne. In the long stretch of country occupied by them, every crown-tenant (that is almost every inhabitant), is obliged to serve from his twentieth to his fiftieth year, when called upon. The younger men, of course, make up the strength of the regiments; the older men, generally, only take their turns at the frontier guard-houses, until called upon to serve in time of war. This explains how a population of about 1,500,000 to 2,000,000 can furnish a contingent, in case of need, of 150,000 to 170,000 men, or from ten to twelve per cent, of the whole number.

The Austrian army has many points of resemblance to the British army. In both there are many nationalities mixed together, though each regiment, generally, belongs to one nation only. The Highland Gael, the Welshman, the Irishman, and the Englishman, scarcely vary more than the German, the Italian, the Croat, and the Magyar. In either, officers of all races, and even a great many foreigners, are to be found. In either, the theoretical instruction of the officers is extremely defective. In either, the tactical forms have retained a deal of the ancient line-formations, and adopted, in a limited degree only, the use of columns and skirmishing. In either, the dress is of an unusual color: with the English, red, with the Austrians, white. But in the efficiency of their arrangements, in the practical experience and competence of the officers, and in tactical mobility, the Austrians by far surpass the British.

The dress of the soldier, leaving apart the absurd white color of the infantry coat, has been adapted in its cut to the modern system. A short tunic, like the Prussians' sky-blue trowsers, a gray capote, a light képi, similar to the French, make a very good and serviceable dress, excepting, always, the tight trowsers of the Hungarian and Croat regiments, which form part of the national dress, but are, for all that, very inconvenient. The accoutrements are not what they should be; the cross-belt system has been maintained. The frontier troops and artillery are dressed in brown coats; the cavalry, either white, brown or blue. The muskets are rather clumsy, and the rifles, with which both the chasseurs and a certain portion of each company are armed, are of a rather antiquated model, and far inferior to the Minié rifle. The common musket is the old flint gun changed, in an imperfect manner, into a percussion musket, and very often misses fire.

The infantry, and in this respect it is similar to the English, is more distinguished by its action in masses, than by its agility in light infantry service. We must, however, except the frontier troops and the chasseurs. The first are, for the most part, very efficient in skirmishing, especially the Serbians, whose favorite warfare is one of ambuscades. The chasseurs are mainly Tyrolians, and first-rate marksmen. But the German and Hungarian infantry generally impose by their solidity, and, during Napoleon's wars, they often showed that in this respect they deserve to be placed along with the British. They, too, have more than once received cavalry, in line, without deigning to form square, and wherever they have formed squares, the enemy's cavalry could seldom break them up—witness Aspern.[311]

The cavalry is excellent. The heavy or "German" cavalry, consisting of Germans and Bohemians,[a] is well horsed, well armed, and always efficient. The light cavalry has, perhaps, lost by mixing up the German chevau-légers with the Polish lancers, but its Hungarian hussars will always remain the models of all light cavalry.

The artillery, recruited mostly from the German provinces, has always stood high; not so much by early and judicious adoption of improvements, as by the practical efficiency of the men. The non-commissioned officers, especially, are educated with great care, and are superior to those of any other army. With the officers, theoretical proficiency is left too much an optional matter, but yet Austria has produced some of the best writers on the subject. In Austria, study is the rule, at least with subalterns, while in England, an officer who studies his profession is considered a disgrace to his regiment. The special corps, staff, and engineers, are excellent, as is proved by the beautiful maps they have made from their surveys, especially of Lombardy. The British ordnance map, though good, is nothing in comparison.

The great confusion of nationalities is a serious evil. In the British army, every man can at least speak English, but with the Austrians, even the non-commissioned officers of the non-German regiments can scarcely speak German. This creates, of course, a deal of confusion, difficulty, and interpreting, even between the officer and the soldier. It is partly remedied by the necessity in which frequent change of quarters places the officers of learning at least something of every language spoken in Austria. But yet, the inconvenience is not obviated.

The severity of the discipline, which is whacked into the men by frequent applications of a hazel stick to their posteriors, and the long time of service, prevent the outbreak of serious quarrels between the various nationalities of the army, at least in time of peace. But 1848 showed how little internal consistency this body of troops possesses. At Vienna, the German troops refused to fight the revolution. In Italy and Hungary, the national troops passed

[a] Czechs.—*Ed.*

over to the side of the insurgents, without as much as a struggle. Here it is that the weak point of this army lies. Nobody can tell how far or how long it will hold together, or how many regiments will leave it in any peculiar case, to fight their former comrades. There are six different nations, and two or three different creeds, represented in this one army; and, as to the sympathies pervading it, they must necessarily clash in a time like the present, when nations are panting for the free use of their forces. In a war with Russia, would the Greek Catholic Serbian, influenced by Panslavist agitation, fight the Russians, his cousins by race, and holding the same creed as he? In a revolutionary war, would the Italian and Hungarian forsake his country, to battle for an emperor foreign to him in language and nationality? It is not to be expected; and therefore, whatever the strength of the Austrian army may be, very particular circumstances are required to bring its full power into play.

[SECOND ARTICLE]

[*Putnam's Monthly*, No. XXXIII, September 1855]

I. THE PRUSSIAN ARMY

The Prussian army deserves special notice, on account of its peculiar organization. While, in every other army, the peace-footing is the groundwork of the entire establishment, and no cadres are provided for the new formations which a great war at once necessitates, in Prussia, we are told, everything, to the minutest detail, is prepared for the war-footing. Thus, the peace establishment simply forms a school, in which the population are instructed in arms and maneuvers. This system, including, as it professes to do, the whole able-bodied male population in the ranks of the army on the war-footing, would appear to render the country which adopts it safe from every attack; yet this is by no means the case. What is attained is, that the country is stronger by about 50 per cent. than under the French or Austrian system of recruiting; by which means it is possible for an agricultural state of some seventeen millions of inhabitants, on a small territory, without a fleet or direct maritime commerce, and with comparatively little manufacturing industry, to maintain, in some respects, the position of a great European power.

The Prussian army consists of two great divisions: of those soldiers who are still being trained—the line; and of those trained men who may be said to have been sent home on indefinite furlough—the landwehr.

The service in the line lasts five years, from the twentieth to the twenty-fifth year of each man's age; but three years of active service are thought sufficient; after which, the soldier is dismissed to his home, and placed for the remaining two years in what is called the war-reserve. During this time he continues to figure on the reserve-lists of his battalion or squadron, and is liable to be called in at any time.

After having been, for two years, in the war-reserve, he passes into the first levy of the landwehr (*erstes Aufgebot der Landwehr*), where he remains up to his thirty-second year. During this period he is liable to be called in, every other year, for the exercises of this corps, which generally take place upon a pretty extensive scale, and in connection with those of the line. The maneuvers generally last a month, and very often from 50,000 to 60,000 troops are concentrated for this purpose. The landwehr of the first levy are destined to act in the field along with the line. They form separate regiments, battalions, and squadrons, the same as the line, and carry the same regimental numbers. The artillery, however, remain attached to the respective regiments of the line.

From the thirty-second to the thirty-ninth year, inclusive, the soldier remains in the second levy (*zweites Aufgebot*) of the landwehr, during which time he is no longer called upon for active duty, unless a war breaks out, in which case the second levy has to do garrison duty in the fortresses, thus leaving available the whole of the line and first levy for field operations. After the fortieth year, he is free from all liability to be called out, unless, indeed, that mysterious body called the *Landsturm*, or levy *en masse*, be required to arm itself. The landsturm includes every man not comprised in the former categories, with all those too small or too weakly, or otherwise liberated from service, between the sixteenth and sixtieth year of age. But this landsturm cannot even be said to exist on paper, for there is not any organization prepared for it, no arms or accoutrements provided; and if it should ever have to assemble, it would not be found fit for anything but police duty at home, and for a tremendous consumption of strong drink.

As in Prussia every citizen is, according to law, a soldier, from his twentieth to his fortieth year, a population of seventeen millions might be expected to furnish a total contingent of at least a million and a half of men. But, in reality, not one half of this number can be got together. The fact is, that the training of such a mass of men would presuppose, at three years' service with the regiments, a peace establishment of at least 300,000 men, while Prussia merely maintains something like 130,000. Thus various devices are employed to liberate a number of men otherwise liable to serve: men fit enough for duty are declared too weak, the medical inspection either selecting the best candidates only, or allowing itself to be moved by bribes in the selection of those considered fit for duty, and so on. Formerly, the reduction of the time of actual service, for the infantry, to two years only, was the means of bringing down the peace establishment to some 100,000 or 110,000 men; but since the revolution,[a] the government, having found out how much an additional year of service will do in making the men obedient to their officers, and reliable in case of insurrection, the three years' service has been generally introduced again.

The standing army, or the line, is composed of nine army-corps—one of guards and eight of the line. Their peculiar organization will be explained presently. They comprise, in all, thirty-six regiments of infantry (guards and line), of three battalions each[b]; eight regiments of reserve, of two battalions each; eight combined reserve battalions, and ten battalions of chasseurs (*Jäger*); in all, 144 battalions of infantry, or 150,000 men.

The cavalry is composed of ten cuirassier, five dragoon, ten lancer, and thirteen hussar regiments, of four squadrons, or 800 men each; in all, 30,000 men.

The artillery consists of nine regiments, each composed, when on the war-footing, of four six-pounder, three twelve-pounder, and one howitzer, foot batteries, and three batteries of horse artillery, with one reserve company to be turned into a twelfth battery; beside four garrison companies, and one company of workmen. But as the whole of the war reserve and landwehr of the first levy (of the artillery) are required to man these guns, and to complete the companies, the line-artillery may be described as consisting of nine regiments, of about 2,500 men each, with about thirty guns in each regiment, fully horsed and equipped.

Thus, the grand total of the Prussian line would amount to about 200,000 men; but from 60,000 to 70,000 men may safely be deducted for the war reserves, dismissed to their homes after three years' service.

The first levy of the landwehr counts, for every regiment of the guards and line, one of landwehr, except for the eight reserve regiments; beside, it has eight reserve battalions, forming a total of 116 battalions, and about 100,000 men. The cavalry has two regiments of guards, and thirty-two of the line, with eight reserve squadrons; in all, 136 squadrons, or about 20,000 men. The artillery is attached to the line regiments, as before stated.

[a] The revolution of 1848-49.—*Ed.*

[b] Not all regiments in the guards corps consisted of three battalions.—*Ed.*

The second levy also counts 116 battalions, 167 squadrons (comprising sundry reserve and dépôt squadrons, whose duties are assimilated to those of the second levy), and some garrison artillery; altogether, about 150,000 men.

With the nine battalions of sappers, several minor corps, about 30,000 pensioners, and an army train amounting, on the war-footing, to no less than 45,000 men, the whole of the Prussian force is stated to amount to 580,000 men; of which, 300,000 are for the field, 54,000 for the dépôts, 170,000 for the garrisons and as a reserve, with about 60,000 non-combatants. The number of field-guns attached to this army should be between 800 and 850, divided into batteries of eight guns (six cannon and two howitzers) each.

For all these troops, not only the complete organization of the cadres, but also the arms and equipments, are provided; so that, in case of a *mobilization* of the army, nothing has to be found but the horses; and as Prussia is rich in horses, and as animals as well as men are liable to instant requisition, no great difficulty is presented by this necessity. So says the regulation; but how the matter stands, in point of fact, was shown when, in 1850, the army was mobilized. The first levy of the landwehr was equipped, though not without great difficulty; but the second levy found nothing provided, neither clothing, nor shoes, nor arms, and thus it offered the most ridiculous spectacle imaginable. Long before this occurred, competent judges, who had themselves served in the Prussian army, had predicted that such would be the case; and that, in point of fact, Prussia could, on an emergency, count upon nothing but the line and a portion of the first levy. Their opinion was fully borne out by the event. No doubt, the equipments for the second levy have since been provided; and this body, if called out now, would, in a month or six weeks, form a very respectable corps for garrison, and even field duty. But then, in time of war, three months' drill is considered quite sufficient to prepare a recruit for the field; and thus, the cumbrous organization adopted by Prussia does not at all insure such enormous advantages as is generally believed. Beside, in a couple of years, the material reserved for the second levy will again have disappeared in the same way as that which had certainly once existed, but was not to be found when needed in 1850.

Prussia, when adopting the principle that each citizen was to be a soldier, stopped half-way, and falsified that principle, thereby falsifying all her military organization. Once the system of conscription abandoned for that of universal compulsory service, the standing army, as such, ought to have been abolished. Mere cadres of officers and non-commissioned officers should have been maintained, through whose hands the young men should have passed for instruction, and the period of instruction should not have lasted longer than was necessary for the purpose. If such had been the case, the time of service, during peace, must have been brought down to a year, for all the infantry, at least. But that would not suit either the government or the military martinets of the old school. The government wanted a disposable and reliable army, to be used, in case of need, against disturbances at home; the martinets wanted an army which, in precision of drill, in general appearance, and in solidity, could rival the remaining armies of Europe, composed of comparatively older soldiers. A body of young troops, serving no more than a single year, would not do for either purpose. Consequently, the middle course of three years' service was adopted, and hence arise all the faults and weaknesses of the Prussian army.

As we have seen, at least one half of the available men are excluded from the army. They are at once inscribed on the rolls of the second levy, which body, swelled thereby nominally to enormous numbers, is completely swamped, in whatever efficiency it might possess, by a mass of men who never handled a musket, and are no better than raw recruits. This reduction of the actual military strength of the country by at least one half, is the first bad effect produced by the protracted time of service.

But the line itself, and the first levy of the landwehr, suffer under this system. Of every regiment, one third has served less than three, one third less than two years, and the remaining third less than one year. Now it is not to be expected that an army composed like this can have those military qualities, that strict subordination, that steadiness in the ranks, that *esprit de corps,* which distinguish the old soldiers of the English, Austrian, Russian, and even the French armies. The English, who are competent judges in this matter, from the long period their soldiers serve, consider that it takes three years completely to break in a recruit.* Now, as, in time of peace, the Prussian army is composed of men none of whom have ever served three years, the natural consequence is that these military qualities of the old soldier, or at least the semblance of them, have to be drummed into the young Prussian recruit by an intolerable martinetism. The Prussian subaltern and sergeant, from the impossibility of the task

* See Sir W. Napier's *Peninsular War.*

imposed upon them, come to treat their subordinates with a roughness and brutality doubly repulsive from the spirit of pedantry with which it is coupled; and this pedantry is the more ridiculous because it is in complete contrast with the plain and sensible system of drill prescribed, and because it constantly appeals to the traditions of Frederick the Great, who had to drill a quite different set of men in a quite different system of tactics. Thus, real efficiency in the field is sacrificed to precision on the parade-ground, and the Prussian line, upon the whole, may be considered inferior to the old battalions and squadrons which, in the first onset, any of the great European powers can bring forward against it.

This is the case, in spite of advantages of which no other army is possessed. The Prussian, as well as the German in general, makes capital stuff for a soldier. A country, composed of extensive plains varied by large groups of mountains, furnishes material in abundance for every different arm. The general bodily aptitude for both light infantry and line infantry duty, possessed equally by the majority of the Germans, is scarcely equaled by other nations. The country, possessing horses in plenty, furnishes numerous men for the cavalry, who, from their childhood, have been at home in the saddle. The deliberate steadiness of the Germans adapts them especially for the artillery service. They are, withal, among the most pugnacious people in the world, enjoying war for its own sake, and often enough going to look for it abroad, when they cannot have it at home. From the *Landsknechte* of the middle age to the present foreign legions of France and England, the Germans have always furnished the great mass of those mercenaries who fight for the sake of fighting. If the French excel them in agility and vivacity of onslaught, if the English are their superiors in toughness of resistance, the Germans certainly excel all other European nations in that general fitness for military duty which makes them good soldiers under all circumstances.

The Prussian officers form by far the best educated body of their class in the world. The general educational tests to which they are subjected are of a far higher standard than those of any other army. Brigade and divisional schools are maintained to complete their theoretical education; higher or more special military knowledge is provided for by numerous establishments. Prussian military literature holds a very high rank; the works it has furnished for the last twenty-five years sufficiently prove that their authors not only perfectly understood their own business, but could challenge, for general scientific information, the officers of any army. In fact, there is almost too much of a smattering of metaphysics in some of them, and this is explained by the fact that, in Berlin, Breslau, or Königsberg, you may see officers taking their seats amongst the students at the university lectures. Clausewitz is as much a standard author in his line, all over the world, as Jomini; and the works of the engineer Aster mark a new epoch in the science of fortification. Yet, the name of a "Prussian lieutenant" is a by-word all over Germany, and, indeed, the caricatured *esprit de corps*, pedantry and impertinent manners inculcated by the general tone of the army, fully justify the fact; while nowhere are there so many old, stiff-necked martinets among the field-officers and generals as in Prussia—most of them, however, relics of 1813 and '15. After all, it must be acknowledged that the absurd attempt to force the Prussian line into what it can never be made to be—an army of old soldiers—deteriorates the quality of the officer as much as it does that of the soldier, and even more.

The drill-regulations in the Prussian army[a] are, undoubtedly, much the best in the world. Simple, consistent, based upon a few common sense principles, they leave very little to be desired. They are owing to the genius of Scharnhorst, who was, perhaps, the greatest military organizer since Maurice of Nassau. The regulations for handling large bodies of troops are equally good. The scientific manuals, however, for the artillery service, which are officially recommended to the officers, are old-fashioned and by no means up to the requirements of the present time; but this blame is confined to works bearing a more or less official stamp, and does not at all bear upon Prussian artilleristic literature in general.

The engineering body enjoy, and deservedly, a very high character. From them proceeded Aster, the first military engineer since Montalembert. They have constructed a series of fortresses, from Königsberg and Posen to Cologne and Coblentz, which has obtained the admiration of Europe.

The equipment of the Prussian army, since the changes effected in 1843 and '44, is not very handsome, but very convenient for the soldiers. The helmet is a very efficient protection against sun and rain, the clothing is loose and comfortable, the adiustment of the accoutrements still better than that adopted in France. The guards and light battalions (one to each regiment) are armed with the rifled needle-gun; the remainder of the line are having their

[a] [G.J.D. von Scharnhorst,] *Kriegs-Artikel für das Preussische Heer.—Ed.*

muskets transformed, by a very simple process, into good Minié rifles; as to the landwehr, they, too, will, in two or three years, receive the Minié gun, but as yet they carry percussion muskets. The saber of the cavalry is too broad and crooked—most of the cuts fall flat. The material of the artillery, both in cannon, carriages, and harness, leave much to be desired.

On the whole, the Prussian army, that is, the line and first levy, forms a respectable body of men, but nothing like what Prussian patriotic authors boast. The line, once in the field, will very soon throw off the fetters of the parade-ground, and, after a few engagements, be equal to their opponents. The landwehr of the first levy, as soon as the old soldier-like spirit has been re-awakened, and if the war be popular, will equal the best old troops in Europe. What Prussia has to fear, is an active enemy during the first period of a war, when troops of superior organization, and of older standing, are brought against her; but in a protracted struggle she will have a greater proportion of old soldiers in her armies than any other European state. In the beginning of a campaign, the line will form the nucleus of the army, but the first levy will very soon push it into the shade, by the greater bodily strength and the higher military qualities of its men. They are the real old soldiers of Prussia—not the beardless youths of the line. Of the second levy we do not speak; it has yet to show what it is.

II. THE RUSSIAN ARMY

In Russia, too, a certain provision has been made for establishing cadres for the war-footing, by a scheme of reserves, similar, in some points, to the Prussian landwehr system. But, on the whole, the Russian reserve comprises such a limited number of men, and the difficulty of bringing them together from all the points of that vast empire is so great, that, as early as six months after the Anglo-French declaration of war,[a] and before a single shot had been fired in the Crimea, the abolition of the system and the formation of new bodies, followed up since by other new formations, at once became necessary. Thus, in Russia, we must distinguish between the army as it was on the breaking out of the war, and the army as it is now.

---

[a] Britain and France officially declared war on Russia on March 27 and 28, 1854, respectively.—*Ed.*

The Russian army, in time of peace, is divided as follows:—1. The active army—six corps of the line, Nos. 1 to 6; 2. The reserve army—one corps of guards, one corps of grenadiers, two corps of cavalry of the reserve; 3. The special corps—that of the Caucasus, that of Finland, that of Orenburg, that of Siberia; 4. The troops for inland duty—veterans, inland guards, invalids, and so forth; 5. The irregular troops. To these must be added the reserves, consisting of soldiers dismissed on furlough.

The composition of each of the six corps of the line is as follows:—it includes three divisions of infantry, consisting each of a brigade of the line and one of light infantry, each brigade consisting of two regiments, each regiment of four service-battalions; in all, six brigades or twelve regiments, comprising forty-eight battalions, with one battalion of rifles, and one of sappers; total, fifty battalions. There is also one division of light cavalry, containing one brigade of lancers, and one brigade of hussars, each of two regiments, or sixteen squadrons; total, thirty-two squadrons. The artillery consists of one division [of artillery] of three foot brigades, and one horse brigade; total, fourteen batteries or 112 guns; total, per corps, fifty battalions, thirty-two squadrons, 112 guns; grand total, 300 battalions, 192 squadrons, 672 guns.

The guards contain three divisions, or six brigades, comprising twelve regiments (nine of grenadiers, and three of carabineers, or light infantry); in all, thirty-six battalions, for the regiments of guards and grenadiers count three service-battalions only. There is also one battalion of rifles and one of sappers and miners, beside three divisions of cavalry (one cuirassiers, one lancers, one hussars), comprising six brigades or twelve regiments, and making in all seventy-two squadrons of cavalry. There is one division of five brigades and fifteen batteries (nine foot, five horse, one rockets); in all, 135 guns. The grenadier corps consists of three divisions or six brigades, comprising twelve regiments or thirty-six battalions of infantry, one battalion of rifles, and one of sappers and miners. This corps also counts one division of cavalry, including two brigades (lancers and hussars), made up of four regiments or thirty-two squadrons. The artillery consists of three foot and one horse brigade, with fourteen batteries; in all, 112 guns.

The reserve cavalry is organized as follows:—1st corps: three divisions (two of cuirassiers, one of lancers), comprising six brigades or twelve regiments; in all, eighty squadrons (forty-eight of cuirassiers, thirty-two of lancers). There is also one division of horse artillery, containing three brigades, with six batteries; in all, forty-eight guns.—2d corps: three divisions (one lancers, two dragoons) or six brigades; including twelve regiments or 112 squadrons (thirty-two of lancers, eighty of dragoons). There are also two squadrons of mounted sappers and pontoniers, and six batteries of horse artillery, comprising forty-eight guns.

The Caucasian corps is composed of one reserve grenadier brigade, containing two regiments or six battalions; three divisions of infantry, containing twelve regiments or forty-eight battalions; one battalion of rifles, one of sappers; forty-seven battalions of the Caucasian line (militia); total, 103 battalions. The cavalry consists of one regiment of dragoons, of ten squadrons. Of artillery there is one division, with ten common and six mountain batteries, of 180 guns in all.

The Finland corps consists of one division, comprising two brigades or twelve battalions of infantry; that of Orenburg, of one division, likewise of two brigades, but of only ten battalions; that of Siberia, of one division, comprising three brigades; making fifteen battalions. Finally, the grand total of the regular troops, actually under arms in time of peace, may be stated as follows:—

	Battal.	Squad.	Guns.
6 corps of the line	300	192	672
Guards	38	72	135
Grenadiers	38	32	112
Reserve cavalry	—	194	96
Caucasian corps	103	10	180
Finland corps	12	—	—
Orenburg do.	10	—	—
Siberia do.	15	—	—
Total	516	500	1,195

The troops for inland service consist of fifty-two battalions of inland guards, 800 companies of veterans and invalids, eleven and a half squadrons of gens d'armes, and ninety-eight companies of artillery. These troops can hardly be counted in an estimate of the available force of the country.

The irregular troops, mostly cavalry, form the following divisions:—

1. The Don Cossacks:—fifty-six regiments, each of six sotnias; in all, 336 sotnias, thirteen batteries.

2. The Tshornomor (Black Sea Cossacks):—seventy-two sotnias, nine battalions, three batteries.

3. The Caucasian line Cossacks (on the Kuban and Terek):—120 sotnias and three batteries.

4. The Astrachan Cossacks:—eighteen sotnias, one battery.

5. The Orenburg Cossacks:—sixty sotnias, three batteries.

6. The Ural Cossacks:—sixty sotnias.

7. The Bashkir levy:—eighty-five sotnias, almost all Bashkirs and Kalmyks.

8. The Siberian Cossacks:—twenty-four battalions, eighty-four sotnias, three batteries, composed partly of Tungusians, Buriates, &c.

9. The Azov Cossacks, engaged in naval service.

10. The Danubian Cossacks in Bessarabia: twelve sotnias.

11. The Baikal Lake Cossacks, but recently formed, of unknown organization and strength.

The total would amount to 847 sotnias (squadrons of 100 men each, from *sto*, hundred), thirty-three battalions, twenty-six batteries. This would make about 90,000 men of cavalry, and 30,000 infantry. But, for actual war purposes on the western frontier, perhaps 40,000 to 50,000 cavalry, a few batteries, and none of the infantry are available.

Thus, in time of peace, the Russian army (exclusive of the inland service troops) should consist of 360,000 infantry, 70,000 cavalry, and 90,000 artillery; in all, 500,000 men; beside a number of Cossacks, varying according to circumstances. But of these 500,000 men, the local corps of the Caucasus, of Orenburg, and Siberia cannot be made available for any war on the western frontier of the empire; so that, against western Europe, not more than 260,000 infantry, 70,000 cavalry, and 50,000 artillery, with about 1,000 guns, can be used, beside some 30,000 Cossacks.

So far for the peace establishment. For the event of a war, the following provisions were made: the full time of service was twenty, twenty-two, or twenty-five years, according to circumstances. But after either ten or fifteen years, according to circumstances, the soldiers were dismissed on furlough, after which they belonged to the reserve. The organization of this reserve has varied very much, but it appears, now, that the men on furlough belonged, during the first five years, to a reserve battalion (the fourth of each regiment in the guards and grenadiers, the fifth in the line), a reserve squadron, or a reserve battery, according to their respective arms. After the lapse of five years they passed to the dépôt (fifth or respectively sixth) battalion of their regiment, or to the dépôt squadron or battery. Thus, the calling-in of the reserve would raise the effective strength of the infantry and artillery about fifty per cent., of the cavalry about twenty per cent. These reserves were to be commanded by retired officers, and their cadres, if not in full organization, were nevertheless, to a certain degree, prepared.

But when the war broke out, all this was altered. The active army had to send two divisions to the Caucasus, though it was destined to fight on the western frontier. Before the Anglo-French troops embarked for the east, three corps of the active army (the third, fourth, and fifth) were engaged in the campaign against the Turks. At that period, indeed, the reserves were concentrating, but it took an enormous length of time before the men could be brought up to their respective headquarters from all points of the empire. The allied armies and fleets in the Baltic and Black Seas, as well as the wavering policy of Austria, necessitated more vigorous measures; the levies were doubled and tripled, and the motley mass of recruits, thus got together, were formed, along with the reserves, into fourth, fifth, sixth, seventh, and eighth battalions for all the infantry regiments, while a similar increase was made in the cavalry. Thus, the eight corps of guards, grenadiers, and line, instead of 376 battalions, now muster about 800, while, for every two squadrons or batteries of the peace establishment, at least one of reserve has been added. All these figures, however, look more formidable on paper than in reality; for, what with the corruption of the Russian officials, the mal-administration of the army, and the enormous length of the marches from the homes of the men to the dépôts, from the dépôts to the points of concentration of the corps, and from thence to the seat of war, a great proportion of the men are lost or invalided before they come to meet the enemy. Besides, the ravages of disease, and the losses in battle, during the two last campaigns, have been very serious, and, altogether, we do not think that the 1,000 battalions, 800 squadrons, and 200 batteries of the Russian army, can much exceed, at present, 600,000 men.

But the government was not satisfied with this. With a promptitude which shows how fully it is aware of the difficulty of bringing together large masses of men from the various portions of this vast empire, it decreed the levy of the militia as soon as the organization of the seventh and eighth battalions was completed. The militia, or *opoltshenie*, was to be organized in *druginas* (battalions) of 1,000 each, in proportion to the population of each province; twenty-three men out of every 1,000 males, or nearly one-quarter per cent. of the population were to serve. For the time being, the opoltshenie was called out in the western provinces only. This levy, made upon a population of 18,000,000, comprising about 9,000,000 males, must have produced about 120,000 men, and this agrees with what the reports from Russia state. There is no doubt that the militia will prove, in every respect, inferior even to the newly formed reserve, but, at all events, it is a valuable addition to the forces of Russia, and, if employed to do garrison duty in Poland, it can set free a good many regiments of the line.

On the other hand, not only many Cossacks, but even considerable numbers of Bashkirs, Kalmyks, Kirghiz, Tungusians, and other Mongol levies have arrived on the western frontier. This shows how early they were ordered westwards, for many of them had above a twelve-month's march to make before they could arrive at St. Petersburg, or on the Vistula.

Thus, Russia has taxed her military resources almost to the utmost; and, after two years' campaigning, during which time she has lost no decisive battle, she cannot muster more than 600,000 to 650,000 regular troops, with 100,000 militia, and perhaps 50,000 irregular cavalry. We do not mean to say that she is exhausted; but, there is no doubt, that now, after two years' war, she could not do what France did after twenty years' war, and after the total loss of her finest army in 1812: pour forth a fresh body of 300,000 men and arrest, for a time, at least, the onslaught of the enemy. So enormous is the difference, in military strength, between a densely and a thinly populated country. If France bordered on Russia, the 66,000,000 inhabitants of Russia would be weaker than the 38,000,000 French. That the 44,000,000 Germans are more than a match for the 66,000,000 subjects of the orthodox Czar, there is not the slightest doubt.

The Russian army is recruited in various ways. The great body of the men is raised by the regular levy, which takes place one year in the western, and the next in the eastern provinces of Russia in Europe. The general percentage is four or five men levied out of every 1,000 (male) "souls;" for in the Russian census the males only are counted, as, according to the orthodox belief of the east, the women do not constitute "souls." Those from the western half of the empire serve twenty, those from the eastern half twenty-five years. The guards serve twenty-two years; young men from the military colonies twenty years. Beside these levies, the soldiers' sons are a fertile source of recruits. Every son born to a soldier while in service is obliged to serve; and this principle is carried so far that children borne by soldiers' wives are claimed by the state, though the husband may have been at the other end of the empire for five or ten years. These soldiers' children are called *cantonists*, and most of them are educated at the expense of the government; from them most of the non-commissioned officers are taken. Finally, criminals, vagabonds, and other good-for-nothing individuals, are sentenced, by the courts of law, to serve in the army. A nobleman has the right of sending a serf, if otherwise able-bodied, into the army; and every father, when dissatisfied with his son, can do the same. "*S'bogom idi pod Krasnuyu shapkoo.*" Begone, then, with God, and put the red cap on—that is to say, go into the army—is a common saying of the Russian peasant to a disobedient son.

The non-commissioned officers, as we have said, are mostly recruited from the soldiers' sons, educated in government establishments. From early boyhood subject to military discipline, these lads have nothing whatever in common with the men whom they are, subsequently, to instruct and direct. They form a class separate from the people. They belong to the state—they cannot exist without it: once thrown upon their own resources, they are fit for nothing. To get on, then, under the government, is their only object. What the lower class of employés, recruited from the sons of employés, are in the Russian civil service, these men are in the army: a set of cunning, low-minded, narrowly-egotistical subordinates, endowed with a smattering of elementary education, which almost renders them more despicable; ambitious from vanity and love of gain; sold, life and soul, to the state, and yet trying, daily and hourly, to sell the state, in detail, whenever they can make a profit by it. A fine specimen of this class is the feldjäger or courier who accompanied M. de Custine during his travels in Russia, and who is admirably portrayed in that gentleman's account of Russia.[a] It is this class of men, both in the civil and military branches, which principally foments the immense corruption pervading all branches of the public service in that country. But as it is, there is no doubt that, if this system of total appropriation of the children, by the state, were done away with, Russia would not be able to find a sufficient number of civil subaltern employés and military non-commissioned officers.

With the class of officers it is, perhaps, still worse. The education given to a future corporal or sergeant-major is a comparatively cheap article; but to educate officers for an army of one million (and that is the number for which the Russian cadres, officially speaking, should be prepared) is a costly affair. Private

[a] A. de Custine, *La Russie en 1839*, T. IV, pp. 283-85.—*Ed.*

establishments do nothing or little for the purpose. The state, again, must do everything. But it evidently cannot educate such a mass of young men as are required for this use. Consequently, the sons of the nobility are, by a direct moral compulsion, induced to serve for at least five or ten years in the army or the civil service; for every family in which three consecutive generations have not "served," loses its privilege of nobility, and especially the right to own serfs—a right without which, in Russia, extensive landed property is worse than valueless. Thus, vast numbers of young men are brought into the army with the rank of ensign or lieutenant, whose entire education consists, at the best, in a certain fluency in French conversation on the most ordinary topics, and some little smattering of elementary mathematics, geography and history—the whole drummed into them for mere show. To them, to serve is an ugly necessity, to be gone through, like a prolonged medical treatment, with unfeigned disgust; and as soon as the prescribed time of service has elapsed, or the grade of major is attained, they retire, and are inscribed on the rolls of the dépôt battalions. As to the pupils of the military schools, they, too, have almost all been crammed so as to pass the examinations; and they are, even in mere professional knowledge, far behind the young men from the Austrian, the Prussian, or French military schools. On the other hand, young men of talent, application, and passion for their special branch, are so rare in Russia that they are seized upon wherever they show themselves, be they foreigners or natives. With the greatest liberality, the state provides them with all the means for completing their studies, and gives them rapid promotion. Such men are used to show off Russian civilization before Europe. If they are inclined to literary pursuits, they meet with every encouragement so long as they do not overstep the bounds of Russian government requirements, and it is they who have furnished what little there is of value in Russian military literature. But up to the present time, the Russians of all classes are too fundamentally barbarous to find any enjoyment in scientific pursuits or head-work of any kind (except intrigues), and, therefore, almost all their distinguished men in the military service are either foreigners, or, what nearly amounts to the same, "ostzeïski," Germans from the Baltic provinces. So was the last and most distinguished specimen of this class, General Todtleben, the chief engineer at Sebastopol, who died in July from the effects of a wound.[312] He was certainly the cleverest man at his trade in the whole siege, either in the Russian or the Allied camp; but he was a Baltic German, of Prussian extraction.

In this manner the Russian army has among its officers the very best and the very worst men, only that the former are present in an infinitesimally small proportion. What the Russian government thinks of its officers it has plainly and unmistakably shown in its own tactical regulations. These regulations do not merely prescribe a general mode of placing a brigade, division, or army-corps in action, a so-called "normal disposition," which the commander is expected to vary according to the ground and other circumstances, but they prescribe different normal dispositions for all the different cases possible, leaving the general no choice whatever, and tying him down in a manner which, as much as possible, takes all responsibility from his shoulders. An army-corps, for instance, can be arranged, in battle, in five different ways, according to the regulations; and, at the Alma, the Russians were actually arrayed according to one of them—the third disposition—and, of course, they were beaten. This mania of prescribing abstract rules for all possible cases, leaves so little liberty of action to the commander, and even forbids him to use advantages of ground to such an extent, that a Prussian general in criticising it says:

> "Such a system of regulations can be tolerated in an army, only, the majority of whose generals are so imbecile, that the government cannot safely intrust them with an unconditional command, or leave them to their own judgment."

The Russian soldier is one of the bravest men in Europe. His tenacity almost equals that of the English and of certain Austrian battalions. As John Bull boasts of himself, he does not know when he is beaten. Russian squares of infantry have resisted, and fought hand to hand, a long while after the cavalry had broken them; and it has always been found easier to shoot them down than to drive them back. Sir George Cathcart, who saw them in 1813 and '14,[a] as allies, and in 1854 in the Crimea, as enemies, gives them the honorable testimonial that they are "incapable of panic." Beside this, the Russian soldier is well made, healthy, a good marcher, a man of few wants, who can eat and drink almost anything, and more obedient to his officers than any other soldier in the world. And yet the Russian army is not much to boast of. Never, since Russia was Russia, have the Russians won a single battle against either Germans, French, Poles, or English, without being vastly superior in numbers. At even odds, they have always been beaten by any army, except Turks or Prussians; and at Citate

---

[a] G. Cathcart, *Commentaries on the War in Russia and Germany in 1812 and 1813.—Ed.*

and Silistria,[313] the Turks, though inferior in numbers, defeated them.

The Russians are, above all things, the clumsiest soldiers in the world. They are not fit either for light infantry or for light cavalry duty. The Cossacks, capital light cavalry as they are in some respects, are so unreliable generally, that before the enemy a second line of out-posts is always placed in the rear of the line of Cossack out-posts. Beside, the Cossacks are totally unfit for a charge. As to the regular troops, infantry and cavalry, they are not fit to act in skirmishing order. The Russian, imitator as he is in everything, will do anything if ordered or compelled, but will do nothing if he has to act upon his own responsibility; in fact, this term can hardly be applied to a being who never knew what responsibility was, and who will go to be shot at with the same passive obedience as if he were ordered to pump water, or to whip a comrade. To expect from the Russian soldier, when acting on out-post duty or in skirmishing order, the rapid glance of the Frenchman, or the plain common sense of the German, would be an insult to him. What he requires is command—clear, distinct command—and if he does not get it, he will perhaps not go backwards, but he will certainly not go forwards, nor use his own senses.

The cavalry, though a deal of expense and care has been bestowed upon it, has never been excellent. Neither in the wars against the French, nor in that against Poland, did the cavalry distinguish itself. The passive, patient, enduring obedience of the Russians is not what is wanted in cavalry. The first quality of the horseman is just what the Russian lacks most: "*dash*." Thus, when the 600 English dragoons, with all the daring and pluck of real horsemen, dashed at the numerically far superior Russians at Balaklava, they rode down before them Russian artillery, Cossacks, hussars, lancers, until they came to the solid columns of the infantry; then they had to turn back; yet, in that cavalry action, it is still doubtful who deserves to be called the victor. If such a senseless charge had been made against any other army, not a man would have returned; the enemy would have taken them in flank and rear, and cut them down singly. But the Russian horsemen actually awaited them standing, and were ridden down before they thought of moving their horses! Surely, if anything should condemn the Russian regular cavalry, it is such a fact as this.

The artillery is provided with a material of unequal quality, but where it has good guns, it will do its duty well. It will display great bravery in the field, but it will always be found wanting in intelligence. A Russian battery which has lost its officers is good for nothing; and while the officers live, it can only take the positions, often absurd, prescribed by the regulations. When besieged in a fortress where patient endurance and constant exposure to danger are required, the Russian artillery will distinguish itself, not so much by precision of aim, as by devotion to duty and steadiness under fire. The whole of the siege of Sebastopol proves this.

In the artillery and engineers, however, are to be found those well-educated officers whom Russia shows off before Europe, and who are really encouraged to use their talents freely. While in Prussia, for instance, the best men, when subalterns, have usually been so thwarted by their superiors, and while all their proposed improvements have been snubbed as presumptuous attempts at innovation, so that many of them have had to seek employment in Turkey, where they have made the regular artillery one of the best in Europe—in Russia, all such men are encouraged, and, if they distinguish themselves, make a rapid and brilliant career. Diebitsch and Paskiewitsch were generals at twenty-nine and thirty years of age, and Todtleben, at Sebastopol, in less than eight months was advanced from a captain to a major-general.

The great boast of the Russians is their infantry. It is of very great solidity, and, used in line or column, or behind breastworks, will always be awkward to deal with. But here its good qualities end. Almost totally unfit for light infantry duty (the so-called chasseurs are light infantry in name only, and the eight battalions of rifles attached to the line corps are the only real light infantry in the service), usually bad marksmen, good but slow marchers, their columns are generally so badly placed that it will always be possible to pound them well with artillery before they are charged. The "normal dispositions," from which the generals dare not deviate, contribute a great deal toward this. At the Alma, for instance, the British artillery made terrible havoc amongst the Russian columns long before the equally clumsy British line had formed, defiled across the river and re-formed for the charge. But even the boast of solid tenacity must be taken with a considerable grain of salt, since at Inkermann 8,000 British infantry, surprised in a position but incompletely and slovenly occupied, resisted, in hand to hand fight, the 15,000 Russians brought against them for more than four hours, and actually repelled every renewed attack. This battle must have shown the Russians that, upon their own favorite ground, they had found their masters. It was the bravery of the British soldiers and the intelligence and presence of mind of both non-commissioned officers and soldiers which defeated all the attempts of the Russians; and from this battle we must consider as justified, the claim of the British to the title of the first infantry *of the line* in the world.

The clothing of the Russian army is a pretty close imitation of that of the Prussians. Their accoutrements are very badly adjusted; not only the belts for bayonets and cartridge pouch are crossed over the chest, but also the straps which hold the knapsack. There are, however, some alterations being made just now, but whether they affect this point, we do not know. The small arms are very clumsy, and have only been lately provided with percussion caps; a Russian musket is the heaviest and most unwieldy thing of its kind. The cavalry swords are of a bad model and badly tempered. Of the guns, the new ones taken in the Crimea, are described as very good and of excellent workmanship; but whether that is uniformly the case is very doubtful.

Finally, the Russian army still bears the stamp of an institution in advance of the general state of civilization of the country, and has all the disadvantages and drawbacks of such hot-house creations. In petty warfare, the Cossacks are the only troops to be feared, from their activity and indefatigability; but their love of drink and plunder makes them very unreliable for their commander. In grand war, the slowness with which the Russians move will make their strategic maneuvers little to be feared, unless they have to deal with such negligent opponents as the English were last autumn. In a pitched battle, they will be obstinate opponents to the soldiers, but not very troublesome to the generals who attack them. Their dispositions are generally very simple, founded upon their prescribed normal rules, and easy to be guessed at; while the want of intelligence in both general and field officers, and the clumsiness of the troops, make it a matter of great risk for them to undertake important maneuvers on a battle field.

III. THE SMALLER ARMIES OF GERMANY

Bavaria has two army-corps, of two divisions each. Each division contains two brigades of infantry (four regiments of infantry and one battalion of rifles), one brigade of cavalry, containing two regiments, and three foot and one horse batteries. Each army-corps has, beside, a general reserve of artillery, of six foot batteries, and a detachment of sappers and miners. Thus, the whole army forms sixteen regiments of three battalions each, with six battalions of rifles, in all, fifty-four battalions; two regiments of cuirassiers, and six of light dragoons, in all, forty-eight squadrons; two regiments of foot artillery (of six six-pounder and six twelve-pounder batteries each), and one of horse artillery (four six-pounder batteries), in all, twenty-eight batteries of eight guns each, making 224 guns, beside six companies of garrison artillery, and twelve train companies; there are also one regiment of engineers, of eight companies, and two sanitary companies. The whole strength, on the war-footing, is 72,000 men, beside a reserve and landwehr, the cadres of which, however, do not exist.

Of the army of the Germanic Confederation,[314] Austria furnishes the 1st, 2d, and 3d corps; Prussia the 4th, 5th, and 6th; Bavaria the 7th. The 8th corps is furnished by Württemberg, Baden, and Hesse-Darmstadt.

Württemberg has eight regiments (sixteen battalions) of infantry, four of cavalry (sixteen squadrons), one regiment of artillery (four foot and three horse-batteries, with forty-eight guns). Total, about 19,000 men on the war-footing.

Baden keeps four regiments (eight battalions), two fusileer battalions, one rifle battalion; in all, ten battalions of infantry, with three regiments, or twelve squadrons of cavalry, and four foot and five horse-batteries, containing together forty guns. Total, on the war-footing, 15,000 men.

Hesse-Darmstadt has four regiments or eight battalions of infantry, one regiment or six squadrons of light horse, and three batteries of artillery (one mounted) of eighteen guns. Total, 10,000 men.

The only peculiarity of the 7th and 8th army-corps is, that they have adopted the French gun-carriage for the artillery. The 9th federal army corps is formed by the kingdom of Saxony, which furnishes one division, and Electoral Hesse and Nassau, which furnish the second.

The quota of Saxony is four brigades of infantry, of four battalions each, and one of rifles, of four battalions; beside four battalions of the line, and one battalion of rifles as a reserve, still unorganized; four regiments of light horse, of five squadrons each; one artillery regiment, six foot and two horse-batteries. Total, twenty battalions of infantry, twenty squadrons and fifty guns; or 24,500 men on the war-footing. In Electoral Hesse there are four regiments or eight battalions, with one battalion of fusileers and one of rifles; two squadrons of cuirassiers, seven squadrons of hussars; three batteries, of which one of horse artillery. Total, ten battalions, nine squadrons, nineteen guns, and 12,000 men on the war-footing. Nassau affords seven battalions, 2 batteries, or 7,000 men, and twelve guns, on the war-footing.

The 10th army-corps consists of Hanover and Brunswick, which maintain the first division; and of Mecklenburg, Holstein, Oldenburg, and the Hanse towns,[a] which furnish the second division. Hanover furnishes eight regiments or sixteen battalions, and four battalions of light infantry; six regiments or twenty-four squadrons of cavalry, and four foot and two horse-batteries. Total, 22,000 men, and thirty-six guns. The artillery is on the English model. Brunswick furnishes five battalions, four squadrons, and twelve guns, in all, 5,300 men. The small States of the second division are not worth mentioning.

Finally, the smallest of the small fry of German States form a reserve division, with which the entire army of the German Confederation, on the war-footing, may be summed up in a table, as follows:—

	I. CONTINGENTS.				II. RESERVE CONTINGENTS.			
	Inf.	Cav.	G'ns	Total.	Inf.	Cav.	G'ns	Total.
Austria,	73,501	13,546	192	94,822	36,750	6,773	96	47,411
Prussia,	61,629	11,355	160	79,484	30,834	5,660	80	39,742
Bavaria,	27,566	5,086	72	35,600	13,793	2,543	36	17,800
Eighth Corps,	23,369	4,308	60	30,150	11,685	2,154	32	15,075
Ninth Corps,	19,294	2,887	50	24,254	9,702	1,446	25	12,136
Tenth Corps,	22,246	3,572	58	28,067	11,107	1,788	29	14,019
Reserve Division,	11,116			11,116	5,584			5,584
Total,	238,721	40,754	592	303,493	119,455	20,364	298	151,767

This of course does not represent the real armed force of the Confederation, as, in case of need, Prussia, Austria, and Bavaria would furnish far more than the above contingents. The troops of the 10th corps and reserve division, perhaps, also, those of the 9th corps, would form the garrisons, so as not to interfere, by their

[a] The free cities of Bremen, Hamburg and Lübeck.—*Ed.*

multifarious organizations and peculiarities, with the rapidity of field operations. The military qualities of these armies are more or less the same as those of the Austrian and Prussian soldiers; but, of course, these small bodies furnish no occasion for developing military talents, and many old-fashioned arrangements exist among them.

In a third and concluding article, we shall consider the Spanish, Sardinian, Turkish and other armies of Europe.

[THIRD ARTICLE]

[*Putnam's Monthly*, No. XXXVI, December 1855]

I. THE TURKISH ARMY

The Turkish army, at the beginning of the present war, was in a higher state of efficiency than it had ever reached before. The various attempts at reorganization and reform made since the accession of Mahmud, since the massacre of the Janissaries, and especially since the peace of Adrianople, had been consolidated and systematized.[315] The first and greatest obstacle—the independent position of the pashas in command of distant provinces—had been removed, to a great extent, and, upon the whole, the pashas were reduced to a discipline somewhat approaching that of European district commanders. But their ignorance, insolence, and rapacity remained in as full vigor as in the best days of Asiatic satrap rule; and if, for the last twenty years, we had heard little of revolts of pashas, we have heard enough of provinces in revolt against their greedy governors, who, originally the lowest domestic slaves and "men of all work," profited by their new position to heap up fortunes by exactions, bribes, and wholesale embezzlement of the public money. That, under such a state of things, the organization of the army must, to a great extent, exist on paper only, is evident.

The Turkish army consists of the regular active army (Nizam), the reserve (Redif), the irregular troops, and the auxiliary corps of the vassal states.

The Nizam is composed of six corps (Orders), each of which is raised in the district it occupies, similar to the army-corps in Prussia, each of which is located in the province from which it recruits itself. Altogether the organization of the Turkish Nizam and Redif is, as we shall see, copied from the Prussian model. The six Orders have their head-quarters in Constantinople, Shumla, Toli-Monatzir, Erzeroum, Bagdad, and Aleppo. Each of them should be commanded by a Mushir (field marshal), and should consist of two divisions or six brigades, formed by six regiments of infantry, four of cavalry, and one of artillery.

The infantry and cavalry are organized upon the French, the artillery upon the Prussian system.

A regiment of infantry is composed of four battalions of eight companies each, and should count, when on its full complement, 3,250 men, inclusive of officers and staff, or 800 men per battalion; the general strength, however, before the war, seldom exceeded 700 men, and in Asia was almost always much less.

A cavalry regiment consists of four squadrons of lancers, and two squadrons of chasseurs, each squadron to contain 151 men; in general, the effective strength was here even more below the standard than in the infantry.

Each artillery regiment consists of six horse and nine foot batteries, of four guns each, thus representing a total of sixty guns.

Every order was thus expected to number 19,500 infantry, 3,700 cavalry, and sixty guns. In reality, however, from 20,000 to 21,000 men in all is the utmost ever reached.

Beside the six Orders, there are four artillery regiments (one of reserve, and three of garrison artillery), two regiments of sappers and miners, and three special detachments of infantry sent to Candia, to Tunis, and Tripoli, of a total strength of 16,000 men.

The total strength of the Nizam, or regular standing army, before the war, should, therefore, have been as follows:

36	reg. of infant. averaging	2,500—	90,000
24	" cavalry "	660-670—	16,000
7	" field artillery		9,000
3	" garrison "		3,400
2	" sappers and miners		1,600
Detached corps			16,000
			136,000

The soldiers, after having served five years in the Nizam, are dismissed to their homes, and form, for the seven following years, part of the Redif or reserve. This reserve counts as many orders, divisions, brigades, regiments, etc., as the standing army; in fact, it is to the Nizam what in Prussia the first levy of the landwehr is to the line, with the sole exception, that in Prussia, in larger masses than brigades, line and landwehr are always mixed, while in the Turkish organization they are to be kept separate. The officers and non-commissioned officers of the Redif are constantly assembled at the dépôts, and once a year the Redif are called in for exercise, during which time, they receive the same pay and rations as the line. But such an organization, presupposing a well-regulated civil administration, and a civilized state of society, far from having been reached in Turkey, must in a great degree exist on paper only, and if we count, therefore, the Redif as equal in numbers to the Nizam, we shall certainly put it down at its highest possible figure.

The auxiliary contingents consist of troops from:

1. The Danubian Principalities,	6,000	men.
2. Servia,	20,000	"
3. Bosnia and Herzegovina,	30,000	"
4. Upper Albania,	10,000	"
5. Egypt,	40,000	"
6. Tunis and Tripoli,	10,000	"
Total, about	116,000	"

To these troops must be added the volunteer Bashi Bazouks, whom Asia Minor, Kurdistan, and Syria can furnish in great numbers. They are the last remnant of that host of irregular troops which, in past centuries, flooded Hungary, and twice appeared before Vienna.[316] Mostly cavalry, their inferiority, even to the worst-equipped European horseman, has been proved by two centuries of all but constant defeats. Their self-confidence has disappeared, and now they serve no other purpose than to swarm around the army, eating up and wasting the resources upon which the regular body should subsist. Their love of plunder and unreliable temper make them even unfit for that active outpost duty which the Russians expect from their Cossacks; for the Bashi Bazouks, when most wanted, are least to be found. In this present war, it has, therefore, been found desirable to keep their numbers down, and we do not think that there were ever collected more than 50,000 of them.

Thus the numerical strength of the Turkish army, at the beginning of the war, may be estimated as follows:

Nizam,	136,000
Redif,	136,000
Auxiliaries, regulars from Egypt and Tunis,	50,000
Do. irregulars, Bosnia and Albania,	40,000
Bashi Bazouks,	50,000
Total,	412,000

But again, from this sum total several deductions have to be made. That the Orders stationed in Europe were in pretty good condition, and as near their full complement as can be expected in Turkey, seems pretty certain; but in Asia, in the distant provinces where the Mussulman population predominates, the men might be ready, while neither arms, nor equipments, nor stores of ammunition were forthcoming. The Danubian army was formed from the three European Orders principally. They were the nucleus around which the European Redifs, the Order of Syria, or, at least, a good part of it, and a number of Arnauts,[a] Bosnians, and Bashi Bazouks were collected. Yet the excessive caution of Omer Pasha—his constant unwillingness up to the present time to expose his troops in the field—is the best proof that he has but a limited confidence in the capabilities of this, the only good regular army Turkey ever possessed. But in Asia, where the old Turkish system of embezzlement and laziness was still in full blossom, the two Orders of the Nizam, the whole of the Redifs, and the mass of the irregulars were unable to withstand a Russian army vastly inferior in numbers; in every battle they were beaten, and, at the end of the campaign of 1854, the Asiatic army of Turkey had all but ceased to exist. There, then, it is clear that not only the details of the organization, but a great proportion of the troops themselves had no real existence. The want of arms, equipments, ammunition, and provisions, was the constant complaint of the foreign officers and newspaper correspondents in Kars and Erzeroum; and they plainly stated that nothing but the indolence, incapacity, and rapacity of the Pashas was the cause of it. The money was duly sent to them, but they always appropriated it to their own uses.

[a] Turkish name for Albanians.—*Ed.*

The equipment of the Turkish regular soldier is on the whole imitated from the western armies, the only distinction being the red fez or skull-cap, which is about the worst head-gear possible in that climate, where, during the heats of summer, it causes frequent sun-strokes. The quality of the articles furnished is bad, and the clothing has to stand longer than can be expected, in consequence of the officers generally pocketing the money destined for its renewal. The arms are of an inferior description, both for the infantry and cavalry; the artillery alone has very good field-guns, cast at Constantinople, under the direction of European officers and civil engineers.

The Turk, in himself, is not a bad soldier. He is naturally brave, extremely hardy and patient, and, under certain circumstances, docile. European officers who have once gained his confidence, can rely upon him, as witness Grach and Butler at Silistria, and Iskender Bey (Ilinski) in Wallachia. But these are exceptions. On the whole, the innate hatred of the Turk for the "Giaour" is so indelible, and his habits and ideas are so different from those of a European, that, so long as his remains the ruling race in the country, he will not submit to men whom he inwardly despises as incommensurably his inferiors. This repugnance is extended to the very organization of the army, ever since it has been put upon a European footing. The common Turk hates Giaour institutions as much as the Giaours themselves. Then the strict discipline, the regulated activity, the constant attention required in a modern army are things utterly hateful to the lazy, contemplative, fatalist Turk. The officers, even, will rather allow the army to be beaten than exert themselves, and use their own senses. This is one of the worst features in the Turkish army, and alone would suffice to make it unfit for any offensive campaign.

The private and non-commissioned soldiers are recruited by volunteers and the ballot; the lower grades of officers are sometimes filled by men promoted from the ranks, but generally by the camp-followers and domestic servants, the tshibukdjis and kafeidjis of the higher officers. The military schools at Constantinople not very good in themselves, cannot furnish young men enough for the vacancies. As to the higher ranks, a system of favoritism exists, of which the western nations have no idea. Most of the generals were originally Circassian slaves, the *mignons* of some great man in the days of their youth. Utter ignorance, incapacity, and self-sufficiency rule supreme, and court-intrigue is the principal means of advancement. Even the few European generals (renegades) in the service would not have been accepted, if they had not been absolutely necessary to prevent the whole machine from falling to pieces. As it is, they have been indiscriminately taken, both from men of real merit and mere adventurers.

At present, after three campaigns, no Turkish army can be said to exist, except the 80,000 men of Omer Pasha's original army, part of which is stationed on the Danube, and part in the Crimea. The Asiatic army consists of about 25,000 rabble, unfit for the field, and demoralized by defeat. The remainder of the 400,000 men are gone nobody knows where; killed in the field or by sickness, invalided, disbanded, or turned into robbers. Very likely this will be the last Turkish army of all; for, to recover from the shock received by her alliance with England and France, is more than can be expected from Turkey.

The time is gone by when the contests of Oltenitza[317] and Citate created an exaggerated enthusiasm for Turkish bravery. The stubborn inactivity of Omer Pasha sufficed to raise doubts as to their other military qualifications, which not even the brilliant defense of Silistria could entirely dispel; the defeats in Asia, the flight of Balaklava, the strictly defensive attitude of the Turks in Eupatoria, and their complete inactivity in the camp before Sebastopol have reduced the general estimate of their military capabilities to a proper level. The Turkish army was so constituted that a judgment on its general value was hitherto completely impossible. There were, no doubt, some very brave and well-managed regiments, capable of any duty, but they were greatly in the minority. The great mass of the infantry lacked cohesion, and was, therefore, unfit for field-duty, though good behind intrenchments. The regular cavalry was decidedly inferior to that of any European power. The artillery was by far the best portion of the service, and the field-regiments in a high state of efficiency; the men were as if born for their work, though no doubt the officers left much to desire. The Redifs appear to have suffered from a general want of organization, though the men no doubt were willing to do their best. Of the irregulars, the Arnauts and Bosnians were capital guerrillas, but nothing more, best used in defending fortifications; while the Bashi Bazouks were all but worthless, and even worse than that. The Egyptian contingent appears to have been about on a level with the Turkish Nizam, the Tunisian nearly unfit for anything. With such a motley army, so badly officered and subject to such maladministration, no wonder it is all but ruined in three campaigns.

II. THE SARDINIAN ARMY

This army is composed of ten brigades of infantry, ten battalions of rifles, four brigades of cavalry, three regiments of artillery, one regiment of sappers and miners, a corps of carabineers (police troops), and the light horse in the island of Sardinia.

The ten brigades of infantry consist of one brigade of guards, four battalions of grenadiers, two battalions of chasseurs, and nine brigades of the line, equal to eighteen regiments of three battalions each. To these are added ten battalions of rifles (bersaglieri), one for every brigade, thus constituting a proportion of light infantry, actually trained, far stronger than in any other army.

There is, besides, a dépôt battalion for every regiment.

Since 1849, the strength of the battalions has been very much reduced, from financial motives. On the war-footing, a battalion should number about 1,000, but on the peace-footing there are no more than about 400 men. The remainder have been dismissed on indefinite furlough.

The cavalry counts four regiments of heavy, and five of light cavalry. Every regiment has four field and one dépôt-squadron. On the war-footing, a regiment should count about 800 men in the four field-squadrons, but on the peace-footing there are scarcely 600.

The three regiments of artillery consist of one regiment of workmen and artificers, one of garrison artillery (twelve companies), and one of field-artillery (six foot, two horse, two heavy batteries of eight guns each). The light batteries have eight lb. guns and twenty-four lb. howitzers, the heavy batteries sixteen lb. guns; in all eighty guns.

The regiment of sappers and miners has ten companies, or about 1,100 men. The carbineers (horse and foot) are very numerous for such a small kingdom, and number about 3,200 men. The light horse, doing duty as police troops in the island of Sardinia, figure about 1,100 strong.

The Sardinian army, in the first campaign against Austria, in 1848, certainly reached the strength of 70,000 men. In 1849, it was very near 130,000.[318] Afterwards it was reduced to about 45,000 men. What it is now it is impossible to say, but there is no doubt that, since the conclusion of the treaty with England and France,[319] it has been again increased.

This great elasticity of the Piedmontese army, which allows it to increase or diminish the numbers present under arms at any time, arises from a system of recruiting very nearly akin to that of Prussia; and, indeed, Sardinia may be called, in many respects, the Prussia of Italy. There is in the Sardinian states a similar obligation for every citizen to serve in the army, though, unlike Prussia, substitutes are allowed; and the time over which this obligation extends, consists, as in Prussia, of a period of actual service and another period, during which the soldier dismissed from the ranks remains in the reserve, and is liable to be called in again in time of war. The system is something between the Prussian method and that of Belgium and the minor German states. Thus, by calling in the reserves, the infantry, from about 30,000 men, may be raised to 80,000, and even more. The cavalry and field artillery would undergo but a small augmentation, as in these arms the soldiers generally have to remain with the regiments during the whole period of their service.

The Piedmontese army is as fine and soldier-like a body of men as any in Europe. Like the French, they are small in size, especially the infantry; their guards do not average even five feet four inches; but what with their tasteful dress, military bearing, well-knit but agile frames, and fine Italian features, they look better than many a body of bigger men. The dress and equipments are, with the infantry of the line and guards, upon the French principle, with a few details adopted from the Austrians. The bersaglieri have a costume of their own, a little sailor's hat with a long hanging plume of cock-feathers and a brown tunic. The cavalry wear short brown jackets, just covering the hip-bone. The percussion-musket is the general arm of the infantry; the bersaglieri have short Tyrolese rifles, good and useful weapons, but inferior to the Minié in every respect. The first rank of the cavalry used to be armed with lances; whether this is still the case with the light-horse we cannot say. The eight lb. calibre for the horse and light-foot batteries gave them the same advantage over the other continental armies which the French had while they preserved this calibre; but their heavy batteries, carrying sixteen pounders, rendered them the heaviest field artillery of the continent. That these guns, when once in position, can do excellent service, they have shown on the Chernaya,[320] where their accurate firing contributed a great deal to the success of the Allies, and was universally admired.

Of all the Italian states, Piedmont is the best situated for creating a good army. The plains of the Po and its tributaries produce capital horses, and a fine, tall race of men, the tallest of all Italians, exceedingly well-adapted for cavalry and heavy artillery service. The mountains, which surround these plains on three sides, north, west, and south, are inhabited by a hardy people, less in size, but strong and active, industrious and sharp-witted, like all mountaineers. It is these that form the staple of the infantry, and especially of the bersaglieri, a body of troops nearly equaling the Chasseurs de Vincennes in training, but certainly surpassing them in bodily strength and endurance.

The military institutions of Piedmont are, upon the whole, very good, and, in consequence, the officers bear a high character. So late as 1846, however, the influence of the aristocracy and the clergy had a great deal to do with their appointment. Up to that period, Charles Albert knew but two means of governing—the clergy and the army; in fact, it was a general saying in other parts of Italy, that in Piedmont, out of three men you met in the street, one was a soldier, the second a monk, and only every third man a civilian. At present, of course, this has been done away with; the priests have less than no influence, and, though the nobility preserve many officers' commissions, the wars of 1848 and '49 have stamped a certain democratic character upon the army which it will not be easy to destroy. Some British Crimean newspaper correspondents have stated that the Piedmontese officers were almost all "gentlemen by birth," but so far from this being the case, we know, personally, more than one Piedmontese officer who rose from the ranks, and can safely assert that the mass of the captains and lieutenants are now composed of men who either gained their epaulettes by bravery against the Austrians, or who at least are not connected with the aristocracy.

We think that the greatest compliment that can be paid to the Piedmontese army is contained in the opinion expressed by one of its late opponents, General Schönhals, quarter-master-general of the Austrian army in 1848 and '49. In his "Recollections of the Italian Campaigns", this general, one of the best officers of the Austrian army, and a man violently opposed in every way to anything smacking of Italian independence, treats the Piedmontese army throughout with the highest respect.

"Their artillery [...]," he says, "consists of picked men, under good and well-informed officers; the matériel is good, and the calibre is superior to ours [...]." "The cavalry is no contemptible arm; the first rank carry lances, but as a very adroit rider only can well manage this arm, we should not like to say that this innovation was exactly an improvement. Their school of equitation, however, [...] is very good." "At Santa Lucia, both parties fought with astonishing bravery. The Piedmontese attacked with great vivacity and impetuosity—both Piedmontese and Austrians performed many feats of great personal valor." "The Piedmontese army [...] has a right to mention the day of Novara without a blush,"—and so on.[a]

In the same way, the Prussian General Willisen, who assisted in part in the campaign of 1848, and who is no friend of Italian independence, speaks highly of the Piedmontese army.[b]

Ever since 1848, a certain party in Italy has looked upon the king of Sardinia as the future chief of the whole peninsula. Though far from participating in that opinion, we still believe that whenever Italy shall reconquer her freedom, the Piedmontese forces will be the principal military instrument in attaining that object, and will, at the same time, form the nucleus of the future Italian army. It may undergo, before that happens, more than one revolution in its own bosom, but the excellent military elements it contains will survive all this and will even gain by being merged in a really national army.

III. THE SMALLER ITALIAN ARMIES

The papal army hardly exists except on paper. The battalions and squadrons are never complete, and form but a weak division. There is, besides, a regiment of Swiss guards, the only body on which the government can place any reliance. The Tuscan, Parmesan and Modenese armies are too insignificant to be mentioned here; suffice it to say that they are organized, upon the whole, on the Austrian model. There is, besides, the Neapolitan army, of which, too, the least said the sooner mended. It has never shone conspicuously before the enemy, and, whether fighting for the king, as in 1799, or for a constitution, as in 1821, it always distinguished itself by running away.[321] Even in 1848 and '49, the native Neapolitan army was everywhere beaten by the insurgents, and, had it not been for the Swiss, King Bomba[c] would not now be on his throne. During the siege of Rome, Garibaldi advanced with a handful of men against the Neapolitan division and beat it twice.[322] The army of Naples, on the peace-footing, is estimated at 26,000 or 27,000 men, but in 1848 it is stated to have numbered nearly 49,000 men, and the full footing should raise it to 64,000. Of all these troops, the Swiss are alone worth mentioning.

---

[a] Engels is quoting from the anonymously published book by C. Schönhals, *Erinnerungen eines österreichischen Veteranen aus dem italienischen Kriege der Jahre 1848 und 1849*, Bd. I, S. 166, 167 and 223; Bd. II, S. 239.—*Ed.*

[b] A reference to W. Willisen's book *Der Italienische Feldzug des Jahres 1848.*—*Ed.*

[c] Ferdinand II. He was nicknamed King Bomba after the bombardment of Messina by Neapolitan troops in 1848.—*Ed.*

They consist of four regiments, of two battalions each, and should number, when complete, 600 men per battalion, or 4,800 men. But the cadres are now overfilled, so that each battalion is about 1,000 strong (the fourth, or Bernese regiment, alone mustering 2,150), and the whole number may be estimated at nearly 9,000. These are really first-rate troops, commanded by officers of their own country, and independent, in their internal organization and administration, from the government of Naples. They were first taken into pay in 1824 or '25, when the king,[a] no longer trusting the army that so shortly before had revolted, found it necessary to surround himself with a strong body-guard. The treaties or "capitulations," as they were called, were concluded with the different cantons for thirty years; the Swiss articles of war and the Swiss military organization were secured to the troops; the pay was three-fold that of the native Neapolitan soldiers; the troops were recruited by volunteers from each canton, where recruiting offices were established. Pensions were secured to retiring officers, veterans, and the wounded. If, at the expiration of the thirty years, the capitulation was not renewed, the regiments were to be broken up. The present Swiss constitution[323] forbids recruiting for foreign service, and the capitulations, therefore, were canceled after 1848; recruiting was stopped, at least ostensibly, in Switzerland, but at Chiasso and other points of Lombardy, dépôts were established, and many a recruiting agent secretly continued his business on Swiss soil. So eager was the Neapolitan government for recruits, that it did not refuse to accept the refuse of the political refugees then in Switzerland. The King of Naples, under these circumstances, confirmed the privileges granted to the Swiss soldiers by the capitulations, and in August last, when the thirty years had elapsed, by a special decree again prolonged these privileges for so long a time as the Swiss should remain in his service.

IV. THE SWISS ARMY

In Switzerland no national standing army exists. Every Swiss is compelled to serve in the militia, if able-bodied; and this mass is divided into three levies (*Auszug, erstes* and *zweites Aufgebot*[b]), according to age. The young men, during the first years of service, are called out separately for drill, and collected from time

---

[a] Ferdinand I.—*Ed.*
[b] Men under arms, first levy and second levy.—*Ed.*

to time in camps; but whoever has seen the awkward gait and uncomfortable appearance of a Swiss squad, or heard the jokes they crack with the drill-sergeant while under drill, must at once see that the military qualities of the men are but very poorly developed. Of the soldierly capabilities of this militia we can only judge by the one example of the Sonderbund war, in 1847,[324] which campaign is distinguished by the extremely small number of casualties in proportion to the forces engaged. The organization of the militia is almost entirely in the hands of the various cantonal governments; and, though its general form is fixed by federal laws, and a federal staff is at the head of the whole, this system cannot fail to create confusion and want of uniformity, while it must almost necessarily prevent a proper accumulation of stores, the introduction of improvements, and the permanent fortification of important points, especially on the side where Switzerland is weak, toward Germany.

The Swiss, like all mountaineers, make capital soldiers when drilled; and, wherever they have served as regular troops under foreign banners, they have fought exceedingly well. But being rather slow-headed, they need drilling much more, indeed, than either French or North Germans, to give them confidence in themselves, and cohesion. It is possible that national feeling might possibly replace this in the case of a foreign attack upon Switzerland, but even this is very doubtful. An army of 80,000 regular troops, and less, would certainly be a match for all the 160,000 and more men which the Swiss say they can congregate. In 1798, the French finished the business with a few regiments.[325]

The Swiss boast a great deal of the rifles of their sharp-shooters. There are, certainly, in Switzerland, comparatively more good shots than in any other European country, the Austrian Alpine possessions excepted. But when one sees how these dead shots, when called in, are almost all armed with clumsy common percussion muskets, the respect for the Swiss sharp-shooters is considerably lessened. The few battalions of rifles may be good shots, but their short, heavy pieces (*Stutzen*) are antiquated and worthless compared with the Minié, and their awkward, slow method of loading, with loose powder from a horn, would give them but a poor chance when opposed to troops armed with less superannuated weapons.

Altogether, arms, accoutrements, organization, drill, everything is old-fashioned with the Swiss, and very likely will remain so as long as the cantonal governments have anything to say on the subject.

V. THE SCANDINAVIAN ARMIES

The Swedish and Norwegian armies, though united under one crown, are as separate as the two countries to which they belong.[326] In contrast to Switzerland, both give us the example of an Alpine country with a standing army; but the Scandinavian peninsula is altogether, by the nature of the soil, and the consequent poverty, and thin population of the country, so much akin to Switzerland, that even in the military organization of both, one system, and that the militia system, predominates.

Sweden has three sorts of troops,—regiments raised by voluntary enlistment (*Värfvade truppar*), provincial regiments (*Indelta truppar*), and Reserve troops. The Värfvade consist of three regiments of infantry, containing six battalions, two of cavalry and three of artillery, with thirteen foot and four horse batteries, altogether 96 six lb., 24 twelve lb., and 16 twenty-four lb. guns. This makes a total of 7,700 men, and 136 guns. These troops contain all the artillery for the whole army.

The Indelta form twenty provincial regiments of two battalions, with five separate battalions of infantry, and six regiments of a strength varying from one to eight squadrons. They are estimated at 33,000 men.

The Reserve troops form the mass of the army. When called in they are expected to reach 95,000 men.

There is, besides, in the province of Götaland, a sort of militia constantly under arms, numbering 7,850 men, in twenty-one companies and sixteen guns. Altogether, therefore, the Swedish army comprises about 140,000 men with 150 field guns.

The volunteers for the enlisted regiments are generally engaged for fourteen years, but the law allows engagements of three years. The Indelta are a sort of militia, living, when once trained, in farms apportioned to them and their families, and called in only once a year for four weeks' drill. They have the revenues of their farms for pay, but when assembled they receive a special compensation. The officers also receive crown-lands on tenure in their respective districts. The Reserve consists of all able-bodied Swedes from twenty to twenty-five years of age; they are drilled a short time, and afterwards called in a fortnight in every year. Thus, with the exception of the few Värfvade and the Gothland troops, the great body of the army—Indelta and Reserve—are, to all intents and purposes, militia.

The Swedes play a part in military history which is beyond all proportion to the scanty population which furnished their renowned armies. Gustavus Adolphus, in the thirty years' war,[327] marked a new era in tactics by his improvements; and Charles XII, with his adventurous foolhardiness which spoiled his great military talent, actually made them do wonders—such as to take entrenchments with cavalry. In the later wars against Russia, they behaved very well; in 1813, Bernadotte kept them as much as possible out of harm's way, and they were scarcely under fire, unless by mistake, except at Leipsic,[328] where they formed but an infinitesimal part of the allies. The Värfvade, and even the Indelta, will, no doubt, always sustain the character of the Swedish name; but the Reserve, unless assembled and drilled a long time before brought into action, can only figure as an army of recruits.

Norway has five brigades of infantry containing twenty-two battalions and 12,000 men; one brigade of cavalry, of three divisions of chasseurs, containing 1,070 men; and one regiment of artillery of about 1,300 men; beside a reserve of militia, of 9,000 men; altogether about 24,000 men. The character of this army does not vary much from that of Sweden; its only distinguishing feature is a few companies of chasseurs, provided with flat snow-shoes, on which, with the assistance of a long pole, they run, Lapland fashion, very rapidly over the snow.

The Danish army is composed of twenty-three battalions of infantry (one of guards, twelve line, five light, five chasseurs) in four brigades, each battalion numbering about 700 men on the peace-footing; three brigades of cavalry (three squadrons of guards, six regiments of dragoons, of four squadrons each, the squadron containing 140 men in time of peace), and one brigade of artillery (two regiments and twelve batteries with 80 six lb. and 16 twelve lb. guns), and three companies of sappers. Total, 16,630 infantry, 2,900 cavalry, 2,900 artillery and sappers with ninety-six guns.

For the war-footing, each company is raised to 200, or the battalion to 800 men, and each squadron to 180 men, raising the line in all to 25,500 men. Besides, thirty-two battalions, twenty-four squadrons, and six batteries of the reserve can be called in, representing a force of 31,500 men and raising the total of the force to about 56,000 or 57,000 men. Even these, however, can be increased in case of need, as during the late war Denmark proper alone, without either Holstein or Schleswig, could muster from 50,000 to 60,000 men,[329] and the Duchies are now again subject to the Danish conscription.

The army is recruited by ballot, out of the young men of from twenty-two years and upwards. The time of service is eight years, but actually the artillery remain six years, the line four years only with the regiments, while for the remainder of the time they belong to the reserve. From the thirtieth to the thirty-eighth year the men remain in the first, and then up to the forty-fifth year in the second levy of the militia. This is all very nicely arranged, but, in any war against Germany, nearly one-half of the troops—those from the Duchies—would disband and take up arms against their present comrades. It is this strong admixture of Schleswig-Holsteiners which forms the great weakness of the Danish army, and, in reality, almost nullifies it in any complications with its most powerful neighbor.

The Danish army, since its reorganization in 1848-'49, has been well equipped, well armed, and brought altogether to a very respectable footing. The Dane, from Denmark proper, is a good soldier and behaved very well in almost every action of the three years' war; but the Schleswig-Holsteiner proved himself decidedly his superior. The corps of officers is good upon the whole, but there is too much aristocracy and too little scientific education in it. Their reports are slovenly made, and similar to those of the British, to which army the Danish troops likewise appear related in their want of mobility; but they have not shown of late that they possess such immovable steadiness as the victors of Inkermann. The Schleswig-Holsteiners are, without any dispute, among the best soldiers in Europe. They are excellent artillery men, and as cool in action as the English, their cousins. Though inhabitants of a level country, they make very good light infantry; their first rifle-battalion in 1850 might have vied with any troop of its class.

VI. THE ARMY OF HOLLAND

The Dutch army numbers thirty-six battalions of infantry in nine regiments, containing 44,000 men in all; four regiments of dragoons composed of twenty squadrons; two squadrons of mounted chasseurs; and two squadrons of gens d'armes; in all, twenty-four squadrons, comprising 4,400 cavalry, with two regiments of field artillery (five six lb. and six twelve lb. foot, two six lb. and two twelve lb. horse batteries, of 120 guns in all), and one battalion of sappers, making a total of 58,000 men, beside several regiments in the colonies. But this army does not always exist in time of peace. There is a nucleus remaining under arms, consisting of officers, subalterns, and a few voluntarily enlisted men. The great mass, though obliged to serve for five years, are drilled during a couple of months, and then dismissed so as to be called in for a few weeks in each year only. Besides, there is a sort of reserve in three levies, comprising all the able-bodied men from twenty to thirty-five years of age. The first levy forms about fifty-three, and the second twenty-nine battalions of infantry and artillery. But this body is not at all organized, and can hardly be accounted even as militia.

VII. THE BELGIAN ARMY

The Belgian army has sixteen regiments of infantry, containing forty-nine battalions, beside a reserve battalion for each regiment; comprising in all 46,000 men. The cavalry consists of two regiments of chasseurs, two of lancers, one of guides, two of cuirassiers, making thirty-eight squadrons, beside seven reserve squadrons, in all 5,800 men. There are four regiments of artillery (four horse, fifteen foot batteries, four dépôt batteries, twenty-four garrison companies), with 152 guns, six and twelve pounders; and one regiment of sappers and miners, numbering 1,700 men. The total, without the reserve, is 62,000 men; with the reserve, according to a late levy, it may be raised to 100,000. The army is recruited by ballot, and the term of service is eight years, but about one half of that time is passed on furlough. On the peace-establishment, therefore, the actual force will scarcely reach 30,000 men.

VIII. THE PORTUGUESE ARMY

The Portuguese army consisted, in 1850, of the following troops:—

	Peace footing.	War footing.
Infantry, ...	18,738	40,401
Cavalry, ...	3,508	4,676
Artillery, ...	2,707	4,098
Engineers and Staff		495
	25,681	49,670

The artillery consists of one field-regiment, of one horse and seven foot batteries; three regiments of position and garrison artillery, and three detached battalions in the islands. The calibre is six and twelve pounds.

IX. THE SPANISH ARMY

Of all European armies, that of Spain is, from peculiar circumstances, most a matter of interest to the United States. We give, therefore, in concluding this survey of the military establishments of Europe, a more detailed account of this army than its importance, compared with that of its neighbors on the other side of the Atlantic, might seem to warrant.

The Spanish military force consists of the army of the interior, and of the colonial armies.

That of the interior counts one regiment of grenadiers, forty-five regiments of the line, of three battalions each, two regiments of two battalions each in Ceuta, and eighteen battalions of cazadores or rifles. The whole of these 160 battalions formed, in 1852, an effective force of 72,670 men, costing the state 82,692,651 reals, or $10,336,581, a year. The cavalry comprises sixteen regiments of carabineers, or dragoons and lancers, of four squadrons each, with eleven squadrons of cazadores, or light horse, in 1851; in all 12,000 men, costing 17,549,562 reals, or $2,193,695.

The artillery numbers five regiments of foot artillery, of three brigades each, one for each division of the monarchy; beside five brigades of heavy, three of horse, and three of mountain artillery, making a total of twenty-six brigades, or, as they are now called, battalions. The battalion has in the horse artillery two, in the mountain and foot artillery four batteries; in all ninety-two foot and six horse batteries, or 588 field guns.

The sappers and miners form one regiment of 1,240 men.

The reserve consists of one battalion (No. 4) for every infantry regiment, and a dépôt-squadron for each cavalry regiment.

The total force—on paper—in 1851 was 103,000 men; in 1843, when Espartero was upset, it amounted to 50,000 only; but at one time Narváez raised it to above 100,000. On an average 90,000 men under arms will be the utmost.

The colonial armies are as follows:

1. The army of Cuba; sixteen regiments of veteran infantry, four companies of volunteers, two regiments of cavalry, two battalions of four batteries foot, and one battalion of four batteries of mountain artillery, one battalion of horse artillery with two batteries, and one battalion of sappers and miners. Beside these troops of the line, there is a *milicia disciplinada*[a] of four battalions and four squadrons, and a *milicia urbana* of eight squadrons,

[a] Disciplined militia.—*Ed.*

making a total of thirty-seven battalions, twenty squadrons and eighty-four guns. During the last few years this standing Cuban army has been reinforced by numerous troops from Spain; and if we take its original strength at 16,000 or 18,000 men, there will now be, perhaps, 25,000 or 28,000 men in Cuba. But this is a mere approximation.

2. The army of Porto Rico; three battalions of veteran infantry, seven battalions of disciplined militia, two battalions of native volunteers, one squadron of the same, and four batteries of foot artillery. The neglected state of most of the Spanish colonies does not allow any estimate of the strength of this corps.

3. The Philippine Islands have five regiments of infantry, of eight companies each; one regiment of chasseurs of Luzon; nine foot, one horse, one mountain battery. Nine corps of five battalions of native infantry, and other provincial corps, previously existing, were dissolved in 1851.

The army is recruited by ballot, and substitutes are allowed. Every year a contingent of 25,000 men is levied; but, in 1848, three contingents, or 75,000 men, were called out.

The Spanish army owes its present organization principally to Narváez, though the regulations of Charles III, of 1768,[a] still form the groundwork of it. Narváez had actually to take away from the regiments their old provincial colors, different in each, and to introduce the Spanish flag into the army! In the same manner he had to destroy the old provincial organization, and to centralize and restore unity. Too well aware, by experience, that money was the principal moving lever in an army which had almost never been paid and seldom even clad or fed, he also tried to introduce a greater regularity in the payments and the financial administration of the army. Whether he succeeded to the full extent of his wishes, is unknown; but any amelioration introduced by him, in this respect, speedily disappeared during the administration of Sartorius and his successors. The normal state of "no pay, no food, no clothing," was reestablished in its full glory; and while the superior and general officers strut about in coats resplendent with gold and silver lace, or even don fancy uniforms, unknown to any regulations, the soldiers are ragged and without shoes. What the state of this army was ten or twelve years ago, an English author thus describes:—

"The appearance of the Spanish troops is, to the last degree, unsoldierly. The sentry strolls to and fro [...] on his beat, his shako almost falling off the back of his

[a] *Ordenanzas de S. M. para el regimen, disciplina, subordinacion, y servico de sus ejercitos*, T. I-II.—*Ed.*

head, his gun slouched on his shoulders, singing outright [...] a lively seguidilla with the most *sans façon* air in the world. He is, not unfrequently, destitute of portions of his uniform; or his regimental coat and lower continuations are in such hopeless rags, that, even in the sultry summer, the slate-colored great-coat is worn as a slut-cover [...]; the shoes [...], in one case out of three, are broken to pieces, disclosing the naked toes of the men—such in Spain are the glories of the *vida militar.*"[a]

A regulation, issued by Serrano, on Sept. 9, 1843, prescribes that:—

"All officers and chiefs of the army have in future to present themselves in public in the uniform of their regiment, and with the regulation sword, whenever they do not appear in plain clothes; and all officers are also to wear the exact distinctive marks of their rank, and no other, as prescribed, without displaying any more of those arbitrary ornaments and ridiculous trimmings by which some of them have thought proper to distinguish themselves."

So much for the officers. Now for the soldiers:—

"Brigadier General Cordoba has opened a subscription in Cadiz, heading it with his name, in order to procure funds for presenting one pair of cloth trousers to each of the valiant soldiers of the regiment of Asturias!"

This financial disorder explains how it has been possible for the Spanish army to continue, ever since 1808, in a state of almost uninterrupted rebellion. But the real causes lie deeper. The long continued war with Napoleon, in which the different armies and their chiefs gained real political influence, first gave it a pretorian turn. Many energetic men, from the revolutionary times, remained in the army; the incorporation of the guerrillas in the regular force even increased this element. Thus, while the chiefs retained their pretorian pretensions, the soldiers and lower ranks altogether remained inspired with revolutionary traditions. In this way the insurrection of 1819-23 was regularly prepared, and later on, in 1833-43,[330] the civil war again thrust the army and its chiefs into the foreground. Having been used by all parties as an instrument, no wonder that the Spanish army should, for a time, take the government into its own hands.

"The Spaniards are a warlike but not a soldier-like people," said the Abbé de Pradt.[b] They certainly have, of all European nations, the greatest antipathy to military discipline. Nevertheless, it is possible that the nation, which for more than a hundred years was celebrated for its infantry, may yet again have an army of which it can be proud. But, to attain this end, not only the military system, but civil life, still more, requires to be reformed.

---

[a] Here and below Engels quotes from the anonymously published book by T. M. Hughes, *Revelations of Spain in 1845,* Vol. I, pp. 326 and 329.—*Ed.*

[b] Dominique de Pradt, *Mémoires historiques sur la révolution d'Espagne,* p. 189.—*Ed.*

Karl Marx

GENERAL SIMPSON'S RESIGNATION. —FROM PARLIAMENT

London, August 3. The day before yesterday *The Morning Post*, in obviously embarrassed phraseology, informed the British public that General Simpson will soon resign his command under the pretext of weakened health and will have *no* successor.[a] In other words: *the English army is to be placed under French general command*. In this way the Government would shift the responsibility for the conduct of the war from itself onto "our great and glorious ally". Parliament forfeits the last semblance of control. At the same time an infallible means for transforming the alliance between England and France into the most acrimonious dissension between the two nations has been discovered. We see the same master hand at work in whose all too robust grasp the Entente Cordiale[331] broke into pieces in 1839.

Parliament concludes its present session in a fitting manner—with scandals.[b] *First scandal*: the withdrawal of the Bill for limited liability in *private* (not joint-stock) commercial companies at the bidding of the *big* capitalists before whose frowns even the Olympian Palmerston trembles. *Second scandal*: the adjournment *in infinitum* of the Bills regulating lease-hold tenure in Ireland, which have been moving to and fro in both Houses of Parliament for 4 years—a cowardly compromise in which the House of Commons has consented to take back its own work, the Cabinet to break its word and the Irish Brigade[332] to hold the question open

[a] "The Command of the Army in the East", *The Morning Post*, No. 25455, August 2, 1855.—*Ed.*

[b] The reference is to the sittings of the House of Commons of July 24, July 30 and August 2. *The Times*, No. 22115, July 25; No. 22120, July 31 and No. 22123, August 3, 1855.—*Ed.*

for exploitation on the hustings.[a] *Final scandal*: Major Reed's motion obliging the Cabinet to recall Parliament in the event of peace being concluded during the recess. Reed is a buffoon, notoriously in Palmerston's pay. His aim was to deceive the House into passing a *vote of confidence* as a result of his "distrustful motion". But the House laughed his motion down, laughed Palmerston down and laughed itself down. It has reached the stage where "laughter" remains the last recourse for depravity to repudiate itself.

Written on August 3, 1855

First published in the *Neue Oder-Zeitung*, No. 361, August 6, 1855

Marked with the sign ×

Printed according to the newspaper

Published in English for the first time

[a] Marx uses the English word.—*Ed.*

Karl Marx

COMMENTARY ON THE PARLIAMENTARY PROCEEDINGS

London, August 8. The financial report on the British Empire in Asia presented by Vernon Smith (at present Great Mogul and Manu in one person) and Bright's motion to bring this important subject before the Commons at a "debatable" time in the future prompted yesterday's Commons debate on *India*,[a] which we shall leave to one side for the time being since we intend to provide a detailed sketch of conditions in India[333] during the parliamentary recess.

Lord *John Russell* will hardly allow the impending conclusion of this Parliamentary session to pass off without an attempt to make political capital out of his awkward situation. He is *no longer* in the Government, and *not yet* a member of the opposition—this constitutes his awkward situation. The position of leader in the Tory opposition is already occupied, and Russell has nothing to gain from this side. In the liberal opposition Gladstone is pressing to the fore. In his latest and, from his point of view, exemplary speech—on the occasion of the Turkish loan—Gladstone skilfully advocated peace with Russia, by showing the war to be a war at the expense of Turkey and the fighting nationalities, especially Italy.[b] Russell senses that dreadful misfortunes will occur during

[a] The speeches of Smith, Bright, Russell and Palmerston in the House of Commons on August 7, 1855, were published in *The Times*, No. 22127, August 8, 1855.—*Ed.*

[b] Gladstone's speech in the House of Commons on July 20, 1855. *The Times*, No. 22112, July 21, 1855.—*Ed.*

the recess, implying a great clamour for peace when Parliament reassembles. He senses that this peace must be demanded on liberal pretexts, all the more so since the Tories have run themselves into the position of the war party *par excellence.* Italy—the pretext for making peace with Russia! Russell envies Gladstone this brainwave and since he is unable to *anticipate* him with this plausible position, he has decided to *absorb* him by translating Gladstone's speech from the sublime style into the trivial. The circumstance that he is no longer in the Government as Palmerston is, and not yet, like Gladstone, in the opposition, promises to make the plagiarism profitable. Thus Russell rose yesterday evening and began by assuring the House that he did "not wish either to diminish or to aggravate the responsibility [...] of the Government". This responsibility was great, however. This year alone £49,000,000 had been voted for war expenses, and it would soon be time to account for this enormous sum. In the Baltic the fleet had done nothing and would probably do still less. The prospects in the Black Sea were no more promising. Austria's change of policy permitted Russia to send its armies from Poland, etc., to the Crimea. On the Asiatic coast catastrophes were impending for the Turkish army. The prospect of sending a foreign legion of twenty to thirty thousand men there as a replacement had disappeared. He regretted that his Viennese despatches had not been laid before Parliament. The Turkish ambassador[a] had completely agreed with him concerning the acceptability of a peace on the basis of the latest Austrian proposals. Should the war be pursued any further against the will of Turkey then in future it would no longer be a question of underwriting loans but of subsidies. Piedmont had joined the Western Powers, but for this it was demanding, and rightly so, a change in the conditions of Italy. Rome was occupied by the French, the Papal States by the Austrians, an occupation which maintained despotism there and in the two Sicilies and prevented the people of Italy from following the example of Spain. Russia's occupation of the Danubian principalities was the excuse for the present war. How to square with this the Franco-Austrian occupation of Italy? The independence of the Pope[b] and thus the balance of Europe was endangered. Could an understanding not be reached with Austria and France concerning changes in the Papal form of government which would permit the evacuation of

---

[a] Arif Bey.—*Ed.*
[b] Pius IX.—*Ed.*

the Papal States? Finally the hackneyed advice: the Ministers should not conclude a dishonourable peace, but should also let no opportunity for peace negotiations slip through their hands.

Palmerston replied that "he was not like other people who took upon themselves the responsibility of declaring a war and then shrank back before the responsibility of conducting it. He was not such a man as that". (He indeed knows what "responsibility" involves.) Conditions for peace depended upon the results of war, and the results of war depended upon all sorts of circumstances, i.e., upon chance. (Thus chance is responsible for the results of war and the results of war are responsible for the conditions of peace.) As far as he (Palmerston) knew, Turkey was in complete agreement with the views of France and England. Even if this were not so, Turkey was *merely a means*, not an end in the struggle against Russia. The "enlightened" Western Powers must know better what was advantageous than the decaying Eastern Power. (This is a splendid commentary on the declaration of war against Russia, in which the war is described as a purely "defensive war" on Turkey's behalf; on the notorious Vienna Note which the "enlightened" Western Powers wished to force upon Turkey, etc.) As for Italy, that was a ticklish question. A dreadful state of affairs reigned in Naples, but why? Because it was the ally of Russia, a *despotic* state. As for the condition of Italy occupied by Austria and France (not despotic states?), "the governments there are not, to be sure, in accordance with the feelings of the people", but the occupation was necessary to maintain "order". Besides, France had reduced the number of troops in Rome and Austria had evacuated Tuscany completely. Finally Palmerston congratulated England upon the alliance with France, which was now so intimate that actually only "*one Cabinet*" was governing on both sides of the Channel. And he had just been denouncing Naples for its alliance with a despotic state! And now he congratulated England on the same thing! The point of Palmerston's speech was that he used military tirades to conclude a session he had been able to keep so free of military deeds.

Using Italy as a false pretext for peace, in the same way as he had used Poland and Hungary as a false pretext for war after his return from Vienna, was naturally a matter of no consequence to Russell. It did not embarrass him to forget that as premier in 1847-1852 he had allowed Palmerston, first to help stir up Italy with false promises, only to abandon it later on to Bonaparte and King Ferdinand, to the Pope and the Emperor.[a] [334] That did not

[a] Francis Joseph I.—*Ed.*

matter to him. What mattered to him was snatching the "Italian pretext" from Gladstone and making it his own.

Written on August 8, 1855

First published in the *Neue Oder-Zeitung*, No. 371, August 11, 1855

Marked with the sign ×

Printed according to the newspaper

Published in English for the first time

Karl Marx

THE MILITARY FORCES AGAINST RUSSIA

London, August 11. At the moment the armies mustered by the allies against Russia are limited, apart from their own troops, to:

1. a small Piedmontese auxiliary corps of 15,000 men—a corps extorted from Piedmont by the concerted threats of England, France and Austria. This bloodletting of Piedmont was one of the conditions Austria made for selling its adhesion to the "Treaty of 2 December"[335];

2. the *Foreign Legion*, amounting to a few thousand troops—an *olla podrida*[a] of occidental mercenaries enticed bit by bit surreptitiously and illegally away from their respective countries;

3. an *Italian Legion* of 4,000 to 5,000 men, still in the process of formation;

4. a *Polish Legion*, existing in the form of a project;

5. finally, in the distant future, a *Spanish* auxiliary corps, to represent "dire financial necessity".

This motley sample card of volunteer corps and diminutive armies provides a map of the Europe England and France have in their retinue at this moment. Can one conceive of a more consummate caricature of the army of nations which the first Napoleon rolled into motion against Russia?

Written on August 11, 1855

First published in the *Neue Oder-Zeitung*, No. 375, August 14, 1855

Marked with the sign ×

Printed according to the newspaper

Published in English for the first time

---

[a] Hotchpotch (literally: rotten stew).—*Ed.*

Karl Marx

THE POLAND MEETING[336]

London, August 13. The repeated angry sallies of the Government newspapers against the great Poland meeting which took place last Wednesday in St. Martin's Hall[a] necessitate some marginal notes. The initiative for the meeting evidently originated with the Government itself. The "Literary Association of the Friends of Poland",[337] an association composed of Czartoryski's supporters on the one hand and English aristocrats with a friendly disposition towards Poland on the other, was pushed forward as a front. From its inception this association has been a blind tool in the hands of Palmerston, who manipulated and controlled it through the mediation of the recently deceased Lord Dudley Stuart. The addresses concerning Poland and deputations which it sent to Palmerston each year were one of the most significant aids he had in keeping his "anti-Russian" reputation alive. For their part Czartoryski's supporters gained important advantages from this connection: they figured as the only respectable, so to say "official" representatives of the Polish emigration, they could keep down the democratic party among the emigrants and they had the association's significant material means of relief at their disposal as recruiting funds for their own party. The controversy between the Literary Association and the "Centralisation"[338] of the Democratic Polish Association has been fierce and long-lived. In 1839 the latter held a great public meeting in London, exposing the intrigues of the "Literary" Association, unfurling the past history of the Czartoryskis (this was done by Ostrowski, the author of a

[a] The meeting was held on August 8, 1855. Reports on it were published in *The Times,* No. 22128, August 9, 1855, and in *The People's Paper,* No 70, August 11, 1855.—*Ed.*

history of Poland written in English[a]) and openly declaring its opposition to the diplomatic-aristocratic "restorers" of Poland. From this moment the position which the "Literary" Association had usurped was undermined. In passing, it should be noted that the events of 1846 and of 1848-49[339] added a third element to the Polish emigration, a socialist group, but this, together with the democrats, opposes the Czartoryski party.

The purpose of the meeting held at the instigation of the Government was threefold: to form a Polish legion and thus get rid of part of the "Polish foreigners" by sending them to the Crimea; to refurbish Palmerston's popularity; and finally to deliver any potential Polish movement into his own hands and those of Bonaparte. The government press claims that a deeply laid conspiracy inspired by Russian agents thwarted the purpose of the meeting. Nothing could be more ridiculous than this assertion. The majority of the audience in St. Martin's Hall was made up of London Chartists. The anti-Government amendment* was moved by an Urquhartist and seconded by an Urquhartist—Collet and Hart. Leaflets distributed in the hall said that

> "the meeting had been called by English aristocrats simply trying to maintain the old British system of government, etc.". "Poland, which condemned every alliance with the present rulers of Europe, did not wish to be restored by any of the existing governments, nor sink to being a tool of diplomatic intrigue, etc."

These leaflets were signed by the president and the secretary of the "Polish Democratic Committee". Now considering that in London all three factions, Chartists, Urquhartists and the really "democratic" Polish emigration are on anything but friendly terms with one another, every suspicion of a "conspiracy" vanishes. The noisy interruptions of the meeting were provoked exclusively by the unparliamentary refusal by the chairman, Lord Harrington, to read out Collet's amendment and put it to the vote. They were aggravated by the secretary of the "Literary

* The following is the wording of Collet's amendment, which was adopted by the meeting: "That this meeting, cordially desiring the restoration of Polish nationality, cannot forget that the destruction of that nationality was mainly owing to the perfidious conduct of Lord Palmerston from 1830 to 1846; that so long as Lord Palmerston is a servant of the Crown, no proposal for the restoration of Poland can be anything but a sham and a delusion, and that the truth of this proposition is shown by the fact that Lord Palmerston has carried on the war in such a way as to avoid, as far as possible, injuring Russia, while he has proposed terms of peace which utterly destroy the integrity and independence of Turkey."

---

[a] J. B. Ostrowski, *The History of Poland,* Vols. I-II.—*Ed.*

Association of the Friends of Poland" Colonel *Szulszewski's* notion of shouting for a constable to have Collet arrested. The tumult naturally reached its climax when Lord Harrington, Sir Robert Peel and their friends fled the platform and quit the premises. With the appointment of George Thompson as president in place of Harrington tranquillity was instantly restored.

The specimens of England's ruling class prominent at this Poland meeting were by no means calculated to instil any special respect for the patriciate. The Earl of *Harrington* may perhaps be a very good man, but he is indubitably a very bad speaker. It would be impossible to witness a more embarrassing performance. Only by means of supreme exertion could his lordship stammer forth two connected words. To this moment he failed to conclude a single sentence of his speech. In the meantime this was done for him—by the stenographers. His lordship is a military man and undoubtedly brave, but judging from the way he conducted the Poland meeting, he is better fitted for any other vocation than for that of being a leader. As a speaker Lord *Ebrington,* the midwife of the Sunday Bill, is only a little better than the Earl of Harrington. His physiognomy betrays obstinacy, his skull has the form of a battering ram. He has one undeniable merit. Arguments cannot defeat him. Napoleon once declared that Englishmen did not know when they were beaten. In this respect Ebrington is a model Englishman.

After the lords came the baronets. Lord Ebrington proposed the government motion on the restoration of Poland; Sir Robert Peel followed him and spoke as his seconder. In many respects no greater contrast can be imagined than exists between the "Member for Tamworth" (Peel) and the "Member for Marylebone" (Ebrington). The former is a roguish and natural humbug, the latter an affected and puritanical chicken heart. The one amuses, the other disgusts. Sir Robert Peel gives the impression of a traveller in wines who has been raised to the nobility, Lord Ebrington of an inquisitor converted to Protestantism. Tony Lumpkin and Beau Brummell rolled into one would, more or less, produce the incongruity exhibiting itself in Peel's person, dress and manner. An extraordinary mixture of clown and dandy. Palmerston is extremely partial to this oddity from Tamworth. He finds it serviceable. Whenever he wants to know which way the popular wind is blowing, he hoists aloft Sir Robert Peel to act as his weather-vane. When he desired to know if public opinion in England would sanction the expulsion of Victor Hugo, etc., he let Sir Robert Peel deliver a denunciation of the refugees and an apology for Bonaparte.[340] So once again in relation to Poland. He exploits him as a "feeler". Peel is extraordinarily fitted for this not particularly dignified role. He is what the English call "a chartered libertine",[a] a dashing madcap, a privileged eccentric, for whose impulses and outbursts, erratic manoeuvrings, words and deeds no Government is held responsible, nor any party. Sir Robert came to the Poland meeting padded out and, it is said, made up in the artistic fashion. He appeared to be girdled, wore a crimson rose in his buttonhole, was as perfumed as a milliner and in his right hand he flourished a huge umbrella with which he beat time as he spoke. By a highly ironic coincidence the ex-vicepresident of the Association for Administrative Reform,[341] Mr. *Tite*, followed hard on the heels of the lords and the baronets. Since the influence of this association gained him the designation of the Solon of Bath he has begun his parliamentary career, as is well known, by voting *against* Scully's motion for a piece of administrative reform and *for* Palmerston's Turkish loan, while *abstaining*, with great moderation, from voting on Roebuck's motion.[b] The lords and the baronets seemed to be pointing at him and snickering: There you have our substitute! It is unnecessary to describe Mr. Tite in detail. Shakespeare did so when he invented the immortal Shallow, compared by Falstaff to one of the little men made out of cheese-parings after supper.[c]

In contrast to all these gentlemen the very first words of an unknown young plebeian named *Hart* gave the impression that he was a man able to inspire and to govern great masses. Now we can understand the Government's vexation at the Poland meeting. It was not only a defeat for Palmerston, but even more so for the class he represents.

Written on August 13, 1855

First published in the *Neue Oder-Zeitung*, No. 379, August 16, 1855

Marked with the sign ×

Printed according to the newspaper

Published in English for the first time

[a] Shakespeare, *Henry V*, Act I, Scene 1, quoted by Marx in English.—*Ed.*

[b] Scully submitted his motion to the Commons on July 10, 1855; Palmerston's motion on the Turkish loan was submitted on July 20; for Roebuck's motion, submitted on July 17, see this volume, pp. 337-38, 355-57 and 363.—*Ed.*

[c] Shakespeare, *Henry IV*, Second Part, Act III, Scene 2.—*Ed.*

Karl Marx

ON THE CRITIQUE OF AUSTRIAN POLICY IN THE CRIMEAN CAMPAIGN[342]

London, August 15. Bratiano recently addressed a letter to *The Daily News* in which he depicts the suffering of the inhabitants of the Danubian principalities under the Austrian army of occupation, alludes to the equivocal attitude of the French and English consuls and then puts this question:

"Is Austria acting as an ally or even as a *neutral party* when she maintains an army of 80,000 in the principalities thereby, as the official despatches prove, preventing the Turks entering Bessarabia and also the formation of a Romanian army which could have taken an active part in the war, while withdrawing 200,000 men from Galicia thus enabling Russia to send a similar number to the Crimea?"

Austria's ambiguous position arose the moment when neither neutral nor an ally, she set herself up as a *mediator*. The following extract from a despatch of Lord Clarendon to the Viennese Cabinet, dated June 14, 1853, seems to prove that *England* in part forced her into this role:

"If the Russian army proceeded beyond the Principalities, and other provinces of Turkey were invaded, a general rising of the Christian population would ensue, not in favour of Russia, nor in support of the Sultan,[a] but for their own independence; and it would be needless to add that such a revolt would not be long in extending itself to the Danubian Provinces of Austria but it would be for the Austrian Government to judge of the effect it might produce in Hungary and in Italy, and the encouragement it must give to the promoters of disorder throughout Europe whom Austria has reason to fear, and who even now would appear to think that the moment is at hand for the realisation of their projects. It was these considerations, I said, that rendered Her Majesty's[b] Government most anxious to unite with Austria for an object so essential to the best interests of society, and to endeavour with her to discover some mode by which the just claims of Russia may be reconciled with the sovereign rights of the Sultan."

---

[a] Abdul Mejid.—*Ed.*
[b] Queen Victoria's.—*Ed.*

Another question concerning Austrian policy remains as unanswered at the conclusion of the parliamentary session as at the start. What was Austria's position with regard to the *Crimean expedition*? On July 23 this year Disraeli asked Lord John Russell on what authority he had declared that "*one of the principal causes of the Crimean expedition was the refusal of Austria to cross the river Pruth*".[a]

Lord John Russell could not remember—i.e., he said "his authority was a vague recollection, a general recollection". Disraeli then addressed the same question to Palmerston, who said

"he would not answer questions taken piecemeal from a long course of negotiations between Her Majesty's Government and the Government of one of the Sovereigns[b] who was *to a certain degree* in alliance with Her Majesty."

With this apparently evasive answer Palmerston was evidently only indirectly confirming Russell's claim, pleading delicacy with regard to the "ally to a certain degree". Let us now move from the House of Commons to the House of Lords. On June 26 this year Lord Lyndhurst delivered his philippic against Austria:

"Early in June" (1854) "Austria resolved on making a demand upon Russia to evacuate the principalities. That demand was made in very strong terms with something like an intimation that if it were not complied with Austria would resort to forcible means to secure this object."

After some historical remarks Lyndhurst continues:

"Well, did Austria then immediately carry into effect any attack upon Russia? Did she attempt to enter the principalities? Far from it. She abstained from doing anything for a period of several weeks, and it was only when the siege of Silistria had been raised and the Russian army was in retreat, and when Russia herself had served a notice that she would within a certain time leave the principalities and retire behind the Pruth [...]—that Austria again remembered her engagements."[c]

In reply to this speech Lord *Clarendon* declared:

"When Austria entered into these successive engagements with England and France and when she made those extensive and costly preparations for war, when, moreover she urgently proposed that military commissioners should be sent by France and England to the head-quarters of General Hess, I have no doubt she intended and expected war. But she also expected that long before the season for military operations began the allied armies would have obtained decisive victories in the Crimea, that they would be free, and would be able to undertake other

[a] Disraeli's questions and the replies by Russell and Palmerston were published in *The Times*, No. 22114, July 24, 1855. Disraeli quotes from Russell's speech in the House of Commons on July 19, 1855.—*Ed.*

[b] Presumably Francis Joseph.—*Ed.*

[c] The speeches of Lyndhurst and others who took part in the debate in the House of Lords on June 26, 1855, were published in *The Times*, No. 22091, June 27, 1855.—*Ed.*

operations in concert with her own forces. That, unfortunately, was not the case; and if Austria had at our invitation declared war, she would in all probability have had to wage that war *single-handed.*"

Still more astonishing is *Ellenborough*'s later statement in the House of Lords, which to this moment has not been challenged by any minister:

"*Before* the expedition to the Crimea was despatched, Austria proposed to communicate with the allied Powers on the subject of future military operations; acting, however, upon preconceived opinions, the allies sent that expedition, and *then* Austria at once said that she could not meet the Russians single-handed, and that *the expedition to the Crimea rendered it necessary for her to adopt a different course of action.* At a subsequent period, just at the commencement of the conference at Vienna, when it was of the greatest possible importance that Austria should act with us—at that time, still looking to nothing but the success of your operations in the Crimea, you withdrew from the immediate vicinity of Austria 50,000 good Turkish troops, thus depriving Austria of the only assistance on which she could rely in the event of a military expedition against Russia. It is clear, therefore, my lords, and also from the recent statements of the noble earl, Clarendon, that it is our ill-advised expedition to the Crimea which has paralysed the policy of Austria, and which has reduced her to her present difficult position. *Before* that expedition sailed to the Crimea I warned the Government. [...] I warned them of the effect which that expedition would produce upon the policy of Austria."

Here then we have a direct contradiction between the statement of Clarendon, the Foreign Secretary, between his statement and the statement of Lord John Russell and the statement of Lord Ellenborough. Russell says: the Crimean expedition sailed because Austria refused to cross the Pruth, i.e., to take sides against Russia with arms in hand. No, says Clarendon. Austria could not take sides against Russia because the Crimean expedition did not have the desired result. Finally, Lord Ellenborough: the Crimean expedition was undertaken against the will of Austria, and forced her to abstain from the war with Russia. These contradictions—however one may interpret them—prove in any case that the ambiguity was not merely to be found on the side of the Austrians.

Written on August 15, 1855

First published in the *Neue Oder-Zeitung,* No. 383, August 18, 1855

Marked with the sign ×

An enlarged English version was published as a leading article in the *New-York Daily Tribune,* No. 4493, September 13, 1855 and reprinted in the *New-York Semi-Weekly Tribune,* No. 1075, September 14, 1855

Printed according to the newspaper

This version is published in English for the first time

Karl Marx and Frederick Engels

THE ANGLO-FRENCH WAR AGAINST RUSSIA[343]

[*Neue Oder-Zeitung*, No. 385, August 20, 1855]

London, August 17. The Anglo-French war against Russia will undoubtedly always figure in military history as "the *incomprehensible* war". Big talk combined with minimal action, vast preparations and insignificant results, caution bordering on timidity, followed by the foolhardiness that is born of ignorance, generals who are more than mediocre coupled with troops who are more than brave, almost deliberate reverses on the heels of victories won through mistakes, armies ruined by negligence, then saved by the strangest of accidents—a grand ensemble of contradictions and inconsistencies. And this is nearly as much the distinguishing mark of the Russians as of their enemies. If the British have destroyed an exemplary army through the maladministration of the civil servants and the slothful incompetence of the officers; if the French have had to run useless risks and suffer enormous losses simply because Louis Napoleon affected to run the war from Paris, the Russians for their part have suffered similar losses as a result of maladministration and foolish but peremptory orders from Petersburg. Ever since the Turkish wars of 1828-29 Tsar Nicholas's military talents have been "passed over in silence" even by his most servile eulogists. If the Russians have Todtleben, who is *not a Russian*, they have on the other hand Gorchakov and [other]... *ovs* who in no respect yield to the S[ain]t-Arnauds and Raglans in the matter of incompetence.

One would have supposed that now, at any rate, when so many minds are occupied in drawing up plausible plans for attack and defence, and given this ever increasing mass of men and material, some breath-taking idea must needs be born. Not a bit of it, however. The war drags on and its prolongation serves only to enlarge the area over which it is being fought. The greater the proliferation of new theatres of war, the less the activity in each of them. We now have six: *the White Sea, the Baltic, the Danube, the Crimea, the Caucasus* and *Armenia*. What has been happening throughout this stupendous area can be told in the space of one column.

Of the *White Sea*, the Anglo-French wisely say nothing at all. Here they have only two practicable military aims: to prevent the coastal and other trade of the Russians in these waters and, if possible, to capture Archangel. The former has been attempted, but only up to a point; this year as well as last the Allied squadrons always arrived too late and sailed away too soon. The second object, the seizure of Archangel, has never been embarked upon. Instead of carrying out this, its real task, the blockading squadron has scattered to carry out slovenly attacks on Russian and Lapp villages and the destruction of what little the needy fishermen possess. The excuse proffered by English correspondents for these ignominious goings-on is the morose irritability of a squadron that feels itself incapable of getting down to serious work! Some defence!

On the *Danube* nothing is happening. The delta of this river is not even being cleared of the brigands who infest it. Austria holds the key to the door that leads into Russia from this side and seems determined to hang on to it.

In the *Caucasus* all is quiet. The formidable Circassians, like all barbarian and independent mountain-dwellers, seem to be perfectly content with the withdrawal of the Russian mobile column from their valleys and to have no desire to descend into the plain save on looting forays. They know how to fight only on their own territory and seem, furthermore, far from delighted at the prospect of annexation by Turkey.

In *Asia* Turkey may be seen as she reall is—her army there fully reflects the decayed state of the empire. It was deemed necessary to call on the Frankish *giaour* for assistance; but the Franks[a] could do nothing there save throw up field-works. All their attempts at making the troops adopt civilised methods of warfare failed utterly. The Russians have invested Kars and are apparently prepared to attack it systematically. It is difficult to see how the town can be relieved, unless Omer Pasha lands at Batum with 20,000 men and attacks the Russians in the flank. It is incomprehensible, and by no means a feather in the Russians' cap,

[a] A name frequently applied to West Europeans in the Middle East.—*Ed.*

that they should have acted so cautiously and hesitantly in the face of such an ill-disciplined adversary, when they had 20,000-30,000 good troops at their disposal. Whatever successes they may score in this theatre of war, the most they can achieve is the capture of Kars and Erzerum, for a march on Constantinople through Asia Minor is quite out of the question. For the time being, therefore, the war in Asia is of no more than local interest and, since it is hardly possible, given the inaccuracy of existing maps, to express from afar an accurate tactical and strategical opinion, we shall not pursue the matter further. There remain the two principal theatres of war, the Crimea and the Baltic.

[*Neue Oder-Zeitung*, No. 387, August 21, 1855]

London, August 18. In the Crimea the siege drags on lethargically.[a] The French and British were at work throughout the whole month of July on the new *approaches* to the Redan and the Malakhov and, though we were repeatedly given to understand that they had moved "quite close" to the Russians, we now learn that on August 4 the head of the sap was no closer than 115 metres to the Russian main ditch, and perhaps not even as close as that. It is certainly satisfactory to see Hotspur Pélissier[b] brought down to the acknowledgement that his "system of assault" has failed, and that regular siege works must pave the way for his columns; but for all that, to leave 200,000 men quiet in their tents to wait for the completion of these trenches, and to die in the

[a] Instead of this sentence the *New-York Daily Tribune* has: "Our files of English, French and German journals, received yesterday morning by the mail of the *Canada*, shed no additional light on the battle of August 16, on the Chernaya, where Liprandi was repulsed by the Allied forces and a number of Russian prisoners taken. With regard to this affair, we must wait for the next steamer before we can receive any satisfactory details. It is rather suspicious, however, that so little was known about it at Paris and London previous to the sailing of the *Canada*. Had it been really as decisive as the English journals represent, something more than the very incomplete statements now in our possession would naturally have been made public.

"It appears that the assault on the Malakoff, which was expected to have taken place on the 15th, had to be postponed, and that the preliminary bombardment did not commence till the 17th. Indeed, there is reason to suspect that the siege works are not in so forward a state as the journals of Paris and London have reported."—*Ed.*

[b] Pélissier is ironically compared to Sir Henry Percy (1364-1403) called Hotspur, the eldest son of the first earl of Northumberland, as portrayed in Shakespeare's *Henry IV*, Part 1.—*Ed.*

meantime of cholera and fever, is singular management. If—as the Paris papers maintain—the Chernaya cannot be crossed in view of the impregnable Russian position on the far side, something useful might at least be achieved by a sea-borne expedition to Eupatoria and an attempt to force the Russians on this side into the open field and to find out their real strength and the state of their resources. As matters now stand the Turkish, Sardinian and half the French and British armies have been reduced to the role of passive onlookers. Hence a large part of them could be used for diversions. But the only diversions we have heard of are those created every evening at Astley's Amphitheatre, in Surrey Gardens and Cremorne Gardens where, amidst a storm of applause from the patriotic cockneys,[a] the Russians suffer frightful defeats.

The Russians must by now have received all their reinforcements and will be at maximum strength during the period that lies immediately ahead. The British are sending out a few more regiments, the French have despatched 10,000-15,000 men with more to follow and all in all 50,000-60,000 fresh troops are to be added to the allied forces in the Crimea. On top of that the French Government has registered or bought a large number of river steamers (variously put at between 50 and 100), all of which are to be used for an expedition in the Black Sea. Whether they are intended for the Sea of Azov or the entry to the Dnieper and the Bug, where Ochakov, Kinburn, Kherson and Nikolayev would constitute objects of attack, remains to be seen. We mentioned on a previous occasion that some bloody affrays might be expected towards the middle of August, for at that time the Russians, after receiving reinforcements, would again seize the *initiative*.[b] Under General Liprandi they have in fact carried out a sortie directed against the French and Sardinians on the Chernaya and been beaten off with heavy loss.[344] Allied losses have *not* been stated and must therefore have been very considerable. Something more than telegraphic reports will be needed if this affair is to be discussed in greater detail.[c]

---

[a] Marx uses the English word.—*Ed.*

[b] See this volume, pp. 363-64.—*Ed.*

[c] Instead of this paragraph and the greater part of the preceding one, beginning with the words "If—as the Paris papers maintain—the Chernaya cannot be crossed", the *New-York Daily Tribune* has: "It must be confessed that from first to last, this has been a war of incapacities on both sides. Todtleben is the only man in either camp who has shown a spark of genius."—*Ed.*

Finally, in the *Baltic,* "a great blow has been struck"[a]! *Vide* the English press. Bombardment of Sweaborg[345]! Destruction of Sweaborg! Earthworks and all other installations lie in ruins! Sweaborg has actually ceased to exist! Glorious triumph for the Allies! The Navy is in an indescribable state of enthusiasm! And now let us consider the facts as they are.[b] The Allied fleets, six liners, four or five large frigates (blockships[c]), and about thirty mortar-vessels and gunboats, crossed over from the Revel to Sweaborg on August 7. On the 8th they took up their positions. The vessels of light draft passed through the shoals and rocks west of the fortress, where no large ship can pass, and apparently drew up at long range from the islands on which Sweaborg is situated. The large vessels remained outside, and as far as we can judge out of range of the forts. Then the gunboats and mortar-vessels opened fire. No direct firing appears to have been attempted. It was all shelling from mortars or shell guns at the highest elevation practicable. The bombardment lasted forty-five hours. As to the amount of damage inflicted it is not possible to estimate without detailed accounts from both parties. The arsenal and various magazines of powder (apparently small ones) were destroyed. The "*town*" of Sweaborg (so far as we know, only a few houses inhabited by people connected with the fleet or the works) was burnt. As to the fortifications themselves, the damage done to them cannot but be insignificant, for the fleets, as both Admirals state, had *not a man killed,* only a few wounded, and no loss whatever in *matériel.*[d] No better proof could be given that they kept out of harm's way. In that case they might bombard, but could not act by direct fire, by which alone fortifications can be destroyed. Dundas, who is far more honest and collected in his report than the French Admiral, according to the *Moniteur*'s rendering of the text which may have been coloured in Paris, avers that the damage inflicted was confined to the three islands (out of the seven constituting Sweaborg) which are situated west of the main entrance to the bay of Helsingfors. An attack on the

---

[a] The words in quotation marks are given both in German and in English in the original.—*Ed.*

[b] Instead of the preceding part of this paragraph the *New-York Daily Tribune* has: "With regard to the attack on Sweaborg, we are also still without full official reports or newspaper correspondence. The facts, however, appear on a careful examination of all the information at hand to be as follows."—*Ed.*

[c] Marx uses the English term.—*Ed.*

[d] The reference is to the report of Admiral Dundas, which was published in *The Times,* No. 22134, August 16, 1855, and that of the French Admiral Penaud, published in *Le Moniteur universel,* No. 227, August 15, 1855.—*Ed.*

main entrance does not even seem to have been attempted. It seems that the large vessels looked on and did nothing, and the decisive act in such an attack—the landing of troops to possess themselves of the works and destroy them—was entirely out of the question. Thus the damage inflicted falls upon stores and storehouses exclusively—that is, upon matters easily replaced; and if the Russians avail themselves of their time and means, Sweaborg may in three weeks be in as good a condition as ever. Militarily speaking, it has not suffered at all; the material results of the whole affair are hardly worth its cost; and it seems to have been undertaken merely because the Baltic fleet must do something before it comes home for the season, partly because Palmerston wanted to conclude the parliamentary session with a firework. Unfortunately the event occurred 24 hours too late for this purpose. Such was the glorious destruction of Sweaborg by the Allied fleets. We shall revert to the matter as soon as detailed reports are to hand.[a]

Written on August 17 and 18, 1855

First published in the *Neue Oder-Zeitung*, Nos. 385 and 387, August 20 and 21, 1855

Marked with the sign ×

An abridged English version of the second part of the article was published as a leading article in the *New York Daily Tribune*, No. 4483, September 1, 1855, and reprinted in the *New-York Semi-Weekly Tribune*, No. 1072, September 4, 1855

Printed according to the *Neue Oder-Zeitung*

Published in English in full for the first time

[a] The end of this paragraph from the words "partly because Palmerston wanted..." is omitted in the *New-York Daily Tribune*.—*Ed.*

Karl Marx

EVENTS AT THE THEATRES OF WAR

London, August 22. The reports of Admirals Penaud and Dundas[a] confirm the assessment which we have made of the "glorious destruction of Sweaborg, the Gibraltar of the North" (*Times* terminology). Thus we read today in one of the London newspapers:

"The great bombardment of Sweaborg was such that one can only say that it has perhaps inflicted considerable damage on the enemy owing to the spread of fire. We do not, however, seem to have gained much by it. The success was neither brilliant nor substantial. As much remains undone in the Baltic as before."[b]

Of course *The Times*, needing fair weather and good tidings during the Queen's trip to France,[346] having painted nothing but *couleur de rose* for the last few days and pretending to be suffering from a fit of optimism—*The Times* stubbornly insists on dreaming of the destruction of the "town" of Sweaborg.

As far as the Chernaya affair[347] is concerned, further reports, above all, are required for its proper evaluation. For everything depends on how far the battle was centred on the narrow passes of the Chernaya and to what extent the depth of the water made the river a real obstacle. If the battle took place in front of the French lines without such an obstacle then this would cast great discredit on the Russians. If, on the other hand, it was a case of forcing narrow passes which could not be circumvented, this would explain the large Russian losses, and both sides may have

---

[a] The report of Penaud was published in *Le Moniteur universel*, No. 230, August 18, 1855, and that of Dundas in *The Times*, No. 22138, August 21, 1855.—*Ed.*

[b] In a report from Paris of August 15 published in *The Times*, No. 22135, August 17, 1855.—*Ed.*

acquitted themselves honourably. But in any case it is not clear why the Russians failed to attempt a detour through the Baidar Valley. It is, however, certain that if the allies do not voluntarily move out, the Russians have now proved their inability to expel them from the plateau and the Chernaya line. And so the old dilemma has cropped up again.

The storming of Malakhov may be expected any day now. If it fails, the Allies are in a difficult position. If it succeeds, which is after all possible, though only with tremendous losses, this still does not mean that the south side is lost, unless evacuation should be necessary due to lack of provisions. But at any rate the Allies would have achieved the prospect of driving out the Russians before winter. The reports about the state of health of the English army in the Crimea are contradictory. According to one account every month 1,000 English soldiers in the trenches become unfit for duty. It is certain that out of a single regiment, the 10th Hussars, with a force of 676 men, 161 are sick. Dr. Sutherland, head of the health commission despatched to the Crimea by the government, writes in a letter to Lord Shaftesbury inter alia:

> "Week ending July 7. Strength of the British army 41,593, total deaths 150, deaths from cholera 71, deaths from fever 17, deaths from diarrhoea 19, deaths from dysentery 2. Week ending July 14. Strength of the army 42,513, total deaths 123, deaths from cholera 55, deaths from fever 18, deaths from diarrhoea 10, deaths from dysentery 5. The deaths from wounds for these two weeks were 44 and 30, making a total of 74."[a]

The ratio of deaths due to disease to deaths due to injuries during the first two weeks of July is thus almost 4:1. Dr. Sutherland makes the following contrast between the Army's state of health last winter and this summer:

> "The winter mortality was a far different thing from the summer mortality. Hardly any of the causes—namely, bad food, want of rest, overwork, want of clothing and shelter, and exposure to the elements, which caused scorbutis over the whole army—exist now. [...] All the cases then were scorbutic, and hence the awful mortality in the hospitals at Scutari; it was exactly like the Irish famine fever" (1847); "now we have [...] fever and cholera, the intensity of which in our camp has been, no doubt, most materially lessened by the great care bestowed on the men."

The besieged army's state of health is at present indisputably worse than that of the besiegers. Dr. Sutherland's letter can, however, by no means command full confidence since, as a recent

---

[a] The letter was printed in *The Times*, No. 22139, August 22, 1855.—*Ed.*

incident has shown, criticism within the English camp is *punished*. Approximately six weeks ago *The Times* published an anonymous letter denouncing the unforgivable treatment of the wounded after the bloody carnage of June 18.[a] The War Office demanded the name of the correspondent from *The Times*. The demand was rejected, unless Mr. Frederick Peel expressly promised that the correspondent would not suffer any reprisals because of his revelations. Peel would not accept this condition but denounced the refusal of *The Times* in Parliament. Mr. Bakewell (assistant surgeon[b]), the author of the letter in question, had in the meantime been sent on sick-leave to Scutari. This occurred in the middle of July. The authorities in the camp discovered somehow or other that he had written the letter. Behind his back, and *during his absence*, a court of inquiry was set up consisting of superior medical officials, for the most part personally compromised by Bakewell's letter. This court condemned him, without giving him the chance to defend himself or submit evidence to substantiate his charges. On August 3 his dismissal[c] was announced in the general *ordre du jour* of the army. One should gauge the credibility of the official or semi-official English reports on the state of health of the army, care of the injured, etc., with this incident in mind.

Written on August 22, 1855

First published in the *Neue Oder-Zeitung*, No. 395, August 25, 1855

Marked with the sign ×

Printed according to the newspaper

Published in English for the first time

[a] [R. H. Bakewell,] "The Wounded before Sebastopol. To the Editor of *The Times*", *The Times*, No. 22098, July 5, 1855.—*Ed.*

[b] Marx uses the English term.—*Ed.*

[c] *The Times*, No. 22139, August 22, 1855.—*Ed.*

Karl Marx

NAPIER'S LETTER

London, August 24. Today's newspapers have published a letter from Sir *Charles Napier*, in which our view of the Sweaborg affair[a] is substantially confirmed. We give the following excerpt from it.

"It will be seen by what I have written and by Admiral Dundas's despatch,[b] had my plan been followed up to the letter, Sweaborg would have been annihilated. It appears that the allies had only 43 gun and mortar boats, and many mortars have been disabled; they ought at least to have had 100—Sir James Graham in a letter to me" (1854) "said 200. Had that number been there the bombardment would have been continued by means of reliefs, as men are relieved in the trenches. The mortars would have had time to cool, and the bombardment continued till not one stone was left on another, and an opening made for the ships to go in and finish the work. Instead of that, the Admiralty do not seem to have foreseen that mortars could not stand for ever, though they must have had reports from Sebastopol; and thus an operation which appears to have been managed with great judgment has only met with partial success, for Admiral Dundas, in his report, admits the sea defences were little injured. [...] Had Admiral Dundas's means been greater he might have continued the bombardment as long as the weather remained fine, and the fleets, instead of returning to Nargen, might have been at anchor in Sweaborg.

"The first year there might have been some excuse for the Admiralty not having means, but none the second. [...] Instead of building gun and mortar boats they built a parcel of *iron* floating batteries which could hardly swim and, if they could, they would have been useless, for, had they been placed within 400 yards of Sweaborg they would have been annihilated, and at 400 yards[c] they would have done no harm.

"The first experiment on iron cost the country a million, and where are they? The second experiment not much less than half a million, and they have not yet left our ports, and probably never will. This is because incapable men are at the head.

---

[a] See this volume, pp. 485-87. Napier's letter was published in *The Times*, No. 22141, August 24, 1855.—*Ed.*

[b] Published in *The Times*, No. 22138, August 21, 1855.—*Ed.*

[c] In *The Times:* "at 800 yards".—*Ed.*

The Ministers have been driven to reform the War Department—when will they think of reforming the Admiralty? Till they do the people's money will be thrown away. The Admiralty do not seem to have contemplated the effect of a bombardment, though I told them upwards of a year ago what would happen and if they had read history they would have known that Martinique was taken by mortars; there were not casemates for all the garrison, nor were there at Sweaborg. Admiral Dundas says it formed no part of his plan to attempt a general attack by the ships on the defences, and his operations were confined to such destruction of the fortress and arsenals as could be accomplished by mortars.

"Had Admiral Dundas been furnished with sufficient means he would have contemplated an attack on the defences, and assembled the whole of his fleet, ready to take advantage of the terror and confusion occasioned by the gun and mortar boats. The heat of the conflagration alone would have kept the garrison from the guns, and the fleet would have been in Sweaborg, and the whole of the fortifications, islands, and all blown to the Devil; instead of that, the wooden buildings and magazines are destroyed, and the work will have to be begun again next year."

Napier concludes his letter thus:

"Sir James Graham was one of the Ministers who sent a British army to Sebastopol in the middle of last September, without means of moving, without food, proper tents, or clothing, and without hospitals, to pass a dreary winter and perish; and he was the Minister who wanted me to take a British fleet, in the end of October, to perish among the rocks of Sweaborg, and, to their shame, got two naval officers to put their names to the insulting letter he wrote me; and these men still remain in the Admiralty, and that is the way the navy of this country is managed. The two summers in the Baltic will be a lesson to them. They are in possession of my plans of attacking Kronstadt, and I dare say are in possession of Admiral Dundas's; and Sir James Graham and his two coadjutors had better go next summer and carry them into execution."

Written on August 24, 1855

First published in the *Neue Oder-Zeitung*. No. 397, August 27, 1855

Marked with the sign ×

Printed according to the newspaper

Published in English for the first time.

Karl Marx

AUSTRIA AND THE WAR[348]

We communicate to our readers on another page an account by an Austrian officer of a tour of inspection of the Galician Army recently made by the Emperor Francis Joseph. The writer, in narrating the events of this tour, and in stating the dislocation of the Imperial forces, confirms the opinion we have on former occasions taken care to explain, that in the preparations she last year made for war Austria was by no means engaged in a comedy for the delusion of the Western Powers. Certainly she could never have made such sacrifices merely to throw dust in the eyes of the world.

It is true that the utmost necessity alone induced her to arm against Russia; and indeed, as long as it was possible to procrastinate, Austria clung to the cobweb thread of a prospective peace which Russian diplomacy held out for a bait. At last, however, her patience was exhausted, and St. Petersburg learned with surprise, not unmingled with terror, that the Austrian columns were drawn up along the Galician frontier. This was before the bare possibility of such an armament had been admitted; and to concentrate an army of equal strength on the Russian side, within an equally short time, was altogether out of the question. The arts of diplomacy had therefore again to be resorted to. In what manner, and with what success this was done, need not be repeated. The whole of the immense army lately gathered on the Galician frontiers was dissolved at once, and the apprehensions of Russia in that quarter were partly allayed.[349] We say partly, because two important elements have risen with that army which are not dissolved along with it. These are the fortifications and railways erected, renewed, or completed, during the stay of the army in Galicia.

While in all other parts of the Empire the Government was guided by the principle of abandoning railway enterprise to private speculators, while the Western Railway, intended to connect Vienna with Munich, was even strikingly neglected, Baron Hess, the commander-in-chief in Galicia, was employing thousands of soldiers in the construction of a line of which however great the strategical value the commercial advantages are questionable, at least for the present—a line, too, which otherwise might have remained in the desks of private engineers for thirty years to come. To Russia nothing could have been more disagreeable than the construction of these railways, by which Austria is now able to reconcentrate the army just dissolved within less than a fifth part of the time required by Russia to bring up a similar army. Whoever will take the pains to inquire into the statistics of Austrian railway enterprise, and compare what has been done in the east to meet purely political views with the little attention paid to the interests of commerce in the west, he cannot fail to disbelieve that these Galician railways were thus hurried into premature existence for the mere deception of the world. Indeed, it is plain that such a purpose would have been much better answered by the speedy completion of the western lines connecting Austria with Bavaria.

Our opinion is also confirmed in a still higher degree by the recent extensive improvements and additions in the fortifications of the eastern provinces of Austria. If railways may or may not be constructed from strategical considerations, the erection and completion of a system of fortifications, and the unproductive outlay occasioned by such works, certainly admit of no explanation beyond the immediate necessities of the case. What we have said about the comparative extent of railway-works in the east and west of Austria applies with much greater force to these fortifications. Of the thirty-six fortresses of the Austrian Empire seven belong directly, and nine indirectly, to the eastern line of defense, most of them having only recently been raised to a high perfection—as for instance Cracow, Przemysl and Zaleszczyki. The two former, together with Lemberg, which on account of its situation cannot be made of great strength, command the road to Warsaw; the latter is at the easternmost extremity of Galicia, opposite the important Russian fortress of Chotin. Cracow has been made a fortress of the first order, and all the works of this, as well as of the other

Galician fortifications, have been put in complete readiness for war. It was once the custom in the Austrian army to give the command of fortresses to old worn-out generals, as a sort of honorable retirement; and such places were looked upon as a sort of exile for officers in disgrace at the Court; but we now find in the whole east and north-east really efficient men, generals of merit and distinguished staff-officers in command of fortresses. Cracow is commanded by Field-Marshal Wolter; Przemysl by Major-General Ebner; Zaleszczyki by Major-General Gläser; Carlsburg, in Transylvania, by Field-Marshal Sedlmayer; and Olmütz, on the north-western flank, by General von Böhm. At the same time the state of things in the west is the very reverse—men and things all but ruins tranquilly made over to further decay. How different would be the aspect there if the Western Powers could even pretend to call Austria's policy ambiguous! How the Austrian authorities would hasten to restore Linz with its forty Maximilian towers, now scarcely treated as a fortress—and Salzburg, once a stronghold of the first order! Instead of this, what do we behold?—dead quiet and perfect absence of all military preparations. The very soldiers returning from the East, where they expected to reap their laurels, are invalided as fast as they approach the Bavarian frontier.

These being facts which speak for themselves, there remains only one question to be settled: namely, through whose fault was the policy of Austria baffled and that country saddled with an enormous additional debt, without any immediate advantage either to itself or to its ostensible allies? We know it to be an opinion current at Vienna and reechoed throughout Germany, that Austria shrank back for fear of creating a second adversary in Prussia, and because a war undertaken without the aid of Germany, offered no guaranty of as speedy a termination as the exceptional position of the empire requires. We must however insist upon the contrary view. It is our judgment that if Austria had boldly attacked the Russian army, Prussia and the rest of Germany would have been compelled to follow, more or less slowly and reluctantly, in her track.

Who, then, is to be held responsible for the present Austrian policy?—England, under the guidance of that brilliant boggler and loquacious humbug, Lord Palmerston. To prove this proposition it is necessary to leave the military camp and to enter the diplomatic labyrinth. On the 23d of July Mr. Disraeli asked Lord John Russell the authority for his statement that "one of the principal causes of the expedition to the Crimea was the refusal of

Austria to cross the River Pruth."[a] Lord John could not recollect—that is he said his "authority was his general recollection." Mr. Disraeli then put the question to Lord Palmerston, who

"would not answer questions like these, picked out piecemeal from a long course of negotiations between her Majesty's Government and the Government of one of the Sovereigns[b] in alliance to a certain degree with her Majesty. All he could say with regard to himself was, that he had always thought the Crimea was the place where the most effective blow could be struck at the preponderance of Russia in the Black Sea; and if there had been no other reason [...] that would, in his mind, be amply sufficient for the expedition." "My opinion," he declared, "was that the expedition to the Crimea was the best step to take."

Thus we learn from Lord Palmerston that the Crimean campaign originated not with Austria, not with Bonaparte, but with himself. On June 26 Lord Lyndhurst, making a fierce onslaught on Austria, stated that

"early in June [1854] she resolved on making a demand upon Russia to evacuate the Principalities. That demand was made in very strong terms, with something like an intimation that if it were not complied with Austria would resort to forcible means to secure this object."

After some historical observations, the learned lord went on to say:

"Did Austria then immediately carry into effect any attack upon Russia? Did she attempt to enter the Principalities?—Far from it. She abstained from doing anything for a period of several weeks, till the moment when the siege of Silistria had been raised and the Russian army was in retreat, and when Russia herself had served a notice that she would within a certain time leave the Principalities and retire behind the Pruth."[c]

Lord Lyndhurst thus reproaches Austria for saying one thing and doing another. He was followed in the debate by Lord Clarendon, and from him we may get some idea of the genius which transformed the Austria of May and June into the Austria of July and August. He says that

"when Austria entered into those successive engagements with England and France, and when she made those extensive and costly preparations for

[a] The House of Commons debate (Disraeli's questions and the replies by Russell and Palmerston) was reported in *The Times*, No. 22114, July 24, 1855. Russell's statement quoted by Disraeli is from the former's speech in the House of Commons on July 19, 1855.—*Ed.*

[b] Presumably Francis Joseph.—*Ed.*

[c] The House of Lords debate of June 26, 1855 was reported in *The Times*, No. 22091, June 27, 1855.—*Ed.*

war—when, moreover, she urgently proposed that military commissions should be sent by France and England to the headquarters of Gen. Hess, I have no doubt she intended and expected war. But she also expected that long before the season for military operations began the allied armies would have obtained decisive victories in the Crimea—that they would be free, and would be able to undertake other operations in concert with her own forces. That unfortunately was not the case; and if Austria had at our invitation declared war, she would in all probability have had to wage that war single-handed."

The explanation of Lord John Russell is thus in direct opposition to the statement of Lord Clarendon. Lord John stated that the Crimean expedition sailed because Austria refused to cross the Pruth—that is, to take part against Russia. Lord Clarendon tells us that Austria could not take part against Russia because of the expedition to the Crimea.

Next, we may consult with profit an uncontradicted statement of Lord Ellenborough:

"Before the expedition to the Crimea was dispatched, Austria proposed to communicate with the allied Powers on the subject of future military operations; acting, however, upon preconceived opinions, the Allies sent that expedition, and then Austria at once said that she could not meet the Russians single-handed, and that the expedition to the Crimea rendered it necessary for her to adopt a different course of action. At a subsequent period, just at the commencement of the Conferences at Vienna, when it was of the greatest possible importance that Austria should act with us—at that time, still looking to nothing but the success of your operations in the Crimea, you withdrew from the immediate vicinity of Austria 50,000 good Turkish troops, thus depriving Austria of the only assistance on which she could rely in the event of a military expedition against Russia. It is clear, therefore, my lords, and also from the statements of the noble earl [Clarendon], that it is our ill-advised expedition to the Crimea which has paralyzed the policy of Austria, and which has reduced her to a position of such difficulty as to prevent her at once adopting a course which is essential for her honor, her dignity, and her interest. Before that expedition sailed to the Crimea I ventured to counsel the Government as to what the necessary consequences of it would be. I counseled them as to the effect which that expedition would produce upon the policy of Austria."

The advice of Lord Ellenborough was not heeded. Palmerston sent off the Sevastopol expedition at the very moment when its sailing was best calculated to prevent and avert Austrian hostilities against Russia. It almost looks as if he had meant to render aid to the great enemy of England, and as if he had purposely entrapped Austria into her present ambiguous position in the Principalities, delivered her over to Russian diplomacy, and crowded her still nearer to the brink of that abyss into which she must ultimately sink. In this matter, as in so many others during his long and inglorious career, Palmerston has brilliantly succeeded, whatever may have been his real purpose, in serving the interest of Russia alone.

Written in the second half of August 1855

First published in the *New-York Daily Tribune,* No. 4493, September 13, 1855, reprinted in the *New-York Semi-Weekly Tribune,* No. 4502, September 14, 1855 as a leading article; the German version of the second half of this article was published in the *Neue Oder-Zeitung,* No. 383, August 18, 1855, marked with the sign ×

Reproduced from the *New-York Daily Tribune*

Karl Marx and Frederick Engels

THE PUNISHMENT OF THE RANKS[350]

London, August 28. A single institution of the British army is sufficient to characterise the class the British soldier is recruited from. We refer to the *punishment of flogging*. Corporal punishment no longer exists in the French, the Prussian or several smaller armies. Even in Austria, where the recruits for the most part are semi-barbarians, its abolition is evidently being striven for; for instance, the punishment of running the gauntlet was recently expunged from the military law of Austria. In England, on the other hand, the "cat-o'-nine-tails"[a] has remained in full operation—an instrument of torture quite on a par with the Russian knout. Whenever a reform of military legislation has been mooted in Parliament all the old plumed hats have waxed passionate on behalf of the "cat", and none more zealously than old Wellington. For these men an unflogged soldier was an incomprehensible creature. In their eyes bravery, discipline and invincibility were the exclusive attributes of men bearing the scars of at least 50 lashes on their backsides like liegemen of old bearing a coat of arms.

The only reform has been the limitation of the number of strokes of the lash to 50. The efficacy of this reform may be judged from the fact that in Aldershot about a week ago a private expired shortly after receiving 30 strokes of the lash. On this occasion the favourite method of soaking the "cat-o'-nine-tails" in urine was employed. The application of urine on raw and bleeding flesh is an infallible recipe for tormenting the patient beyond the bounds of sanity. The nine-tailed cat is not only an instrument of torture, it leaves behind ineradicable scars, it brands

[a] Here and below Marx and Engels use the English term.—*Ed.*

a man for life. Even in the English army such a branding entails a constant oppressive burden of shame. The flogged soldier falls below the level of his comrades! But under the British military code punishment before the enemy consists almost exclusively of flogging, and thus the punishment lauded by its defenders as the only means of maintaining discipline in decisive moments becomes the surest means of destroying discipline, by breaking the moral composure and the *point d'honneur* of the soldier. This explains two strange facts. Firstly: *the great number of British deserters before Sevastopol.* During the winter when the British soldiers had to make superhuman efforts in guarding the trenches, those unable to keep awake for 48-60 hours at a stretch were flogged. Just imagine it! Floggings for heroes like the British soldiers, who had proved themselves in the trenches before Sevastopol and in the open before Inkerman[351]! But the articles of war left no choice. Floggings were meted out to the best men in the army if they were overcome by fatigue, and dishonoured as they were they deserted to the Russians. It is impossible to conceive of a better motivated condemnation of this system than is provided by these facts. In no previous war have the troops of any nation deserted to the Russians in any numbers worth mentioning. They knew they would receive worse treatment than in their own national ranks. It was left to the British army to provide the first strong contingent of such deserters, and according to the evidence of the Englishmen themselves it was the "cat-o'-nine-tails" which recruited these deserters to Russia.

The second fact is the difficulty England encounters in all its attempts at forming foreign legions. As early as the anti-Jacobin war, even though the British articles of war nominally apply to the foreign corps, corporal punishment had to be abandoned in fact. At the beginning of this century some heterodox British generals, Sir Robert Wilson among others, published pamphlets criticising the corporal punishment of soldiers. For more than ten years Sir Francis Burdett thundered against the "cat-o'-nine-tails" in Parliament and called the British "a flogged nation".[a] In the Commons he found energetic seconds in Lord Folkestone and the famous Lord Cochrane (now Admiral Earl of Dundonald). In the press Cobbett conducted a strenuous campaign against the "cat", atoning for it with two years' imprisonment. At one point, during the last years of war against Napoleon, exasperation in the nation

[a] The English phrase is used in the original and the German translation is given in brackets.— *Ed.*

and in the army reached such heights that the Duke of York, equally notorious for his bigoted attachment to square-bashing, his bolting from the French and his amours with Madame Clarke, was forced to issue an order of the day in which all officers received notice that were flogging a frequent occurrence in their respective commands it would hinder their promotion.

How then can we explain the fact that the "cat-o'-nine-tails" has victoriously survived all these storms of half-a-century? Very simply. It is the instrument by which the aristocratic character of the British army is preserved, by which all higher positions, starting with ensign, remain secure as the apanage of the younger sons of the aristocracy and the gentry. With the disappearance of the "cat-o'-nine-tails" the extraordinary distance between the soldiers and the officers, which splits the army into two virtually separate races, would also disappear. At the same time the army's ranks would be opened to sections of the population higher than those from which they have hitherto been recruited. And that would seal the fate of the old constitution of the British army. It would be revolutionised through and through. The nine-tailed cat is the Cerberus guarding the treasure of the aristocracy.

Written on August 28, 1855

First published in the *Neue Oder-Zeitung*, No. 405, August 31, 1855

Marked with the sign ×

Printed according to the newspaper

This version is published in English for the first time

Frederick Engels

THE BATTLE OF THE CHERNAYA[352]

Contrary to our expectation the mail of the *Africa*, which we received late on Wednesday night, failed to bring the report of Prince Gorchakoff concerning the battle of the Chernaya, fought on the 16th ult. However, the French and English accounts which we printed yesterday afford sufficient information for a tolerably correct judgment of the affair.[a] In the French report one is struck by the absence of that tendency to bluster which but too often is innate in a French *sabreur*, and which was so prominent in Pélissier's first Bulletins. The old General is now uncommonly clear, business-like, and to the point[b]; he even gives the Russians full credit for the bravery they displayed on that occasion; and his report very favorably contrasts with General Simpson's amusing calculations as to the numbers engaged, by which it would appear that without any great effort some 15,000 French and Sardinians defeated 60,000 Russians. The facts of the case appear to have been as follows:

On the morning of Aug. 16, before daybreak, the Russians descended from the Mackenzie hights and took up a position on

[a] Instead of these two sentences the *New-York Semi-Weekly Tribune* and *New-York Weekly Tribune* have: "At last we have received the reports of the several commanding Generals in the Crimea concerning the battle of the Chernaya, fought on the 16th ult."—*Ed.*

[b] In the *Neue Oder-Zeitung* of September 3, 1855 the beginning of the article reads as follows: "Although we still have no detailed Russian report on the battle of the Chernaya (fought on August 16), the French and English reports this time allow a fairly accurate judgment of the affair. The defeat of June 18 seems to a certain degree to have held in check the tendency to bluster which was so prominent in Pélissier's first Bulletins. His report on the Chernaya affair is uncommonly clear, business-like, and to the point."—*Ed.*

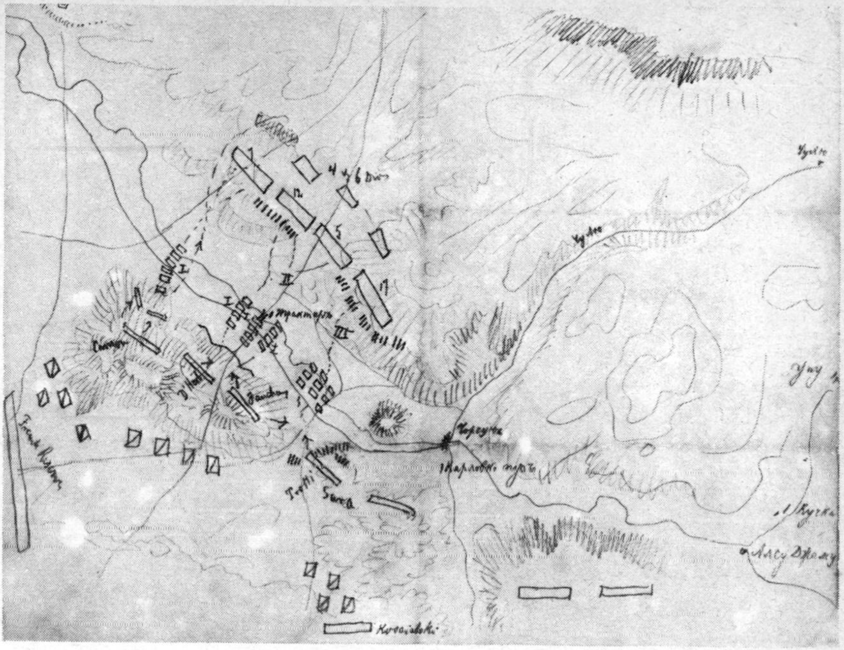

Chart of the Battle of the Chernaya
(August 16, 1855) made by Engels

the edge of the hills descending toward the Chernaya. They were commanded by Prince Gorchakoff in person, under whom Gen. Read commanded the right wing (7th and 12th divisions), while Liprandi with the 5th division appears to have occupied the center, while the 17th division formed the Russian left. Portions of the 4th and 6th divisions were also present, and seem to have acted as reserves. The 5th division, along with the troops belonging to the 4th and 6th, form part of the second (Paniutin's) corps, which had but just arrived in the Crimea; the remainder were old Crimean troops, and must have figured with effective numbers very much reduced.

The ground on the opposite side of the Chernaya is mostly level, a continuation of the plain of Balaklava toward the river; but close to its banks this plain is interrupted by two groups of hillocks, rising gradually from the Balaklava side, but falling off toward the Chernaya, thus offering a good defensible position against an enemy crossing the river. Between these two groups of hillocks lies the valley into which the British Light Cavalry charged in the battle of Balaklava.[353] The eastern group of hillocks, forming the right wing of the position, was occupied by La Marmora with his two Sardinian divisions; the other, toward the northwest, by three French divisions, which thus formed the center and left of the position. The French were commanded by General d'Herbillon, who had disposed Camou's division to the left, his own in the center, and Faucheux's division to the right, where it joined the Sardinian division of Trotti. The position gained additional strength from the two obstacles in its immediate front: first, the Chernaya, which river at the time was certainly fordable, but still obliged the Russians to cross at certain places only, and with a small front; and secondly, the aqueduct, cut in most places into the rock, and thus offering, even after its passage, a steep wall of scarped rock to be climbed. On the brink of the hills the French and Piedmontese had thrown up some light breast-works just sufficient to shelter their cannon. The two groups of hillocks formed, so to speak, several bastions flanking each other with their artillery. Beyond the Chernaya, which was crossed by bridges at Chorgun, on the Sardinian extreme right, and at an inn (in Russian Traktir) in front of the French center, the Piedmontese had two companies as outposts, while the bridge of Traktir was covered by a slight bridge-head occupied by the French. The French outposts were still beyond this.

On the morning of the 16th the Russians having got their artillery in position on the hights east of the Chernaya, sent their advanced troops down into the valley. Day had not yet broken and a dense fog facilitated a surprise, as at Inkerman. The allied outposts were driven in in a moment, and by daybreak the bridge-head and the whole eastern side of the river were in their hands, while they were fighting for the passage of the bridges with two French regiments. Then the 7th and 12th Russian divisions, placed exactly opposite the French divisions of Camou and d'Herbillon, descended in two close columns into the valley; and here they formed their columns of attack and advanced in two distinct masses—the 7th division, passing river and aqueduct, partly by fords, partly by flying-bridges constructed in all haste, against Camou; while the 12th division, part of which remained in reserve, advanced against d'Herbillon by the bridge of Traktir, the defenders of which were in an instant thrown back by the overwhelming masses of the Russians. They advanced with greater rapidity and spirit than were ever shown by Russians through the aqueduct and up the hill-side. The 7th Russian division came up nearly to the brink of the hill, when Camou's troops, deployed in line, gave them a volley and charged them in flank and rear with such vehemence that the Russians instantly turned, recrossed the river under a murderous fire, and, if we may believe Pélissier, that 7th division never showed itself again during the battle. In the center, the 12th division succeeded in scaling the hights and driving in several French regiments. The fate of the battle appeared uncertain for a moment, when d'Herbillon ordered a brigade from Faucheux's division to attack the left flank of the Russian columns, and after a short struggle, the Russians were driven down the declivity, followed by the French, who for a moment retook the bridge.

Gorchakoff, however, had prepared a fresh attack. The remainder of the 12th division and the 5th division had descended into the valley, where they sheltered the fugitives who re-formed; and now the whole of the 12th and 5th divisions moved forward for a second charge. They passed by the bridge, and close to the right and left of it, and advanced with great vivacity against the allied center (d'Herbillon's and Faucheux's divisions). But by this time the French had got all their artillery into position; it fired in front against the Russian columns, while the Sardinian artillery took them in flank. In spite of this murderous fire they advanced steadily and rapidly, and again reached the hights. There they found the French collected, deployed in line a little behind the edge of the hill. As soon as the heads of the columns were fairly on the edge, the French gave them a volley, and charged them with the bayonet in front and flank. The struggle was as short as before. The Russians gave way and fled in disorder across the river, pursued by the musketry and artillery-fire of the Allies. This second defeat of the Russians virtually decided the battle. They had three-fifths of their infantry engaged, and could not hope to see any fresh reenforcements arrive on the field; the Allies, too, had three divisions out of five engaged, but fresh troops were hurrying to support them from the camp before Sevastopol. Pélissier had sent for two more divisions of the line and one of the Guards, and they were coming up. It was now about 8 o'clock in the morning.

Gorchakoff, in spite of these odds, resolved upon another attack. The 17th division now had to come forward and to form a nucleus for such part of the beaten troops as were still fit to be brought against the enemy. The line of attack was again shifted to the left; it was Faucheux's division upon which the Russians fell this time. But in vain. The cross-fire of the French and Sardinian artillery decimated them before they could reach the summit of the hills, and again the French lines broke their columns and drove them back to the other side of the river, while the Piedmontese (Trotti's division) took them in flank and completed the victory. There remained but the troops of the 4th and 6th divisions intact, amounting to the effective strength of about one division. To launch these would have served no purpose whatever. The defeat was unmistakable; and accordingly the Russians, bringing forward their artillery, commenced the retreat. Their own position was so strong that Pélissier deemed an attack upon it out of the question; and therefore they were molested by the artillery and rifles only.[a] The loss of the Russians in this affair was enormous in comparison with that of the Allies. The former lost about 5,000 in killed, wounded and prisoners; the latter about 1,500 only. The reason of this was, that the Russians had to make all their charges under the most effective fire of the allied artillery, especially the Piedmontese, whose 16-pounders, though slow to move, are of the highest effect when once in position.

The Russian attack was here made exclusively in front. To turn the French left by Inkerman, appeared impossible from the command exercised by the French batteries on the spur of the

---

[a] Instead of the last two sentences the *Neue Oder-Zeitung* of September 4, 1855, where the end of this article is published, has: "Yesterday we described the mere progress of the battle of the Chernaya. For an accurate assessment of the number of troops engaged on both sides we shall have to wait for the Russian reports."—*Ed.*

ridge opposite that place. To turn the Allies by their right would have necessitated that the main body of the Russians should descend into the valley of Baidar, where the ground is evidently too intricate for such clumsy troops. Thus the front attack was chosen, and very properly a surprise attempted. The surprise partially succeeded, but was not carried out with the necessary energy. When the Russians were once masters of the passages of the Chernaya, they should have pushed forward their masses just as they happened to be at hand, in order to follow up their advantage before the French could recover from the first blow.[a] Instead of that, they allowed their opponents the time necessary to bring their troops and artillery into position, and the effect of the surprise which might have brought into their hands the hights occupied by the French ceased almost as soon as the Russians had reached the Chernaya. This is another proof of the difficulty of moving Russian troops under circumstances where they should be expected to act rapidly and where inferior commanders must use their own judgment.

The French have always been notorious for a certain contempt of outpost duty. Even in their best estate an active enemy could any night surprise their outposts and alarm their camps without any great risk. On this occasion they showed that even the slowly-moving Russians might do it. Their main position was so close on the Chernaya that their advanced troops should have been either pushed much further forward, or, if the ground did not allow this, that they should have been reenforced so strongly as to be able to hold out until the camp could be got under arms. As it was, the French were encamped without any proportionate advanced guard, and in consequence the Russians were able to advance on their main position before they had time to bring their full powers of resistance into play. More active opponents than the Russians would have brought forward superior numbers so rapidly that the hights occupied by the French must have been carried before any regular and systematic resistance could have been made.[b] But the Russians themselves were afraid of risking a

---

[a] This sentence does not occur in the *Neue Oder-Zeitung*.—*Ed.*

[b] Instead of the passage beginning with the words "On this occasion they showed..." the *Neue Oder-Zeitung* has: "That omission was all the more striking this time as Pélissier had repeatedly been informed of the plans of the Russians, even on the eve of the battle, by Russian deserters. As it was, the French were encamped on the hills without any proportionate advanced guard, so that the enemy could have advanced before they had had time to bring their full powers of resistance into play. This could have decided the outcome had the French been confronted by an active opponent."—*Ed.*

division or two of their troops in twilight-fighting, and thus they lost every advantage the surprise had gained for them.

The decisive and easily-bought successes of the French in repelling the Russian columns when they had already scaled the hights, were due to a system of tactics hitherto not often followed by them. They have evidently learnt this mode of fighting from the English, who are masters in it. In defending a range of hills, the great advantage consists in concealing your troops just behind the crest, where they are fully sheltered, deploying them in line, and awaiting the appearance of the hostile columns. As soon as the heads of the columns appear on the crest, your line pours a volley into them, to which but a few muskets can reply, and then you rush upon them, in front and flank, with the bayonet. The English fought thus at Busaco, Pampeluna, Waterloo,[354] and other battles, with constant success. Yet the continental troops of Europe appear to have lost all trace of this all but infallible mode of defending a range of hights. In the manuals of tactics it figured, but in practice it had almost disappeared before the universal predilection for columns covered by skirmishers. The French deserve great credit for having adopted from their old opponents this plain and effective maneuver. Had they been disposed in columns there is little doubt the Russians would have had greater advantages over them and perhaps even carried the day. But as it was, the fire of a deployed line of infantry, acting upon an enemy disorganized by a telling artillery fire and the fatigue of mounting a steep hill, proved overwhelming; and a hearty advance with the bayonet was quite sufficient to hurl back the masses that had already spent their spirits before the glittering steel was close upon them.[a]

This is the third pitched battle of this war, fought in the open field, and like Alma and Inkerman,[355] it is distinguished by its comparatively short duration. In Napoleon's wars a great deal of preliminary skirmishing characterized a battle; each party sought to feel the enemy before engaging him on decisive points and with decisive masses; and it was after each party had engaged the greater number of its troops only that the decisive blow was attempted. Here we see, on the contrary, no time lost, no fencing to tire out the enemy; the blow is struck at once, and upon the result of one or two attacks the fate of the battle depends. This looks a great deal braver than Napoleon's mode of fighting; yet, if

---

[a] The concluding part of this paragraph beginning with the words "but in practice it had almost disappeared" does not occur in the *Neue Oder-Zeitung*.—*Ed.*

a superiority of two to one, as the Allies possessed on the Alma, or if the known clumsiness of the Russians in maneuvering may seem to justify such straightforward action, the fact is that it shows in both parties a great want of generalship; and whenever the *sabreurs* who act upon this principle happen to be opposed to a general who properly understands how to occupy their troops, how to lay snares for them and invite them to run into them, they will very soon find themselves in a very unenviable position.

Finally, we repeat what we have often said; bravery in the soldiers and mediocrity in the generals are the chief characteristics, on both sides, of the present war.[a]

Written about August 31, 1855

First published in the *New-York Daily Tribune,* No. 4494, September 14, 1855, reprinted in the *New-York Semi-Weekly Tribune,* No. 1076, September 18, 1855 and the *New-York Weekly Tribune,* No. 732, September 22, 1855 as a leading article; the German version was published in the *Neue Oder-Zeitung,* Nos. 409 and 411, September 3 and 4, 1855, marked with the sign ×

Reproduced from the *New-York Daily Tribune*

[a] Instead of the last two paragraphs the *Neue Oder-Zeitung* has: "The battle of the Chernaya is the third 'great' battle of the Crimean campaign alongside the battles of the Alma and Inkerman. Characteristic of all these battles is their extraordinary simplicity, we would almost say primitiveness. No long manoeuvring, several strong blows, rapid decision. In Napoleon's battles we find, on the contrary, a great deal of skirmishing, all sorts of manoeuvres, and the decisive blow dealt unexpectedly only after the greater part of the troops has temporarily been engaged. The Crimean mode of procedure looks braver but in fact only shows the mediocrity of the generals on both sides and bears out our view that in modern times the art of war has been developing in reverse proportion to war material. If the battle of the Chernaya by no means provides as strong evidence of the Russians' inability as the battle of Inkerman, it undoubtedly proves anew the superiority of the Western armies. It shows to those prophets who on the pretext of having discovered a 'new' element in history are merely giving modern colour and shape to their school recollections of the decline of the Roman Empire that the substitutes for the Goths should be looked for not among the Muscovites but elsewhere.

"In *The Morning Advertiser* Sir Charles Napier is publishing his correspondence with Sir James Graham, something he has threatened to do for a long time."—*Ed.*

Karl Marx

ANOTHER BRITISH REVELATION[356]

With the single exception of the posthumous papers of Sir A. Burnes, published by his father in order to clear his memory from the false imputation, cast upon him by Lord Palmerston, of having initiated the infamous and unfortunate Afghan war, and proving to evidence that the so-called dispatches of Sir A. Burnes, as laid before Parliament by Lord Palmerston, were not only mutilated to the entire perversion of their original sense, but actually falsified and interpolated with passages forged for the express purpose of misleading public opinion[357]—with this single exception, there has, perhaps, never appeared a series of documents more damaging to the reputation of the British Government and of the caste which enjoys a hereditary tenure of office in that country, than the correspondence between Sir James Graham and Sir Charles Napier, just published[a] by the old Admiral with a view to vindicate his own character.

In this controversy Sir James Graham possesses one great advantage over his adversary—no revelation whatever is likely to lower his character in the world's judgment. The man who loudly boasted of having been an accomplice in the murder of the Bandieras; who stands convicted of having regularly opened, and tampered with, private letters at the London Post-Office for the mere benefit of the Holy Alliance; who spaniel-like licked the hands of the Emperor Nicholas, when he landed on the English shore; who even exaggerated the atrocious cruelty of the new English Poor Laws by his peculiar method of administering them;

[a] *The Times*, Nos. 22149, 22150, 22152 and 22154, September 3, 4, 6 and 8, 1855.—*Ed.*

and who, but a few months ago, vainly attempted in a full House to throw upon Mr. Layard the odium of the injuries he had himself inflicted upon poor Captain Christie[a] [358]—such a man may be fairly considered character-proof. There is something mysterious in his public career. Possessed neither of the uncommon talents which allow Lord Palmerston to belong to no party, nor of the hereditary party influence which enables Lord John Russell to dispense with uncommon talents, he has nevertheless succeeded in acting a prominent part among British statesmen. The clue to this riddle is to be found, not in the annals of the history of the world, but in the annals of *Punch*. In that instructive periodical there occurs, year after year, a picture drawn from the life, and adorned with the laconic inscription: "Sir Robert Peel's Dirty Boy." Sir Robert Peel was an honest man, though no great man; but above all, he was a British statesman, a party leader, forced by the very exigencies of his position to do much dirty work, which he was rather averse to doing. Thus, Sir James proved a true godsend to him, and thus Sir James happened to become an inevitable man, and a great man too.

Sir Charles Napier belongs to a family alike distinguished by their gifts and their eccentricities. The Napiers, amid the present tame race of men, impress one with the notion of some primitive tribe, enabled by their natural genius to acquire the arts of civilization; but not to bow before its conventionalities, to respect its etiquette, or to submit to its discipline. If the Napiers have always done good service to the English people, they have always quarreled with and revolted against their government. If they possess the value of Homeric heroes, they are also somewhat given to their swaggering mood. There was the late General Sir Charles Napier—undoubtedly the most ingenious soldier England has possessed since the times of Marlborough, but not more noted for his conquest of Scinde[359] than for his quarrels with the East India Company, which were prolonged beyond the grave on the part of his family. There is General Sir W. Napier, the first writer in the military literature of England, but not less famous for his eternal feuds with the British War-Office—whose regard for the narrow prejudices of his countrymen is so small that, at first, his celebrated history of the Peninsular War was unanimously denounced by the British reviews as "the best French account ever given of that War." There is also the antagonist of Sir James

[a] This refers to Graham's speech in the House of Commons on May 18, 1855. *The Times*, No. 22058, May 19, 1855.—*Ed.*

Graham, old Admiral Napier, who made his renown by unmaking the orders of his superiors. As for this last burly scion of the Napiers, Sir James fancied he had wrapped him in boa-constrictor folds, but they finally prove to be mere conventional cobwebs.

Sir James Graham, as First Lord of the Admiralty, deprived Sir Charles Napier, on his return to England, of his command; in the House of Commons he pointed to him as the responsible author of the Baltic failure, in proof of which he quoted some passages from his private letters[a]; he accused him of having shrunk from the execution of the bold orders he had received from the Admiralty Board; he expressed a hope that no other Lord of the Admiralty would at any future time be inconsiderate enough to hoist Sir Charles Napier's flag; and he ridiculed him in the papers at his disposal as "Fighting Charley," who, like the mythological King of France, "marched up the hill with twenty thousand men, and then marched down again." Sir Charles, to use his own words,

> "demanded inquiry on his conduct, which was refused; he appealed to the Cabinet, but received no reply, and finally to the House of Commons. The papers were refused, under the plea that it would be injurious to her Majesty's service."[b]

After the bombardment of Sweaborg that plea was of course at an end.

Sir James thought his game the more sure, as he had taken the precaution of marking all his letters "private" which were likely to expose himself and to vindicate his intended victim. As to the meaning of that sacramental word "private," Sir James himself, when giving his evidence before the Sevastopol Committee, stated that a British First Lord of the Admiralty is wont to mark public instructions "private" whenever he has good reason to withhold them not only from the public, but even from Parliament.[c]

With a man like Sir James, who thinks himself entitled to turn private letters into public ones, it is quite natural to convert public documents into private property. But this time he reckoned without his host. Sir Charles Napier, by boldly breaking through the shackles of "private instructions," is perhaps exposed to the chance of being struck from the British Navy list, and has probably disabled himself from ever again hoisting his flag; but, at

---

[a] Graham's speech in the House of Commons on March 8, 1855. *The Times*, No. 21997, March 9, 1855.—*Ed.*

[b] "Sir Charles Napier on the Bombardment of Sweaborg. To the Editor of *The Times*", *The Times*, No. 22141, August 24, 1855.—*Ed.*

[c] "State of the Army before Sebastopol", *The Times*, No. 22054, May 15, 1855.—*Ed.*

the same time, he has not only barred the entrance of the Admiralty Board to Sir James, but also shown to the English people that their navy is as rotten as their army. When the Crimean campaign stripped from the British army its time-honored reputation, the defenders of the ancient régime pleaded not guilty on the plausible ground that England had never pretended to be a first-rate military power. However, they will not dare to assert that Great Britain has laid no claim to be the first naval power of the world. Such is the redeeming feature of war; it puts a nation to the test. As exposure to the atmosphere reduces all mummies to instant dissolution, so war passes supreme judgment upon social organizations that have outlived their vitality.

This correspondence between Sir James Graham and Admiral Napier, extending from the 24th of February to the 6th of November, 1854, and denied a place in full in our columns only from its great length, may be summed up very briefly. Up to the end of August, when the Baltic season, as is generally known, has reached its close, all went very smoothly—although Sir Charles Napier, on the very outset of the expedition, had told Sir James his opinion that

"the means which the Admiralty had provided for fitting out and manning the North Sea fleet [...] were insufficient for the occasion and unequal to an encounter with the Russians on fair terms."

During all this time Sir James in his letters does nothing but smile upon his "Dear Sir Charles." On March 12 he "congratulates" him on the "order " in which the fleet had left the English shores; on April 5 he is "satisfied with his movements;" on April 10 he is "entirely satisfied with his proceedings;" on June 20 he calls him "a consummate Commander-in-Chief;" on July 4 he is "sure that whatever man can do will be done by Sir Charles;" on August 22 he "congratulates him sincerely on the success of his operations before Bomarsund;" and on August 25, seized with a sort of poetical rapture, he breaks forth:

"I am more than satisfied with your proceedings; I am delighted with the prudence and sound judgment you have evinced."

During the whole time Sir James feels only anxious lest Sir Charles,

"in the eager desire to achieve a great exploit and to satisfy the wild wishes of an impatient multitude, should yield to some rash impulse, and fail in the discharge of one of the noblest of duties—which is the moral courage to do what you know to be right, at the risk of being accused of having done wrong."

As early as May 1, 1854, he tells Sir Charles:

"I believe both Sweaborg and Kronstadt to be all but impregnable from the sea—Sweaborg more especially—and none but a very large army could operate by land efficiently in the presence of such a force as Russia could readily concentrate for the immediate approaches to her capital."

If Sir Charles tells him on June 12 that

"the only successful manner of attacking Sweaborg that he could see after the most mature consideration, assisted by Admiral Chads [...], was by fitting out a great number of gun-boats [...]" [a]—

Sir James answers him on July 11:

"With 50,000 troops and 200 gun-boats you might still do something great and decisive before the end of September."

But hardly had the Winter set in, the French army and navy sailed away, and the heavy equinoctial gales begun to furrow the Baltic waves—hardly had Sir Charles reported

"that our ships have already been parting their cables; the *Dragon* was reduced to one anchor, and the *Impérieuse* and *Basilisk* lost one each the other night; and the *Magicienne* was obliged to anchor in a fog, and when she weighed in the night from off Nargen found herself obliged to anchor off Renskar Lighthouse, having drifted among the rocks; and that the *Euryalus* had been ashore on the rocks, and that it was a mercy she was not lost"—

when Sir James all at once discovered that "war is not conducted without risks and dangers," and Sweaborg, therefore, must be taken without a single soldier or a single gun or mortar-boat! Indeed, we can only repeat with the old Admiral: "Had the Emperor of Russia been First Lord of the Admiralty he would have written just such letters."

At the Admiralty Board, as is clearly shown by this correspondence, anarchy reigned as supreme as at the War-Office. Sir James approved of Napier's movement inside the Belt, while the Board disapproved of it. In August, Sir James writes him to prepare for an early retreat from the Baltic, while the Board sends dispatches in a contrary sense. Sir James takes one view of Gen. Niel's report, and the Board an opposite one. But the most interesting point presented by the correspondence is, perhaps, the new light it throws upon the Anglo-French Alliance. The French admiral [b] showed Sir Charles his orders of recall on the 30th of August. The

[a] "Sir Charles Napier on the Bombardment of Sweaborg. To the Editor of *The Times*", *The Times*, No. 22141, August 24, 1855.—*Ed.*

[b] A. F. Parseval-Deschênes.—*Ed.*

French army sailed on the 4th of September, and the rest of the French fleet left on the 19th; while Sir James Graham informs Sir Charles that he only knew of their withdrawal on the 25th September. Sir James, therefore, erroneously supposed "the decisions to have been taken on the spot, with Napier's consent," but, as he emphatically adds: "without any reference to the English Government." On the other hand, it seems that Niel, the French General of Engineers, and Louis Bonaparte's intimate friend, gave the advice to "destroy Sweaborg in two hours, by sail-of-the-line." This would seem to show clearly that he intended goading the English fleet into a desperate attack, in which they would uselessly knock their heads on the forts and sunken rocks of the Russian defenses.

Written about September 8, 1855

First published in the *New-York Daily Tribune*, No. 4502, September 24, 1855 as a leading article

Reproduced from the newspaper

Frederick Engels

THE FALL OF SEVASTOPOL[360]

After a year of varying fortunes and terrible suffering, the Crimean campaign has at last reached its turning-point.[a] From the 1st inst. to the 8th the Russian telegraphic dispatches admit that considerable damage had been done to the lines of Sevastopol by the allied fire, and that the damage had been repaired "as much as possible," and no more. Finally, on the 8th about noon the Allies stormed four of the bastions—were defeated at one, carried two, but were again compelled to leave them, though they finally maintained themselves in the fourth, and what was most important, on the Malakoff Hill. The loss of this point forced the Russians on the 9th to march their troops from the southern to the northern side, and thus to abandon the town of Sevastopol, after having exploded their magazines, blown up the buildings, ruined the defensive works by springing mines under them, and converted, to use Gen. Pélissier's words, the whole place into an immense blazing furnace[b]; they also burnt their steamers, sunk their last ships-of-war, and finally broke up the bridge near Fort Paul.[c]

---

[a] In the *Neue Oder-Zeitung* the article begins as follows: "*London*, September 11. At 9 o'clock last night the guns of James's Park and the *Tower* announced the fall of the southern side of Sevastopol. At the Lyceum, Haymarket and Adelphi theatres the managers at last had the satisfaction of soliciting the hurrahs, the 'God save the Queen' and the 'Partant pour la Syrie' on the strength of official dispatches rather than, as hitherto, of false rumours.

"The Crimean campaign has at last reached its turning-point."—*Ed.*

[b] A. Pélissier, "Crimée, 9 septembre, huit heures du soir", *Le Moniteur universel*, No. 254, September 11, 1855.—*Ed.*

[c] Instead of the last sentence the *Neue Oder-Zeitung* has: "the loss of which forced the Russians to lay waste to and abandon the southern side".—*Ed.*

The arrival of considerable reenforcements after the battle of the Chernaya, must have relieved the allied Generals from any apprehension on the score of the Russian army at Inkerman; for, though even the remainder of the 4th and 6th Russian divisions, beside the two divisions of grenadiers, had joined that army, the Allies were now in a position to oppose successfully any number of men the Russians could throw across the Chernaya; while enough of allied troops would remain to carry on the siege, and even to attempt an assault. It must be confessed that the French Government has now been exceedingly prompt in sending to the Crimea a number of troops fully adequate to the Russian reenforcements already there, or on the march from Poland and Volhynia; for the number of the French forces dispatched to the East since the beginning of July, must amount to at least 50,000.

Under these circumstances, the English and French advanced mortar batteries being in good working condition, the trenches were pushed up to the ditch, under the protection of a vigorous fire. How near the advanced trenches were established, and whether a complete crowning of the glacis, *secundum artem*,[a] was accomplished, we do not yet know. The firing more and more assumed the character of a regular bombardment and vertical fire was successfully made use of to render the place untenable for large bodies of troops, till finally the assault was ordered.

On the Mamelon, the Russians had last Spring constructed a number of fireproof and shellproof compartments with the aid of traverses and blindages. These contrivances gave capital protection against the enemy's fire, but when the assault was made, it was found that no room had been left for concentrating a sufficient number of troops for the defense of the work. Compartment after compartment, defended by a few men only, was carried by the French, and at once formed a ready-made lodgement for them. The same mistake appears to have been made in the completion of the defenses of the Malakoff. The thing was overdone, and when the French once got hold of the commanding point of the hill, the Russian works themselves must have afforded them protection against the Russian fire.

The Redan (Bastion No. 3) and the Redan of the Careening Bay (Bastion No. 1 of the Russians) being situated on more level ground, did not admit of the terraced batteries and complicated defenses applicable to the Malakoff. Here, therefore, a simple coupure appears to have been made in the interior of the bastion,

---

[a] According to the rules of art.—*Ed.*

cutting off the salient angle and exposing its interior to an overwhelming fire. The troops for its defense could thus be placed further to the rear, and the interior of the work protected by sallies from the coupure. In consequence of this arrangement, which was of the kind generally adopted in such cases, the English lines and the French columns ordered to the assault of these positions could indeed penetrate beyond the all but abandoned outer wall; but when there, face to face with the coupure, they were crushed by its grape and musketry, and had to give up the assault.

As soon as the Malakoff was carried, Gen. de Salles, on the French left attack, made an attempt to establish himself in the Central bastion (No. 5, between the Flagstaff and Quarantine bastions). He was repulsed. We are not informed whether this assault was undertaken on his own responsibility or whether it formed part of the original plan. Nor do we know how far the proximity of the French trenches to the bastion justified such a detached and hazardous attempt.

The fact of the Malakoff hill being taken, at once formed the turning point of the struggle. From all the preceding events of this remarkable siege, it was to be anticipated that the French, if properly alive to their business, were not in the remotest danger of being driven out of their new position.[a] The Malakoff completely commands the Karabelnaya and the eastern slope of the hill on which the town of Sevastopol was built. Taking in the rear the sea forts on the southern side of the harbor, it made the whole of the inner harbor and the greater part of the outer harbor untenable to the Russian ships of war. By the fall of the Malakoff the continuity of the defensive lines of Sevastopol became interrupted at that very point upon which the security of the whole was dependant. The possession of the Malakoff, therefore, meant the possession of Karabelnaya, the destruction of the town by bombardment, the taking in flank and rear of the Flagstaff bastion, and the disappearance of the last chance of the town's holding out. Sevastopol had hitherto been a fortified camp for a large army, as indeed are all modern fortresses. By the capture of the Malakoff it had sunk to the rank of a mere bridge-head to the Russian garrison of the north side, and more than this, of a bridge-head without a bridge. It was therefore wise to abandon it. It is true we had heard a good deal of new works constructed on the inner slope of the Malakoff, with a view to maintain the

[a] In the *Neue Oder-Zeitung* this sentence does not occur.—*Ed.*

defense of the Karabelnaya, after the loss of that fortification; but they do not seem to have been of value enough to induce Prince Gorchakoff to continue the defense. However, we shall now soon know what was their real nature.[a]

Some Russian ships had already been burned in the harbor by shells from the allied batteries. The Malakoff once armed with French guns would have made it difficult for the remaining Russian vessels to find a safe anchorage, except just at the foot of Forts Nicholas and Alexander, and there is not room for a great many; hence the burning and sinking of the remainder of the fleet.

The Karabelnaya side being completely in the hands of the Allies, they are in a position to undertake operations in the field. Though they will not be able to establish many batteries or many troops in that suburb, on account of the fire from the northern shore of the harbor, they have succeeded in reducing the Russian portion of Sevastopol to less than one-half its extent before the 8th inst., and to a fortress capable of holding but a limited number of defenders. Not only is the offensive power of the garrison completely crushed, but its defensive strength is greatly reduced. A far smaller number of men will suffice to carry on the siege, and the troops thus set free, with the reenforcements now on the road or at the camp of Maslak, will be available for an expedition to Eupatoria. The more we examine the relative position of both Russians and Allies on the Chernaya, the more evident it becomes that neither party can drive the other away hence without great superiority and enormous sacrifices. The opinion in the allied camp would seem to be that from 60,000 to 70,000 men should be sent to Eupatoria, in order to march upon the communications of the Russians at Sympheropol. Suppose the Russians to have 200,000 men in the Crimea (which they certainly have not), 80,000 men would be required for the defense of the North Forts, 60,000 for the position on the Chernaya, and 60,000 to meet the allied army of Eupatoria. In the present spirit of the allied forces, it is certain that with equal numbers and in an equally divided field, they will beat the Russians; and as by taking up a position on the Russian line of communications they can force them to give battle, there does not seem to be any risk in such an undertaking. On the contrary, it is probable that the Russians would be able to oppose this expeditionary army with but 60,000 men at the very outside.

[a] The passage beginning with the words "It was therefore wise to abandon it" does not occur in the *Neue Oder-Zeitung*.—*Ed.*

The sooner, however, such a movement is undertaken the better for the Allies, and if they act vigorously they may expect great results. They now have both moral and numerical superiority, and we doubt not they will profit by it before another winter on the plateau has reduced their numbers and damped their spirits. Indeed the latest report is that by the 13th 25,000 men had already sailed for Eupatoria, and we shall doubtless hear of a still greater force following.

Of these important events we have as yet only the meagre information conveyed by telegraphic dispatches. When more complete details reach us we shall return to the subject again.[a]

Written about September 11, 1855

First published in the *New-York Daily Tribune,* No. 4506, September 28, 1855 and the *New-York Semi-Weekly Tribune,* No. 1079, September 28, 1855, reprinted in the *New-York Weekly Tribune,* No. 734, October 6, 1855 as a leading article; the German version was published in the *Neue Oder-Zeitung,* No. 429, September 14, 1855, marked with the sign ×

Reproduced from the *New-York Daily Tribune*

---

[a] Instead of the passage beginning with the words "Suppose the Russians to have 200,000 men" the *Neue Oder-Zeitung* has: "This would force the Russians to fight a battle in the open field in which, under the present circumstances, success would seem to be guaranteed to the Allies. But everything depends on the latter's taking advantage of the present situation with dispatch and energy."—*Ed.*

Karl Marx

O'CONNOR'S FUNERAL

London, September 11. Yesterday afternoon the funeral of O'Connor, the late Chartist leader, took place. A procession of 20,000 people, practically all of them from the working class, moved from Finsbury Square and Smithfield to Notting Hill, from where the coffin was taken to Kensal Green Cemetery (one of the most magnificent burial-grounds in London).

Four-horse hearses, decorated with enormous plumes in the English fashion, took their place at the head of the procession. Hard on their heels followed flag-bearers and standard-bearers. In letters of white the black flags bore the inscription "He lived and died for us".[a] A gigantic red flag magnificently displayed the inscription "Alliance des peuples". A red liberty cap was swaying at the top of the main standard.[361] When the service in the beautiful, cloistered cemetery chapel was over, William Jones made a funeral oration at the grave of the deceased. The singing of a hymn concluded the ceremony. All the requirements for a great demonstration were at hand, but the finishing touch was missing because Ernest Jones was prevented from appearing and speaking by the fatal illness of his wife. As the procession moved back into the city at about half past five in the afternoon it had the ironic satisfaction of meeting five detachments of constables marching out, and greeted them each in turn with a "too late".[b] Since O'Connor died as a pauper in the true sense of the word, the burial expenses were met by the working class of London.

Written on September 11, 1855

First published in the *Neue Oder-Zeitung,* No. 430, September 15, 1855

Marked with the sign ×

Printed according to the newspaper

Published in English for the first time

[a] Marx quotes the English text of the inscription and gives the German translation in brackets.— *Ed.*

[b] Marx uses the English words and gives the German translation in brackets.— *Ed.*

Frederick Engels

CRIMEAN PROSPECTS[362]

Beyond an imperfect list of the British officers killed and wounded, the journals brought by the steamer *America*—and we have examined them with care—add scarcely anything to our previous knowledge of the circumstances attending the capture of the southern side of Sevastopol. It is true that there is a plenty of speculation as to both the causes and the consequences of Gorchakoff's sudden abandonment of a place so long and so desperately defended; and among such speculations those of our correspondents at London and Paris are eminently worthy of attention. But there are some points of view and some considerations which neither of these writers, opposite as are their views, seems to have dwelt upon with the necessary care, or to have given the due amount of importance.

Precisely what turn matters now will take in the Crimea depends to a great extent on the causes which induced the Russians to give up the south side. That purely tactical and strategical motives were completely foreign to this sudden resolution, is evident. Had Gorchakoff considered the south side, and even the Karabelnaya, untenable as soon as the Malakoff should have fallen, he would not have thrown up so many internal defenses in that suburb. Though the ultimate success of the siege might be considered assured by the taking of that commanding point, yet from four to six weeks breathing time might have been gained by a stubborn defense, first of the inner rocks of the suburb, and then of the town proper. To judge from the best maps, plans and models, there was no necessity whatever in a mere tactical or strategical light to abandon so hastily what had been fended with such tenacity. Military science alone cannot account for a step which can yet scarcely be attributed to the confusion and fright caused by an unexpected and decisive defeat. Necessities of a different nature must have been active to force Gorchakoff to a step which compromises his military position and career so seriously as this.

There are two possibilities only. Either the *morale* of the Russian soldiers was so completely broken up that it would have been impossible to rally them in anything like order behind the inner lines of defense, so as to continue the struggle, or else they had begun to run short of provisions, not only within Sevastopol but in the camp without. The all but uninterrupted series of defeats to which the Russian army had been exposed, from Oltenitza and Chetatea to the Chernaya, and the assault of Sept. 8, must certainly have completely destroyed the spirit of the defenders of Sevastopol; and all the more, as they consisted principally of the same troops who were beaten on the Danube and later at Inkerman.[363] The Russians have rather dull moral feelings, and can stand defeats longer than most troops; but no army in the world can hold together forever when it is beaten by every enemy it meets, and when to a long list of defeats it can oppose nothing except the negative satisfaction of its tenacious and lengthened resistance, and a solitary example of successful, active defense, like that of the 18th June.[364] But such a resistance in a besieged place is of itself demoralizing in the long run. It implies hardships, want of rest, sickness, and the presence, not of that acute danger which braces, but of that chronic danger which must ultimately relax the mind. The rapidly succeeding defeats on the Chernaya and at the Malakoff must have completed the demoralization, and it is more than likely that Gorchakoff's troops in the town were no longer fit to be led against the enemy. And as the Malakoff commanded the bridge to the other side, and the French guns might any day have destroyed it, relief became impossible, while retreat might at least save the troops. It is not astonishing that this demoralization should at last seize the garrison; it is astonishing that it had not done so long before.

There are also some very strong symptoms that want of provisions for the army generally had a great deal to do with Prince Gorchakoff's sudden retreat. The interruption of Russian navigation in the Sea of Azoff, though it had not that immediate effect which the British and French Press, then so much in want of some success, expected it to have, must nevertheless in the long run prove troublesome to the Russians, as it confined them to one single line of operations, and thereby limited their supplies. The immense difficulty of transporting victualing stores, ammunition and forage from Kherson through a thinly-populated steppe country must have been greatly increased when this road became the only one by which the army could be provided. The means of transport, brought together by requisition from the Ukraine and Don Provinces, must finally have been used up; horses and draft-oxen must have been sacrificed in great numbers, both by overwork and scantiness of provender; and the nearest provinces once being exhausted, it became more and more difficult to replace the necessary stock. This shortness of supplies would show itself at first, not so much in Sevastopol (where reserve stores must have been kept up for the event of the place being invested on the north side too), as in the camp above Inkerman, at Bakshiserai, and on the line of march of the reenforcements. The reports of the allied commanders had more than once adverted to this being the case; but other circumstances too indicate that such must have been the fact. By this impossibility of feeding even the troops now in the Crimea, we can alone explain why the two divisions of grenadiers so long on the march, and now said to be about Perekop, were not allowed to advance and to partake in the battle on the Chernaya, and why, notwithstanding the better half of the troops advancing to relieve Sevastopol was thus kept back, that battle was yet ventured, though with a force ridiculously small in proportion to the task expected from it.

Thus all indications point to this, that both demoralization of the greater portion of the Russian troops, and want of supplies for the army in the field, induced Gorchakoff not to stake too much on delaying, for a few days, the fall of a fortress which had become untenable. He profited by the last chance of saving the garrison, and he would seem to have done right; for according to all appearances he would have had to leave it to its fate, to collect his field-army, and to retire into the interior of the Crimea, if not to Perekop. In this case, the garrison of the south side would soon have been compelled either to cross stealthily to the north side or to capitulate; and the north side, too, once cut off from all chance of ever being relieved, and garrisoned by demoralized troops, would have been starved into submission.

So long as the Russians had a chance not only of keeping their army in the Crimea up to something like a force equaling that of the Allies but were even expecting reenforcements which would make it far outnumber its opponents, the north side of Sevastopol was a position of immense importance.[365] To hold the north side by a garrison while the field army stood where it did up to the latest news we have received, was to bring the allied army on the plateau of the Heracleatic Chersonese. It was to exclude their ships from Sevastopol Bay, and to deprive them of a proper naval base of operations nearer than the Bosphorus, for neither Kamiesh nor Balaklava can pass for such a thing. So long as the Russians were able to keep the field in the Crimea the north side was as much the key to the whole of the Crimea and to what gives the whole country any military and naval importance as the Malakoff was to the south side. But from the moment the Russians are unable to hold the field, the north side has no longer any great importance. It is a fortified position of a certain strength, but which if regularly besieged by sufficient forces is doomed to fall, for relief there can then be none.

This may seem astonishing after the great importance ascribed, and rightly too, to the north side. And yet it is quite correct. The whole of this war has been, in appearance, a war of fortifications and sieges, and has in the eyes of superficial observers completely annihilated the progress made by Napoleon's rapid maneuver, thus carrying back the art of warfare to the days of the Seven Years' War.[366] But in reality nothing is more contrary to fact. Fortresses and groups of fortresses have no other importance now-a-days than as the fixed points on which an army in the field supports itself in its movements. Thus the camp at Kalafat was a bridge-head allowing Omer Pasha to menace the Russians in flank; thus Silistria, Rustchuk, Varna, Shumla, were the four salient angles, so to say, of a large fortified camp into which he could always retreat, and where he could not be followed unless two at least of those salient angles were taken or neutralized. Thus Sevastopol formed the pivot of the Russian army in the Crimea, and whenever that army was outnumbered or otherwise checked, Sevastopol allowed it breathing time until fresh reenforcements had come up. To the Allies Sevastopol was a Russian naval center to be destroyed, a naval base of operations to be gained; to the Russians it was the possession of the Crimea, because it was the only position to be held against far superior numbers until relieved. Thus the ultimate decision always rested with the armies in the field, and the importance of fortresses depended, not on their natural or artificial strength or intrinsic value, but on the protection and support (*appui*) they could give to the field army.

Their value has become relative. They are no longer independent factors in the game of war, but merely valuable positions which it may or may not be expedient to defend by every means and to the last extremity. This the Sevastopol affair proves more than any previous occurrence. Sevastopol, like all really modern fortresses, takes the place of a permanently-fortified camp. As long as the disposable force is sufficient to defend that camp, as long as supplies are plentiful, the communications with the main base of operations secure, especially as long as that camp held by a strong army prevents the enemy from going past it without exposing his own safety—so long that camp is of first-rate importance and may baffle the enemy for a whole campaign. But if such is no longer the case; if the defending force suffers check after check, runs short of provisions, risks having its communications cut off and being reduced to the fate of the Austrians at Ulm in 1805[367]—then it is high time to prefer the safety of the army to the abstract value of the position and to retreat at once to another place offering greater advantages.

This seems to be now the situation of the Russians. The greater part of their original active army—fourteen divisions out of twenty-four—is engaged, and has been partly destroyed in the Crimea, and what they have of reserves and militia, or other new formations, can stand no comparison with the troops they have lost. They will certainly do well not to send any more men to that dangerous peninsula, and indeed to abandon it as soon as they can. The Allies are far superior to them in numbers and especially in spirit. With Gorchakoff's present army to risk a battle in the field would be to solicit defeat. He may be turned either by the south coast and the valley of the Salghir, or by Eupatoria. Either operation would force him to give up his communication with the north side, never to regain it, for the numerical superiority of the Allies is increasing every day. It would seem that the best he can do is to make as bold a front as possible, while he prepares everything for blowing up the northern forts, and to steal a march or two on his opponents. The sooner he gets to Perekop the better. This is especially the case if the report we have from Paris be true that the Allies began sending an army to Eupatoria immediately after getting possession of Sevastopol. If they act with vigor, either in that direction or along the south coast and the passes of the Chatyr Dagh, the campaign must speedily close, leaving them in possession of the Crimea. So far as we can see the only mistakes now in their power are a serious front attack on the Russian position above Inkerman, or a week's inaction. The next steamer, due here to-morrow night, can hardly fail to settle the question as to what they mean to do.

Written about September 14, 1855

First published in the *New-York Daily Tribune,* No. 4508, October 1, 1855, reprinted in the *New-York Semi-Weekly Tribune,* No. 1080, October 2, 1855 as a leading article; an abridged German version was published in the *Neue Oder-Zeitung,* No. 435, September 18, 1855, marked with the sign ×

Reproduced from the *New-York Daily Tribune*

Karl Marx and Frederick Engels

EVENTS IN THE CRIMEA[368]

London, September 14. "The ringing of bells and the thunder of cannon" is the slogan of the day in England at the moment. The world seems full of happiness and every building of the slightest importance, public or private, is full of Anglo-French flags. The same scene in Manchester as in London, despite the "Manchester School"; in Edinburgh as in Manchester, despite the Scottish philosophy. At the moment, nothing is able to dampen the general enthusiasm, not even the extraordinary list of fatalities flashed to London by the telegraph. The defeat of the British before the Redan bastion and the capture of the decisive point, fort Malakhov, by the French—this *contrast* alone muffles the clamour of victory and sets some bounds to the boastfulness. Anyone sharing the old prejudice—one owed like so many others to the uncritical confusion of modern and ancient conditions of society—the prejudice that industry and commerce destroy the martial character of a people may now inform himself of the contrary in England, and even in Manchester, its industrial metropolis. It is a very simple matter. In modern society the wealth of a nation, though not the wealth of the individual, increases with increased *labour*; in ancient society it increased with the increased *laziness* of the nation. *Steuart,* the Scottish economist, who published his important work ten years *before* Adam Smith, had already discovered and developed this point.[a]

---

[a] The reference is to Sir James Steuart's *An Inquiry into the Principles of Political Œconomy,* published in London in 1767 (the point in question is discussed in Volume I, Book I, Chapter VII) and Adam Smith's *An Inquiry into the Nature and Causes of the Wealth of Nations,* published in London in 1776.—*Ed.*

But public enthusiasm is vainly seeking nourishment in the latest telegraphic despatches. They are as meagre as the first was rich. Pélissier writes that a *"matériel immense"* has fallen into the hands of the Allies at Sevastopol.[a] We suspect—a heap of old iron whose price is bound to fall.

The turn that will be taken by events now depends mainly on the motives which induced the Russians to abandon the South Side so suddenly. This much is clear. Purely tactical and strategic reasons played no part in this decision. If Gorchakov had considered the surrender of Karabelnaya and the town to be inseparable from the fall of fort Malakhov, then why the huge mass of defence works within the suburb? In spite of the commanding position of the Malakhov 5-6 weeks could have been won by a stubborn defence, first of the inner defence works of the suburb and then of the town itself. Judging from the best maps, plans and models there are no purely strategic or tactical reasons for the sudden surrender of what has so far been held so tenaciously. There remain only two feasible explanations: the moral self-confidence of the Russian army was broken to a point which made it inadvisable to take a new stand behind the inner defence works of the town. Or the lack of provisions was beginning to make itself felt, not only in the town but also in the camp, or, finally, both these reasons.

The almost unbroken series of defeats suffered by the Russian army from Oltenitza and Chetatea to the battle on the Chernaya and the assault of September 8 can only have had a demoralising effect on the besieged troops, all the more so as a great number of them had witnessed the defeats on the Danube and at Inkerman.[369] Certainly, the Russians possess an obtuse sense of morale and as a result they can endure defeats better than other troops. However, even this is bound to have its limits. Resistance stretched over an unusually long period of time in a besieged location has in itself a demoralising effect. It comprises suffering, exertion, lack of rest, disease and the constant presence, not of acute danger, which steels, but of that chronic danger which breaks men down. The defeat on the Chernaya, where half the reserve army was engaged, precisely those reinforcements which were to rescue the South Side, and the seizure of the Malakhov, the key to the whole position, these two defeats must have consummated the demoralisation. Since the Malakhov commanded the bridge to the

---

[a] Pélissier's report of September 10, 1855, *Le Moniteur universel,* No. 256, September 13, 1855.—*Ed.*

other side and the French could destroy it at any moment, all access became problematic and retreat became the last resort of the troops. As for the lack of provisions, there are signs that it was beginning to make itself felt. The interruption of Russian shipping in the Sea of Azov restricted the Russians to a single line of operations and thus shortened their supplies. The enormous difficulty of transporting food, munitions, etc., over a thinly-populated steppe naturally grew as soon as the road from Kherson alone remained open. The means of transport requisitioned and collected from the Ukraine and the Don provinces had to become used up sooner or later, and for the adjacent provinces, since they were exhausted, it became more and more difficult to replace them. This lack of supplies must first of all have revealed itself, not in Sevastopol, where great stocks were heaped up, but in the camp at Inkerman, at Bakhchisarai and along the reinforcements' line of march. This is the only possible explanation why the two infantry divisions which have been on the march for so long and are now said to be at Perekop, did not advance and take part in the battle on the Chernaya, and also, on the other hand, why in spite of the absence of this, the better, half of the replacement troops the battle was risked with a fighting force which was entirely disproportionate to its task. If these points of view are correct then Gorchakov had indeed no alternative but to use the capture of fort Malakhov as a respectable pretext for saving his garrison.

Written on September 14, 1855

First published in the *Neue Oder-Zeitung*, No. 435, September 18, 1855

Marked with the sign ×

The English version was published in the *New-York Daily Tribune*, No. 4508, October 1, 1855, and reprinted in the *New-York Semi-Weekly Tribune*, No. 1080, October 2, 1855 as a leading article

Printed according to the *Neue Oder-Zeitung*

Published in English for the first time

Karl Marx

THE COMMERCIAL AND FINANCIAL SITUATION

London, September 24. Public opinion at the moment is occupied almost as much with the commercial and financial situation, not only in Great Britain but especially in *France,* as with the war in the Crimea. As we know, the Bank of France has raised its discount on government bonds and similar securities to 5 per cent, while it discounts commercial bills of exchange at 4 per cent. The directors of the French bank, worried by the flow of precious metal from its vaults, had already decided to increase the discount for commercial bills of exchange to 5 per cent as well when the Minister of Finance[a] intervened directly and forbade them to carry out this operation. The concern of the government is naturally to maintain the appearance of an easy money market and overflowing credit for as long as possible and to keep the shopkeeping world in a good mood.

The *Manchester Examiner* has stated that

"The drain during the last two years on the wealth of France has been enormous. [...] But, in two years, the Government of Louis Napoleon has spent £200,000,000—the municipality of Paris has lavished vast sums of borrowed money on the adornment of his capital—projects requiring great wealth have been formed, at the instigation and under the patronage of the Government—the *Crédit Mobilier*[370] alone has been the parent of no less than half a dozen great companies, each of which has had its shares puffed up to an enormous premium—the capital of these companies has yet to be paid up, and an immense mass of every sort of share paper is passing from hand to hand without any reference to the reckoning day. The financial state of the Government, the purely speculative character of much of that enterprise, the present position of the French money market, and the burden of another indifferent harvest both on the people and

[a] P. Magne.—*Ed.*

the Bourse, all points to chances of disaster which may prove as embarrassing to the war in the East[a] as to the internal peace and prosperity of France herself."[b]

With regard to the *grain market* the above-quoted newspaper comments in particular:

"There can be no doubt that both France and England will be large importers of grain; and the orders which have already been sent out to the Danube from this country will [...] cause extensive shipments of grain to be made from the United States in place of gold to Europe. Last year's was the best harvest ever known in this country, and yet we imported, from August, 1854, to August, 1855, 2,335,000 quarters of wheat, and 1,588,892 cwts. of flour, and the average price, nevertheless, of the whole year was above 70s. [...] During the coming year [...] we shall require much larger imports [...] to prevent prices rising very considerably. Where supplies are to be obtained if not from North America? [...] The crops in Northern Germany also are a failure, [...] and the United States even are shipping flour to the Baltic, whence we have been accustomed to import no inconsiderable portion of wheat in times of need. Austria, it has been announced by the Government, has average crops, but it is doubtful whether she will have any surplus for export, and throughout Southern Italy a serious scarcity is felt, which cannot, as heretofore, be relieved by imports from the [...] ports in the Black Sea."

Thus in demand for grain France will not only have to compete with England but also with a large part of the European continent. Nothing shows how distasteful this situation is for its Government better than the half consolatory, half didactic article in the *Moniteur*.[c]

As for the numerous new joint-stock companies in France which are mentioned by the *Manchester Examiner*, a work recently published in Paris, *Opérations de Bourse*,[d] shows that in one branch alone—that of the *joint-stock banks*—their numbers have increased six-fold in Paris alone since the February Revolution. Before 1848 only two were in existence; now there are twelve of these banks in Paris, namely the *Banque de France*, the *Caisse Commerciale*, the *Comptoir d'Escompte*, a commandite bank under the firm of Lediheur and Co., the *Crédit Foncier de France*, the Martinique Bank, the *Banque de Guadeloupe*, the *Banque de l'île de la Réunion*, the Bank of Algiers, the *Crédit mobilier*, the *Société Générale du crédit maritime*, the *Caisse et journal des chemins de fer*, the *Comptoir central*,

[a] The *Manchester Daily Examiner and Times* has "our policy in the East".—*Ed.*
[b] "The condition of the money market...", *Manchester Daily Examiner and Times*, No. 193, September 24, 1855.—*Ed.*
[c] The article, dated September 19, was published in *Le Moniteur universel*, No. 263, September 20, 1855.—*Ed.*
[d] A. Courtois fils; *Des opérations de Bourse ou Manuel des fonds publics français et étrangers et des actions et obligations de sociétés françaises et étrangères négociés à Paris*, Paris, 1855.—*Ed.*

the *Crédit industriel* and the *Banque de Sénégal*. The *paid-up* capital of these banks amounts only to 151,230,000 francs and their total bank capital only to 252,480,000 francs, or about £10,000,000, which does not equal the capital of the Bank of England alone.

"...The large superstructure which is built by the credit system on this small foundation", writes the London *Economist*, a journal which supports the Government, "is anything but satisfactory. Against the capital of the *Bank of France*, 91,250,000f, are issued notes to the amount of 542,589,300f, or six times the amount. [...] The *Crédit mobilier* [...] is empowered to issue bonds to ten times the amount of its capital. The *Crédit Foncier de France* [...] whose nominal capital is 30,000,000f has issued bonds to the amount of 200,000,000f. We may anticipate, therefore, that a panic, or a depreciation of this mass of obligations, would cause in Paris and France very considerable distress...."[a]

Written on September 24, 1855

First published in the *Neue Oder-Zeitung*, No. 453, September 28, 1855

Marked with the sign ×

Printed according to the newspaper

Published in English for the first time

[a] "Paris Banks", *The Economist*, No. 630, September 22, 1855.—*Ed.*

Frederick Engels

THE STATE OF THE WAR[371]

It is plain from the advices of the last Liverpool steamer that the Czar[a] has no intention of making peace under the circumstances now existing. His sudden departure for Odessa instead of going to Warsaw, where he had arranged to meet the King of Prussia[b]; the transfer of the residence of the Empress[c] from St. Petersburg to Moscow,[d] the heart and center of Holy Russia; the leaving the administration of affairs in the hands of the Grand Duke Constantine, the most warlike of his brothers; and the taking of the other brothers with him to the seat of war—all this indicates a determination to prosecute the contest to some other end than can now be realized. At the same time extensive preparations are making for the defense of South Russia.[e] Nikolaieff and Kherson, the two most important fortified points, form the centers for an army of reserve now collecting in the government of Kherson, and that portion of Taurida situated north of Perekop. Beside a number of army reserves (Fifth, Sixth, Seventh and Eighth battalions of the line-regiments), whose number it is impossible to fix even approximately, forty thousand men of the militia are reported to be collected at Nikolaieff. About twenty-five thousand men are said to be at Odessa. Whether these rumors are exact or not, the fact of the Emperor's departure shows that a considerable force must be concentrating there.

---

[a] Alexander II.—*Ed.*

[b] Frederick William IV.—*Ed.*

[c] Maria Alexandrovna.—*Ed.*

[d] In the *Neue Oder-Zeitung* the article begins as follows: "The Emperor's departure from Russia to Odessa; the transfer of the residence of the Empress from St. Petersburg to Moscow...."—*Ed.*

[e] In the *Neue Oder-Zeitung* this sentence does not occur.—*Ed.*

The plan of operations of the Russians seems to be elaborated with the same foresight for which all their grand strategic schemes are generally distinguished. Not only is the complete loss of the Crimea taken into account as a possible event, but even a campaign in South Russia. For this purpose the line of the Dnieper is chosen, very naturally, as the main line of defense; and Kherson and Nikolaieff as the first, and Ekaterinoslav as the ulterior base of operations. Nikolaieff is within reach of an attack by water; therefore, against an enemy in possession of the Black Sea, an inland base is absolutely necessary. Now, Ekaterinoslav is a position of great strategical importance.[a] Situated on the very point where, by a bend in its course, the Dnieper forms an angle of about seventy-five degrees, it is a capital center for an army which, in its retreat toward the interior, intends to cover itself first behind the southern course (N. E. to S. W.) and later on behind the middle course (N. W. to S. E.) of that river. An army advancing from Perekop into the interior of Russia would first have to force the passage of the Dnieper somewhere about Kherson, and then, advancing toward Ekaterinoslav, to pass the same river again at that place. Any detachments advancing on the left bank of the Dnieper could easily be stopped a few leagues south of Ekaterinoslav, on the line of the Voltschya, a river which there empties into the main stream. Beside these advantages, the whole country to the south of Ekaterinoslav is one vast steppe, two hundred miles in width, through which it is extremely difficult to convey and to feed an army; while that town itself, situated on the northern range of the steppe, and in close proximity to the rich and comparatively densely populated provinces of Kieff and Poltava, can receive any amount of provisions without difficulty. And lastly, Ekaterinoslav maintains the communication with the army of the center at Kieff and covers the road to Moscow.

Ekaterinoslav, as we learn from trustworthy sources, is now being fortified and provided with the reserve magazines for the southern army.[b] Stores of food, equipments, ammunition are

---

[a] Instead of the last two sentences the *Neue Oder-Zeitung* has: "As Kherson and Nikolayev lie within the range of operation not only of gun-boats but even of sloops of war, an inland base is needed. This is provided by Ekaterinoslav."—*Ed.*

[b] Instead of the text following this sentence the *Neue Oder-Zeitung* has: "If on the one hand this testifies to the Russians' strategic foresight—and it is certainly not in vain that the old general and deserter Jomini has schooled them for such a long time—it just as much shows, on the other hand, that they expect no successes for a considerable time to come. If the Allies ventured to advance into Russia's interior (via

collected there; and if ever the Allies should venture to advance into the interior, they would have to force this point before they could proceed any further. But even under circumstances very unfavorable to the Russians, the chances are that the forces of either party would be at least pretty equally matched at Ekaterinoslav. Such an advance, however, is out of the question in this campaign, and nearly so in that of 1856. Indeed, any movement of the Allies into the interior of Russia would be a blunder, unless the Crimea and all the countries south of the Caucasus, nay, even of the Kuban and Terek, were freed from Russian dominion, all the Russian coasts devastated, Ismail taken, the mouths of the Danube up to Galatch opened to trade, and, in short, everything done which could be attempted against the extremities of Russia on that side. Then even it would be a mistake to advance into the interior of the steppe, until the passive resistance of Russia, successfully maintained, left no other choice. It is evident that the probability of such an event occurring is not very great; but if the Russians are already preparing against it, we have another proof of that comprehensive foresight which has of late distinguished the chief strategical management of their forces, and which is apparently due to the commanding influence of General Jomini.

For the present, the conquest of the Crimea is still the great task

---

Perekop) they would of course have to force Ekaterinoslav. That, however, is out of the question in this campaign, and nearly so in that of 1856. First the Russians would have to evacuate the Crimea, the whole of Trans-Caucasia and the Caucasus up to the Terek and Kuban, Odessa would have to be burnt down, the port of Nikolayev destroyed and the Danube cleared up to Galatz. All these extremities of Russia would have to be amputated before the Allies could so much as think of undertaking a campaign into Russia's interior. So the long-range strategic plan of the Russians seems to bode nothing good.

"The allied troops are moving towards the valley of the Upper Chernaya in order to turn the Russians' extreme right wing at Aitodor or the upper Belbek. Both Gorchakov and Pélissier say so in their dispatches. It seems to us the Allies are executing this manoeuvre with too much show really to pursue that end.

"Clearly the object of the Allies is to drive the Russians from their entrenched position on Mackenzie's heights. Once they have succeeded in this, the Russians will have to abandon the northern fort and therefore evacuate the Crimea. For there is not a single position between Mackenzie's heights and Simferopol which cannot be turned, and beyond Simferopol the steppe, being untenable for large armies, offers no positions whatever. Whether the Russians will be able to maintain the Crimea therefore depends on their ability to maintain, in particular, their present position on Mackenzie's heights."—*Ed.*

of the Allies. On that head our latest intelligence[a] was that they had sent a strong column of infantry and cavalry into the valley of the upper Chernaya, threatening to turn, by Aitodor or the upper Belbek, the Russian extreme right. Gorchakoff had telegraphed, besides, that the Allies were daily concentrating additional troops on the Chernaya. Now, this movement of the Allies toward the Russian right has evidently been made with such a degree of show, the Russians themselves having noticed it at once, that it cannot prelude a serious attempt at turning the Russians on that side. It may serve either to draw away from the camp at Mackenzie's farm a portion of the troops defending that intrenched position, or else to mask a great expedition to Eupatoria. The first supposition hardly seems likely, from the concentration of the allied troops on the Chernaya, noticed at the same time by Gorchakoff; the second supposition is more likely; and though, as we have before stated, a flank movement by the south coast would seem preferable,[b] such an expedition, suddenly transporting a large force on the flank and rear of the Russians, cannot but be of great effect, and must decide the campaign.

As to the actual position of the Russians in the Crimea we have no clear information. They are doing their best to maintain a bold front, and if the state of their stores allows, it is certainly the best they can do. Still we remain of opinion that they must soon leave the Crimea unless the Allies make great mistakes and they, themselves, receive provisions more plentifully than they have a right to expect. The great object of the Allies is to drive them away from the position of Mackenzie's hights, for that position once lost, the north side of Sevastopol, defended by a small garrison, must be abandoned to its fate, and the Crimea must be evacuated; because between Mackenzie's farm and Sympheropol there is not a single tolerable position which cannot be turned with the greatest ease, and beyond Sympheropol the steppe, being untenable for large armies, offers no positions whatever.

One thing however is certain, namely, that there can be little delay in the decision of this question. The *Atlantic*, due here to-day, will most probably bring us intelligence of a battle in the field, which, if

---

[a] As can be seen from the version published in the *Neue Oder-Zeitung*, the reference is to Pélissier's dispatch of September 11, published in *Le Moniteur universel*, No. 268, September 25, 1855, and Gorchakov's dispatch of September 17, published in *The Times*, No. 22169, September 26, 1855.—*Ed.*

[b] See this volume, p. 529.—*Ed.*

unfavorable to the Russians, must be followed by their prompt retreat from the peninsula.

Written on September 26, 1855

First published in the *New-York Daily Tribune,* No. 4522, October 17, 1855, reprinted in the *New-York Semi-Weekly Tribune,* No. 1085, October 19, 1855 as a leading article; an abridged German version was published in the *Neue Oder-Zeitung,* No. 455, September 29, 1855, marked with the sign ×

Reproduced from the *New-York Daily Tribune*

Karl Marx and Frederick Engels

THE REPORTS OF GENERALS SIMPSON, PÉLISSIER AND NIEL

London, September 27. The reports of Generals Simpson, Pélissier and Niel,[a] and especially the despatches from British newspaper correspondents in the Crimea, form a vast and complex documentary material, and it is a time-consuming process to sift it judiciously. For this reason we shall be able to examine the events of September 7 and 8 in detail only in our next report.[b] We may note, however, that the British press is almost unanimous, and rightly so, in its condemnation of General Simpson and the higher English commanders acting under him. The joke making the rounds of the Russian army, that "*L'armée anglaise est une armée des lions, commandée par des ânes*" (The English army is an army of lions led by asses) has been thoroughly vindicated by the assault on the Redan. A London newspaper is demanding a new Sevastopol committee, forgetting that the miserable leadership of the British army is the inevitable result of rule by an antiquated oligarchy. All preparations miscarried from the very start. The English trenches were still so far (250 yards) from the Redan ditch that the troops had to run the gauntlet of enemy fire without cover for a quarter of an hour and were out of breath when they arrived. French engineers had drawn attention to this defect

---

[a] Simpson's report of September 9 (*The Times*, No. 22166, September 22, 1855), Pélissier's of September 11 and 14 and Niel's of September 11 (*The Times*, No. 22170, September 27, 1855).—*Ed.*

[b] The assault on the southern side of Sevastopol was analysed by Engels in the article promised here. There are two versions of this article, one was published in the *New-York Daily Tribune* (see this volume, pp. 546-52) and another in the *Neue Oder-Zeitung* (wherever the latter differs from the English version this is pointed out in footnotes to the English text).—*Ed.*

beforehand; however, the answer they received from the English was:

"If we were to advance another couple of yards then we should come to an angle which would expose us to enfilading fire by the Flagstaff bastion and thus great losses."

In the first place this risk of losses was undeniably smaller than that incurred by the exposure of the troops during the assault. Furthermore the enfilading fire could have been countered partly by traverses and bends in the trenches and partly by setting up counter-batteries. All the remonstrations of the French foundered against Simpson's thick-skinned obstinacy, however. What is more, whereas the French trenches were broad, spacious and capable not only of absorbing vast military forces but also of concealing them, the British trenches were narrow and so constructed that every Briton with a touch of corpulence immediately attracted the attention of the Russian commanders to himself. The wide stretch of ground the British troops had to run across meant that, instead of directly throwing themselves upon the enemy after reaching the object of their attack, they first of all sought cover and engaged in musket fire, which gave the Russians time to rally. The miserable inadequacy of the British preparations is also revealed by the fact that once their troops had gained control of the rampart, no one thought of spiking the Russian cannon positioned there. They had with them neither workers with the necessary instruments nor artillery troops who could have done the job with no extra instruments. General Simpson's tactical arrangements before and during the assault take the cake, however. (During the assault, as we learn from the [report] of a *Daily News* correspondent, Simpson, who suffered from a cold in the head, sat wrapped in a wide cape, in an easy chair in the Greenhill[a] battery.) He had detailed an assault party of 200 men, a covering party of 320 men and a total operational force of not more than 1,000 men against the fearsome Redan, against which the English attacks had broken for six months. When the English had broken through the salient of the Redan they were exposed to murderous fire from the redoubt, which had been transformed into a stronghold, and from the casemates positioned behind it on the flanks. With sufficient numbers they could have by-passed the redoubt, which would have put a speedy end to the battle. No reinforcements arrived on the scene, however, even though Colonel Windham sent for them urgently three times and eventually had to go

---

[a] The reference is to the Mamelon.—*Ed.*

himself to search for them. Thus the troops remained on the parapet for three fatal hours, twice forcing their way inside only to be slaughtered uselessly one by one, and finally had to retreat in great disorder. The inadequate number of troops with which Simpson, disposing of masses which would have sufficed twenty-fold, originally undertook the assault, the holding back of the necessary reserves during the action, the useless and wanton sacrifice of the brave assault troops—all this amounts to one of the greatest scandals known to modern military history. Simpson would inevitably have faced a court martial under the first Napoleon.

On the Continent the evil of *patrimonial jurisdiction* has been attacked, and rightly. However, the *unpaid English magistracy*[372] is nothing but a modernised, constitutionally flavoured version of patrimonial jurisdiction. Read the following literal extract from an English provincial newspaper:

"Last Tuesday[a] Nathaniel Williams, an elderly labourer, [...] was brought before a bench of magistrates, at Worcester and fined 5s., with 13s. costs, for cutting a small amount of wheat, belonging to himself, on Sunday, the 26th of August. He pleaded that it was a work of necessity—that the wheat would have been spoilt if he had not cut it—that he was employed from morning till night in farm labour. Nothing helped. The magistrates liberally interlarded with Reverends[b] were inexorable".[c]

Just as here the priests judge their own case, so do the factory-owners, the squires[d] and the other privileged estates which compose the unpaid magistracy.

We have taken the following extract from the private letter of an Englishman (a Whig) at present in Paris:

"Today's warlike article (dated September 24) in the *Constitutionnel*[e] seems to have discouraged the Paris bourgeoisie a great deal; and in three different districts, all of great commercial importance, however, I heard the same comments, almost in the same words: There you have it! For almost a year they told us that once Sevastopol were taken it would be possible to open peace negotiations. Now that Sevastopol has been taken we are told that this is a purely military matter and that peace cannot be contemplated before the whole Crimea has fallen. Things will carry on in this way and heaven knows when peace will come. All this is expressed

---

[a] September 18, 1855.—*Ed.*

[b] Marx and Engels use the English word and give the German translation in brackets.—*Ed.*

[c] This quotation coincides almost word for word with a passage in a letter to the editor from Worcester, signed "No Bitter Observer" (published in *The Times*, No. 22165, September 21, 1855). The letter was probably also published in a local newspaper.—*Ed.*

[d] The English word is used in the original.—*Ed.*

[e] Signed by the editor A. de Césena.—*Ed.*

in the most dejected manner. To be just, one has to admit that apart from the question of national glory, the present war has come at an inopportune time for France for many reasons. Every week the autumn reports turn out to be worse than was assumed the preceding week. At the moment for instance the price of bread in Rouen is 26 sous the four-pound loaf, which is the same as 3 francs or 60 sous in Paris. In Bordeaux the municipal council has already been forced to approve a large sum for subsidies should the price of a four-pound loaf rise to 1 franc, considered a famine price in the Gironde. This situation is gradually spreading over the whole area of the country. The internal situation in France is thus extremely delicate, the partisans of the revolution are scattered over the country in terrifying numbers, and if the emergency becomes unbearable they may well gather thousands around their banners. The new organisation of the departmental and municipal councils was an enormous blunder. The system has fatal effects.[373] In many departments at this moment no departmental council exists; and the mayors appointed by the Government are now constantly forced to dissolve their municipal councils. Almost every day you can read an official announcement that the mayor of this or that town has dissolved the municipal council; or that Prefect N.N. has dissolved the general council. The reasons are not made public; but, although all comments in public are prohibited, the fact itself nevertheless agitates the department in which it takes place. In many respects this would make the presence of older and more experienced soldiers desirable."[a]

Written on September 27, 1855

First published in the *Neue Oder-Zeitung*, No. 457, October 1, 1855

Marked with the sign ×

Printed according to the newspaper

Published in English for the first time

[a] Retranslated from the German.— *Ed.*

Frederick Engels

THE GREAT EVENT OF THE WAR[374]

The details of the successful general assault at Sevastopol, on the 8th ult., are now fully known to us, through the official reports of the allied commanders, and the correspondence of the European journals, the most important of which have already occupied a place in our paper. Of course these interesting statements have been read quite universally, and it is not necessary that we should recapitulate the facts they contain. What we desire to do is to give our readers a clear idea of the conditions under which the assault took place, and to explain why, on that occasion, the Allies met with such opposite results at different points of the attack.[a]

According to Gen. Niel,[b] the French had pushed their trenches at all points quite close to the Russian works. Opposite the Little Redan of the Careening bay (Bastion No. 1), and the Malakoff (Bastion No. 2), the head of the sap was no more than twenty-five yards distant from the Russian ditch. At the Flagstaff (Bastion No. 4), the distance was thirty; at the Central (Bastion No. 5), forty yards. On all these points, therefore, the storming columns were close to the works to be stormed. The English, on the other hand, had given up sapping as soon as they had arrived at 240 yards from the Great Redan (Bastion No. 3).[c] This was due to the spirit

[a] Instead of this paragraph the *Neue Oder-Zeitung* has: "Five French divisions and units of two English divisions were engaged on September 8. According to their own admission, the Allies lost 10,000 men out of about 45,000, i.e. almost one man in four. The Russian losses cannot be estimated."—*Ed.*

[b] General Niel's report of September 11, 1855, published in *The Times*, No. 22170, September 27, 1855.—*Ed.*

[c] In the *Neue Oder-Zeitung:* "Despite remonstrations by French engineers, the English had given up sapping 240 yards from the Great Redan (Bastion No. 3). The stupidity of this has already been discussed."—*Ed.*

of routine still predominant in the English army. As soon as they had pushed their trenches to that distance, they found that on going any further they would be enfiladed from the Flagstaff bastion, which projects a good deal beyond the other Russian works. Now, there is a general rule in the theory of sieges not to trace any portion of the trenches so that its prolongation will meet any point occupied by the enemy, as this would lay it open to enfilading fire.

This is of course right enough when one can do without such faulty tracing. But here, where this enfilading fire could not be avoided (the general plan of the siege and the nature of the ground precluding the idea of taking the Flagstaff bastion separately beforehand), it was evidently better to make faulty trenches than none at all. The theoretical rules in fact provide plenty of remedies for such an unavoidable evil. Traverses and the compound sorts of sap are prescribed in such a case. The French engineer officers, it seems, remonstrated with their English comrades, telling them that, although they might lose many men in pushing their trenches under such adverse circumstances, yet it was better to lose them now in completing a work which would all but secure the success of an assault, than to lose them during an assault, the result of which might be very doubtful from the want of covered approaches. But the British engineers knew better. The result shows them to have been grossly in the wrong.[a]

The French general distributed his forces as follows: Against the key of the whole position, the Malakoff, M'Mahon's division; to its right, against the curtain connecting it with Bastion No. 1, the division of La Motterouge; on the extreme right, against Bastion No. 1 itself, Dulac's division. The Malakoff being the only point which, in case of serious resistance, it was necessary to force at all risks, M'Mahon had for his reserve a division of Guards under Mellinet.[b] So much for the French attack on the Karabelnaya side. On the town-side, the Flagstaff bastion forming a sort of advanced citadel on very strong ground, and having interior works of considerable strength, was not to be immediately attacked in front; but the Central bastion was to be assaulted by Levaillant's division, which, in case of success, was to be followed up by d'Autemarre's division, ordered to turn the gorge of the Flagstaff

[a] This paragraph and part of the preceding one beginning with the words "This was due to the spirit of routine" do not occur in the *Neue Oder-Zeitung*.—*Ed.*

[b] The beginning of this sentence up to and including the words "at all risks" does not occur in the *Neue Oder-Zeitung*.— *Ed.*

bastion, to assail which in front, at that moment, Cialdini's Piedmontese brigade was concentrated in the trenches. The position between the Malakoff and the Flagstaff bastion was held by the English. They were to attack the Redan.

The Malakoff was to be assailed first, and after its capture, the remaining columns were to advance on their respective objects of attack. The Malakoff was a large redoubt on the top of the commanding hill of that name, closed on all sides, but having wide apertures to the rear for admitting reenforcements. It was connected by a curtain with the Great and Little Redans to its right and left; they, too, were closed redoubts, containing smaller works, intended for reduits; while the rear faces, the embrasures of which looked into the interior of the redoubts, formed a coupure. The gorges of these coupures were again connected with the Malakoff by a second or interior curtain, forming a second line of defense. The interior of the Great and Little Redans was pretty free from obstructions, and therefore completely commanded by the artillery of the coupures and reduits. But the Malakoff redoubt, on which the fire of the enemy had been concentrated ever since the Mamelon was taken, was crammed, alongside the ramparts, with hollow traverses. affording bomb-proof shelter to the gunners and troops on duty, while the interior was filled with large blockhouses, roofed bomb-proof, serving as barracks, and completely unfit for defense. When first the news of the taking of the Malakoff arrived, we stated that undoubtedly the Russians had committed the same error as in the construction of the Kamtchatka redoubt on the Mamelon, viz.: that in order to save themselves from the enemy's fire, they evidently had made the interior of the fort unfit for defense against an assault, by cutting it up into small compartments.[a] Our opinion is now fully borne out.[b] The labyrinth of the Malakoff, like that of the Mamelon, proved quite indefensible; in ten minutes it was taken, never to be recaptured.

The arrangements of the French for this assault on the Malakoff were admirable. Everything was foreseen and provided for. A new sort of bridges, the description of which is not forthcoming, was used to cross the ditch; they were laid down in less than a minute. No sooner had the assault commenced than the sappers constructed a flying sap from the trenches to the ditch, cut large passages through the Russian breastworks, filled

---

[a] See this volume, pp. 519-23.—*Ed.*

[b] In the *Neue Oder-Zeitung*: "This view has now been fully borne out by General Niel's report."—*Ed.*

up the ditch opposite, and formed a practicable road into the interior of the Malakoff redoubt by which supports, reserves and even field-guns could move up. As soon as the whole of the redoubt was taken, the passages in the gorge were rapidly closed, embrasures cut, field-guns brought up, and in a couple of hours, before the Russians could seriously attempt to reconquer the work, it was completely turned against them, and they came too late. Gunners were ready to spike the guns if necessary, and the detachments of infantry carried short-handled trenching-tools in their waist-belts.

This attack was under the immediate superintendence of Marshal Pélissier and Gen. Niel. Whether the other attacks were equally well organized we are not told; but they were generally unsuccessful, and that of the Central bastion especially. This assault seems to have been undertaken by Gen. de Salles with quite insufficient forces, for as soon as the French arrived at the Russian parapet they were compelled to seek shelter behind it; the assault degenerated into a skirmishing fire, and was necessarily repulsed. What this means Gen. Simpson has taken good care to show us in his assault on the Redan.[a] The attack on the Little Redan was most bloody, and the position well defended by the Russians, who here alone defeated five French brigades.

We have on former occasions noticed the absurd system prevalent in the British army, of forming their storming columns so weak that they can but count as forlorn hopes in case they meet with anything like serious resistance.[b] That blunder was conspicuous in Lord Raglan's plan of attack on the 18th of June[375]; and it seems Gen. Simpson was determined even to outdo his late chief.[c] The salient angle of the Redan had suffered from the English fire, and it was determined to direct the assault against this portion as soon as the Malakoff should be fully secured by the French. Accordingly, Gen. Simpson had storming parties told off from the second and light divisions, amounting, all in all, to about 1,800

---

[a] This sentence does not occur in the *Neue Oder-Zeitung*.—*Ed.*

[b] See this volume, pp. 313-19 and 328-32.—*Ed.*

[c] Instead of this sentence the *Neue Oder-Zeitung* has: "That method of procedure stems from the fact that most of the fortresses the English had to deal with, including Wellington in Spain, were built according to the Italo-Spanish system and therefore could seldom accommodate more than 500 men. Everything is traditional with the English and so is their method of assault, even though the conditions for it disappeared long ago. Thus Lord Raglan emulated the old Wellington method on June 18, we know with what success. Instead of drawing a lesson from his misfortune Simpson deemed it his duty not only to emulate Raglan but even to outdo him."—*Ed.*

men—or the half of two brigades! The other two brigades of these divisions were to act as supports, and the third and fourth divisions were to form the reserves; and beside these, the Guards and Highland divisions were on the spot—altogether a force of 25,000 men; and out of these the actual assault was confided to about 1,800, supported later on by about 2,000 more! Now, these 1,800 men, unlike the French, who could jump out of their trenches into the Russian ditch, had to perform a journey of 250 yards across open ground, exposed to the flanking fire from the curtains of the Redan. They fell in heaps, but they advanced, passed the ditch by escalade, penetrated into the salient angle, and here they found themselves at once opposed to a tremendous fire of grape and musketry from the coupure and reduits in the rear of the Redan. The consequence was that they dispersed, seeking shelter behind the traverses, and commenced firing on the Russians exactly as the French did at the Central bastion. This would not have done any harm, had the supports and reserves only advanced and followed up, in close attack, the advantages already gained. But hardly a man came, and those who came, came in driblets and irregularly. Three times Brigadier Windham, who commanded, sent officers to ask for the advance of troops in regular formation, but none were brought. All the three officers were wounded in crossing the plain. At last he went himself, and prevailed upon Gen. Codrington to send another regiment; when all at once the British troops gave way, and abandoned the Redan. The Russian supports had come up, and swept the place clean out. Then Father Simpson, who still had 20,000 men intact, resolved to attempt another assault next morning!

This feeble attack of the English on the Redan stamps their Crimean generals with the indelible mark of incapacity. They appear to have an innate tendency to surpass each other in blundering. Balaklava and Inkerman[376] were great feats in that respect; but the 18th of June and the 8th of September, outstrip them by far. So carelessly was the assault arranged that while the English held the salient of the Redan, not even the guns found in it were spiked, and therefore these very guns plied the English on their retreat as lustily with grape and case-shot as they had done during their advance. As to attempts at forcing a proper lodgment, neither Simpson nor the newspaper correspondents mention any such thing. In fact the first precautions appear to have been neglected.[a]

[a] Instead of the passage beginning with the words "The salient angle of the Redan had suffered from the English fire" (third sentence of the preceding

The attacks on the Redan, Central bastion and Little Redan were, it is true, mere demonstrations to a certain degree. But the attack on the Redan still had an importance of its own. That was a position by which the conquest of the Malakoff became immediately decisive, because if the Malakoff commands the Redan by its hight, the Redan commands the access to the Malakoff, and when once taken, would have taken in flank all Russian columns marching to recapture that hill. The conquest of the Malakoff induced the Russians to quit the whole of the south side; the conquest of the Redan would have obliged them to evacuate at least the Karabelnaya in haste, and before they could organize that well-arranged system of destruction by fire and explosion under shelter of which they made good their retreat. The English, then, have actually failed to do what their allies had a right to expect from them, and on a very important point, too.[a] And not only have the generals failed, but the soldiers, too, were not what they had formerly been. Mostly young lads recently arrived in the Crimea, they were too eager to look out for shelter, and to fire instead of attacking with the bayonet. They lacked discipline and order; the different regiments got mixed, the officers lost all control, and thus the machine was out of train in a few minutes. Yet it must be acknowledged that, for all that, they held out in the Redan for nearly two hours in dogged, passive resistance while no support was coming up; but then we are not accustomed to see the British infantry sink down to the level of the Russians, and seek their only glory in passive bravery.

The palm of the day belongs to Generals Bosquet and M'Mahon. Bosquet commanded the whole of the French assault on the right, and M'Mahon had the division which took and held the Malakoff. This was one of those rare days in which the French really out-did the English in the point of bravery. In every other point they had shown their superiority over them long before. Are we, then, to conclude that the English army has degenerated, and that its infantry cannot boast any longer of being, in close order, the first infantry of the world? It would be premature to say so; but certainly, of all men in the world, the British generals in the Crimea are the best fitted to ruin the physical and moral character

---

paragraph) the *Neue Oder-Zeitung* has: "On September 8, Simpson had 25,000 men on the spot. Out of these he confided the actual assault to 1,800."—*Ed.*

[a] Instead of this sentence the *Neue Oder-Zeitung* has: "Through the blunders of its general the English army made a full victory impossible." The rest of this paragraph is omitted.—*Ed.*

of the army; and on the other hand, the raw material for soldiers which has now been for some time introduced into the ranks, is far inferior to what it used to be. The British people had better look to this; two defeats in three months form a novel feature in British military history.

Of the Russians we can only say that they fought with their accustomed passive bravery, and in the assault made to retake the Malakoff even displayed great active courage. What their tactical arrangements were, we have no means of judging until their report is published. One thing is certain, namely, that the Malakoff was completely taken by surprise. The garrison were enjoying their dinner, and not any portion of them, except the artillery at the guns, appear to have been under arms and ready to meet an attack.

If we now look at what has been done since the taking of the south side, we find from Gorchakoff's reports[a] that 20,000 allied troops (of what nation is not said) have gone to Eupatoria, and that at the same time strong reconnoitering parties are pushed against the Russian left in the valley of Baidar, where the Russian advanced troops were compelled to retire towards Urkusta, in the direction of the valley of the upper Chulin, another tributary to the Chernaya. The corps of 30,000 men, now at Eupatoria, are rather weak, and could not venture to any great distance from the place. But others may follow. At all events, field operations have commenced, and another fortnight must decide whether the Russians can hold their ground, or whether they must leave the whole of the Crimea a prey to the Allies.[b]

Written on September 28, 1855

First published in the *New-York Daily Tribune*, No. 4519, October 13, 1855, reprinted in the *New-York Semi-Weekly Tribune*, No. 1084, October 16,1855 as a leading article; the German version was published in the *Neue Oder-Zeitung*, No. 463, October 4, 1855, marked with the sign ×

Reproduced from the *New-York Daily Tribune*

---

[a] Report of September 11, 1855 in *Russky Invalid*, No. 211, September 16, 1855.—*Ed.*

[b] Instead of the last three paragraphs the *Neue Oder-Zeitung* has: "The palm of the day belongs to generals Bosquet and Mac-Mahon. Bosquet commanded the whole of the French assault on the right, and Mac-Mahon was in charge of the division that held the Malakhov.—The Russians fought with their usual passive bravery. The Malakhov was obviously taken by surprise. The garrison were having dinner, and only the artillery were at their guns, ready to meet an attack."—*Ed.*

Karl Marx

A DIPLOMATIC IMPROPRIETY

London, October 2. Considerable surprise has been caused here by a speech of Sir Alexander Malet, the British envoy accredited to the German Federal Diet.[377] For in the speech,[a] which was made at a dinner in Homburg given on the occasion of the capture of Sevastopol, he launched into a strong attack on the King of Prussia[b] and his Ministers. The British envoy said bluntly that the British people were entitled to expect a different policy from Prussia, especially since the majority of the Prussian people had never concealed their sympathies for the Western Powers. Sir Alexander is of the opinion that if Prussia had sided with the Western Powers, Austria would have acted energetically and it would have been impossible for Russia to oppose the Prussian coalition. Prussia is thus, as it were, made directly responsible for the war. As the King of Prussia is a member of the German Confederation, at which Sir Alexander is accredited as British envoy, it is widely believed that this attack will in any case give rise to serious representations. If he is defended by his government, it will be a pointer to Britain's future policy; if the contrary is the case one can certainly expect the recall of the envoy.

Written on October 2, 1855

First published in the *Neue Oder-Zeitung*, No. 465, October 5, 1855

Marked with the sign ×

Printed according to the newspaper

Published in English for the first time

[a] An account of it was published in *The Times*, No. 22172, September 29, 1855.—*Ed.*

[b] Frederick William IV.—*Ed.*

Karl Marx

THE OFFICIAL FINANCIAL REPORT

London, October 2. We now have before us the official report on the national revenues for the past year, half-year and quarter (according to Gladstone's innovations the English financial year ends for both expenditure and revenue on September 30).[a] On the one hand it demonstrates the elasticity of English resources, on the other that the probabilities calculus is not the forte of English financiers. With regard to the past financial year the net surplus amounts to £8,344,781, with regard to the past half-year to £2,929,699, and to the past quarter £1,924,124. The significance of these figures is transformed at once if one takes into consideration on the one hand the increase in taxation which has taken place under Gladstone and Lewis and on the other the disproportion between the tax increases as calculated and as realised. This is incontrovertibly revealed as soon as we look into details. In the customs we find an increase of £1,290,787 for the year, of £608,444 for the half-year, and of £364,423 for the quarter. This is due entirely to the new taxes on tea, sugar and coffee. It needs the bourgeois optimism of *The Daily News* to use this statistical premise to deduce that prosperity within the working classes has increased. As we know, Gladstone suspended the tax reductions on tea and sugar which the House of Commons had decreed at his suggestion in 1854. His successor Lewis added 3 shillings per cwt. on sugar, which according to his estimate was to bring in £1,200,000 in taxes; 3d. per pound of tea, which according to his calculations was to add £750,000 to the customs; and finally 1d. per pound of coffee, which should be equivalent to

[a] The report was published in *The Times*, No. 22173, October 1, 1855.—*Ed.*

a financial surplus of £150,000. The total surplus revenue from the customs for the last quarter, however, only amounts to £364,423, that is far less than even half of the additional return expected from the increased tax on sugar alone. From the taxation lists we see that the consumption of coffee has fallen by almost 2 per cent as against 1853. The customs revenue from wine and tobacco has fallen significantly.

In England the excise is regarded as the barometer of the "comforts"[a] the lower classes of the people enjoy. Here we find a reduction of £266,006 in the best quarter, although Sir George Cornewall Lewis' new tax on distilled liquors was in full operation in Scotland and Ireland. He counted on receiving an increase of £1,000,000 from his additional tax. Instead of this he has lost £266,006 over the quarter. As for the stamp-duty, there is an increase over the year of £100,472 but a loss over the half-year of £48,402 and for the last quarter a loss of £103,344. This is all the more striking when one considers that Gladstone's newly introduced inheritance tax is in full operation. In the postal revenue, which belongs to this category (of stamp revenues), we find a deficit of £206,819 over the year, of £175,976 over the half-year and of £81,243 for the last quarter. The landed property tax shows an increase of £6,484,147 for the year, £2,195,124 for the half-year and £1,993,590 for the quarter. But we must not forget that Gladstone doubled the former rate of taxation and expected this to yield an increase of £6$^1/_2$ million, while Sir George Cornewall Lewis moreover passed a new additional tax of twopence in the pound, from which he anticipated another tax increase of £4,000,000. Thus with regard to the revenue from landed property the increase in revenue has in no way corresponded to the increase in taxation, either.

The swindles and the probable future of the Crédit Foncier and the Crédit mobilier[378] and other Bonapartist creations in banking and in bankruptcy constantly occupy the public here. In this connection one may recall that Émile Péreire and other directors of these institutions were originally *Saint Simonists*. These gentlemen always expected the salvation of the world from the *banks*, perhaps also from *bankruptcy*. In any case they have found their *own salvation* therein. In so far as one abstracts from the great general ideas of the master, St. Simonism has been realised under Bonaparte in the only form in which it was possible. What more could one want! Péreire is Bonaparte's chief financial humbug and

[a] Marx uses the English word.—*Ed.*

M. Michel Chevalier is one of his editors-in-chief, he is the principal economist of the *Journal des Débats. Habent sua fata libelli*[a]. But great ideas too have their "*fata*".

Written on October 2, 1855

First published in the *Neue Oder-Zeitung*, No. 467, October 6, 1855

Marked with the sign ×

Printed according to the newspaper

Published in English for the first time

[a] Books have their fate—a saying by the Roman grammarian and poet Terence, from his work *De litteris, syllabis et metris* (*Carmen heroicum*, verse 258).—*Ed.*

Karl Marx

THE BANK OF FRANCE.—REINFORCEMENTS TO THE CRIMEA.— THE NEW FIELD MARSHALS

London, October 1. The Bank of England has once again raised the rate of interest, from 5 per cent to $5^1/_2$ per cent. In the first instance this measure is directed against the *Banque de France*, which—by way of bills of exchange drawn on London and discounted there—has shipped gold to the value of £4,600,000 from England to France in the course of the last six weeks. The most disturbing rumours are circulating on the stock exchange here concerning the financial state of the *Banque de France*. According to some of them a suspension of cash payments is imminent, according to others the notes of the *Banque de France* will receive a guarantee of increase "for additional security". This latter measure would then infallibly lead to a "run"[a] on the bank and to the immediate depreciation of its paper currency. Finally, it is claimed that the *Banque de France* will attempt to increase its capital to double the present amount by means of a subscription. However protean these rumours may appear as far as their details are concerned, they all indicate that the *Banque de France* is heading towards a crisis and that this institution, which has always been regarded as unshakeably solid since its foundation during the reign of Napoleon I, has become under Napoleon III just one more of the *inverted* credit pyramids which must be regarded as the most characteristic monuments of his reign. That section of French society which demanded more than anything else the *appearance* of abundant credit and of a "*prospérité toujours croissante*"[b] cannot complain when it is time to pay the price for

[a] Marx uses the English word.—*Ed.*
[b] Constantly growing prosperity.—*Ed.*

this pleasant deception. In any case the financial operations, stock exchange manoeuvres and bank speculations which caused such a tremendous sensation in the last years of Louis Philippe's reign and gave rise to a whole polemical literature of the type of *Juifs rois de l'époque,*[a] *La dynastie Rothschild,*[b] etc., appear as mere child's play when they are compared with what has been achieved in this line from 1852 to the present time.

At this moment there are approximately 6,000 men under orders for shipment to the Crimea, among them 800 artillerymen, 900 cavalrymen and the rest infantry. In addition to these about 4,000 infantrymen are supposed to be despatched from Gibraltar, Malta, the Ionian Islands and Piraeus to the theatre of war. These reinforcements—even taking the Foreign Legion into account—are far from sufficient to restore the active English army even to its original strength. This brought the following comment from *Bright* at a meeting in Rochdale yesterday:

> "Were I an advocate of the war I should adopt a quite different policy with regard to our internal military establishment. I should introduce a proper system of conscription, such as exists in Russia, Austria and France, and thus compel people from all classes to play their due part in what is called the task of the nation."[c]

The appointment of the superannuated lords and earls Combermere, Strafford and Hardinge as field marshals as a reward for General Simpson's defeat before the Redan bastion (he is to be recalled, incidentally) is one of the many poor jokes and frivolous jests with which Palmerston is wont to brighten the evening of his life. The first two generals may fittingly be considered *deceased,* so their promotion has rather the character of a retroactive canonisation. Their earthly career long since finished, they have been raised to military sainthood. Lord Hardinge holds the antediluvian rank of *Commander in Chief* of the English army and has amply earned his field marshal's baton for his determined and indefatigable sycophancy and fawning upon field marshal Prince Albert. What makes the business still more piquant is the circumstance that a victory gained with the French over the Russians is celebrated by the promotion of forgotten officers who

---

[a] Written by Alphonse Toussenel.— *Ed.*

[b] A reference to Georges-Marie Dairnvaell's pamphlets *Grand procès entre Rothschild Ier, Roi des Juifs, et Satan Dernier, Roi des Imposteurs, Histoire édifiante et curieuse de Rothschild I-er, Roi des Juifs...* and *Rothschild I-er, ses valets et son peuple,* all published in Paris in 1846 (the first one anonymously).— *Ed.*

[c] Marx gives a free rendering of Bright's speech made on October 3, 1855. Cf. the report published in *The Times,* No. 22177, October 5, 1855.— *Ed.*

have fought against the French with the Russians. Thus for instance Lord Strafford's merit consists in having led a brigade of Guards at Waterloo,[379] commanded the first army corps in the march on Paris and taken possession of Paris by occupying the heights of Belleville and Montmartre.

Written about October 4, 1855

First published in the *Neue Oder-Zeitung*, No. 469, October 8, 1855

Marked with the sign ×

Printed according to the newspaper

Published in English for the first time

Karl Marx

THE COMMITTEE AT NEWCASTLE-UPON-TYNE

London, October 6. The Committee set up at Newcastle-upon-Tyne for the purpose of investigating the "Action of Diplomacy", has just published a very remarkable report.[380] We quote the most important passages from it and for the present we shall merely mention that Mr. *Porter*, who is a prominent figure in the following documents, was Vice-President of the British Board of Trade[a] and has a place in English literature as the author of *The Progress of the Nation*.

No. 1. *Report of the Committee at Newcastle-upon-Tyne*. The committee [...] have to report—1. That Mr. Porter, whilst in office at the Board of Trade, during the administration of Lord Melbourne, and whilst Lord Palmerston was Foreign Minister, formed and expressed the conviction, as the result of his own observation, and of facts within his own knowledge, that Lord Palmerston systematically sacrificed the interests of England to those of Russia, in matters relating to commercial treaties. 2. That Mr. Porter did not conceal this conviction from his official chief, the President of the Board of Trade,[b] Lord Palmerston's colleague; but that, on the contrary, when, in 1840, he was offered a mission to Paris, for the purpose of negotiating a commercial treaty with France, he declined to accept that mission, except on the express condition that he should have no communication to make to the Foreign Office; assigning as a reason for this demand, his conviction that his endeavours to conclude such a treaty would be treacherously thwarted by the chief of that department. 3. That this condition was submitted to; and Mr. Porter, in consequence, [...] undertook the mission to Paris. 4. That whilst in office, under Mr. Gladstone, during Sir R. Peel's administration, Mr. Porter adhered to his former convictions, and in addition charged Lord Palmerston with having received Russian money; alleging that the agent in this transaction was a Jew, by name Jacob James Hart, who formerly kept a gambling-house, in St. James's street, and who was

[a] Here and below Marx uses the English term.—*Ed.*
[b] Labouchere.—*Ed.*

subsequently appointed British Consul at Leipsic, by Lord Palmerston; and that he had ascertained this in consequence of enquiries made by the government, with a view of getting rid of Hart. 5. That, independently of Mr. Porter's evidence, it is an indubitable fact, to be ascertained by any who will take the trouble to enquire, as we have done, that Jacob James Hart did keep a gambling-house, and was appointed by Lord Palmerston to be British Consul at Leipsic, where he was universally shunned as a most disreputable character.

The committee subjoin evidence which they have taken.

Newcastle, September 20th, 1855 *G. Crawshay* and others

We publish the following *extracts* from that evidence:

No. 2. Mr. Porter heard of the transaction concerning the gambling-house only later, under Sir Robert Peel's Administration.

The circumstances, as related by Mr. Porter to me, are as follows:

There was a Jew, a British Consul at Leipsic, who was considered, both by natives and British merchants, as a most discreditable representative of England, particularly as it was ascertained that he had been the keeper of a gambling-house somewhere about St. James's street. An attempt was made to get him removed, and the matter was brought before Sir R. Peel's government. But that government experienced such fierce and violent opposition from Lord Palmerston, who had made the appointment originally, that they gave way. The secret of Lord Palmerston's adherence to such a disreputable character came then to be inquired into, and it was found that Lord Palmerston, at a time when he was in great pecuniary embarrassment, I think about 1825, was told by Princess Lieven to go to the gambling-house kept by this Jew, where a foreigner was [...] to lose to him £20,000 in two nights.

Mr. Porter spoke of this openly to many persons, amongst others to Mr. Bright.

April 7th, 1855 *D. Ross,* of Bladensburg

No. 3. Hart's appointment was made in 1841, when Palmerston was just about to leave the Cabinet. A letter of Palmerston's which expressed regret that at the moment he did not have a more advantageous post for Hart at his disposal was flaunted by Hart before several people in Leipsic.

Worthling, April 28, 1855 *D. Urquhart*

No. 4. It would be as impossible for me, as it is unnecessary, to recall all private conversations with Mr. Porter. I shall confine myself to one incident. An important treaty had been concluded with a European state (Naples) under which, if it had been ratified, this country would in an amicable way have obtained considerable commercial advantages. Those in official positions who knew about the Russian action in the Cabinet and opposed it, feared that the treaty would be wrecked, if there remained any pretexts for discussion, formalities or preliminaries. Accordingly to avoid this danger, the treaty was entirely completed and only presented to the Government after having been approved of and signed by Naples. It was received in silence in Britain. No government organ was permitted to welcome this event. The Foreign Office ignored it completely. Those who had brought about the treaty induced a Member of Parliament to ask whether Naples had given its approval to such a treaty. Palmerston replied that this was a complete misunderstanding, no such treaty existed, there existed merely a few rough notes for a treaty. I recollect that Porter, after referring to this reply of the Minister, opened a depository of public documents in my presence, laid hold of one, handed it to me and exclaimed, "*Here is the treaty*". It is probably still where it was. This treaty had been negotiated by MacGregor, now M.P. for Glasgow. Even more astonishing was Porter's assertion about the sacrifice of a commercial treaty which he had himself negotiated with France, and whose conclusion was baulked by Palmerston.

May 4, 1855 *R. Monteith*

No. 5. I remember having heard of the appointment of Mitchely (or some similar name), a Jew or a former Jew, who was joint owner and also joint editor of *The Morning Post.* Palmerston secured him the consulate at St. Petersburg, a position which he retained until the outbreak of the war, and which yielded £4,000 to £5,000 per annum. It was just after the general election, in 1847, that *The Morning Post,* then strictly Derbyite and Conservative, published an article about the Ministry, which with regard to Palmerston said that Urquhart could make charges against Palmerston which made one's hair stand on end. *Shortly afterwards* Mitchely received this appointment. It is true that the management of the newspaper passed into different hands, but from that moment *Palmerston was not included* in its general attacks on the Government but was on the contrary praised and assisted by the newspaper, even while it continued to support Derby and the Corn Laws. During the last twelve months it openly deserted the Conservative camp and became not only a Palmerstonian paper but also a pro-Government one.

Charles Attwood[381]

Written on October 6, 1855

First published in the *Neue Oder-Zeitung,* No. 475, October 11, 1855

Marked with the sign ×

Printed according to the newspaper

Published in English for the first time

Frederick Engels

PROGRESS OF THE WAR[382]

The news from the war is abundant. In addition to the report of Gorchakoff, on which we comment elsewhere, we have by the steamer of Saturday, the official accounts of the cavalry action at Kurulu near Eupatoria, before reported; the intelligence of an unsuccessful assault of the Russians on Kars, of the destruction by the Allies of Taman and Phanagoria, and of the landing of a body of allied troops in the peninsula of Kinburn.

The cavalry action near Eupatoria was fought by twelve French squadrons (fourth hussars, sixth and seventh dragoons). According to Gen. d'Allonville's report,[a] which is plain and intelligible, the French and Turks made an extensive reconnoissance toward the interior on three different roads—one to the south and two to the north of Lake Sasik. The two latter columns met at a village called Dolshak, where they discovered the approach of the Russian cavalry. Here the reports begin to disagree. Gen. d'Allonville maintains that eighteen squadrons of Russians—while the French were dismounted, baiting their horses—tried to turn them by the south and cut off their retreat to Eupatoria; that he then ordered his men to mount, fell upon the flank of the Russians, routed and pursued them for two leagues. Gorchakoff says that the Russians were only one regiment (eighteenth lancers) or eight squadrons; that they were surprised by the French after having dismounted in

[a] A. Pélissier, "Grand quartier général, à Sébastopol, le 1er octobre 1855", *Le Moniteur universel*, No. 289, October 16, 1855.—*Ed.*

order to unlimber a battery of artillery, and that under these circumstances they had to run for their lives. He makes Gen. Korff responsible for this mistake. Now what business a whole regiment of lancers had to dismount and assist in unlimbering a battery of eight guns, and how it was that the gunners, whose business it was to do this work, were not at hand, we are left to guess for ourselves. The whole report of Gorchakoff is so confused, so unmilitary, so impregnated with the desire to palliate this first cavalry disaster, that it is impossible to treat it as a serious statement of facts. At the same time we see Gen. Korff made responsible for this defeat, as Selvan was made responsible for Silistria, Soimonoff for Inkerman, Read for the Chernaya.[383] Gorchakoff, though defeated in every action, is still invincible. It is not he who is beaten, far from it; it is some unlucky subaltern who upsets the general's wise plans by some clumsy mistake, and who generally gets killed in action in punishment for this crime. In this instance, however, the blunderer is unfortunate enough to preserve his life. Perhaps he may, later on, have something to say to Gorchakoff's dispatch. In the mean time he has the satisfaction that his opponent represents him in a far better light than his infallible commander-in-chief does. Since then, the British light cavalry division has been sent to Eupatoria to reenforce the French.

Two other expeditions have been undertaken on the extreme flanks of the Crimean theater of war. One of these was from Kertch and Yenikale to the opposite side of the straits. The small fortresses of Taman and Phanagoria have been destroyed, about one hundred guns captured, and thus the entrance to the Sea of Azoff has been completely secured by the Allies. This operation was merely one of precaution; its immediate results are of no great consequence.

The second expedition is of greater importance. The allied fleets, with about ten thousand troops, first made a demonstration off Odessa, where, however, not a shot was fired, and then sailed to Kinburn. This place is situated near the extremity of a tongue of land which on the south encloses the estuary of the Dnieper and Bug. At this point, the estuary is about three miles wide; a bar with fifteen feet of water (according to the best charts) closes its entrance. On the north side of this entrance is situated Otshakoff, on the south side Kinburn. Both these places first came into notoriety during the Russo-Turkish campaign of 1787, when the Bug formed the frontier of the two empires, and consequently Otshakoff belonged to the Turks and Kinburn to the Russians.[384]

At that time, Suvaroff commanded the left wing of the Russian army (under Potemkin), and was stationed at Kinburn. The Turks, then masters of the Black Sea, crossed over from Otshakoff. They first made a diversion by landing behind the town of Kinburn, to the south-east; but when they saw that Suvaroff was not to be led astray by this false maneuver, they landed with their main body at the north-western extremity of the spit, exactly opposite Otshakoff. Here they entrenched themselves, and attacked the fortress; but Suvaroff sallied forth with a far inferior number of men, engaged them, and, with the help of reenforcements coming up, drove them into the sea. Their loss was enormous. Suvaroff himself, however, was wounded during this action, which was followed up in the following year, 1788, by the storming of Otshakoff.

This time the Allies landed, not below, but about four miles above the town of Kinburn, so as to intercept its communications by land with Kherson and the interior of Russia. Their gun-boats will very likely soon intercept the communications by water also. The spit of Kinburn, for six miles above the town, is extremely narrow, like that of Arabat, and so low and sandy that on digging a few feet below the surface water is found. Thus, strong fortifications with deep ditches cannot be constructed there in a hurry; and the works thrown up by the Turks in 1787 were either stockades or sand-bag batteries. The fortifications of Kinburn themselves cannot, for the same reason, be very formidable, no good foundation for masonry scarps being possible, though since that time broad wet ditches have no doubt been constructed. Nevertheless, we think that Kinburn cannot long hold out against the Allies if energetically attacked; and once in their hands, it opens to them a perspective of important operations in the direction of Cherson and Nikolaieff—that is, the direction of the base of operations of the Russian army in the Crimea. This descent, then, may prove very important if properly followed up. But up to the departure of the steamer no news of anything decisive had arrived, and thus we are led to conclude that this expedition is also to be conducted in the habitual, easy, jog-trot style of the Allies.

The defeat of the Russians before Kars will very probably prove to be the crowning event of the campaign in Armenia. The Turks, badly organized and short of every requisite for war, had played but a poor part in this portion of the seat of war. Unable to hold the field, they confined themselves to the occupation of Kars, Erzeroum and the country immediately under the command of these fortresses. Gen. Williams, who had entered the Turkish service, commanded at Kars and superintended the construction of proper defensive works. For the greater part of the Summer the whole campaign on either side was confined to skirmishes, forays and foraging expeditions in the hill country; the general and first result of which was that the Russians, gradually gaining ground, succeeded in blockading Kars and even in cutting off its communications with Erzeroum. Kars is situated in a lateral valley of the Upper Araxes; Erzeroum at the sources of the Euphrates; Batoum, on the mouth of the Churuk Su (Bathys), the upper course of which passes near, both to Kars and to Erzeroum, so that one of the roads between these two places follows the basin of the Churuk Su as far as Olti, whence it strikes off across the hills toward Kars. Olti was, therefore, the central point for the Turks, as a road from Batoum there joins the one mentioned above, and Batoum was the place from which the nearest and strongest reenforcements were to be expected. Had the Russians succeeded in taking Kars, their first step would have been to establish themselves at Olti thereby cutting off Erzeroum from its nearest and best communication with the Black Sea and Constantinople. The Turks, however, were so dispirited that they retired as far as Erzeroum, merely occupying the mountain pass between the Upper Euphrates and the sources of the Araxes, while Olti was all but completely neglected.

At last, when Kars was more closely hemmed in, they attempted to form a convoy of provisions at Olti, and with a strong escort to force an entrance into Kars. Part of the cavalry from Kars having been sent away, as it was useless there, actually fought its way through the Russians as far as Olti, and the convoy started shortly afterward; but this time the Russians were better on the alert—the Turks were completely defeated, and the convoy was captured by the Russians. Kars, in the mean time, began to run short of provisions; Omer Pasha was, indeed, sent to take the command in Asia and to organize at Batoum an army fit to act in the field; but this creation of a new army takes a deal of time, and a march direct to the relief of Kars by Olti would not have been the best course he could take, as Kars might any day be compelled to surrender from want of provisions before relief could arrive.

In this difficult position the Turks stood at the end of September; Kars was considered as good as lost, and the Russians were sure, by merely blockading the town, to starve it out. But the Russians themselves appear not to have been willing to wait until the last flour was baked and the last horse cooked in Kars. Whether from the fear of approaching Winter, the state of the roads, shortness of provisions, superior orders, or the fear of Omer Pasha's relieving corps, they at once made up their minds to act vigorously. Siege-guns arrived from Alexandropol, a fortress on the frontier but a few leagues from Kars, and after a few days of open trenches and cannonading, Kars was assaulted by the concentrated main body of the Russian army under Muravieff. The combat was desperate, and lasted eight hours. The Bashi-Bazouks and foot irregulars, who had so often run before the Russians in the field, here fought on more congenial ground. Though the attacking forces must have been from four to six times more numerous than the garrison, yet all attempts to get into the place were in vain. The Turks had here at last recovered their courage and intelligence. Though the Russians, more than once, succeeded in entering the Turkish batteries (very likely lunettes open at the gorge, so as to be commanded by the fire of the second line of defense), they could nowhere establish themselves. Their loss is said to have been immense; four thousand killed are stated to have been buried by the Turks; but before crediting this, we must have more detailed and precise information.

As to Omer Pasha's operations, he had a double choice. Either to march up the Churuk Su, by Olti, to the relief of Kars, where he would run the risk of arriving too late for this object, while he would have led his army to the Armenian plateau, where the Russians are secure from effective front attack by a strong line of fortresses, and where Omer Pasha could have no opportunity to fall on their flanks; or he would have to march up the Rion to Kutais, and thence across the hills into the valley of the Kura toward Tiflis. There he would meet with no fortified posts of any consequence, and menace at once the center of Russian power in the South Caucasian country. A more effective means for recalling Muravieff from Armenia could not be found, and our readers may recollect that we have over and over again referred to this line of operations as the only one fit to deal a great blow at the strength of the Russians in Asia.[a] The proper basis of operations for this march would be Redout Kaleh; but as there is no safe harbor, Omer Pasha has chosen Sukum Kaleh, where there is a good harbor and a better road along the coast. Whether the

---

[a] See this volume, p. 269.—*Ed.*

season is not too far advanced for any serious operations there we shall soon learn.[a]

Written about October 19, 1855

First published in the *New-York Daily Tribune,* No. 4538, November 5, 1855, reprinted in the *New-York Semi-Weekly Tribune,* No. 1090, November 6, 1855 and, in a revised and enlarged form, in the *New-York Weekly Tribune,* No. 739, November 10, 1855 as a leading article

Reproduced from the *New-York Daily Tribune*

[a] For a description of the further fighting in the Kars area after the abortive Russian assault of September 29, 1855, and of the fall of Kars see this volume, pp. 588-94 and 595-98.— *Ed.*

Frederick Engels

ASPECTS OF THE WAR[385]

"Of what use are allies to thee, O Russian?
Stride forth, and thine is the whole world!"[a]

Times appear to be changed since Derjavin, the poet-laureate of Catherine II, could venture this proud appeal to his people. At that period, indeed, the Russians had made giant strides. The whole of South, or New Russia, from the Don to the Dniester, and the whole of West Russia, from the Dniester to the Niemen, were added to the Empire. Odessa, Cherson, Kharkov, Ekaterinoslav, and Sevastopol were founded; and indeed so long as the "great nation" of the East had no more dangerous opponents to fight than Turkish janissaries and Polish volunteers, every march appeared to imply a conquest and every declaration of war to be a sure guarantee of a speedy and glorious treaty of peace. It is true the Russian legions, on venturing beyond their favorite and favorable ground received a terrible lesson at Zorndorf, and were saved from even a severer one at Kunersdorf by the intervention of the Austrian Loudon only.[386] It is true that in 1798-99 even Suvaroff found his match in Masséna, and had to pay dearly for his Italian victories with the defeat of Zurich and the disastrous retreat across the Saint Gothard.[387] But for all that, the time of Catherine and Suvaroff was the great and glorious epoch of the Russian arms, and never since then has a similar splendor surrounded them. At Austerlitz, at Friedland, the inferiority of the Russian army, as compared with the French, was signally manifested; and if at Eylau they were saved from similar disgrace, it was because Lestocq, with the remnants of the Prussian army, rendered them the same service Loudon had done at Kunersdorf.[388] At Borodino an inferior number of Frenchmen defeated

[a] G. R. Derzhavin, *On the Capture of Warsaw.—Ed.*

them[389]; and had not Napoleon kept his guards in reserve, the defeat would have been decisive. The battles fought by the Russians during the French retreat from Moscow were far more glorious to the latter than to the former. And in the campaigns of 1813 and 1814, it was the Germans who had not only to supply the numerical force, and to bear the brunt of every battle, but to find the generals who could plan them.

Of the campaigns against Napoleon, however, it might be said that there was no disgrace in being beaten by a man who was in himself a host; but when the campaign of 1828-29, against the Turks, and of 1831, against the Poles,[390] showed again what superiority of numbers and what great efforts and waste of time it cost the Russians to overcome opponents far less formidable than Napoleon and his well-seasoned troops, the decline of Russian military glory was evident. It cannot be denied that at the very time when Russian influence in European politics was stronger than ever, the actual feats of the Russian army justified anything but such a political position. And though Russia, in consequence of the events of 1848-50, was actually raised to the position of arbiter and protector of all Europe east of the Rhine, the campaign which seemingly elevated her to such omnipotence, the Hungarian campaign, was positively disgraceful to Russian generalship, and did not add a single laurel leaf to the crown of victory of the "invincible" Russian army.

This "young, powerful, irresistible nation," this "people of the future," as the Russians modestly called themselves, in a military sense at least culminated long ago, and was even declining when the present war began. The Russian army was ranked as a respectable force from the tenacity and solidity of its infantry, though with many shortcomings which more than made up for these advantages. It appeared imposing by its numbers, professedly ready for war at any moment, and by the implicit obedience which held this vast machine together. But alas! what has become of this mighty army, this "stern fact" which so frightened Western Europe! Three of its eight corps, on the Danube, were checked by what Turkey could find to oppose to them; and when the Crimean campaign began, division after division, corps after corps was drawn into the insatiable whirlpool, never to disentangle themselves again. Indeed the army was drained to its very reserves and *élite* troops. The innate bravery as well as the innate clumsiness of the Russian soldiers was aided by the engineering skill of a truly gifted man, Todtleben; it was favored by the sins of omission and commission of the allied generals; it achieved a passive defense, glorious and even unparalleled of its kind, kept up full eleven months; but with all that, there was not a single actual success, not a single victory, and, indeed, invariable and inglorious defeat wherever the Russians attempted to take the initiative, no matter against what sort of enemies.

Except the truly incredible bravery displayed by the French and English soldiers, and in some instances by the Turks, also, the whole of this war does not afford to the Allies much matter for bragging; from the Alma[391] to the present day, their generalship has been worse than indifferent, and in no single instance have they ever seized time by the forelock. But such days as Inkerman and the Chernaya prove irretrievably the superiority of western armies over the Russians, while the repelled assaults on Silistria and Kars prove that under certain circumstances even the Turks are more than a match for them.[392] This war has been distinguished by more hand to hand encounters than all the wars of Napoleon together. Not an action but the troops have actually closed, even in the open field. Everywhere the bayonet has decided in the last instance. Now the bayonet—*Russki styk*—always was the great boast of the Russians. And precisely with the bayonet have the Russians been beaten in every instance, and by inferior numbers too. *Russki styk* belongs to bygone days, and the men who had to shrink back at Silistria, Kars, and even from the small bridge-head of Oltenitza, are no longer the same as those who took Akaltzik, Erzeroum and Warsaw, much less the same whom Suvaroff made to storm Ismail and Praga.[393] "Stride forth a Russian" is bitter irony when applied to the step of the soldiers retiring over the bridge from South to North Sevastopol.

That the position of the Russians in the Crimea is not very enviable is proved by the Emperor Alexander's return to the north without having gone to see the army before the enemy. Had there been any improvement in its position, any possibility of encouraging it by prospects of speedy reenforcements, of increased supplies, and of changes in the fortune of war, surely Alexander would not have lost the opportunity to visit that army which at all events has exhibited more patience and more passive resisting force than any previous army, even in Russia. As he has not done so, there is an increased probability that the rumors are true according to which the Russians are resolved to retire by small detachments from Sympheropol toward Perekop, leaving a rear-guard only to make a bold front against the enemy as long as may be necessary. There are, indeed, other circumstances tending to confirm these rumors. The fire of the north forts against

Sevastopol, though not very effective, is on the increase, as if they intended to expend all their ammunition before leaving. The troops about Inkerman are daily diminishing; and at the same time, as if to make up for this, fresh batteries are daily erected on the north shore. The camp about Mackenzie's even is reported to be peopled by diminished numbers. On the other hand, it is true, stronger columns have appeared on the Upper Belbek as soon as the French showed themselves there, and no progress of any note has been made by the Allies on that side.

It is, however, not to be forgotten that the road through the steppe from Sympheropol by Perekop to Cherson, offers no means of subsistence whatever to a marching army, and very often not even water. Thus small detachments only can pass at a time, as everything for their consumption has to be brought from a distance; consequently the slower Gorchakoff effects his retreat, the more regularly supplied will be his columns and the fewer men will he lose on the long march. On the other hand, the allied generals will commit an unpardonable military sin if they allow this gradual retreat of the Russians, without even ascertaining, by strong reconnaissances, whether it is actually taking place or not. As far as we can judge, Pélissier is noways satisfied on this point, but it is his own fault exclusively. Should he go on with his offensive movements at the present slow rate, he may have finished his preliminary operations for an attack upon the Russian position by the time the last Russian passes the lines of Perekop. But the "conqueror of Sevastopol" has now a reputation to lose, and this has made him even more cautious than the defeat of the 18th of June did.[394] Napoleon finished his campaign of 1796 in the maritime Alps, in six days and four battles, and that was ground far more difficult than the Crimean chalk-hills; but then he was not an understrapper to his own nephew.[a] One attempt has, indeed, been made on the part of the Allies which displays a little more energy. The corps at Eupatoria, reenforced by Gen. de Failly's French division, consisting of nine battalions, and Paget's British light dragoon brigade, which counts four regiments, has now extended its feelers as far as half way to Sympheropol, but very soon retreated again. Gorchakoff, who sends this piece of news,[b] states the strength of the Allies at from thirty thousand to forty thousand men. We shall be nearer the mark if we take the first number. But with thirty thousand men disposable in the field,

[a] Napoleon III.—*Ed.*
[b] "Paris, Wednesday Evening", *The Times*, No. 22200, November 1, 1855.—*Ed.*

the Eupatoria corps might attempt far bolder movements, especially as its line of retreat to Eupatoria, either north or south of Lake Sasik, cannot be cut off. Thus, after all, we find the same languor at Eupatoria as on the Chernaya; and that this languor, instead of being lashed up into action, will rather become more languid, there can be no doubt, if it be certain, as the whole British press asserts, that Gen. Codrington is to succeed old Father Simpson in the command of the British forces. Codrington distinguished himself at the Redan on the 8th of September, where he commanded the assaulting divisions, by his magnificent imperturbability. So imperturbable was he that he could afford to look with the marble placidity of Horace's honest man—*si fractus illabatur orbis*[a]—on the defeat of his vanguard, without so much as even suspecting that it might not be amiss to send the reserves to their support! Codrington, no doubt, is the man for the moment—the great general who has been looked for so long in vain—and if he gets the command the British are safe from defeat, as he never would allow more than his outpost troops to be beaten in a single day.

That the Russians are actually retreating from the Crimea is also indicated by another fact. When Alexander was at Nikolaieff, he inspected the 31st, 32d, 33d, 34th, 35th and 36th marine equipages recently arrived from Sevastopol. These marine equipages are battalions of sailors and marines, each of which serves at sea to man a ship-of-the-line, and one or more smaller vessels. That these troops left the Crimea when they could neither be missed nor replaced if any lengthened resistance was intended, clearly shows what is to be expected. The mission of Generals Benkendorf and Stackelberg to headquarters in the Crimea, in order to inquire into and report on the state of the army there is also significant, and from what we know of the doings of the allied generals, it may be expected that the Russian retreat, on the whole, will be effected unmolested and without any great loss.

The London *Times* of course knows better than this.[b] If Pélissier does not act now, it is merely to induce the Russians to *stop* in the Crimea. If they were to retreat now, while the season is tolerable, what could he do to prevent them? what great injury could he inflict on them? No; Pélissier's plan is far deeper.

[a] Part of Horace's dictum "si fractus illabatur orbis, impavidum ferient ruinae" (if the world were to crumble into atoms, the ruins would strike him undismayed). Horatius Flaccus Quintus, *Carmina*, Lib. III, III.—*Ed.*

[b] This refers to the leading article in *The Times,* No. 22195, October 26, 1855.—*Ed.*

Pélissier not only intends to conquer the Crimea, but also to make the Russians perform a counterpart to the French retreat from Moscow. He is waiting for Winter to set in, and then he will pounce upon them, expel them from their position, drive them in heedless flight across the frozen steppe, or, as the Russians say of 1812, turn against them "His Excellency Gen. Hunger, and his Excellency Gen. Frost;" and then have them stopped in their march by the flanking corps falling upon them from Eupatoria, from Kertch, from Kinburn, so that what cold and hunger have left, will have to surrender at discretion, and not a man escape to tell the tale of the Crimean catastrophe to his countrymen.

Such is the strategy of the London *Times*.

Written in late October 1855

First published in the *New-York Daily Tribune*, No. 4543, November 10, 1855 as a leading article

Reproduced from the newspaper

Frederick Engels

THE RUSSIAN ARMY

At the time the war between the Western Powers and Russia was declared, the Anglo-French press was of opinion that Russia would have no lack of men to fight, but that she would soon be short of money. Financial difficulties were counted on to counteract the strength and to impede the movements of those millions of soldiers which Russia could, it was said, send forth at any time against her enemies. But what has been the actual fact? Russia, though ostensibly banished from all the great European Stock exchanges, has found no difficulty in contracting a loan[395]; her paper money, in spite of repeated fresh issues, maintains its credit; and her troops on their marches are fed, and the means of transport are furnished by the population in a manner impossible in any other less exclusively agricultural country. Blockaded as her ports are, she has managed hitherto to weather all those financial shoals upon which the London wiseacres were sure she would founder. As to the inexhaustible supply of men, however, matters look far different. While England with voluntary enlistment at home and abroad has managed gradually to increase her Crimean army to some forty thousand men, while France has only called in for the present year one hundred and forty thousand men instead of eighty thousand, and yet could send to the East an army numerous enough for more work than Pélissier could cut out for it, what has Russia had to do? Two general levies have been ordered on the whole extent of territory subject to the conscription, each averaging ten men to every one thousand male souls; then a general levy for the militia of twenty-three men to each one thousand souls, and now a fresh general levy for the line of ten men to each one thousand souls is again decreed. The average levy, in time of peace, is about five per one thousand for one-half of the empire, the other half furnishing recruits the year following. Thus two-and-a-half per one thousand male souls on the whole empire (except, of course, in the provinces not subject to conscription) is the yearly average. The two years of war, however, have now already caused levies to be made amounting in the whole to fifty-three to each one thousand souls, or about two-and-a-half per cent of the entire population, male and female—that is, in each of the two years, ten times the amount of the regular peace recruiting. If we suppose France to have, during the two years of the war, recruited for her army altogether three hundred thousand men, which is certainly beyond the mark, that would make, for a population of thirty-six millions, five-sixth per cent in two years, or five-twelfths per cent per annum—that is, just one-sixth of the numbers which Russia has had to incorporate in her army. It is true that in Russia about one-ninth per cent, and in France two-ninths per cent, of the entire population are taken annually in time of peace, for military service; but then, as the time of actual service in Russia is more than twice as long as in France, that circumstance is more than balanced.

That this continuous drain upon the able-bodied male population begins to tell in Russia, while its counterpart is hardly felt in France, we learn from all quarters. In Poland particularly we are informed that hands are wanted for the tillage of the soil; and the great discontent of the nobles at the general abstraction of their most valuable serf-property is another proof of the fact. The appointment of an out-and-out aristocrat, Lanskoy, to the ministry of the Interior, and his circular to the nobility,[a] stating that the Emperor Alexander, by a ukase, has guaranteed to them all their rights and privileges, shows how seriously alarmed the Court is at these symptoms of discontent among the owners of serfs.

The most remarkable feature, however, in these quickly-renewed recruitings, is the insignificance of the actual numerical increase gained, through them, for the army. Reckoning the total number of male souls subject to conscription at twenty-two millions, which is certainly low, in two years no less than six hundred and sixty thousand men have been enrolled in the ranks of the line, and five hundred and six thousand in those of the militia. Of the latter, indeed, a portion only have been mobilized, amounting perhaps to two hundred thousand men; so that the actual drain on the able-bodied male population has been about

[a] Issued on August 28, 1855.—*Ed.*

eight hundred and sixty thousand men. Beside these should be counted the soldiers of the reserve, dismissed on furlough for the last five or ten years of their term of service, and called in before the war broke out; but as most of these were called in as far back as 1853, we will not take them into account here.

In spite of these reserves, forming the fifth and sixth battalions of each infantry regiment—in spite of the six hundred and sixty thousand recruits incorporated partly in the first four line-battalions of each regiment, partly in the newly-formed second reserve (seventh and eighth) battalions of these regiments, the various bodies of the line are still far short of their full complement of men. The most curious proof of this is afforded by a proclamation issued at Nikolaieff, by the commander of the army of the south, Gen. Lüders.[a] He declares that by imperial order, twenty-three *druginas*[b] of the militia (twenty-three thousand men) attached to the army of the south, are to be incorporated with the line, and that they are to join the third and fourth battalions of each regiment. Now this measure cannot possibly have any other signification than that the regiments forming the army of the south are so reduced in numbers, that the mass of the soldiers of the third and fourth battalions are to be transferred to the first and second battalions while their places are to be filled by the militia. In other words, before the incorporation of the militia with them, the four battalions of these regiments were scarcely as strong as two battalions of the full complement. If such losses have taken place in an army the greater portion of which has never been before the enemy, and no portion of which has been engaged since Silistria, what must have been the losses in the Crimea and in Asia! We gain at once an insight into the actual state of the Russian army, and the conjecture which this insight allows us to make as to its wear and tear, explains the possibility of two-thirds of a million of men being absorbed into it without visibly increasing its numbers.

But how is this immense and disproportionate wear and tear brought about? First, by the enormous marches the recruits have to make from their respective homes to the chief towns of the provinces, thence to their depots, and finally to their regiments—not to count the marches these regiments have to make afterward. It is no trifle for a recruit to march from Perm to Moscow, from

[a] Lüders' proclamation was reported in *The Times*, No. 22200, November 1, 1855.—*Ed.*

[b] See this volume, p. 440.—*Ed.*

Moscow to Wilna, and finally from Wilna to Odessa or Nikolaieff. And if such interminable marches are hurried on by the supreme will of a man like Nicholas, who fixes the hour of arrival as well as the hour of departure, and punishes every deviation from his order; if brigades, divisions, army-corps, are precipitated in hot haste from one end of the empire to the other, regardless of the numbers left behind on account of sickness and fatigue; if a march from Moscow to Perekop has to be made at the rate of an ordinary forced march, which elsewhere is never continued beyond two days—a great deal of this wear and tear is explained. But to this overstraining of the physical powers of the soldier must be added the confusion necessarily arising from the notorious mal-administration of every department in the Russian service, especially in the army commissariat. Then comes the method of having the soldiers fed on the march as far as possible by the inhabitants of the country on the line of march—a method quite practicable if well managed, in an exclusively agricultural country, but illusory and open to the greatest inconvenience wherever, as in Russia, the commissariat and the commanding officers make good their embezzlements out of the stores stolen from the peasantry. And finally come the formidable miscalculations which necessarily must occur wherever armies disseminated over such a vast extent of ground are made to move by orders from one center, and are expected to execute them with the regularity of clockwork, while all the premises upon which these orders are based are false and unreliable. It is not the sword and the shot of the enemy, it is not the sickness inevitable in many parts of Southern Russia, it is not even the necessity of long marches which so decimates the Russian army; it is the special circumstances under which the Russian soldier is enlisted, drilled, marched, treated, fed, clad, lodged, commanded and fought, which can account for the terrible fact that very nearly the whole of the Russian army, as it existed in 1853, has already disappeared from the face of the earth without having made its opponents suffer more than one third of such a loss.

The order of the day of General Lüders is remarkable for another circumstance. It confesses openly that the militiamen are anything but fit to be led against the enemy. It implores the old soldiers not to laugh at or despise these young troops for their awkwardness under arms; it admits that they hardly know anything about drill, and introduces an alteration in the drill-regulations which must have been expressly sanctioned by the Emperor. The men are not to be "disgusted" by useless parade-drill; the most indispensable movements only are to be practiced with them; handling, loading, firing their muskets, firing at the target, movements in column, and skirmishing—everything else is declared to be useless parade-drill. Thus a Russian general, under the express sanction of the Emperor, condemns two-thirds of the whole Russian drill-regulations as useless stuff, fit for nothing but to disgust the soldier with his duties; and these regulations were the very work of which the late Emperor Nicholas was most proud!

The "young soldiers", whose very gesture and step are thus described as provoking the laughter of their comrades, would not in any other country be called recruits. They have been under arms from six to ten months, and yet they are as clumsy as if they came straight from the plow. It cannot be said that the long marches they have had to make have left them no time for drill. Napoleon in his latter campaigns incorporated his recruits in their respective battalions after a fortnight's drill, and then dispatched them to Spain, to Italy, to Poland; they were drilled during the march, both while marching and when arrived in quarters; and when they joined the army, after six or eight weeks' marching, they were expected to be fit for active service. Never did Napoleon allow his recruits more than three months' drill to become soldiers; and even in 1813, when he had to create a fresh army, fresh cadres, and everything, he brought his conscripts down to the battlefields of Saxony in three months from the time they had joined their depots; and his opponents soon learned what he could do with these "raw recruits." What a difference between this quickness of adaptation with the French and this clown-like clumsiness of the Russian! What a certificate of incapacity in the officers of this Russian militia! And yet, Lüders says, these officers have nearly all served in the line, and many of them have smelt powder.

The restriction of the drill to the most indispensable movements, too, shows what Lüders expects from his new reenforcements. Skirmishing and movements in column alone are to be practiced; no deployments into line, no formations of columns out of the line. The Russian soldier, indeed, is of all the least fit for line movements, but he is quite as unfit for skirmishing. Close column-fighting is his forte, that formation in which blunders of commanding officers are followed by the least possible disorder and derangement of the general order of battle, and where the cohesive instinct of the brave but inanimate mass may make up for these blunders. The Russian soldiers, like the wild horses of the steppe when persecuted by wolves, throng together in a shapeless mass, immovable, unmanageable, but which will hold its ground until a supreme effort of the enemy forces it asunder. But, anyhow, line formations are necessary in many circumstances, and even the Russians have recourse to them, though in a moderate degree. What then is to become of an army which cannot form in line at all, or which when got into line with a deal of trouble, cannot reform in column without throwing everything into confusion?

Written about November 2, 1855

First published in the *New-York Daily Tribune,* No. 4548, November 16, 1855, reprinted in the *New-York Semi-Weekly Tribune,* No. 1094, November 20, 1855 as a leading article

Reproduced from the *New-York Daily Tribune*

Karl Marx

BIG MEETING IN SUPPORT OF POLITICAL REFUGEES[396]

London, November 13. An exceptionally well attended meeting was held in St. Martin's Hall last night. The notices announcing the meeting spoke of "a joint demonstration against the recent expulsions from Jersey, the proposed Alien Bill[397] and the present war policy".[a] The last point, however, was dropped to ensure concord on the other two points. The chairman, Mr. *Edward Miall*, M.P., gave a survey of the events which led to the expulsion and then continued:

"The simple object of this meeting is to protest both against the past and against the future. We claim on behalf of political exiles here the right of asylum (cheers) on the simple ground that they are *political* exiles (cheers), whose misfortunes suffice to secure our sympathy and protection (cheers). We do not ask what politics they profess or what might be the party in their own country to which they belong. We make no distinction between prince and plebeian in this respect. (Cheers.) We want the right of sanctuary to be accorded equally to all who come to these shores. Hitherto we have done this impartially. We have extended our hand to Prince Louis Napoleon, just as we sheltered a forgotten monarch under the name of John Smith.[b] (Cheers and laughter.) We have granted the protection of our laws to Orleanists, Fusionists,[308] Royalists and Republicans not according to the policy of the rulers of the country from which they fled, but according to the laws of this country. (Cheers.) Our national hospitality has bid them all a cordial welcome. Among others we have held in high esteem *Kossuth* (prolonged applause) whom *The Times* recently called the noble Magyar, we have likewise afforded *Mazzini* the protection he sought. (Loud applause.) We had not thought it necessary to inquire whether the political views of these men were in accordance with our own; it sufficed that they were exiles from their own country for political causes, and their misfortunes were a sufficient passport

---

[a] Below follows a summary of a report of this meeting published in *The Times*, No. 22210, November 13, 1855.—*Ed.*

[b] Louis Philippe.—*Ed.*

to our sympathies. (Cheers.) This is what we claim for the Jersey [...] refugees. (Hear, hear!) This is what we claim for all who come to these shores and we will not bate one jot of our national hospitality at the bidding of any one. (Loud and prolonged cheers.) It is therefore fitting that those who come here should be welcomed to the full enjoyment of British liberty and not merely to a prison. (Hear, hear!) There must be no registration of political refugees, no police surveillance. (Hear, hear!) The freedom of these persons, just as our own, must not be placed in the hands of any minister or the Crown", etc.

After *Miall's* fairly long speech, which was greeted with tremendous applause and did not pass off without fierce attacks on Louis Napoleon and Austria, Mr. *Washington Wilks* read the following letter from *Cobden*:

"My dear Sir,—I cannot, I am sorry to say, take a part in your demonstration against the arbitrary treatment of M. *Victor Hugo* and his brethren in exile. But although distance from town and other engagements prevent me from being present, I sympathize very cordially with the promoters of the meeting. Surely such proceedings as those which you are meeting to protest against ought to open the eyes, of at least that part of the public which is supporting the war (cries of oh, oh) from a sympathy with liberalism abroad, as to the gross delusion that has been practised on their credulity (cries of oh, oh) by those who have told them that in the hands of our present Government the war in which we are engaged is a struggle for liberty. (Hisses and cheers.) Depend on it, the tendency, both at home and abroad, ever since the peace of Europe was broken, has been the very reverse; and give us but a few years more of war, and we shall find ourselves retrograding to the dark political doings of Sidmouth's evil days.[399] (Cries of no, no, hissing and cheering.)"

R. Cobden

The meeting then passed the following resolution:

"That this meeting utters its indignant protest against the recent expulsion of refugees from Jersey, and affirms that foreigners landing in the dominion of the British Crown become at once entitled to the natural and legal right of Englishmen—a public examination and trial by jury before exposure to any penal consequences. That this meeting pledges itself and calls upon the country to resist by all lawful means the apprehended attempt to carry through Parliament an act invalidating or restricting the right of sanctuary."

This demonstration will be followed by quite a number of similar ones. Incidentally I cannot refrain from observing that the whole refugee question consists of much smoke and little fire. Public opinion has definitely turned against the government, but I also believe that this uproar was allowed for in the government's calculations. The government responded to Louis Napoleon's first demands so clumsily, tragi-comically and blusteringly merely to demonstrate the fact to him that *further* concessions were beyond the power of a British government. Had it been in earnest, the government would have proceeded more skilfully and would not have struck in such a grotesque way and so long before the opening of Parliament. Palmerston does not love the refugees, but he regards them as a means which he must keep at hand so as to be able to threaten the Continent with them when the occasion arises. I am convinced that just now the refugees have less reason for anxiety than ever before.

Written on November 13, 1855

First published in the *Neue Oder-Zeitung*, No. 537, November 16, 1855

Marked with the sign ×

Printed according to the newspaper

Published in English for the first time

Karl Marx

TRADITIONAL ENGLISH POLICY[400]

Concerning the foreign policy of English Whigs a most erroneous impression prevails; it is supposed that they have been ever the sworn foes of Russia. History clearly establishes the contrary. In the diary and correspondence of James Harris, first Earl of Malmesbury—for several years, under both Whig and Tory administrations, English Minister at the Court of St. Petersburg—and in the Memoirs and Correspondence of Charles James Fox, edited by Lord John Russell, we find astounding revelations of Whig policy as inspired and inaugurated by Fox, who is still the political hierophant of the Whigs, being in fact as much revered by them as Mohammed is by the Osmanlis. To understand, therefore, how England has been ever[a] subservient to Russia, we will revert for a moment to facts antecedent to the accession of Fox to the Cabinet.

In the diary of the Earl of Malmesbury we perceive the anxious, impatient haste with which England pressed her diplomacy on Russia during our War of Independence.[401] Her Embassador was instructed to conclude by any means an alliance offensive and defensive. The reply of the Czarina in the first instance was evasive: the very word "offensive" was odious to Catherine; and it was necessary first to wait the course of events. Finally the English diplomat discerned that the obstacle was Russia's desire of English support for her Turkish policy; and Harris advised his Government of the necessity of nourishing the Russian appetite, if her aid against the American Colonies was to be secured.

---

[a] The *New-York Daily Tribune* has "even".—*Ed.*

The following year the proposition of Sir James Harris assumes a milder form; he does not ask for an alliance. A Russian protest to hold France and Spain in check, if backed by a naval armament, will be acceptable to England. The Empress replies that she can perceive no occasion for such a measure. The Embassador, with servile flattery, remonstrates that

"A Russian Sovereign of the seventeenth century [...] might well have spoken so, but since that epoch Russia has become a leading power in Europe, [...] and the concerns of Europe are hers also. [...] If Peter the Great could behold the Russian navy [...] allied to that of England [...] he would confess himself no longer the first of Russian rulers"

—and so on in the same strain.

The Empress accepted this flattery, but rejected the Embassador's proposals. Two months later, on November 5, 1779, King George wrote to his "lady sister," the Czarina, an autograph letter in old-fashioned French. He no longer insisted on a formal protest, but would be satisfied with a simple demonstration.

"The apparition merely"—such were his royal words—"of a portion of the Imperial fleet will suffice to restore and confirm the peace of Europe, and the league joined against England will at once vanish."

Has ever another power of the first order so abjectly supplicated?

But all this wheedling on the part of England failed of its object, and in 1780 the armed neutrality was proclaimed.[402] England patiently swallowed the pill. To sweeten the dose her Government had previously proclaimed that the merchant-vessels of Russia should not be stopped or hindered by English cruisers. Thus, without compulsion England at that time surrendered the right of search. Soon afterward the English diplomat assured the Cabinet at St. Petersburg that British vessels of war should not molest the subjects of the Empress in their commercial pursuits; and in 1781 Sir James Harris claimed as a merit for the English Board of Admiralty that it overlooked the frequent case of Russian vessels conveying naval stores to the enemies of England, and that wherever such vessels had been by mistake arrested or hindered, liberal indemnity for the detention had been awarded by the Board. Every inducement was employed by the English Cabinet to detach Russia from the neutrality. Thus, Lord Stormont writes to the Embassador at St. Petersburg:

"Is there no dear object with which to tempt the ambition of the Empress—no concession advantageous to her navy and her commerce, which may move her to help us against our rebellious colonies?"

Harris replies that the cession of Minorca will be such a bait. In 1781 Minorca was proffered to Catherine—but not accepted.

In March, 1782, Fox entered the Cabinet, and immediately the Russian Minister at London[a] was advised that England was ready to treat with Holland, with whom the previous Ministry had declared war on the strength of the treaty of 1674[403]— wherein it was conceded that Free ships make Free goods—and would at once conclude an armistice. Harris is instructed by Fox to represent these advances as an evidence of the deference which the King desires to pay to the wishes and opinions of the Empress. But Fox does not stop here. A Cabinet Council advises the King to make known to the Russian Minister residing near his Court that his Majesty is desirous of sharing the views of the Empress, and of forming the most intimate relations with the Court of St. Petersburg, making the declaration of neutrality the basis of stipulations between the two countries.

Soon after this Fox resigned. His successor, Lord Grantham, certified that the rather favorable disposition of St. Petersburg toward London was the fruit of Fox's policy; and when Fox reentered the Cabinet, the idea was proclaimed by him that an alliance with the Northern Powers was the policy for an enlightened Englishman, and should continue to be so forever. In one of his letters to Harris he admonishes him to regard the Court of St. Petersburg as the one whose friendship is of the first importance to Great Britain, and avers that the proudest aim of his first brief administration was to make plain to the Empress how sincerely the English Ministry desired to follow her counsels and win her confidence. The partiality of Fox to a Russian alliance was extreme. He advised the King to write to the Empress and invite her to lend her condescending attention to the affairs of England.

In 1791, Fox, being then in the Opposition, said in Parliament[b] that

> "it was something new for a British house to hear the growing greatness of Russia presented as matter for anxiety. [...] Twenty years before, England had introduced Russian vessels into the Mediterranean. He (Fox) had advised the King not to impede the annexation of the Crimea to Russia. England had confirmed Russia in her scheme to found her own aggrandizement on the ruin of Turkey. It were madness to betray jealousy of Russia's increased power in the Black Sea."

---

[a] I. M. Simolin.—*Ed.*

[b] Fox's speech in the House of Commons on March 29, 1791.—*Ed.*

In the course of the same debate, Burke, then a Whig, observed:

"It is something new to consider the Turkish Empire as a part of the European equilibrium;"

and these views were urged in still stronger language, again and again by Burke—who is held by every party in England as the paragon of British statesmen—down to the close of his political life; and they were caught up by the great leader of the Whigs,[a] who succeeded in command of that party.

During Lord Grey's administration in 1831 and 1832, he took occasion in a discussion on foreign policy to state his conviction that it would be for the advantage of Turkey herself and the happiness of Europe if that Power were merged in the Russian Empire. Was Russia less barbarous then than she is pictured now? Was she less then that hideous despotism which modern Whigs in such terrible color portray her? And yet not alone was her alliance coveted with fawning servility, but she was encouraged by English liberal statesmen to that very design for which she is now so vehemently denounced.

Written about December 28, 1855

First published in the *New-York Daily Tribune*, No. 4597, January 12, 1856 as a leading article

Reproduced from the newspaper

---

[a] Fox.—*Ed.*

Frederick Engels

THE WAR IN ASIA

Little by little we are getting at the details of the fall of Kars[404]; and so far they fully confirm what we have habitually asserted to be the case with respect to the Turkish army in Asia Minor.[a] It is now beyond the possibility of denial that that army has been systematically ruined by the neglect of the Turkish Government, and by the unchecked sway of Turkish indolence, fatalism and stupidity. Indeed, the facts now disclosed go a great way to prove that even direct treason, as is commonly the case in Turkey, has had much to do with the fall of Kars.

As far back as the beginning of last year's campaign, we had occasion to show to our readers the wretched condition of the Turkish army at Erzeroum and Kars, and the flagrant peculation from which that state of things proceeded.[b] There were concentrated for the defense of the Armenian highlands the two army-corps of Asia Minor and Mesopotamia, beside part of the corps of Syria. These corps had been reenforced by their redifs or reserve battalions, and formed the nucleus of a numerous host of Kurdish and Bedouin irregulars. But the four or five unfortunate battles of 1853 and 1854, from Akaltzik to Bayazid, had destroyed the cohesion and spirit of this army, while the want of clothing and provisions during the Winter completely ruined it. A motley assemblage of Hungarian and Polish refugees, adventurers as well as men of decided merit, had been collected at its headquarters,

---

[a] See this volume, pp. 484-89.— *Ed.*

[b] See the section "The Turkish Army" in Engels' series of articles *The Armies of Europe* (this volume, pp. 451-56).— *Ed.*

without any officially-recognized position. Before the ignorant, jealous and intriguing Pashas the adventurers could pass themselves off as first-rate men, while the really useful men among these refugees were treated as adventurers; in the end it was a race of vanity and intrigue, discreditable to the refugees as a mass, and destroying almost every vestige of their influence. Then came the British officers, who were received with great respect, backed as they were by the consideration due to an allied Government, and by the utter helplessness of the Turkish commanders. But they, too, failed in their attempts to infuse anything like military spirit into the Armenian army. Their efforts might now and then rouse a Pasha from his stolid apathy for a moment, secure the construction of the most indispensable defensive works at Kars, and prevent, from time to time, some of the grossest instances of peculation and even connivance with the enemy; but this was all. When Gen. Williams, last Spring, strained every nerve to procure the most indispensable stores of provisions at Kars, he was constantly checked. The Turkish commissariat thought a siege out of the question; it had no horses to move stores with. When asses were found to be abundant, they thought it derogatory to the Sultan's[a] stores to be transported by asses, and so forth; so that in the end Kars, the bulwark of Armenia, at only two marches from the Russian stronghold of Gumri, was, in fact, left without any provisions at all, and had to forage for itself in the environs. It was the same with regard to ammunition. After the Russian attack of Sept. 29, there remained but three days' ammunition for the artillery, though it is to be remembered that no actual siege took place—the 29th September being the only real fighting-day during the blockade. The medicine-chests sent to the army contained all sorts of rubbish, and the surgeons were provided from Constantinople with obstetrical instruments to probe wounds and amputate limbs with!

This was the state of things in Kars. That with such scanty resources a garrison composed of the demoralized troops of Anatolia should have made such a desperate resistance on the 29th of September, and held out so long afterward against hunger, is one of those redeeming facts in Turkish history which abound in the present war. The same fatalism which leads to apathetic indolence in the superiors produces this stubborn resistance in the masses. It is the last remnant of the spirit that bore the banner of Islam from Mecca to Spain and was only

---

[a] Abdul Mejid.—*Ed.*

checked at Poitiers.[405] Its offensive strength is gone, but a trace of its defensive power has remained. This stubbornness of resistance behind walls and ramparts is essentially Turkish; it would be a great mistake to attribute the credit of it to the presence of European officers. If such were present at Kars and Silistria in 1855 and 1854, they were not so at Varna, at Braila, at Silistria in 1829, when the same feats of heroism were exhibited.[406] What European officers could do in such instances was to correct mistakes, to strengthen redoubts, to give unity to the system of defense, and to prevent direct treachery. But the individual bravery of the soldiers has always been the same, whether they were present or not; nor was it wanting at Kars, even among the disorganized troops of the all but destroyed army of Anatolia.

This leads us to the merits of the British officers who played a conspicuous part in the defense of Kars, and who are now prisoners of war at Tiflis. That they did a great deal toward preparing the means of resistance, that to them is due all the credit for having fortified the place, provisioned it as well as possible, lashed the Turkish Pashas out of their dreamy indolence, and conducted the defense on the 29th of September, cannot be doubted. But it is preposterous to ascribe to them, as the British press now does, all the credit of the 29th September, and of the defense generally, and to set them down as a parcel of heroes, abandoned in the hour of danger by the cowardly Turks, for whose sake they sacrificed themselves. That during the assault they were foremost in the ranks of the defenders, we do not intend to deny; the Englishman is of so pugnacious a nature that the greatest and most common fault of the British officer, in a battle, is to forget his duty as an officer and to fight as a private soldier. Indeed, when he does this he is sure of the applause of his countrymen, although in any other army he would risk being cashiered for loss of presence of mind. But on the other hand, the Turkish soldier is so accustomed to see his own officers run away that when once his spirit is up, he cares nothing at all for officers or command, but fights where he happens to stand, and is not at all the man to notice or much less to be inspired by the fact of half a dozen Englishmen beside him, attempting to display their bravery. That the fortifications of Kars were planned in an exceedingly faulty manner we fully demonstrated immediately after the assault of September 29[a] was known here, and the

---

[a] See this volume, pp. 563-68, 694-702.—*Ed.*

judgment we then passed upon them has since been completely confirmed by the official map of these fortifications published by the British Government. Finally, then, the merits of these British officers at Kars must be measured by the French proverb: "In the kingdom of the blind, the one-eyed is a king." Many a man who cannot muster the knowledge necessary to pass the examination for Sub-Lieutenant in France, would make a great General among the Cochin-Chinese; and if British officers are notorious in their own country for professional incompetence, it must not be expected that they will be illuminated by sudden floods of knowledge or genius on taking service in Turkey. For our part, we believe that Kmety deserves as much credit as any man who partook in the defense of Kars.

While this was the state of things at Kars, what was going on at Erzeroum? A dozen old Pashas passed their days in smoking their chibouks, quite unconscious that any responsibility rested upon them, that Kars was hard pressed, or that the enemy was within a few marches, on the other side of the Dewe Boyun hills. A few thousand regular troops, accompanied by some irregulars, marched to and fro, never risking an attack on the enemy, and returning as soon as they had descried his outposts. There was neither the force nor the spirit to relieve Kars, and consequently Kars was starved out while the army of Erzeroum scarcely dared to demonstrate in its favor. General Williams must have known that he could not expect any assistance from that quarter. But what reports, what promises he received respecting the effect of Omer Pasha's movements, we have no means of guessing. It has been said that Williams intended, at the last extremity, to force his way with the garrison through the Russian army; but we doubt whether such a plan was seriously entertained. The hilly ground, offering but very few passes by which Erzeroum could be gained, was all in favor of the Russians; if a few defiles were well occupied by them, this plan was not feasible. On the other hand, movements of troops become almost impossible toward the latter end of October in a country elevated from 5,000 to 8,000 feet above the sea, where Winter sets in very early and lasts from six to nine months. If Kars could hold out till Winter, the loss of a garrison of 6,000 regular troops would be nothing in comparison to the time gained by the prolonged defense. Erzeroum, the great center of all the Turkish stores in Armenia, was almost without fortifications, and would thereby be made safe till May, 1856; while the actual advantage gained by the Russians would be confined to the virtual possession of the villages of the Kars Chai and the Upper Araxes, neither of which could have been disputed to them, even if the garrison of Kars had succeeded in reaching Erzeroum. This town was scarcely fortified at all; if the garrison of Kars had actually found its way thither toward the middle of October, there would not have been a sufficient force to defend it. As an open town only can Dewe Boyun be defended, by a battle in front of it, in the Pass.[a] Thus the patience of the garrison of Kars saved Erzeroum.

Again, the question is asked, whether Omer Pasha could not have saved Kars, and almost every European correspondent in the East has an answer of his own to it. It is even now attempted to lay all the blame of the fall of Kars on Omer Pasha, and that by the very parties who formerly were full of his praise. The fact is, that in the first instance, Omer Pasha was retained in the Crimea, against his own will, until it was almost too late to undertake anything on a grand scale before Winter. When finally he went to Constantinople to settle his plan of operations, he had to spend his time in counteracting intrigues of all kinds. When at last everything was ready, the promised British transports were not forthcoming; and when the army was concentrated near Batoum, and later on at Sukum Kaleh, no stores, ammunition and means of transport were provided. How, under such circumstances, Omer Pasha was expected to march to the direct relief of Kars, it is not easy to make out. We find that during his Mingrelian expedition, he could never venture to go more than two or three days' march from the coast, and yet there he had good Russian military roads to march on. But in going to Kars, either by Erzeroum or Ardahan, he would have had to march either twenty or twelve days from the coast, using for his roads the beds of rivers and paths across the hills, where nothing more clumsy than a pack-horse can pass. The caravans from Trebizond to Erzeroum have no other roads to travel over, and the fact that they never use vehicles is the best proof of what ground they have to traverse. And this is the only track which is at all beaten; as to the so-called roads from Batoum into the interior, their existence is still more problematical, as no great traffic passes over them. The wise military critics who reproach Omer Pasha with not having marched straight upon Kars should first study the accounts of men who have traveled over the ground—such as Curzon and

[a] The *New-York Semi-Weekly Tribune* and *New-York Weekly Tribune* have: "As an open town only can be defended by a battle in front of it, in the Dewe Boyun Pass."—*Ed.*

Bodenstedt.[a] As to the allegation of the London *Times,* that Gen. Williams had pointed out to Omer Pasha Batoum as a starting point for a direct march on Kars,[b] we can only say that Williams knows Armenia, where he has lived many years, far too well to propose such a thing.

All things considered, Omer Pasha could not do better than menace the communications of the Russians before Kars. How far he might be enabled to do this effectively depended upon the mobility of his own army and on the Russian forces opposed to him. Leaving out of the question the first consideration, as a matter to be judged of after the fact, we concluded from the beginning, that in all probability the Russians would prove too strong for the invading army. Our very first statement of the forces at the disposal of Bebutoff, and which has turned out quite exact, showed that even at Kutais, the Russians, with a little management, might oppose a superior force to the Turks. And so they did. Had Omer Pasha been ever so free in his movements, he could not have forced, with the army at his command, the passage of the Rioni. But beside this, the slowness and uncertainty with which his supplies were brought up, hampered his operations from the start. After every two or three marches he had to halt nearly a week in order to form the most indispensable depots of provisions; and when at last he had advanced three days' march from Redout Kaleh into the interior, he was completely paralyzed. Finding at the same time a superior army before him, he could but retreat to the coast, where the Russians followed him, harassing his rear very severely. The Turkish army now bivouacs on the coast and is being transported to Batoum, Trebizond, and other places, having suffered severely both from the enemy and from sickness. Mingrelia, with the exception of the coast forts, is again in the hands of the Russians.

This concludes the third lucky campaign of the Russians in Asia: Kars and its Pashalik conquered; Mingrelia freed from invasion; and the last body of Turkish troops remaining in the field, Omer Pasha's army, considerably weakened numerically and morally—these results are not to be despised in a country like that south-west of the Caucasus, where all operations are necessarily slow in consequence of the ground and of the want of roads. And

---

[a] The reference is to F. Bodenstedt's book *Die Völker des Kaukasus und ihre Freiheitskämpfe gegen die Russen,* published in Frankfurt am Main in 1848, and R. Curzon's book *Armenia: A Year at Erzeroom, and on the Frontiers of Russia, Turkey and Persia.—Ed.*

[b] *The Times,* No. 22254, January 3, 1856.—*Ed.*

if these successes and positive conquests are placed as a set-off against the occupation of the south side of Sevastopol, of Kertch, Kinburn, Eupatoria, and a few Caucasian forts by the Allies, it will be seen that the advantages actually gained by the latter are not so overwhelming as to justify the rhodomontade of the British press. It is a very significant fact that the Paris *Constitutionnel*, in an article inspired by the French Court, directly charges Lord Redcliffe with being the principal cause of the Asiatic disasters, by his not only withholding from the Porte the subsidies granted to it on the part of the Allies, but also inducing it to keep back, as long as possible, the reenforcements intended for the theater of war.[a]

Written about January 11, 1856

First published in the *New-York Daily Tribune*, No. 4608, January 25, 1856, reprinted in the *New-York Semi-Weekly Tribune*, No. 1114, January 29, 1856 and the *New-York Weekly Tribune*, No. 751, February 2, 1856 as a leading article

Reproduced from the *New-York Daily Tribune*

[a] L. Boniface, "D'après les nouvelles qui viennent de Constantinople...", *Le Constitutionnel*, No. 8, January 8, 1856.—*Ed.*

Frederick Engels

THE EUROPEAN WAR

The system of warfare carried on hitherto by the Western Powers against Russia, has completely broken down. It will not do to carry on this year's campaign, if campaign there is to be, upon the plan which has, so far, been followed up. To concentrate the whole forces of France, England, Turkey and Sardinia, against one particular point in the Crimea, a point which, by using indirect means, might have been gained as an accessory; to fight for that point eleven long months, and then to obtain only one half of it; to neglect all other opportunities for dealing effective blows at the enemy to such an extent that Russia could obtain by the conquest of Kars, a counterpart to the loss of the south side of Sevastopol—all that might do for a campaign or two, in a war where the most vulnerable points of the opposing parties were covered by the neutrality of Central Europe. But it will do no longer. The Council of War which has just been sitting in Paris, is the best proof that now we shall have something like war in earnest if the war is to continue at all.[407]

The war, as hitherto carried on, has been a state of official hostilities, mitigated by extreme politeness. We do not here allude to civilities marking the unavoidable intercourse of flags of truce, but to the civilities which the very councils of war of the contending parties displayed to their opponents. That the war arose at all, is the fault of a miscalculation on the part of the Emperor Nicholas. He never expected that France and England would join to oppose his designs upon Turkey; he looked out for a quiet little war of his own with the Sultan,[a] which might lead his troops for a second time to the walls of Constantinople,[408] arouse European diplomacy when it would be too late, and finally give his

[a] Abdul Mejid.—*Ed.*

own diplomatists a chance of gaining, as usual, twice as much in conferences and congresses as his troops could have gained by the sword. Unfortunately, unexpectedly, unwillingly, Russia and the Western Powers were entangled into war over this business before they were aware of it, and to war they had to go, though none of them liked it. Now, either party had a last means of warfare in perspective which it thought would frighten the other from resorting to extremities. It was expected to be a war of principles, and of a more or less revolutionary character in which Germany and her dependencies, Hungary, Poland, Italy would have to partake. The *ultima ratio*[a] of the West was to be the setting loose of the oppressed nationalities of Hungary, Poland, Italy, and more or less of Germany also. The *ultima ratio* of Russia, on the other hand, was the appeal to Panslavism, the realization of the dreams fostered by enthusiasts for the last fifty years, among the Slavonic population of Europe.

But neither the Russian Government, nor that of Louis Bonaparte (not to speak of Palmerston) chose to appeal to such means of action before the last extremity had arrived; and in consequence the war has been carried on with a mutual forbearance and urbanity scarcely habitual between legitimate monarchs of ancient lineage, much less between such upstarts and usurpers as the Romanoffs, the Hanoverians, and the Pseudo-Bonapartes. The Baltic coast of Russia was scarcely touched; no attempts at permanent lodgment were made there. There, as in the White Sea, private property was much more assailed than Government property; and on the coast of Finland, especially, the British fleets seemed to have no other end in view than to reconcile the Fins to the Russian rule. In the Black Sea similar principles were acted upon. The Allied troops sent there appeared to have come for the purpose of making the Turks long for a Russian invasion; for that is the only conclusion to be drawn from their conduct, ever since 1854 till now. The most innocent portion of the time they spent in Turkey was during their stay at Varna, when, incapable of doing good, they did at least no considerable harm except to themselves. When at last they started for the Crimea. They managed to carry on the war in such a way that the Russian Government had every reason to be highly satisfied with them. The Duke of Cambridge has been, lately, distributing plenty of medals to the French troops returned from the Crimea; but no medals, crosses, grand-crosses, stars and ribbons the Russian

[a] Final argument or last resort.—*Ed.*

Government can bestow will adequately express the gratitude it owes to the directors of the campaign of 1854 and '55. Indeed, when the south side of Sevastopol was abandoned by its Russian garrison, it had cost the Allies in dead and invalid 250,000 men, beside millions on millions of money. The Russians, always worsted in battle, had regularly defeated their enemies in resolution, activity, and the skill of their commanding engineer.[a] If Inkermann was an indelible disgrace to the Russians, the building up of the redoubts on Sapun and the Mamelon by the Russians, under the very nose of their opponents, was an indelible disgrace to both English and French. And, after all, it appears that Sevastopol did not so much exhaust the forces of Russia as those of the Allies, for it did not prevent the Russians from taking Kars.

This taking of Kars is, in fact, the most disgraceful thing which could have happened to the Allies. With the enormous naval armaments at their disposal, with a number of troops superior, ever since June, 1855, to the Russians in the field, they never attacked the weakest points of Russia, the Transcaucasian provinces. Nay, they even allowed the Russians to organize in that part an independent base of operations, a sort of vice-royalty, capable of holding out some time against a superior attack, though the communications with the mother country might be interrupted. Not satisfied with that, not forewarned by the continuous defeats the Asiatic-Turkish army had suffered in 1853 and '54, they prevented the Turkish army of Omer Pasha from doing any good in Asia, by keeping it in the Crimea, and in the Crimea they gave it nothing to do except hewing wood and drawing water for its Allies. Thus, after the whole coast from the straits of Kertch to Batoum had been carefully cleared of all Russian settlements, after thereby a line had been gained on which ten or fifteen points could be chosen as capital bases for any operations against Caucasia or Transcaucasia—the weakest part of Russia as we have often shown[b]—nothing was done, until at last Kars being hard pushed, and the army at Erzeroum being fit for nothing, Omer Pasha was allowed to undertake his unfortunate expedition to Mingrelia—too late to do any good.

This obstinacy in concentrating the pith of the war in a Peninsula about the size of Long Island, has certainly served to keep aside all unpleasant questions. No nationalities, no Panslav-

---

[a] Todtleben.—*Ed.*

[b] See Engels' article "The Progress of the Turkish War" (present edition, Vol. 12, pp. 450-56) and the article by Marx and Engels, "State of the Russian War" (present edition, Vol. 13, pp. 246-52).—*Ed.*

ism, no trouble with Central Europe, no necessities for conquest, no great decisive results which might embarrass ulterior negotiations by implying the necessity of imposing real sacrifices on any party, have appeared upon the scene. But to the men engaged in the actual campaign this is not agreeable. To them, at least from the Sergeant-Major downward, the war has been a matter of stern, stubborn fact. Never, as long as there have been wars, has such brilliant bravery been thrown away for such inadequate results as in this Crimean campaign. Never have such numbers of first-rate soldiers been sacrificed, and in such a short time, too, to produce such indecisive successes. It is evident that such sufferings cannot be imposed again upon the armies. There must be some more palpable gain than barren "glory." You cannot go on fighting at the rate of two great battles and four or five general assaults per annum, and yet remain always on the same spot. No army stands that in the long run. No fleet will stand a third campaign of the modest nature of the two last, in the Baltic and Black Seas. If the war is to continue, we hear, accordingly, of the invasion of Finland, of Esthonia, of Bessarabia; we are promised Swedish auxiliaries, and Austrian demonstrations. But at the same time we are informed that Russia has accepted the Austrian proposals as a basis for negotiation,[409] and while this is far from settling the question of peace, it opens a possibility of that consummation.

There is, then, a chance that there may not be another campaign; but if one does come, we may presume that it must be much more extensive and fruitful than those that have preceded it.

Written about January 18, 1856

First published in the *New-York Daily Tribune*, No. 4616, February 4, 1856 as a leading article

Reproduced from the newspaper

Karl Marx

THE AMERICAN DIFFICULTY.—AFFAIRS OF FRANCE[410]

London, Friday, Feb. 8, 1856

Except the venal gentry of the Ministerial press, nobody in England seems to believe much in our Anglo-American difficulty.[411] Some people consider it a trick to withdraw attention from the peace negotiations. Others pretend that Palmerston will push on to a mutual recall of Embassadors, when he will go out, as Pitt did before the peace of Amiens,[412] to return when a truly English Minister is again wanted. From the manner in which the dispute is maintained very clever people look upon the whole as a simple election dodge of the President.[a] The Democratic press beholds Bonaparte behind the scenes, delighted in fanning internecine war between the Anglo-Saxons on either side of the Atlantic. Everybody else is quietly convinced that there is not the least chance of hostilities, however high official language may run. This view, we observed, is entertained also by the French Government paper, the *Constitutionnel*, which offers its master as pacificator for the New as well as for the Old World.[b]

The principal circumstance not to be lost sight of in estimating this affair is the almost virtual extinction of the *entente cordiale* between England and France,[413] more or less openly confessed by the English press. Take, for instance, the London *Times*, the paper which not long ago proclaimed this Bonaparte a much greater man than the real Napoleon, and proposed to expel all the vicious people who would not bow to that creed. In a leading article it now suggests that the only obstacle to peace is Bonaparte's

[a] Pierce.—*Ed.*

[b] L. Boniface, "Une question intéressante...", *Le Constitutionnel*, No. 37, February 6, 1856.—*Ed.*

over-eagerness for it. This is followed up by another article hinting that the "chosen instrument of Providence" is, after all, a mere *pis-aller* of French society, accepted "because there was not to be found one single man in whom the nation could place its confidence and esteem." In a third article it denounces his whole staff of generals, ministers, functionaries, &c., as a motley band of stockjobbing desperadoes.[a] The language of the provincial press of England is even less reserved. Observe, on the other hand, the altered tone of the French journals—their fulsome adulation and flattery to Russia; so singularly contrasting with their moderate antipathy for England. Further, observe the very confident menaces of a general Continental coalition held out by the Austrian, Belgian and Prussian papers. Lastly, take the Russian press which in its peace homilies ostentatiously addresses itself to France alone, without as much as mentioning England.

"A rainbow of peace," says the *Nordische Biene,* "has appeared in the horizon, and has been joyfully hailed by all friends of civilization.... In these two years of war with Four Powers, the Russian people has given a striking proof of its great and noble character, and has earned the respect of its enemies. [...] As regards France, it may be positively affirmed that the French nation loves and respects the Russians, admires their courage and self-denial, and takes every opportunity of expressing its sympathy, as it did when there was a short suspension of hostilities in the Crimea, as also when Russian prisoners passed through France. The French prisoners, on their part, have been treated by the Russians like brothers."[b]

Le Nord of Brussels bluntly intimates that Bonaparte cultivated the Austrian mediation from the beginning with the view to throw off the English alliance at the first opportunity.[c]

The alliance with France then being about to be supplanted by a rupture with that country, England, still at war with Russia, evidently cannot mean to embark in a war with America, and it is plain that no importance, beyond what has been pointed out, can attach to the present difficulty between the two Governments.

Peace in Europe itself is by no means certain. With regard to the conditions presented by the Allies to Russia[414]: the fact is there is hardly the appearance of a concession in their acceptance. The cession of a problematic strip of land in Bessarabia, marked out by a mysterious chain of mountains not to be discovered on any map, is more than counterbalanced by the obdurate silence on the Russian acquisition of Kars, suspiciously mentioned since in a

---

[a] The articles in question were published in *The Times,* Nos. 22277, 22278 and 22275, January 30, 31 and 28, 1856. *Pis-aller* means "last resort".— *Ed.*

[b] *Severnaya Pchela,* No. 11, January 14, 1856.— *Ed.*

[c] *Le Nord,* No. 19, January 19, 1856.— *Ed.*

Petersburg paper as a Russian province. Meanwhile, the advantages of an armistice, together with the other opportunities in the course of turning up, do not make it improbable that Russia, having had the time to concentrate her forces on all the decisive points, may wish to continue the war. The great pledge of peace, however, is the absolute necessity for Bonaparte to conclude it at any price. On the one hand the means for carrying on the war are failing him; on the other hand there is growing up a necessity of repeating the Crimean expedition, as Montalembert said of the expedition against Rome, in the interior of France.[415]

Shortly before the acceptance of the preliminaries of peace by Russia, it was generally current at Paris that Bonaparte contemplated a forced loan, to be borne proportionately to the amount of direct taxes. The *vacuum* in his exchequer is forcibly demonstrated by the condition of his army in the Crimea. For some time past the lamentable state of the troops under Pélissier has been alluded to by correspondents. The plain statement which follows is given by a British non-commissioned officer writing to *The Birmingham Journal*, under date of Sevastopol, January 5:

"To-day was very fine. About 3 o'clock a strong north wind blew, and it froze very hard, which soon made us button up. Our men do not feel the cold; but you would pity the poor French. They are eternally dragging fuel from Sevastopol. They are miserably clad and, I think, are worse fed. Every hour of the day there are some of them looking for biscuit. Our men pity them, and are very kind. Our sentries have orders not to allow them in the camp, because some were in the habit of selling *cognac*, which caused some of our men to get drunk. But the poor French manage to elude the sentries occasionally, and introduce themselves with *bono Inglis*. Of course, our men know what they want, and never send them away empty-handed. The poor fellows have not so much as a glove to put on their hands. The only article I see they have got more than they had in Summer is a hood to their great-coat, and a pair of common, coarse cloth gaiters, which reach the knee, and are buckled round the knee with a few straps. They do not wear socks, and they generally *have had* boots. The fact is, they are the picture of misery, and indeed they feel it when they see the British soldier with his fine seal-skin cap, tweed coat, lined with fur, a fine, large comforter round his neck and one round his waist, and a fine, strong pair of ox-hide boots which come to the knee."

The state of Napoleon's finances must be wretched enough, when he leaves his army, his one and all, in the condition just described; at the same time, an inference as to their administration may be drawn from the fact that these two years of war have cost already more than all his uncle's[a] campaigns, from 1800 to 1815, together. Even Bonapartist generals, returned from the Crimea, are said to have commented indignantly on the impudent robberies of Morny & Co., at the expense of the army. These

[a] Napoleon I.—*Ed.*

remonstrances have found publicity in a semi-official paper, which has the following:

> "If peace be concluded, the emperor will turn his whole attention to the finances, and especially to certain abuses too inherent to great movements of speculation, such as certain accumulations of incompatible offices, and certain fortunes a little too rapidly acquired."

Meanwhile revolutionary symptoms manifest themselves in the youth of the universities, in the working-classes, in a portion of the middle class, and what is the worst for Bonaparte, in the army.

On the affair of the *Ecole Polytechnique*, we are informed that Bonaparte, although sufficiently exasperated at their taciturn attitude on the 29th of December when he played the Roman Senate with this army (as he likes to play the Roman Imperator with his Senate),[416] at first meditated a compromise with the *Ecole*. The students were given to understand that the Emperor was inclined to maintain that institution, if they consented, as an opportunity would be given them to manifest sympathy for the dynasty. To this the *Ecole* replied by their delegates that not only they would not cry *vive l'Empereur*, but would drive any of their comrades from school who should utter that cry. It was upon this reply that the dissolution of the anarchical establishment was determined. One-half, composed of the pupils destined for military service, will be transferred to Vincennes, there to form a simple school of artillery. The other half, destined to the civil service, will be in the *Ecole Normale*.[a] The building itself is to be converted into barracks. Such is the end of the pet institute of Napoleon the Great.

The prison of Mazas is filled with pupils of the University of Paris, and with other young men who, at the funeral of David, the sculptor, had raised the cry of *Vive la liberté*. There was a circumstance connected with the demonstration against Nisard peculiarly annoying to Bonaparte. The police having made their razzia among the students for having hissed Nisard's apotheosis of Tiberius as the savior of Roman society, the rest formed in a body, and, traversing all Paris, went to Nisard's residence, *Rue Courcelles*, and summoned him to put their comrades at liberty. A detachment of soldiers of the line dispatched after them arrived there almost at the same time. Received with cries of *Vive la ligne*,[b] they immediately stood at ease, and refused to act. To prevent a further fraternization, they were at once withdrawn, and sup-

---

[a] Pedagogical higher school in Paris.—*Ed.*

[b] Long live the Army!—*Ed.*

planted by *sergents de ville.*[a] The students removed in a body to the Odéon, where they invaded the pit, and kept singing the "*Sire de Franc Boissy,*"[417] shouting the more offensive verses right into the ears of Bonaparte and Eugénie, who were present in their box.

The Bonapartist press confess that the number of arrests effected in the departments amount to 5,000; the figure given elsewhere of 15,000 is therefore probably the whole truth. This conspiracy of the laborers,[418] it now appears, had its ramifications in the midst of the army. It became necessary to break up the whole school for non-commissioned officers at La Flèche, and to change all the garrisons of the center of France. In order to suppress this dangerous spirit in the army, Bonaparte is having recourse to that most dangerous experiment of the Restoration, setting up a complete system of espionage through all ranks of the army. This new legion of honor has led to some very lively altercations between Marshal Magnan and certain superior officers who do not think it much to the taste of the troops.

The movement of the working classes of Paris, as in all times preceding a crisis, is betokened by *quod libets,*[b] the greatest favorite of which is the

"Voilà qu'il part, voilà qu'il part,
Le petit marchand de moutarde,
Voilà qu'il part pour son pays
Avec tous ses outils," etc.[c]

To leave no doubt as to who is meant by the little mustard-vendor, the police has prohibited the song.

The esteem in which Bonapartist institutions are held, is illustrated by an anecdote related in the *Nord.* Some Senators did not hesitate to approve of the act of M. Drouyn de Lhuys in resigning his senatorship, but took good care not to imitate him. Morny being asked if any of them were likely to follow the example, replied that he had excellent reasons to believe the contrary. "But what reasons have you?" asked his interlocutor. "I have thirty thousand very good reasons, *one franc* a piece," coolly answered Morny.[d]

---

[a] Police.—*Ed.*
[b] Medleys.—*Ed.*
[c] "He is leaving, he is leaving,
The little mustard-vendor.
He is leaving for his country
With all his belongings," etc.—*Ed.*
[d] *Le Nord,* No. 37, February 6, 1856.—*Ed.*

One more circumstance may be mentioned of immense meaning in the present condition of the French people. I don't revert to the stock-jobbers, for whom peace and war are equally convenient. The first time in their history the mass of the French people have shown themselves indifferent to their old hobby "la gloire." This ominous fruit of the revolution of 1848 proves in a manner not to be mistaken, that the epoch of Bonapartism has passed its climax.

Written on February 8, 1856

First published in the *New-York Daily Tribune,* No. 4634, February 25, 1856, reprinted in the *New-York Semi-Weekly Tribune,* No. 1123; February 29, 1856 as a leading article

Reproduced from the *New-York Daily Tribune*

Karl Marx

THE FALL OF KARS[419]

The papers relating to the fall of Kars, as laid before the British House of Commons, have been described by our London correspondent as arranged with a view to conceal, rather than disclose the truth; and a careful examination of the Blue Book in which they are contained[a] evinces the correctness of that judgment. Hardly less remarkable and significant than the papers themselves, are the comments they have elicited from the leading press of London. *The Times*, for instance, has devoted three consecutive articles to the subject,[b] selecting, however, as the special marks of its flourishes, invectives and arguments, the dispatches covering the interval from August 2, 1854, the day of General Williams's appointment as British Commissioner at the head-quarters of the Turkish army in Asia, to the latter part of January, 1855, when his personal quarrels with Lord Stratford de Redcliffe had, at last, died away. The real aim of *The Times*, in giving this exaggerated importance to that portion of the documents which do not even touch on the epoch of actual warfare, is transparent. On the one hand, public attention was to be diverted from the darkest pages in this most melancholy Blue Book; and on the other, Lord Redcliffe is to be made the scapegoat of the Government at home. The rest of the daily

---

[a] *Papers Relative to Military Affairs in Asiatic Turkey, and the Defence and Capitulation of Kars*. London, 1856. Below Marx quotes documents included in this collection.— *Ed.*

[b] This refers to the series of articles published under the heading "The Capitulation of Kars" in *The Times*, Nos. 22320, 22322 and 22323 on March 20, 22 and 24, 1856. The last, fourth, instalment in this series appeared in *The Times*, No. 22325 on March 26, after Marx had written this article.— *Ed.*

London press, with the exception of *The Morning Herald*, are but too happy to follow in the track beaten by *The Times*.

To become initiated in the mysteries of that disastrous Asiatic campaign, we must start from a quite different point, and commence by inquiring into the action of the Allied Governments during the decisive epoch, beginning with the first advance of the Russians from Gumri, in May, and ending with the capitulation of Kars, on November 24, 1855.[420] Carefully concocted as it is, mutilated by omissions, falsified by extracts, beautified by patches and plasters, even this Government publication, if put to the critical rack, may be forced to speak truth.

Toward the end of May, 1855, Gen. Williams reports to Lord Redcliffe, who reports to Lord Clarendon, that a large Russian force, consisting of 28,000 infantry, 7,500 cavalry, and 64 pieces of artillery was assembled around Gumri; that the Mushir[a] had received information of their intention to attack Kars, and that their own (Turkish) force concentrated in the intrenched camp consisted of 13,900 infantry, 1,500 cavalry, 1,500 artillerymen, and 42 field-pieces. When Redcliffe received this letter from Williams, and Clarendon from Redcliffe, both already held in their hands another letter from Williams, in which he makes the following statement:

"I left Erzeroum yesterday (2d June) en route for Kars, which place the enemy has announced, in an order of the day, his intention to attack.... I have now *four months' provision in that garrison*" (viz.: at Kars), "and [...] trust the central Government and the Allies will soon prove to this remnant of an army that it is not absolutely forgotten by them."

The English Government, then, was informed that if Kars should be cut off from Erzeroum, and a blockade be established by the Russians, the fortress could not hold out much longer than Oct. 3, 1855. If it did fall rather more than a month after, it was because the garrison were Turks, and not beef-eaters.

On the receipt of the dispatches from General Williams, Redcliffe makes urgent recommendations to the Porte that reenforcements with fresh supplies and money should be sent forthwith to the army of Kars. He even invites the Seraskier,[b] now that Circassia is cleared of the Russians, to unite the army of Batoum with that of Kars. Why the Porte objected to this proposal, the following dispatch from Gen. Williams explains:

---

[a] Vassif Pasha.—*Ed.*
[b] The Turkish War Minister, Rushdi Pasha (Mehemet).—*Ed.*

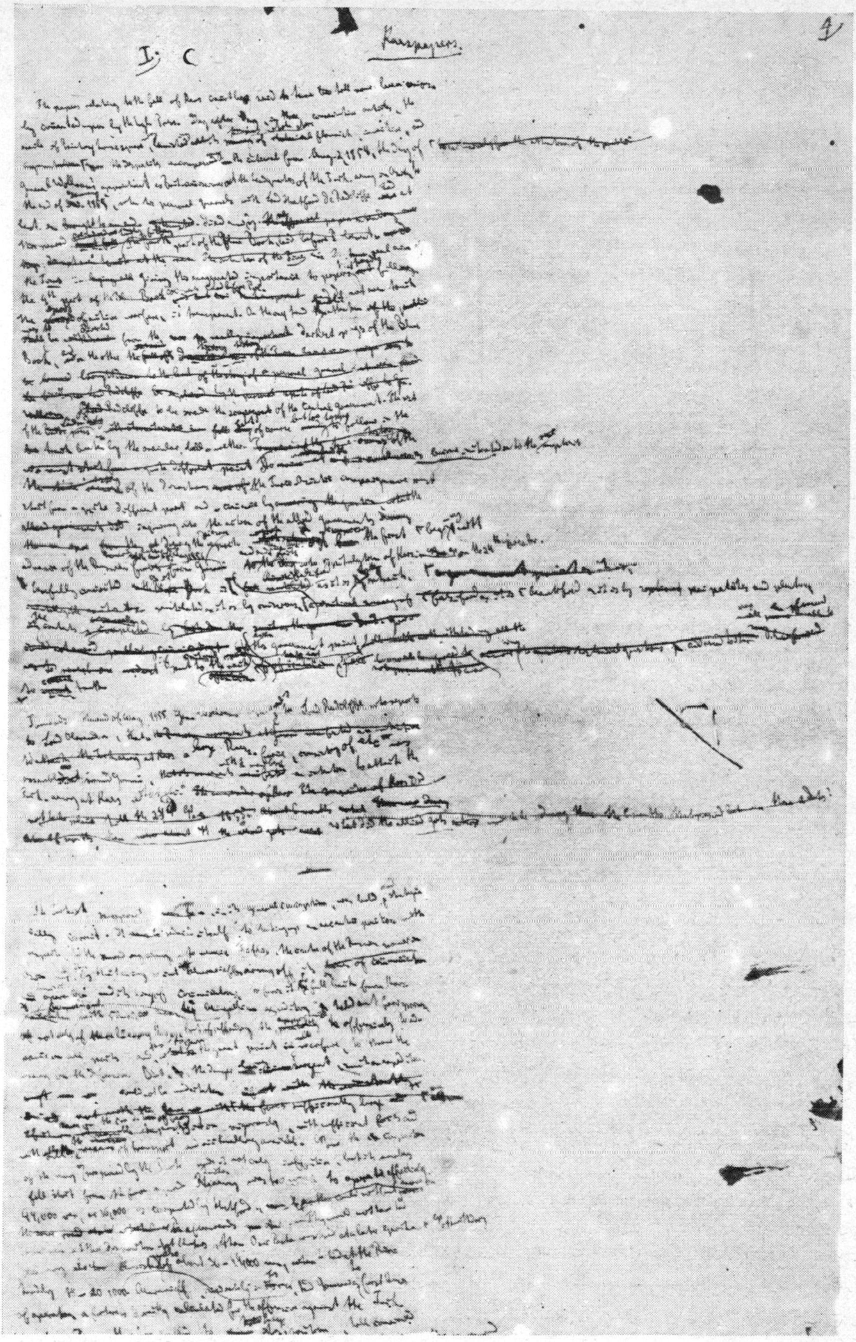

Fragment of the first page of Marx's notes for his articles on the fall of Kars

"*Kars,* June 28, 1855.—Mustapha Pasha of Batoum has [...] recently written to me to say that he had only 3,772 regular troops, and was pressed by the enemy."

On June 28, Lord Redcliffe reports to Lord Clarendon that:

"It is some consolation to him [...] that even at this eleventh hour the Porte has recognized the necessity of listening to his advice, and sending out reenforcements without further delay."

The only difficulty avowed by Redcliffe himself was to decide where those reenforcements were to come from.

"How are they to be provided with the necessary supplies? [...] Nothing can with prudence or consistency be detached from the army under Omer Pasha in the Crimea. At Batoum, Sukum Kaleh, and other neighboring stations on the coast, it would be extremely difficult to muster more than 11,000 men. [...] The other parts of the Empire afford no additional reserves, with the exception of Bosnia, where it is still possible that a few thousand men might be detached. I speak of regulars. Bashi-Bazouks may be procured, but your lordship knows what little dependence is to be placed on such undisciplined hordes. There remains the half-formed corps of Gen. Vivian, and the irregular cavalry collected by Gen. Beatson and his officers. [...] In Bulgaria I question the existence of more than 50,000 men, including garrisons.... Austria, it is true, has declared her intention of considering the passage of the Danube by Russia a *casus belli,* and she also stands pledged to the exclusion of that power from the Danubian Principalities; but the resolution which in such an emergency would enable the Porte to take its line upon those assurances, and to overlook the awkwardness of leaving an important position inadequately defended, is more fit to be admired than to be embraced."

According, then, to the avowal of Redcliffe himself, he urges the Porte to send to Kars "reenforcements of every description," while he is quite aware that there exist none of any description whatever.

On June 30 there took place at the Grand-Vizier's[a] house, on the Bosphorus, a meeting between the Grand-Vizier, the Seraskier, and Fuad Pasha on the one side, and Redcliffe, attended by Brigadier Mansfield, on the other. The Turkish Ministers proposed, as they had done before, to collect an army at Redout Kaleh, which was to advance to Kutais, and to make from there an excursion into Georgia. They proposed that the expeditionary force should be composed as follows:

Vivian's Contingent	20,000	To be drawn fm Bulgaria	5,000
Beatson's	3,000	Egyptian Cavalry	800
Batoum garrison	12,000	Tunis Horse	600
Albanians	2,000		
Total			43,400

[a] Ali Mehemet Pasha.—*Ed.*

The Turkish Ministers expressed their readiness to intrust the direction of the expedition to a British commander, and to accept General Vivian in that capacity. Gen. Vivian at once raised difficulties as to the means disposable for this plan, and considered the employment of his contingent as premature and interfering with the arrangements for its organization. Two weeks later Redcliffe communicated to his Government that—

"Preparations for the said expedition are in progress, and that it might save much valuable time if he was informed at once by telegraph whether Government was prepared to sanction a powerful diversion, by Redout Kaleh and Kutais into Georgia."

On July 13th, 1855, Lord Clarendon sends a dispatch wherein he first repeats the objections raised by General Vivian, and then adds his own:

"Her Majesty's government are of opinion that the wiser course would be to send reenforcements to the rear of the Turkish army, instead of sending an expedition to the rear of the Russian army. The reenforcements might go to Trebizond, and be directed from thence upon Erzeroum. The distance from Trebizond to Erzeroum is less than from Redout Kaleh to Tiflis, and the march is through a friendly instead of through a hostile country; and at Erzeroum the army would meet supporting friends instead of opposing enemies, and supplies instead of famine.

"If the army of Kars cannot maintain that position against the Russians, *it should fall back upon Erzeroum*, and the whole Turkish force should be concentrated there. If the Russians are to be defeated" (are they?), "it will be easier to defeat them by the whole force collected than by divided portions of that force: and *a defeat would be the more decisive the further it took place within the Turkish frontier*."

On the following day, July 14, Clarendon also addresses the following telegraphic answer to Lord Redcliffe's telegraphic question:

"The plan for reenforcing the army at Kars, contained in your dispatches of the 30th June and 1st inst., is disapproved. The reasons will be sent by the messenger to-day against employing the Turkish contingent until it is fit for service. Trebizond ought to be the base of operations, and if the Turkish army of Kars and Erzeroum cannot hold out *at the latter place* against the Russians, it might *fall back on Trebizond*, where it would easily be reenforced."

It is very curious that this telegraphic dispatch, dated London, July 14, had not arrived at Constantinople on July 19, on which day we find Redcliffe writing again to Clarendon:

"An appeal has [...] been made by means of the electric telegraph to her Majesty's Government, who were entreated to lose no time in making known their pleasure as to the proposed diversion."

In fact, this answer from London only reached Constantinople on the 30th of July, six days after the arrival there of the London mail of the 14th of July. On July 15 the Seraskier informs Lord Redcliffe, through Gen. Mansfield, that:

"The 15,000 men in Bulgaria destined to form part of the expedition were in readiness to march to the coast with sufficient means of transport, and that, in general, *his preparations were so advanced as only to require the assent of Her Majesty's Government to carry them into effect.*"

Meanwhile, appeals from Gen. Williams for assistance followed upon appeals. On June 23 he announces that—

"The enemy [...] has pushed forward large bodies of cavalry, [...] and urgently recommends the immediate landing of troops at Trebizond, and if the season admit of it, strong demonstrations from Redout Kaleh."

On June 26, he writes that the Turkish army in Kars was surrounded by the Russians, who had established themselves on the high road between that fortress and Erzeroum, and cut off a portion of the provisions collected for the army. On June 27, he states that the Russian army was master of the surrounding country. On June 28, that the enemy was master of all beyond the reach of their guns, and that the troops at Kars were twenty-three, twenty-seven and twenty-eight months respectively in arrear of their pay; and on July 7, that the united forces of the Russians were ready either to assault or to more closely invest Kars, by cutting off their only remaining communication with Erzeroum via Olti. It is true that these latter dispatches did not arrive in London till July 26; still the use of the telegraph occurred to the British Government only on August 9—not indeed to advise what should be done in consequence of this news, but only to raise fresh difficulties against what the Porte was preparing to do. On the same day on which Lord Clarendon addressed Lord Redcliffe by telegraph, Lord Panmure addressed General Vivian as follows:

"*War Department,* July 14, 1855.

"Sir: I transmit herewith, for your information, a copy of a dispatch which the Earl of Clarendon has addressed to her Majesty's Embassador at Constantinople, on the subject of the plan proposed by the Porte for the relief of the Turkish army at Kars, and I have to acquaint you that I entirely concur in all that is said in that dispatch as to the objectionable character of the plan proposed by the Porte. I place such full reliance on your professional ability that I feel no anxiety lest you should undertake any expedition of a nature so wild and indigested as that contemplated by the Porte. While it is your duty to give every aid in your power, not simply as commanding the Contingent, but as a British officer enjoying the confidence of her Majesty's Government, to our allies, the Turks, it is at the same time necessary that you should be cautious in not risking the honor of the British name and your own reputation by undertaking military operations for which proper bases have not been laid down, communications opened, supplies arranged, and transport provided. A *coup de main* by means of suddenly throwing an army on the coast to threaten, or even to attack an enemy's stronghold, is one thing; but a deliberate expedition to invade an enemy's country, and on his own territory to make war against him, is quite another. In the first case something may be hazarded; but in the other every preparation must precede action. Moreover, from all the information which has reached me, I have every reason to believe the army of Batoum to be in a deplorable state. I know the Contingent to be scarcely organized; of the Bulgarian troops you can have no knowledge; and I presume that Beatson's troops are as little reduced to control and discipline as your own troops. In short, I am assured that it would be madness to attempt to succor Brigadier-General Williams in this way. It is too late to regret the policy which has left that gallant officer and his army exposed to such straits; but it would only be opening the way to fresh failure to follow out such schemes as have been proposed for the purpose of relieving him. You must, as I have no doubt you feel, lose no time in getting your force into order for service, which will be sure to await you somewhere as soon as you are ready for it; but organization is as necessary for an army as endurance and valor, and without the former the latter qualities are utterly unavailing.

"*Panmure.*"

The plan proposed by the Porte was, in its general conception, bold and strategically correct; it amounted, in fact, to the adoption of an eccentric position with respect to the invading army, menacing Tiflis, the center of the Russian power in Asia, and thus, by threatening to cut off Muravieff's basis and line of operations, forcing him to retreat from before Kars. A Mingrelian expedition held out fair prospects not only of relieving Kars, but of affording ample opportunity to gain the great point in all warfare, viz.: throwing the enemy on the defensive. But, the urgency of the danger being admitted, such an expedition could hardly be undertaken save on the condition of its being pushed on with rapidity, with a numerically sufficient force, and with an abundance of supplies and means of transport. Now, the army proposed by the Porte for this service, apart from its motley composition and the unfinished drill of certain portions, was to muster 43,000, or, as Redcliffe computes them, only 36,000 men. It was with about the same force that Omer Pasha afterward undertook the expedition; still, when he arrived at the Rioni (Phasis), his army had dwindled down to 18,000 or 20,000 men. Muravieff had, in his immediate rear, Gumri, as his nearest support, a fortress expressly calculated for the offensive against the Turkish territory; he was therefore enabled to keep his position till informed of the advance on Tiflis being near its accomplishment. However, for the expedition to assume this dangerous turn, there was required the descent of at least 55,000 to 60,000 men on the Circassian coast, the capture of Kutais, and the forcing of the pass of Gori. The Turks not having that force at their disposition, there remained but the alternative of marching via Trebizond on Erzeroum, thence to relieve, reenforce and provision Kars and limit themselves to the defensive. An army of 20,000 men was, at all events, more useful at Erzeroum than one of only 40,000 in Mingrelia. There were also difficulties in the way of that operation; the roads being extremely bad, a considerable force with its artillery and ammunition could hardly reach Erzeroum in less than three months, and thus the crisis might have been over long before the army could arrive on the scene of action. If, on the other hand, a small force were sent, it might succeed in reestablishing the communication between Erzeroum and Kars, but would be insufficient to guard Erzeroum if Kars had fallen. It is clear, then, that the Turks had hit on the best plan for the relief of Kars; but that the Allies, by locking up in the Crimea the only Turkish army capable of carrying it out, prevented its execution.

Let us now come to the objections raised by the British Government. Lord Clarendon commences his attack, not upon the weak points, but on the strategically correct points of the Turkish plan. He thinks it wiser for an army to strengthen its defensive basis in its own rear than to undertake offensive operations in the rear of the enemy. We will leave him to settle this point with old Napoleon or Jomini, while we can quite understand his anxiety for a safe retreat. He thinks it better for an army to march through a friendly country than through a hostile one, if march it must. In his first dispatch he says that if the Turkish army could not maintain its position at Kars, it should fall back on Erzeroum. Did he not know Kars was the key of Erzeroum, and that but for the prolonged defense of Kars, Erzeroum in its then state of defense would have fallen in the same year? But, as his Lordship entertains peculiar views as to the offensive and the marching of armies, so he holds opinions of his own with regard to defensive warfare. A defeat of the Russians, he says, would be the more decisive, the nearer it took place to the gates of Constantinople. In his telegraphic dispatch of July 14, he goes a step further, and coolly recommends the Porte to withdraw its army not only from Kars, but also from Erzeroum, falling back on Trebizond, "where it could easily be reenforced." He would have the Turkish army come to its reenforcements, if the reenforcements would not come to it. Not choosing to recollect, before the fall of Kars, the importance of Erzeroum as the center not only of the commercial but also of the military resources of Anatolia, he discovers, after the fall of Kars (when writing to Lord Cowley in December, 1855), that that alone was sufficient—

"to bring about the worst consequences, if prompt and decisive measures are not taken. Masters of that strong fortress, threatening Erzeroum, and commanding all the mountain passes, the Russians might be able to force the whole of Kurdistan and the Armenian population to assist them against the Sultan[a]; and the Allies might in a few months learn that far greater dangers threatened the Ottoman Empire on the side of Asia than on that of Europe."

From the same telegraphic dispatch (14th July) we also see that the Turkish contingent was formed for no other purpose than to remove from the control of the Porte the only reenforcements of its armies.

This much would seem to result from the dispatches of Clarendon, namely: that it was a settled point with the British Government as early as July, 1855, that Kars and Erzeroum should fall into the hands of the Russians. This strange and indeed almost impossible view of the case is further confirmed by the dispatch of Lord Panmure to General Vivian. Nothing could be more curious than the distinction drawn by this English Minister between his own Crimean expedition and the Mingrelian expedition intended by the Porte. Because the civilized Governments of the West had ventured upon a headlong *coup de main* against Sevastopol, the barbarians of the East must not undertake a "deliberate" expedition against Georgia. The forces enumerated in the Turkish plan he scatters to the winds, and laughs at the notion that Turkey possessed any army fit for operations, except the one pent up in the Crimea. What, then, after all, was the meaning of the hectoring and bullying instructions as to reenforcements with which the British Government worried the poor Porte? Was it to read well in a Blue Book on "The fall of Kars?"

Written about March 25, 1856

First published in the *New-York Daily Tribune*, No. 4671, April 8, 1856 as a leading article

Reproduced from the newspaper

[a] Abdul Mejid.—*Ed.*

The People's Paper.

...ST ALWAYS BE FOLDED TO EXPOSE THE STAMP. } LONDON, SATURDAY, APRIL 5, 1856. { STAMPED COPY TRANSMISSIBLE UNSTAMPED COPY (TRANSMISSIBLE BY

Karl Marx

THE FRANCE OF BONAPARTE THE LITTLE[421]

The France of Bonaparte the Little, revelling at the birth of a son[a] of a Montijo, lavishing the treasures of a nation on a ludicrous pageantry, "all clinquant, all in gold, like heathen gods,"[b] that France is terribly contrasting with the France tortured at Cayenne, smarting at Lambessa, lingering at Belle-Île,[422] and rotting in the Bagne—with the France starving in the Crimea and the France in France reeling on the brink of bankruptcy.

In the letter of Citizen Tassilier, literally translated from the original,[c] the reader will find the genuine and soul-stirring story of the French citizens transported to Cayenne. The press of true-born British flunkeyism, it is true, trumpets into the ears of the drowsy world in most hyperbolical flourish the great news of the boundless magnanimity and rather superhuman clemency of the sausage-hero of the camp of Satory[423] proclaiming a general amnesty[d] and deafening the first screams of his testy baby by the shouts of thousands of Frenchmen given back to their families and to liberty.

But turning away from the paid exaltation of the sycophant, let us harken to the unbribed language of facts. Boustrapa[e] offers the men he has tortured during four years, to tear asunder their chains, on the condition of their consenting to brand themselves

[a] Prince Eugène, titled King of Algeria (born March 16, 1856).—*Ed.*

[b] Shakespeare, *Henry VIII*, Act I, Scene 1.—*Ed.*

[c] *The People's Paper* has the following editorial note here: "M. Tassilier's letter we are forced to postpone till next week, from want of space. We direct the particular attention of all our readers to it." Marx's translation of the letter was published in *The People's Paper*, No. 206, April 12, 1856.—*Ed.*

[d] The *New-York Daily Tribune* has: "superhuman clemency of Louis Bonaparte, proclaiming a general amnesty".—*Ed.*

[e] A nickname of Louis Bonaparte, formed of the first syllables of Boulogne, Strasbourg and Paris, the cities where Bonapartist coups were staged in August 1840, October 1836 and December 1851, respectively. The *New-York Daily Tribune* everywhere has "Bonaparte" instead of "Boustrapa".—*Ed.*

with indelible infamy, and to pass through the *furcae Caudinae* of the lower empire.[424] If they will declare *loyal submission* to the empire, that is, sanctify the *coup d'état*, and abnegate the Republic—if they will sell their souls, Boustrapa is ready to sell them their lives.

"Already," says the *Moniteur*,[a] "at the inauguration of the empire, this generous appeal has been made."

Thus, the *Moniteur* itself[b] avows that the general amnesty, now puffed as a stupendous novelty, is but a repetition of a stale farce played off four years ago. The genius of corruption flatters himself that his victims are now brought down to his own level, that they are sufficiently broken in to accept[c] as a grace in 1856 what they indignantly resented as an affront in 1852.

The *Moniteur* decks its "generous appeal" to meanness with wisely calculated forgeries and falsifications. It pretends that after the events of June 1848, 11,000 persons having been condemned to transportation to Algiers, the clemency of the President left only 306 in Africa. Now, with the same *Moniteur* in our hand, we assert that from the 11,000 prisoners made in June 1848, there remained in November 1848, at the time when the *Assemblée Constituante* discussed the execution of the decree of transportation, only 1,700; that 1,500 of them were sent to Belle-Île, and on the 8th March, 1849, under the ministry of O. Barrot, 700 out of these 1,500 were directed to Bona, in Africa. It is then this last figure of 700 that the grace of Boustrapa has reduced to 306, and not as his lying *Moniteur* has it, the enormous number of 11,000, and that small grace itself was only a trick played off against the assembly. However, we are obliged to thank the *Moniteur* for having reminded France of the atrocious infamies committed by Cavaignac and the Bourgeois Republic.[d]

As to the transported and exiled of December, the same *Moniteur* computes their number at 11,201, and affirms that this is now reduced to 1,058. Now, the *coup d'état* made more than 11,000 victims in the sole departments of the Lower Alps, Hérault, Var and Nièvre, and at this very moment there remain at least 12,000 victims doomed to exile or deportation. It is notorious that the *coup d'état* has affected more than 50,000 persons. It should be further remarked that the "generous appeal" of the *Moniteur* is exclusively addressed to those deported to Algiers and other

[a] *Le Moniteur universel*, No. 80, March 20, 1856.—*Ed.*
[b] The *New-York Daily Tribune* has: "the official journal itself".—*Ed.*
[c] The *New-York Daily Tribune* has: "to humbly accept".—*Ed.*
[d] This sentence does not occur in the *New-York Daily Tribune*.—*Ed.*

foreign possessions, the slightest allusion being avoided to the condemned of Angers, the incarcerated for participation in secret societies, to those thrown into the Bagne by the ambulant war councils of 1851, to the prisoners of Belle-Île, to the students locked up for hissing the paid white-washers of Boustrapa, etc. By way of compensation, the *Moniteur* announces an unsophisticated and unconditional amnesty for poachers, smugglers, forgers, thieves, deserters, convicts, and *id genus omne.*[a] It is quite in keeping with the character of the Lower Empire and the precedents of the Brummagem[b] Bonaparte, that the birth of a son should prove a holiday for all the lower relations of the father.

From the victims of the *coup d'état* we pass now to its tools, from the men who opposed it to the slaves that executed it, from the soldiers of liberty to the army of the Crimea. If it is a great historical sign that Bonaparte, in midst of the fresh delusions of a new fangled dynasty, and the supreme triumph of his admittance into the embalmed air of rancid legitimacy, still wants to be acknowledged by his wretched victims, and, therefore, hypocritically bids for their adhesion to the empire,[c] it is a trait of historical irony, not less notable that at the very time the head and the members of the society of the 10th December[425] are feasting the success of the *coup d'état* in pompous profusion at Paris, the army that imposed this disgusting rule upon France is expiating its crime in the Crimea by denudation, starvation, agony and death in their most dismal and hideous forms.

In the first period of the Oriental campaign, from November 1854, to March 1855, the upstart of December was extolled as a second providence and in every tune was sung the admirable military administration of the empire of all the glories, in contrast to the scandalous sufferings that befell the English army from intentional treason at home and[d] the natural working of a superannuated system. But, as in every other feat of the Lower Empire, what was taken for a substance, was but a theatrical phantasmagoria calculated for immediate stage effect. During two years Bonaparte had been exclusively bent on preparing for war. He had strained every nerve of the immense power of centralised

---

[a] *Le Moniteur universel,* No. 81, March 21, 1856. *Id genus omne* means "all persons of that sort".—*Ed.*

[b] This word does not occur in the *New-York Daily Tribune.*—*Ed.*

[c] Instead of the words "for their adhesion to the empire" the *New-York Daily Tribune* has "the acknowledgement".—*Ed.*

[d] The words "intentional treason at home and" do not occur in the *New-York Daily Tribune.*—*Ed.*

France to provide for the first movement of his army.[a] Indeed, it is not to be wondered at, that even the wretched adventurer of Strassburg and Boulogne should not succeed, during the first two years of his misrule, in breaking down the admirable organisation of the French army, bequeathed by the first revolution. It is a miracle that he has contrived that point in the first two years of actual warfare. Having lavished more wealth on a Batrachomyomachia[426] of his own, than the Great Napoleon in fifteen years of his Iliad,[b] he finds at the beginning of the third year the resources of France drained, her military administration broken up, and her very army dwindling away from misery. The cancer that eats up the French army is the organic principle of the Lower Empire—theft and embezzlement; and but two years were needed to make its work appear on the surface.

The wretched state of the French army was for a long time carefully concealed not only in the French but also in the English press.[427] Now-a-days it has become a secret running the streets and encumbering the thoroughfares. It has become a truth no longer controverted after Bonaparte's own *Moniteur* has given it the lie direct.[c] For the present purpose it will suffice to quote from the last letter of the *Times'* Sebastopol correspondent:—

"The French army, however, numerous as they may show it to be on paper, is dwindling sadly; scurvy and fever are playing havoc in its ranks: I recently stated its daily loss at 170 men ... now the French admit the daily mortality in their army to be 120 men, and in some days considerably more. The right wing of the army, in the Baidar valley, suffers the most.... When the mild weather sets in, a great increase of disease is to be anticipated.... The sick returns of the French will be terrible.... The French army is being expended at least as rapidly as it was by shell and shot during the severest part of the siege."[d]

Insufficiency of shelter, want of covering, and the scarcity of food[e] are pointed at as the principal causes of their trials. Having described the rigour of the weather, "tubs of water in the huts having frozen to a depth of 3 inches," and the prevalence of

[a] The *New-York Daily Tribune* has: "He had strained every nerve of the centralized power of France to provide for the first movements of his army—then the main prop of his usurpation and which had not yet served his turn."—*Ed.*

[b] The *New-York Daily Tribune* has: "Having lavished more wealth in that short struggle than the great Napoleon in the fifteen years of his warfare...."—*Ed.*

[c] This refers to reports published in *Le Moniteur universel,* Nos. 84 and 85, March 24 and 25, 1856. In the *New-York Daily Tribune* this sentence does not occur.—*Ed.*

[d] Here and below Marx quotes from a report by W. H. Russell published in *The Times,* No. 22324, March 25, 1856.—*Ed.*

[e] In the *New-York Daily Tribune* the words "principally of wine and vegetables" are added here.—*Ed.*

snow-storms which "allowed few huts to remain in which the snow did not make its appearance in great quantities," the correspondent puts the question what the French army must have suffered in tents not huts carefully fitted out, not double tents well dug out, but single and unprotected tents. He concludes by stating that "it is really painful to meet the French convoys of sick," and that Marshal Pélissier is more anxious to hide them from the English army than to mitigate their sufferings.

We add another quotation from *The Morning Advertiser*, the very paper that shared with *The Morning Post* the infamous privilege of hailing Bonaparte's advent in 1851 and of still trumpeting Lord Palmerston as the truly English minister:—

"There are 3,000 sick in the French camp of the Chernaya—the ambulances are choked and the medical staff decimated by disease and exhaustion—the commissariat has broken down, and is unable to feed the troops—the men are actually begging biscuits from the soldiers at the outposts—scurvy from the want of vegetables, and typhus from the want of meat, rage with indomitable virulence—and the contrast between the two armies is the source of open discontent on the part of the French soldiery. The transports are insufficient to convey the sick to Constantinople—the hospitals there have more than 12,000 patients in them—the epidemic is a positive pestilence—and the mortality frightful—the troop-ships arriving from the east at Marseilles are loaded with the dregs of fever, and the vessels and the typhoid patients are consigned to the lazaretto at Frioul." [a]

What is to be done with this withering army? [b] are they to be soothed by recitals of the Arabian tale of the King of Algiers' "nativity"? or by the description of the embroidered and gold-laced uniforms of the cautious hero's pampered guards? It should be recollected that French soldiers have no stomach for undergoing injuries like English privates. Proof, if proof be wanted, the several attempts made in the French army to shoot General Pélissier, a fact recorded by the *Gazette de Milan*,[c] Radetzky's *Moniteur*. Nor must it be imagined that the army of the line in France remains a dull spectator of the Crimean tragedy. The razzias of the Paris police are beginning to affect the barracks.[d] The Zouaves ordered to Paris to chafe public en-

[a] The quotation from *The Morning Advertiser* and the preceding paragraph do not occur in the *New-York Daily Tribune*.—*Ed.*

[b] Instead of this sentence the *New-York Daily Tribune* and *New-York Semi-Weekly Tribune* have: "What is to be done with these discontented legions, dying from a wretched commissariat, scandalous neglect, and notoriously organized plunder?"—*Ed.*

[c] *Gazzetta Ufficiale di Milano.*—*Ed.*

[d] Instead of this sentence the *New-York Daily Tribune* has: "The razzias of the Paris police have lately been directed at two barracks situated on the right bank of the Seine."—*Ed.*

thusiasm by their exhibition are already removed from the capital, they having become suspicious. Two other regiments returned from the Crimea have also been banished into the provinces. The antagonism between the guard and the line is daily growing more embittered, Bonaparte being about to create at this very moment new guard regiments in sufficient numbers to enable this privileged corps to keep the garrison of Paris, exclusive of the regiments of the line. Having bribed the army into antagonism to the country, he is now trying to bribe an army within the army—a rather dangerous experiment this.

The Finances—we would not call them the heels of this strange Achilles, he being rather tall at his heels—require a separate article for a full exposition. For the present it may suffice to state[a] that the funds falling somewhile hence, it was consequently expected the announced conclusion of peace, and the birth of another Bonaparte could not fail to send them up. Such an issue was not quite left to chance. Not only the Government gave orders to freely use the public chests at its disposal for the purchase of public funds, but the *crédit mobilier*, and similar mushrooms of Bonapartist credit were, during two consecutive days, largely employed in buying stock. All these manoeuvres notwithstanding, on the very news of the "nativity," instead of rising, the funds went down, and continue to go down. Bonaparte, in great rage now, prohibited the sale on Change of any but governmental quoted papers, and had then the principal stockjobber summoned to the *Préfecture de Police*.

When the statuary of Pallas Athene tumbled down in the Parthenon, such an accident told fatal tidings to the Republic of Athens. Bonaparte's bust, tottering on its pedestal in the Synagogue,[b] where the marketable value of governments is settled, and the peoples' history discounted, presages the downfall of the Empire of Agio.

Written about April 1, 1856

First published in *The People's Paper*, No. 205, April 5, 1856 (signed: K. M.) and simultaneously in the *New-York Daily Tribune*, No. 4676, April 14, 1856, reprinted in the *New-York Semi-Weekly Tribune*, No. 1136, April 15, 1856 as a leading article

Reproduced from *The People's Paper*

[a] The preceding sentence does not occur in the *New-York Daily Tribune*. The paragraph begins as follows: "As for the finances of France, it may suffice to state...."—*Ed.*

[b] The *New-York Daily Tribune* has: "in the temple".—*Ed.*

Karl Marx

THE FALL OF KARS[428]

Written in late March and April 1856

First published in *The People's Paper*, Nos. 205, 206, 207 and 208, April 5, 12, 19 and 26, 1856

Signed: *Karl Marx*

Reproduced from the newspaper

[I]

[*The People's Paper*, No. 205, April 5, 1856]

The fall of Kars is the turning-point in the history of the sham-war against Russia. Without the fall of Kars no Five Points, no Conferences, no treaty of Paris, in one word: no sham peace.[429] Then if we can prove from the Government's own Blue Book[a]—carefully cooked, as it is mutilated by extracts, deformed by omissions, plastered and patched up by falsifications—that Lord Palmerston's cabinet has planned from the beginning, and systematically carried out to the end, the fall of Kars, the veil is lifted and the drama of the Oriental War with all its startling incidents emerges from the mist diplomatically wrapt around it.

Towards the end of May, 1855, General Williams reports to Lord Redcliffe, who reports to Lord Clarendon, that

"a large force, consisting of 28,000 infantry, 7,500 cavalry, and 64 pieces of artillery, was assembled round Gumri, and that the Mushir[b] had received information of the intention of the enemy to attack Kars. We have in that entrenched camp 13,900 infantry, 1,500 cavalry, 1,500 artillerymen and 42 field pieces."

Seven days later, on June 3rd, Williams informed Clarendon:

"I have now four months provisions in the garrison of Kars, and I trust the central government, and the allies, will soon prove to this remnant of an army that it is not absolutely forgotten by them."

This despatch (see Kars papers, No. 231) was received in Downing-street,[c] on June 25th. On that day, consequently, the

[a] *Papers Relative to Military Affairs in Asiatic Turkey, and the Defence and Capitulation of Kars*, London, 1856. Documents from this book are quoted below.—*Ed.*

[b] Vassif Pasha.—*Ed.*

[c] 10 Downing Street is the official residence of the British Prime Minister.—*Ed.*

British government knew that on Oct. 3rd, Kars must fall if not relieved; and this knowledge became the basis of its operations.

On July 11th, Lord Clarendon receives three despatches from General Williams, dated June 15th, 17th, and 19th, stating severally that a skirmish of the advanced posts had taken place; that on the 16th of June a regular attack of the entrenched camp by the Russians had been gallantly repulsed by the Turks, and lastly that the enemy had made a flank march upon the entrenched camp, and established himself in force (30,000) within an hour's march of the weakest point of the Turkish position. Williams concludes the last of these despatches with the following words:

"Unfortunately we have no irregular cavalry. ... The enemy has already partially interrupted our communications with Erzeroum."

When the same news reached Constantinople, Lord Redcliffe was invited to a Conference at the Grand Vizier's[a] house on the Bosphorus. It was proposed by the Turkish ministers to relieve Kars by an expedition from Redout Kaleh by Kutais into Georgia, the force to consist of—

Vivian's Contingent	20,000
Beatson's	3,000
Batoum Garrison	12,000
Albanians	2,000
From Bulgaria	5,000
Egyptian Regular Cavalry	800
Tunis Horse	600
Total	43,400

The Porte expressed its readiness to entrust the direction of this expedition to a British commander, and to accept General Vivian in that capacity. This proposition reached Lord Clarendon on July 11th. On July 12th, Lord Redcliffe further informed him by telegraph that

"Preparations for an eventual expedition [...] are in progress. It might save much valuable time if you would inform me at once by telegraph whether government is prepared to sanction a powerful diversion by Redout Kaleh and Kutais into Georgia."

From June 25th to July 12th the British government, apprised of the danger of Kars, moved not a finger to come to the rescue,

[a] Ali Mehemet Pasha.—*Ed.*

not once was the telegraph set in motion; from the very day, however, when there is some Turkish plan for the relief of Kars to be thwarted, they suddenly are all activity. On July 13th (see No. 248 of Kars papers) Clarendon addresses a despatch to Redcliffe to this effect:

"Her Majesty's government are of opinion that the wiser course would be to send reinforcements to the rear of the Turkish army, instead of sending an expedition to the rear of the Russian army. The reinforcements might go to Trebizond, and be directed from thence upon Erzeroum. The distance from Trebizond to Erzeroum is less than from Redout Kaleh to Tiflis, and the march is through a friendly instead of through a hostile country; and at Erzeroum the army would meet supporting friends instead of opposing enemies, and supplies instead of famine. If the army at Kars cannot maintain that position against the Russians, it should fall back upon Erzeroum, and the whole Turkish force should be concentrated there. If the Russians are to be defeated, it will be easier to defeat them by the whole force collected than by divided portions of that force; and a defeat would be the more decisive, the further it took place within the Turkish frontier."

On the day following the receipt of Redcliffe's telegraphic despatch, Clarendon becomes still more liberal, adding Erzeroum also to the list of places to be fallen back from.

(Telegraphic.)

"The Earl of Clarendon to Lord Stratford de Redcliffe,

Foreign Office, July 14th, 1855.

"The plan for reinforcing the army at Kars contained in your despatches of 30th June, and 1st instant (should be the 12th inst.) is disapproved. The reasons will be sent by the messenger to-day against employing the Turkish Contingent until it is fit for service. Trebizond ought to be the base of operations, and if the Turkish army of Kars and Erzeroum cannot hold out at the latter place against the Russians, it might fall back upon Trebizond where it would easily be reinforced."

If Kars is the key to Erzeroum, Erzeroum is the key to Constantinople, and the central point of the strategical and commercial lines of Anatolia. Kars and Erzeroum once in the hands of Russia, the British land-trade, *via* Trebizond to Persia, is cut off. The British Government, aware of all these circumstances, coolly advises the Porte to surrender the keys of its house in Asia, when scarcely one of the two was in danger, and invites the besieged army of Kars to come to the reinforcements forbidden to come to the besieged army. "If," says his lordship, "the Russians are to be defeated" (where is the necessity? he seems to ask) he thinks a defeat would be the more decisive and easy the further it took place within the Turkish frontier, i.e., the more strong places and territory are surrendered to the Russians, and, in fact, the nearer behind Constantinople.

These despatches of Lord Clarendon are worthily backed by the following despatch from my lord "Take care of Dowb" Panmure,[430] the English Carnot, to Lieutenant-General Vivian:—

"Lord Panmure, to Lieut.-General Vivian,
"War-Department, July 14, 1855.

"Sir,—I transmit, herewith, for your information, a copy of a despatch which the Earl of Clarendon has addressed by the present opportunity to her Majesty's embassy at Constantinople, on the subject of the plan proposed by the Porte for the relief of the Turkish army at Kars, and I have to acquaint you that I entirely concur in all that is said in that despatch as to the objectionable character of the plan proposed by the Porte. I place such full reliance on your professional ability, that I feel no anxiety lest you should undertake any expedition of a nature so wild and undigested as that contemplated by the Porte. Whilst it is your duty to give every aid in your power, not simply as commanding the Contingent, but, as a British officer enjoying the confidence of her Majesty's Government, to our allies the Turks, it is at the same time necessary that you should be cautious in not risking the honour of the British name and your own reputation, by undertaking military operations for which proper basis has not been laid down, communications opened, supplies arranged, and transportation provided. A *coup de main* by means of suddenly throwing an army on the coast to threaten, or even to attack, an enemy's stronghold is one thing; but a deliberate expedition to invade an enemy's country, and on his own territory, to make war upon him, is quite another. In the first case something may be hazarded; but in the other every preparation must precede action. Moreover, from all the information which has reached me, I have every reason to believe the army of Batoum to be in a deplorable state. I know the Contingent to be scarcely organised; of the Bulgarian troops you have no knowledge, and I presume that Beatson horse are as little reduced to control and discipline as your own troops. In short I am assured that it would be madness to attempt to succour Brigadier-General Williams in this way. It is too late to regret the policy which has left that gallant officer and his army exposed to such straits; but it would only be opening the way to fresh failures to follow out such schemes as have been proposed for the purpose of relieving him. You must, as I have no doubt you feel, lose no time in getting your force into order for service which will be sure to await you somewhere, as soon as you are ready for it; but organisation is as necessary for an army as endurance and valour, and without the former, the latter qualities are utterly unavailing."

This despatch puts down Lord Palmerston's war minister a regular clown, useful only for the amusement of his master. To threaten, "or even" to attack, the stronghold of Sebastopol, where Russia had accumulated the defensive labour of twenty years, appears to him one thing very sensible, because it was a needless *coup de main* on the part of the allies; but a "deliberate invasion" on the part of the Porte, of an enemy's country with the purpose of beating him—"Dowb" never heard of such a thing. He entirely concurs with Clarendon in opinion that, to strengthen the rear of one's own army, instead of acting in the rear of the enemy, is the true essence of strategy—a point we may leave him to settle with

Napoleon I, Jomini, and all other great strategists. He also concurs with his friend in thinking, that in warfare an army must never march through hostile, but always through friendly countries—"with supplies instead of famine"—the true philosophy of the trencher-knife. But through the complacent silliness of the clown we catch a glimpse of the mind that moves him! or could it be given to poor Dowb, to make the discovery that Georgia was a hostile, instead of a friendly country—Georgia, Russia's Poland in the Caucasus.

The Turkish proposal which Dowb styles wild and ill-digested, was, in its general conception, bold, correct, we may say the only strategical idea given birth to in the whole war. It reduced itself to taking up an eccentric position with respect to the besieging army, to menace Tiflis, the centre of the Russian power in Asia, and to force Muravieff to retreat from Kars by the threat of becoming cut off from his basis of operations and line of communications. Such a Mingrelian expedition bade fair not only to relieve Kars, but to afford the opportunity of advancing offensively on all parts, and thus to gain the greatest point in all warfare—viz., to throw the enemy on the defensive. But the danger being urgent, such a plan, to result in success, required to be pushed on vigorously, with a sufficient force, and abundant means of supply and transport. Having in his immediate rear Gumri, as his first base of operations, a fortress directly calculated for the defensive against the Turkish territory, Muravieff was enabled to keep his position, till convinced of an advance upon Tiflis really becoming dangerous. To assume that character there was required a descent on the Circassian Coast of at least 55,000, the capture of Kutais, and the forcing of the pass of Gori. Omer Pasha, who, at a later period, undertook the same expedition at the head of 36,000 men, mustered on the Rioni hardly 18,000 to 20,000.

There can exist no doubt that an army of 20,000 men at Erzeroum would have been more useful than one of only 40,000 in Mingrelia. On the other hand it should not be forgotten that at the time when the Porte made its proposal, the Russians at Tiflis, according to the Blue Book itself, amounted to only 15,000 men, and Bebutoff with his reinforcements had not yet arrived. Besides, the movement of an army sufficiently large for its purposes from Trebizond to Erzeroum, and thence to Kars, with supplies, ammunition, and guns, would have cost, on Omer Pasha's assurance, exactly four months. Lastly, if the Porte proposed a right plan, with insufficient means, it was the part of its ally to provide the right means, and not to suggest a false plan. Sixty-thousand Turks were at that time pent up in the Crimea, in inactivity—and those the only effective troops of Turkey.

"At Batoum, Sukum Kaleh, and other neighbouring stations on the coast," writes Lord Redcliffe, under date 28th June, "it would be extremely difficult to muster more than 11,000 men.... The other parts of the empire (Bulgaria excepted), afford no additional reserves, with the exception of Bosnia, where it is still possible that a few thousand men might be detached; I speak of regulars, Bashi-bazouks may be procured, but your lordship knows what little dependency is to be placed on such undisciplined hordes.... In Bulgaria I question the existence of more than 50,000 men, including garrisons. [...] Austria, it is true, has declared her intention of considering the passage of the Danube by Russia a *casus belli*—and she also stands pledged to the exclusion of that power from the Danubian Principalities; but the resolution which in such an emergency would enable the Porte to take its line upon those assurances, and to overlook the awkwardness of leaving an important position inadequately defended is more fit to be admired than likely to be embraced."

What troops, then, remained at the disposal of the Porte, save the Anglo-Turkish Contingent? and this, as results from the despatches of Clarendon and Panmure, was only a contrivance to withhold from the Porte its last available force.

But did the British Government oppose any plan of theirs to the Turkish one? Was it in any way bent on sending the Anglo-Turkish Contingent to Trebizond, and thence to Erzeroum or Kars? In his despatch dated July 14th, Clarendon declares himself "against employing the Turkish Contingent until it is fit for service." If unfit for service, it was as unfit for the Erzeroum expedition as for the Mingrelian one. Clown Panmure, in his despatch of the same day, writes to Vivian, the commander of the Contingent:—"You must lose no time in getting your force into order for service, which will be sure to await you *somewhere*, as soon as you are ready for it"—thus summoning him to be ready not for an immediate service, not for Erzeroum, but *somewhere*—that is, *nowhere*. Still, on Sept. 7th (see No. 302 of Papers), Clarendon considers the Anglo-Turkish Contingent so little organised as to be unfit to encamp in the entrenched lines before Sebastopol. It is thus evident that the British Government brings forth the Erzeroum plan, not to execute it, but to thwart the Mingrelian expedition of the Porte. It was not opposed to a certain plan for the relief of Kars, but to any plan. "It would be madness to attempt to succour the army of Brigadier-General Williams.... It is too late to regret the policy"(Palmerston's policy) "which has left that gallant officer and his army exposed to such straits," said Panmure to Vivian. It is too late to do anything but surrender Kars to Russia, and Erzeroum into the bargain, says Clarendon to Redcliffe. Not only was this plan settled by the Palmerstonian Government as early as July 13th, but it is confessed in the Blue Book, and not a moment shall we see them swerving from it.

From No. 254 to 277 of the Kars Papers every despatch of Redcliffe during July exhibits the Porte busily engaged in the preparations for Vivian's Mingrelian expedition. How came this to pass?

On the 12th July, 1855, as will be remembered, Lord Redcliffe telegraphed to the Earl of Clarendon that the preparations for the Mingrelian expedition, under General Vivian were in progress, and "to save much valuable time," he applied for Government instructions to be sent by telegraph. Consequently, by telegraph, Clarendon despatches his protest against the Turkish plan, but, although this message bears the inscription of July 14th on its front, it does not reach Constantinople till July 30th, when we find Lord Redcliffe writing again to Clarendon:—

> The unfavourable judgment passed by Her Majesty's Government on the plans which have lately been under discussion, with a view to the relief of the Sultan's[a] army at Kars, has naturally increased the Porte's embarrassment. It was my duty to make it known to the Turkish Ministers, not only as an opinion, but, with respect to General Vivian's Contingent, as a veto. A most serious dilemma is the immediate result. Her Majesty's Government not only withhold the Contingent, but express a decided preference for the alternative of sending reinforcements to Erzeroum by way of Trebizond. This opinion is not adopted by the Porte, or indeed by any official or personal authority here. The Seraskier,[b] Omer Pasha, General Guyon, and our own officers,[...] agree with the Porte, and the French Embassy, in preferring a diversion on the side of Redout Kaleh, as offering better chances of success, supposing, of course, the necessary means of transport, supply, and other indispensable wants, can be sufficiently provided.... Meanwhile, the advices from Kars are not encouraging, and time of precious value is unavoidably wasted in doubt and uncertainty.

The way from Constantinople to London being not a whit longer than the way from London to Constantinople, it is a very curious fact indeed that Redcliffe's telegraphic despatch, leaving Constantinople on July 12th, should reach London on the 14th of that month, while Lord Clarendon's despatch, leaving London on July 14th, should reach Constantinople only on the 30th, or about that date. Redcliffe, in his despatch of July 19th, complains of the silence of the Government whom he had entreated "to lose no time in making known its pleasure." From a later despatch, dated

[a] Abdul Mejid.—*Ed.*
[b] Rushdi Pasha. "Seraskier" means "War Minister".—*Ed.*

July 23rd, we learn that he had received no answer even then. In fact, the receipt of the answer is not acknowledged, as we have said, before the 30th. There can exist, then, no doubt that the London date of the Clarendon despatch is *false*, and that it was not sent until weeks after the date given in the Blue Book. This falsification betrays the aim of the delay. Time of precious value was to be wasted, doubt and uncertainty were to be engendered, and above all, the Porte was to kill the whole of the month of July with preparations for Vivian's expedition, which the British Government was determined should not take place.

[II]

[*The People's Paper*, No. 206, April 12, 1856]

The strategical scruples of the British Government not allowing it to settle, during the interval of three months, its views of the great operations to be undertaken by the Porte, nothing would seem more fair and urgent than that it should have sent in the meantime, on its own responsibility, a small detachment *via* Erzeroum, to re-open the communications between that town and Kars. The allies were masters of the Black Sea, and the British Government had at its uncontrolled disposition General Beatson's 4,000 Bashi-bazouks, the only effective corps of Turkish irregular horse. Once landed at Trebizond they might have reached Erzeroum in ten days, escorting provisions to Kars, and thus enabling that fortress to prolong its resistance to from four to six weeks, when the severe Armenian winter setting in, all offensive movements on the part of the besiegers would have been stopped. General Beatson wrote to Redcliffe on the 7th July, applying to be sent on active service.

No notice was taken of his memorial. On the 14th of August petitions were presented by the troops themselves, praying that they might not be inactive, but be despatched to Asia. They received no answer whatever. Beatson ventured upon a third remonstrance on September 12. The forbearance of the British Government being now exhausted by the harassing importunities of the indiscreet petitioner, some diplomatic-military intrigues were set on foot, crowned by Beatson's dismissal from the service. As Beatson himself was dismissed from the service, so all his communications with the Government are dismissed from the Blue Book.

We have seen how stubbornly the British Government was bent on an expedition to Erzeroum *via* Trebizond. On the news of the Russians having established themselves on the high-road between Erzeroum and Kars, and cut off a portion of the provisions collected for the Kars army, some spontaneous efforts at immediate relief were risked from Trebizond, behind the back of the British Embassy. In Redcliffe's despatch, dated July 16th, 1855, is enclosed a report from Vice-Consul Stevens, to this effect:

"Trebizond, July 9, 1855. My Lord,—I have the honour to report that [...] Hafiz Pasha left for Erzeroum yesterday with 300 artillerymen and 20 field-pieces. A large force of irregulars, which may reach the number of 10,000, is now assembling, and will march to-day for the same place. (signed, Stevens.)"

Redcliffe, as in duty bound, forthwith asks for explanations, on the Seraskier's silence with regard to the collection of 10,000 irregulars at Trebizond, and the advance of Hafiz Pasha for Erzeroum.

"All that I had heard on the subject from his Excellency," he complains, "is that Toussoum Pasha was directed to go to Trebizond, and thence perhaps to Sivas, where he would assemble 4,000 irregulars, and proceed with them to the theatre of war."

By drawing lines between Trebizond, Sivas and Erzeroum, it will be seen that they form an isosceles triangle—the basis of which, viz., the line from Trebizond to Erzeroum, is about one-third shorter than either of the sides. To send, then, reinforcements direct from Trebizond to Erzeroum instead of sending Toussoum Pasha from Constantinople to Trebizond, from Trebizond, "perhaps," to Sivas, there to waste time in collecting an irregular force, with the view of advancing perhaps upon Erzeroum, was too rash a course not to be rebuked by the British Ambassador. Not daring to tell the Seraskier that the relief of a besieged town depends on a well calculated dilatoriness, he puts him the question:

"May it not be doubtful whether so large a body of Bashi-bazouks suddenly and loosely brought together, may be of any use to any party but the enemy?"

The Seraskier very properly replying,

"that he had insisted on having the necessary funds wherewith to pay them, which was the main instrument of control, and that he had threatened to retire from office, if his demand was not complied with."

Lord Redcliffe turns at once hard of hearing.

In entering upon the second plan of operations proposed by the Porte, and baffled by its Allies, we tread a maze, where all is meander and no forth-right.

From a despatch of Lieut.-Colonel Simmons's, the British commissioner in Omer Pasha's camp, dated July 15th, addressed to Lord Clarendon, and from Omer's memoranda enclosed in it, the following facts may be collected. On June 23rd Omer Pasha received a letter from General Williams, stating that the communication with Erzeroum was cut off, and requiring in the most pressing terms that reinforcements might be sent to Kars with the least possible delay, or that a powerful diversion might be made on the side of Redout Kaleh. Under date of July 7, Omer Pasha addressed a memorandum to the allied commanders—Simpson and Pélissier—requesting them to assemble a council of the allied generals and admirals commanding-in-chief, in order to come to an immediate resolution. In his memorandum he proposes that,

"he should throw himself, with the part of his army which is here"(at Balaklava) "and at Kertch—25,000 infantry, 3,000 cavalry from Eupatoria, and a proportional artillery—upon some point of the Coast of Circassia, and by menacing from thence the communications of the Russians, oblige them to abandon the siege of Kars."

In support of this proposal, Omer argues that the Ottoman army in Asia, to the number of 10,000 men blockaded in the entrenched camp of Kars by a superior Russian force, is in a position in which it is probable that from want of food it may be obliged to capitulate; that the garrison in Kars is in fact the Ottoman army in Asia; that if the garrison of Kars should yield, Erzeroum, a town, from its situation, difficult to fortify, will fall into the hands of the enemy, by which means he would become master of the communications with Persia, and of a great part of Asia Minor; that by accepting his proposal the Allies will make use of the chief advantages which they possess, viz., the facility of sea transport, and of the only Turkish army that is effective and capable of marching, viz., his own. In answer to that memorandum, Marshal Pélissier and General Simpson write that, "in absence of further information, they consider a conference would be premature." Omer Pasha, however, on July 12th, addresses them again, to inform them that,

"in the meanwhile he had received from his Government a despatch, according to which, the whole of Turkey in Asia, up to the gates of Constantinople itself, is undefended, and entreating him, as every hour is of the greatest value, immediately to find the means, and put in execution the resources necessary to avert the great danger in which the Government of Turkey, and in consequence the cause of the Allies, are placed." "Under these circumstances," he adds, "since I have in the Crimea 60,000 Turks, of whom the greater part are Asiatics, and whose families and property are exposed to the ravage of the enemy, and since I find that that army is inactive in the Crimea, without prospects of any immediate service that

I can discover, I consider it my duty to my sovereign and the common cause to repeat my former proposal."

Accordingly he invites them to a conference at the English head-quarters. Simultaneously with this common note to the allied generals he caused [Lieut.-]Colonel Simmons to address a confidential letter to General Simpson and Admiral Lyons, of which we give the following extract:—

The Porte have proposed to General Vivian to take the Turkish Contingent to Redoût Kaleh.... Omer Pasha, however, thinks there will be great risk in sending them there, as the men are not yet acquainted with their officers, the officers do not speak their language, and consequently cannot command them in the field, and the Contingent, although it might form a garrison, cannot yet be in a condition to march into the interior. The force of the Contingent also is small to make the contemplated operation. Omer Pasha also thinks that possessing, as he does, the confidence of the Turks, and being well-known in Asia, where he has had several campaigns, he is more likely to gain the sympathies and assistance of the inhabitants in provisioning and gaining information, [...] than strangers who do not know the language or country.

On July 14th the Conference took place, attended by Omer Pasha, [Lieut.-]Colonel Simmons, Generals Simpson, Pélissier, and Martimprey, and Admirals Lyons, Bruat, and Stewart. Omer Pasha went into a detailed statement of the Russian forces in Asia, and their operations in the vicinity of Kars. He amply developed the arguments above quoted, and forcibly stuck to the opinion that

"no time was to be lost in preparing a movement to check the progress of the Russians in Asia."

However, as [Lieut.-]Col. Simmons reports to Clarendon,

"the generals and admirals having received no information from their respective ambassadors at Constantinople, which should lead them to believe that the affairs of Asia were in that precarious state in which Omer Pasha, from the information received from his Government, believed them to be," decided that "in the absence of such information they would give no opinion on the subject."

In this instance, then, the allied generals declined giving any opinion on the subject, because they had received no information from their respective Governments. Afterwards, the allied Governments declined giving their orders because their generals had not given their opinion. Rather startled at the cool behaviour of the allied commanders, at their curious tactics of making their incredulity in facts a reason for giving no opinion on them, and at the incivility of giving the lie to his Government, the only one immediately interested in the matter, Omer Pasha, rose at once, and peremptorily declared that, "under the circumstances, he felt it his duty to proceed to Constantinople for a few days to confer with his Government."

Accordingly, two days later, July 16th, he proceeded to Constantinople, taking with him [Lieut.-]Colonel Simmons, but being accompanied also by one [Lieut.-]Colonel Suleau, "ostensibly travelling for the purpose of restoring his health" (see enclosure 1 in No. 270 of the Kars papers), but really charged by Pélissier and Simpson with the mission of thwarting Omer Pasha's project. This Suleau, attached to the staff of Simpson, conveyed a letter to Redcliffe from poor General Simpson—the most unlucky warrior ever heard of, as General Evans has it[a]—in which that general tells his ambassador not that he and his colleagues did not believe in Omer Pasha's statements, but that "they entertained the strongest objection to the withdrawal of any troops from the Crimea at this moment"—not that they had thought fit to withhold their opinion from Omer Pasha, but that he

"earnestly begs his Excellency to use his powerful influence with the Porte to cause their opinion to prevail over that of his Highness,[b]" for "great public interests were at stake," and "serious consequences might result from his success."

Success indeed! It was Omer Pasha's success that troubled Pélissier's sleep, who, up to that period, had nothing to boast of but the disgraceful battle of the 18th of June.[431] Poor Simpson, the unlucky warrior, naturally obtuse, as General Evans affirms his mind to be, was clever enough to catch the uneasiness of his co-commander, and to manage an intrigue in the rear of Omer Pasha, the only manoeuvre he can be said to have executed during the whole Crimean campaign.

In a despatch, dated July 19th, Redcliffe writes to Clarendon that

"the night before last (July 17th) he was surprised to hear that Omer Pasha had arrived suddenly from the Crimea [...] and went straight to the Seraskier."

He chuckles at the rumour reported by the fanariot[432] Pisani, that

"the generalissimo's arrival without the orders of his Government had created some feelings of dissatisfaction," and is under "a strong impression that Omer will best consult the interests of the alliance by returning without unnecessary delay to the command of his forces in the Crimea."

---

[a] Evans' speech in the House of Commons on February 29, 1856. *The Times*, No. 22304, March 1, 1856.—*Ed.*

[b] Omer Pasha.—*Ed.*

Notwithstanding Redcliffe's strong impression, Omer Pasha's stay at Constantinople was prolonged from the 17th of July to the beginning of September. It will be seen, by and by, how this waste of time was occasioned.

On July the 23rd, Redcliffe informs Clarendon that

"Omer Pasha [...] had proposed [...] to the Porte to make himself an incursion towards Georgia, starting from Redout Kaleh, and turning Kutais to good account."

This idea had been debated the night before (July 22) in a council at the Grand Vizier's,[a] and the result of the deliberations had been

"that the troops to be employed in the above-mentioned manner, under the command of Omer, should be taken from Eupatoria, to the amount of 20,000, and from Bulgaria to the amount of 5,000, and that the Contingent, with its numbers completed, should occupy the vacant space at Eupatoria. By way of alternative, it is proposed, that if the above-mentioned plan be objectionable, it might be so far modified as to take only 10,000 men from the Crimea, and 15,000 from Bulgaria, including those destined to form part of the Contingent."

Now, this despatch, which Clarendon is said to have received on August lst, on the arrival of which he immediately took occasion to address a despatch to Lord Cowley, the British Ambassador at Paris, is evidently and wilfully misconstrued in its main passage—viz., the passage in which the Porte is stated to have proposed the withdrawal from Eupatoria of 20,000 men, to be placed under the command of Omer Pasha, and their replacement at Eupatoria by the Turkish Contingent. It is this very passage to which Clarendon points in his despatch to Lord Cowley, stating "Her Majesty's Government to be favourably disposed to it," and expressing "his hope that the Government of the Emperor will concur in it." In this passage Eupatoria is interpolated for Balaklava. From the despatch of [Lieut.-]Colonel Simmons, dated 15th July, received by Clarendon on the 30th July, it will have been seen that Omer Pasha, in his memoranda to the allied generals, and in the war council, insisted upon taking with him that part of his army which is here (Balaklava), which he had brought from Eupatoria, and which he declared the only one fit for the Asiatic campaign. Did Omer Pasha alter his opinion, after arriving at Constantinople? The contrary is shown from a despatch dated August 2nd, in which Simmons states:—

"His Highness Omer Pasha informed me that he should be happy to give over to complete the contingent any of the Turkish troops under his command, except

[a] Ali Mehemet Pasha.—*Ed.*

the division which is now at the camp before Sebastopol, which being composed of his best troops, he is naturally desirous to have with him, if he make the proposed movement to Asia."

Will it be asserted that the Porte in the council of the night of July 22nd, arrived at a resolution contrary to Omer's proposal? In the very despatch of 23rd July in which Redcliffe reports the Porte's resolution, he tells Clarendon that,

"Omer Pasha has been most graciously received and most generously rewarded by the Sultan," and adds, "I need not add that he is on excellent terms with his Majesty's ministers, and particularly with the Seraskier Pasha."

Any discrepancy, therefore, between the Porte and its commander-in-chief, is out of the question; both of them appear equally startled on receiving from London the injunction of placing the troops at Eupatoria under Omer's command, and withdrawing from it the troops at Sebastopol and Kertch. What, then, was the intention of the British Government in forging the above passage? To conceal from the public that while exhibiting themselves as the patrons of Omer's project before the French Government, by a mere shuffling of words they substituted for the Porte's own proposal, one directly hostile to it. Thus a new subject of dispute was provided. Matters were embroiled still further, and the occasion was afforded to waste August and September with orders and counter-orders. The false play of the British Government is apparent even in the arrangement of the Blue Book. To confound the reader, Clarendon's despatch to Cowley figures on page 248, followed up from page 248 to 252 by an extract from Redcliffe's despatch of July 19th, Simpson's letter to Redcliffe of July 16th, Omer Pasha's letters and memoranda, and only in the last place by Redcliffe's despatch of July 23rd, of which Clarendon's instruction to Cowley pretends to be the sequel.

We must now stay for a moment in the Foreign-office, Downing-street, there beholding the Earl of Clarendon busily engaged in acting the head clerk of great Palmerston. Two days after the despatch of his message to Redcliffe on July the 16th, he is forwarding to Redcliffe another despatch concluding with the following words:

"Her Majesty's Government would still recommend that whatever force is sent for the relief of the army of Kars should proceed to Trebizond. If, indeed, Omer Pasha, who, we understand, is about to proceed to Constantinople, should determine to take any part of his own army with Tunisians and Albanians, to Redout Kaleh, her Majesty's Government would have nothing to say to that proceeding."

Redcliffe's despatch dated Constantinople, 23rd July, having reached London on August lst, in exactly nine days, the despatch of Clarendon dated 16th July, again wants more than half a month to reach Constantinople. It had not arrived on July 30th, when Redcliffe wrote that

> "her Majesty's Government insisting upon having the reinforcements sent via Trebizond placed the Porte in the most serious dilemma."

Redcliffe, then, was not in possession of Clarendon's despatch, according to which her Majesty's Government have nothing to say to the Redout Kaleh expedition, if undertaken by Omer Pasha himself. It is a feature peculiar to the chronology of this strange diplomatic-military drama that all despatches sure to create delay arrive with the most admirable speed, while all those pretending to recommend speed arrive with the most inexplicable delay. But there is another point quite as startling in Clarendon's last-quoted despatch. While Lord Redcliffe writes from Constantinople, dated July 19th, that he was surprised to learn of Omer Pasha's sudden arrival at Constantinople, on the 16th of July, on the very day Omer Pasha left the Crimea, Clarendon informs Redcliffe, from London, that "he understands Omer to be about to proceed to Constantinople." Omer Pasha himself, we know, adopted this resolution only on July 14th, after the breaking up of the war-council. In the interval from July 14th to the 16th no vessel left Sebastopol for Constantinople, so that Omer was obliged to request Admiral Lyons to place at his disposition her Majesty's ship *Valorous*. Are we then to understand that while the despatches, the Foreign-office telegraph, from London, require seventeen days to arrive at Constantinople, the despatches it receives from the Crimea convey intelligence of events even before they do happen? Not quite so. There was the submarine telegraph from Sebastopol to Varna, and the telegraph from Varna to London; so that Clarendon may have had direct intelligence the very day of the war-council's sitting. But where is this telegraphic despatch dated Sebastopol? Certainly not in the Blue Book. It is simply suppressed. And why? The same electric wire which informed Clarendon of Omer Pasha's intended departure must have informed him of the resistance he met with on the part of Pélissier, that is on the part of the French Government. Thus the question would naturally arise why Clarendon quietly waited from 16th July to the lst of August to break the matter to the French Government, and to commence negotiations with it on the point on which the whole campaign depended? To prevent this question the telegraphic despatch has disappeared. But having suppressed that despatch from the Crimea, why did he insert his own despatch, from London, dated the 16th July? As no trace can be discovered of the latter ever having reached Constantinople, its omission would have caused no palpable blank in the Blue Book. A double-edged end was aimed at. On the one hand the readiness of the English Government to relieve Kars was to be paraded in contrast to the difficulties raised by Bonaparte, and the whole odium of the delay to be shifted to his shoulders. On the other hand, Clarendon's belief in the spurious despatch of the 23rd July, was to be proved by his willingness to leave to Omer Pasha any part of his army, before he was aware of the resolution of the Porte to clog him with the Eupatoria army; having once become aware of this resolution, Clarendon, it is true, did stand upon it, Omer Pasha's and the Porte's protests notwithstanding. All the proceedings of Clarendon, his encouraging the Porte to occupy July with Vivian's expedition, his deferring the negotiations with Bonaparte to August, his substitution in the despatch to Paris a spurious proposition of the Porte, the very acceptance of which by Bonaparte was sure to become a source of further imbroglio in this comedy of errors—all these proceedings tended to the same end—to kill time.

[III]

[*The People's Paper*, No. 207, April 19, 1856]

On August 2nd, 1855, Lord Cowley telegraphs from Paris that "Count Walewski foresees objections to the proposal" made by Clarendon in the name of the Porte. Thus the occasion is afforded to the clever Earl of displaying, in a despatch dated August 3rd, his patriotic zeal, and of pressing on the French Government the enormous consequences likely to arise from Kars and Erzeroum falling into the hands of Russia. The following day, Aug. 4th, he receives a despatch from Paris to this effect:

"Telegraphic—Lord Cowley to the Earl of Clarendon.

"Paris, August 4, 1855.—The French Government will not oppose the projected expedition to Asia Minor under Omer Pasha, provided that the numbers of the Turkish contingent before Sebastopol are not diminished."

Notwithstanding its conditional form, this is the unconditional acceptance of the proposal made by Clarendon on August lst in the name of the Porte according to which the troops stationed at Eupatoria were to be given over to Omer Pasha, and General Vivian's contingent to replace them there. On the same day Clarendon despatched the following to Redcliffe:

"August 4th.—Omer Pasha can go to relieve Kars, provided he does not diminish his Turkish troops before Sebastopol or disturb the garrison at Yenikale."

The French government had only protested against the diminution of the Turkish troops before Sebastopol. The English government add another clog by sequestrating the Turkish troops at Yenikale too. On August 8th, Clarendon received a letter from General Williams dated Kars, July 14th, stating that General

Muravieff had made close reconnaissances on the 11th and 12th July, and that on the 13th

"he appeared with his whole army on the southern heights above Kars which form the key of our defences, and by the crowning of which Kars was taken in 1828."[433]

The letter concludes with the words,

"I have just heard that the Russian general expects reinforcements from Bayazid via Gumri, and that those troops recently expelled from the garrisons of the coast of Circassia are also marching into the interior of Georgia, and may take part in the future operations of Asia Minor." (No. 276)

Having become aware of the reinforcement of the Russians, the zeal of Clarendon for the diminution of the Turkish forces receives a fresh impulse. He immediately sits down to complete his *index militum prohibitorum*[a]:

"Telegraphic—The Earl of Clarendon to Lord Redcliffe.

"Foreign-office, Aug. 9, 1855.—General Vivian's contingent to go immediately to Eupatoria. The Turkish troops there 10,000 or 12,000 to go with Omer Pasha to Redout Kaleh. The Turkish troops at Balaklava and Kertch not to be diminished in number. The Turkish force to go to Redout Kaleh under Omer Pasha, to be completed to its proper number by troops from Bulgaria or elsewhere, not from the Crimea."

Here, then, we behold Clarendon again extending the circle of interdiction. Recollecting, from [Lieut.-]Colonel Simmons's despatch of July 15th, that Omer Pasha intended taking with him "the part of his army which is here (Balaklava) and at Kertch—25,000 infantry, 3,000 cavalry from Eupatoria and artillery," he now forbids the Porte to touch the garrison at Kertch, and extends Bonaparte's objection to the removal of Turkish troops from Sebastopol to the whole Crimea—save Eupatoria; and even the number of troops at the latter place dwindles down to 10,000 or 12,000, instead of the 20,000 mentioned in his despatch to the French Government, dated August 1. With a sort of clownish humour he leaves the Porte at liberty to look out for troops "elsewhere." Having filled the bomb at London, he may now quietly await its bursting at Constantinople.

In Clarendon's despatch to Redcliffe of July 16th, we were struck by this passage: "If, indeed, Omer Pasha, who, we understand, is about to proceed to Constantinople, should

---

[a] List of withheld troops.—*Ed.*

determine to take any part of his own army to Redout Kaleh, Her Majesty's Government have nothing to say to that proceeding." Now, from a letter of Fuad Effendi to Redcliffe, dated July 31, from Redcliffe's answer of August 4, and from Redcliffe's letter of August 8 (see No. 282 and enclosures), it results that Clarendon's despatch, dated July 16th, had not yet reached Constantinople on August 8. Fuad Pasha states in his letter that what has been begun of the measures (relating to the Mingrelian expedition) had been suspended, in consequence of "the official and categorical answer expected (from London) having not yet been received," and defends the Turkish plan of a Mingrelian expedition against "the substance of the English despatches," according to which "the succours *must* be sent through Erzeroum by way of Trebizond." Redcliffe, in his answer, dated Aug. 4, tells us that

"when latterly called upon to declare the opinions of his Government, he performed that duty with a painful sense of the embarrassments which surrounded the Porte,"

increased as they would be by the opinion "he was called upon to declare," and adds:

"Though Her Majesty's Government have declared their decided preference for a more direct operation by Trebizond and Erzeroum, their objections to a diversion on the side of Circassia would in all likelihood be modified if the force employed were of a compact or reliable character."

In his despatch to Clarendon, dated August 8, he complains that the Government

"still leans with all its weight on Trebizond as the only true chance of relief.... The military authorities are decidedly in favour of it"(the Mingrelian expedition).... "Amidst so many motives to vigorous support of the only practicable scheme of relief, [...] I made no reserve in communicating the adverse opinions of Her Majesty's Government to the Porte."

Clarendon's answer to this latter despatch of Redcliffe's (August 20) must be considered from a double point of view—with respect to Redcliffe's assertion that in his opinion the English Government had resisted the Mingrelian expedition up to August 8, and with respect to the plan which Clarendon forwarded to Paris on August 1 as the Porte's own plan. As to the first point, Clarendon declares (see No. 283):—

"My various messages by telegraph, and my despatch of the 4th inst., which you will have received since the date of your despatch, will have shown you that Her Majesty's Government, in conjunction with that of the Emperor of the French, were willing that Omer Pasha should proceed to Asia to effect a diversion for the relief of Kars, and Her Majesty's Government in that case no longer insists upon the view they had entertained at first, that the relief should be given by way of Trebizond."

With the exception of the despatch of July 14, in which Clarendon protested against the Mingrelian expedition, and summoned the Turks to fall back from Erzeroum and Kars, and his despatch, dated August 9, which Redcliffe, of course, could not have received on August 8, Clarendon had, according to the Blue Book, sent no telegraphic despatch at all. It is therefore a palpable falsehood when he speaks of his "various messages by telegraph" withdrawing the veto of the British Government against the Mingrelian expedition. Why does he not refer to his despatch dated July 16? Because it figures only in the Blue Book, was written only for the Blue Book, and has never left the Foreign-office at Downing-street. Redcliffe, as if aware of the trap laid for him, writes to Clarendon, dated August 13 (No. 286):—

"I have just learnt the contents of your lordship's telegraphic message dated the 9th inst. The sanction given by Her Majesty's Government to the experiment of a diversion on the side of Redout Kaleh will, I doubt not, afford the highest satisfaction as well to the Turkish Ministry as to Omer Pasha. The disappointment occasioned by the terms of the preceding message, which appeared to favour exclusively an advance upon Kars by Trebizond, was evident [...]."

Redcliffe knows nothing of Clarendon's various "despatches by telegraph;" he knows only of the preceding message being "exclusively" in favour of a Trebizond expedition. He means the message of the 13th, backed by the telegraphic message of the 14th of July. He ignores altogether the existence of the message of the 16th of July. We insist upon this point for a simple reason. One glance at the Kars papers will satisfy everybody as to the constant efforts made by the British Government to thwart the projects of the Porte. But the falsifications, forgeries, and lies which we reveal, prove the British Government to have been conscious of foul play, and betray on its part a preconcerted plan, which it dares not openly confess.

Let us now consider Clarendon's despatch of Aug. 20, from another point of view:—

"Omer Pasha," he says, "as commander of the Sultan's troops, will be free to direct his movements in a manner most beneficial to the common cause; and the only limitation placed by the two governments on his proceedings is the condition that the movement in Asia shall not lead to any diminution of the Turkish force employed before Sebastopol and Yenikale, while the Turkish Contingent, under General Vivian, may be made available for filling up the room of the Turkish troops whom Omer Pasha may take with him from Eupatoria."

According to Clarendon's despatch to Paris, dated August 1, the Porte had proposed to place the Eupatoria troops under Omer Pasha while not meddling with the Turkish army before Sebastopol. How can he call the simple acceptance of the Porte's own proposal, "putting a limitation on Omer Pasha's proceedings?" But, on the other hand, could he do otherwise? Since the very despatch of Redcliffe he is answering, reminds him that the Pasha reckons on "17,000 men from Balaklava," 3,000 from Kertch, etc. Thus, what figured in his despatch to Paris as the Porte's own proposal, is now enjoined to the Porte, as the advice of its Western allies.

Up to the 13th of August—just a month after Omer Pasha had proposed to the Allied commanders his Mingrelian expedition—the Porte was labouring under the painful conviction that the British Government objected to it, and all its preparations for the relief of Kars were consequently kept in deadly suspense. On the 13th, at last, it is delivered from that nightmare, and has the satisfaction to understand that its Western allies have accepted the resolution it had come to on July 22nd. It would now, at last, be free to turn its energies against Muravieff, instead of against Clarendon. On the 15th of August, the Ottoman Council was assembled for deliberation as to the most effectual means of succouring Kars. The result of their deliberations is quite as startling as it is unexpected.

"Omer Pasha," Redcliffe says in his despatch to Clarendon, dated August 16th (No. 294), "objects most positively to the plan transmitted from London by telegraph, of stationing the contingent at Eupatoria, and he is not prepared to assume the responsibility of commanding the expedition, unless the Turkish troops before Sebastopol be allowed to form part of it."

Thus we see the Eupatoria plan, pretended to have been sent on the 23rd July to London, is now asserted to have been transmitted on August 9 from London to Constantinople.

On the 16th of August, [Lieut.-]Colonel Simmons also addressed a despatch to Clarendon (No. 297):

"I have to inform your Lordship that the Seraskier having received [...] a communication from Lord Stratford de Redcliffe, to the effect that her Majesty's Government had ordered the Turkish contingent to Eupatoria, placed the communication into the hands of his Highness Omer Pasha, who conceiving that this movement would not enable the Porte to provide the necessary force to make any operation in Asia to save the army of Kars, has drawn up a report for the Seraskier.... Omer Pasha, while insisting upon taking with him his troops [...] from Sebastopol, will hand over part of them and the Turkish troops at Kertch to the Anglo-Turkish contingent, such as are required to complete its full complement.... The proposal of the Pasha appears to me the only one which holds out any hope of saving the army of Kars, subject to the condition which His Highness understands has been imposed by the English and French Governments—that there is to be no material reduction of force in the Crimea, and therefore that the first proposal made by Omer to the Generals, reported in my despatch of July 15th, cannot be put in execution.[...] The Pasha doubts if the expedition will now be in time to save the garrison of Kars, but if not, it will at any rate prevent the enemy from establishing himself in the government of Erzeroum, and there organizing measures for another advance into the interior in the next campaign."

Omer Pasha's memorandum to the Seraskier, alluded to in the above despatch of [Lieut.-]Colonel Simmons, is enclosed in Redcliffe's letter to Clarendon, dated August 16th. We extract from it the following considerations made by Omer Pasha:

"The troops now at Eupatoria, are composed of different materials, Tunisians and Egyptians,[a] and are deficient of the means of land transport.... They are not capable of taking the field or of manoeuvring.... If the Egyptians were to go to Asia, as it will be necessary to keep the field during the commencement of the winter, coming as they do from a hot climate [...], they could not perform the necessary manoeuvres, and the army being composed of different materials there would be but little chance of success. By the execution of this project the unity of the Ottoman as well as of the English army will be destroyed, and it is to be observed that much of the energy, if not the existence, of an army in warfare depends upon its unity.... The Pasha observes, that every general in warfare ought to consider beforehand the most difficult circumstances in which he may be placed by the events of war, and to provide as far as possible against misfortune. He supposes the case, that the army of Kars is destroyed before his arrival in Asia, and that the Russians had advanced beyond that place, and states that in such a case, being with an army composed of different materials, in which he could not place entire confidence, he would find himself in similar difficulties in which the army of Asia is now placed ....

"Every general to whom an operation is confided, ought to consent to the operation, and its mode of execution, in order that he may be made responsible for its conduct [...]. The Anglo-Turkish contingent, if supplied with its full complement from the detachments about to be drafted from Bulgaria and from Kertch, will be almost equal in numbers to the divisions under his command. [...] As far as the numbers of the Allied armies are concerned, there need be no diminution, if his views were acceded to. On the contrary, if the plan, sent from London, were acted upon, the permanent arrangements made by the Seraskier for the supply of the garrison of Eupatoria [...] would be broken up, unavoidable delay must ensue, absolutely new establishments would have to be organized."

The destruction of the last effective Turkish army, the loss of the unity of the English as well as the Ottoman army, the wilful sacrifice of the Egyptians and Tunisians, the breaking up of the permanent arrangements made for the supply of the Turkish troops at Eupatoria, the creation of unavoidable delay, the ruin of his own military representation, the exposure of the Mingrelian

[a] In *Kars Papers*: "Turks and Egyptians".—*Ed.*

army to the fate of the garrison of Kars—these are, according to Omer Pasha, the natural consequences of the plan sent from London. While communicating to Clarendon this strong protest, Lord Redcliffe evinces not the least suspicion of having himself been the channel through which the Porte is made to have transmitted the identical project to Lord Clarendon.

We have, thus, new and irrefutable proof that the proposal of the Porte, as figuring in the despatch dated July 23rd, is a London forgery, and that Clarendon in submitting it to the acceptance of the French Government in his despatch of August lst was fully aware of committing an atrocious fraud.

His scheme worked exactly up to his intention, the Porte, at last informed that the British Government consents to the Turkish expedition in general, learns simultaneously, that it objects to all the details required for carrying it out. Having been compelled to waste one month with struggling against Clarendon's Erzeroum plan, it has now to waste the still more precious month of August with resisting his Eupatoria scheme.

In a despatch dated August 20, addressed by Redcliffe to Clarendon, he encloses another memorandum of Omer Pasha, similar in substance to the former one, but with the addition (see No. 296):

> "any general undertaking such an operation against all military rules, would sacrifice his military reputation, and he would, moreover, imperil the general alliance. I intend doing neither.
>
> "If I were even to accept this service, it would not serve the object in view."

He represents the troops at Eupatoria "as undisciplined, mixed, and inexperienced soldiers."

On the 20th of August (see No. 298, Simmons to Clarendon) Omer Pasha informs Simmons of the state of things at Kars as reported by an aide-de-camp of the Seraskier, who left Kars on the 5th, and arrived at Constantinople on August 19th,

> "At the time of his departure the stores within the town of Kars did not contain more than sufficient provisions for the garrison for one month or five weeks at the outside, and they were not well provided with ammunition. This, however, does not appear of much consequence, as General Muravieff had proclaimed to his army, which, by the reinforcement it has received, is stated now to number about 50,000 men, to reduce the town of Kars by starvation, and to capture the town without firing a shot.... The Russians have caused the inhabitants to remove everything in the shape of provisions throughout a district within a radius of 8 hours (28 miles) round Kars as a centre.... The forts at Erzeroum consist of 6,000 regular troops, and 12,000 irregulars; but many of the latter are leaving and dispersing." "From Omer Pasha's conversations [...]," says Simmons, "it is evident that the Porte is deeply impressed with the deplorable state of affairs in Asia, and

is almost in despair at the apparent certainty of losing, towards the end of this month or early in September, the garrison of Kars, sixteen thousand men with nearly two hundred pieces of artillery, of which about seventy are field guns.... They are very much grieved and disappointed at the time which has been lost [...]—and that the cabinets of Paris and London, as well as the military authorities in the Crimea, have not considered the subject in that serious aspect in which it presents itself to the Porte, but have objected to the propositions which have hitherto been made with a view to retrieving their position and their preventing the disaster."

On August 21st, at a meeting of the Porte's council (No. 299—Simmons to Clarendon, dated August 23),

"a decision was arrived at to proceed with the utmost vigour and all the means at the disposal of the Porte to carry into execution the plan proposed by Omer Pasha.... A note was agreed upon, to be addressed to the ambassadors of France and England,[a] informing them of the decision of the Porte, and inviting them to obtain the assistance of the fleets of their respective Government to transport the Ottoman troops, with their artillery, baggage, and means of land-transport, to the coast of Asia.... Having done all in their power to effect a movement for the relief of the army of Kars, to recover their position in Asia, they" (the Porte) "considered themselves relieved from the responsibility of any disaster which might happen from the non-execution of any of the plans proposed with that view. The Turkish Government, in order to commence the movement, are now sending their ships to Sizopolis, to begin the embarkation of the troops, etc., but they evidently have entertained some doubt as to taking this decided course, in consequence of the Anglo-Turkish Contingent having received orders from London to proceed to Eupatoria."

Thus the end of August was approaching, the Porte still finds itself clogged in its movements by Clarendon's Eupatoria plan, and its anxiety waxing with the dismal news from Kars, it extorts at last from Redcliffe, who in the meantime had made a trip to Sebastopol, the following telegraphic despatch (No. 290):—

"Lord Redcliffe to the Earl of Clarendon.

"Before Sebastopol, Aug. 26.—I request to be informed definitively and immediately here, whether Omer Pasha may take Turkish troops in whole or in part from Balaklava, provided they be replaced by others of the same numerical force, and whether General Vivian's Contingent is in that case at liberty to take position before Sebastopol, instead of going to Eupatoria. Omer Pasha is expected from day to day. He makes his expedition conditional on the power of acting as above. He has stated plausible reasons for this. If transport can be spared by us the troops may land, it would seem, at Redout Kaleh in about a month. The Russians who threatened Erzeroum have retired by the road to Kars; the Turkish army there is stated to have nearly two months provisions early in August."

[a] É. A. Thouvenel and Stratford de Redcliffe.—*Ed.*

[IV]

[*The People's Paper*, No. 208, April 26, 1856]

Clarendon had now succeeded in thwarting, by his Eupatoria plan, all action on the part of the Porte during the whole month of August. Redcliffe's despatch confirmed the statement of General Williams, that "the provisions of Kars will hardly last to the beginning of September." By what extraordinary devotion the Turkish garrison at Kars contrived to prolong its existence beyond the term assigned by Williams, will be seen from the following memorandum:—

(Enclosure in No. 315.)

Kars, September 1st, 1855.—"The most is made of our provisions; the soldiers are reduced to half-allowances of bread and meat, or rice-butter. Sometimes 100 drachmas of biscuit instead of bread; nothing besides. No money. Mussulman population, 3,000 rifles, will soon be reduced to starvation. Armenians are ordered to quit the town to-morrow. No barley, scarcely any forage. Cavalry reduced to walking skeletons, and sent out of garrison; artillery horses soon the same. How will the field pieces be moved after that?... What is being done for the relief of this army?

(Signed) *Williams.*

Clarendon having made sure that the provisions of Kars could not last beyond the first days of October, and being on the other hand assured by Redcliffe that even with the succour of the allied transports Omer Pasha's troops would not arrive at Redout Kaleh before the first days of October, thinks it no longer dangerous to press on the French Government the acceptance of the Turkish plan. He was informed besides that at the very moment he addressed that Government the assault of Sebastopol was imminent, and Pélissier, therefore, had good reasons not to allow any change in the composition of the troops before Sebastopol. To hide this knowledge, the despatch of Redcliffe is given in the mutilated shape of an extract. The following is Clarendon's despatch to Lord Cowley:—

Foreign Office, Aug. 28, 1855.—"Her Majesty's Government trusts that the Government of the Emperor will agree to the following answer to the despatch from Viscount Stratford de Redcliffe, dated Balaklava, Aug. 26th, in which case your excellency will send it on immediately from Lord Panmure to General Simpson, who will inform Viscount de Redcliffe, if he is still at Balaklava:

"'Omer Pasha is to be at liberty to take such of his own troops as he pleases, from Balaklava to Asia. They must be replaced in equal numbers by General Vivian's Contingent, or by troops from Eupatoria, as the allied generals may decide; and instructions accordingly must be given in conjunction with the admirals as to transporting them.'"

(Signed *Clarendon.*)

Even in this despatch, Clarendon cannot abstain from playing a trick on the Porte. Informed as he was by Omer Pasha's various memoranda that the replacement of his troops before Sebastopol by troops from Eupatoria, would go a great length to spoil his whole plan, he proposes to the French Government, quite *en passant,* to replace the troops before Sebastopol by Vivian's contingent, or by troops from Eupatoria. The answer from Paris was this:—

"Telegraphic.—Lord Cowley to the Earl of Clarendon.

"Paris, Aug. 29, 1855.—The Emperor has no objection to the removal of the Turkish troops from Balaklava, and to their being replaced by others, provided that the allied commanders-in-chief have no objection; but he will not take the responsibility upon himself of saying more under these circumstances. I send the telegraphic despatch to General Simpson, inserting, after the word 'Asia,' 'provided that General Pélissier and you have no objection'."

Lord Clarendon's sincere anxiety to hasten the Mingrelian expedition at this supreme moment, shines in overpowering brightness in his despatch of September 7th, sent by ordinary mail to [Lieut.-]Colonel Simmons, so that it did not arrive till September 23rd. On September 5th he had received the following despatch from [Lieut.-]Colonel Simmons. (No. 301.)

"I have to inform your lordship that Omer Pasha has stated to me that he will not be able to leave Constantinople for five or six days, as he is occupied in making the necessary arrangements for the expedition to Asia, and his presence here is absolutely required to complete them." According to the arrangements accepted by the Porte "Omer Pasha hoped to land 50,000 men[a] and 3,400 horses in Asia, in

[a] In *Kars Papers*: "15,000 men".—*Ed.*

two trips of the Turkish fleet alone, the operation occupying from three weeks to one month, or for each voyage from ten days to a fortnight.... Omer Pasha is most desirous that assistance should be given by the allies in conveying the troops and their material from before Sebastopol, and baggage-horses from Sizopolis, and he considers the most practicable way in which this could be done, would be by allowing the English fleet to convey the troops from before Sebastopol to Asia, after having conveyed the Contingent to Balaklava to replace them."

To this despatch, Clarendon answers in the following strain:—

"The Earl of Clarendon to Lieutenant-Colonel Simmons.

"Foreign Office, Sept. 7, 1855.

"Sir,—The account of the arrangements proposed by Omer Pasha for the relief of the army in Asia, which is contained in your despatch of the 26th ult., is inconsistent with subsequent statements which have reached her Majesty's Government. In your despatch you report that Omer Pasha reckons upon taking a portion of the Turkish troops from before Sebastopol, and replacing them by General Vivian's Contingent. But it appears, by a despatch of a later date from General Simpson, that Omer Pasha has given it as his opinion that General Vivian's Contingent would not be fit to take up a position before Sebastopol until next spring; and, in consequence of that opinion, and by reason of General Simpson's protest against having the Contingent sent to him, which protest was founded upon that opinion, her Majesty's Government have determined that the Contingent shall not go to join the army before Sebastopol."

Clarendon.

Let it be remarked that Simpson's, the poor warrior's despatch, is omitted from the Blue Book, that Omer Pasha's "opinion" is a changeling, and that the "later date" when Omer expressed his new opinion contradicting his opinion of the 26th of August, happens to be the beginning of July—as will be seen from the following extract from [Lieut.-]Colonel Simmons's despatch, dated, camp of Kamara, Sep. 23rd, 1855:—

"On this subject I beg to inform your lordship that this opinion was given by Omer Pasha in a letter to General Simpson early in the month of July ... and before he was aware of the critical position of the army in Asia. He then stated that he was strongly of opinion that General Simpson could not contemplate making use of the Contingent in the open field (en rase campagne) in front of the enemy.... Lord Raglan had, on several occasions, asked whether I thought it would be possible to make use of the Contingent to hold the lines of Balaklava, and upon consulting Omer Pasha upon the subject, he told me that he saw no objection to it, if his lordship considered it absolutely necessary."

In excavating an opinion of Omer Pasha, given before the Mingrelian expedition was mooted, in falsifying that opinion and in founding upon this falsification a protest, Simpson's "obtuse mind" followed, of course, the secret instructions received from London. Poor Simpson was an invention of Palmerston, one of his golems. Golems, as the German poet Arnim has it,[a] are earth clods, shaped in the human form and infused with a factitious life by the spell of capricious wizards. Supposing Simpson to have written exactly as he is represented to have done in Clarendon's despatch—a point that becomes questionable from the suppression of his despatch in the Blue Book, Clarendon could not be for a moment in doubt either as to the date or as to the substance of Omer Pasha's opinion. As early as July 15, Simmons had informed him that in Omer's opinion "the Contingent, although it might form a garrison, cannot yet be in a condition to march into the interior;" and in a later despatch that "in Balaklava and Kertch the troops of the Contingent will be within fortified lines" and, therefore, not "in the open field."

The history of Omer Pasha's Mingrelian campaign is not given in the Blue Book, but enough transpires to denounce the obstacles thrown in its way by the allied governments even at the too late epoch, when they had reluctantly given their consent and captured the south side of Sebastopol.

Simmons writes to Clarendon from the camp at Kamara on Sept. 21, 1855.

> "On the 18th inst. General Pélissier consented to the departure of three battalions of Turkish chasseurs hence for Asia. [...] They will be embarked in a day or two for Batoum. Up to the present time General Pélissier has not signified his assent to the departure for Asia of any more of the Ottoman troops now stationed here."
>
> "In answer to my inquiries at the Porte," says Redcliffe on Sept. 26th, "I am assured [...] that the passage of troops and the conveyance of provisions are in progress, though slowly, in consequence of the limited command of transport for those purposes. It is impossible not to apprehend that the many changes of plan, the exigencies of our operations at Sebastopol, and heavy demands on the transport-service, concur to diminish the hope of relieving Kars."

Now the many changes of plan were the work of the British ministry; the exigencies of the operations before Sebastopol a mere pretext, as the allies, after the capture of the town, confined themselves to guarding its ruins; and lastly the want of sufficient transport was produced by the orders issued from Downing-street for the useless transmissions of the Contingent from Varna to Yenikale, Kertch, Eupatoria, and back to the Bosphorus.

The gloom of these forebodings was dispelled for a moment by the meteorlike flash of the victory gained by the Turks over the Russian assaulting columns before Kars on September 29th. In

---

[a] L. A. Arnim, *Isabella von Ägypten. Kaiser Karl des Fünften erste Jugendliebe*.—*Ed.*

his despatch of the same date General Williams calls it "a day glorious for the Turkish arms." In his despatch of October 3rd (No. 342), he tells Clarendon,

"During the combat, which lasted nearly seven hours, the Turkish infantry, as well as artillery, fought with the most determined courage; and when it is recollected that they had worked on their entrenchments, and guarded them by night, throughout a period extending to nearly four months—when it is borne in mind that they were ill-clothed and received less than half a ration of bread—that they have remained without pay for 29 months, I think your lordship will admit that they have proved themselves worthy of the admiration of Europe, and established an undoubted claim to be placed among the most distinguished of its troops."

On the receipt of these glad tidings the Porte issued an address to the defenders of Kars (No. 345), in which the following words occur:

"We were conscious of the zeal and intrepidity which animated your excellency, and of the infinite mercy of God, and found consolation in this reflection. On the other hand, we worked day and night in devising means to oblige the enemy to raise the siege, and the joyful tidings of this victory have infused new life into us."

And what an exuberance of life will they not infuse into Clarendon's breast? He who worked day and night in devising means to thwart the means devised by the Porte, how will he not at least profusedly scatter the cheap flowers of his rhetorical sympathy! Nothing of the sort. Rather disappointed in his calculations he vents his spleen upon the Porte, in the following short and provokingly ironical despatch (see No. 346)[a]:

"...The neglected garrison of Kars will at least have the satisfaction of knowing that their sufferings troubled the ... repose of the Turkish ministers, who, in default of all ordinary means of relief, never ceased to pray for their safety and success."

Clarendon, formerly the silent friend of Aberdeen, figures here as Palmerston's twanging mouthpiece.

From the repulse of the Russians before Kars, on September 29th, to the day of its capitulation, on November 24th,[434] there elapsed again nearly two months. How was this time improved by the British Government? First, by withholding from Omer Pasha the necessary transports. On October 6th Mr. Oliphant, the correspondent of the *Times*, writes from Omer Pasha's camp:

"The Turkish army is gradually assuming a more imposing aspect, and the assent which the allied generals have at length reluctantly given to the despatch of

[a] The quotation that follows is from Clarendon's dispatch to Stratford de Redcliffe of November 21, 1855.—*Ed.*

10,000 Turks from Balaklava, will swell it to about 50,000 strong. The principal delay is caused by the slackness of our authorities in the Crimea, who do not provide transport for the conveyance of the troops here, nor seem to care in the least whether they ever get here or not. It is certainly unfortunate that the only serious cause of annoyance which Omer Pasha has felt with respect to this expedition [...], is to be attributed to the same source which has already been so fruitful of disaster."[a]

But this was not all. As early as July, Lord Palmerston had stated in the Parliamentary debates on the Turkish loan, that the Porte was lamentably deficient in money, and that all its operations depended upon receiving a supply of it at once. The Parliament having consented to the loan, the British Government advertised it in August, 1855, but from a paper laid before Parliament it appears that out of the five millions sterling granted something short of two millions was but paid to the Porte on January 29th, 1856, and that even this sum had been sent in dribblets of one hundred thousand pounds. Still, on Nov. 24, 1855, the Porte declares (see No. 353, inclosure 4):—

"In conclusion, his Excellency"(the Seraskier[b])"turned round to me, and said that I was as well aware as he of the continuous exertion, made by him to help the garrison of Kars[...]. That Omer Pasha had been delayed by causes over which he, unfortunately, could not exercise any control. It was an affair of the alliance. It had all along been understood that such measures as it was in their power to take without the army which had been retained in the Crimea, would not suffice for the object in view.... His Excellency then proceeded to tell me with much force that the Turks were absolutely debarred from executing what was necessary for the prosecution of the campaign by the delay in giving them the advantage of the loan. The grain to the amount of one million of kilos bought by them for the service of the army, was not forwarded, because they could not pay for it.... He had written to the Grand Vizier,[c] that if money was not forthcoming from that source (the loan) in a week from this date, he would resign his office." (Letter of General Mansfield to Lord de Redcliffe.)

It is a rather curious coincidence that on the very day on which Kars surrendered, the Seraskier was forcibly stating to the British military commissioner the true reasons of that disaster—the delay of Omer Pasha's expedition by the Allies retaining from the Porte its own troops, and then the stoppage of all operations during October and November by the British Government retaining from the Porte its own money.

---

[a] Report from Sukum Kaleh published in *The Times*, No. 22195, October 26, 1855.—*Ed.*

[b] Rushdi Pasha (Mehemet).—*Ed.*

[c] Ali Mehemet Pasha.—*Ed.*

When the capitulation was resolved upon at Kars, on Nov. 24th,

"the soldiers were dying by hundreds a day, of famine. They were mere skeletons, and were incapable of fighting or flying. The women brought their children to the general's[a] house for food, and there they left them, and the city was strewed with dead and dying." (No. 366.)[b]

During the whole epoch that Clarendon systematically thwarts the plans of the Porte, paralyses its forces, and retains its own money, we behold him dinning the ears of the manacled man with the counsel to move on vigorously, and abusing him for his slackness. History exhibits, perhaps, no parallel more bitterly ludicrous than that between the British Government making England the laughing-stock of Europe by its adventures in the Crimea, the Baltic, and the Pacific, and the rewards lavished on the tools of its miscarriages—and the same Government upbraiding the Porte in the severest tones of antique Catonism for the blunders of its military officers and administrators. The Government of Sadleirism, morally indignant at pasha-corruption; the patrons of a Codrington and an Elliot, insisting on the punishment of a Selim Pasha and a Tahir Pasha; the *improvisatori* of a Simpson sullenly frowning on the promoters of an Omer Pasha; "Take-care-of-Dowb" Panmure doctoring the Seraskier; Downing-street with its doctors Smiths, its Filders, its Aireys, and its Gordons, during the very sittings of the Sebastopol Committee, censuring a pasha at Trebizond for a load of sponges and rammers not having been packed in bundles and covered with matting:—this is the true picture of the Oriental war. And, above all, the brave Clarendon's soul-stirring complaints of the Porte's apathy!—think of an official Thersites tasking the Danaides for not filling the sieve.

[a] W. F. Williams.—*Ed.*

[b] Message of J. Brant, British Consul in Erzeroum, to Clarendon of November 27, 1855.—*Ed.*

Karl Marx

SPEECH AT THE ANNIVERSARY OF *THE PEOPLE'S PAPER*

DELIVERED IN LONDON, APRIL 14, 1856[435]

The so-called revolutions of 1848 were but poor incidents—small fractures and fissures in the dry crust of European society. However, they denounced the abyss. Beneath the apparently solid surface, they betrayed oceans of liquid matter, only needing expansion to rend into fragments continents of hard rock. Noisily and confusedly they proclaimed the emancipation of the Proletarian, *i.e.* the secret of the 19th century, and of the revolution of that century. That social revolution, it is true, was no novelty invented in 1848. Steam, electricity, and the self-acting mule were revolutionists of a rather more dangerous character than even citizens Barbès, Raspail and Blanqui. But, although the atmosphere in which we live, weighs upon every one with a 20,000 lb. force, do you feel it? No more than European society before 1848 felt the revolutionary atmosphere enveloping and pressing it from all sides. There is one great fact, characteristic of this our 19th century, a fact which no party dares deny. On the one hand, there have started into life industrial and scientific forces, which no epoch of the former human history had ever suspected. On the other hand, there exist symptoms of decay, far surpassing the horrors recorded of the latter times of the Roman Empire. In our days, everything seems pregnant with its contrary. Machinery, gifted with the wonderful power of shortening and fructifying human labour, we behold starving and overworking it. The new-fangled sources of wealth, by some strange weird spell, are turned into sources of want. The victories of art seem bought by the loss of character. At the same pace that mankind masters nature, man seems to become enslaved to other men or to his own infamy. Even the pure light of science seems unable to shine but on the dark background of ignorance. All our invention and progress seem to result in endowing material forces with intellectual life, and in stultifying human life into a material force. This antagonism between modern industry and science on the one hand, modern misery and dissolution on the other hand; this antagonism between the productive powers and the social relations of our epoch is a fact, palpable, overwhelming, and not to be controverted. Some parties may wail over it; others may wish to get rid of modern arts, in order to get rid of modern conflicts. Or they may imagine that so signal a progress in industry wants to be completed by as signal a regress in politics. On our part, we do not mistake the shape of the shrewd spirit that continues to mark all these contradictions. We know that to work well the new-fangled forces of society, they only want to be mastered by new-fangled men—and such are the working men. They are as much the invention of modern time as machinery itself. In the signs that bewilder the middle class, the aristocracy and the poor prophets of regression, we do recognise our brave friend, Robin Goodfellow,[a] the old mole that can work in the earth so fast, that worthy pioneer—the Revolution. The English working men are the first-born sons of modern industry. They will then, certainly, not be the last in aiding the social revolution produced by that industry, a revolution, which means the emancipation of their own class all over the world, which is as universal as capital-rule and wages-slavery. I know the heroic struggles the English working class have gone through since the middle of the last century—struggles less glorious, because they are shrouded in obscurity, and burked by the middle-class historian. To revenge the misdeeds of the ruling class, there existed in the middle ages, in Germany, a secret tribunal, called the "Vehmgericht."[b] If a red cross was seen marked on a house, people knew that its owner was doomed by the "Vehm." All the houses of Europe are now marked with the mysterious red cross. History is the judge—its executioner, the proletarian.

First published in *The People's Paper*, No. 207, April 19, 1856

Reproduced from the newspaper

---

[a] A character in Shakespeare's *A Midsummer Night's Dream*.—*Ed.*

[b] The *Vehmgericht*, derived from *Vehme* (judgment, punishment) and *Gericht* (court), was a secret tribunal which exercised great power in Westphalia from the end of the twelfth to the middle of the sixteenth century.—*Ed.*

Karl Marx

PRUSSIA[436]

The strange frenzy which has converted France into a gambling-house, and identified the Napoleonic Empire with the Bourse, has by no means been confined within Gallic boundaries. That plague, unrestrained by political frontiers, has crossed the Pyrenees, the Alps, and the Rhine, and, wonderful to say, has seized upon solid Germany, where speculation in ideas has given way to speculation in stocks, the *summum bonum*[a] to the bonus, the mysterious jargon of dialectics to the no less mysterious jargon of the Exchange, and the aspiration for unity to the passion for dividends. Rhenish Prussia, from its proximity to France, as well as from the high development of its industry and commerce, was the first to catch the disease. Not only did the Cologne bankers enter into a formal alliance with the great swindlers at Paris, by purchasing with them the *Indépendance belge* as their common organ, and establishing an international bank at Luxemburg; not only did they drag into the whirlpool of the Crédit Mobilier[437] all South-Western Germany, but in the limits of Rhenish Prussia and in the Duchy of Westphalia they succeeded so well that at this moment every layer of society, except that formed by the working classes and smaller peasantry, is permeated by the gold mania, so that even the capital of the small middle class, diverted from its customary channels, seeks for wild adventure, and every shopkeeper is turned into an alchemist. That the rest of Prussia has not escaped the contagion will be seen by the following extract from the *Preussische Correspondenz*, a ministerial paper.

---

[a] Supreme good.—*Ed.*

"Observations recently made on the money market justify the assumption that there is again approaching one of those frightful commercial crises which return periodically. The feverish movement of an immoderate spirit of speculation, first prompted abroad, has, since last year, pervaded Germany to a great extent, and not only the Berlin Bourse and the Prussian capitalists have been dragged into this whirlpool, but also whole classes of society, which, at every former time, endeavored to shun any immediate participation in the hazards of the stock market."

On this apprehension of an imminent financial crisis, the Prussian Government grounded its refusal to allow the establishment of a Crédit Mobilier, the dazzling colors of which were suspected to conceal a swindling purpose. But what is not permitted under one form may be allowed in another; and what is not permitted at Berlin will be tolerated at Leipsic and Hanover. The latest phase of the speculative mania has set in at the close of the war,[a] which, apart from the commercial excitement inseparable from any conclusion of peace—as witnessed in 1802 and 1815—is this time marked by the peculiar feature that Prussia has formally expressed her wish to throw open her markets to the importation of western capital and speculation. We shall, accordingly, soon hear of the grand Irkutsk trunk-line with branches to Pekin, and other not less monstrous schemes, the question being not what is really designed for execution, but what fresh material may be offered for the spirit of speculation to feed upon. There was nothing wanting but the peace to hurry the great crash apprehended by the Prussian Government.

This uncommon participation by Prussia in the speculative movement of Europe would have been impossible but for the great strides made by its industry of late years. The capital invested in railways alone has been increased from 19,000,000 to 154,000,000 Prussian thalers, in the interval from 1840 to 1854-55. Other railroads at an estimated cost of 54,000,000, are in progress; and the Government have further authorized the construction of new lines at a cost of 57,000,000. Eighty-seven joint-stock companies, with a capital of 83,000,000, have sprung into life since 1849. From 1854-56, nine insurance companies, with a capital of 22,000,000, have been registered. In these last two years, likewise, six joint-stock companies, with a capital of 10,500,000, have commenced to run spinning-mills. From the Cotton Report it will be seen that the quantity of cotton received by the different ports of Europe, has, from 1853-56, varied in the

[a] The Crimean war (1853-56).—*Ed.*

following proportions, according to the return of the first seven months of the year the export of bales being as follows:

	1853	1854	1855	1856
To England	1,100,000	840,000	963,000	1,131,000
France	255,000	229,000	249,000	354,000
Other European ports	204,000	179,000	167,000	346,000

Hence it follows that the Continent, which in 1853 received only about one third of the cotton exported to England, received in 1856 as much as five eighths of it. To this must be added the cotton reshipped by England to the Continent. The great export to France is only so in appearance, considerable quantities being transported from Havre to Switzerland, Baden, Frankfort and Antwerp. The development of Continental industry as exhibited by the above figures denotes therefore, above all, the increase of German, and chiefly of Prussian industry. The wealth accumulated by the industrial middle classes of late years, is nearly rivaled by the appreciation of land-owners' profits during the war period of dearth and high price. Horses, cattle, live-stock in general, and not least corn, have kept so high in Germany itself, that the influence of foreign markets has hardly been needed to enable the great landholders to roll in gold. It is wealth—the rapid increase of wealth never before experienced by these two classes—which has furnished the basis for the present speculative murrain in Prussia.

The bursting of the bubble will put the Prussian State to a severe test. The different counter-revolutions it has undergone since 1849 have ended in placing the Government in the power of the narrow class of noble landowners, with respect to whom the King, who has done everything to create their supremacy, now finds himself in the same situation as did Louis XVIII toward the *Chambre introuvable*.[438] Frederick William had never the sense to put up with the dry bureaucratic machinery of Government bequeathed him by his father. He has all his life been dreaming of beautifying the Prussian State edifice by some romantico-gothic decoration. The short experience which he has had of his *Herrenhaus*,[a] however, must have satisfied him that in reality the landocracy or *Krautjunkers*, as they are called in Prussia, so far from deeming themselves happy in serving as a mediaeval ornament to the bureaucracy, are striving with all their might to degrade the bureaucracy and make it the simple executor of their class-interests. Hence the split between the Junkers and the

[a] The First Chamber of the Prussian Diet.—*Ed.*

Administration; between the King and the Prince of Prussia.[a] To show the Government how much they are in earnest, they have just refused to renew the grant of an additional tax which had been levied during the war—a thing unheard of in constitutional Prussia. They have coolly and deliberately proclaimed the doctrine that they are as much kings over their little estates as the King himself is over the country at large. They insist that the Constitution, while it is to remain a sham for all other classes, must be a reality for themselves. Emancipating themselves from all control of the bureaucracy, they wish to see it weigh with double force on the classes below.

The middle class, who betrayed the revolution of 1848, have now the satisfaction, even while they are accomplishing their social triumph by the unrestrained accumulation of capital, of seeing themselves politically annihilated. Moreover, the *Krautjunkers* delight in every day finding fresh occasions to make them feel their humiliation, even setting aside the common laws of etiquette. When the middle-class spokesmen get up in the House of Deputies, the Junkers leave their benches *en masse*, and when requested at least to listen to opinions contrary to their own, they laugh in the faces of the gentlemen of the Left. When the latter complain of the obstructions put in the way of elections, they are informed that it is simply the duty of the Government to protect the masses from seduction. When they contrast the licentiousness of the aristocratic, with the shackled condition of the liberal press, they are reminded that liberty in a Christian State is not to do as one pleases, but as pleases God and the authorities. One day they are given to understand that "honor" is the monopoly of an aristocracy; the next day they are stung to the quick by a practical illustration of the exploded theories of a Haller, a de Bonald and a de Maistre. Proud of his philosophical enlightenment, the Prussian citizen has the mortification of seeing the first scientific men driven from the universities, education handed over to a gang of obscurants, ecclesiastical courts meddling with his family concerns, and the police taking him to church on a Sunday. Not content with exempting themselves from taxes so far as they could, the Junkers have packed the middle class in guilds and corporations, adulterated their municipal institutions, abolished the independence and immovability of their Judges, cancelled the religious equality of the different sects, and so forth. If at times their choking anger breaks through their fears, if they occasionally muster enough

[a] William.—*Ed.*

courage to threaten, from their seats in the Chamber, the Junkers with a coming revolution, they are sneeringly answered that the revolution has as heavy an account to settle with them as with the nobility.

Indeed, the higher middle class is not likely to find itself again, as in 1848, at the head of a Prussian revolution. The peasantry in Eastern Prussia have lost not only all that the revolution of 1848 had brought them in the shape of emancipation, but have been reduced once more, both administratively and judicially, under the direct yoke of the nobility. In Rhenish Prussia, by the attraction of capital toward industrial enterprise, they have sunk deeper into the bondage of the mortgagee, at the same rate at which the interest on loans has risen. While in Austria something, at least, has been done to conciliate the peasantry, in Prussia nothing has been left undone to exasperate them. As to the working classes, the Government has prevented them from participating in the profits of their masters by punishing them for strikes, and has systematically excluded them from taking part in political affairs. A disunited dynasty, a Government broken up into hostile camps, the bureaucracy quarreling with the aristocracy, the aristocracy with the middle class—a general commercial crisis, and the disinherited classes brooding in the spirit of rebellion against all the upper layers of society: such is the aspect of Prussia at this hour.

Written on April 15, 1856

First published in the *New-York Daily Tribune*, No. 4694, May 5, 1856 as a leading article

Reproduced from the newspaper

Karl Marx

THE HOUSE OF LORDS AND THE DUKE OF YORK'S MONUMENT[439]

At the very time that Lord John *Russell*

"The minimus of hind'ring knot-grass made,"[a]

amused the House of Commons with one of his dwarfish mock-schemes for the education of that giant called the people, his fellows in the House of Lords were exhibiting a practical specimen of the education enjoyed by the heaven-born rulers of Great Britain. The subject of their debates was a report of the Committee of the House of Commons, recommending for local purposes, the removal of the Duke of York's monument from Waterloo Place.[b] On that occasion the Marquis of *Clanricarde* said,

"The Duke of *York* was not only eminent from his illustrious birth, but he had performed great professional services to the Crown and the country.... The regret for his death was not confined merely to the circle of his friends, but was universally felt. All parties concurred in bearing testimony to the zeal which he had displayed in the discharge of the duties committed to him."[c]

According to the Marquis of Lansdowne

"a memorial erected some years ago to the memory of an illustrious individual whom they all respected, should not be lightly disposed of or set away."

Aberdeen, the travelled Thane, called the monument "in a certain manner *sanctified*." The Earl of Malmesbury

"concurred entirely in what had fallen from the noble earl with respect to what might be called the sentimental view of the case."

---

[a] Shakespeare, *A Midsummer Night's Dream*, Act III, Scene 2.—*Ed.*

[b] A road was to be built across St. James's Park.—*Ed.*

[c] The speeches of Clanricarde, Lansdowne, Aberdeen and Malmesbury in the House of Lords on April 10, 1856 were reported in *The Times*, No. 22339, April 11, 1856.—*Ed.*

Let us cast a retrospective view at the life of the royal hero thus canonized by the Lords.

The most memorable event in the Duke of York's lifetime—his birth—happened to occur in 1763. Twenty-six years later he contrived to draw the attention of the world to his person by renouncing the state of single blessedness, and getting a married man. The Anti-Jacobin war afforded the royal prince an opportunity of becoming a royal captain. If, during his ever-famed campaign of Flanders, and his no less famed campaign of the Helder, the English army was regularly beaten, it had the constant satisfaction of beholding its royal commander returning to his home again in a whole skin. It is known how cleverly he ran away before Houchard at Hondscho, and how his siege of Dunkirk in some sort outjested the siege of Troy.[440] Such was the distinguished celebrity he won in his Flanders campaigning that Pitt, growing jealous of his renown, caused the war-minister Dundas, to send despatches to his Royal Highness with the urgent intimation to come home, to reserve the display of his personal bravery to times of greater hazard, and to remember the old Fabian maxim: *famae etiam jactura facienda est pro patria.*[a] An officer of the name of Cochrane Johnstone, to whom by and by we shall return, was the person selected to be the bearer of these despatches and—says an author of those bygone times—

"Johnstone performed this service with a degree of celerity and resolution that entitled him to the admiration of the army."[b]

Greater still than the Duke's military exploits during this same campaign, turned out his financial ones, a convenient fire at every depot, settling for ever the accounts of all his commissaries, contractors, and in-supers. These successes notwithstanding, we find his Royal Highness again in 1799 at the head of the Helder expedition which, in the British papers under Pitt's avowed patronage, was represented as a mere holiday march, it being thought a rather preposterous idea that an army of 45,000 men, with the squadron commanding the Zuyder Zee at its back, with an offspring of the royal house of Brunswick at its head, was not by its mere appearance to scatter to the winds a rabble of about 20,000 Frenchmen,

"commanded by a printer's boy of Limousin, one Brune, who had received his military and political education in the Tennis Courts of the French Revolution."

---

[a] Even glory should be sacrificed for the Fatherland.—*Ed.*

[b] [W. Cobbett,] "Mr. Cochrane Johnstone" [I], *Cobbett's Weekly Political Register,* Vol. X, No. 1, July 5, 1806.—*Ed.*

However, with that blunt cynicism peculiar to those Jacobin generals, the printer's boy of Limousin had the impudence to beat his Royal Highness hollow, whenever he happened to board him, and when his Royal Highness, considering it still more meritorious to live for one's country than to die for it, strove to get back to the Helder, Brune was so discourteous as not to let him before he had signed the famous capitulation of Alkmaar,[441] stipulating the surrender of eight thousand French and Dutch seamen then prisoners of war in England.

The Duke of York had now had enough in the shape of campaigns, and wisely condescended for a while to shroud his name in the obscurity naturally enveloping the commander-in-chief at the Horse-Guards.[a] Yet in that position he found himself placed over a department costing the nation £23,000,000 a year, and entrusting to him, under the King's sole control, the absolute power of promoting or cashiering any number of about 12,000 commissioned and staff officers.

His Royal Highness did not fail to engross a very large portion of public gratitude by his enlightened general orders regarding the cashiering the *queues* of all the privates and non-commissioned officers; the addition of a sponge to their appointments, for the purpose of keeping their heads clean, the dressing right and left, the quick and slow step; the locking up and the opening of ranks, the wheeling and facing, the tossing of the firelock, the hair-cutting and the black-legging, and the polishing of arms and accoutrements; the screwing up of John Bull's broad chest in tight jerkins, and the crowning his blockhead with an Austrian cap, and the covering his large back with a faceless coat—and all that sort of important affairs, making up the drill-serjeant's science. At the same time he exhibited the higher qualities of a strategist and a tactician in his domestic campaign against Colonel Cochrane Johnstone, the officer who had been commissioned by Pitt to cut short his victorious campaigns in Flanders. Johnstone, in the year 1801, Colonel of the 8th West India regiment (blacks) and Governor of the island of Dominica, was called home in consequence of a mutiny that had broken out in the regiment. He preferred charges against John Gordon, the major of his regiment, who was in immediate command of it at the time of the mutiny. This Major Gordon, as well as a Colonel Gordon, the Duke's secretary, belonged to that distinguished family that has stocked the world with great men—such as Gordon, the Ad-

[a] I.e., the headquarters of the British army.—*Ed.*

rianople treaty-monger,[442] the travelled Thane Aberdeen, and his no less illustrious son, Colonel Gordon, of Crimean memory. The Duke of York, then, had to wreak his vengeance, not only on a slanderer of the Gordons, but above all on the bearer of the delicate despatch. Notwithstanding Colonel Johnstone's importunities, John Gordon was not brought to a court-martial till the month of January 1804. Although the court pronounced his conduct to have been irregular, culpably negligent, and highly censurable, the Duke of York maintained him in full possession of his rank and pay, while he omitted from a promotion of brevet-major-generals in Oct. 1803, the name of Colonel Johnstone, who saw the names of officers, his juniors, preferred to him. On his complaints to the Duke, Johnstone, at the end of nine weeks, on Dec. 10, 1803, received the answer from his Royal Highness that he was not included in the general brevet-promotion because

"there existed charges against him, the merit of which had not been decided."[a]

He failed to obtain any further satisfaction until 28th of May, 1804, when he became informed that Major Gordon was his accuser. His trial was put off from one term to the other; the court-martial which was to try him being ordered now to Canterbury, now to Chelsea, and it only took place in March 1805. Johnstone being fully and honourably acquitted by the court, applied for restoration to his rank, but met with a refusal from his Royal Highness on May 16, 1805. On June 28th General Fitzpatrick, one of the Fox *coterie*,[443] announced in Parliament that in the interest of Johnstone, the injuries inflicted upon whom "had spread the greatest alarm throughout the whole army," he should propose a specific proceeding at the commencement of the next session of parliament.[b] The next session came, but having in the meantime been transformed into a war-minister, Fitzpatrick stated from the Treasury-bench that he should not bring forward the threatened motion. Some time afterwards this Secretary of war—a carpet-knight who had never seen an enemy, who had sold his company in the guards twenty years before, and never served a single day since—had a regiment given to him by the Duke of York; Fitzpatrick, the war-minister, having thus to audit the account of Fitzpatrick the Colonel. By dint of such stratagems

[a] [W. Cobbett,] "Mr. Cochrane Johnstone" [I], *Cobbett's Weekly Political Register*, Vol. X, No. 1, July 5, 1806.—*Ed.*

[b] Fitzpatrick's speech in the House of Commons, June 28, 1805. *Hansard's Parliamentary Debates* [First Series], Vol. V, London, 1812.—*Ed.*

the Duke of York succeeded in crushing Colonel Johnstone and thus asserted his strategical talents.

That notwithstanding a certain dullness, hereditary in the illustrious house of Brunswick, the Duke was a sharp fellow in his own way, is sufficiently shown by the fact that he figured as the chief of George III's "domestic cabinet," the closet and family-council, and as the head of the court-party, called the King's friends.[444] It is not less shown by the fact that, with an annual income of £61,000 he contrived to squeeze £54,000 as a loan out of the ministry, and in spite of this public credit not to pay his private debts. To perform such feats, a man must needs be of nimble spirits. As it is generally known how "upon place and greatness many eyes are stuck,"[a] it will be easily understood that the Grenville Administration was not ashamed to propose to his Royal Highness to relieve him from some subordinate duties of his office—which relief, as is complained in a pamphlet paid by the duke,[b] would have reduced the commander-in-chief to a mere cipher. Lansdowne, be it remarked, served in the same cabinet, under the name of Lord Henry Petty. That same administration threatened to clog the illustrious warrior with a military council, falsely pretending that "the nation" would be lost, unless the inexperience of the commander-in-chief was assisted by a body of officers. Thus far was the duke pressed by this unworthy cabal as to demand an inquiry into his conduct at the Horse Guards. Happily this intrigue of the Grenville party was defeated by the immediate interposition, or rather command, of George III who, although a notorious idiot, had wit enough to understand the genius of his son.

In the year 1808 the brave and patriotic sentiments of the royal captain induced him to solicit the command of the British armies in Spain and Portugal, but then the general dread of the masses to behold England bereft of such a home-commander, at so critical a moment, burst out in most noisy, indiscreet, and almost indecent demonstrations. He was warned to remember his former ill-fortune abroad, to keep him in reserve for the enemy at home, and to beware of public execration. Nothing daunted, the magnanimous duke had a pamphlet published, to prove his hereditary claim to be beaten in Portugal and Spain, as he had

---

[a] Shakespeare, *Measure for Measure*, Act IV, Scene 2 (paraphrased).—*Ed.*

[b] This refers to the anonymous pamphlet, *A Plain Statement of the Conduct of the Ministry and the Opposition, towards His Royal Highness the Duke of York*, London, 1808.—*Ed.*

been in Flanders and Holland. But, alas! the *Morning Chronicle* of that period states that,

"in the present instance it is notorious that ministers and people, ins and outs, are fully agreed in opinion."

Yea, the talked-of appointment of the duke seemed to threaten England with a regular row. Thus, one may read in a London weekly paper of that time:—

"Not to the inns, the coffee-houses, the marts, the malls, and the settled gossiping-shops, has the conversation upon the subject been confined. It has entered into all private circles; it has been a standing dish at the dinner and tea-table; men stop each other to talk about the Duke of York's going to Spain; the eager Londoner stops even on his way to Change, to ask whether it be really true that the Duke of York is going to Spain; nay, in the very church porches of the country, among the smock frocked politicians, whose conversation as to the public matters seldom went beyond the assessed taxes, you see half a score faces thrust almost to the point of contact, in order to know for 'zarten if the Duke of York be a gooen to be zent to Spain.'"[a]

It is evident, then, in spite of the numerous efforts of his envious deprecators, that it was impossible to keep the past deeds of the Duke hidden from the world. What a satisfaction for one single man, this unanimous anxiety of a whole people to keep him at home. The Duke, of course, could not but give his gallant mind the extreme pain of chilling his martial ardour, and quietly staying at the Horse Guards.

Before passing to the brightest period of this monumental life, we must stop a moment and show that as early as 1806, the Duke was fully and publicly appraised by his father's loyal subjects. In his *Political Register* of that year, Cobbett says:

"He rendered himself famous for nothing but running away, and bringing infamy upon the arms of England [...]; [...] at once half an idiot, and yet master of the utmost degree of low cunning; [...] equally conspicuous for feminine weakness and fiendlike cruelty, for pride and for abjection, for prodigality and rapaciousness. [...] While he had the command of the soldiers, he made a vile job of his trust, and, through the means thereof, shamefully robbed the people whom he was amply paid to defend. [...] Having previously bribed or intimidated every one, from whom he might apprehend exposure, he gave way to his numerous and conflicting vices, and rendered himself the object of universal, though whispering, execration."[b]

[a] [W. Cobbett,] "Duke of York", *Cobbett's Weekly Political Register,* Vol. XIV, No. 8, August 20, 1808.—*Ed.*

[b] [W. Cobbett,] "Mr. Cochrane Johnstone" [II], *Cobbett's Weekly Political Register,* Vol. X, No. 8, August 23, 1806.—*Ed.*

On the 27th January, 1809, Colonel Wardle rose in the House of Commons, to make a motion "for the appointment of a Committee to inquire into the conduct of the Commander-in-chief, with regard to promotions and exchanges in the army."[a] In a speech lacking all sense of delicacy, detailing all the cases he had to bring forward in support of his motion, and giving the names of all the witnesses he was to call upon for substantiating his cases, he accused the pet hero of the present House of Lords that his concubine, a certain Mrs. Clarke, possessed the power of military promotion, that the military exchanges also were at her disposal, that her influence extended to appointments in the staff of the army, that she was endowed with the privilege of augmenting the military force of the country, that she received pecuniary consideration from all these sources, that the Commander-in-chief was not only a secret party to all her transactions, did not only save his own purse by her supplies, but had even endeavoured to derive himself, through her means, pecuniary accommodations, independently of Mrs. Clarke's advantages. In one word, he contended that the royal captain not only kept his mistress at the expense of the British army, but allowed himself to be kept by her in return. Upon this motion the house resolved[b] to have an examination of the witnesses at the bar. The examination having lasted to the 22nd Feb., confirmed point for point the ungracious slander of Colonel Wardle. It was proved that the real office of the Horse Guards did not exist at Whitehall[c] but at Mrs. Clarke's establishment in Gloucester Street, consisting of a splendid house, with a variety of carriages, and a long retinue of footmen, musicians, singers, players, dancers, parasites, pimps, and bawds. This Horse Guard of his own, the Royal captain had mounted in 1803. Although such a house could not be maintained for £20,000 a year—and there was besides a country establishment at Wybridge—it was proved from the witnesses' evidence that Mrs. Clarke never got from the duke's own pocket, more than £12,000 a year, a sum scarcely sufficient to pay wages and purchase liveries. The rest was procured from the wholesale traffic in petticoat commissions. There was produced before the House a

---

[a] *Hansard's Parliamentary Debates* [First Series], Vol. XII, London, 1812. This volume also contains material of the House of Commons inquiry proposed by Wardle and held in February 1809. Excerpts from it are quoted below in this article.—*Ed.*

[b] On January 31, 1809.—*Ed.*

[c] The seat of a number of government offices in London, including the army headquarters, the Admiralty and various ministries.—*Ed.*

written scale of Mrs. Clarke's prices. The regular price for a majority being £2,600, Mrs. Clarke sold it at 900; a company for £700, instead of the regulation price of £1,500, etc. Nay there existed actually in the city, a public office for the sale of Commissions at the same reduced prices, and the managing agents of that office stated to be the commissioners of the favourite mistress. Whenever she complained of pecuniary embarrassments, the duke told her "she had greater interest than the queen, and she ought to use it." In one case the zealous commander-in-chief punished an individual by reducing him to half-pay for non-performance of a nefarious contract with his mistress; in another he reserved to himself a bonus of £5,000; in another case, he appointed on her interference boys actually at school to lieutenancies, and surgeons who were never called upon to leave their shops to join their companies. One Colonel French obtained from Mrs. Clarke a letter of service, *i.e.* an authority for raising 5,000 men for the army. On this occasion the following dialogue between the Duke and his mistress was stated before the house to have taken place.

> *The Duke.*—I am continually worried by Mr. French about this levy. He is always wanting something more to be done in his favour. [...] How does he behave to you darling?
>
> *Mrs. Clarke.*—Middling, not very well.
>
> *The Duke.*—Master French must mind what he is about, else I will soon cut up him and his levy too.

There were also produced some love letters of the illustrious duke mixed up with mercantile-military transactions. One of them dated Aug. 4, 1803 commences thus.

> "How can I sufficiently express to my sweetest, my darling love, the delight which her dear, her pretty letter gave me, or how much I feel all the kind things she says to me in it; millions and millions of thanks for it my angel."

After this sample of the Duke's style it is not to be wondered at that the learned gentlemen of St. John's College, Oxford, presented his Royal Highness with the diploma of an L.L.D. Not content with military commission, the lovers also hit upon trafficking in bishoprics and deaneries.

Other points turned up not less honourable to the illustrious scion of the House of Brunswick; for instance that an officer, named Dowler, had for years been Mrs. Clarke's paramour, and that in his company she sought for a compensation for the grudgery, the disgust, and loathing experienced in the duke's society.

The Duke's friends scolding his angel "an infamous woman, an impudent baggage,"[a] pleaded for their tender juvenile of about 50, for the husband of twenty years' standing, the paramount power of passion. Which passion, by the by, did not prevent the duke, 7 months after his separation from Mrs. Clarke, withholding from her the annuity convened between them, and on her demands becoming urgent, threatening her with the pillory and the bastile. This very threat became the next cause of Mrs. Clarke's disclosures to Colonel Wardle.

It would be tedious to wade through the whole proceedings of the Commons, with all its sordid incidents, or to expostulate on the gallant duke's begging letter dated 23rd February (1809) in which he solemnly declared, to the House of Commons "on the honour of a prince," that he knew of nothing, even of what was proved by letters in his own handwriting. It may suffice to say that General Ferguson declared in the House "that it was not for the honour of the army that the duke should remain in command;" that the Chancellor of Exchequer, Mr. Perceval, announced on March 20th, the Duke's resignation of his office, and that upon this announcement the House accepted Lord Althorp's motion that "his Royal Highness the Duke of York, having resigned the command of the army, the House did not now think it necessary to proceed any further," etc. Lord Althorp grounded his motion on his wish

> "to place the duke's resignation on the journal of the House, in order to record that the Duke had forfeited the confidence of the country for ever, and in consequence he must abandon all hopes of ever returning again to that situation."

As a tribute for his bold proceedings against the duke, Colonel Wardle was deluged with thanks—addresses transmitted from every county, city, town and borough of Great Britain.

One of the first acts of the Regency of the Prince of Wales—afterwards George the Fourth—in 1811, was York's restoration to his position as commander-in-chief—an initiatory step quite in keeping with the whole reign of that royal Caliban[b] who, because the last of mankind, was called the first gentleman of Europe.

---

[a] From Beresford's speech in the House of Commons on February 3, 1809. Excerpts from it and also from the speeches of Ferguson on March 17, 1809 and Perceval and Althorp on March 20, 1809 are quoted according to *Hansard's Parliamentary Debates* [First Series], Vols. XII and XIII, London, 1812.—*Ed.*

[b] A character in Shakespeare's *The Tempest.*—*Ed.*

This Duke of York, then, whose monument would grace a dung-hill, is the Marquis of Clanricarde's "eminent commander-in-chief," Lord Lansdowne's "illustrious and all-respected individual;" and the very same personage represented by the Earl of Aberdeen's "sanctified monument"—in one word the guardian angel of the House of Lords. The worshippers are worthy of the saint.

Written about April 25, 1856

First published in *The People's Paper*, No. 208, April 26, 1856

Reproduced from the newspaper

The Free Press.

Karl Marx

TO THE EDITOR[a] OF *THE FREE PRESS*

Sir,—I have the honour to enclose a copy of a paper[b] which you may perhaps think proper to communicate to your readers.

Your obedient Servant,

Dr. Karl Marx

London, 26th April,
28, Dean street, Soho

Written on April 26, 1856

First published in *The Free Press* and *The Sheffield Free Press*, May 3, 1856

Reproduced from *The Free Press*

[a] G. Crawshay.—*Ed.*

[b] See this volume, pp. 673-80.—*Ed.*

Karl Marx

KARS PAPERS CURIOSITIES[445]

1. *Falsification.*—In a telegraphic despatch dated Constantinople, July 12, 1855, Lord Redcliffe summons the Foreign Office, "in order to save much valuable time," to send "by telegraph" its decision as to the Mingrelian expedition which the Porte had proposed to undertake with the Anglo-Turkish contingent, under General Vivian's command. In No. 249 of the Blue Book,[a] we find Lord Clarendon's answer, a despatch dated "London, July 14, 1855," bearing on its frontispiece the sacramental word "telegraphic," rejecting the Porte's proposal, and inviting the Turkish army to fall back from Kars and Erzeroum on Trebizond. Lord Redcliffe's telegraphic question being dated Constantinople, July 12th, and Lord Clarendon's telegraphic answer, London, July 14th, it appears that to run between Constantinople and London a telegraphic message wants at the most, two days. Accordingly, Lord Clarendon's telegraphic despatch, dated London, July 14th, should have reached Constantinople on July 16. However, in a despatch dated July 19th, Lord Redcliffe complains of the silence of his Government which he had entreated "to lose no time in making known his pleasure." From Lord Redcliffe's later despatch dated July 23rd, it results that he had received no answer even then. In fact, the receipt of any answer from the Foreign Office, is not acknowledged before July 30th. (See No. 277.) One is thus reduced to the dilemma either that the way from London to Constantinople is about seven times longer than the way from Constantinople to London, or that

[a] *Papers Relative to Military Affairs in Asiatic Turkey, and the Defence and Capitulation of Kars,* London, 1856.—*Ed.*

the London date of Lord Clarendon's despatch, as given in the Blue Book, is *false.* The delay in Lord Clarendon's answer caused time of precious value to be wasted. The falsification of the Blue Book date of that answer would denote, that delay was intended. To conceal that intention, a spurious date had to be prefixed to the despatch, instead of the true one.

2. *Suppression.*—I do not allude to the numerous mutilations pointed at in the Blue Book under the convenient term of "Extract"; nor to the total suppression of the whole correspondence between General Beatson and the British Government, but rather to a telegraphic despatch sent from Sebastopol, on July 14, 1855, and received in London on July 16, 1855. On July 14th, in a conference held at the English head-quarters with the Allied Commanders-in-Chief and the Admirals, Omer Pasha proposed to make an incursion from Redout Kaleh, *via* Kutais, into Georgia, at the head of that part of the Turkish army then

> "at Balaklava or at Kertch—25,000 infantry, 3000 cavalry from Eupatoria, and a proportional artillery."

The allied commanders, refusing to give any opinion on the subject—(see [Lieut.-]Colonel Simmons' despatch to Clarendon, dated July 15)—Omer Pasha broke up the conference by declaring that "under these circumstances, he felt it his duty to proceed to Constantinople;" and so he did. *On the very same day* when Omer Pasha left the Crimea—on July 16th—Lord Clarendon, according to the Blue Book, wrote a despatch to Lord Redcliffe, stating that

> "we" (the Government) "understand that Omer Pasha *is about to proceed to Constantinople.*"

This intelligence Lord Clarendon could only have derived from a telegraphic despatch dated Balaklava, July 14. Where is this despatch? Certainly, not in the Blue Book. The same electric wire which informed Lord Clarendon of Omer Pasha's intended departure, must have informed him of the cause of that departure, viz., the resistance he met with on the part of Pélissier, *i.e.*, on the part of the French Government. Thus the question would naturally arise why Lord Clarendon quietly waited from July 16th to August 1st, a fact shown by the Blue Book, to break the matter to the French Government, and to commence negotiations with it, on a point on which the whole campaign depended. To prevent this question, the telegraphic despatch has disappeared.

3. *Fraud*.—In Lord Clarendon's above-mentioned despatch to Lord Redcliffe, dated July 16th, the following passage occurs:

> "Her Majesty's[a] Government would still recommend that whatever force is sent for the relief of the army of Kars, should proceed to Trebizond. If, indeed, *Omer Pasha* [...] should determine to take *any part of his own army*, with Tunisians and Albanians, to Redout Kaleh, her Majesty's Government would have *nothing to say to that proceeding*."

Now, Omer Pasha having just determined to take a certain part of his own army to Redout Kaleh, the unconditional sanction given to such a plan, in Lord Clarendon's despatch, must have removed all difficulties; or, if new ones arose, at all events prove them to have not originated with the British Government. Unfortunately, this despatch, dated London, July 16th, figures only in the Blue Book, was written only for the Blue Book, and has never left the shelves of the Foreign Office. No trace of its ever having reached Constantinople is to be discovered. On the contrary, it results from Lord Redcliffe's despatch, dated Constantinople, July 30th, that he had not received it on that date, when he complained of "the most serious dilemma" in which "the unfavourable judgment passed by her Majesty's Government" on the Turkish plans had placed the Porte. Nor had Lord Clarendon's despatch, dated July 16th, arrived on July 31st, when Fuad Effendi, in a letter to Lord Redcliffe, defended the plan of a Mingrelian expedition against "the substance of the English despatches," according to which "the succours *must* be sent through Erzeroum by way of Trebizond." Nor had it arrived on August 4th, when Lord Redcliffe, in answer to Fuad Effendi, told him that

> "when latterly called upon to declare the opinions of his Government, he performed that duty with the painful sense of the embarrassments which surrounded the Porte,"

increased as they would be by the opinion "he was called upon to declare;" and added,

> "though her Majesty's Government have declared their decided preference for a more distinct operation by Trebizond and Erzeroum, their objections to a diversion on the side of Circassia, would in all likelihood be modified, if the force employed were of a compact or reliable character."

Lord Redcliffe was, then, on Aug. 4th, not possessed of Lord Clarendon's despatch dated July 16th, in which her Majesty's Government *had* already *modified* its objections to a diversion on the side of Circassia, "*if*" Omer Pasha himself should undertake it

---

[a] Queen Victoria's.—*Ed.*

with "any part of his own army." On August 8th, Lord Redcliffe was *not yet* blessed with the mysterious despatch, as we find him again complaining to Lord Clarendon—(see No. 282 and enclosures)—that the British Government "still *leans* with all its weight to Trebizond, as the *only* true channel of relief;" and bewailing his own ambiguous position.

"Amidst so many motives," says he, "to vigorous support of *the only practicable scheme of relief*, I made no reserve in communicating the *adverse* opinions of her Majesty's Government to the Porte."

Yea, still, on *August 13th*, Lord Redcliffe did not even suspect the existence of the London despatch, dated July 16th, as he informs Lord Clarendon that "the disappointment occasioned by the terms of *the preceding despatch*"—according to the Blue Book, the despatch dated July 16th, should have been *the preceding* despatch—"which appeared to favour *exclusively* an advance upon Kars by Trebizond, was evident." Now, however Blue Book time and space may be allowed to differ from common time and space, nobody will venture to believe that the despatch leaving London on July 16th, should not have reached Constantinople on August 13th. But that Lord Clarendon's despatch, dated London, July 16th, has actually *never left London*, and was *never* intended to do so, results from a despatch of his own, dated London, 20th August. In this despatch (No. 283), purporting to answer Lord Redcliffe's complaints, dated August 8th, Lord Clarendon endeavours to show that her Majesty's Government, in *different* previous despatches had renounced its resistance to the Porte's proposal, and

"were willing that Omer Pasha should proceed to Asia to effect a diversion for the relief of Kars."

But, strange to say, while the various messages which the noble lord refers to, in proof of his assertion, have left no trace whatever in the Kars papers, his despatch, dated July 16th, so ostentatiously paraded in the Blue Book, is most discreetly ignored in his justification to Lord Redcliffe. Thus, while baffling every Turkish attempt for the relief of Kars, the British Foreign Office was carefully preparing its *pièces justificatives* for the fall of Kars.

4. *Forgery and Shuffle.*—According to Lord Redcliffe's despatch, addressed to the Foreign Office, and dated Constantinople, July 23rd,

"Omer Pasha [...] had proposed [...] to the Porte to make himself an incursion towards Georgia, starting from Redout Kaleh, and turning Kutais to good account."

This idea had been debated on the night of July 22nd, in a council at the Grand Vizier's[a] [...], and the result of the deliberation had been,

> "that the troops to be employed in the above-mentioned manner, under the command of Omer, should be taken from *Eupatoria*, to the amount of 20,000, and from Bulgaria to the amount of 5500, and that the (Anglo-Turkish) contingent, with its numbers completed, should occupy the vacant place at Eupatoria."

Lord Clarendon having received this despatch on August lst, instantly forwarded it to Lord Cowley. Pointing at the just quoted "passage," he states "Her Majesty's Government to be favourably disposed to it," and expresses "his hope that the Government of the Emperor will concur in it." Here, at last, one is forced to acknowledge *bonne foi*[b] zeal and expedition on the part of Lord Palmerston's Cabinet. But, alas! while exhibiting itself as the patron of Omer Pasha's project before the French Government, by a mere shuffling of words, it substituted for the Porte's own proposal one directly hostile to it. This *tour de passe-passe*[c] was played off by the simple substitution in Lord Redcliffe's despatch, dated July 23rd, of the word *Eupatoria*, in the place of the word *Balaklava*.

From the despatch of [Lieut.-]Colonel Simmons, dated July 15th, it will be seen that Omer Pasha, in his *memoranda* to the allied generals, and in the war council at the English headquarters, insisted upon taking with him that part of the Turkish infantry which was then stationed at Balaklava, which he had brought from Eupatoria, and which he declared the only fit one for the Asiatic campaign. Did Omer Pasha, after his arrival at Constantinople, alter his opinion? The contrary is shown by a despatch, dated Constantinople, August 2nd, in which [Lieut.-] Colonel Simmons states:

> "His Highness, Omer Pasha, informed me that he should be happy to give over, to complete the contingent, *any* of the Turkish troops under his command, *except* the division which is now at the camp before Sebastopol, which being composed of his best troops, he is naturally desirous to have with him if he make the proposed movement to Asia."

Will it be asserted that the Porte, at the council of the night of July 22nd, arrived at a resolution contrary to Omer Pasha's proposal? In the very despatch of July 23rd, in which Lord

[a] Ali Mehemet Pasha.—*Ed.*
[b] Honest.—*Ed.*
[c] Trick.—*Ed.*

Redcliffe reports the Porte's resolution, he tells Lord Clarendon that

"Omer Pasha has been most graciously received and most generously rewarded by the Sultan[a];" and adds: "I need not add that he is on excellent terms with His Majesty's ministers, and particularly with the Seraskier Pasha."

Any discrepancy, therefore, between the Porte and its commander-in-chief is out of the question. The false play of Lord Palmerston's cabinet is apparent even from the arrangement of the Blue Book. To confound the reader, Lord Clarendon's despatch to Lord Cowley, dated August lst, figures on page 248, followed up, from 248 to 252, by an extract from Lord Redcliffe's despatch of July 19th, General Simpson's letter to Lord Redcliffe of July 16th, Omer Pasha's letters and memoranda, and only in the last place by Lord Redcliffe's despatch of July 23rd, of which the instruction to Lord Cowley pretends to be the sequel. On August 4th, Lord Clarendon received the acceptance by the French Government of the proposal he had made on August lst, in the name of the Porte, according to which 20,000 men were to be withdrawn from Eupatoria, to be placed under the command of Omer Pasha, and to be replaced at Eupatoria by General Vivian's contingent. On August 13th the Porte is at last informed of the acceptance of its own proposal by its Western Allies. Accordingly, on August 15th the Ottoman council is assembled for deliberation, and what was the result of that deliberation?

"Omer Pasha," writes Lord Redcliffe to Lord Clarendon, dated August 16th (No. 294), "*objects most positively to the plan transmitted from London by telegraph*, of stationing the contingent at *Eupatoria*, and *he is not prepared to assume the responsibility of commanding the expedition*, unless the Turkish troops before Sebastopol be allowed to form part of it."

Thus, then, it oozes out that the Eupatoria plan, pretended to have been forwarded on July 23rd from Constantinople to London, has, on the contrary, been transmitted on August 9th from London to Constantinople.

In the same despatch of Lord Redcliffe is enclosed a memorandum of Omer Pasha. The destruction of the last effective Turkish army, the loss of the unity of the English as well as the Ottoman army, the wilful sacrifice of the Egyptians and Tunisians, the breaking up of the permanent arrangements made for the supply of the Turkish troops at Eupatoria, the creation of unavoidable delay, the ruin of his own military reputation, and the exposure of

[a] Abdul Mejid.—*Ed.*

his Mingrelian army to the fate of the garrison of Kars—such were, according to Omer Pasha, the natural consequences of "the plan trasmitted from London." While communicating to Lord Clarendon this strange protest, Lord Redcliffe evinces not the slightest suspicion of having ever been himself the channel through which the Porte had transmitted that identical plan to Lord Clarendon; a sufficient proof this that the forgery, the interpolation of Eupatoria for Balaklava, was committed at London and not at Constantinople. During the whole month of August and part of September, we behold the Porte struggling against the *spurious* proposition Lord Clarendon had pressed in its own name on the French Government.

5. *Falsehoods.*—Under this head we can, of course, only give a few examples, as the whole Blue Book is sprinkled with them. In answer to Lord Redcliffe's despatch, dated August 8th, Lord Clarendon addressed him a despatch, dated August 20th (No. 283); in which he declares

> "*my various messages by telegraph*, and my despatch of the 4th inst. ... will have shown you that her Majesty's Government ... were willing that Omer Pasha should proceed to Asia," &c.

With the exception of his despatch of July 14th, in which Lord Clarendon protested against the Mingrelian expedition, and summoned the Turks to fall back from Kars and Erzeroum on Trebizond, and of his despatch dated August 9th, which Lord Redcliffe could, of course, not have received on August 8th, Lord Clarendon had, according to the Blue Book, sent no telegraphic despatch at all to Constantinople. He would be sure not to put his own light under a bushel. His *various* messages by telegraph, withdrawing the *veto* of the British Government against the Mingrelian expedition, are only so many lying phantoms.

In a despatch dated August 26th, [Lieut.-]Colonel Simmons informs Lord Clarendon that Omer Pasha reckoned upon taking a portion of the Turkish troops from before Sebastopol, and replacing them by General Vivian's contingent. In his answer to [Lieut.-] Col. Simmons, dated September 7th (No. 302), Lord Clarendon writes:—

> "It appears by a despatch, of a *later date*, from General Simpson, that Omer Pasha had given it as *his opinion* that Gen. Vivian's contingent would not be fit to take a position before Sebastopol, until next spring; and, *in consequence of that opinion*, and by reason of Gen. Simpson's protest against having the contingent sent to him, *which protest was founded upon Omer Pasha's opinion*, her Majesty's Government have determined that the contingent shall not go to join the army before Sebastopol."

Now, from a despatch of [Lieut.-]Col. Simmons, dated September 23rd (No. 307), it may be seen that Omer Pasha's opinion "*of a later date,*" refers to an opinion given by him

> "in a letter to Gen. Simpson, early in the month of July, [...] before he was aware of the critical position of the army in Asia;" and that he had not declared Gen. Vivian's contingent to be unfit "to take up a position before Sebastopol," but only "to make use of it *in the open field* (*en rase campagne*) *in front of the enemy.*"

In excavating at the beginning of September an opinion tendered by Omer Pasha at the beginning of July, in perverting the substance of that opinion, and in founding on this perversion, and that anachronism a protest against Omer Pasha's project, Gen. Simpson, the lucky warrior, would, of course, only have acted up to secret instructions received from London. Supposing Gen. Simpson's despatch to have been exactly, such as it is represented by Lord Clarendon—a fact that becomes rather doubtful from the *suppression* of that despatch in the Blue Book—the noble lord could not have one moment hesitated as to the true date or substance of Omer Pasha's "*opinion.*" He was fully informed of it on July 30, the day when he received [Lieut.-]Col. Simmons's despatch, dated Balaklava, July 15. His quibble then, about Omer Pasha's "inconsistency;" his making Omer Pasha's "own opinion" the reason for rejecting his proposal, were ludicrously false pretences. In point of fact, Lord Palmerston and his subordinates carried to the last their system of bullying the Porte for its want of activity, and baffling all its attempts at action. From the very beginning, we behold them devising—not means for the relief of Kars, but objections to the means devised by the Porte, carefully preparing subjects of dispute, anxiously bent on embroiling matters, huddling imbroglio upon imbroglio in this tragic comedy of errors—all their proceedings tending to one and the same end—to kill time, and thus to ensure the fall of Kars.

Written about April 26, 1856

First published in *The Free Press* and *The Sheffield Free Press,* May 3, 1856

Signed: *Karl Marx*

Reproduced from *The Free Press*

FROM THE PREPARATORY MATERIALS

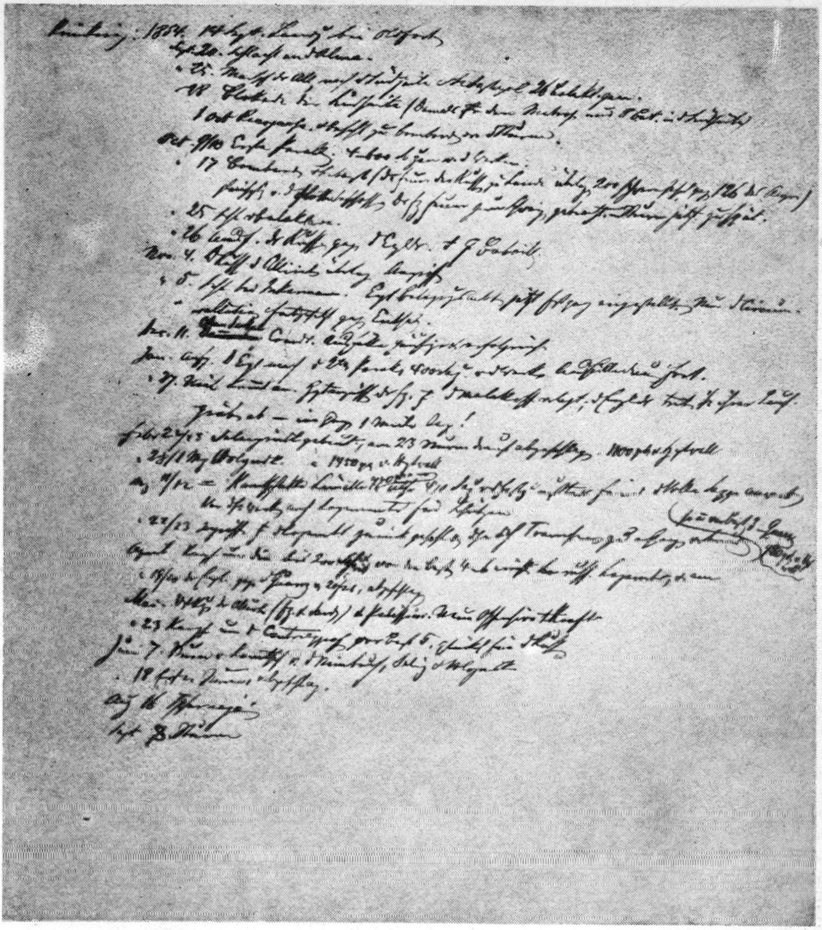

Engels' summary "Crimean War"

Frederick Engels

CRIMEAN WAR[446]

1854

September 14.	Landing at Old Fort [near Eupatoria].
" 20.	Battle of the Alma.
" 25.	Allies march on Sevastopol (south side).
" 26.	Balaklava taken.
" 28.	South side blockaded. (Apart from bluejackets only 8 battalions on the south side at that time.)
October 1.	Reconnaissance; decision taken to bombard prior to the assault.
" 9-10.	First parallel 4-600 *sagenes* in front of the fortifications.
" 17.	Bombardment of Sevastopol (the shelling of the Russians on land is superior, 200 heavy guns against the attackers' 126), simultaneously bombarded by the fleet. French guns silenced.—Now too late for assault.
" 25.	Battle of Balaklava.
" 26.	Russian sortie against British with 9 battalions.
November 4.	Russians superior in strength to Allies. Attack.
" 5.	Battle of Inkerman. Construction of British siege-works now virtually at a standstill. The circumvallation against a relieving force alone going ahead.
December 11.	Osten-Sacken in command. Successful and more frequent sorties.

[1855]

January. Beginning	British construct 2nd parallel 400 *sagenes* in front of the works. Sorties continue.
" 27.	Niel arrives. Main French attack switched to the Malakhov; British abandon half their approach trenches—one mile in all!
February 22-23.	Selenghinsk constructed; assault on it on the 23rd beaten off. 1,100 yards from main rampart.
28 [Feb.]-1 March	Volhynsk constructed, 1,450 yards from main rampart.
March 11-12.	Kamchatka lunette 770 yards, i.e. 470 *sagenes* in front of the fortress the enemy had to use the zigzag sap. Further entrenchments for riflemen in front of this work.
" 22-23.	Attacks on the entrenchments repulsed; these linked by trenches to form a whole; similarly before Bastion 3—Quarry[a] 430 yards from the main rampart.
April	Assault on the entrenchments established by the Russians up to 200 paces before Bastions 4-6, and
" 19-20.	[attack] by the British on the Quarry;
" 20-21.	[both] repulsed.
May	Reinforcement for the Allies (French and Sardinians) and Pélissier. New offensive in strength.
" 23.	Battle for the counterapproaches in front of Bastion 5; fortune favoured Russians.
June 7.	Assault before Kamchatka and the Quarry, Selenghinsk and Volhynsk.
" 18.	First assault, repulsed.
August 16.	Chernaya.
September 8.	Assault.

Written after September 8, 1855

First published in facsimile in: Marx and Engels, *Works*, Second Russian Edition, Vol. 11, Moscow, 1958

Printed according to the manuscript

Published in English for the first time

[a] Here and below the English word is used. Towards the end Engels uses the German equivalent: "Steinbruch".—*Ed.*

APPENDICES

AUSTRIA'S WEAKNESS[447]

The great points of weakness in Austria are usually supposed to be her bankrupt treasury and the revolutionary elements of Italy and Hungary. It is true that in a war with France and England those elements might be employed with great effect against her; but in a war with Russia her vulnerable point lies in another quarter. Though this point was always plain to be seen, and, indeed, has been indicated by Austrian statesmen themselves, we had, during the life of the Emperor Nicholas, no menace to show that he had firmly resolved, in any contingency, to take advantage of it. His successor,[a] however, appears to be less scrupulous, or at any rate less reserved. He has clearly announced to Austria that in the event of her finally joining the Allies he shall put himself officially at the head of the great Slavonic brotherhood, and call to his aid all the slumbering sympathies of race or religion which naturally impel the Slavonians of Austria and Turkey to Russia, as well as all the deep-seated animosities they cherish against the nations and governments that now hold them in more or less complete subjugation.

Panslavism as a political theory has had its most lucid and philosophic expression in the writings of Count Gurowski. But that learned and distinguished publicist, while regarding Russia as the natural pivot around which the destinies of this numerous and vigorous branch of the human family can alone find a large historical development, did not conceive of Panslavism as a league against Europe and European civilization. In his view the legitimate outlet for the expansive force of Slavonic energies was Asia. As compared with the stagnant desolation of that old continent, Russia is a civilizing power, and her contact could not be

[a] Alexander II.—*Ed.*

other than beneficial. This manly and imposing generalization has, however, not been accepted by all the inferior minds which have adopted its fundamental idea. Panslavism has assumed a variety of aspects; and now, at last, we find it employed in a new form, and with great apparent effect, as a warlike threat. As such, its use certainly does credit to the boldness and decision of the new Czar. And how just the fear with which the threat has inspired Austria, we now propose to show.

Of the seventy millions of Slavonians living east of the Bohemian forest and the Karnic Alps, about fifteen millions are subject to the Austrian Emperor, comprising representatives of almost every variety of Slavonic speech. The Bohemian, or Tshekh branch (six millions), falls exclusively in the Austrian dominions; the Polish branch is represented by about three millions of Galicians; the Russian by three millions of Malo-Russians (Red Russians, Ruthenes[448]) in Galicia and the north-east of Hungary—the only Russian tribe out of the pale of the Russian Empire; the South Slavonic branch by about three millions of Slovenes (Carinthians and Croats)[449] and Serbians, including some stray Bulgarians. These Austrian Slavonians are of two different kinds. One part of them consists of the remnants of tribes whose history belongs to the past, and whose present historical development is attached to that of nations of different race and speech; and to complete their unfortunate position, these hapless relics of former greatness have not even a national organization within Austria, but are divided among different provinces. Thus the Slovenes, although scarcely 1,500,000 in number, are spread over the different provinces of Krain, Carinthia, Styria, Croatia, and South-western Hungary. The Bohemians (Tshekhs), though the most numerous tribe of Austrian Slavonians, reside partly in Bohemia, partly in Moravia, and partly (the Slovak branch) in North-western Hungary. These tribes, therefore, though living exclusively on Austrian soil, are far from being recognized as constituting separate nations. They are considered as appendages, either to the German or the Hungarian nation, and in reality they are nothing else.

The second portion of Austrian Slavonians is composed of fragments of different tribes, which, in the course of history, have become separated from the great body of their nation, and which, therefore, have their center of gravity out of Austria. Thus the Poles have their natural center of gravity in Russian-Poland; the Ruthenes in the other Malo-Russian provinces united with Russia; the Serbians in the Serbian principality. That these fragments, torn from their respective nationalities, will continue to gravitate, each toward its natural center, is a matter of course, and becomes more and more evident as civilization, and with it the want of historical, national activity, is spread among them. In either case, the Austrian Slavonians are *disjecta membra*,[a] seeking their reunion either among each other, or with the main body of their separate nationalities.

This is the cause which formerly rendered Panslavism so active in Austria. In order to secure the restoration of each Slavonian nationality, the different tribes of Slavonians in Austria long since began to work for a union of all the Slavonic tribes. The first appearance of Austrian Panslavism was merely literary. Dobrowsky, a Bohemian, the founder of the scientific philology of the Slavonic dialects, and Kollár, a Slovak poet from the Hungarian Carpathians, were its originators. With Dobrowsky it was the enthusiasm of a scientific discoverer; with Kollár, political ideas soon became predominant; but still he ventured to complain only; the greatness of the past, the disgrace, the misfortune and foreign oppression of the present, were the themes of his poetry. The dream of the Panslavic Empire dictating laws to Europe was at that time hardly hinted at.

But the lamenting period soon passed away, and historical research upon the political, literary and linguistic development of the Slavonic race, made great progress. Šafařík, Kopitar and Miklosich as linguists, Palacký as a historian, took the lead, followed by a host of lesser men like Hanka and Gaj. The glorious epochs of Bohemian and Serbian history were glowingly depicted in their contrast to the present degraded and broken state of those nations. While in Germany philosophy formed the pretext under the protection of which the most revolutionary doctrines in politics or theology were propounded, in Austria, and under the very nose of Metternich, historical and philological science was used by the Panslavists as a cloak to teach the doctrine of Slavonic unity, and to create a political party with the unmistakable aim of upsetting Austria, and instituting a vast Slavonian empire in its place.

Austrian Panslavism was destitute of the most essential elements of success. It wanted both force and unity; force, because the Panslavic party consisted of a portion of the educated classes only, had no hold upon the masses, and withal no strength capable of

---

[a] Scattered limbs, dismembered parts—paraphrase of Horace's expression "disjecti membra poetae".—*Ed.*

resisting both the Austrian Government and the German and Hungarian nationalities against which it entered the list; unity, because its uniting principle was a mere ideal one, which, at the very first attempt at realization, was broken up by the fact of diversity of language. Of this diversity, a ludicrous illustration was afforded by the famous Slavonian Congress at Prague, in 1848.[450] There, after various attempts to make out a Slavonic language that should be intelligible to all the members, they were obliged to resort to the tongue most hated by them all—the German.

In fact, so long as the movement was limited to Austria it offered no great danger, but that very center of unity and strength which it wanted, was very soon found for it. The national uprising of the Turkish Serbians, in the beginning of this century,[451] had called the attention of the Russian Government to the fact that there were some seven millions of Slavonians in Turkey, whose speech, of all other Slavonic dialects, most resembled the Russian. Their religion too, and their ecclesiastic language—old Slavonic or Church-Slavonic—were exactly the same as in Russia. It was among these Serbians and Bulgarians that the Czar for the first time began an agitation supported by appeals to his position as the protector of the Eastern Church. It was therefore only natural that as soon as this Panslavist movement in Austria had gained consistency, Russia should extend thither the ramifications of her agencies. Where Roman Catholic Slavonians were met with the religious side of the question was dropped; Russia was merely held up as the proper head of the Slavonic race, and the strong and united people which was to realize the great Slavonic Empire from the Elbe to China, and from the Adriatic to the frozen ocean.

Metternich, in the latter years of his power, very well appreciated the danger and saw through the Russian intrigues. He opposed the movement with all the means in his power. But the only proper means—general freedom of expansion—did not belong to his system of policy. Accordingly, on Metternich's downfall in 1848, the Slavonic movement broke out stronger than ever, and embraced a large proportion of the population. But here its reactionary character at once came to light. While the German, Hungarian and Italian movements were decidedly progressive and revolutionary, the Slavonic party turned to the conservative side. It was the Slavonians that saved Austria from destruction, and enabled Radetzky to advance on the Mincio, and Windischgrätz to conquer Vienna. And to complete the drama, in

1849 the Russian army had to descend into Hungary and settle the war for Austria there.

While thus driven by her own want of vitality to depend on Slavonic aid for her very existence, Austria seized the first moment of security to react against the Slavonians in her own territory. For this purpose she had to adopt a policy at least partially progressive. The special privileges of the Provinces were broken down; a centralized empire took the place of a federal one; and instead of all the different nationalities a fictitious Austrian nationality was created. Though these changes were in some degree against the German, Italian and Hungarian nationalities, they yet fell with far greater weight on the less compact Slavonian tribes, and more especially gave the German element a considerable preponderance.

But the sentiment of race and of attachment to Russia has been strengthened rather than weakened by this process. Austrian Panslavism possesses, perhaps, at this moment a greater latent force than ever. It represents the only element in Austria which was not broken down in the late revolutionary struggle. The Italians, the Hungarians, the Germans even, all came debilitated and discouraged out of that vehement convulsion. The Slavonians alone felt themselves unconquered and unreduced. Is it surprising that Francis Joseph should hesitate before setting on foot a war in which Russia would find millions of devoted and fanatical allies within his own Empire?

Written about April 17, 1855

First published in the *New-York Daily Tribune*, No. 4383, May 7, 1855 as a leading article; reprinted in the *New-York Semi-Weekly Tribune*, No. 1038, May 8, 1855 and the *New-York Weekly Tribune*, No. 713, May 12, 1855

Reproduced from the *New-York Daily Tribune*

PROGRESS OF THE WAR[452]

The news from the war is abundant. We have the official accounts of the cavalry action at Kurulu, near Eupatoria, before reported—the intelligence of an unsuccessful assault of the Russians on Kars, of the destruction by the Allies of Taman and Phanagoria, and of the capture of Kinburn at the mouth of the Dnieper.

The cavalry action near Eupatoria was fought by twelve French squadrons (fourth hussars, sixth and seventh dragoons). According to Gen. d'Allonville's report,[a] which is plain and intelligible, the French and Turks made an extensive reconnaissance toward the interior on three different roads—one to the south and two to the north of Lake Sasik. The two latter columns met at a village called Dolshak, where they discovered the approach of the Russian cavalry. Here the reports begin to disagree. Gen. d'Allonville maintains that eighteen squadrons of Russians—while the French were dismounted, baiting their horses—tried to turn them by the south and cut off their retreat to Eupatoria; that he then ordered his men to mount, fell upon the flank of the Russians, routed and pursued them for two leagues. Gorchakoff says that the Russians were only one regiment (eighteenth lancers) or eight squadrons; that they were surprised by the French after having dismounted in order to unlimber a battery of artillery, and that under these circumstances they had to run for their lives. He makes Gen. Korff responsible for this mistake. Now what business a whole regiment of lancers had to dismount and assist in unlimbering a

[a] A. Pélissier, "Grand quartier général à Sébastopol, le 1er octobre 1855", *Le Moniteur universel*, No. 289, October 16, 1855.—*Ed.*

battery of eight guns, and how it was that the gunners, whose business it was to do this work, were not at hand, we are left to guess for ourselves. The whole report of Gorchakoff is so confused, so unmilitary, so impregnated with the desire to palliate this first cavalry disaster, that it is impossible to treat it as a serious statement of facts. At the same time we see Gen. Korff made responsible for this defeat, as Selvan was made responsible for Silistria, Soimonoff for Inkermann, Read for the Chernaya.[453] Gorchakoff, though defeated in every action, is still invincible. It is not he who is beaten, far from it; it is some unlucky subaltern who upsets the general's wise plans by some clumsy mistake, and who generally gets killed in action in punishment for this crime. In this instance, however, the blunderer is unfortunate enough to preserve his life. Perhaps he may, hereafter, have something to say to Gorchakoff's dispatch. In the mean time he has the satisfaction that his opponent represents him in a far better light than his infallible commander-in-chief does. Since then, the British light cavalry division has been sent to Eupatoria to reenforce the French.

The defeat of the Russians before Kars will very probably prove to be the crowning event of the campaign in Armenia. The Turks, badly organized and short of every requisite, had played but a poor part in this portion of the seat of war. Unable to hold the field, they confined themselves to the occupation of Kars, Erzeroum and the country immediately under the command of these fortresses. Gen. Williams, who had entered the Turkish service, commanded at Kars and superintended the construction of proper defensive works. For the greater part of the Summer the whole campaign on either side was confined to skirmishes, forays and foraging expeditions in the hill country; the general and first result of which was that the Russians, gradually gaining ground, succeeded in blockading Kars and even in cutting off its communications with Erzeroum. Kars is situated in a lateral valley of the Upper Araxes; Erzeroum at the sources of the Euphrates; Batoum on the mouth of the Churuk Su (Bathys), the upper course of which passes near both to Kars and to Erzeroum, so that one of the roads between these two places follows the basin of the Churuk Su as far as Olti, whence it strikes off across the hills toward Kars. Olti was, therefore, the central point for the Turks, as a road from Batoum there joins the one mentioned above; and Batoum was the place from which the nearest and strongest reenforcements were to be expected. Had the Russians succeeded in taking Kars, their first step would have been to establish themselves at Olti, thereby cutting off Erzeroum from its nearest and best communication with the Black Sea and Constantinople. The Turks, however, were so dispirited that they retired as far as Erzeroum, merely occupying the mountain pass between the Upper Euphrates and the sources of the Araxes, while Olti was all but completely neglected.

At last, when Kars was more closely hemmed in, they attempted to form a convoy of provisions at Olti, and with a strong escort to force an entrance into Kars. Part of the cavalry from Kars, having been sent away, as it was useless there, actually fought its way through the Russians as far as Olti, and the convoy started shortly afterward; but this time the Russians were better on the alert—the Turks were completely defeated, and the convoy was captured by the Russians. Kars, in the mean time, began to run short of provisions; Omer Pasha was, indeed, sent to take the command in Asia and to organize at Batoum an army fit to act in the field; but this creation of a new army takes a deal of time, and a march direct to the relief of Kars by Olti would not have been the best course he could take, as Kars might any day be compelled to surrender from want of provisions before relief could arrive.

In this difficult position the Turks stood at the end of September; Kars was considered as good as lost, and the Russians were sure, by merely blockading the town, to starve it out. But the Russians themselves appear not to have been willing to wait until the last flour was baked and the last horse cooked in Kars. Whether from the fear of approaching Winter, the state of the roads, shortness of provisions, superior orders, or the fear of Omer Pasha's relieving corps, they at once made up their minds to act vigorously. Siege-guns arrived from Alexandropol, a fortress on the frontier but a few leagues from Kars, and after a few days of open trenches and cannonading, Kars was assaulted by the concentrated main body of the Russian army under Muravieff. The combat was desperate, and lasted eight hours. The Bashi-bazouks and foot irregulars, who had so often run before the Russians in the field, here fought on more congenial ground. Though the attacking forces must have been from four to six times more numerous than the garrison, yet all attempts to get into the place were in vain. The Turks had here at last recovered their courage and intelligence. Though the Russians more than once succeeded in entering the Turkish batteries (very likely lunettes open at the gorge, so as to be commanded by the fire of the second line of defense), they could no where establish themselves. Their loss is said to have been immense; four thousand killed are stated to have been buried by the Turks; but before crediting this we must have more detailed and precise information.[a]

The capture of Kinburn was effected by the same fleet which made a demonstration before Odessa, whence, however, they sailed away without firing a shot, on their real errand, which was the reduction of Kinburn. This place is situated near the extremity of a tongue of land which on the south incloses the estuary of the Dnieper and Bug. At this point, the estuary is about three miles wide; a bar with fifteen feet of water (according to the Russian charts) hinders its entrance. On the north side of this entrance is situated Otshakoff, on the south side of Kinburn. Both these places first came into notoriety during the Russo-Turkish campaign of 1787, when the Bug formed the frontier of the two empires, and consequently Otshakoff belonged to the Turks and Kinburn to the Russians. At that time, Suvaroff commanded the left wing of the Russian army (under Potemkin), and was stationed at Kinburn. The Turks, then masters of the Black Sea, crossed over from Otshakoff. They first made a diversion by landing behind the town of Kinburn, to the south-east; but when they saw that Suvaroff was not to be led astray by this false maneuver, they landed with their main body at the north-western extremity of the spit, exactly opposite Otshakoff. Here they intrenched themselves, and attacked the fortress; but Suvaroff sallied forth with a far inferior number of men, engaged them, and, with the help of reenforcements, drove them into the sea. Their loss was enormous. Suvaroff himself, however, was wounded during this action, which was followed up in the following year, 1788, by the storming of Otshakoff.

The few details yet known respecting the taking of Kinburn confirm the experience of former episodes in this war, while they again tend to prove the intentional incorrectness of the Russian charts. On all their best charts there is no water of sufficient depth for ships-of-the-line or heavy frigates to be found anywhere within some miles of Kinburn. Yet when the allied fleets sent out gun-boats to take soundings within easy range of Kinburn, they found fully four and a half fathoms at sixteen hundred yards from the walls—at least, so it appears—on the north side within the estuary. Nine heavy steam-frigates could approach to that distance and shell the place; and while the mortar-boats did the

---

[a] For an account of the further fighting in the Kars area after the abortive Russian assault on the fortress on September 29, 1855, and of the fall of Kars see this volume, pp. 588-94 and 595-98.—*Ed.*

same from much nearer stations, the gun-boats enfiladed the faces of the bastions, and the floating batteries—which must have approached to some six hundred or seven hundred yards, if not closer—succeeded in making several breaches in the sea-walls.

What the precise nature of the defenses of Kinburn was, we cannot as yet make out very distinctly. The small town stretching right across the narrow spit was defended by a sort of continuous rampart of masonry, something like a bastioned pentagon or square, with guns firing on barbette, or through masonry embrasures. The guns for the most part stood uncovered, but on the points where their fire was to act with the greatest force there were two tiers, the lower one casemated, the upper one firing through masonry embrasures in a wall erected on the flat roof of the casemates. As at Bomarsund,[454] the masonry, as soon as it was acted upon by a vastly superior fire from the ships, crumbled away, and three breaches, it appears, were formed by the floating batteries in from six to eight hours. This is explained by the very small number of guns in the fortress, of which there were only seventy; and, as the attack could be expected from any side, every front of the fortress had to be armed, so that against the main attack no more than from sixteen to twenty guns could be brought to bear. That their fire should soon have been silenced by the vertical fire of the mortar-boats, the enfilading shots of the gun-boats, the shell-storm of the steam-frigates, and the breaching front fire of the floating batteries, bringing into action at least eight to tenfold their number of guns, is not to be wondered at. And as the day was exceedingly calm, the fire from the floating batteries was as steady as it would have been from any shore battery; it therefore could really act as breaching fire. These unwieldy, floating masses, helpless and useless as soon as the least amount of swell destroys their steadiness, must necessarily be able to do great execution in perfectly calm weather, and in situations where the large vessels can approach within range and thereby draw upon themselves the principal fire of the enemy. Such favorable circumstances, however, occur but seldom; and where fortresses like Kronstadt, Sweaborg, or the sea-forts of Sevastopol, were the objects of their attack, the floating batteries would prove more cumbersome than useful. Thus on the whole, the affair at Kinburn cannot be said to have proved anything in favor of these clumsy sea-monsters.

The allied troops who landed to the south-east of Kinburn must have amounted to a couple of thousand: for of the English alone there were six battalions on board the fleet numbering, with artillery, nearly four thousand men, of which but a portion, however, was landed; while the French had another brigade on board their ships. The part taken by the troops in this action was very inconsiderable; they sent skirmishers and field guns against the place, but as there was a broad wet ditch in front of it, the Russians appear to have treated this impotent demonstration with sovereign contempt, not even opening a heavy fire on them, for we do not hear that the allied troops lost anything to speak of. It was the overwhelming fire of the fleets alone which forced the place to surrender, and as soon as its guns had been silenced, the fleets offered a capitulation, which was accepted. The garrison marched out with the honors of war and surrendered themselves prisoners. Then it was found that the whole force in the fortress consisted of thirteen hundred or fourteen hundred men; and this at once proves what sort of a fortress Kinburn was. In bastioned fortresses, especially small ones, it is generally considered that one weak battalion, or from five hundred to six hundred men, is required for every bastion; a bastioned square, the smallest fortification possible in the bastioned system, requiring from two thousand to two thousand five hundred men for its defense. Here a little over one-half of that number only were present, and yet they had to defend not only plain ramparts, but also to serve the guns in the casemates. Thus, either the fortifications, then, must have been very insignificant indeed, or else very weakly defended; and in either case, the success of the allied fleets before Kinburn does not in any way affect the generally adopted opinion that one gun ashore, well sheltered behind earth ramparts, is worth more than six on board ship coming to attack it.

The entrance to the estuary of the Dnieper once having been forced by the Allies, and the pretended existence of a bar of great shallowness at that point having been proved to be a mere Russian stratagem, the whole estuary is opened to the action of the French and English fleets. The interior of the estuary is known to have a great depth of water, at least in the central channel, though nearer to the shores it abounds in sand-banks, none of which, however, are formidable to gun-boats and other light vessels. Thus Otshakoff, Glubokoye and other points on the shores of the estuary are exposed to the attacks of the Allies and very likely will have to suffer from them.

That the entrance to the estuary is not the shallow channel indicated on the charts, the allied admirals might have inferred from the history of the campaign of 1788. And here we may be allowed to refer again to that campaign, not only because it gives us a clear insight into what the nature of this estuary is with reference to naval warfare, but also because it was then the scene of some of the exploits of our Revolutionary hero, Paul Jones.

At that time, Kinburn and the south shore were held by the Russians, and Otshakoff and the north shore, by the Turks. The Russians had a fleet at Glubokoye, between the mouths of the Dnieper and the Bug; its sailing vessels of deep draught were commanded by Rear-Admiral Paul Jones, and consisted of five ships of the line of eighty guns, and eight frigates, while the rowing flotilla of sixty-five light vessels was under the orders of the Prince of Nassau-Siegen. The Turks had about Otshakoff, under Hassan-Pasha, ten ships of the line, six frigates and fifty-three vessels of light draught. A second Turkish fleet of eight sail of the line, eight frigates, and twenty-four smaller sail was cruising in the offing. After a few preliminary engagements, Hassan-Pasha, on the 27th of June, entered the estuary with the whole of his first fleet, sailed up as far as Glubokoye (thus proving that ships of the line, with their full armament on board, could come up so far), and formed in order of battle, the large vessels in the first line. The Russians, on the contrary, covered their liners and frigates with the row-boats. On the morning of the 28th the battle began. The Turkish line advanced, and soon came up within range of the Russian liners. Within an hour a Turkish ship of seventy guns was aground; the admiral's flag-ship, carrying eighty guns, was ashore a few moments after. Two frigates of forty guns went to succor them, but one of them struck on a shoal almost immediately; while Paul Jones's large vessels kept the remainder of the Turkish vessels engaged, the row-boats closed up with the stranded vessels, boarded and set fire to them. The remainder of the Turkish fleet soon retired in no enviable state; but still their large ships made such a bold front that their retreat was pretty nearly unmolested by the Russian gun-boats and galleys.

But the measure of their disaster was not yet filled. Hassan-Pasha, having collected the remains of his fleet at Otshakoff, resolved to join the fleet cruising in the Black Sea, and to effect this, he had to pass round the point of the Kinburn spit. Here Suvaroff, who commanded in the peninsula, had constructed a masked battery of twenty-four guns; and when the Turks, on the night of the 30th of June, 1788, attempted to double that cape, the battery opened upon them with great effect. Before daybreak, the fire of the Russians, favored by a bright moonlight, had brought the Turkish fleet into great distress, whose ships had to pass one after the other through the narrow channel, and were all the while within easy range of the battery. Several vessels got ashore, others showed signals of distress, some went down or were in flames; and as day broke the Russian fleet bore down upon them. Paul Jones very wisely kept his large ships back, as there was no room for them to maneuver; and indeed the liner *Vladimir,* venturing too much forward, was lost on a shoal. But the rowing flotilla closed with the Turks, and destroyed a great many of their ships, so that before noon the whole action was at an end. Three sail of the line, five frigates, and seventeen smaller sail were destroyed, and one liner and two frigates were taken by the Russians. Of the two sail of the line which were saved by the Turks, one went down before it could reach Constantinople, and a frigate sank as soon as she had reached the island of Poresan. A portion of the Turkish fleet sought shelter under the guns of Otshakoff, but even here Prince Nassau-Siegen attacked and destroyed them on the 1st and 2d August.

This campaign shows clearly what sort of a naval battle-field the Dnieper estuary is. The smaller sort of ships of the line, or at least the large fifty and sixty gun frigates, can enter it; but whether they will be able to maneuver in it with any degree of safety, though they be propelled by steam, remains doubtful. But that corvettes, sloops and vessels of lighter draught, especially steamers, can easily maneuver in these waters, while the larger vessels may serve, when once moored, as stationary batteries, there is not the slightest doubt whatever. And with the means of naval warfare now in the possession of the Allies, with due activity they should be able to scour the estuary from Otshakoff to the mouth of the Dnieper and the Bug.

But it is not only with a view to naval operations alone that the possession of this place is of great importance to the Allies. It gives them an unassailable position on the peninsula between the Dnieper and the Crimea; a position commanding the entrance of the estuary of that river and menacing at the same time the communications between Perekop and Kherson. There is a rumor mentioned in the Vienna papers that the Allies had landed thirty thousand men on the spit of Tendra, a long, narrow island stretching within a few miles distance along the southern shore of the peninsula of Kinburn. If the fact of the landing be true, the numbers are evidently exaggerated. But if even a small body only of the allied troops had occupied this spit, it would show their intention of establishing themselves on the peninsula, and of seriously menacing the Russian lines of communications. They might from this position prove as troublesome to Russian convoys as the corps of Gens. d'Allonville and Paget, from Eupatoria, might to the convoys coming down from Perekop to Sympheropol. They might even, by rapidly concentrating a strong force on this peninsula, make a dash at Kherson, and burn everything with the exception of the small citadel—unless, indeed, the Russians have fortified that town too, and can spare a strong garrison to defend it. Anyhow, Kinburn and the long, flat sandy islands along the shore of the gulf leading to Perekop, form a series of positions which the Allies can easily hold with small bodies of troops, and each of which they can turn at any moment into a base for ulterior and rapid operation. The Russians may thus be obliged, by a few battalions, to disseminate a great number of their troops in order to secure most important points from sudden irruptions; and so long as the allied fleets hold command of the sea, these newly gained possessions cannot be attacked by any Russian land force.

Written in the second half of October 1855

This version of the article was first published in the *New-York Weekly Tribune*, No. 739, November 10, 1855 as a leading article

Reproduced from the newspaper

NOTES
AND
INDEXES

NOTES

[1] "The Struggle in the Crimea" is one of the many articles on the Crimean War written by Engels at Marx's request for the *New-York Daily Tribune.*

Marx contributed to this newspaper from August 1851 to March 1862, but not until August 1852 did he begin sending articles of his own. His first were written in German and translated into English by his friends, mostly Engels. By late January 1853, his knowledge of English had improved sufficiently for him to begin writing them in English.

Marx's and Engels' articles in the *New-York Daily Tribune* dealt with key issues of foreign and domestic policy, the working-class movement, the economic development of European countries, colonial expansion and the national liberation movement in colonial and dependent countries. They immediately attracted attention by their profundity, political insight and literary merits. The *New-York Daily Tribune* editors publicly acknowledged their high quality. For instance, in a leading article on April 7, 1853, they saw fit to "pay a tribute to the remarkable ability of the correspondent... Mr. Marx has very decided opinions of his own, with some of which we are far from agreeing; but those who do not read his letters neglect one of the most instructive sources of information on the great questions of current European politics." In a letter to Jenny Marx of July 1, 1853, Charles Dana, one of the editors, wrote that the owners of the *Tribune* and the reading public had a high opinion of her husband's articles.

Many articles by Marx and Engels were reprinted in the *Tribune*'s special issues—the *New-York Weekly Tribune* and *New-York Semi-Weekly Tribune,* and some were reproduced in the Chartist *People's Paper.* Other newspapers, including the *New-York Times,* quoted from them. Their articles reached Europe too. For example, in his speech in the House of Commons on July 1, 1853, John Bright, leader of the Free Traders, specially noted Marx's article on Gladstone's budget published in the *Tribune* (see present edition, Volume 12, p. 176).

The *Tribune* editors sometimes took liberties with the articles, printing them unsigned, in the form of editorials, especially from September 1854 onwards. In some cases they tampered with the text, making insertions, some of which were in direct contradiction to the content of the articles. Marx repeatedly protested against these practices. In the autumn of 1857 he was forced to reduce the number of his contributions in view of the *Tribune's* weak financial position, the result of the economic crisis in the U.S.A. He ceased contributing to the paper altogether after the outbreak of the American Civil War, mainly because the *Tribune* had come under the sway of people advocating a compromise with the slave-owning states.

"The Struggle in the Crimea" is one of the series of reviews of the Crimean War of 1853-56 which Engels began to write for the *New-York Daily Tribune* in the autumn of 1853 and the *Neue Oder-Zeitung* in January 1855 (in the latter case the reviews were either German versions of articles written for the *Tribune* or special reports included by Marx in his articles for the *Neue Oder-Zeitung*). The *New-York Daily Tribune* published these reviews as leading articles without giving the name of the author (see present edition, Vols. 12 and 13). p. 3

2 The *battle of the Alma* took place on September 20, 1854. The Russian forces were commanded by A. S. Menshikov, and the numerically superior forces of the French, British and Turks by Saint-Arnaud and Raglan. It was the first battle after the Allies' landing in the Crimea (at Eupatoria) on September 14. The defeat and withdrawal of the Russian troops opened up the way to Sevastopol for the Allies. Later Engels also described this battle in his article "Alma" written for the *New Americana* (see present edition, Vol. 18). p. 3

3 Piedmont (the Kingdom of Sardinia) joined the anti-Russian coalition at Napoleon III's insistence in January 1855 and sent a corps of 15,000 troops to the Crimea. Count Camillo Cavour, the head of the Piedmontese government, who wanted to unite Italy under the aegis of the Savoy dynasty that ruled Piedmont, hoped thus to win France's support in the future struggle of the Kingdom of Sardinia for the North Italian provinces of Lombardy and Venice, which had been captured by Austria. This support was to help him avenge Piedmont's defeat in the war against Austria in 1848-49. p. 4

4 On May 4, 1811, in the course of the Peninsular War (1808-14) British, Spanish and Portuguese forces commanded by Wellington laid siege to the French-held fortress of Badajoz (south-western Spain). However, on May 14 Wellington was forced to lift the siege in order to engage the French army sent to relieve the besieged garrison. The siege was resumed on May 25, but lifted again for the same reason on June 17. The fortress was captured by Wellington's troops on April 6, 1812, after a new siege which began on March 16. p. 6

5 This article belongs to the series written by Marx for the *Neue Oder-Zeitung*, which gave a systematic coverage of the home- and foreign-policy debates in the British Parliament in 1855. It includes material from Engels' review "The Struggle in the Crimea" written for the *New-York Daily Tribune*. The series began with the article "The Opening of Parliament" (see present edition, Vol. 13, pp. 600-02).

The *Neue Oder-Zeitung* was a democratic daily published in Breslau (Wrocław) from 1849 to 1855. In the autumn of 1854 Marx was invited to contribute to it by Ferdinand Lassalle, whose cousin, Max Friedländer, published the newspaper. Originally Marx was very critical of the *Neue Oder-Zeitung*. During the revolution of 1848-49 he criticised the Breslau democrats grouped round it for their vacillations and conciliatory policy, and the "Address of the Central Authority to the League" (March 1850) stressed the hostility of the *Neue Oder-Zeitung* towards the working-class movement (see present edition, Vol. 10, pp. 277-87). However, Marx's attitude to the newspaper changed in later years, when it became the most radical opposition organ in Germany and was persecuted by the censorship and the Prussian government. At that time, the editorial board was headed by the bourgeois democrats Temme, Stein and Elsner. In September 1855 Elsner became Editor-in-Chief.

In a letter to Elsner of November 8, 1855, Marx noted that the *Neue Oder-Zeitung* was publishing "the maximum of what is possible under the present condition of the press". In these circumstances he considered it necessary to give the newspaper every possible support. When its financial position deteriorated in the autumn of 1855, he offered to write for it without payment.

Marx began to contribute to the *Neue Oder-Zeitung* as its London correspondent at the end of December 1854, sending two or three reports a week. His articles were marked with the sign ×. Given the almost total absence of a working-class press in Germany during the years of reaction Marx and Engels thought it important to use the bourgeois-democratic press for the struggle against reaction. Marx's work for the *Neue Oder-Zeitung* enabled him to keep in touch with Germany and familiarise German readers with key issues of foreign and domestic policy, the working-class and democratic movement and the economic development of capitalist countries, above all Britain and France. He regularly sent reports on the progress of the Crimean War. Sometimes he used for this purpose Engels' military reviews written for the *New-York Daily Tribune,* translating them into German (in the present edition both Marx and Engels are given as their authors). Sometimes Marx abridged Engels' articles or introduced changes and additions. In October 1855 the *Neue Oder-Zeitung* found itself almost without means to pay its correspondents. At the end of the year the paper closed down. The last article definitely known to have been written by Marx appeared in the *Neue Oder-Zeitung* on November 16, 1855. p. 8

6 The *Peelites* were a group of moderate Tories supporting Robert Peel, who advocated economic concessions to the commercial and industrial bourgeoisie as a means of maintaining the political rule of the big landowners and financiers. In 1846, he secured the repeal of the Corn Laws (see Note 14). This move, favouring the industrial bourgeoisie, was bitterly resented by the Protectionist Tories and led to a split in the Tory party and the emergence of the Peelites as an independent group. The Peelites were represented in Aberdeen's coalition government (1852-55) and joined the Liberal party in the late 1850s and early 1860s. p. 8

7 The *Manchester School*—a trend in political economy reflecting the interests of the industrial bourgeoisie. It favoured free trade and non-interference by the state in the economy. The Free Traders' stronghold was Manchester, where the movement was led by Cobden and Bright, two textile manufacturers who founded the Anti-Corn Law League in 1838. In the 1840s and 1850s the Free Traders were an independent political group which later formed the Left wing of the Liberal Party. p. 8

8 The *Mayfair Radicals* were a group of aristocratic politicians (Molesworth, Bernal Osborne and others) who flirted with democratic circles. The name derives from Mayfair, an aristocratic district on the edge of Hyde Park in London. p. 8

9 Palmerston's resignation from the post of Foreign Secretary in Russell's Whig Cabinet occurred on December 19, 1851, and was caused by his approving, in a conversation with the French Ambassador, of the Bonapartist *coup d'état* of December 2, 1851, without consulting other Cabinet members. On the whole, however, the British government shared Palmerston's attitude and was the first in Europe to recognise the Bonapartist regime. p. 9

10 The *battle of Balaklava* took place on October 25, 1854. Units of the Russian army tried to cut off the British and Turkish troops taking part in the siege of Sevastopol from their base in Balaklava. They succeeded in inflicting serious losses on the enemy, especially on the British cavalry, but failed to achieve their main objective. For a description of this battle see Engels' article "The War in the East" (see present edition, Vol. 13, pp. 518-27). p. 12

11 The articles "Lord Palmerston" were written by Marx for the *Neue Oder-Zeitung* in connection with the formation of the Palmerston government on February 6, 1855, and are essentially a résumé of Marx's well-known pamphlet *Lord Palmerston* written for the *New-York Daily Tribune* in the autumn of 1853 and also published, in fuller form, in the Chartist *People's Paper* (see present edition, Vol. 12, pp. 341-406). p. 14

12 *Carbonari*—members of secret political societies in Italy and France in the first half of the nineteenth century. In Italy they fought for national independence, the unification of the country and liberal constitutional reforms. In France the movement was above all directed against the restored monarchy of the Bourbons (1815-30). In the first half of the nineteenth century the word "carbonari" was synonymous with "revolutionary". p. 15

13 In 1847 in Athens the house of the merchant Pacifico, a Portuguese Jew and British citizen, was burnt down. Palmerston used this as a pretext for sending units of the British Navy to Greece and presenting the Greek government with an ultimatum. The actual purpose of this move was to force Greece to cede several strategic islands in the Aegean. During the discussion of the Anglo-Greek conflict in the British Parliament in June 1850 the government's foreign policy was approved by the House of Commons. The House of Lords, on the contrary, rejected Palmerston's policy by a majority of 37. France and Russia indicated their displeasure through their ambassadors in London: the French Ambassador left the British capital, the Russian Ambassador failed to attend a dinner given by Palmerston. p. 15

14 The *Corn Laws,* the first of which were passed as early as the fifteenth century, imposed high import duties on agricultural products in order to maintain high prices for these products on the domestic market. The Corn Laws served the interests of the big landowners. The struggle between the industrial bourgeoisie and the landed aristocracy over the Corn Laws ended in their repeal in June 1846. p. 16

15 The *blockade of the River Scheldt* and the Dutch coast by the British and French navies was undertaken in 1832 with a view to forcing Holland to cease hostilities it had resumed in 1831 against Belgium, which had overthrown Dutch rule. As a result, both Holland and Belgium were compelled to agree to a compromise peace treaty (1833) drawn up by Britain, France, Russia, Prussia and Austria.

The *blockade of the mouths of the rivers Tagus and Douro* was undertaken by Britain during the civil war in Portugal (1828-34). In this war the feudal-clerical party led by the pretender to the Portuguese throne, Dom Miguel, fought against the liberal bourgeois party of Constitutionalists. In an attempt to strengthen its influence in the Iberian Peninsula, the British government sent its navy to the Portuguese coast and thereby tipped the scales in favour of the Constitutionalists. p. 16

16 The *blockade of Mexico*—under the pretext of protecting French citizens in Mexico a French squadron blockaded several Mexican ports on April 16, 1838. The blockade affected British commercial interests. Despite numerous petitions from the commercial bourgeoisie urging the British government to intervene and ensure the free passage of British ships, in the Parliamentary debate of March 19, 1839, Palmerston defended the position of the government, which did not want a conflict with France.

The *blockade of Buenos Aires* and the Argentine coast by the British and French navies (1845-50) aimed at forcing the Argentine government to open the rivers Paraná and Uruguay to foreign ships (they had been closed to foreign shipping in 1841 in connection with the war between Argentina and Uruguay) and recognise Uruguay's independence. These demands were granted in 1850 and 1851. p. 17

17 In 1838 the King of Naples granted a French company a monopoly to mine sulphur in Sicily. This move evoked a sharp protest from the British government, which regarded it as an infringement of Britain's commercial interests, guaranteed by the Anglo-Neapolitan treaty of 1816. In 1840 the British Navy in the Mediterranean was ordered to open hostilities. Naples was forced to comply with Britain's demands.

For details of the *Pacifico* affair see Note 13.

In 1837 Mohammed Shah of Persia laid siege to the Afghan fortress of Herat, a junction of important trade routes. In 1838 the British government declared his actions to be hostile to Britain and demanded an end to the siege. Later it dispatched a naval squadron to the Persian Gulf, threatening war. The Shah was compelled to lift the siege and conclude an unequal trade agreement with Britain (1841). p. 17

18 A reference to Britain's intervention in the Carlist War in Spain (1833-40) in which the feudal Catholic forces, led by pretender to the throne Don Carlos, fought against the bourgeois liberals who supported the government of Regent María Cristina. Britain sent its navy and a legion of volunteers to Spain. The latter took part in the fighting on María Cristina's side in 1835-37. These moves were designed to consolidate Britain's influence in the Iberian Peninsula.

The *war with China for the importation of opium*—a reference to the so-called First Opium War (1839-42), Britain's war against China which marked the beginning of the latter's transformation into a semi-colony. Britain used as a pretext for this war the confiscation by the Chinese authorities in Canton of opium stocks owned by foreign merchants. As a result of this war the Treaty of Nanking was imposed on China (August 29, 1842) which obliged it to open five ports (Canton, Amoy, Foochow, Ningpo and Shanghai) to British trade, cede the island of Hongkong to Britain "in perpetuity" and pay Britain a huge indemnity. Under a supplementary treaty signed in 1843 China was forced to grant extraterritoriality to foreigners. In 1844 unequal treaties were imposed on China by the USA and France. p. 17

[19] This refers to Anglo-American clashes on the US-Canadian border over disputed territories, one to the north of the American State of Maine, the other—Oregon—on the Pacific coast. These clashes became especially sharp in the late 1830s and early 1840s. p. 17

[20] The *Afghanistan campaigns*—during the first Anglo-Afghan war (1838-42) in which Britain strove to establish colonial rule in Afghanistan, British troops invaded Afghan territory twice (in 1838 and 1842). Both invasions failed to achieve their purpose.

At the insistence of the British government, Britain, Russia, Austria and Prussia signed a convention in London on July 15, 1840, on military assistance to Turkey in its war against Egypt (1839-41). In the autumn of 1840 British and Austrian warships bombarded Beirut, Saint-Jean-d'Acre and other fortresses on the Syrian coast, which had been captured by Mehemet Ali, the ruler of Egypt, between 1831 and 1833. Eventually Mehemet Ali was forced to relinquish his possessions outside Egypt and submit to the supreme authority of the Sultan. p. 17

[21] Evidently a reference to the inspection of ships by the British in connection with the slave trade. At the beginning of the nineteenth century Britain, in its drive against the slave trade, claimed the right to inspect all suspect ships even in peacetime. This was strongly opposed by the U.S. government because many ships carrying slaves from West Africa sailed under the U.S. flag.

Britain's right to inspect Portuguese ships was recognised by the Anglo-Portuguese treaties of 1810, 1815 and 1817. In return for Britain's waiving of Portugal's debts the latter undertook to allow her own ships to carry only a limited number of African slaves and only to Brazil, then a Portuguese colony, and to ban the use of her flag by slavers of other countries. This agreement was often violated, especially after Brazil won independence in 1822. In 1839 the British Parliament passed a law allowing British ships to detain ships engaged in the slave traffic. p. 17

[22] The *Treaty of Adrianople* was concluded by Turkey and Russia in September 1829 following the war of 1828-29. Under the treaty Russia obtained the Danube delta including the islands, and a considerable part of the eastern Black Sea coast south of the Kuban estuary. Turkey was to recognise the autonomy of Moldavia and Wallachia, granting them the right to elect their own hospodars (rulers). Their autonomy was to be guaranteed by Russia. The Turkish government also undertook to recognise the independence of Greece, whose only obligation to Turkey was to pay an annual tribute to the Sultan, and abide by all the previous treaties relating to the autonomy of Serbia, which was to be formalised by a special firman.

The *Balta-Liman Treaty,* concluded by Russia and Turkey on May 1, 1849, laid down conditions for the continued presence of their troops in Moldavia and Wallachia, which had been occupied to suppress the revolutionary movement. Under the treaty, the occupation was to continue until the threat of revolution had been fully eliminated (the foreign troops were not withdrawn until 1851); for a certain period the hospodars were to be appointed by the Sultan in agreement with the Tsar. A series of measures by Russia and Turkey, including another occupation, were envisaged to provide for the eventuality of another revolution. p. 17

[23] On May 8, 1852, Russia, Austria, Britain, France, Prussia, Sweden and Denmark signed the London Protocol on the integrity of the Kingdom of

Denmark. It was based on the protocol adopted by the same states (except Prussia) at a conference in London on July 4, 1850 and signed on August 2, 1850, which established the principle of the indivisibility of the Danish Crown possessions, including the duchies of Schleswig and Holstein. The London Protocol mentioned the Russian Emperor among the lawful claimants to the Danish Crown who had renounced their rights in favour of Duke Christian of Glücksburg, proclaimed successor to King Frederick VII (the Russian Emperor descended from Duke Charles Peter Ulrich of Holstein-Gottorp, who was Russian Tsar as Peter III). This created a precedent for Russian claims to the Danish Crown in the event of the Glücksburg dynasty dying out. p. 17

24 Under an agreement signed by Russia, Britain and the Netherlands in London on May 19, 1815, Britain and the Netherlands had undertaken to compensate Russia's military expenses connected with the expulsion of Napoleonic troops from the Dutch and Belgian provinces by gradually repaying part of Russia's debt to the Dutch bankers Hope & Co. and the interest on that debt. A special clause stipulated that the payments would be discontinued in the event of a secession of the Belgian provinces from the Netherlands. After the 1830 revolution and the establishment of an independent Belgian state, the Netherlands stopped its payments. However, Palmerston signed a new agreement with Russia on November 16, 1831, confirming Britain's financial commitments. p. 18

25 The *Treaty of Unkiar-Skelessi* was signed by Russia and Turkey on July 8, 1833. Prior to that, in the spring of the same year, Russian troops had landed in Unkiar-Skelessi, on the Bosphorus, to help protect the Turkish capital from the army of Ibrahim Pasha, son of Mehemet Ali, the ruler of Egypt who had rebelled against the Turkish Sultan. In May 1833, the Porte concluded peace with Mehemet Ali through the mediation of Britain and France, ceding Syria and Palestine to Egypt. However, the Tsarist government, taking advantage of the tense situation and the presence of Russian troops in Turkey, induced the Porte to conclude a defence treaty with Russia which contained a secret clause obliging Turkey to close the Straits to all foreign warships except Russian vessels. This clause remained in force until the Turko-Egyptian war of 1839-41, when Nicholas I reached agreement with Britain and other Powers on joint action against Mehemet Ali, but was compelled to agree to the closure of the Straits to the warships of all states in peacetime. p. 18

26 A reference to the attempt by Mohammed Shah of Persia to gain possession of Herat in 1837-38 (see Note 17). Russia gave him diplomatic support in that campaign. p. 19

27 The Treaty of Adrianople (1829) (see Note 22) gave Russia control of the islands in the Danube delta but guaranteed freedom of navigation on the Danube to the merchant ships of all countries. However, in the spring of 1836 a Russian quarantine post was set up in the Sulina arm of the Danube which in effect acted as a customs office controlling passing vessels. When the question was discussed in the British Parliament in April 1836, Palmerston declared that Russia's actions were not prejudicial to Anglo-Turkish trade and therefore he saw no grounds for diplomatic intervention by Britain. p. 19

28 A reference to the national liberation insurrection in Poland in 1830-31. It started on November 29, 1830, when Polish patriots occupied the Belvedere Palace in Warsaw, the residence of Grand Duke Constantine, the Tsarist Commander-in-

Chief (virtually vice-regent) in the Kingdom of Poland. By November 30 the whole of Warsaw was in the hands of the insurgents. p. 19

29 On February 14, 1855, *The Times* (No. 21977) published a letter signed "A Colonial Reformer" which asked why Sidney Herbert was not being allowed to continue as Secretary of War if he really possessed the merits attributed to him by his supporters, and was, instead, being offered a high post in the Colonial Office if he really was responsible for the plight of the British wounded in the Crimea, as claimed by his opponents. p. 22

30 See Note 8. p. 25

31 This refers to the Great Exhibition held in London in 1851. A special building of metal and glass, known as the Crystal Palace, was erected for it in Hyde Park. p. 29

32 A reference to the lawsuit over the inheritance of Eliza Josephine Handcock, the mistress of the Earl of Clanricarde, that took place in the Irish Court of Chancery in January 1855. The action had been brought by John Stratford Handcock, the rightful heir of Josephine's daughter Honoria who died on December 12, 1853. His rights were contested by John de Burgh, son of Josephine and the Earl of Clanricarde. In the course of the proceedings public attention was drawn to the mysterious circumstances attending the death of Josephine's husband, William Handcock, and of their three daughters, none of whom had come of age. Some witnesses hinted that the Earl of Clanricarde was implicated in these events.

Marx draws a parallel between this case and that of Altarice-Rosalba-Fanny, the Duchess of Praslin, who was found murdered in her home in August 1847. Suspicion fell on her husband, the Duke of Praslin, who was arrested and poisoned himself during the investigation. p. 31

33 This article was written by Engels for the *New-York Daily Tribune*. The section relating to the British army was included by Marx, in free translation and with a number of alterations, in his report "Parliamentary and Military Affairs" (February 20, 1855) written for the *Neue Oder-Zeitung* (see this volume, pp. 40-42; the corresponding passage is indicated in Engels' article by a footnote). Both Marx and Engels are therefore given as the authors of this report in the present edition. A considerable part of Engels' article was reproduced by Marx, with cuts and minor alterations, in another report for the *Neue Oder-Zeitung* entitled "Zustand der Armeen" ("The State of the Armies"), dated by him February 21 and published on February 24, 1855. As it entirely consists of material taken from the article "The War That Looms on Europe", this report has not been included in the present edition. The most significant alterations made by Marx have been indicated in footnotes. p. 32

34 A reference to the talks between the British, French and Russian Ambassadors and Austrian Foreign Minister Buol sponsored by Emperor Francis Joseph, which opened in December 1854. Their official purpose was to work out a basis for peace negotiations between the belligerents in the Crimean War. They were a sequel to an earlier round of talks between diplomats of the Western Powers, the Prussian Ambassador and the Austrian Minister (the Russian Ambassador refused to participate) held in Vienna in 1853-54 by way of mediation in the Russo-Turkish conflict. The second round failed to resolve the differences between the belligerents in the Crimean War. In mid-March 1855 representatives of Austria, Britain, France, Turkey and Russia met at a higher level at the

Vienna Conference (Britain was represented by Special Envoy Lord John Russell, France by Foreign Minister Drouyn de Lhuys). That conference also produced no results (see Note 88). p. 32

35 In the *battle of Inkerman* in the Crimea (November 5, 1854) the Anglo-French forces defeated the Russian army, but the Russians' vigorous action compelled the enemy to refrain from storming Sevastopol and instead lay siege to the city. Engels described the battle in detail in his article "The Battle of Inkerman" (see present edition, Vol. 13, pp. 528-35). p. 34

36 On January 29, 1855, Nicholas I issued a manifesto calling for the formation of a people's militia. It was to be recruited in 18 gubernias of Central Russia (not Southern Russia, as the article says) after the regular levy. p. 38

37 See Note 10. p. 40

38 *Blue Books*—periodically published collections of documents of the British Parliament and Foreign Office. Their publication began in the seventeenth century. p. 40

39 See Note 88. p. 41

40 At the end of January 1855, John Roebuck submitted a motion in the House of Commons calling for the establishment of a committee to inquire into the condition of the British army in the Crimea and the work of the government departments responsible for its maintenance. Discussion of the motion led to a government crisis and the resignation of Aberdeen's Cabinet (see Marx's article "Comments on the Cabinet Crisis", present edition, Vol. 13, pp. 603-04). After forming a new ministry in February 1855 Palmerston approved Roebuck's motion, but the Peelites Graham, Gladstone and Herbert, who had belonged to the former coalition government, resigned their posts in the new cabinet. As a result, Palmerston's government in its final form consisted mainly of Whigs. p. 43

41 See Note 7. p. 43

42 This remark shows that Marx may have attended the sitting of the House of Commons on February 23, 1855. This would have enabled him to compare the speeches made there with the reports on the sitting published in *The Times*, No. 21986, February 24, 1855, and in other newspapers. p. 44

43 The *Four Points*—demands made by the Western Powers on Russia as preliminary conditions for peace talks in their Note of August 8, 1854. Russia was required to renounce her protectorate over Moldavia, Wallachia and Serbia, which was to be replaced by an all-European guarantee; to grant freedom of navigation on the Danube; to agree to a revision of the London Convention of 1841 on the closure of the Bosphorus and Dardanelles to the warships of all nations in peacetime, and to renounce its protection of Christians in Turkey. The Tsarist government at first rejected the Four Points but in November 1854 was forced to accept them as the basis for future peace talks. The Four Points were discussed at the Vienna conferences of Ambassadors (see Note 34) but the attempts of the Western Powers to link the question of the Straits with demands for a reduction of the Russian Navy in the Black Sea caused the Russian Ambassador in Vienna, A. M. Gorchakov, to walk out of the talks. p. 44

44 This refers to the debates in the British Parliament in 1845 on proposals to raise subsidies to the Catholic College in Maynooth (Ireland) which was

founded in 1795 with the assistance of Pitt the Younger. By supporting this college the British government sought to ingratiate itself with the Irish landlords, certain sections of the bourgeoisie and the clergy and thus split the Irish national movement. p. 45

45 This refers to the Reform Bill passed by the British House of Commons in 1831 and finally approved by the House of Lords in June 1832. It gave the vote to owners and tenants of houses rated at £10 or over. The working class and the petty bourgeoisie—the main force in the struggle for reform—were denied suffrage. p. 47

46 The *People's Charter,* which contained the demands of the Chartists, was published in the form of a Parliamentary Bill on May 8, 1838. It contained six points: universal suffrage (for men of 21 and over), annual parliaments, vote by ballot, equal electoral districts, abolition of the property qualification of MPs and payment of MPs. Petitions urging the adoption of the People's Charter were turned down by Parliament in 1839, 1842 and 1848. p. 47

47 A reference to a radical political trend among the Free Traders which in 1849 founded the National Parliamentary and Financial Reform Association. Its purpose was to agitate for the "Little Charter", a reform bill repeatedly submitted to Parliament by Joseph Hume between 1849 and 1851. In contrast to the People's Charter, it contained three points: voting rights for every tenant of a house or part of a house (Household Suffrage), triennial parliaments, and vote by ballot. By counterposing this programme to the demands of the Chartists while at the same time adopting, in an extremely curtailed form, some of these demands, the bourgeois radicals hoped to gain control of the working masses at a time when the Chartist movement was declining. However, most of the politically active workers, except for the reformist elements in the Chartist movement, including O'Connor's supporters, refused to support the Little Charter. In 1855 the National Parliamentary and Financial Reform Association disintegrated. p. 47

48 This article was first published in English in Karl Marx and Frederick Engels, *On Britain,* Moscow, 1953 under the title "Palmerston and the English Oligarchy". The title was provided by the editors. p. 49

49 The Roman Emperor Caligula (A.D. 12-41) bestowed the consulship on his favourite horse.

The *Grand Moguls* was the name given by Europeans to the rulers of an empire founded in Northern India in 1526 by Turkic conquerors then considered to be descendants of Genghis Khan's Mongolian warriors (hence the name "Moguls"). Although the empire fell into decline in the eighteenth century and came under British domination, its rulers retained nominal sovereignty until 1858. p. 49

50 This refers to Russell's appointment as Britain's representative at the Vienna Conference, which was to open in March 1855 (see Note 88). p. 50

51 *Emancipation of the Catholics*—in 1829 the British Parliament, under pressure of a mass movement in Ireland, lifted some of the restrictions curtailing the political rights of the Catholic population. Catholics were granted the right to be elected to Parliament and hold certain government posts. Simultaneously the property qualification for electors was increased fivefold. With the aid of this manoeuvre the British ruling classes hoped to win over to their side the upper

crust of the Irish bourgeoisie and Catholic landowners and thus split the Irish national movement.

Repeal of the Corn Laws—see Note 14.

The mass movement for *Parliamentary reform* in Britain (see Note. 45) developed in the late 1820s and early 1830s during Wellington's Tory Ministry. The reform was carried out by Grey's Whig Government (November 1830 to July 1834). p. 51

52 *Court of Queen's (King's) Bench*—Britain's oldest judicial institution. In the nineteenth century (up to 1873) it was an independent high court for criminal and civil cases and also supervised the lower courts. Subsequently its competence was limited to civil disputes. p. 51

53 This version of the article first appeared in English translation in Karl Marx and Frederick Engels, *Articles on Britain,* Moscow, 1971. The other version entitled "The Crisis in England" was written by Marx for the *New-York Daily Tribune* in English. It is reproduced in this volume in its original form. p. 53

54 A reference to the overthrow of the Stuart dynasty and the enthronement, together with his wife Mary, daughter of the deposed Stuart King James II, of William III of Orange, after which constitutional monarchy was consolidated in Britain on the basis of a compromise between the landed aristocracy and the finance bourgeoisie. p. 54

55 The term "millocracy" (*mill*+the Greek *kratia*) was first used by Thomas Carlyle in his work *Past and Present,* published in 1843.

Reform Bill of 1831—see Note 45. p. 54

56 The 1834 Poor Law (an Act for the amendment and better administration of the laws relating to the poor in England and Wales) permitted only one form of aid to needy able-bodied persons—their enrolment in prison-type workhouses where they were engaged in monotonous and exhausting unproductive labour. The people nicknamed them Bastilles for the Poor. The law aimed at making the poor accept hard working conditions in industry, thus increasing the supply of cheap labour.

Repeal of the Corn Laws—see Note 14. p. 54

57 A reference to one of the biggest strikes by British workers in the 1850s. In August 1853, the weavers and spinners at the cotton mills of Preston and its environs walked out demanding a 10 per cent increase in wages. They were supported by workers in other trades. In September the Associated Masters retaliated by organising a lockout. About 25,000 of Preston's 30,000 workers stayed away from work. Thanks to the relief given them by workers in other cities, they were able to hold out for more than 36 weeks. In February 1854, the lockout was lifted but the strike continued. To bring it to an end the Associated Masters began importing workers from Ireland and the English workhouses. In March, the leaders of the strike were arrested. As their funds ran out, workers were forced to return to the mills. The strike ended in May. p. 55

58 The *Irish Brigade* was the name given to the Irish faction in the British Parliament from the 1830s to 1850s. Up to 1847, the Irish Brigade was led by Daniel O'Connell. As neither the Tories nor the Whigs had a decisive majority the Brigade was able to tip the balance in Parliament and sometimes even decide the fate of the government.

In the early fifties, a number of MPs belonging to this faction formed an alliance with the radical Irish Tenant-Right League and set up what they called an Independent Opposition in the House of Commons. However, the leaders of the Irish Brigade soon made a deal with the British ruling circles, securing some secondary posts in Aberdeen's Coalition Government and refusing to support the League's demands. This demoralised the Independent Opposition and ultimately led to its collapse (1859). p. 58

59 By altering the beginning of this article the editors of the *New-York Daily Tribune* gave the impression that it had been written in America. Some other contributions by Marx and Engels published as leading articles in this newspaper were also edited in this way. p. 59

60 See Note 32. p. 62

61 The sale of commissions in the English army dated back to the late seventeenth century and was maintained up to 1871. It ensured that members of the English aristocracy held a dominant position in the army. p. 63

62 The *Mutiny Act* was passed by Parliament annually from 1689 to 1881, empowering the Crown to maintain a standing army and navy of a fixed size, prescribe manuals and regulations for the army and navy, set up courts martial and establish a system of punishment for mutiny, refusal to obey orders, infringements of discipline, etc. The first Mutiny Act was passed in connection with riots in the British Army. p. 63

63 *Simony* (from Simon Magus, an allusion to his offer of money to the Apostles, Acts 8, 9:24)—the practice of selling or buying ecclesiastical preferments, etc. in the Middle Ages. Advocates of ecclesiastical reform challenged it as early as the twelfth century. p. 64

64 Revolutionary action by gold-diggers took place in Victoria in November and December 1854. On November 29, licences were burnt at a gold-diggers' meeting. On December 2, an armed clash occurred between the insurgents and troops. Also in December the Ballarat Reform League was set up which formulated the insurgents' demands: abolition of gold-digging licences, release of the gold-diggers arrested for setting fire to the hotel, and political reforms including four of the six Chartist points. Although the uprising was suppressed and martial law introduced, some of the insurgents' demands had to be granted. p. 64

65 An allusion to the system of extortionate taxes levied by the British Parliament and Government on the North American colonies—the high tariff on sugar imports (introduced in 1764), the stamp duty (1765), the exorbitant customs duties on imports from England, etc. It was bitterly resented by the local bourgeoisie and the masses in the colonies and was one of the factors that led to the War of Independence (1775-83) in the course of which the United States of America was formed. p. 65

66 The *Riot Act*—an Act passed in 1715 on the maintenance of public peace and order. It empowered the local authorities to disperse assemblages of "trouble-makers" by force and charge them with felony. The Act obliged the authorities to read part of it to those assembled and to open fire if the latter refused to disperse within an hour. p. 66

67 On March 5, 1855, *The Times* published a letter by the English doctor Augustus Bozzi Granville (later reprinted by other London newspapers) in

which he maintained that he had predicted the imminent death of the Tsar in a conversation with Palmerston as early as July 6, 1853. The letter was reported in the *Neue Oder-Zeitung* on March 9, 1855. p. 68

68 The Pythia—a priestess and prophetess of Apollo at Delphi. p. 68

69 A reference to the aggravation of Anglo-French differences in the Middle East during the Turko-Egyptian war of 1839-41. The conclusion, without French participation, of the London Convention of July 15, 1840 (see Note 20) on aid by the Western Powers to the Sultan in his struggle against the Egyptian ruler Mehemet Ali created the danger of war breaking out between Britain and France. Fearing the formation of an anti-French coalition, France was forced to discontinue its support for Egypt. p. 71

70 In 1846 the Guizot Government managed to arrange the marriage of the Spanish infanta María Luisa Fernanda to Louis Philippe's youngest son, the Duke of Montpensier, and thwart Britain's plans to marry Leopold of Coburg to Queen Isabella II of Spain. The tension between the British and French governments over these marriage projects became very acute and after the failure of British diplomacy Palmerston sought a pretext to take revenge. p. 71

71 The *Treaty of Utrecht of 1713* was one of a series of peace treaties concluding the war of the Spanish succession, which had been waged from 1701 between France and Spain, on the one hand, and the countries of the anti-French coalition (Britain, the Netherlands, Portugal, Prussia, Savoy and Habsburg Austria), on the other. Austria did not sign the treaty and made peace with France at Rastatt in 1714. Under the terms of the treaty, Philip V, the Bourbon King of Spain and Louis XIV's grandson, retained the Spanish crown. The King of France was to renounce his right and that of his successors from the Bourbon dynasty to the Spanish crown. Several French and Spanish possessions in the West Indies and North America, as well as Gibraltar, passed into Britain's hands.

When he accused France in 1846 of violating the treaty of Utrecht, Palmerston had in mind Louis Philippe's plans for uniting the two monarchies through the marriage of his youngest son and the Spanish infanta. p. 71

72 This article was first published in English in Marx, Engels, *Ireland and the Irish Question,* Moscow, 1971. p. 78

73 See Note 58. p. 78

74 A reference to the agreement concluded in February 1835 by Daniel O'Connell, leader of the liberal wing of the Irish national movement, with the leaders of the Whig party. The negotiations had been held in the house of Lord Lichfield in London. Under the agreement, Irish liberals were to get certain administrative posts. O'Connell, for his part, promised to call off the mass campaign for the repeal of the Anglo-Irish Union of 1801 which abolished the autonomy of the Irish Parliament, and to support the Whigs in the British Parliament. p. 78

75 The repeal of the Anglo-Irish Union of 1801. In the 1820s repeal became the most popular slogan in Ireland. In 1840 the Repeal Association was set up. Its leader, Daniel O'Connell, sought a compromise with the British ruling circles. In January 1847 a group of radicals broke away from the Association and

formed the Irish Confederation. Its left, revolutionary wing led the national liberation movement and became the target of severe reprisals in 1848. Eventually, the Repeal Association broke up completely. p. 78

76 See Note 7. p. 78

77 See Note 51. p. 79

78 Between 1845 and 1847 potato blight was the occasion of widespread famine in Ireland. The poverty of the small tenants ruthlessly exploited by the big landowners made the mass of the population almost entirely dependent on a diet of potatoes grown on their own little patches. Meanwhile the British Government not only withheld any effective form of relief, but exported large quantities of grain and other agricultural products from Ireland to England. About one million people starved to death, and the wave of emigration caused by the famine swept away another million. Large areas of Ireland were depopulated. The abandoned land was turned by English and Irish landlords into pasture.

In 1848 a popular national liberation uprising was being prepared in Ireland by the revolutionary wing of the Irish Confederation (Mitchel, Lalor, Reilly and others). In May 1848 the British authorities took severe reprisals against the movement, leaving it virtually leaderless. The vacillating Confederation leaders (Smith O'Brien and others) missed the right moment for action. Instead of a country-wide insurrection, isolated and often unprepared uprisings occurred in a number of towns and agricultural areas in late July 1848, which were quickly put down by troops.

In 1849 Parliament passed the Encumbered Estates Act for Ireland, which was supplemented by a series of other Acts in 1852 and 1853. The 1849 Act provided for the sale of mortgaged estates by auction if their owners were proved to be insolvent. As a result, the lands of many ruined landlords passed into the hands of usurers, middlemen and rich tenants. p. 80

79 A version of this article headlined "Krimsche Angelegenheiten" ("Crimean Affairs") and dated March 16, 1855 appeared in the *Neue Oder-Zeitung*, No. 131, on March 19, 1855. It was marked with the sign ×. In translating Engels' article into German Marx abridged it slightly and made a few changes (the more important ones are indicated in the footnotes). p. 81

80 This refers to the landing in Eupatoria on February 9, 1855 of Turkish troops transferred from Bulgaria and commanded by Omer Pasha. They comprised two Turkish and one Egyptian divisions, two squadrons and two field batteries with a total strength of 21,600. p. 83

81 The text of this article, written by Engels for the *New-York Daily Tribune*, was included by Marx, in his own translation and with a number of alterations and additions, in his report "Criticism of the French Conduct of the War" published in the *Neue Oder-Zeitung* on March 20, 1855. Marx's version is published in this volume on pages 90-93.

The *New-York Daily Tribune* version was reproduced in full by Marx's daughter, Eleanor Marx-Aveling, and Edward Aveling in the collection *The Eastern Question. A Reprint of Letters written 1853-1856 dealing with the events of the Crimean War*, London, 1897. Marx was given as the author of all the articles in the collection as they were published in the *New-York Daily Tribune* either with his signature or unsigned. The publication of the Marx-Engels correspondence in 1913 (*Der Briefwechsel zwischen F. Engels und K. Marx*, Stuttgart,

1913) revealed that a considerable number of the articles sent by Marx to the *Tribune* had been written by Engels.

The first sentence in this article was supplied by the editors of the *New-York Daily Tribune.* The reference is to the extracts from the pamphlet *De la conduite de la guerre d'Orient* which were reprinted in English translation in the *New-York Daily Tribune,* No. 4350, on March 29, 1855 under the heading "Secret History of the Crimean Expedition. Its Origin and Blunders. Revelations of Prince Napoleon". p. 86

82 Engels is referring to the battles of Balaklava and Inkerman (see notes 10 and 35). p. 87

83 On May 21 and 22, 1809 at *Aspern,* on the left bank of the Danube near Vienna, Napoleon I's troops lost a battle to the Austrian army commanded by Archduke Charles. However, Napoleon succeeded in saving his troops from destruction by withdrawing from the left bank. On July 5 and 6 he defeated the Austrians at Wagram. Napoleonic France won the war against the Fifth Coalition (Austria, Britain, Spain and Portugal). p. 88

84 In a full-scale battle fought at *Leipzig* from October 16 to 19, 1813, the forces of the coalition of European Powers formed after Napoleon's expulsion from Russia in 1812 (Russia, Austria, Prussia, Britain, Sweden and others) inflicted a decisive defeat on the army of Napoleonic France and her allies. p. 88

85 An allusion to Louis Bonaparte's abortive putsch in Strasbourg on October 30, 1836. Aided by several Bonapartist officers he succeeded in persuading two artillery regiments of the Strasbourg garrison to mutiny. The mutineers were disarmed in a matter of hours. p. 88

86 On the *Eighteenth Brumaire* (November 9) 1799 a coup d'état was staged in France which resulted in the establishment of Napoleon Bonaparte's military dictatorship. On June 14, 1800 Napoleon's troops defeated an Austrian army at *Marengo* (Northern Italy). This first major victory by Napoleon after the coup consolidated his power.

The second edition of the Eighteenth Brumaire—Louis Bonaparte's counter-revolutionary coup d'état of December 2, 1851—led to the establishment of the Bonapartist Second Empire in France. p. 91

87 The memorandum handed by Britain, France and Austria to Russia's Ambassador in Vienna, Prince Alexander Gorchakov, during the Vienna Conference on the terms for peace negotiations (see Note 34). p. 94

88 The Vienna Conference was to work out the terms for peace between the participants in the Crimean War. It was attended by Russia, Britain, France, Austria and Turkey and lasted, with intervals, from March 15 to June 4, 1855. The negotiations centred on the Four Points (see Note 43). While agreeing, with certain reservations, to Points 1, 2 and 4, Russia emphatically rejected Point 3 which, as interpreted by the Western Powers, called for a reduction of the Russian Navy in the Black Sea. Britain and France insisted on its acceptance and turned down Austria's compromise proposal that Russia and Turkey should be allowed to agree between themselves on the size of their naval forces in the Black Sea. The Conference ended without adopting any decisions. p. 94

89 The *Peace Society* (the Society for Promoting Permanent and Universal Peace)—an organisation founded by the Quakers in London in 1816. It was

strongly supported by the Free Traders, who believed that, given peace, free trade would enable Britain to make full use of her industrial superiority and thus gain economic and political supremacy. p. 96

90 The *Ten Hours Bill,* passed by the British Parliament on June 8, 1847, applied only to adolescents and women and was ignored by many manufacturers.

In February 1850 the Court of Chancery (one of Britain's high courts) acquitted a number of manufacturers accused of infringing the Ten Hours Bill. This ruling caused protests from the workers. On August 5, 1850 Parliament passed a new Bill which stipulated a ten-and-a-half-hour working day for women and adolescents and fixed the beginning and end of the working day. p. 97

91 This article was first published in English in the collection Karl Marx and Frederick Engels, *Articles on Britain,* Moscow, Progress Publishers, 1971, pp. 229-32. p. 98

92 For details on the *People's Charter* see Note 46. Echoing the Chartist speakers at the meeting, Marx further mentions the Charter's five basic demands, omitting the sixth—payment of MPs. p. 99

93 See Note 10. p. 102

94 See Note 35. p. 102

95 See Note 88. p. 102

96 See Note 7. p. 103

97 A reference to the protocols signed by Britain, France, Austria and Prussia at the Vienna Conferences.

The protocol of December 5, 1853 proposed that Turkey enter into peace talks with Russia through the mediation of the four Powers (for details see Note 170).

The protocol of January 13, 1854 urged Russia to settle its military conflict with Turkey and informed the Russian government of the Porte's readiness for peace talks.

The protocol of April 9, 1854 demanded from Russia the immediate evacuation of its troops from the Danubian Principalities and a guarantee of the continued existence of the Ottoman Empire. p. 104

98 This refers to the London conventions of 1840 (see Note 20) and 1841. The latter was signed, on July 13, 1841, by Britain, Russia, Austria, Prussia and Turkey, and also by France which, faced with the prospect of an anti-French coalition, was forced to withdraw its support for the Egyptian ruler Mehemet Ali, who had attacked the Sultan, and join the Powers in backing the latter. The convention also stipulated that the Bosphorus and Dardanelles were to be closed to the warships of all Powers in peacetime. p. 105

99 See Note 43. p. 106

100 The treaty of alliance between Britain, France and Austria signed in Vienna on December 2, 1854. The signatories undertook not to enter into any agreements with Russia without preliminary consent between themselves and not to allow the occupation of the Danubian Principalities by Russian troops. Negotiations with Russia were to be based on the Four Points. By means of this treaty Britain and France sought to draw Austria into the war against Russia. Austria,

for its part, hoped to use the alliance to strengthen its influence in the Balkans and subjugate the Danubian Principalities. p. 106

101 An extract from this article by Engels, and his next article, "The Battle at Sevastopol", were included by Marx, in abridged form, in the report "Ueber die letzten Vorgänge in der Krim" ("On the Latest Events in the Crimea"), which was dated March 23, 1855 and published in the *Neue Oder-Zeitung*, No. 143, on March 26. The more important different readings in the English and German versions are indicated in the footnotes.

The present article was included in *The Eastern Question.* p. 109

102 "Les singes", which means "monkeys" and also "buffoons" and "superiors", was the name given to pro-Napoleonic generals. Marx mentioned the fact in a letter to Engels of September 13, 1854 and in several articles for the *New-York Daily Tribune* (see present edition, Vols. 13 and 39). p. 109

103 Prince Jerome Bonaparte, Junior, commanded a division in the Crimea in 1854. Disapproving of the Crimean expedition, lacking military talent and unpopular with the army, he feigned sickness to stay away from directing military operations and later returned to Paris without permission. p. 109

104 On the German version of this article see Note 101. The first paragraph was presumably supplied by the editors of the *New-York Daily Tribune.* p. 113

105 Marx is presumably referring to the visit of Lord Malmesbury, the former Foreign Secretary in Derby's Tory Cabinet, to Paris in March 1853 during which he was invited to dinner by Napoleon III and had a confidential talk with him on strengthening Anglo-French relations. p. 118

106 *St. James's Palace*—royal residence in London since the late seventeenth century. Festive ceremonies and receptions were frequently held there. p. 121

107 The *Kuchuk-Kainarji peace treaty* was concluded by Russia and Turkey on July 21, 1774, following the former's victories in the Russo-Turkish war of 1768-74. Russia obtained part of the Northern shore of the Black Sea between the South Bug and the Dnieper with the fortress of Kinburn; she also got Azov, Kerch and Yenikale and compelled Turkey to recognise the independence of the Crimea, which facilitated its eventual incorporation into Russia. The Sultan undertook to grant a number of privileges to the Greek Orthodox Church. Article 14, in particular, provided for the building of an Orthodox church in Constantinople. p. 122

108 See Note 6. p. 122

109 The *Demagogues* were members of an opposition movement of German intellectuals. The word gained wide currency following the Carlsbad conference of Ministers of German states in August 1849, which adopted a special resolution against the intrigues of "demagogues". Here the reference is to the opponents of the counter-revolutionary monarchies restored in Europe after Napoleon's fall. p. 123

110 *Exeter Hall*—a building in London, meeting place of religious and philanthropic societies.

Puseyism—a trend within the Anglican Church between the 1830s and 1860s. It was named after the Oxford theologian E. B. Pusey, who called for

the restoration of certain Catholic rites and dogmas. The Puseyites represented the interests of the aristocracy, which strove to retain its influence in opposition to the industrial bourgeoisie, which was on the whole Protestant. In particular, the Puseyites upheld the Catholic view of the Eucharist as the "transubstantiation" of bread and wine into the true body and blood of Christ. In contrast to this, the other Anglican and Protestant trends regarded the bread and wine merely as symbols of the "true presence" of Christ's body and blood.
p. 126

111 See Note 35. p. 126

112 This is an altered English version of Marx's article "The Committee of Inquiry" written for the *Neue Oder-Zeitung* (see this volume, pp. 124-27).
p. 128

113 A reference to Aberdeen's coalition ministry of 1852-55. This "Cabinet of All the Talents" included Whigs, Peelites (see Note 6) and representatives of the Irish faction in the British Parliament. p. 130

114 This paragraph, especially its concluding part, shows signs of interference by the editors of the *New-York Daily Tribune*. p. 132

115 The *siege of Silistria* (Silistra)—a fortress on the south bank of the Danube in Bulgaria—by Russian troops was one of the major operations in the Danubian theatre during the Crimean War. The siege began in the first half of May 1854, but in the fourth week of June the Russian troops withdrew beyond the Danube in view of the hostile attitude of Austria, which had concentrated considerable forces behind the Russian lines. A description of the fighting in this area was given in the articles "The Russian Retreat" by Marx and Engels and "The Siege of Silistria" by Engels (see present edition, Vol. 13, pp. 253-57 and 234-45). p. 134

116 This is an altered German version of Engels' article "Progress of the War". The text was translated and edited by Marx. p. 136

117 This would seem to refer to the fighting between the Turkish and Russian forces that took place at Kalafat, in the Danubian theatre of war, in mid-January 1854. p. 136

118 *Bashi-bazouks*—irregular detachments of the Turkish army in the eighteenth and nineteenth centuries; the name was also given to troops noted for their lack of discipline and for their cruelty and looting. p. 136

119 The system of recruitment in force in France until 1872 (abolished by the French Revolution but reintroduced by Napoleon I) enabled members of the propertied classes called up for the army to hire substitutes. In an attempt to tighten its control over the armed forces the Bonapartist government in April 1855 introduced the law of "dotation", under which substitutes, unless close relations of the draftee, were to be provided by the state. In return the person exempted from service was to contribute a fixed sum to the "army dotation" fund p. 139

120 Under the heading "Prospect in France and England" this article (minus the first sentence) was included in *The Eastern Question*.

The opening sentence was presumably contributed by the editors of the *New-York Daily Tribune* in an attempt to provide some sort of explanation for the long absence of articles signed by Marx. At the time, most of Marx's articles

were published as editorials. It may be assumed that in this particular case the editors printed the article under Marx's name as they did not want to be identified with the revolutionary proletarian attitude clearly expressed in the article.
p. 141

121 See Note 88.
p. 141

122 See Note 6.
p. 143

123 The *Peace Society*—see Note 89. By "peace party" Marx means the Free Traders or the Manchester School (see Note 7).
p. 143

124 See Notes 2, 35 and 10.
p. 144

125 A reference to the heroic uprising of Paris workers in June 1848. It was the first civil war between the proletariat and the bourgeoisie in history. The defeat of the uprising was followed by a counter-revolutionary offensive in many European countries, including France itself.
p. 145

126 A German version of this article dated April 14, 1855 was published in the *Neue Oder-Zeitung*, No. 177, on April 17 under the heading "Kritik des napoleonischen 'Moniteur'-Artikels" ("A Critique of Napoleon's Article in *Le Moniteur*"). The article was translated into German and edited by Marx. The more important changes are indicated in the footnotes.

Under the heading "Napoleon's Apology" the English version was included in *The Eastern Question*.

The first sentence of the article in the *New-York Daily Tribune* shows editorial interference. It was evidently the editors who added the lines concerning the reprinting in the *Tribune* of passages from the *Moniteur* leading article (actually there was only a brief summary of the article in the "Letters from Europe" column of the *New-York Semi-Weekly Tribune*, No. 1035, April 27, 1855).
p. 146

127 See Notes 22 and 107.
p. 147

128 In the battle of *Baylen* on July 20, 1808, during the Spanish war of independence (1808-14), the French troops commanded by General Dupont were encircled by the Spaniards and laid down their arms.

At Culm (Bohemia) on August 29 and 30, 1813, during the war of the coalition of European Powers against Napoleonic France, the Austrian troops encircled and captured the French forces commanded by General Vandamme.
p. 147

129 A reference to Mivart's (Claridge's) Hotel, 42 Brook Street, London, where Louis Napoleon stayed from 1838 to 1840, during his banishment from France after the abortive coup in Strasbourg on October 30, 1836.
p. 148

130 A German version of this article dated April 15, 1855 appeared in the *Neue Oder-Zeitung*, No. 179, on April 18 under the heading "Die Affäre vom 23. März" ("The March 23 Affair"). The text was translated and edited by Marx. Footnotes indicate the passages where the German version differs from the English.

The reference to the publication of the French and English reports on the events of March 23, 1855 (second paragraph of the English version) was added by the editors of the *New-York Daily Tribune*.
p. 151

131 This article was written by Engels at Marx's request for simultaneous publication in the *Neue Oder-Zeitung* and *New-York Daily Tribune*. It was based

on Engels' studies of the language, literature and history of many Slav peoples, which he began after moving to Manchester in 1850. He read Pushkin's *Eugene Onegin* and *Bronze Horseman* and Griboyedov's *Wit Works Woe* in the original. His notes on the vocabulary of these works are extant, together with the passages he copied from a reader in Russian literature, and his notes on the history of Russia and Serbia. These preparatory materials and the references in Engels' articles to the works of many noted Slavists—Dobrowsky, Kollár, Mikloszić, Palacký, Šafařík and others—bear witness to the intensity and fruitfulness of his studies, which enabled him to draw on numerous sources, including some in Slavic languages, in his analysis of the history, culture and national movements of the Slavs.

As can be seen from the closing sentence of the second instalment of this article, Engels intended to continue his discussion of the subject, laying special emphasis on exposing the reactionary character of the Pan-Slavist ideas. He regarded them as an instrument of the great-power policies of the Habsburgs (Austro-Slavism) and a means of vindicating the aggressive tendencies of Russian Tsarism. In sending Engels' article to Elsner, the editor of the *Neue Oder-Zeitung*, Marx wrote on April 17, 1855 that it was "the *beginning* of a polemic against *Pan-Slavism*" (see present edition, Vol. 39). However, no further articles on this subject appeared in the newspaper.

Marx attached particular importance to publishing a critique of Pan-Slavist ideas in the *New-York Daily Tribune* because he considered it vital to counteract the influence of A. Gurowski, a propagandist of Pan-Slavism and apologist for Tsarist Russia, who contributed to the *Tribune* and had published several pamphlets on the subject, including the brochure *Russia as It Is* (1854). The two instalments of the present article were published in the *New-York Daily Tribune* on May 5 and 7 as separate articles under the headings "The European Struggle" (for this version, which differs considerably from that of the *Neue Oder-Zeitung*, see pp. 163-65 of this volume) and "Austria's Weakness". In the second English article several unwarranted changes were made by the *Tribune* editors who, among other things, inserted a whole paragraph extolling Gurowski's ideas. This version is therefore published in the Appendices, with the necessary explanations given in the notes (see pp. 689-93 and Note 447).

Between January and April 1856 Engels wrote fifteen articles on Pan-Slavism for the *New-York Daily Tribune*, but the editorial board turned them down and in September sent them back to Marx. The manuscripts have not been preserved. Engels' plan for a pamphlet on Pan-Slavism, to be published in Germany, was not realised. p. 156

132 The *Ruthenians*—the name given in nineteenth-century Western ethnographical and historical literature to the Ukrainians of Galicia, the Eastern Carpathians and Bukovina, who were cut off at the time from the rest of the Ukrainian people. p. 157

133 In listing the Carinthians and Croats with the Slovenes, Engels was basing himself on the then current system of classification of the South Slav peoples, which singled out an "Illyrian branch", comprising the Slavs who inhabited the north-western part of the Adriatic coast of the Balkan Peninsula and the adjoining areas captured in the Middle Ages by the Austrian Habsburgs (Styria, Carinthia, Carniola and others). A considerable section of the Slav population of these areas, including the Carinthians, does belong to the Slovenes, but the Croats are a Slav people in their own right. p. 157

[134] The *Slav Congress* met in Prague on June 2, 1848. It was attended by representatives of the Slav countries forming part of the Austrian Empire. The Right, moderately liberal wing, to which Palacký and Šafařík, the leaders of the Congress, belonged, sought to solve the national problem through autonomy of the Slav lands within the framework of the Habsburg monarchy. The Left, radical wing (Sabina, Frič, Libelt and others) wanted to act in alliance with the revolutionary-democratic movement in Germany and Hungary. Radical delegates took an active part in the popular uprising in Prague (June 12-17, 1848), directed against the arbitrary rule of the Austrian authorities, and were subjected to cruel reprisals. On June 16, the moderate liberal delegates declared the Congress adjourned indefinitely. p. 159

[135] The Serbian insurrection against the arbitrary rule and brutal reprisals of the Turkish janissaries, which flared up in February 1804, developed into an armed struggle for Serbia's independence from Turkey. In the course of the insurrection a national government was set up and in 1808 Georgi Petrovič (Karageorge), the leader of the insurgents, was proclaimed hereditary supreme ruler of the Serbian people. The Serbian movement was greatly advanced by the successful operations of the Russian army in the Balkans during the Russo-Turkish war of 1806-12. Under the Bucharest peace treaty of 1812 Turkey was to grant Serbia autonomy in domestic affairs, but taking advantage of Napoleon's invasion of Russia, the Sultan sent a punitive expedition to Serbia in 1813 and restored Turkish rule there. It was overthrown in 1815 as a result of a new Serbian insurrection and diplomatic support from Russia. After the Russo-Turkish war of 1828-29, which ended in the signing of the Adrianople peace treaty of 1829, Turkey recognised the autonomy, i.e. virtual independence, of the Serbian Principality by a special firman of the Sultan issued in 1830. p. 160

[136] This article is an altered version of part of the article "Germany and Pan-Slavism". The latter was written for the *Neue Oder-Zeitung*. Under the heading "Panslavism" the English version was printed in *The Eastern Question*. See Note 131. p. 163

[137] A reference to the adjournment of the Vienna Conference caused by disagreement between the participants on the Third Point of the terms presented to Russia (see Note 88). It was adjourned on April 26, 1855, following Russia's rejection of the Western Powers' demand that it should limit its naval forces in the Black Sea. It met for the last time on June 4, 1855. p. 163

[138] The *Reform Movement*—see Note 51.

The *Anti-Corn Law movement*—see Note 14.

The *Bank Restriction Act,* passed in 1797, introduced a compulsory rate for notes and abolished their convertibility into gold. These measures were re-introduced virtually in full in 1821 on the basis of an Act passed in 1819. p. 166

[139] The *Association for Administrative Reform* was set up in London in May 1855 on the initiative of liberal circles in the City. Taking advantage of the outcry caused in the country by press reports and the findings of the Parliamentary Committee of Inquiry on the plight of the British army in the Crimea, the Association hoped by means of mass rallies to bring pressure to bear on Parliament and win broader access for members of the commercial and finance bourgeoisie to government posts, monopolised by the aristocracy. In their

campaign the Association's leaders sought to obtain the support of the Chartists. However, at rallies organised by the Association and at their own rallies the Chartists refused to back the moderate bourgeois demands for administrative reform and instead urged a Parliamentary reform based on the People's Charter (see Note 46). The administrative reform campaign was a failure, and the Association soon ceased to exist. In his subsequent reports Marx frequently touched on the Association's activities and relations with the Chartists. p. 167

140 In Christoph Martin Wieland's *Die Abderiten, eine sehr wahrscheinliche Geschichte* a trifling dispute causes the population of the ancient Thracian city of Abdera to divide into two parties, the struggle between which nearly leads to the city's destruction. The first edition of the novel appeared in Weimar in 1774, the second, enlarged one, in 1781. p. 167

141 In the 1806 general election the Radical James Paull, a friend of William Cobbett's, was put forward as a candidate for Westminster. However, the authorities refused to endorse his nomination because of his denunciations of the Viceroy of India, Richard Wellesley. The Westminster electorate retaliated by returning to Parliament another Radical, Francis Burdett, who had actively defended Paull. p. 168

142 The *Thirty Years' War* (1618-48)—a war in which the Pope, the Spanish and Austrian Habsburgs and the Catholic German princes fought against the Protestant countries: Bohemia, Denmark, Sweden, the Republic of the Netherlands and a number of German states. The rulers of Catholic France—rivals of the Habsburgs—supported the Protestants. Germany was the main arena of this struggle, the object of pillage and territorial claims. The Treaty of Westphalia (1648) sealed her political dismemberment. p. 168

143 Marx is referring to Pius IX, who between 1846 and early 1848 introduced a number of moderate liberal reforms in the Papal States in the interests of the nobility and the commercial and industrial bourgeoisie. In this way he sought to counteract the mounting revolutionary movement in Italy. p. 168

144 A group of French deputies (called the Dynastic Opposition) headed by Odilon Barrot took part in the campaign of banquets for electoral reform conducted by the bourgeois and petty-bourgeois opposition in France on the eve of the February 1848 revolution. The group had joined the movement in an attempt to render it innocuous to the July monarchy. The Dynastic Opposition favoured moderate electoral reform as a means of preventing revolution and preserving the Orleans dynasty. p. 168

145 An abridged and altered version of this article by Engels was published in the *Neue Oder-Zeitung,* No. 217, on May 11, 1855, under the heading "Die Belagerung von Sebastopol" ("The Siege of Sevastopol"). It was marked with the sign × and dated May 8. The translation and editing were done by Marx. Footnotes indicate the passages where the German version differs from the English. p. 170

146 The report turned out to be false. Engels stated this on the basis of verified data in his article "The Crimean War" (see this volume, pp. 201-07). The Russian fortifications mentioned were taken by the Allies on June 7, 1855. p. 170

147 On April 28, 1855, Giovanni Pianori, an Italian revolutionary and associate of Garibaldi, shot at Napoleon III when the French Emperor was riding on

horseback in the Champs Elysées. The abortive attempt was provoked, among other things, by the part Louis Bonaparte played in 1849, when still President, in sending an expeditionary corps against the Roman Republic and crushing the Italian revolution. Pianori was executed in May 1855. p. 177

148 A German version of Engels' article "The New Move in the Crimea" appeared in the *Neue Oder-Zeitung* under the heading "Der Feldzug in der Krim" ("The Campaign in the Crimea"), dated May 11. The translation and editing were done by Marx.

The opening lines and further passages in the English version show alterations made by the editors of the *New-York Daily Tribune*. A comparison of the two versions reveals changes in the estimate of the strength of the Allied forces in the Crimea and a somewhat different presentation of figures, which was probably based on the reports of other *Tribune* correspondents, including A. Pulszky. However, the overall conclusions in the two versions are identical. p. 180

149 The second half of this article beginning with the words "The *anti-aristocratic* movement" was first published in English under the heading "The Character of the Whigs and Tories" in Karl Marx, *Surveys From Exile, Political Writings*, Vol. 2, Harmondsworth, 1973. p. 186

150 On May 14, 1855, Ellenborough moved in the House of Lords that a message be sent to the Queen informing her that the House was dissatisfied with the conduct of the Crimean War and that the success of the campaign could only be ensured by appointing deserving people to government posts. The proposal was discussed and rejected on the same day. p. 187

151 The *Anti-Corn Law League* was founded by the Manchester factory owners Cobden and Bright in 1838. By demanding complete freedom of trade, the League fought for the abolition of the Corn Laws (see Note 14). In this way it sought to weaken the economic and political position of the landed aristocracy and lower the cost of living thus making possible a lowering of the workers' wages. The repeal of the Corn Laws under Peel's Tory government led to a split in the ranks of the Tories and facilitated the coming to power of the Whigs (1846). Having achieved its end, the League ceased to exist. p. 187

152 See Note 139. p. 187

153 The Act for a Seven-Year Parliament (the *Septennial Act*), passed by Parliament in the interests of the Whig oligarchy in 1716, extended the term of Parliament from three to seven years.

By the latest Workhouse and Factory legislation the 1834 Poor Law is meant (see Note 56). p. 188

154 A reference to the British naval expedition to the mouth of the Scheldt in 1809, during the war waged by the Fifth Coalition (Austria, Britain, Portugal and Spain) against Napoleonic France. The British captured Walcheren Island, but were unable to launch further operations and had to evacuate the island after about 10,000 of their landing party of 40,000 had died of hunger and disease. p. 190

155 The *rotten boroughs* were sparsely populated constituencies which had retained the right to a seat in Parliament from the Middle Ages. In practice the election of MPs from the rotten boroughs depended on the landlords who controlled them. The 1832 Reform Act (see Note 45) deprived most of the rotten

boroughs of Parliamentary representation, but the old system of demarcating electoral districts, which favoured the landed aristocracy, was largely preserved. p. 192

156 A reference to the *London Chartist Organising Committee* set up in February 1855 as a successor to the Welcome and Protest Committee. The latter had been formed by Ernest Jones in October 1854 to arrange a festive welcome to London for Armand Barbès, a participant in the 1848 revolution in France who had been released from prison, and to organise a demonstration of protest against the proposed visit to London of Napoleon III, who was expected to come at about the same time. Together with the Executive of the National Charter Association the London Organising Committee worked for the revival of the Chartist movement in London and for closer international co-operation of democratic forces. The Committee included Ernest Jones, George Harrison, James Taylor and other noted Chartists. It set up a seven-man commission charged with the task of establishing international ties. Together with representatives of French, German and other refugees in London the commission formed an International Committee. At the end of 1855 the London Organising Committee was disbanded, and the International Committee was set up as an independent organisation. Renamed the International Association in 1856, it operated until 1859. p. 196

157 In the *battle of Jena* (October 14, 1806) the French army, commanded by Napoleon, routed the Prussian army, thus forcing Prussia to surrender. p. 204

158 This article was first published in English under the heading "On the Reform Movement" in Karl Marx, *Surveys from Exile, Political Writings,* Vol. 2, Harmondsworth, 1973. p. 208

159 See Note 47. p. 209

160 In July 1854, a French force commanded by Espinasse invaded the Dobruja. The expedition was a total failure. Many French soldiers died of cholera and other diseases. p. 212

161 On the night of December 1, 1851, a battalion of the regiment commanded by Espinasse was on guard duty at the National Assembly. On December 2 Espinasse, bribed by the Bonapartists, ordered his troops to occupy the Assembly building, thereby contributing to the success of Louis Bonaparte's coup d'état. p. 212

162 A reference to Disraeli's statement in the House of Commons on May 22, 1855, that he would shortly submit for discussion a draft message to the Queen censuring the Palmerston government's vacillating policy on the issue of war and peace. A motion to this effect was in fact tabled on May 24 and evoked a lively debate in Parliament. Marx described this debate in a number of his articles (see this volume, pp. 227-36, 245-48 and 257-59). p. 213

163 See Notes 88 and 137. p. 214

164 Marx included this article in an abridged and somewhat revised form in his report for the *Neue Oder-Zeitung* headlined "Prologue at Lord Palmerston's.—Course of the Latest Events in the Crimea", which is published in this volume as a joint article by Marx and Engels (see pp. 218-21). p. 215

165 The section of this article dealing with the latest events in the Crimea (up to

the last but one paragraph, which describes the circumstances of Pélissier's appointment) is an abridged German version of Engels' article "The New French Commander", published in the *New-York Daily Tribune,* No. 4414, on June 12, 1855 (see this volume, pp. 215-17). The editing and translation were done by Marx. p. 218

166 See Note 162. p. 218

167 See Note 162. p. 222

168 On May 11, 1855, T. M. Gibson stated in the House of Commons that he was going to submit for discussion a draft message to the Queen expressing the desire for a successful conclusion of the Vienna Conference and for an honourable peace. p. 223

169 A reference to the third of the Four Points put forward by the Allies as terms for peace talks with Russia (see Note 43). It was interpreted by Western diplomats as calling for a limitation of the Russian naval forces in the Black Sea and was rejected by Russia's representatives at the Vienna Conference (see Notes 88 and 137). p. 228

170 On December 5, 1853, the British, French and Prussian representatives at the Vienna Conference and the Austrian Foreign Minister Buol signed a protocol under which Notes were sent to Turkey and Russia offering Western mediation in settling the Russo-Turkish dispute. The following terms were stipulated as a basis for negotiations: evacuation by Russia of Moldavia and Wallachia, renewal of the former Russo-Turkish treaties, a guarantee of the rights of Christians by all European powers, and reform of Turkey's administrative system. p. 228

171 See Note 107. p. 229

172 See Note 43. p. 229

173 *Probabilism*—a theory that, truth being unattainable, all knowledge can only be probable. According to it, any action is permissible since some kind of plausible justification can always be found for it. p. 231

174 See Note 43. p. 232

175 See Note 110. p. 233

176 See Note 107. p. 235

177 *Categorical imperative*—the basic concept of the ethics of the German philosopher Immanuel Kant (1724-1804). It denotes the moral obligation of the individual to act according to rules that could serve as principles of universal legislation. p. 236

178 See Note 43. p. 238

179 This article was first published in English under the heading "The Association for Administrative Reform.—People's Charter" in Karl Marx and Frederick Engels, *On Britain,* Moscow, 1962. p. 240

180 See Note 139. p. 240

181 The alignment of class forces in France after the defeat of the uprising of Paris workers in June 1848 enabled the Bonapartist circles to take advantage of universal suffrage in order to get Louis Napoleon elected President (December 10, 1848). On May 31, 1850, the French Legislative Assembly abolished

universal suffrage. Louis Napoleon demagogically used the slogan of its restoration in staging his coup d'état on December 2, 1851. An analysis of these events is given in Marx's *The Class Struggles in France, 1848 to 1850* (see present edition, Vol. 10) and *The Eighteenth Brumaire of Louis Bonaparte* (Vol. 11). p. 242

182 In 1842 the radical and liberal Free-Trade circles made several attempts to enlist the working-class movement in the campaign for the repeal of the Corn Laws and for moderate reforms. To distract the workers from the struggle for the implementation of the Chartists' social and political programme, they put forward the vague demand for "full suffrage". With the aid of some conciliatory Chartist leaders (Lovett, Vincent and others) the radicals succeeded in convening in Birmingham two conferences of representatives of the bourgeoisie and Chartists (in April and December 1842) which discussed joint campaigns for electoral reform. However, on December 27 the Chartist majority at the conferences rejected the proposal to replace the People's Charter with a new "Bill of Rights" and the demand for "full suffrage". From then onwards the Charter was the exclusive demand of the proletarian masses. p. 243

183 See Note 88. p. 245

184 On the *Peelites* see Note 6.
On the *Manchester School* see Note 7. p. 246

185 The works of Thomas Hobbes were published in 1839-45, eleven volumes in English and five in Latin, by Molesworth. p. 247

186 A reference to the Protocol of December 5, 1853 (see Note 97).
On the *Four Points* see Note 43. p. 248

187 The opening lines of the first and third paragraphs (the references to the reports brought by the *Asia* and to those received from Halifax, as well as to the publication in the preceding issue—No. 4424, June 22, 1855—of reports on the fighting in the Crimea) were added by the *Tribune* editors. The article was reproduced by Marx in German translation and with some alterations in his report published in the *Neue Oder-Zeitung* on June 11, 1855, under the heading "Zur Kritik der Vorgänge in der Krim" ("A Critique of the Events in the Crimea"). p. 249

188 This article is, in part, a German version of Engels' report "From the Crimea" written for the *New-York Daily Tribune* (see this volume, pp. 249-52). The translation and editing were done by Marx. The description of the Allies' expedition to the Sea of Azov, their landing of May 25, 1855, and the capture of Kerch and Yenikale may have been taken from the same report, the relevant passage of which might have been left out by the *Tribune* editors because reports on this expedition had been published in the paper earlier (see the leading articles "From the Crimea" and "The Crimean War" in the *New-York Daily Tribune*, Nos. 4415 and 4422, June 14 and 21, 1855). p. 253

189 See Note 151. p. 259

190 The first paragraph of this article (the reference to the publication of the dispatches by General Pélissier and Lord Raglan under the common heading "The Recent Successes Before Sevastopol" in the *New-York Daily Tribune*, No. 4428, June 28, 1855) was added by the *Tribune* editors.

An abridged version of this article with a few editorial changes by Marx (dated June 12, 1855 and marked with the sign ×) was published in the *Neue Oder-Zeitung* on June 15 under the heading "Kritik der Krimschen Unternehmungen" ("Criticism of the Operations in the Crimea"). p. 260

191 After the defeat of the Prussian troops by Napoleon's army at Jena and Auerstadt in the autumn of 1806, many Prussian fortresses surrendered to the advancing French without a fight. However, the garrison of Colberg (Polish name: Kolobrzeg) on the Baltic coast offered staunch resistance. The siege began in mid-March 1807 and lasted for three and a half months. The defence, directed by Gneisenau, was supported by Schill's guerrilla detachment, operating behind the French lines.

The fortress of Danzig (Gdansk), occupied by the French after their defeat in Russia in 1812, was besieged by the Russians and Prussians from land and sea in early 1813. The garrison withstood three regular sieges, but was ultimately forced to surrender. On January 2, 1814, the Allied troops entered the city. p. 261

192 After the successful start of the North Italian campaign by General Bonaparte's army in the spring of 1796—a series of victories over the Austrians, the defeat of their allies, the Piedmontese, and the capture of Lombardy's capital, Milan—its advance was arrested by the resistance of Mantua. In June the French beleaguered the fortress. At the same time, Napoleon had to use some of his men for active operations against the Austrian troops attempting to relieve the city. It was only after a nine-month siege and the defeat of the Austrian relief army that the Mantua garrison surrendered (February 2, 1797).

Danzig (Gdansk) was besieged by the French in March 1807, in the course of Napoleonic France's war against the Fourth European coalition (Prussia, Russia, Britain and Sweden). The garrison, consisting of Prussian troops and a Russian detachment, offered stiff resistance, supported by the attempts of another Russian detachment to break the siege from without. The fortress surrendered to the superior French forces at the end of May 1807. p. 262

193 The text of this article by Engels was translated by Marx into German and included, with a certain amount of editing, in two reports for the *Neue Oder-Zeitung:* "The Debate on Layard's Motion.—The War in the Crimea", dated June 16 and published June 19, 1855 and "The Local War.—Debate on Administrative Reform.—Report of the Roebuck Committee, etc.", dated June 20 and published June 23, 1855. The two reports are therefore published here as written jointly by Marx and Engels (see this volume, pp. 277-79 and 287-91) p. 267

194 A reference to the French intervention against the Roman Republic which led to the latter's fall (July 1849) and the restoration of the temporal power of the Pope. Louis Napoleon, as President of the French Republic, was one of the organisers of the intervention. p. 267

195 See Note 43. p. 268

196 The *Treaties of Tilsit*—the peace treaties concluded on July 7 and 9, 1807 by Napoleonic France with Russia and Prussia, members of the Fourth anti-French coalition which was defeated in the campaigns of 1806 and 1807. In an attempt to divide the defeated powers, Napoleon made no territorial claims on Russia and even managed to have part of Prussia's Eastern possessions (the Bialystok region) transferred to it. At the same time, harsh terms were imposed on

Prussia, who lost nearly half its territory to the German states dependent on France, was obliged to pay an indemnity, had its army limited, etc. However, Russia, as well as Prussia, had to sever its alliance with Britain and, to its own disadvantage, join the Continental System. Napoleon formed the vassal Duchy of Warsaw on Polish territory seized by Prussia during the partitions of Poland in the late eighteenth century, and planned to use the duchy as a bridgehead in the event of war with Russia. The further aggravation of Russo-French differences led to Napoleon's campaign against Russia in 1812. p. 269

197 A reference to the Austro-Prussian treaty of April 20, 1854, obliging the two states to take joint action against Russia in the event of her refusing to evacuate the Danubian Principalities or of the Russian troops' advancing further in the Balkans. p. 271

198 *Lower Empire* (Bas Empire)—the name given in historical literature to the Eastern Roman Empire (Byzantine Empire); also used with reference to states at the stage of decline or disintegration. Here an allusion to the Second Empire in France. p. 271

199 Acting on instructions from the Home Secretary James Graham, the British authorities in 1844 opened the correspondence of a number of Italian revolutionary refugees, including letters from the Bandiera brothers to Mazzini in which they set forth their plan for an expedition to Calabria to organise an uprising against the Neapolitan Bourbons and Austrian rule in Italy. In June 1844 the members of the expedition, betrayed by one of their number, were arrested. The Bandiera brothers were shot. p. 273

200 See Note 139. p. 274

201 This article has not been found. p. 274

202 In this report Marx drew on Engels' article "Napoleon's War Plans" written for the *New-York Daily Tribune* (see this volume, pp. 267-72). p. 277

203 In his House of Commons speech on June 15, 1855, Layard tabled a resolution stating that the traditional practice of appointing members of influential families to government posts had caused incalculable harm to the country and was discrediting the nation. Layard's motion, discussed on June 15 and 18, was rejected. p. 277

204 See Note 43. p. 278

205 The *Vienna Congress* of European monarchs and their Ministers (September 1814 to June 1815) concluded the wars of the European coalition against Napoleonic France. It was attended by representatives of all European states, except Turkey. The congress revealed sharp differences between the principal participants: Russia and Prussia, on the one hand, and Austria, Britain and France, on the other. The extremely protracted negotiations were accompanied by endless balls, masquerades and theatrical events. The decisions of the congress (further in the text Marx calls them the Vienna treaty, meaning the sum total of international acts, including the Final Act of June 9, 1815) helped re-install several royal dynasties overthrown during the French Revolution and the Napoleonic wars, sealed the political disunity of Germany and Italy, sanctioned the annexation of Belgium by Holland and the partition of Poland, and outlined measures to combat the revolutionary and national liberation movement, thereby preparing the ground for the Holy Alliance, a counter-revolutionary union of European monarchs. p. 283

206 Marx is referring to the secret treaty of alliance against Russia and Prussia signed by France, Austria and Britain in the Austrian capital on January 3, 1815, during the Congress of Vienna. Along with Chancellor Metternich of Austria and British Foreign Secretary Castlereagh, an important part in preparing the treaty was played by Talleyrand-Périgord, the French representative at the Congress, who sought to exploit the differences between the members of the former anti-Napoleonic coalition. The formation of the Anglo-Austro-French alliance forced Prussia to reduce her claims on the Kingdom of Saxony and with regard to the Polish lands. p. 283

207 The treaties signed by Russia, Prussia and Austria in Vienna on May 3, 1815, and the Final Act of the Congress of Vienna, signed on June 9, 1815, sanctioned the abolition of the Duchy of Warsaw, set up by Napoleon in 1807, and a new partition of the Polish lands between Austria, Prussia and Russia. p. 284

208 See Note 198. p. 286

209 The last paragraph of this article was presumably added by the *New-York Daily Tribune* editors. p. 286

210 In this report Marx drew on Engels' article "Napoleon's War Plans", which was written for the *New-York Daily Tribune* (see this volume, pp. 267-72). p. 287

211 See Note 196. p. 288

212 Speaking in the House of Commons on June 15, 1855, Edward George Bulwer-Lytton tabled a proposal (in the form of an amendment to a proposal by Layard) urging stricter regulations for the filling of government posts and a number of other administrative reforms. The proposal, largely aimed at depriving the Administrative Reform Association (see Note 139) of its *raison d'être*, was discussed by the House on June 15 and 18 and adopted on June 20. p. 289

213 On May 26, 1855, the British frigate *Cossack* stopped off Gange (Hangö) in the Gulf of Finland and sent a boat under a flag of truce to treat with the Russians. Mistaking the envoys for an intelligence party, the Russian commanding officer, an ensign, laid an ambush. In the ensuing clash half the British sailors were killed and the others wounded and taken prisoner. The incident was discussed by the British Parliament. Marx describes the debate in question in his next report for the *Neue Oder-Zeitung* (see this volume, pp. 292-96). p. 291

214 The beginning of Marx's article (the part concerning the false report about the seizure of Sevastopol) appeared in the *Neue Oder-Zeitung* on June 25 with an editorial note saying that the conclusion would be published in the next morning issue of the paper. p. 292

215 On June 18, 1855, one of the major battles of the Crimean War was fought at Sevastopol, ending in defeat for the Allies. The nearly nine-month-long siege of the city, the destruction caused by the bombardment, and the capture by French and British troops on June 7, 1855 of the outlying fortifications, the Selenghinsk and Volhynsk redoubts and the Kamchatka lunette (which had been erected by the defenders in the course of the siege) induced the Allied command to undertake a full-scale assault on the Southern (Korabelnaya) part

of the city. It was launched on the fortieth anniversary of the battle of Waterloo, fought on June 18, 1815. The assault was preceded by massive bombardment of the city from land and sea. Despite the Allies' substantial superiority in numbers, their attack, launched along the whole line of Russian fortifications at dawn on June 18, 1855, was repulsed at every point. The attackers suffered heavy losses. The fighting on June 18 showed the strength of Sevastopol's defences and the staunchness of the Russian troops. Marx gave a detailed account of the battle in his report "The Mishap of June 18.—Reinforcements"; Engels described it in his articles "From Sevastopol" and "The Late Repulse of the Allies" (see this volume, pp. 297-301, 313-19 and 328-32). p. 292

216 During an inspection of troops in Boulogne at the end of September 1854 Napoleon III declared that the Allies had taken Sevastopol. This statement was based on false reports. p. 292

217 A reference to the law on a new internal loan passed by the Legislative Corps on June 20, 1855. The loan was to total 750 to 800 million francs. p. 293

218 See Note 213. p. 293

219 In the battle of Waterloo fought on June 18, 1815, the Anglo-Dutch and Prussian forces commanded by the Duke of Wellington and Blücher defeated Napoleon's army. p. 297

220 The *Treaty of Unkiar-Skelessi*—see Note 25.

The *Dardanelles Treaty*—a reference to the London Straits Convention signed on July 13, 1841 (see Note 98). p. 300

221 Marx's description of the mass demonstration held in Hyde Park on June 24, 1855, in protest against a series of anti-popular measures adopted by Parliament (in particular, the prohibition of Sunday trading) is based mainly on his own observations. Wilhelm Liebknecht writes in his memoirs that Marx and other German revolutionary democrats took part both in this demonstration and in one organised by the Chartists at Hyde Park on the following Sunday, July 1, 1855. According to Liebknecht, in the course of the latter demonstration, which was dispersed by the police, Marx was very nearly arrested. Two days after the events of June 24, Marx wrote to Engels: "The demonstration held at Hyde Park on Sunday afternoon looked very revolutionary." The present article was first published in English in Karl Marx and Frederick Engels, *On Britain*, Moscow, 1953. It was printed together with another article by Marx, describing the demonstration on July 1 (see this volume, pp. 302-07 and 323-27) under the joint editorial heading: "Anti-Church Movement. [—Demonstration in Hyde Park"]. p. 302

222 The *High Church*—a trend in the Anglican Church which stressed the latter's derivation from Catholicism, maintained the traditional rituals and originally drew its following mainly from the aristocracy.

The *Low Church*—a trend in the Anglican Church which laid special emphasis on Christian morality; its following originally consisted predominantly of members of the bourgeoisie and the lower clergy.

Dissidents or *dissenters* were members of various Protestant sects and trends in England who to some degree or other rejected the dogmas of the Established Church. p. 302

223 According to British Parliamentary procedure the House of Commons, when discussing certain important questions, may declare itself a Committee of the

Whole House. Each of its sittings is presided over by one of a list of chairmen who is appointed by the Speaker. p. 303

224 A reference to the Executive Committee of the National Charter Association. Founded in July 1840 and numbering nearly 50,000 members in its heyday, the Association was the first mass working-class party in the history of the labour movement. In 1848, the defeat of the Chartists and division in their ranks drastically reduced the Association's following. Nevertheless, in the 1850s the Association, headed by Ernest Jones and other revolutionary leaders, launched a campaign for the revival of Chartism on a revolutionary basis. It urged the implementation of the People's Charter and the socialist principles proclaimed by the Chartist Convention in 1851.

In 1855 widespread discontent with the policy of the ruling oligarchy induced the revolutionary Chartists to make another attempt to reorganise Chartism. In the summer of that year a number of local Chartist committees were elected, and in August the Executive Committee of the National Charter Association was formed. It included Ernest Jones, Abraham Robinson and James Finlen. The Association ceased its activities in 1858. p. 305

225 See Note 213. p. 308

226 See Note 139. p. 309

227 An Act passed in Britain in the early eighteenth century obliged newly elected Members of Parliament to swear what was known as the Oath of Abjuration, which was a solemn denial of the right of James II's descendants to the Crown. The Oath included a statement of devotion to Christianity. Refusal by an MP to take the Oath virtually debarred him from participation in Parliamentary proceedings. Despite repeated motions for amending the text of the Oath, it was not until 1866 that the passage on devotion to Christianity was omitted.

Lord John Russell's Jewish Disabilities Bill (1853) to allow elected Jews to swear a non-Christian oath had been carried in the Commons but rejected by the Lords. p. 311

228 An abridged German version of this article dated June 29, 1855 was published in the *Neue Oder-Zeitung* on July 2, 1855 under the title "Über die Ereignisse in der Krim" ("On the Events in the Crimea"). The translation and editing were done by Marx. The first paragraph in the *New-York Daily Tribune* version shows signs of editorial interference. p. 313

229 See Note 219. p. 316

230 On Marx's participation in the second mass demonstration against the Anti-Sunday Trading Bill, held in Hyde Park on Sunday, July 1, 1855, see Note 221. On July 3, 1855 Marx wrote to Engels about this demonstration: "The scenes in Hyde Park last Sunday were disgusting, firstly because of the constables' brutality and secondly because of the purely passive resistance put up by the huge crowds. Meanwhile things are clearly seething and fermenting and we can only hope that great disasters in the Crimea will bring them to a head."

The article was first published in English in: Karl Marx and Frederick Engels, *On Britain*, Moscow, 1953, pp. 420-25, as Part II, together with Marx's article on the demonstration of June 24, 1855 (see this volume, pp. 302-07) under the common editorial heading "Anti-Church Movement—Demonstration in Hyde Park". p. 323

231 A reference to the battle of Inkerman (November 5, 1854) in which the British suffered heavy losses (see Note 35). p. 326

232 The text of this article by Engels was used by Marx in two reports for the *Neue Oder-Zeitung*: "Clashes between the Police and the People.—The Events in the Crimea" (published in this volume as a joint work by Marx and Engels, see pp. 333-36) and "Über den Sturm vom 18. Juni" ("On the Assault of June 18"). The latter has not been included in this volume as it is an almost word for word translation of part of Engels' article "The Late Repulse of the Allies".

The first paragraph of the *New-York Daily Tribune* version of this article shows signs of editorial interference. p. 328

233 A reference to the defeat of the British and Turkish forces in the battle of Balaklava (see Note 10). Particularly heavy losses were suffered by the British cavalry. p. 332

234 The section of this article dealing with military events is part of Engels' article "The Late Repulse of the Allies" which was written for the *New-York Daily Tribune* (see this volume, pp. 328-32). p. 333

235 *Maine Law*—the first law passed in the US banning the production and sale of alcoholic beverages. It was first adopted in the State of Maine in 1841 and renewed in amended form in 1851. p. 333

236 Napoleon III and Empress Eugénie visited London in April 1855. p. 334

237 Marx and Engels used this phrase with reference to Max Stirner in *The German Ideology* (see present edition, Vol. 5, p. 355). p. 334

238 See Note 139. p. 334

239 "Infantry Balaklava"—see Note 233.

Marx continued his analysis of the military events of June 18, 1855 in a report dated July 7 and headlined "Über den Sturm vom 18. Juni" ("On the Assault of June 18"). It was published in the *Neue Oder-Zeitung* on July 11. The report reproduced in German a large section of Engels' article "The Late Repulse of the Allies" (see this volume, pp. 328-32). p. 335

240 *Quakers* (or *Society of Friends*)—a religious sect founded in England during the seventeenth-century revolution and later widespread in North America. The Quakers rejected the Established Church with its rites and preached pacifist ideas. The "wet" Quakers, so called in opposition to the orthodox or "dry" Quakers, were a trend which emerged in the 1820s and sought to renew the Quaker doctrines. p. 335

241 See Note 51. p. 337

242 Part of this article, beginning with the words "For two years..." and up to the end, was first published in English in Marx, Engels, *Ireland and the Irish Question*, Moscow, 1971. p. 340

243 *Court of Chancery*—one of England's highest courts, a division of the High Court of Justice following the Judicature Act of 1873. It was presided over by the Lord Chancellor and dealt with matters relating to inheritance, observance of contracts, joint-stock companies and similar legal problems. It was notorious for red tape and procrastination. p. 340

244 *Committee of Supply* (or *Committee of Ways and Means*)—in accordance with parliamentary procedure, the House of Commons, when discussing major questions concerning the national budget, declares itself a Committee of Ways and Means. This is one of the cases when the House sits as a Committee of the Whole House (see Note 223). p. 341

245 For the *Irish Brigade* see Note 58.

The Bills in question were submitted by Aberdeen's coalition Government in June 1853 to reduce the class struggle in the Irish countryside by granting the tenants certain rights and protecting them from landlord arbitrariness. Marx discussed the Bills in his article "The Indian Question.—Irish Tenant Right" (see present edition, Vol. 12, pp. 157-62). As Marx had foreseen, the British Parliament, reluctant to impinge on the interests of the landed aristocracy, refused to grant even minor concessions to the tenants. Even in curtailed form, the Bills were virtually quashed. p. 342

246 The text of this article was reproduced by Marx in an abridged and altered German version (dated July 14) which was published in the *Neue Oder-Zeitung* on July 17 under the heading "Russell's Resignation.—The Events in the Crimea". In the present edition the *Neue Oder-Zeitung* version is given as a joint article by Marx and Engels (see this volume, pp. 348-51). p. 344

247 The nickname of Gebhard Leberecht von Blücher, the Prussian field marshal, who advocated active offensive tactics during the 1813 campaign against Napoleon. For more on this see the article "Blücher" by Marx and Engels in Volume 18 of the present edition. p. 344

248 The section of this article relating to the events in the Crimea is a somewhat abridged and altered version of Engels' article "The Great Crimean Blunder" (see this volume, pp. 344-47). p. 348

249 See Note 247. p. 349

250 I. e. from the sittings of the Vienna Conference (see Note 88). p. 353

251 *Previous question*—(in British parliamentary procedure) the question as to whether a vote shall be taken on a question or issue, debated before the main question is put. A vote on the previous question—whether it was expedient "that this question be now put"—was often taken to avoid a division on some important matter. If the vote was negative the question was postponed, if positive it was put without further debate. p. 355

252 According to custom, Ministers and Members of Parliament accused of illegal actions may be tried before the House of Lords at the instance of the House of Commons, a judicial process known as impeachment. This custom, which enabled the House of Commons to supervise the activities of Ministers, was frequently resorted to in the seventeenth and eighteenth centuries, but was practically abandoned in the nineteenth. p. 357

253 Marx included the text of this article, in an abridged German translation, in his report of July 20 for the *Neue Oder-Zeitung*. It appeared on July 23 under the heading "From Parliament.—From the Theatre of War" (see this volume, pp. 363-66). In the present edition this report is given as a joint item by Marx and Engels. p. 358

254 For the *battle of Inkerman* (November 5, 1854) see Note 35.

On the fighting for the Mamelon (the Kamchatka lunette) and other outlying Russian fortifications at Sevastopol in June 1853 see Engels' article "From Sevastopol" (this volume, pp. 313-19).

On the assault of June 18, 1855 see Engels' article "The Late Repulse of the Allies" (this volume, pp. 328-32) and Note 215. p. 358

255 Marx's report reproduces in an abridged and altered form Engels' article "War Prospects" written for the *New-York Daily Tribune* (see this volume, pp. 358-62). p. 363

256 See Note 251. p. 363

257 See Note 254. p. 363

258 A reference to the dismissal on January 3, 1851 by President Louis Bonaparte of General Changarnier from the posts of commander of the Paris garrison and chief of the Paris National Guard. The General was a placeman of the Party of Order, which comprised the two monarchist factions—the Legitimists and the Orleanists—in the Legislative Assembly, whose conflict with the Bonapartists was growing increasingly acute. As a pretender to dictatorial power Changarnier was also a personal rival of Louis Bonaparte. p. 364

259 On June 27, 1855 Britain, France and Turkey concluded an agreement by which the British and French governments undertook to grant Turkey a loan of £5 million. In July the British Government tabled a Bill in the House of Commons calling for a guarantee of the loan. It encountered strong opposition and was only passed by an insignificant majority. In August the Bill was sanctioned by Queen Victoria. p. 367

260 See Note 88. p. 367

261 By the *Wakefield School* Marx means the supporters of the plan for "systematic colonisation" advanced by the British economist and statesman Edward Gibbon Wakefield in his work *England and America* (Vols. 1 & 2, London, 1833) and in other writings. Wakefield advocated colonisation through emigration, but held that there should be restrictions on the purchase of land by resettlers. This was to ensure the colonies an ample supply of wage labour and reduce social conflicts in the home country by providing an outlet for redundant labour.

Wakefield's theory of colonisation attracted Marx's attention as early as the beginning of the 1850s, when he made a number of notes from Wakefield's book *A View of the Art of Colonisation* (London, 1849). Later he gave a detailed critique of this theory in the last chapter of the first volume of *Capital* (see present edition, Vol. 31). p. 368

262 Marx later used the findings of the parliamentary committee in question ("First Report from the Select Committee on Adulteration of Food. Ordered, by the House of Commons, to be printed, 27 July, 1855) in a number of notes to the first volume of *Capital* (see present edition, Vol. 31, Index of Quoted and Mentioned Literature). p. 369

263 Marx subsequently discussed the problem of industrial accidents stemming from employers' neglect of safety precautions in the first volume of *Capital*, notably the chapter "Machinery and Modern Industry" (see the section "The Factory"). As in the present article, he compared industrial accident reports to military bulletins, pointing out that the development of capitalist machine industry "with the regularity of the seasons, issues its list of the killed and wounded in the industrial battle". Characteristically, there too Marx corrobo-

rated his conclusions with quotations from reports of factory inspectors, notably that of Leonard Horner for the second half of 1855 ("Reports of the Inspectors of Factories for the Half Year Ending 31st October, 1855." London. 1856). The "Reports of the Inspectors of Factories for the Half Year Ending 30th April, 1855", which he analyses in the present article, were also used by him, but in a different context, in the chapter in *Capital* on the rate of surplus value (see present edition, Vol. 31. Index of Quoted and Mentioned Literature). p. 370

264 The satirical pamphlet *Lord John Russell*, which Marx wrote in connection with the crisis of Lord Palmerston's Cabinet and John Russell's resignation, was intended as a series of articles for the *Neue Oder-Zeitung* and the *New-York Daily Tribune*. It was to be a portrait of this Whig leader, presenting all the major aspects of his activity. While he was collecting the relevant material for the pamphlet—Parliamentary reports, political brochures, articles in periodicals and Russell's own writings—Marx wrote to Engels (July 17, 1855): "Do you know of any book about the *êtres* of little Johnny Russell?" By the beginning of August 1855 a considerable part of the pamphlet had been written, and its publication began in the *Neue Oder-Zeitung*. On August 7 Marx wrote to Engels: "In the last few weeks I have sent the *Tribune* a series of articles—to be precise, three—reviewing the career of this little man from the outset."

However, the pamphlet was published in full only in the *Neue Oder-Zeitung*, as a series of six articles under the common heading "Russell". The *New-York Daily Tribune* published one big article (August 28) under the heading "Lord John Russell", which was an abridged English version of instalments II to VI of the series that appeared in the *Neue Oder-Zeitung*. The cuts may have been by the *Tribune* editors, who condensed the series into a single article. It appeared unsigned.

Instalment I of the *Neue Oder-Zeitung* series was first published in English in Karl Marx and Frederick Engels, *On Britain*, Moscow, 1953. It was followed by the condensed version of articles II to VI reproduced from the *New York Daily Tribune*.

In the present edition the pamphlet is published in full, according to the *Neue Oder-Zeitung*, but under the heading given in the *New-York Daily Tribune*. Where the German version differs substantially from the English the relevant passages are given in the footnotes. p. 371

265 On the *Utrecht Peace* (1713) see Note 71.

Marx knew some of Russell's historical works earlier. For instance, in July 1843 he familiarised himself with the German edition of his constitutional history of Britain (*Geschichte der englischen Regierung und Verfassung von Heinrichs VII bis auf die neueste Zeit*, Leipzig, 1825). Excerpts from it are contained in one of his Kreuznach notebooks on world history (Notebook III). p. 374

266 On the Reform Bill (submitted by Russell in the House of Commons on March 1, 1831) see Note 45. p. 374

267 The English version, which was published in the *New-York Daily Tribune* and reproduced in abridged form instalments II to VI of the *Neue Oder-Zeitung* series, has no date at the beginning and starts with the following paragraph, in all probability added by the editors: "We have recently had occasion to notice the funeral obsequies of this politically departed statesman, and to utter a few farewell words above his grave. The part which his birth, and his position as

the only presentable member of the great revolutionary family and old Whig house of Bedford enables him to play in the drama of European Affairs, and the connection of his name with some of the great progressive measures of the day, seem to us to entitle him to a somewhat more lengthened and analytic obituary." p. 376

268 Following the massacre of workers at a mass meeting in support of electoral reform on St. Peter's Field near Manchester on August 16, 1819, the British Parliament passed the Six Acts, proposed by Lord Castlereagh, which virtually abolished Habeas Corpus and the freedom of the press and assembly. They became known as the "gagging acts", and Marx uses the phrase in the English version of the article where he speaks of "Castlereagh's six gagging acts". p. 376

269 *Boroughs* (in the English version: "nomination boroughs")—a reference to the rotten boroughs (see Note 155).

Copyholders, leaseholders—types of tenant farmers in England whose legal status was formalised as early as the Middle Ages. The former held land by copy of the manorial court roll and were liable to the payment of a fixed rent. The latter held land under a lease, the terms of which were agreed upon by the landlord and the tenant. p. 377

270 This refers to the widespread movement of farm labourers throughout the south of England in late 1830 and early 1831. The movement, which began apparently spontaneously in the south-east, was largely directed against the use of threshing machines, which the labourers held responsible for growing impoverishment and unemployment. As it spread rapidly from county to county to embrace the whole of southern England there were definite signs of some sort of collective plan behind it, and the participants claimed to represent a legendary "Captain Swing"—whence the name of the "Swing" movement. Large gangs went out at night systematically destroying all the threshing machines in the neighbourhood, and also burning down ricks and sometimes the houses of landlords and of parsons, whom they held to be in league with the landlords. The majority of tenant farmers, however, appear to have had a certain sympathy with the labourers, since they preferred the old methods and felt themselves obliged to purchase threshing machines only under pressure from landlords and of competition from other farmers who had been persuaded to buy one. Thus the farmers put up little resistance to the destruction of the machines, and on occasion even encouraged it. The Swing uprisings were crushed by the authorities. Nevertheless, they succeeded in their aims in as much as the destroyed machines were not restored and the threshing machine virtually disappeared from British agriculture for twenty years, until the 1850s. p. 377

271 *Tenants-at-will*—tenants holding land on conditions dictated by the landlord at the given moment and dependent on his arbitrary will. p. 378

272 *Freeholders*—a category of small landowners in England dating back to the Middle Ages. p. 379

273 In keeping with English parliamentary tradition, the speaker of the House of Lords, the Lord Chancellor, sits on a *woolsack*, symbolising what once used to be the main source of England's national wealth. p. 379

274 See Note 6. p. 381

275 In April 1833 the British Parliament adopted a police law for Ireland. This was caused by the spread of peasant unrest, in particular, the refusal of Irish peasants, the vast majority of whom were Catholics, to pay tithes to the Anglican Church in Ireland. The British Government was also forced to resort to other measures to control the profound social conflict in Ireland and safeguard the position of the Established Church. Marx discusses them further on in the text. Despite the mass movement, it was not until 1838 that tithes were abolished (by the Commutation Act). However, under the new regulations too the peasants continued to pay for the maintenance of the Anglican Church, now indirectly in the form of an increase in rents which the landlords were obliged to transfer to the church funds. p. 383

276 See Note 74. p. 384

277 See Note 75. p. 385

278 The Bill introduced by Peel into the House of Commons in the spring of 1846 to legalise the arbitrary police regime in Ireland under the guise of prohibiting the bearing of arms. The bill was lost because of the opposition of the Whigs, who took advantage of the situation to overthrow the Peel ministry. When they came to power the Whigs themselves tried to take police measures against the Irish national liberation movement. In 1847 they passed on emergency law for Ireland which ushered in a new regime of atrocious repression of the Irish people. p. 385

279 A writ of *Habeas Corpus*—the name given in English judicial procedure to a document enjoining the appropriate authorities to present an arrested person before a court on the demand of the persons interested to check the legitimacy of the arrest. Having considered the reasons for the arrest, the court either frees the arrested person, sends him back to prison or releases him on bail or guarantee. The procedure, laid down by an Act of Parliament of 1679, does not apply to persons accused of high treason and can be suspended by decision of Parliament. The British authorities frequently made use of this exception in Ireland. p. 386

280 See Note 14. p. 386

281 The sliding scale, so called, was adopted by the British Parliament at the proposal of the Tory Government in 1828. According to it import tariffs on grain were raised when grain prices on the home market fell and lowered when they went up. p. 388

282 See Note 151. p. 389

283 The *Corporation Act*, adopted by the British Parliament in 1661, required that persons holding elective posts (mainly members of municipal bodies) should take the sacrament according to the rites of the Church of England.

The *Test Act* of 1673 required the same of all persons holding government posts.

Originally directed against the Catholic reaction, these Acts later became instruments for fighting every form of opposition to the Established Church, including the various sectarian movements (the dissidents or dissenters), and protecting its privileges. p. 390

284 See Note 51. p. 391

285 I. e. the anniversary of the Gunpowder Plot, a Catholic conspiracy to blow up

Parliament. It was uncovered on November 5, 1605. Guy Fawkes was one of the plotters. Their aim was to restore Catholicism in England. p. 392

286 The *Ecclesiastical Titles Bill*, which became law in August 1851, declared invalid the Pope's edict of 1850 on the nomination of Catholic bishops and archbishops in Britain. p. 392

287 *Irish Brigade*—see Note 58.

Manchester men, Manchester school—see Note 7. p. 392

288 A German version of the article, dated July 27 and 28, 1855, was published in the *Neue Oder-Zeitung* under the heading "Birmingamer Konferenz.—Die dänische Erbfolge.—Die vier Garantien" ("The Birmingham Conference.—The Danish Succession.—The Four Guarantees") on July 30 and 31. It differs slightly from the English version in content and the way of quoting (as a rule, the quotations are more condensed and treated more freely). Where the German differs substantially from the English this is indicated in the footnotes. Marx's main sources were the reports of the committees of the Birmingham Conference, which were published soon after it ended on June 23, 1855.

Under the heading "The Birmingham Conference" the article was included in *The Eastern Question*. p. 394

289 A reference to the London Protocol of May 8, 1852 on the integrity of the Danish monarchy (see Note 23). p. 394

290 The *State Reform Association* was set up by the Left, radical wing of the bourgeois opposition in July 1855. In contrast to the Administrative Reform Association, it urged Parliamentary reform based on universal suffrage. The Radicals leading the Association sought an agreement with the Chartists, hoping to bring the working-class movement under their ideological and political influence. Jones, Finlen and other Chartist leaders became members of the Association's Executive Committee, but soon resigned under pressure from the Chartist rank and file, who realised the danger of the Radicals' gaining control of the Chartist organisation. p. 394

291 See Note 43. p. 396

292 *London Treaty of July 6, 1827*—a reference to the convention signed by Britain, Russia and France confirming the St. Petersburg Russo-British protocol of April 4, 1826 which recognised Greece's right to autonomy. Like the protocol, the convention included an agreement on the diplomatic recognition of Greece and on armed mediation in the Greco-Turkish conflict. The contracting parties confirmed the commitment recorded in the protocol to seek no territorial or commercial benefits for themselves in pacifying Greece except such as were common to all European states.

The *Treaty of Adrianople*—see Note 22. p. 398

293 The *London convention of 1841*—see Note 98. p. 399

294 *Russo-Dutch loan*—see Note 24.

The *Treaty of Unkiar-Skelessi*—see Note 25.

The *Treaty of the Dardanelles*—presumably the London convention on the Straits of 1841 (see Note 98).

On the *Balta-Liman Treaty* see Note 22. p. 400

295 Engels wrote this survey at the request of Marx, who received an order for it from the US journal *Putnam's Monthly* through Charles Dana, editor of the

New-York Daily Tribune. In forwarding Dana's letter to Engels on June 15, 1855, Marx asked him to write "one printed sheet on all the European armies for *Putnam's Monthly*". However, Engels' survey turned out much longer and took a considerable time to write. Marx helped Engels by collecting data on various European armies, the Spanish and the Neapolitan, in particular, at the British Museum library. After receiving the first article of the series for forwarding to New York, Marx wrote to Engels (August 7, 1855): "The article on the 'Armies' is excellent." On September 1 he informed Engels of the *New York Times*' review—on the whole, favourable—of this article, which had been published in the August issue of *Putnam's Monthly,* and of the reviewer's awkward attempts to dispute the instances of corporal punishment of the lower ranks in the British Army cited by Engels. The continuation and conclusion of the series were published in the September and December issues of the journal. They were numbered articles two and three (the first article appeared without a number). By printing the survey unsigned, the editors tried to suggest that the author was an American. This may also have been the reason for the minor editorial changes in the text, in particular the use of the pronoun "our" with reference to the US army (see p. 407). p. 401

296 *Putnam's Monthly* has the following note here, in all probability supplied by the editors: "We must not omit to state that our own country has produced a military history of the first class for impartiality, becoming language, and even handed justice to friend and foe: we refer to *The War with Mexico,* by Major Ripley." R. S. Ripley's book, published in New York in 1849, was known to Marx and Engels. Marx describes it in letters to Engels of November 30 and December 2 and 15, 1854. No statements by Engels on it have come to light. p. 405

297 See Note 157. p. 405

298 A reference to the operations of the British forces, commanded by Wellington, in the Peninsular War, which was waged by Britain against Napoleonic France on the territory of Spain and Portugal from 1808 to 1814. Simultaneously, throughout the Iberian Peninsula, the Spanish and Portuguese peoples were fighting for independence against the French occupation. In the course of the war Wellington won the battles of Oporto in 1809, Busano in 1810, and Fuentes de Oñoro in 1811. He also took Ciudad Rodrigo and Badajoz in 1812. p. 405

299 *Boulogne Camp*—the bridgehead set up by Napoleon I at Boulogne-sur-Mer on the English Channel between 1803 and 1805 for invading England. The threat of an attack by the forces of the third anti-French coalition (Russia, Austria, Britain and Sweden) formed in 1805 prevented him from carrying out his plan.

At *Austerlitz* on December 2, 1805 Napoleon's troops defeated the Russians and Austrians. p. 405

300 The battle of New Orleans (USA) between the British and American forces coincided with the receipt of a dispatch on the signing of the Ghent Treaty (December 24, 1814) which ended the British-American war of 1812-14 (the Second War of Independence) by restoring the pre-war position. p. 405

301 At *Borodino,* near Moscow, a full-scale battle was fought by the French and Russian forces on September 7, 1812. It turned the tide in the war of 1812 in favour of Russia, even though the Russian army was forced to leave Moscow. p. 407

302 The French Imperial Guards, disbanded after the fall of Napoleon I, were restored by a special decree of Napoleon III on May 1, 1854. p. 410

303 See Note 119. p. 411

304 See Note 2. p. 411

305 The *Seven Years' War*—the war of 1756-63 between Britain and Prussia, on the one hand, and France, Russia and Austria, on the other. It was caused mainly by colonial and commercial rivalry between Britain and France and the clash between Prussia's policy of aggrandizement and the interests of Austria, France and Russia. In the course of the war the Prussian army of Frederick II won a series of victories over the French and Austrians, but suffered a number of serious defeats in battles against the Russian forces. As a result of the war, Britain expanded her colonial empire at the expense of France. Austria and Prussia retained, by and large, their former frontiers. p. 414

306 This section was used by Marx as material for several articles for the *Neue Oder-Zeitung*. The text from the beginning up to the words "a small heroic detachment of Britons was almost lost in the mass of Allied troops" was reproduced in almost literal translation with a few insignificant cuts in the report "Die britische Armee", dated by Marx August 25, 1855 and published in the *Neue Oder-Zeitung,* No. 399, August 28. The continuation up to the paragraph beginning with the words "The uniform and equipment of the British soldiers", edited and enlarged by Marx, provided the basis for the article "The Punishment of the Ranks", dated August 28, 1855 and published in the *Neue Oder-Zeitung,* No. 405, August 31, 1855. In this volume it is given as a joint work by Marx and Engels (see pp. 501-03). The rest of the section beginning with the words "The uniform and equipment of the British soldiers" and up to the end was used by Marx with a few cuts and additions in his article "Uniformirung und Equipirung des britischen Soldaten" ("Uniform and Equipment of the British Soldier"), dated August 23, 1855 and published in the *Neue Oder-Zeitung,* No. 407, September 1, 1855. All these articles in the *Neue Oder-Zeitung* are marked with the sign ×. Where the article "Uniform and Equipment of the British Soldier" differs substantially from the corresponding English text, this is pointed out in the footnotes. p. 416

307 See Note 10. p. 417

308 See Note 35. p. 419

309 Speaking of his personal experience, Engels may have had in mind his service as a volunteer in a brigade of the Guards' Artillery in Berlin in 1841-42. p. 421

310 The *Military frontier* or the *Military Border Area*—the southern border regions of the Austrian Empire where military settlements began to be set up in the sixteenth century for protection against Turkish invasions. The inhabitants of these regions—Serbs, Croats, Romanians, Szeklers, Saxons, and others—were allotted plots of land by the state, for which they had to serve in the army, pay taxes and perform certain public duties. In 1848-49 the *granichary,* as the soldiers from these regions were called, formed part of the Austrian armies deployed against the revolutionary movement in Northern Italy and Hungary. p. 425

311 See Note 83. p. 427

312 Todtleben was actually alive at the time. The statement in the text is based on inaccurate information then circulated by the European press. Wounded on June 20, 1855, Todtleben was forced to leave Sevastopol and was undergoing treatment when Engels wrote his survey. p. 443

313 The *battle of Chetatea*, in the Danubian theatre, between the Turkish and Russian armies, took place in the early period of the Crimean War, on January 6, 1854. It resulted from the Turks' attempts to take the offensive in the Kalafat area, at the juncture of Wallachia, Serbia and Bulgaria. After a stiff fight the Russian detachment was compelled to retreat under pressure from considerable Turkish forces (about 18,000 men), but following the arrival of Russian reinforcements the Turks were forced to go over to the defensive and eventually retreated to Kalafat. For a description of these events see Engels' article "The Last Battle in Europe" (present edition, Vol. 12, pp. 579-82).

On the Russians' siege of Silistria in May-June 1854 see Note 115. p. 445

314 *German Confederation* was an association of German states set up by the Congress of Vienna on June 8, 1815. Initially it included 34 states, mostly with a feudal absolutist system of government, and four free cities. For all practical purposes the Confederation sealed Germany's political and economic fragmentation and retarded her development. After the defeat of the revolution of 1848-49 and the failure of the attempts to establish a more stable political union, the German Confederation was restored in its old decentralised and amorphous form. p. 448

315 In 1826 Sultan Mahmud II brutally suppressed a mutiny of the Janissaries, who rebelled against a reform of the Turkish army aimed at replacing the feudal Janissary forces with regular units. After the mutiny was crushed, the Janissary corps was disbanded.

On the *Treaty of Adrianople* see Note 22. p. 451

316 The Turks besieged Vienna twice, in 1529 and 1683, both times unsuccessfully. In 1683 the Austrian capital was relieved by the troops of Polish King John III. p. 453

317 At *Oltenitza* (south-east Wallachia) in the Danubian theatre, the Russian and Turkish forces fought one of the first battles of the Crimean War (November 4, 1853). A Russian detachment attacked the Turkish forces which had crossed to the left bank of the Danube. The attack failed, but the Turkish troops were soon compelled to withdraw to the right bank. Engels described the battle in his article "The War on the Danube" (see present edition, Vol. 12, pp. 516-22). p. 456

318 Engels is referring to the strength of the Sardinian army at the time of the Austro-Italian war of 1848-49. Sparked off in March 1848 by the national liberation uprising in Lombardy and Venice, then under Austrian rule, the war was fought in two stages. Following the entry into the war of the King of Sardinia (Piedmont), the main fighting took place between the Sardinian and Austrian forces, the latter commanded by Field Marshal Count Josef von Radetzky. On July 25, 1848 the Austrians beat the Italians at Custozza, and on August 9 Sardinia signed an armistice obliging her to withdraw her troops from Lombardy and Venice. The mounting revolutionary movement in Italy forced the King of Sardinia to resume hostilities (March 20, 1849), and the second stage of the war began. However, on March 21-23 the Sardinian army

was defeated at Mortara and Novara. The rout of Sardinia also enabled the Austrians to crush the other centres of resistance in Northern Italy. p. 457

319 This refers to the military convention concluded on January 26, 1855 by Britain and France, on the one hand, and the Kingdom of Sardinia (Piedmont), on the other. Sardinia undertook to send a corps of 15,000 to fight against Russia in the Crimean War, while Britain and France guaranteed the integrity of the Kingdom of Sardinia. By entering the war Sardinia's ruling quarters sought to secure Napoleon III's support for their future struggle for the North Italian territories held by Austria. p. 457

320 On August 16, 1855 Russian troops attacked the French and Sardinians on the river Chernaya about twelve kilometres southeast of Sevastopol in an attempt to weaken the Allies' siege of the city. However, the Russians were repulsed and suffered heavy losses due to inadequate preparation of the attack and errors on the part of the Russian command. Engels analysed this important episode of the Crimean War in his article "The Battle of the Chernaya" (see this volume, pp. 504-12). p. 458

321 In 1796, during France's war against the Second Coalition, which included Naples (the Kingdom of the Two Sicilies), the French defeated the army of the Neapolitan King Ferdinand I and seized Naples.

In July 1820 the carbonari, aristocratic and bourgeois revolutionaries, rose in revolt against the absolutist regime in the Kingdom of Naples and succeeded in having a moderate liberal constitution introduced. However, in 1821 Austria, acting in accordance with a decision of the Laibach congress of the Holy Alliance, invaded Naples. The Austrian troops defeated the Neapolitan army and occupied Naples. The absolutist regime was restored. p. 460

322 This refers to the participation of the Kingdom of Naples in the French and Austrian invasion of the Roman republic in May-July 1849. The republican forces, commanded by Garibaldi, launched two vigorous offensives, putting the Neapolitans to flight. p. 460

323 A reference to the Constitution of the Swiss Confederation adopted on September 12, 1848. It ensured a measure of centralisation for the country, which from a loose union of cantons with an extremely weak central administration was turned into a federative state. In place of the former Diet a central legislative body, the Federal Assembly, consisting of a National Council and a Council of States, was set up. Executive power was vested in the Federal Council, whose chairman acted as President of the republic. p. 461

324 The *Sonderbund*—a separatist union of the seven economically backward Catholic cantons of Switzerland, formed in 1843 to resist progressive bourgeois reforms and to defend the privileges of the church and the Jesuits. The decree of the Swiss Diet of July 1847 dissolving the Sonderbund served as a pretext for the latter to start hostilities against the other cantons early in November. On November 23, 1847 the Sonderbund forces, consisting largely of militia detachments, were defeated by the federal army. p. 462

325 In the spring of 1798 the forces of the French Directory defeated the Swiss army and occupied Switzerland. As a result, Swiss territory became one of the main theatres of operations between France and the Second Coalition (Austria, Britain, Russia, the Kingdom of Naples and Turkey). p. 462

326 Norway was a Danish possession from the late fourteenth century. Under the Treaty of Kiel (1814) Denmark ceded it to Sweden. Early in the same year

Norway made an abortive bid for independence, but was forced to accept union with Sweden. The union had been backed by a number of European powers who wanted Sweden to join the anti-French coalition of 1813-14. The annexation of Norway to Sweden was sanctioned by the Congress of Vienna (1814-15). Under the terms of the union Norway retained its parliament (Storting) and administration and also its officer corps in the army, the King of the united kingdom of Sweden and Norway acting as Commander-in-Chief. In 1905 the union was dissolved and Norway regained its independence. p. 463

327 See Note 142. p. 464

328 See Note 84. p. 464

329 This refers to the Kingdom of Denmark's war against the secessionist duchies of Schleswig and Holstein (1848-50). Prussia entered the war on the side of the duchies, seeking to exploit the national liberation movement there for its own ends. However, the need to combat the revolutionary movement in their own country, and diplomatic pressure from the European powers, compelled Prussia's ruling circles to conclude an armistice with Denmark on August 26, 1848 at Malmö. Hostilities were resumed in the spring of 1849, followed by another armistice on July 10. The Schleswig-Holstein forces, now fighting the Danes single-handed, were defeated. The war ended in the restoration of Danish rule in Schleswig-Holstein. p. 464

330 Engels is referring to the second and third bourgeois revolutions in Spain. The former began with the mutiny of a unit of the Spanish army at Cadiz on January 1, 1820. Preparations for the mutiny started in the previous year. The revolution was suppressed in 1823 by the French occupation army sent to Spain in accordance with the decision of the Verona congress of the Holy Alliance. The third revolution (1834-43) was touched off by the first Carlist war of 1833-40 (see Note 18). p. 469

331 *"Entente cordiale"*—the relations established between Britain and France after the July 1830 revolution by an agreement signed in April 1834, when Britain, France, Spain and Portugal formed an alliance. However, already at that stage differences between Britain and France emerged, which intensified as time went on. Marx is referring here to the strongly anti-French attitude taken by the British Government, in particular Palmerston, during the Turko-Egyptian conflict of 1839-41 (see Note 69). p. 470

332 *Bill regulating lease-hold tenure in Ireland*—see Note 245.

The Irish Brigade—see Note 58. p. 470

333 No articles on India by Marx appeared in any subsequent issues of the *Neue Oder-Zeitung.*

The Parliamentary recess lasted from August 14, 1855 to January 31, 1856. p. 472

334 A reference to Palmerston's flirting with the Italian liberal movement on the eve of and during the revolution of 1848-49. In an attempt to avert a revolutionary crisis in Italy he sent Lord Minto to Rome and Naples in the autumn of 1847 to try and persuade Italy's rulers to make certain concessions to the Liberals and introduce some moderate reforms. During the revolution Palmerston's ambiguous attitude gave the Italian Liberals, and even Republi-

cans, grounds to expect diplomatic and military support from Britain. Actually, however, Britain supported the Austro-French invasion of the Roman Republic, thereby greatly contributing to the victory of the counter-revolutionary forces in Italy. p. 474

335 Marx is referring to the treaty concluded by Britain, France and Austria in Vienna on December 2, 1854 (see Note 100). p. 476

336 Some details in Marx's account of the meeting, in particular his description of the speakers, show that his article was based either on his own impressions or those of eyewitnesses. It is possible therefore that he attended the meeting. He may also have used the report on the meeting published in *The People's Paper*, No. 171, August 11, 1855, which gave the text of the amendment tabled by the Urquhartist Collet and adopted by the meeting (Marx quotes it). Marx also had at his disposal copies of leaflets distributed in the hall, from which he quotes, though their contents were not included in newspaper reports. p. 477

337 The *Literary Association of the Friends of Poland* was set up in London in 1832 and was modelled on the Literary Society established in Paris by the conservative, aristocratic-monarchist wing of the Polish refugee community (Adam Czartoryski's followers) in the same year. p. 477

338 The *Democratic Polish Association* was formed by radical nationalist or democratic Polish refugees—noblemen and bourgeois—in France in 1832. In 1836 the *Centralisation*, the Association's executive committee, was established. The Association worked for a popular revolution involving the peasant masses. It aimed at national independence, the abolition of feudal services and inequality stemming from the existence of social estates, the transfer of plots to the peasants without redemption, and a number of other progressive measures. The Democratic Association took an active part in preparing the 1846 Cracow uprising and in the 1848-49 revolution. In the summer of 1849, after the Association was banned in France, the Centralisation's headquarters were transferred to London. The 1850s were marked by dissent within the Association. After the establishment in Poland of the Central National Committee for the Preparation of a National Liberation Uprising, the Association dissolved (1862). p. 477

339 In 1846 a national liberation uprising took place in the Cracow republic, which by decision of the Congress of Vienna was controlled jointly by Austria, Prussia and Russia, who had partitioned Poland at the end of the eighteenth century. The seizure of power in Cracow by the insurgents on February 22, 1846 and the establishment of a National Government of the Polish republic, which issued a manifesto abolishing feudal services, were part of the plan for a general uprising in the Polish lands, which was inspired mainly by the revolutionary democrats. In March the Cracow uprising, lacking active support in other parts of Poland, was crushed by the forces of Austria and Tsarist Russia. In November 1846, Austria, Prussia and Russia signed a treaty incorporating the "free town of Cracow" into the Austrian Empire.

In 1848 a revolutionary movement again spread in many regions of Poland, in particular, Posen and Silesia, and also among the Ukrainian peasants in Galicia. In 1848-49 Polish revolutionaries were active in the revolutionary struggle in Germany, Austria, Hungary, France and Italy. p. 478

340 Addressing the House of Commons on December 12, 1854, Peel urged the British Government to take repressive measures against the political refugees

and put an end to public criticism by refugees, above all Victor Hugo and Lajos Kossuth, of the governments of their countries. p. 480

341 See Note 139. p. 480

342 Later Marx sent an enlarged English version of this article to the *New-York Daily Tribune.* It appeared as a leading article under the heading "Austria and the War" on September 13, 1855 (see this volume, pp. 495-500). p. 481

343 An English version of the second instalment of this article, written by Engels, appeared in the *New-York Daily Tribune* on September 1, 1855 as a leading article headlined "The War". It is considerably shorter than the German version and in some passages, particularly at the beginning, contains editorial changes. In all probability it was the *Tribune* editors who shortened the text considerably. Where the German differs substantially from the English, this has been indicated in the footnotes in the present volume. p. 484

344 See Note 320. p. 487

345 Sveaborg was a fortress situated on a group of islands at the entrance to the Helsinki harbour in the Gulf of Finland (modern Finnish name: Suomenlinna). The bombardment of Sveaborg by British and French ships described in the article took place on August 9 and 10, 1855. p. 488

346 In August 1855 Queen Victoria visited France. According to the official British press, the visit was meant to strengthen the "Holy Alliance of England and France". p. 490

347 See Note 320. p. 490

348 In the second half of this article Marx included a large section of his report "On the Critique of Austrian Policy in the Crimean Campaign" published in the *Neue Oder-Zeitung* on August 18 (see this volume, pp. 481-83). The first paragraph of the article contains changes made by the editors of the *New-York Daily Tribune,* who may, in particular, have added the reference to the report on Emperor Francis Joseph's inspection tour.

The article was published in *The Eastern Question* under the heading "Austria and England". In a footnote to the first sentence the compilers—Eleanor Marx and Edward Aveling—suggest that the report of the Austrian officer mentioned in it was sent to the *Tribune* by Marx in his own translation. However, no evidence to support this has come to light. p. 495

349 The concentration of Austrian troops on the Austro-Russian border began in May 1854 and was accompanied by large-scale conscription. Prior to this, on April 20, 1854, Austria concluded a defensive and offensive treaty with Prussia. Austria's military preparations were a major factor behind Russia's decision to withdraw its troops from the Danubian Principalities. However, on June 24, 1855 a reduction of the Austrian troops concentrated along the Galician frontier began on the orders of the Austrian Emperor. This was tantamount to an open refusal by Austria to enter the war on the side of the Allies. p. 495

350 This article is a fragment of the section "The English Army" from Engels' survey *The Armies of Europe,* published in *Putnam's Monthly* in August-December 1855 (see this volume, pp. 401-69 and Note 295). Marx translated this fragment into German and made a number of additions and other changes. p. 501

351 See Note 35. p. 502

352 A somewhat altered German version of this article was prepared by Marx for the *Neue Oder-Zeitung*. It was dated August 31 and September 1 and published on September 3 and 4 under the heading "Über die Schlacht an der Tschernaja" ("On the Battle of the Chernaya").

The first paragraph in the *New-York Daily Tribune* version contains changes made by the editors who, in particular, added the reference to the publication of the Pélissier and Simpson reports in the *Tribune* (No. 4493, September 13, 1855). p. 504

353 See Note 10. p. 507

354 The battles mentioned were fought by the British and their allies against the armies of Napoleonic France. The battle of *Bussaco* (Portugal) was on September 27, 1810; the battle of *Pamplona* was during the siege of that Spanish fortress in 1813, and the battle of *Waterloo* was on June 18, 1815 (see Note 219). p. 511

355 See Notes 2 and 35. p. 511

356 This article was published in *The Eastern Question* under the heading "Napier and Graham". p. 513

357 In 1839 the British Parliament issued a Blue Book on Persia and Afghanistan containing, among other documents, a number of letters by A. Burnes, the British representative in Kabul, on the Anglo-Afghan war (see Note 20). The letters had been selected and presented by the Foreign Office in such a way as to conceal Britain's provocative role in unleashing the war. Shortly before his death Burnes sent duplicates of his letters to London. Those not included in the Blue Book were published by his family. p. 513

358 A reference to the following facts connected with James Graham's activities as Home Secretary and First Lord of the Admiralty: the opening, on his instructions, of the letters of Italian revolutionary refugees (see Note 199); his part in the welcome given to Russian Emperor Nicholas I during the latter's visit to Britain in June 1844; his administration of the 1834 Poor Law and especially his responsibility for the notorious scandal at the Andover workhouse in 1845; and the attempt to put Captain Christie, head of port and transport facilities in Balaklava, on trial for neglect of duty, an attempt which caused Christie's premature death. p. 514

359 The Sind, an area in Northwest India bordering on Afghanistan, was seized in 1843. During the Anglo-Afghan war of 1838-42, the East India Company by threats and violence forced the feudal rulers of the Sind to agree to the transit of its troops through their territory. In 1843 the British demanded that the local feudal lords become vassals of the Company. This caused an uprising of the Baluch tribes (the Sind's indigenous population) after whose suppression by British troops under Sir Charles Napier the whole area was annexed to British India. p. 514

360 A German version of this article prepared by Marx and dated September 11, 1855 was published in the *Neue Oder-Zeitung* under the heading "Zur Einnahme von Sebastopol" ("On the Capture of Sevastopol"). In a letter to Engels dated September 11, 1855 Marx wrote that he had made a number of changes on the basis of the latest telegraphic dispatches.

The last two paragraphs in the English version were presumably added by the editors of the *New-York Daily Tribune*. p. 519

361 The *Red Cap* was the headgear of the ancient Phrygians. During the French Revolution it was adopted by the Jacobins and came to symbolise freedom. p. 524

362 Part of this article was reproduced by Marx in his report for the *Neue Oder-Zeitung* published on September 18, 1855 under the heading "Events in the Crimea". In the present edition this version is given as an item by Marx and Engels (see this volume, pp. 531-33).

The first and last paragraphs of the English version contain insertions made by the editors of the *New-York Daily Tribune*. The London correspondent mentioned in them was probably A. Pulszky. p. 525

363 The *battles of Oltenitza and Chetatea*—see Notes 317 and 313.

The *battle of the Chernaya*—see Note 320.

The *battle of Inkerman*—see Note 35. p. 526

364 On the Allies' abortive assault on Sevastopol of June 18, 1855 see Note 215. p. 526

365 Engels discussed the significance of the Northern side of Sevastopol in an earlier article, "The Siege of Sevastopol", published in the *New-York Daily Tribune*, No. 4236, November 15, 1854 (see present edition, Vol. 13, pp. 505-09). p. 528

366 See Note 305. p. 528

367 In October 1805, during the war of the Third Coalition (Austria, Britain, Russia and Sweden) against Napoleonic France, the Austrian army of General Mack was encircled by the French at Ulm and forced to surrender. p. 529

368 This article is Marx's adaptation for the *Neue Oder-Zeitung* of part of Engels' article "Crimean Prospects" published in the *New-York Daily Tribune*, No. 4508, October 1, 1855 (see this volume, pp. 525-29). p. 531

369 On the *battles of Oltenitza and Chetatea* see Notes 317 and 313.

On the *battle of the Chernaya* see Note 320.

On the *battle of Inkerman* see Note 35. p. 532

370 The *Société générale du Crédit mobilier* was a big French joint-stock bank founded by the Péreire brothers in 1852. It was closely associated with Napoleon III's government and under the latter's protection engaged in large-scale speculation. It went bankrupt in 1867 and was liquidated in 1871. p. 534

371 An abridged German version of this article was published in the *Neue Oder-Zeitung* on September 29, 1855 under the heading "Die Widerstandskraft Rußlands" ("Russia's Power of Resistance"). The translation and changes were made by Marx.

The first and last paragraphs of the English version contain changes made by the editors of the *New-York Daily Tribune*. p. 537

372 The *patrimonial court* was a feudal court whose jurisdiction was based on the right of the landowners to try and punish their peasants.

The *unsalaried magistrates* were justices of the peace appointed from among members of the propertied classes. p. 544

373 Under the laws on local administration adopted on July 7, 1852 and May 5, 1855 the general councils of the French departments were deprived of the right to elect their presidents, vice-presidents and secretaries. These were

appointed by the head of state; the general councils were to meet in closed session; the prefects and the head of state had the right to dissolve the municipal councils, whose officials were appointed by the local prefects. p. 545

374 An abridged German version of this article was prepared for the *Neue Oder-Zeitung* by Marx. It was dated September 29, 1855 and appeared under the heading "Zur Erstürmung Sebastopols" ("The Assault on Sevastopol") on October 4, 1855. The first paragraph in the *New-York Daily Tribune* version contains changes made by the editors.

The English version was included, under the same heading, in *The Eastern Question.* p. 546

375 See Note 215. p. 549

376 See Notes 10 and 35. p. 550

377 The *Federal Diet* (Bundestag) was the central representative body of the German Confederation (see Note 314). The Diet consisted of representatives of the German states and met in Frankfurt am Main. Though virtually powerless, it was nevertheless an instrument of feudal and monarchist reaction. The Diet ceased its activities during the revolution of 1848-49 in connection with the drafting of the German Imperial Constitution by the Frankfurt National Assembly and the attempts to unite Germany on this basis. Its powers were restored in March 1851. The formation of the North German Union in 1867 under Prussia's hegemony put an end to the German Confederation and the Federal Diet. p. 553

378 See Note 370. p. 555

379 See Note 219. p. 559

380 The Committee in Newcastle-upon-Tyne was one of the Foreign Affairs Committees set up by Urquhart and his supporters between the 1840s and 1860s with the prime purpose of counteracting the foreign policy of Palmerston. Marx was highly critical of the Urquhartists' conservative views, as can be seen from his articles "David Urquhart" (see present edition, Vol. 12, pp. 477-78) and "The Association for Administrative Reform. [—People's Charter"] (see this volume, pp. 240-44) and other newspaper items, also from his letters to Engels of March 9, 1853, February 9 and April 22, 1854, and others. At the same time he held that their foreign-policy statements could be used by Britain's working-class spokesmen in the struggle against the bourgeois-aristocratic oligarchy.

The report of the Committee in Newcastle-upon-Tyne quoted by Marx was published in *The Sheffield Free Press.* A summary of the documents included in the report was issued by this Urquhartist newspaper in the form of a leaflet entitled "The Case of the Alleged Bribery against Lord Palmerston. (Reprinted from the *Free Press*). Sheffield". Marx probably used *The Sheffield Free Press,* though he may have obtained the report from other sources. p. 560

381 No sequel to this report was published in the *Neue Oder-Zeitung.* This is most probably due to the fact that on October 7, 1855 its editor, M. Elsner, asked Marx by letter to stop sending articles for the time being in view of the newspaper's financial straits and obstacles raised by the censors. That is presumably why Marx left this article unfinished. Available material gives no

indication as to whether Marx resumed his regular contributions to the *Neue Oder-Zeitung* later. Although articles and reports marked with the sign × used by Marx continued to appear in the newspaper until it ceased publication in late 1855, only one of them was definitely written by Marx, the article "Big Meeting in Support of Political Refugees" (published on November 16, 1855; see this volume, pp. 581-82), as is indicated by the fact that its basic propositions coincide with those of Marx's letter to Elsner of November 8, 1855 (see present edition, Vol. 39). p. 562

382 The first paragraph of this article was probably added by the editors of the *New-York Daily Tribune.* This is suggested, among other things, by the reference to the publication in the same issue of comments on Gorchakov's report.

Like many other articles by Marx and Engels, this one was reprinted in the *New-York Semi-Weekly Tribune* and the *New-York Weekly Tribune.* The first reprint reproduced the text unchanged, while in the second, which appeared five days later, the section dealing with the operations of the Anglo-French fleet and landing troops against Kinburn (in the Dnieper estuary) was substantially altered and enlarged. The new information may have been drawn from another report by Engels, received in the meantime and not published in the *Daily Tribune,* containing details of the fall of Kinburn (October 17, 1855) which were not yet available to him when he was writing the present report. At the same time, the new text contained additions clearly made by the *Tribune* editors, who may have drawn on the reports of other correspondents. In view of this the *Weekly Tribune* version of the article is given in this volume in the Appendices and not in the main text (see pp. 694-702).

The *Daily Tribune* version was reprinted in *The Eastern Question* under the heading "Alarums and Excursions". The article was attributed to Marx, as also a number of other articles by Engels included in the collection. p. 563

383 On the battle of *Silistria* see Note 115, on that of *Inkerman*—Note 35, and on that of the *Chernaya*—Note 320. p. 564

384 A reference to the first campaign of the Russo-Turkish war of 1787-91. Austria took part in it on the side of Russia, but concluded a separate peace with Turkey in 1790. In the course of the war the Russian forces inflicted a number of serious defeats on the Turkish army and navy. The war ended in the signing of the Treaty of Jassy, which confirmed the incorporation of the Crimea into Russia (1783) and fixed Russia's Western frontier along the river Dniester. p. 564

385 This article and the next ("The Russian Army") belong to the series of works in which Engels reveals the causes of Tsarist Russia's defeat in the Crimean War, the negative effect of serfdom and economic backwardness on the state of armed forces, and the inadequacy of its military potential to satisfy tsarism's foreign-policy ambitions which increased particularly after its participation in suppressing the revolution of 1848-49 (notably the Tsarist intervention in Hungary in 1849). It is from that angle that Engels considers Russia's military history, and this in great measure explains why he gives a rather one-sided account of some of its episodes. It will be noted that in his later writings, based on more objective sources, including works by Russian authors, Engels modified his views on this subject. For instance, he pointed out that in the eighteenth century Turkey was not Russia's strongest opponent, Sweden being more powerful, that even the Ottoman Empire, though in a state of decline,

still possessed a considerable defence potential, and that Frederick II, the Prussian king, had been placed in a critical position by the advance of Russian troops in Prussia during the Seven Years' War (see Engels' article "The Foreign Policy of Russian Tsarism", 1890, present edition, Vol. 28). He had a high opinion of Suvorov's crossing of the Alps in 1799 ("Po and Rhine", 1859, Vol. 16), the operations of the Russian army and partisans during Napoleon's retreat from Moscow in 1812, and the part played by Russian forces in the campaigns against Napoleonic France in 1813 and 1814 (see his articles "Barclay de Tolly" and "Blücher", 1857, Vol. 18, and "The Position in the American Theatre of War", 1862, Vol. 19). The defence of Sevastopol in the Crimean War was later characterised by Engels as active, not passive (see his article "Saragossa-Paris", and instalment XXXIII of his series "Notes on the War", 1870, Vol. 22).

The article was reprinted in *The Eastern Question* under the heading "The Russians as Fighters". p. 569

386 A reference to two major battles in the Seven Years' War (1856-63), waged by Prussia and Britain against Austria, France and Russia.

At *Zorndorf* (Eastern Prussia) on August 25, 1758 the Russian army suffered heavy losses in a battle with the Prussian forces commanded by Frederick II. However, there was no victor in the battle, nor did it prevent a fresh Russian offensive the following year.

At *Kunersdorf* (east of Frankfurt an der Oder) on August 12, 1759 the Russian and Austrian forces under the joint command of P. Saltykov inflicted a heavy defeat on Frederick II's army. The Russian forces, in particular the infantry, played a decisive part in securing the victory. At the same time, the successful operations of the Austrian cavalry corps under Gideon Ernst von Loudon contributed to the rout of the Prussian cavalry. p. 569

387 During the war of the Second Coalition (it was formed in 1798 and included Austria, Britain, Naples, Russia, Turkey and other states) against France, the Russian and Austrian forces under the command of Alexander Suvorov freed almost the whole of Northern Italy from the French in the spring and summer of 1799. At the insistence of the Austrian government Suvorov's army was then sent to Switzerland to link up with the Russian corps of Rimsky-Korsakov, which was being pressed by the forces of the French General Masséna. After the Russian army had heroically fought its way across the Saint Gotthard and several other mountain passes it was encircled by superior French forces, which had defeated Korsakov's corps at Zurich on September 25. Under extremely hard conditions Suvorov's troops succeeded in making their way through a number of Alpine mountain passes and on October 12 reached the upper Rhine. In his work "Po and Rhine" (see present edition, Vol. 16) Engels wrote: "This passage was the most impressive of all Alpine crossings in modern times." p. 569

388 On the *battle of Austerlitz* see Note 299.

At *Friedland* (Eastern Prussia) the closing battle of the war of the Fourth Coalition (Britain, Prussia, Russia and Sweden) against Napoleonic France was fought on June 14, 1807. After the rout of the Prussian Army by Napoleon in 1806, the main theatre of operations in the war shifted to Eastern Prussia, where the French encountered stiff resistance from the allied armies of Russia and Prussia. In the battle of Friedland Napoleon won a victory over the Russian forces. It was preceded by a bloody battle at Preussisch-Eylau (February 7 and 8, 1807) which ended indecisively. The Prussian General Lestocq distinguished himself in that battle as well as the Russian General Pyotr Bagration, who commanded the rearguard. p. 569

389 On the *battle of Borodino* see Note 301. Engels' judgment of it was based on information drawn from a number of West-European military writers who represented the outcome of the battle as a victory for Napoleon and ignored the fateful consequences it had for the French army even though the Russians did leave Moscow temporarily. Later research produced a substantially different picture of the battle. It was established, in particular, that the French rather than the Russian army was superior in numbers and suffered heavier losses. p. 570

390 A reference to the Russo-Turkish war of 1828-29, which ended in the Treaty of Adrianople (see Note 22) and the suppression by the Tsarist forces of the Polish national insurrection in 1830-31. p. 570

391 See Note 2. p. 571

392 On the battles of *Inkerman* and the *Chernaya* and on the siege of *Silistria* see Notes 35, 320 and 115.

On the Russians' abortive assault on Kars (September 29, 1855) see this volume, pp. 563-68. p. 571

393 On the battle of *Oltenitza* see Note 317.

The Russian troops took the fortresses of Akhaltsikh and Erzeroum in Transcaucasia during the Russo-Turkish war of 1828-29. Under the Treaty of Adrianople (1829) Erzeroum was returned to Turkey.

By capturing Warsaw in September 1831 Tsarist forces dealt the final blow to the Polish national insurrection of 1830-31.

The Turkish fortress of Ismail on the Danube was taken by Russian troops by storm under Alexander Suvorov on December 22, 1790, during the Russo-Turkish war of 1787-91.

On November 4, 1794 Russian troops under Suvorov sent by the Tsarist Government to suppress the Polish national insurrection led by Tadeusz Kościuszko (which started in March 1794) captured Praga, a suburb of Warsaw, thus compelling the Polish capital to surrender. The suppression of the insurrection was followed, in 1795, by the third partition of Poland between Austria, Prussia and Russia, and the final abolition of the Polish state. (The first two partitions took place in 1772 and 1793.) p. 571

394 See Note 215. p. 572

395 In June 1854 Russia contracted a 50 million silver rubles loan at 5 per cent interest through the St. Petersburg bank of Stieglitz & Co. It was mainly intended to finance the Crimean War. p. 575

396 On October 10, 1855 the French petty-bourgeois democrat Félix Pyat addressed an open letter to Queen Victoria in connection with her visit to France in August of that year. It was printed in *L'Homme,* a refugee newspaper published in Jersey. Anti-Bonapartist in content, the letter, like all public statements by Pyat, was adventurist in character and provided Bonapartist circles and the conservative British press with a pretext for launching a sustained attack on the refugees. It was rumoured that the British Government was contemplating repressive measures against the refugees. The Governor of Jersey ordered the publisher of *L'Homme,* Sventoslawski, and some other refugees to leave the island. Victor Hugo too was threatened with expulsion.

This in turn gave rise to an angry protest campaign by the progressive public in Britain.

Concerning Marx's authorship of this article see Note 381. p. 581

397 The *Alien Bill* (Marx uses the English term) was passed by the British Parliament in 1793 and renewed in 1802, 1803, 1816, 1818 and, finally, in 1848, this time in connection with revolutionary developments on the Continent and Chartist demonstrations in Britain. The Bill authorised the Government to expel any foreigner from the Realm at any moment. It remained in force for one year. Subsequently conservative circles repeatedly urged its renewal.

In connection with the developments in Jersey, the proposed expulsion of revolutionary refugees was discussed for several months and finally rejected at the beginning of 1856. On February 1 of that year Palmerston told the House of Commons that the Government would not seek a renewal of the Alien Bill. p. 581

398 The *Fusionists* advocated a merger (fusion) of the Legitimists (supporters of the elder branch of the French house of Bourbons) with the Orleanists (supporters of the younger branch). p. 581

399 The name of Viscount Henry Addington Sidmouth, Home Secretary in Liverpool's Tory Cabinet from 1812 to 1821, was associated with a number of anti-popular laws and reactionary measures: the introduction of the Corn Laws in the interests of the landowners in 1815, the restriction of the right of assembly and the virtual introduction of censorship in 1817, the bloody dispersal of a workers' meeting near Manchester in 1819 (the Peterloo massacre), the passage of the "gagging acts" (see Note 268) and others. p. 582

400 This article was reprinted under the same heading in *The Eastern Question.* p. 584

401 The attitude of the European powers during the American War of Independence (1774-83) was determined by their commercial and colonial rivalry with Britain. France entered the war against Britain in 1778, Spain in 1779, and Holland in 1780. Despite the British Government's attempts to secure the support of Russia, the latter maintained an attitude of benevolent neutrality towards the United States and thereby contributed to the victory of the American republic. p. 584

402 The principle of armed neutrality (the armed protection of the merchantmen of neutral countries trading with Britain's opponents) was proclaimed by Catherine II in 1780 and recognised by a number of states. It stipulated the right of neutral countries to trade with the belligerents, a ban on privateering, refusal to recognise the blockade of ports access to which was not actually prevented by armed force, and a number of other rules. The declaration of armed neutrality objectively favoured the struggle of the North Americans for independence. p. 585

403 Britain declared war on Holland in December 1780 on the pretext that the latter was violating the Westminster peace treaty of 1674, which ended the Anglo-Dutch war of 1672-74. Holland was accused, in particular, of infringing a secret clause under which the two parties undertook not to aid any powers hostile to either side. Britain objected to Holland's trade with France, Spain and the United States of North America, against which Britain was waging war.

In taking this attitude Britain ignored another clause of the treaty, one guaranteeing freedom of trade and navigation.

The Anglo-Dutch war ended in 1784 in a victory for Britain. Holland was forced to cede the port of Negapatam (Southern India) to it and grant it freedom of navigation in the waterways of the Dutch East India Company. p. 586

404 The capture of Kars on November 28, 1855 concluded the successful operations by the Russian forces against the Turks in the Caucasian theatre of the Crimean War. Assisted by the British, the Turks had turned Kars into a bridgehead for the invasion of Transcaucasia. In the course of the fighting the Russian forces inflicted a series of defeats on the Turks (at Akhaltsikh on November 26, 1853, at Bash-Kadyklar on December 1, 1853, at Cholok on June 15, 1854, at Bayazid on July 20, 1854 and at Kuruk-Dar on August 5, 1854), thus thwarting their attempts to force their way into Armenia and Georgia. In October 1855 Omer Pasha's army was transferred from the Crimea to the Caucasus and marched from Sukhum-Kaleh to Mingrelia in an unsuccessful attempt to relieve the Turkish garrison. The capture of Kars, the last important event of the war, accelerated the conclusion of peace. p. 588

405 A reference to the campaigns of the Arab tribes of the Arabian Peninsula in the course of which the Arabian Caliphate subjugated and annexed the countries of the Middle East, Northern Africa and Southwest Europe. The Arabs' advance in Europe was stopped in 732 as a result of the battle of Poitiers, in which the Franks under Charles Martel, the virtual ruler of the Merovingian state, defeated the Arabs who had invaded France from Spain. p. 590

406 Engels is referring to the sieges of the Balkan fortresses of Varna, Brăila and Silistria during the Russo-Turkish war of 1828-29. Despite stiff resistance from the Turks, these fortresses were taken by the Russian troops. p. 590

407 A reference to the secret meetings of the military representatives and diplomats of Britain, France and Sardinia held under Louis Bonaparte's chairmanship in Paris in January 1856. According to press reports, they discussed co-ordinated action by the Allies in the event of another military campaign against Russia. p. 595

408 An allusion to an episode in the Russo-Turkish war of 1828-29: the march of advance units of the Russian army towards Constantinople in the summer of 1829. p. 595

409 A reference to the Five Points, the terms for peace talks presented to Russia by Austria on behalf of the Allied Powers in December 1855. An elaboration of the earlier Four Points (see Note 43), they called for replacement of the Russian protectorate over the Danubian Principalities by a protectorate of all the contracting parties, a revision of the Bessarabian border involving the relinquishing by Russia of the territory along the Danube, the neutralisation of the Black Sea, the closure of the Straits to warships, a ban on the maintenance of arsenals and navies in the Black Sea by Russia and Turkey; and collective protection of the Christian subjects of Turkey by the Great Powers. Presented in the form of an ultimatum, these terms were accepted by the Tsarist Government and provided the basis for the Paris peace talks. p. 598

410 In the second half of this article Marx drew on a letter from Engels of February 7, 1856 describing the position in France. p. 599

411 A reference to the struggle between Britain and the United States for domination in Central America. It found reflection in the sharp differences over the interpretation of the Clayton-Bulwer Treaty of 1850, under which Britain and the United States guaranteed the neutrality of the projected Isthmian canal and undertook to refrain from occupying Nicaragua, the Mosquito Coast and certain other areas. However, Britain, in violation of the Treaty, continued to hold the Mosquito Coast and the territories she captured in the 1840s. The United States supported the adventurer William Walker, who had seized power in Nicaragua in 1855. Relations were further aggravated by Britain's attempts to recruit mercenaries in the United States for her Crimean army. The governments of the two countries each threatened to break off diplomatic relations with the other. In October 1855 Britain sent warships to the American coast. The conflict was settled in October 1856 by the signing of a convention neutralising the Mosquito Coast and the adjacent sea zone. p. 599

412 The *peace of Amiens*—the peace treaty concluded by Napoleonic France and its allies (Spain and Holland) with Britain on March 27, 1802. It was actually a brief truce in these states' armed struggle for supremacy, which was resumed in May 1803. p. 599

413 Marx is ironically comparing the Franco-British alliance of the Crimean War period with the rapprochement between Britain and France in the early years of the July monarchy, which went down in history as the "Entente cordiale" (see Note 331). p. 599

414 This refers to the Five Points (see Note 409). p. 600

415 Speaking in the French Legislative Assembly on May 22, 1850, Montalembert urged the Government to launch a military expedition against the revolutionary and democratic forces in France similar to that undertaken against the Roman Republic in 1849 (see Note 194). p. 601

416 On December 29, 1855, during the ceremony held in Paris to welcome the French army returning from the Crimea, students of the École Polytechnique refused to greet the troops and the Emperor. The Government retaliated by repressive measures.

In his speech to the troops Louis Bonaparte compared himself to the Roman Senate, which usually went out in a body to welcome the victorious legions at the gates of Rome. p. 602

417 *Sire de Franc Boissy*—a French song containing satirical allusions to royalty and the government. p. 603

418 At the end of August 1855 several hundred workers in Angers (north-west France) rose in revolt in an attempt to set up a republic. Their leaders were associated with Marianne, a secret republican society established in 1850. Numerous arrests were made and trials held in late 1855 and early 1856 in connection with unrest in different parts of the country. p. 603

419 This article, written for the *New-York Daily Tribune* in connection with the publication of a number of documents relating to the fall of Kars, was Marx's first public reaction to this event. Soon after that he wrote a serialised pamphlet under the same heading for the Chartist *People's Paper* (see this volume, pp. 621-54). In it he used some of the formulations and developed the content of the present article, virtually the first version of the exposé. As the text of

the article differs substantially from that of the pamphlet, the article is reproduced in full in the present edition.

The first paragraph contains insertions made by the editors of the *New-York Daily Tribune.* p. 605

420 The decision to enter into negotiations with the Russians on the terms of capitulation was taken by the commanding officers of the Kars garrison on November 24, 1855. The fortress surrendered on November 28. p. 606

421 Besides *The People's Paper,* Marx also sent this article to the *New-York Daily Tribune,* which published it as a leading article under the heading "Bonapartean Victims and Tools" on April 14, 1856. It was reprinted under that heading in the *New-York Semi-Weekly Tribune* on April 15. The *Tribune* version differs somewhat from *The People's Paper* one. Certain passages were omitted and a number of—presumably editorial—insertions made. One such insertion, referring to Tassilier's letter, is the phrase "which will be found in another column" at the beginning of the article (the letter, possibly translated by Marx, was published in the same issue of the *New-York Daily Tribune*). Both versions contain numerous misprints in figures, which have been corrected on the basis of the sources used by Marx.

The People's Paper, founded in May 1852, was a weekly published by the revolutionary Chartists. Marx contributed to it without claiming remuneration and helped Ernest Jones, the chief editor, with the editing and organisational matters, especially in the weekly's early years. He also enlisted as regular contributors his associates Adolf Cluss (who lived in the USA), Georg Eccarius and Wilhelm Pieper. In the period between October 1852 and December 1856 *The People's Paper,* in addition to publishing Marx's articles written specially for it, reprinted the most important articles by Marx and Engels from the *New-York Daily Tribune.* At the beginning of 1856 Marx's contributions to *The People's Paper* became especially frequent. However towards the end of the year Marx and Engels temporarily broke off relations with Jones and ceased to contribute to his weekly because of Jones' increasing association with bourgeois radicals. In June 1858 the paper was taken over by J. Baxter Langley, a follower of Richard Cobden, with the proviso that Jones should have two columns in each issue for Chartist news. However, the paper met with no success and ceased publication in September 1858. p. 615

422 The reference is to French Guiana where political prisoners were sent for penal servitude. The high mortality caused by the harsh prison regulations and the unhealthy tropical climate earned Cayenne the nickname of the "Dry Guillotine".

Lambessa (Lambèse) was a French penal colony in North Africa set up on the ruins of the ancient Roman town of Lambaesis. From 1851 to 1860 it was a place of deportation for political prisoners.

Belle-Île is an island in the Bay of Biscay. From 1849 to 1857 political prisoners, including participants in the June 1848 uprising of Paris workers, were confined there. p. 615

423 An allusion to the methods Louis Bonaparte employed to win supporters while preparing the coup d'état of December 2, 1851. At the receptions and military reviews he held as President of the Republic at Satory and elsewhere army officers and men were served sausage, cold meat and champagne (see Marx's *The Eighteenth Brumaire of Louis Bonaparte,* present edition, Vol. 11, pp. 99-197). p. 615

424 *Furcae Caudinae* (Caudine Forks)—a gorge near the Roman town of Caudium, where in 321 B.C., during the second Samnite war, the Samnites defeated the Roman legions and made them "pass under the yoke", which was considered a terrible disgrace to a defeated army. Hence the expression to "pass under Furcae Caudinae"—to be subjected to extreme humiliation.

On the *Lower Empire* (the *New-York Daily Tribune* has *New Lower Empire* everywhere) see Note 198. p. 616

425 The *Society of December 10* was a secret Bonapartist society set up in 1849 consisting mainly of *déclassé* elements. Marx gives a detailed description of it in *The Eighteenth Brumaire of Louis Bonaparte* (see present edition, Vol. 11, pp. 99-197). p. 617

426 The *Batrachomyomachia* (The Battle of the Frogs and Mice) was an Ancient Greek anonymous mock-heroic poem parodying Homer's *Iliad.* p. 618

427 Instead of this sentence the *New-York Daily Tribune* has the following one partly or wholly added by the editors: "The wretched state of the French army in the Crimea was broadly asserted in our columns before the London press dared hint at it." p. 618

428 Marx wrote the pamphlet *The Fall of Kars* for the Chartist *People's Paper* as a series of four articles which were published in four consecutive issues of the weekly in April 1856. The individual instalments appeared under Marx's name, unnumbered (for convenience they have been numbered by the editors of this volume). The second, third and fourth instalments were preceded by a note saying that they were continuations of the instalment published in the previous issue. After the first and third instalments there were notes to the effect that they were to be continued in the next issue. The pamphlet was based on Marx's article on the same subject written for the *New-York Daily Tribune* and likewise entitled "The Fall of Kars" (see this volume, pp. 605-14). The text of this article was thoroughly revised and considerably enlarged. In a letter to Engels of April 16, 1856 (see present edition, Vol. 40) Marx wrote that in the absence of the original he was compelled, in preparing the pamphlet, to restore the *Tribune* article from memory as well as he could. His main source in writing both the article and the pamphlet was a Blue Book on the defence of Kars published soon after the surrender of the fortress on November 28, 1855. In late April and early May 1856 Marx compiled a summary of his pamphlet for *The Free Press* and *The Sheffield Free Press,* two periodicals published by David Urquhart and his supporters (see this volume, pp. 673-80).

The People's Paper version of "The Fall of Kars" was reprinted in *The Eastern Question.* p. 621

429 The *Five Points*—see Note 409.

The Paris Treaty—the peace treaty that concluded the Crimean War (1853-56). It was signed by the representatives of Austria, Britain, France, Prussia, Sardinia and Turkey, on the one hand, and of Russia on the other, at the Congress of Paris on March 30, 1856. Under the treaty, Russia ceded the mouth of the Danube and part of Bessarabia, renounced its protectorate over the Danubian Principalities and its protection of Christians in Turkey, agreed to the neutralisation of the Black Sea (involving the closure of the Straits to foreign warships and a ban on Russia and Turkey maintaining navies and naval arsenals on the Black Sea) and returned the fortress of Kars to Turkey in exchange for Sevastopol and other Russian towns held by the Allies. By skilfully exploiting the differences between Britain and France the Russian diplomats at the congress succeeded in foiling the attempts to impose still more onerous peace terms on Russia.

The Paris Treaty failed to settle the Eastern Question. In the 1870s relations between the European Powers in the Balkans and the Near East became tense again. p. 623

430 *"Take care of Dowb" Panmure*—a nickname for the British Secretary at War Panmure who, in an official dispatch informing General Simpson of his appointment to the post of commander-in-chief in the Crimea, asked him to look after Panmure's nephew, the young officer Dowbiggin. p. 626

431 See Note 215. p. 635

432 The *Fanariots* were inhabitants of the Fanar, the main Greek quarter in Constantinople, mostly descendants of aristocratic Byzantine families. Due to their wealth and political connections many of them held high administrative posts in the Ottoman Empire. p. 635

433 A reference to the capture of Kars by the Russians during the Russo-Turkish war of 1828-29. Under the Treaty of Adrianople of 1829 the fortress was returned to the Turks. p. 641

434 See Note 420. p. 652

435 On April 14, 1856 Marx was invited as an official representative of the revolutionary refugees in London to a banquet commemorating the fourth anniversary of the Chartist *People's Paper*. He used the occasion to demonstrate the internationalist solidarity that united the proletarian revolutionaries, among whom he had established himself as the outstanding leader, with the revolutionary wing of the Chartist movement, and show that in contrast to the French and German petty bourgeois democrats, who were merely flirting with the Chartist leaders, the German Communists were true allies of the Chartists, sharing with them the aim of achieving the rule of the working class in all countries (for more on this see Marx's letter to Engels of April 16, 1856 in Vol. 40 of the present edition). In his address (he was the first speaker) Marx concentrated on the historic role of the proletariat. The banquet was also addressed by another representative of the German Communists, Wilhelm Pieper. The other speakers were mostly Chartists (James Finlen, Ernest Jones and others).

Marx did not intend to publish his speech. It was, however, included in the newspaper report under the heading "Fourth Anniversary Banquet of *The People's Paper*". The following text preceded the speech:

"On Monday last at the Bell Hotel, Strand, Ernest Jones entertained the compositors of *The People's Paper* and the other gentlemen connected with its office, at a supper, which was joined by a large number of the leading Democrats of England, France and Germany now in London. The entertainment was of the choicest description, and reflected the greatest credit on the enterprising proprietor of the Hotel, Mr. Hunter; the choicest viands and condiments of the season being supplied in profusion. The tables were well filled with a numerous company of both sexes, Ernest Jones occupying the chair, and Mr. Fawley, manager of *The People's Paper* office, the vice-chair. The banquet commenced at seven, and at nine o'clock the cloth was cleared, when a series of sentiments was given from the chair.

"The Chairman then proposed the toast: 'The proletarians of Europe', which was responded to by Dr. Marx as follows:"

Then follows the text of the speech. p. 655

436 In this article Marx used information on the economic position of Prussia and other European countries which he had received from Engels in a letter of April 14, 1856. p. 657

437 See Note 370. p. 657

438 *Chambre introuvable* was the name given by King Louis XVIII to the Chamber of Deputies in France, which in 1815-16 consisted of extreme conservatives. It attacked the Government from the right and was eventually disbanded by the King because of its arch-reactionary views. p. 659

439 Marx's authorship of this article, published in *The People's Paper* anonymously, is evident from his letter to Engels of April 26, 1856 (see present edition, Vol. 40) where the article is mentioned in the list of items enclosed. "In it I imitate, *tant bien que mal*, the style of old Cobbett," he writes. p. 662

440 A reference to the Duke of York's part in the wars of the First and Second European coalitions (1792-97 and 1799-1800) against the French republic. In 1793 the British army commanded by the Duke unsuccessfully besieged Dunkirk and, following the defeat of the coalition forces at Hondschoote on September 6-8 of that year, narrowly escaped annihilation by hastily retreating without a fight. Later the Duke of York commanded the British corps of the Anglo-Russian army that landed at Helder (Northern Holland) at the end of August 1799. In October the allied troops were defeated by a Franco-Dutch army commanded by Brune. p. 663

441 The *convention of Alkmaar* was signed on October 18, 1799 after the defeat in Holland (then the Batavian Republic) of the Anglo-Russian forces commanded by the Duke of York. It provided for the withdrawal from Holland of the forces of the anti-French coalition and the release of the French and Dutch prisoners. p. 664

442 See Note 22. p. 665

443 A reference to the group of Whig radicals headed by Charles James Fox. They opposed the war against the French republic and advocated a reform of Parliament favouring the industrial and commercial bourgeoisie. p. 665

444 *"Friends of the King"*—a group of close associates of George III, mostly extreme Tories. They supported George III's attempts to extend the Royal prerogative at the expense of Parliament and establish his personal rule. Members of the group repeatedly headed the government and held ministerial posts between 1760 and the early 1780s. p. 666

445 This article is Marx's summary of his pamphlet *The Fall of Kars*, which was published in April as a series of articles in *The People's Paper* (see Note 428). He substantially abridged and rearranged the text of the pamphlet in preparing the summary. The editors of *The Free Press* published it together with the covering letter (see this volume, p. 672), adding the following note in brackets below the heading: "The subjoined paper has been supplied to us by Dr. Karl Marx". p. 673

446 Engels' summary "Crimean War", written in German, listed in chronological order the major military events in the Crimea beginning with the landing of the

Allied troops in Eupatoria on September 14, 1854 and ending with their capture of the Southern side of Sevastopol by storm on September 8, 1855. We do not know for what particular purpose it was compiled. One may assume, however, that Engels, who continued to cover the war after the capture of Sevastopol, was intending to write a retrospective review of the hostilities in the Crimea and drew up this outline of the fighting for that purpose. The review evidently never materialised.

Engels described the main episodes of the war—the battles of the Alma, Balaklava, Inkerman and the Chernaya, the construction of the Selenghinsk redoubt and the Kamchatka lunette, the abortive assault of June 18, 1855, the assault of September 8, 1855, and others—in a series of articles which will be found in Volume 13 (pp. 492-97, 518-27 and 528-35) and in the present volume (pp. 113-17, 132-35, 151-55, 328-32 and 504-12, 546-52). See also Notes 2, 10, 35, 215 and 320. p. 685

447 This article is the English version of part of Engels' article "Germany and Pan-Slavism", published in full in the *Neue Oder-Zeitung* in April 1855, and—in content—a sequel to the article "The European Struggle", which was the English version of another part of "Germany and Pan-Slavism", published in the *New-York Daily Tribune* on May 5 of the same year (see this volume, pp. 156-62 and Note 131). The *Tribune* editors altered Engels' text considerably. In particular, they added the second paragraph, setting forth the views on Pan-Slavism of the *Tribune* correspondent, A. Gurowski, which were at variance with those of Marx and Engels. The closing paragraph too contains editorial changes. Marx was incensed by this treatment and even considered ceasing to work for the newspaper. On receipt of the issue containing the article he wrote to Engels (May 18, 1855): "The devil take the *Tribune*. It is absolutely essential now that it should come out *against Pan-Slavism*" (see present edition, Vol. 39).

The article was published under the same heading in *The Eastern Question*. p. 689

448 See Note 132. p. 690

449 See Note 133. p. 690

450 See Note 134. p. 692

451 See Note 135. p. 692

452 This is an enlarged version of an article published under the same heading in the *New-York Daily Tribune* and the *New-York Semi-Weekly Tribune* (see this volume, pp. 563-67, and Note 382). It shows clear signs of editorial interference. This applies especially to the passages which do not occur in the *Daily* or *Semi-Weekly Tribune* (the details of the capture of Kinburn by the Allies on October 17, 1855). In all probability, the editors added the second passage on the fighting at Kinburn during the Russo-Turkish war of 1787-91 (on which see Note 384) and the part played in it by Rear-Admiral Paul Jones, a veteran of the American War of Independence (1774-83). p. 694

453 On the battle of *Silistria* see Note 115, the battle of *Inkerman*, Note 35, and the battle of the *Chernaya*, Note 320. p. 695

454 A reference to the destruction of the fortifications of Bomarsund, a fortress on one of the Åland islands in the Gulf of Bothnia, by the Anglo-French navy and a French landing party in August 1854. p. 698

NAME INDEX

D

E

F

G

H

I

J

N

O

R

S

T

Y

Z

INDEX OF LITERARY AND MYTHOLOGICAL NAMES

INDEX OF QUOTED AND MENTIONED LITERATURE

WORKS BY KARL MARX AND FREDERICK ENGELS

WORKS BY DIFFERENT AUTHORS

DOCUMENTS

ANONYMOUS ARTICLES AND REPORTS PUBLISHED IN PERIODIC EDITIONS

INDEX OF PERIODICALS

SUBJECT INDEX

GLOSSARY OF GEOGRAPHICAL NAMES[a]

Adrianople	Edirne
Aitodor	Goristoye
Akaltzik	Akhaltsikh
Aleppo (Haleb)	Aleppo or Haleb-es-Shabba
Alexandropol (Gumri)	Leninakan
Arabat	Rybatskoye
Araxes (river)	Aras
Astrachan	Astrakhan
Austerlitz	Slavkov
Baidar	Orlinoye
Bakshiserai	Bakhchisarai
Batum (Batoum)	Batumi
Bayazid	Doğubayazit
Bazardshik (Bazargic)	Tolbukhin
Berdiansk	Osipenko
Braila (Ibraila, Brailow)	Brăila
Breslau	Wrocław
Busaco	Bussaco
Candia	Crete
Careening Bay	Kilen Bay
Carlsburg	Alba Julia
Ceylon	Sri Lanka
Charkoff	Kharkov
Cherson	Kherson
Chotin	Hotin or Khotin
Coblentz	Coblenz or Koblenz
Colberg	Kolobrzeg
Constantinople	Istanbul
Culm	Chlumcc
Dantzic (Danzig)	Gdańsk
Ekaterinoslav (Yekaterinoslav)	Dnepropetrovsk
Erzeroum	Erzerum or Erzurum
Galatch (Galatz)	Galaţi
Gallipoli	Gelibolu
Gumri—see Alexandropol	
Halys (river)	Kizil Irmak
Helsingfors	Helsinki
Inkermann	Inkerman
Kaffa	Theodosia
Kalafat	Calafat
Kars Chai (river)	Kars
Kamtchatka	Kamchatka
Katsha	Kacha
Kamiesh	Kamysh
Kertch	Kerch
Kieff	Kiev
Königsberg	Kaliningrad
Krain	Carniola
Kurulu	Stolbovoye
Kutais	Kutaisi
Lemberg	Lvov
Malakoff	Malakhov
Memel	Klaipeda
Nasgen (Nargö)	Naisar
Nikolaieff	Nikolayev

[a] The glossary includes geographical names occurring in Marx's and Engels' articles in the form customary in the European and American press of the time but differing from the national names or from those given on modern maps. The left column gives geographical names as used in the original (when they differ from the national names of the time, the latter are given in brackets); the right column gives corresponding names as used on modern maps and in modern literature.—*Ed.*

Olmütz	Olomouc
Oltenitza	Olteniţa
Olti	Oltu
Otshakoff	Ochakov
Pampeluna	Pamplona
Pekin	Peking
Persia	Iran
Porto Rico (isl)	Puerto Rico
Posen	Poznań
Preussisch Eylau	Bagrationovsk
Redout Kaleh	Kulevi
Reval (Revel)	Tallinn
Rioni	Rion
Rustchuk	Ruse or Rusčuk
Saint-Jean-d'Acre	Akka
Scinde	Sind or Sindh
Scutari	Usküdar
Shumla	Shumen (Kolarovgrad)
Sizopolis	Sizeboli or Sozopol
St. Petersburg	Leningrad
Sukhum Kaleh	Sukhumi
Sveaborg (Sweaborg)	Suomenlinna
Tiflis	Tbilisi
Tilsit	Sovetsk
Toli-Monatzir	Bitolya or Bitolj
Trebizonde	Trebizond
Tripoli	Tripolitsa
Tunis	Tunisia
Urkusta	Peredovoye
Wartha (river)	Warta
Wilna	Vilnius